iostream Classes Used in the Book

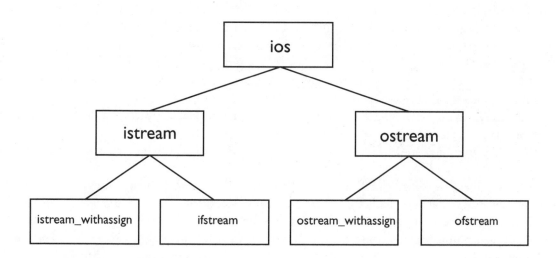

The Visual Workbench Toolbar

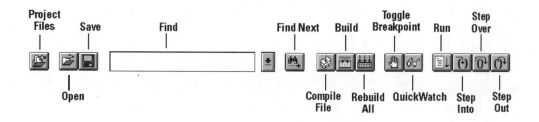

Computer users are not all alike.
Neither are SYBEX books.

We know our customers have a variety of needs. They've told us so. And because we've listened, we've developed several distinct types of books to meet the needs of each of our customers. What are you looking for in computer help?

If you're looking for the basics, try the **ABC's** series. You'll find short, unintimidating tutorials and helpful illustrations. For a more visual approach, select **Teach Yourself,** featuring screen-by-screen illustrations of how to use your latest software purchase.

Running Start books are really two books in one—a tutorial to get you off to a fast start and a reference to answer your questions when you're ready to tackle advanced tasks.

Mastering and **Understanding** titles offer you a step-by-step introduction, plus an in-depth examination of intermeditate-level features, to use as you progress.

Our **Up & Running** series is designed for computer-literate consumers who want a no-nonsense overview of new programs. Just 20 basic lessons, and you're on your way.

We also publish two types of reference books. Our **Instant References** provide quick access to each of a program's commands and functions. SYBEX **Encyclopedias** and **Desktop References** provide a *comprehensive reference* and explanation of all of the commands, features, and functions of the subject software.

Our **Programming** books are specifically written for a technically sophisticated audience and provide a no-nonsense value-added approach to each topic covered, with plenty of tips, tricks, and time-saving hints.

Sometimes a subject requires a special treatment that our standard series doesn't provide. So you'll find we have titles like **Advanced Techiques, Handbooks, Tips & Tricks,** and others that are specifically tailored to satisfy a unique need.

We carefully select our authors for their in-depth understanding of the software they're writing about, as well as their ability to write clearly and communicate effectively. Each manuscript is thoroughly reviewed by our technical staff to ensure its complete accuracy. Our production department makes sure it's easy to use. All of this adds up to the highest quality books available, consistently appearing on best-seller charts worldwide.

You'll find SYBEX publishes a variety of books on every popular software package. Looking for computer help? Help Yourself to SYBEX.

For a brochure of our best-selling publications:

SYBEX Inc. 2021 Challenger Drive, Alameda, CA 94501
Tel: (510) 523-8233/(800) 227-2346 Telex: 336311
Fax: (510) 523-2373

SYBEX®

MASTERING

Microsoft®

VISUAL C++

PROGRAMMING

MASTERING

Microsoft®
VISUAL C++
PROGRAMMING

Michael J. Young

SYBEX®

San Francisco ■ Paris ■ Düsseldorf ■ Soest

Acquisitions Editor: David Clark
Developmental Editor: Gary Masters
Editor: Mark Woodworth
Technical Editor: Amrik Dhillon
Project Editor: Abby Azrael
Book Designer: Suzanne Albertson
Production Artist: Lisa Jaffe
Screen Graphics: John Corrigan
Typesetter: Deborah Maizels
Proofreader/Production Assistant: Janet K. MacEachern
Indexer: Ted Laux
Cover Designer: Archer Design
Cover Illustrator: David Bishop
Cover Photo Art Direction: Ingalls+Associates

Screen reproductions reproduced with Collage Plus.

Collage Plus is a trademark of Inner Media Inc.

SYBEX is a registered trademark of SYBEX Inc.

TRADEMARKS: SYBEX has attempted throughout this book to distinguish proprietary trademarks from descriptive terms by following the capitalization style used by the manufacturer.

SYBEX is not affiliated with any manufacturer.

Every effort has been made to supply complete and accurate information. However, SYBEX assumes no responsibility for its use, nor for any infringement of the intellectual property rights of third parties which would result from such use.

Library of Congress Card Number: 93-60630
ISBN: 0-7821-1282-X

Manufactured in the United States of America
10 9 8 7 6 5 4 3 2

ACKNOWLEDGMENTS

This book is the result of the efforts of many dedicated and talented people at SYBEX. First, I would like to thank Gary Masters, developmental editor, for helping to define the initial concept of the book and for offering his continued enthusiasm and support throughout the project. I would also like to thank Dianne King, acquisitions editor, for turning this concept into a book contract. Thanks, too, to Abby Azrael, project editor, for coordinating the entire effort and patiently waiting for each chapter to arrive; Mark Woodworth, editor, for carefully working through each of these chapters and improving their consistency and style; Amrik Dhillon, technical editor, for verifying the technical accuracy of the text and testing the example programs. Finally, I would like to express my gratitude to all of the other people at SYBEX whose names appear at the front of the book, for their important roles in the project.

CONTENTS AT A GLANCE

	INTRODUCTION	xix
PART I	**Introduction to Microsoft Visual C++**	**1**
	1 Setting Up the Software	3
	2 Creating a Program Using the Visual Workbench	15
PART II	**Introduction to C++**	**35**
	3 Moving to C++	37
	4 Defining C++ Classes	75
	5 Deriving C++ Classes	107
	6 Overloading, Copying, and Converting	133
PART III	**Windows Programming with the MFC Library**	**163**
	7 Generating a Windows Program	165
	8 Implementing the View	199
	9 Implementing the Document	257
	10 Storing Documents	289
	11 Scrolling and Splitting Views	337
	12 Writing MDI Applications	385
	13 Creating Custom Dialog Boxes	415
	14 Including Tool Bars and Status Bars	473
	15 Performing Character I/O	525
	16 Using Drawing Functions	609
	17 Using Bitmaps and Bit Operations	723
	18 Printing and Print Previewing	763
	19 Exchanging Data Using the Clipboard and OLE	825
PART IV	**MS-DOS and QuickWin Programming with the iostream Library**	**885**
	20 Writing MS-DOS and QuickWin Programs	887
	21 Using the iostream Class Library	905
	INDEX	937

TABLE OF CONTENTS

Introduction   xix

PART I   **Introduction to Microsoft Visual C++**   1

1 Setting Up the Software   3

Installing Microsoft Visual C++   4
  Hardware and Software Requirements   4
  Running Setup   5
What Is Included in Visual C++   8
  Microsoft Visual Workbench   8
  Microsoft C/C++ Compiler   8
  Microsoft Foundation Classes   8
  Microsoft App Studio: Resource Editor   9
  Run-Time Libraries   9
  Sample Source Code   9
  Online Help Files   10
  Tools   10
  An Overview of Visual C++   10
Installing the Companion Disk   11
Summary   13

2 Creating a Program Using the Visual Workbench   15

Running the Visual Workbench   16
Creating the Project   18
Editing the Source File   20
Setting Build Options   24
Building the Program   26
Running the Program   28
Debugging the Program   28
Summary   33

PART II	**Introduction to C++**	**35**
	3 Moving to C++	**37**
	Converting from C to C++	38
	New Features of C++	43
	Comments	43
	Declaration Statements	44
	The Scope Resolution Operator	47
	Inline Functions	48
	Default Function Parameters	51
	Reference Types	52
	Constant Types	59
	Overloaded Functions	66
	The new and delete Operators	68
	Summary	72
	4 Defining C++ Classes	**75**
	Defining a Class	76
	Creating a Class Instance	78
	Accessing Class Members	79
	Encapsulation	80
	The Benefits of Encapsulation	84
	Constructors and Destructors	85
	Constructors	85
	Destructors	92
	When Constructors and Destructors Are Called	94
	Inline Member Functions	95
	Organizing the Source Files	97
	The this Pointer	99
	Static Class Members	101
	Summary	104
	5 Deriving C++ Classes	**107**
	Deriving Classes	108
	Providing Constructors for Derived Classes	111

Accessing Inherited Members   112
Creating Hierarchies of Classes   116
    The Advantages of Inheritance   118
Using Virtual Functions   120
    Using Virtual Functions to Handle Class Objects   125
    Using Virtual Functions to Modify Base Classes   127
Summary   129

6   Overloading, Copying, and Converting   **133**

Overloading Operators   134
    Defining Additional Operator Functions   137
    General Guidelines for Overloading Operators   142
    Overloading the Assignment Operator   144
Using Copy and Conversion Constructors   148
    Writing Copy Constructors   149
    Writing Conversion Constructors   152
    Initializing Arrays   159
Summary   160

PART III   Windows Programming with the MFC Library   **163**

7   Generating a Windows Program   **165**

Programming for Windows   166
Creating and Building the Program   167
    1. Generating the Source Code   167
    2. Modifying the Source Code   170
    3. Building and Running the Program   174
The Program Classes and Files   176
How the Program Works   192
    The Flow of Program Control   192
    The InitInstance Function   195
Summary   197

8   Implementing the View   **199**

The MINIDRAW Program   200
    Generating the Source Files   202

Defining and Initializing View Class Data Members   203
Adding Message-Handling Functions   204
Designing the Program Resources   216
Customizing the Window   221
The MINIDRAW Program Source Code   223
The MINIEDIT Program   237
Creating the MINIEDIT Program   238
The MINIEDIT Program Source Code   243
Summary   254

9 Implementing the Document   257

Storing the Graphic Data   258
Redrawing the Window   262
Adding Menu Commands   263
Deleting the Document Data   265
Implementing Menu Commands   266
Handling the Delete All Command   266
Handling the Undo Command   268
The MINIDRAW Source Code   271
Summary   287

10 Storing Documents   289

Adding File I/O to MINIDRAW   290
Adding the File Menu Commands   290
Supporting the File Menu Commands   292
The MINIDRAW Source Code   301
Adding File I/O to MINIEDIT   317
Defining the Resources   318
Adding Supporting Code   319
The MINIEDIT Source Code   321
Summary   334

11 Scrolling and Splitting Views   337

Adding Scrolling Capability   338
Converting Coordinates   340
Limiting the Drawing Size   344
Adding Splitting Capability   352

Updating the Views   356
   Redrawing Efficiently   357
The MINIDRAW Source Code   363
Summary   381

12 Writing MDI Applications   385

The Multiple Document Interface   386
Generating the Program   388
   The Program Classes and Files   390
Modifying the Code   393
Customizing the Resources   395
The MINIEDIT Source Code   401
Summary   413

13 Creating Custom Dialog Boxes   415

Creating a Modal Dialog Box   416
   Generating the Program   418
   Designing the Format Dialog Box   418
   Creating a Class to Manage the Dialog Box   427
   Defining Member Variables   428
   Defining Message Handlers   432
   Modifying the CFormat Code   434
   Displaying the Dialog Box   444
   Setting the Colors   452
   The DIALOG1 Source Code   453
Other Types of Dialog Boxes   467
   Modeless Dialog Boxes   467
   Form Views   468
   Common Dialog Boxes   469
Summary   470

14 Including Tool Bars and Status Bars   473

Adding a Tool Bar and Status Bar to a New Program   474
Adding a Tool Bar to MINIDRAW   476
   Defining the Resources   477
   Modifying the Code   484
Adding a Status Bar to MINIDRAW   496

The MINIDRAW Source Code   499
Summary   523

15 Performing Character I/O   525

Displaying Text   526
    Generating the Program   527
    Writing Code to Display the Lines   527
    Creating the Font Object and Storing the Text 535
    Supporting Scrolling   550
Reading the Keyboard   552
    Reading Keys with a WM_KEYDOWN Message Handler 552
    Reading Keys with a WM_CHAR Message Handler 560
Managing the Caret   567
The TEXTDEMO Source Code   571
The ECHO Source Code   592
Summary   606

16 Using Drawing Functions   609

Creating the Device Context Object   610
Selecting Drawing Tools   612
    Selecting Stock Drawing Tools   612
    Creating Custom Drawing Tools   614
Setting Drawing Attributes   620
    The Mapping Mode   621
Drawing the Graphics   625
    Drawing Points   625
    Drawing Lines   646
    Drawing Closed Figures   650
    Other Drawing Functions   655
The MINIDRAW Program   656
    Defining Classes for the Figures   664
    Other Code Modifications   676
    The MINIDRAW Source Code   683
Summary   720

17 Using Bitmaps and Bit Operations   723

Creating a Bitmap   724
   Loading a Bitmap from a Resource   725
   Creating a Bitmap Using Drawing Functions   727
   Displaying a Bitmap   730
   Other Ways to Use a Bitmap   732
Performing Bit Operations   733
   PatBlt   734
   BitBlt   736
   StretchBlt   741
Displaying Icons   742
The BITDEMO Program   745
   Designing the Bitmap   746
   Modifying the Code   746
   The BITDEMO Source Code   749
Summary   761

18 Printing and Print Previewing   763

Basic Printing and Print Previewing   764
   Modifying the Resources   765
   Modifying the Code   767
Advanced Printing   771
   Changing the Drawing Size   772
   Overriding Virtual Printing Functions   773
   Modifying the OnDraw Function   781
The MINIDRAW Source Code   785
Summary   823

19 Exchanging Data Using the Clipboard and OLE   825

Using the Clipboard   826
   The Clipboard Commands   826
   Using the Clipboard to Transfer Text   830
   Using the Clipboard to Transfer Graphics   841
   Using the Clipboard to Transfer Private Data Formats   847
Using OLE   848
   Generating the Program   850

Defining the Item Class   851
Supporting the Insert New Object Command   853
Displaying the OLE Item   855
Implementing the Paste and Paste Link Commands   856
Supporting the Object Command   861
Implementing the Cut and Copy Commands   862
The OLEDEMO Source Code   864
Summary   880

PART IV   MS-DOS and QuickWin
Programming with the iostream Library   885

20 Writing MS-DOS and QuickWin Programs   887

Creating MS-DOS Programs   888
Building an Example Program   889
Guidelines for Writing MS-DOS Code   893
Creating QuickWin Programs   894
The QuickWin Program Interface   896
Guidelines for Writing QuickWin Programs   899
Enhancing QuickWin Programs   901
Summary   903

21 Using the iostream Class Library   905

The iostream Library   906
Performing Standard Stream I/O   908
Performing Output   909
Performing Input   919
Performing File I/O   922
Performing Output   923
Performing Input   930
Summary   933

Index   937

INTRODUCTION

Visual C++ is Microsoft's most comprehensive and sophisticated program development product to date. It provides an unprecedented level of programming power and convenience, and it offers a diverse set of tools designed to suit almost every programming style.

Learning to use Visual C++, however, can be a daunting task. First, you must deal with the sheer bulk of the product (the Professional Version comes on 20 high-density disks, includes more than 10 bound manuals and 15 online help files, and can consume more than 50MB of hard disk space). Second, you must choose from the variety of programming languages, target environments, and development tools available, ranging from writing C programs for MS-DOS using the run-time library, to writing C++ programs for Windows using the Microsoft Foundation Classes and the code generation tools (the "Wizards").

The purpose of this book is to provide you with a single, comprehensive, step-by-step guide to Visual C++. It is designed to be read through from the beginning and to give you a broad general understanding of the product, enabling you to choose the specific tools you need for particular programming tasks and allowing you to find all the information you need to use these tools. The book, however, provides more than an overview or introduction. The detailed discussions and the tutorial exercises are designed to give you a solid understanding of the key programming tools and techniques, as well as to make you proficient at using these tools and techniques in developing your programs.

How, you might ask, can a single book serve as a comprehensive guide to such an enormous product? *Mastering Microsoft Visual C++ Programming* does this in two ways. First, it focuses on the *newer* software technologies (for example, C++, Windows programming, the Microsoft Foundation Classes, the Wizard code generators, and the `iostream` class library), assuming that you have some knowledge of the older technologies (such as C, MS-DOS programming, and the standard run-time libraries). Second, the book contains many "pointers" to the printed and on-line documentation provided with Visual C++. (These references are described later in the Introduction.) Rather than attempting to discuss every detail of every feature—for example, every parameter passed to every function in a particular group—the book provides an in-depth discussion of the key features and then points you to the exact location in the documentation where you can find additional details.

An Overview of the Book

Part I of the book (Chapters 1 and 2) explains how to install and set up Visual C++ and the companion disk included with this book, and it provides a general description of the components of the Visual C++ product. Part I also introduces you to the basic techniques required to write and build programs using the Visual C++ integrated development environment, the Visual Workbench. You will learn just enough about the Visual Workbench to enable you to write and test simple example programs as you work through Part II.

Part II (Chapters 3 through 6) offers an introduction to the C++ programming language. It covers the general C++ programming techniques that you will use whether you are programming for Windows or for MS-DOS. It also provides detailed explanations of C++ features that are used by the Microsoft Foundation Classes and the `iostream` library, so that you will understand these features when you encounter them in Parts III and IV.

Part III (Chapters 7 through 19) forms the heart of the book. It explains how to write programs for Microsoft Windows, showing you how to use the Visual Workbench, the App Studio (for designing resources), and other Windows development tools. It also illustrates how you can take advantage of the prewritten code supplied by the Microsoft Foundation Classes library, as well as the code generated by the Wizard tools. Chiefly because of the comparative simplicity of programming with these tools, Part III is able to cover not only the basics of Windows programming, but also many relatively advanced topics, such as implementing split window views, displaying status and tool bars, writing MDI (multiple document interface) applications, using drawing functions and bitmaps, print previewing, and exchanging data with OLE (Object Linking and Embedding).

Finally, Part IV (Chapters 20 and 21) explains how to use Visual C++ to write MS-DOS programs, as well as QuickWin programs (which are written using MS-DOS programming techniques, but run as simple Windows applications). In this part, you will also learn how to use the standard `iostream` class library to perform object-oriented I/O from these programs.

The Companion Disk

The companion disk includes all of the source files you need to build the example programs in this book. Chapter 1 describes the contents of this disk, lists the requirements for using it, and explains how to install it.

What Is Required

You can use this book with either the Standard or the Professional Edition of Visual C++. Chapter 1 describes the differences between these two products, and also explains the hardware and software requirements for using Visual C++ and the companion disk.

The book does *not* require knowledge of either the C++ language or Windows programming. The book assumes, however, that you have a basic knowledge of the C language. C++ concepts are frequently explained in terms of—or are contrasted with—C language concepts. If you need to learn or review C, you might consult one of the following books, which are among the many good C programming titles: *The C Programming Language* (second edition) by Kernighan and Ritchie (published by Prentice-Hall) and *C: A Reference Manual* by Harbison and Steele (also published by Prentice-Hall).

Conventions

This section describes several elements that you will find throughout the book: references to the documentation, notes, and sidebars.

The book makes frequent references to the documentation that is provided with Visual C++. Whenever possible, a reference cites *both* the printed documentation *and* the corresponding topic within the online help system. A reference to a *manual* (such as "the *Programming Techniques* manual") designates one of the manuals included with the Visual C++ product. Note that most of the individual manuals are bound together with several other manuals within a single book. A reference to an

SDK manual designates one of the Software Development Kit manuals included only with the Professional Edition of Visual C++ (you can, however, obtain these manuals separately from Microsoft). Chapter 2 (the sidebar labeled "Getting Help") explains how to use the Visual Workbench help system and how to find the online help topics that are cited in the book.

The book contains many notes, which are placed in shaded boxes and labeled "Note" or "Tip." The notes emphasize important points or expand on topics in the main text. The notes are an integral part of the discussions, and you should read them as you proceed through the text.

The book also contains sidebars, which have titles and are separated from the main text by horizontal bars. The sidebars are typically much longer than the notes and provide additional information that is important but not essential for understanding the primary chapter topics. You can therefore safely skip a sidebar, or peruse it before or after reading the main text.

Contacting the Author

You may contact me by sending E-mail to my CompuServe account, number 75156.2572. I welcome your technical questions, feedback, and ideas, as well as inquiries regarding my software development services. (If you have questions about ordering books or disks, please contact the publisher.)

PART I

Introduction to Microsoft Visual C++

In this part of the book, you will learn how to set up and begin using Microsoft Visual C++. Chapter 1 shows you how to install Visual C++ and the companion disk provided with the book, and it provides you with an overview of the Visual C++ product. In Chapter 2 you will learn how to use the Visual C++ tools to edit, build, and debug a simple C++ program.

CHAPTER
ONE

Setting Up the Software

- Installing Microsoft Visual C++

- What is included in Visual C++

- Installing the companion disk

This chapter describes how to install both Microsoft Visual C++ and the companion disk that is provided with this book. It lists the hardware and software requirements for installing and running Visual C++, and describes the installation procedure. It then provides an overview of the components included in Visual C++, to help you choose installation options and to introduce you to the product. The chapter concludes with instructions for installing the companion disk.

Installing Microsoft Visual C++

The requirements and the installation procedure described in this section apply to both the Standard Edition and the Professional Edition of Microsoft Visual C++.

Hardware and Software Requirements

Before you install Microsoft Visual C++, you should check to make sure that you have the hardware and software required to install and run the product. The following are the minimum hardware requirements:

- An IBM-compatible personal computer, with a 80386 or later model processor

- 4MB of RAM (Microsoft recommends having 6MB or more, which will reduce the amount of page swapping to the disk and allow the software to run faster)

- A VGA or higher-resolution video controller and monitor

- A hard disk, with sufficient free space (when you install Visual C++, the setup program displays the total free space on your disk and the exact amount of free space required for the setup configuration you have chosen; the default setup configuration for the Professional Edition requires approximately 50MB)

- A high-density floppy drive (5¼" 1.2MB, or 3½" 1.44MB, depending upon which size disks are included in your Visual C++ package)

- A mouse or similar pointing device

The following are the minimum software requirements for installing and running Visual C++:

- MS-DOS version 5.0 or later
- Microsoft Windows (or Windows for Workgroups) version 3.1 or later; you must run Windows in enhanced mode
- You must install the MS-DOS SHARE program in order to run the Microsoft Visual Workbench; you can do this by including the following line in your AUTOEXEC.BAT file:

    `C:\DOS\SHARE`

    (This line assumes that SHARE.EXE is in the \DOS directory on drive C:. If SHARE.EXE is in a different directory in your system, substitute the correct path.)

To increase the speed of the installation process, you should set the number of MS-DOS buffers to 30 or more. Microsoft also recommends setting the number of files to at least 50. Including the following lines in your CONFIG.SYS file sets the number of buffers to 30 and the number of files to 50:

```
BUFFERS=30
FILES=50
```

Also, the installation will be faster if Microsoft SMARTDrive (provided with Windows), or an equivalent disk-caching program, is installed, and read-caching is enabled for the floppy drive used to install the Visual C++ disks. Including the following line in your AUTOEXEC.BAT file installs SMARTDrive and enables read-caching on all floppy drives:

`C:\WINDOWS\SMARTDRV.EXE`

This example assumes that Windows is installed in the directory C:\WINDOWS. For more information on SMARTDrive, see the *User's Guide* manual included with Windows (Chapter 14, "Optimizing Windows").

Running Setup

To install Visual C++, place the Visual C++ distribution disk labeled "Disk 1— Setup" in a disk drive. Next, in either the Windows Program Manager or Windows

File Manager, choose the Run... command on the File menu. When the Run dialog box appears, enter the following into the Command Line: text box:

A:\SETUP

If the distribution disk is in a drive other than A, substitute the correct drive letter. Once the Setup program begins running, the installation proceeds as follows:

1. The Welcome dialog box appears. While this dialog box is displayed, you can press F1 or click the Help button to view online help describing the dialog box and the installation process. Note that when any of the other dialog boxes is displayed during the installation, you can use this same method to access help that is pertinent to the particular dialog box. Click the Continue button in the Welcome dialog box to proceed with the installation.

2. A message box appears. This dialog box displays some suggestions for enhancing the speed of the installation process. These suggestions were described at the end of the previous section. Click the OK button to continue.

3. The Installation Options dialog box appears. This dialog box, as displayed by the Visual C++ Professional Edition, is shown in Figure 1.1. The dialog box contains a set of check boxes that allow you to choose which of the main Visual C++ components will be installed. These components are briefly described in the next section. By default, all main components are selected. The Installation Options dialog box also displays disk information, including the amount of free space on the proposed installation disk, and the amount of space required for the installation configuration that is currently selected.

4. If you want to change the disk on which the product is installed, or if you want to change the directories in which specific components are installed, click the Directories... button, and specify the desired target locations.

5. If you want to accept the default installation configuration, simply click the Continue button. If you have sufficient hard disk space, it is easiest to accept the default installation; this will ensure that you have all of the tools that are discussed in this book and that are required to build the sample programs provided on the companion disk.

6. If you want to customize the installation, choose the main components that you want to install by selecting the corresponding check boxes in the Installation Options dialog box. If you select the Run-Time Libraries, Sample Source

FIGURE 1.1:

FIGURE 1.1:

The Installation Options dialog box for the Visual C++ Professional Edition

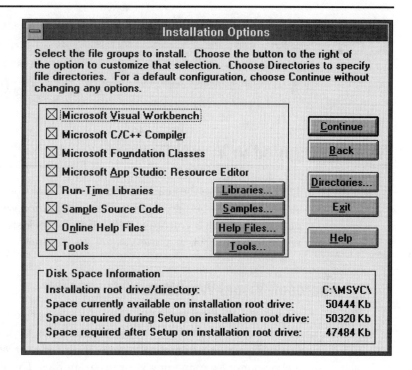

Code, Online Help Files, or Tools check box, you can also click the corresponding button to specify the exact list of items that is to be included. For example, if you select the Run-Time Libraries button to install the code for the run-time library functions, you can click the Libraries... button to specify which versions of the library you want included. The information given in the next section of this chapter will help you make your choices. When you have finished selecting the desired configuration, click the Continue button.

7. Setup prompts you for your name and the name of your organization.

8. Setup creates directories on the target drive and copies all of the Visual C++ files, prompting you each time you need to insert the next distribution disk in the floppy drive.

If you later need to install any additional components, you can simply run Setup again, specifying only the desired components. (You must run Setup rather than copying files directly from the distribution disk, because these files are in a compressed format.)

TIP
For up-to-date information on setting up and using Visual C++, click the Read Me icon that is installed in the Microsoft Visual C++ group of the Program Manager. This will run the Microsoft TechNote Viewer and allow you to access a variety of documentation files.

What Is Included in Visual C++

This section describes each of the main Visual C++ components that may be installed using the Setup program. This information will help you decide which components to install if you are specifying a custom installation, and it will also provide you with an overview of the Visual C++ product.

Microsoft Visual Workbench

The Visual Workbench is the Visual C++ integrated development environment. It provides an editor for entering program source code, *Wizards* (*AppWizard* and *ClassWizard*) for automatically generating code for Windows programs, and a project manager for managing your program files. The Visual Workbench permits you to build and debug programs, as well as to browse through the program source code. The Visual Workbench is introduced in Chapter 2, and it is used throughout the remainder of the book.

Microsoft C/C++ Compiler

You must, of course, install the actual Visual C++ compiler. You generally run the compiler, linker, and other Visual C++ tools *through* the Visual Workbench. (You can, however, run them directly from the MS-DOS command line, although this method is not discussed in the book.)

Microsoft Foundation Classes

The Microsoft Foundation Classes (which will be referred to as the MFC) is an extensive C++ class library designed for creating Windows programs. The MFC simplifies writing Windows programs, and it provides many high-level features that can save you coding effort. Although you can build Windows programs in C or C++ *without* using the MFC, this book (in Part III) teaches Windows programming *with* the MFC.

Microsoft App Studio: Resource Editor

The App Studio is a single, integrated tool for creating all types of resources for Windows programs, such as menus, dialog boxes, and icons. The App Studio works closely with the Visual Workbench (and the ClassWizard code-generating tool) to incorporate resources into your Windows programs. The App Studio is introduced in Chapter 7 and is used throughout the remainder of Part III of the book.

Run-Time Libraries

A run-time library contains the code for the standard run-time functions, such as `strcmp` and `sprintf`, which can be called from C or C++ programs. The library is supplied in several versions. You can specify exactly which versions are installed by clicking the Libraries... button in the Installation Options dialog box and choosing the desired library options. To build the example programs given in this book, you should choose the following options in addition to any other options you select:

- The *Medium* memory model
- The *Windows .EXE Files* and *QuickWin .EXE Files* targets (QuickWin programs are explained in Chapter 20). Also, if you have the Professional Edition of Microsoft Visual C++, select the MS-DOS.EXE files target (for building the example program in Chapter 20).
- A math support option (*Emulation* math support is selected by default)

Sample Source Code

Visual C++ includes a large collection of example programs. You can choose which sets of example programs are installed by clicking the Samples... button in the Installation Options dialog box and choosing the desired types of programs.

Online Help Files

Visual C++ provides extensive online help information. As mentioned in the Introduction, this book makes frequent references to specific topics within the online documentation; Chapter 2 explains exactly how to access online help through the Visual Workbench.

You can specify which help files are installed by clicking the Help Files... button in the Installation Options dialog box and selecting the appropriate check boxes.

> **NOTE**   Although the online help includes most of the reference material required to program in Visual C++, it does not provide much of the information that is discussed in the Visual C++ manuals. For example, it does not include a complete description of the C++ language.

Tools

The Visual C++ Professional Edition provides an additional set of programming tools. Some of these tools run under Windows, while others run under MS-DOS. To choose the specific tools that are installed, click the Tools... button in the Installation Options dialog box, and then select the desired tools in the Tool Options dialog box. For a brief description of the tools, press F1 or click the Help button in the Tool Options dialog box. Note that you do not need any of these tools to build the example programs in this book.

An Overview of Visual C++

Table 1.1 summarizes the features of the main Visual C++ components that were discussed in this section. For each component, it provides the following information:

- Whether the component is included in the Visual C++ Standard Edition

- The target environment of the programs that are created using the component (Windows, QuickWin, or MS-DOS)

- Whether the component is required either for building the example programs given in the book or for working through the techniques that are presented

TABLE 1.1: Basic Components of Visual C++

Component	In Standard Edition?	Target Environment(s)	Required for Book?	Discussed in Chapter(s):
Visual Workbench	Yes	All	Yes	2, 7
C/C++ Compiler	Yes (but not optimizing)	All	Yes	2, 7
Microsoft Foundation Classes	Yes	Windows (primarily)	Yes	7–19 (Part III)
App Studio	Yes	Windows	Yes	7–19 (Part III)
Run-Time Libraries	Yes	All (each target requires special version)	Yes (Medium memory model version)	Discussed throughout book
Sample Source Code	Yes (but not Windows C Samples)	Windows, QuickWin	No	Not discussed
Online Help Files	Yes (but not Pen/ Multimedia Help)	Windows, QuickWin, MS-DOS	No	2
Tools	No	Windows, QuickWin, MS-DOS	No	Not discussed

- The chapter or chapters in the book containing the primary discussion on the component

Installing the Companion Disk

The following are the requirements for installing the companion disk that is supplied with this book:

- You must have 800KB of free space on the hard disk on which you install the disk.

- You need a 5¼" 1.2MB floppy drive. If you have only a 3½" drive, see the instructions printed opposite the disk envelope for obtaining a copy of the companion disk in the 3½" format.

- To build the example programs on the disk, you must install all of the Visual C++ components that are specified as "Required for Book" in Table 1.1.

The companion disk contains all of the files needed to create the example programs presented in the book. It includes all of the source files given in the numbered listings (such as Listing 2.1), plus all of the project (.MAK), resource (.RC), module-definition (.DEF), icon (.ICO), bitmap (.BMP), and other auxiliary files used in building the example programs.

To copy the files from the companion disk to your hard disk, do the following:

1. Insert the companion disk in a floppy disk drive.

2. From the Windows Program Manager or File Manager, choose the Run command on the File menu. Windows will display the Run dialog box.

3. If you placed the companion disk in drive A, type the following line into the Command Line: text box, and click the OK button:

   A:\INSTALL

   If you placed the companion disk in a different drive, substitute the appropriate letter. The Install program will begin running.

4. By default, Install will copy the source files to the directory C:\PMVC. If you want to copy them to a different directory, enter the *full path name* (including the drive) for that directory into the Target Directory: text box within the Install window.

5. Click the OK button in the Install window.

> **NOTE** The files on the companion disk are compressed. The Install program expands each file as it copies it to the target directory. If you want to copy one or more individual files from the companion disk, you can use the Microsoft EXPAND utility included with Windows 3.1. For instructions on using EXPAND, simply run the program from the MS-DOS command line *without* including parameters, and it will display explanatory information.

The Install program copies the source and executable files for each example program to a separate subdirectory within the target directory that you specified. Normally, the name of a subdirectory is the same as the name of the program it contains; for example, if you accept the default target directory (C:\PMVC), Install copies the files for the GREET program given in Chapter 2 to the directory C:\PMVC\GREET.

If, however, there are several versions of a program, Install copies the files for each version into a separate subdirectory; for example, it copies the files for the first version of the MINIDRAW program into C:\PMVC\MINIDRW1, and the files for the second version into C:\PMVC\MINIDRW2. Also, *all* numbered listings from the introduction to C++ in Part II of the book are copied to a single directory, C:\PMVC\CPP (the files in this part do not constitute complete programs).

Summary

This chapter explained how to install both the Microsoft Visual C++ product and the companion disk provided with this book. It listed the hardware and software requirements for installing Visual C++ and the companion disk, and it described the steps required to install both items. It also provided an overview of the components of Visual C++.

The next chapter introduces the Microsoft Visual Workbench, by showing you how to use this integrated development environment to create a simple Windows program.

Creating a Program Using the Visual Workbench

- Running the Visual Workbench

- Creating the project

- Editing the source file

- Setting build options

- Building, Running, and Debugging the program

The Visual Workbench is an integrated development environment that runs as a Windows application and serves as the primary interface for accessing the development tools supplied by Microsoft Visual C++. You can use it to manage programming projects, to create and edit program source files, to generate prewritten code for Windows programs (using the *wizards*), to build and debug programs, and to browse through program symbols. It also works closely with the App Studio, which is used for designing Windows resources. (The wizards and the App Studio are discussed in Part III of the book.)

This chapter introduces you to the Visual Workbench by guiding you through the steps required to build a very simple program. The knowledge you gain here will allow you to enter and run the example code as well as to create simple test programs, while you are reading through the introduction to the C++ language given in Part II of the book. Part III provides detailed information on using the Visual Workbench to create Windows programs, and Part VI explains using the Visual Workbench to generate MS-DOS and QuickWin programs.

Running the Visual Workbench

When you install Visual C++, the Setup program creates a group in the Windows Program Manager named *Microsoft Visual C++*. To run the Visual Workbench, double-click the *Visual C++* icon within this group, as shown below.

Getting Help

Throughout this book, there are many references to the Visual C++ online help. Many of these references cite both a help *file* and a help *topic*. To access the cited information, do the following:

1. On the Visual C++ Help menu, choose the command that corresponds to the cited help file (each command on this menu opens a specific help file). The Windows Help window will appear, displaying a table of contents for the help file.

2. If the reference in the book does *not* cite a particular help topic, you can choose pertinent topics from the table of contents. If it does cite a specific topic, proceed with the following steps.

3. Click the Search button at the top of the Help window, or press the S key. Help will display the Search dialog box.

4. The help topic cited in the book is actually the *search key* for the desired topic. Enter it exactly as it is given in the book into the text box at the top of the Search dialog box. (With each letter you type, Help selects the closest matching key within the list under the text box; you can stop typing as soon as the desired key is selected in this list.)

5. Press Enter or click the Show Topics button. One or more topic titles will appear in the list at the bottom of the Search dialog box, and the first topic will be selected; if necessary, select the desired topic. Press Enter again or click the Go To button. (Usually, step 5 can be accomplished by simply pressing Enter twice.)

For example, a note in Chapter 3 refers you to the *C/C++ Language* online help file and the "new operator, customizing" topic. To access this information, choose the C/C++ Language command on the Visual Workbench Help menu, type S, type "new o" (the "new operator, customizing" key will now be selected in the list), and press Enter twice.

Creating the Project

Once the Visual Workbench begins running, the first step is to create a *project* for the program you are about to write. A Visual Workbench project stores all the information required to build a particular program. This information includes the names and relationships of the program source files; a list of the required library files; a list of all options for the compiler, linker, and other tools used in building the program; and the settings for Visual Workbench options that you use while working on the program.

In this chapter, you will write an example C++ program named GREET. To create a project for this program, perform the following steps:

1. Using the Windows File Manager or other file utility, create a disk directory for storing the project files. For example, you might create the directory C:\SAMPLES\GREET.

2. Choose the New... command on the Visual Workbench project menu. The New Project dialog box will appear.

3. In the New Project dialog box, click the Browse... button. In the Browse dialog box, choose the directory that you created in step 1, and enter the program name, GREET, into the File Name: text box. When you are done, click the OK button.

4. Back in the New Project dialog box, select the QuickWin application (.EXE) project type from the Project Type list. The item you select in this list specifies the general category of the program that you are creating. A Quick-Win application is one that can be written like a text-mode MS-DOS program and yet runs within a window as a Windows application. QuickWin programs are fully described in Chapter 20. Later in the book, you will also learn about several of the other project types. The completed New Project dialog box is shown in Figure 2.1.

5. Click the OK button in the New Project dialog box; the Edit project dialog box will now appear. In this dialog box, the directory you selected in step 3 will already be selected.

FIGURE 2.1:

The New Project dialog box

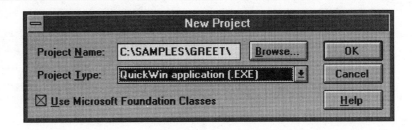

6. Enter the name of the program source file, GREET.CPP, into the File Name: text box within the Edit project dialog box, and click the Add button. The full path name of the file will then appear in the Files in Project: list at the bottom of the dialog box. The completed Edit project dialog box is shown in Figure 2.2. Because GREET.CPP is the only source file for the GREET program, you can now click the Close button to remove the dialog box.

FIGURE 2.2:

The Edit project dialog box

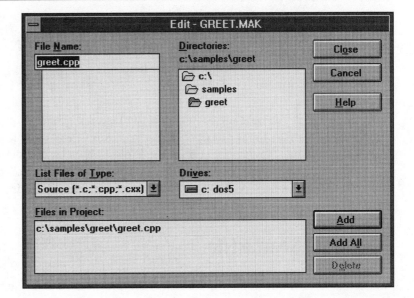

> **NOTE**
>
> Even though the file GREET.CPP does not yet exist, you can add it to the project (of course, it must exist before you can build the program). Most of the example programs given later in the book consist of more than one source file. You can later remove or add source files to a project by choosing the Edit command on the Project menu.

After you have created the new project using these steps, the new project is automatically *opened* within the Visual Workbench (only one project can be open at a given time). As a result, this project will be affected by commands on the Project menu (such as the Build command, which builds the program), and any settings you make through the Options menu will be stored within this project.

> **NOTE**
>
> The Visual Workbench permanently stores most of the project information within the file GREET.MAK, which is known as the *project file*. It also stores the current settings for Visual Workbench options, as well as the current Visual Workbench window setup, in two additional files, GREET.VCW and GREET.WSP, so that these settings can be restored when you reopen the project. These files are all saved in the directory that you selected when you created the project (in step 3 above).

If you quit and then restart the Visual Workbench, it will automatically reopen the project that was open when you quit. If you close the GREET project (by choosing the Close command on the Project menu or by opening another project), you can later reopen it so that you can continue working on the program, by choosing the Open... command on the Project menu and selecting the GREET.MAK project file.

Editing the Source File

The next step is to create the program source file. To do this, choose the New command on the Visual C++ File menu. Visual C++ will open a child window containing an empty, untitled file. Type the following C++ source code into this window:

Listing 2.1

```
// GREET.CPP: The C++ source code for the GREET program.

#include <iostream.h>

char Name [16];

void main ()
   {
   cout << "enter your name: ";
   cin.get (Name, sizeof (Name));
   cout << "\ngreetings, " << Name;
   }
```

Many of the Visual Workbench editing commands should already be familiar to you if you have used other Windows editors (such as Notepad) or other editors that conform to the Common User Access standard (such as the Programmer's Workbench, provided with previous versions of Microsoft C and C++). Table 2.1 summarizes most of the important editing keystrokes. For a complete description of the Visual C++ editing commands and features, see the *Visual Workbench User's Guide* manual (primarily Chapters 5, 6, and 7), or the *Visual Workbench* online help file.

TABLE 2.1: Summary of Visual Workbench Editing Keystrokes

Move the Insertion Point	Keystroke
One character back	←
One character forward	→
One line up	↑
One line down	↓
One word forward	Ctrl+→
One word back	Ctrl+←
To first character in line	Home
To column 1	Home, then Home
One screen up	PgUp
One screen down	PgDn
To beginning of file	Ctrl+Home
To end of file	Ctrl+End

TABLE 2.1: Summary of Visual Workbench Editing Keystrokes (continued)

Select	Keystroke
Any text	Shift + one of the movement keystrokes given above
Cut, Copy, Paste, and Delete Selected Text	**Keystroke**
Copy text to Clipboard and delete it (Cut)	Ctrl+X, Shift+Del
Copy text to Clipboard (Copy)	Ctrl+C, Ctrl+Ins
Paste text from Clipboard (Paste)	Ctrl+V, Shift+Ins
Delete selected text	Del
Delete character to right of insertion point	Del
Delete character to left of insertion point	Backspace
Toggle insert mode	Ins
Undo	**Keystroke**
Undo previous edit	Ctrl+Z, Alt+Backspace
Redo previous edit	Ctrl+A
Tabs	**Keystroke**
Insert tab character (or spaces)	Tab
Move to previous tab position	Shift+Tab
Move several lines one tab to right	Select lines and then press Tab
Move several line one tab to left	Select lines and then press Shift+Tab
Toggle display of tab characters	Ctrl+Alt+T
Find	**Keystroke**
Find text using Find list box	Ctrl+F, enter text, then press Enter or F3
Open Find dialog box	Alt+F3
Find selected text	Ctrl+F3
Find next occurrence	F3
Find previous occurrence	Shift+F3
Find next build error	F4
Find previous build error	Shift+F4
Find matching brace	Place insertion point in front of brace and press Ctrl+]

TABLE 2.1: Summary of Visual Workbench Editing Keystrokes (continued)

Bookmarks	Keystroke
Toggle bookmark on/off	Ctrl+F2
Go to next bookmark	F2
Go to previous bookmark	Shift+F2

Windows	Keystroke
Go to next window	F6
Go to previous window	Shift+F6
Close active window	Ctrl+F4

When you have finished typing in the source code, save the file by choosing the Save or Save As command on the File menu, or by clicking the Save File button shown below. The directory that you specified when you created the project should already be selected within the Save As dialog box. (If this directory is *not* selected, be sure to select it now so that the source file will be stored in the same directory as the other project files.) Enter the file name GREET.CPP into the File Name: text box, and click the OK button. (You must name the file GREET.CPP, because this name was already added to the project.) The .CPP file extension tells the compiler to compile the source code as a C++ program.

Save File

The GREET program uses the C++ *iostream* library. This library provides a comprehensive collection of predefined classes, which QuickWin and MS-DOS programs written in C++ can use for performing basic input and output. C++ classes are explained in Chapter 4, and the iostream library is described in Chapter 21.

The program includes the IOSTREAM.H header file, which contains declarations that are required for using the iostream library. The statement

```
cout << "enter your name: ";
```

displays the string "enter your name: " within the program window. The << operator in this expression is said to be *overloaded*, signifying that it has a special meaning within this context. Overloaded operators are explained in Chapter 6.

The statement

```
cin.get (Name, sizeof (Name));
```

then reads the characters that the user types, and stores them in the character array Name. The first parameter passed to get is the receiving buffer, and the second parameter is the size of this buffer (get is known as a *member function*; member functions are explained in Chapter 4).

Finally, the statement

```
cout << "\ngreetings, " << Name;
```

displays (at the start of a new line in the window) the string "greetings ", followed by the characters that the user entered.

TIP

While the project file and C++ source code file for the GREET program are included in the \GREET subdirectory within the directory in which you installed the companion disk, you will probably find it more instructional to create your own project within a separate directory and manually type in the source code.

Setting Build Options

Before building the program, you will set several options that affect the way the program is built. To do this, choose the Project... command on the Options menu. The Project Options dialog box will appear, as shown in Figure 2.3.

First, the Project Options dialog box allows you to select either the *Debug* or the *Release* build mode. If you select the Debug mode, the Visual Workbench will use a set of compiler and linker options for generating a version of the program that can be debugged with the integrated debugger. Normally, you select this mode while you are developing and testing the program. If you select the Release mode, the Visual Workbench will use a set of options for generating the final, fully optimized version

The Project Options dialog box

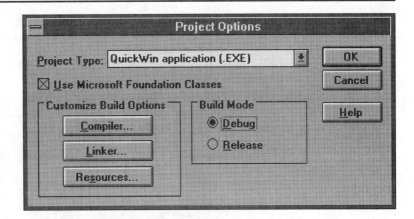

of the program. Because you will be debugging the program later in the chapter, be sure to choose the Debug mode now.

Notice that the QuickWin application (.EXE) project type, which you specified when you created the project, is selected within the Project Type list at the top of the Project Options dialog box. (The Visual Workbench allows you to select a different project type within this list, but you should not do so for the GREET program.) When you first specify a project type, the Visual Workbench chooses a set of default options (for the compiler, linker, and other tools) that are appropriate for generating a program of that type. You can subsequently change any of these options by clicking the appropriate button in the Customize Build Options group. You can click the Compiler... or Linker... button to change the compiler or linker options, or click the Resources... button to change the resource compiler options. (The resource compiler is used to process resources for Windows programs, such as menus, icons, and dialog boxes.)

To gain some practice in setting options, click the Compiler... button. When the C/C++ Compiler Options dialog box appears, choose the Custom Options item in the Category: list at the left of the dialog box. Then, select the Warnings as Errors check box. Choosing this option causes the compiler to treat a warning message (for example, a warning that a local parameter is unused) as an error; accordingly, when a warning condition occurs, the build process stops and you do not have to wait for the executable program to be generated before you can tend to the problem. The completed dialog box is shown in Figure 2.4. Click the OK button in the C/C++

FIGURE 2.4:

The C/C++ Compiler Options
dialog box

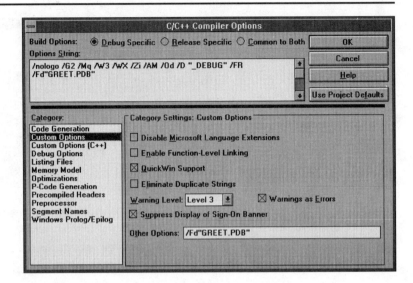

FIGURE 2.4:

The C/C++ Compiler Options
dialog box

Compiler Options dialog box and then click the OK button in the Project Options
dialog box.

Any option you select through the Project Options dialog box is permanently saved
as part of the project (until you explicitly change the option).

> **NOTE** The set of options that you can change through the Project Options dialog box
> depends upon whether you have the Professional Edition or the Standard
> Edition of Visual C++. (Figure 2.4 shows the Compiler Options dialog box for the
> Professional Edition.)

Building the Program

When you are ready to build the program, choose the Build GREET.EXE command
on the Project menu, press Shift+F8, or click the Build button shown below. The Visual Workbench will display a message box stating that the project has changed and
asking whether you would like to build the affected files; click the Yes button to begin the build.

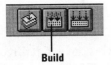

Build

NOTE If a program consists of several source files, the Visual Workbench normally processes only the files that have changed since the last time you built the program. If, however, you have changed one or more project options (for example, switching from the debug to the release build mode, or changing a compiler option), the Visual Workbench will display a message box indicating that the project has changed; if you click the Yes button in this box, it will rebuild all affected program files. You can also force the Visual Workbench to rebuild *all* files in the project by choosing the Rebuild All command on the Project menu, pressing Alt+F8, or clicking the Build All button shown below.

Build All

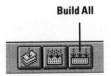

While it is building the program, the Visual Workbench displays the results of each step of the build process within a separate window, which is labeled "Output." The Visual Workbench displays any error or warning messages within this window, and when the build has been completed (successfully or unsuccessfully), it beeps and displays the total number of errors and warnings.

If an error or warning message is displayed in the output window, you can locate the source line that caused the problem by simply double-clicking on the line that contains the message in the output window. Alternatively, you can press F4 (or choose the Next Error command on the View menu) to view the *next* error that occurred when building the program, and you can click Shift+F4 (or choose Previous Error on the View menu) to view the *previous* error. You might want to introduce an error into the GREET.CPP file and rebuild the program to experiment with these features.

Running the Program

After the program has been built successfully, you can run it directly from the Visual Workbench by choosing the Execute GREET.EXE command on the Project menu, or by pressing Ctrl+F5. You can also run it using any of the standard methods for running a Windows program (for example, by double-clicking on the GREET.EXE file name within the Windows File Manager). Figure 2.5 shows the GREET program window after it has finished running.

FIGURE 2.5:

The GREET program

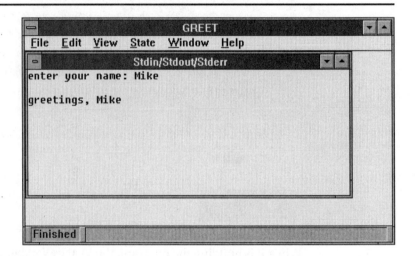

Debugging the Program

One of the most useful features of the Visual Workbench is the integrated debugger, which allows you to quickly and easily debug your programs while you are developing them. This section presents a simple exercise using the GREET program to introduce you to this debugger.

Table 2.2 summarizes most of the important debugging keystrokes. For a complete description of all of the debugger commands and features, see the *Visual Workbench User's Guide* manual (Chapter 11, "Debugging Programs"), or the *Visual Workbench* online help file (several topics discuss the debugger).

TABLE 2.2: Summary of Visual Workbench Debugging Keystrokes

Debugging Action	Keystroke
Toggle breakpoint on line with insertion point	F9
Run program from beginning	Shift+F5
Resume execution from current statement	F5
Execute next statement; include statements within functions (step into)	F8
Execute next statement; skip statements within functions (step over)	F10
Run program, then break at position of insertion point (step to cursor)	F7
Run program until reaching first statement outside of current function (step out)	Shift+F7
Quickly view or modify a variable	Shift+F9
Quickly modify a variable	Ctrl+F9
View call stack	Ctrl+K
End debugging session	Alt+F5

NOTE   The Professional Edition of Visual C++ also includes the CodeView for Windows and CodeView for MS-DOS debuggers (as provided with previous versions of Microsoft C and C++). The Visual Workbench integrated debugger provides almost all of the features of CodeView for Windows, however, and for debugging Windows programs it is more convenient to use.

To get started with the Visual Workbench debugger, perform the following steps:

1. If it is not already open, open the GREET project by choosing the Open... command on the Project menu and selecting the file GREET.MAK.

2. Make sure that you have built the *debug* version of the GREET program. (Choose the Project... command on the Options menu; if the Debug build mode is not selected, select it now and rebuild the program following the instructions given previously.)

3. If it is not already open, open the file GREET.CPP by choosing the Open...
command on the File menu, or by clicking the Open Project File button,
shown below.

Open Project File

4. Choose the Watch command on the Window menu. This will open the Watch
window, which permits you to view the value of any program variable as the
program runs.

5. Choose the Tile command on the Window menu so that both the GREET.CPP
window and the Watch window will be visible.

6. Place the caret on the first line within the main function of GREET.CPP,

```
cout << "enter your name: ";
```

and press F9 or click the Breakpoint button shown below. This will place a
breakpoint on the line; as a result, when you run the program in the debugger,
the program will stop running immediately before executing the code in this
line. To indicate the presence of the breakpoint, the line is highlighted (the default highlight color is red, although you can change the color). Note that if
you press F9 or click the Breakpoint button again, while the caret is still on
the line, the breakpoint is removed.

Breakpoint

NOTE   Following the convention used by the Windows programming interface, the book
uses the term *caret* to refer to the blinking vertical line indicating the text
insertion point, and it uses the terms *cursor* or *pointer* to refer to the mouse
pointer.

7. Choose the Go command on the Debug menu, press F5, or click the Go button (the icon shown below) to begin running the program within the debugger. The GREET program window will appear on the screen (although it may be covered by the Visual Workbench window). The GREET program will stop running immediately before it executes the line containing the breakpoint, and control will return to the debugger. Note that the breakpoint line is now highlighted in yellow to indicate that it is the *next* line that will be executed. (The next line to be executed is known as the *current line*; by default, it is highlighted in yellow, although you can change this color.)

Go

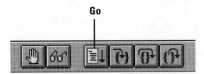

8. You will now begin monitoring the contents of the variable Name, the global character array defined in GREET.CPP. To do this, move the caret to the upper-left corner of the Watch window (for example, by clicking on this spot), type Name, and press Enter. The Watch window will display the array address, but will not immediately display the values of the array elements. To view the elements, move the caret back up to the top line and press Enter again to *expand* the variable so that the values of all members are displayed (as shown in Figure 2.6). Notice that because Name is a global variable, it is initialized to 0.

9. You will now begin single-stepping through the code (that is, executing the code one line at a time). To start, press F10 or click the Step Over button (shown below) to execute the current line. If the GREET window is visible, you will see the prompt string appear in the window. (If the window is initially invisible but you then switch to it, you will *not* see the string, because the program is suspended and therefore cannot redraw its window.) Notice that the second line of code has now become the current line.

Step Over

FIGURE 2.6:

The Watch window displaying the
Name array

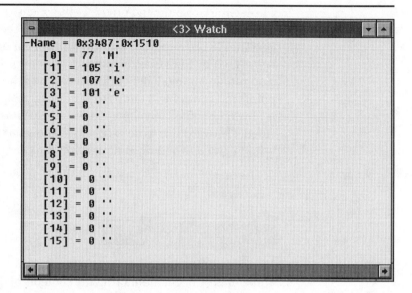

```
 ▭                    <3> Watch                    ▾ ▴
─Name  =  0x3487:0x1510
    [0]  =  77  'M'
    [1]  =  105  'i'
    [2]  =  107  'k'
    [3]  =  101  'e'
    [4]  =  0  ' '
    [5]  =  0  ' '
    [6]  =  0  ' '
    [7]  =  0  ' '
    [8]  =  0  ' '
    [9]  =  0  ' '
    [10]  =  0  ' '
    [11]  =  0  ' '
    [12]  =  0  ' '
    [13]  =  0  ' '
    [14]  =  0  ' '
    [15]  =  0  ' '

 ◄ ▭                                              ►
```

10. Press F10 or click the Step Over button to execute another line of code. When the program executes the next statement—cin.get (Name, sizeof (Name));—it pauses until you enter a name. Therefore, you must now switch to the GREET program window, enter a name, and press Enter. After you press Enter, control returns to the debugger. Notice that the third line of code has now become the current line. Also, observe in the Watch window that Name now contains the string that you just typed.

11. The Watch window also allows you to *alter* the value of a variable. To demonstrate this, move the caret to the Watch window, erase the numeric value for one of the characters contained in Name, type a new number, and press Enter.

12. Choose the Go command on the Debug menu, press F5, or click the Go button to resume execution of the program. The program now displays the Name string, as you just altered it, within the GREET window.

13. Terminate the GREET program (for example, by choosing the Exit command on the File menu). Control now returns to the debugger, which displays a message box indicating that the process has terminated normally.

Once you have finished developing a program, and have debugged and tested it, you will probably want to generate the *release* version, which will be fully optimized and will be contained in a much smaller .EXE file. (The executable file will no longer need to store the debugging information.)

Summary

In this chapter, you learned how to use the Visual Workbench to perform the following tasks:

- To create a *project*, which stores all the information required to develop and build a program
- To enter and edit a program source file
- To set a variety of options that affect the way a program is built
- To build a program
- To run a program
- To debug a program

You can use the simple GREET program that you created in this chapter while you are working through the introduction to C++ in Part II of the book. Whenever you want to enter some example code, or test some code of your own, you can open the GREET.MAK project and modify the GREET.CPP source file. You can then rebuild the program and run it, and the program output will appear in a window on the Windows desktop.

PART II

Introduction to C++

This part of the book introduces the basic concepts of the C++ language as it is implemented in Microsoft Visual C++. The techniques given in these chapters are general; they can be used for Windows, QuickWin, or MS-DOS programming.

Chapter 3 shows you how to make the transition from C to C++. It explains how to convert your C programs to C++, how to begin writing new programs in C++, and how to use many of the simple but helpful enhancements that C++ adds to the C language. The remaining chapters in this part introduce C++ classes, together with the features that depend upon classes. The C++ *class*, which allows you to encapsulate code and data, is the most important new feature of C++ as an object-oriented language. Chapter 4 explains how to define and use classes. Chapter 5 shows how to derive new classes from existing ones, so that you can easily reuse and adapt classes for specific types of objects and efficiently manage hierarchies of related objects. Finally, Chapter 6 explains how to customize the behavior of your classes; specifically, it shows how to define the way that standard C++ operators work with class objects, the way that class objects are initialized, and the way that other data types are converted to class objects.

Although the concepts and techniques presented here apply equally to Windows, QuickWin, and MS-DOS programming, for the sake of simplicity the code examples are written for the QuickWin or MS-DOS target environments. If you want to experiment with a particular C++ feature, you can run the Visual Workbench and open the GREET.MAK project you created in Chapter 2. You can then enter the example code—or your own code—into the GREET.CPP source file and build the program as explained in Chapter 2. (Alternatively, if you have the Professional Edition of Microsoft Visual C++, you can build an MS-DOS program.) Note that the source file for each of the numbered listings given in this part of the book (such as Listing 4.1) is contained in the \CPP subdirectory within the directory in which you installed the companion disk.

Moving to C++

- Converting from C to C++

- New features of C++

This chapter is designed to help you make the transition from C programming to C++ programming. It shows you how to convert your existing C programs, as well as your C programming habits, to C++. It then shows you how to take advantage of some of the convenient new features of C++. The chapter, however, stops short of presenting C++ classes or any of the features that require classes. It may take you a while to master the effective use of classes and restructure your programs to take advantage of them. In the meanwhile, the information given here will allow you to get started quickly by using C++ as simply an enhanced version of C.

Converting from C to C++

If you have written a C program, you have probably already written your first C++ program! With few exceptions, C++ is a superset of C; that is, C++ supports almost all of the features of the C language *in addition to* the many new features that it offers. Therefore, to get started with C++, you can simply compile your existing C programs, as well as the new programs you write, using the C++ compiler rather than the C compiler. You can then gradually begin adding to your code various features that are unique to C++.

To begin using the C++ compiler, you need only name your source file with the .CPP or .CXX extension, rather than the .C extension. There are, however, several programming practices permitted in most versions of C that will not compile using the C++ compiler, or that will compile with C++ but with an altered meaning. The following is a list of some of the most important C constructs that do not work with C++:

- In C, you can freely use any of the following names as identifiers; in C++, however, these are keywords and therefore *you cannot* use them as identifiers:

```
asm
catch
class
delete
friend
inline
new
operator
private
protected
```

```
public
template
this
throw
try
virtual
```

- In C, you are permitted to call a function that is not preceded by the function declaration or definition (although doing so may generate a warning message). In C++, however, the function declaration or definition *must* precede any call to the function within the source file (otherwise, the compiler will generate an *undeclared identifier* error).

NOTE Throughout this book, the term *function declaration* refers to a declaration that specifies only the function name, the return type, and the types of the parameters, while the term *function definition* refers to a declaration that includes the complete function code. Note that both of these items can be described using the general term *declaration;* a declaration simply associates a name with a type.

- In C, you can declare a function that takes one or more parameters without listing these parameters, as in the following declaration:

```
int FuncX ();
```

In C++, however, such a declaration can be used only for a function that has *no* parameters.

- In C, you can use the "old style" function definition syntax, in which the types of the parameters *follow* the parameter list; for example:

```
int FuncX (A, B)    /* OK in C; an ERROR in C++ */
int A;
int B;
    {
    /* code for FuncX */
    return 0;
    }
```

In C++, however, this style is *not* permitted.

- In some versions of C, you can declare a global data object more than once in a given program, without using the extern specifier. In C++, however, you can declare a global data object only once without the extern specifier (to define the data item); all other declarations of the item must include the extern keyword (to make the item accessible within a given scope).

- In C (as defined by the ANSI standard), you can assign a void pointer to *any* pointer type; for example, the following code assigns a void pointer to an int pointer:

```
int A;
int *PInt;
void *PVoid = &A;

PInt = PVoid;   /* OK in C; an ERROR in C++ */
```

In C++, however, the assignment to PInt would generate an error, because the C++ compiler will *not* automatically convert a void pointer to another pointer type in an assignment expression. You could, however, use a cast operation to make the assignment:

```
PInt = (int *)PVoid;   /* OK in C and C++ */
```

- In C, an enum, struct, or union tag can be identical to a typedef name within the same scope. For example, the following code would compile successfully in C:

```
/* this code is OK in C, but erroneous in C++: */

typedef int TypeA;
struct TypeA
    {
    int I;
    char C;
    double D;
    };

typedef int TypeB;
union TypeB
    {
    int I;
    char C;
```

```
     double D;
     };

  typedef int TypeC;
  enum TypeC {Red, Green, Blue};
```

The C compiler is able to distinguish between the duplicate names because the enumeration, structure, or union is always referred to using the `enum`, `struct`, or `union` prefix, as in the following example:

```
/* this code is OK in C, but erroneous in C++: */

typedef int TypeA;
struct TypeA
   {
   int I;
   char C;
   double D;
   };

TypeA X;          /* creates an int */
struct TypeA Y;   /* creates a TypeA structure */

sizeof (TypeA);          /* yields size of an int */
sizeof (struct TypeA);   /* yields size of a TypeA structure */
```

In C++, however, an `enum`, `struct`, `union`, or `class` tag (which in C++ is usually called a *name* rather than a *tag*) must be *different* from any `typedef` name within the same scope. (A `class` is unique to C++; classes will be explained in Chapter 4.) The reason is that the definition creates a new type that you can refer to using the name alone; you are not required to use the `enum`, `struct`, `union`, or `class` prefix (although you can use it if you wish). This feature is illustrated in the following C++ code:

```
/* this code is erroneous in C, but OK in C++: */

struct TypeA
   {
   int I;
   char C;
   double D;
   };

struct TypeA X; /* creates a TypeA structure */
TypeA Y;        /* also creates a TypeA structure */
```

```
sizeof (struct TypeA); /* yields the size of the TypeA
                          structure */
sizeof (TypeA);        /* also yields the size of the TypeA
                          structure */
```

Therefore, if you created a `typedef` with the same name, the C++ compiler would not always be able to distinguish the two types, as shown in the following erroneous code:

```
typedef int TypeA;
struct TypeA /* C++ ERROR: redefinition of TypeA */
   {
   int I;
   char C;
   double D;
   };

TypeA X;    /* should this create an int or a TypeA structure? */
sizeof (X); /* should this yield the size of an int or the size
               of a TypeA structure? */
```

- The following incompatibility is related to the previous one: In C, if an `enum`, `struct`, or union tag is the same as a `typedef` name in an outer scope, you can still refer to the `typedef` within the inner scope (that is, the `typedef` is *not* hidden). In C++, however, the `typedef` name would be hidden. The following code illustrates the difference:

```
typedef int TypeA;

void main ()
   {
   struct TypeA
      {
      int I;
      char C;
      double D;
      };

   TypeA X;  /* in C, X is an int;
                in C++, X is a TypeA structure */

   sizeof (TypeA);  /* in C, yields the size of an int;
                       in C++, yields the size of a TypeA
                       struct */

   }
```

- There are two additional differences in values returned by the `sizeof` operator. First, in C, `sizeof ('x')` equals `sizeof (int)`, but in C++ it equals `sizeof (char)`. Second, assume that you have defined the enumerator

  ```
  enum E {X, Y, Z};
  ```

  In C, `sizeof (X)` equals `sizeof (int)`, but in C++ it equals `sizeof (E)`, which is not necessarily equal to `sizeof (int)`.

You will have to remove any of these incompatible constructs from an existing C program so that the code will compile—and have the same meaning—when using the C++ compiler. The C++ compiler will flag any of these incompatibilities except the last two. The last two (specifically, the differences in values supplied by the `sizeof` operator), do not generate compiler errors, but rather *change the meaning* of the program; they are exceptions to the general rule that if a program compiles successfully under either the C compiler or the C++ compiler, then it will have the same meaning in either language.

New Features of C++

This section describes several of the useful new features of C++ that do not pertain to classes. After reading this section, you might conclude that these features alone justify changing from C to C++. Some of these features are also provided by recent versions of C—specifically, the new comment style, inline functions, and constant types (although there may be syntactic differences from C++). The other features described here are unique to C++.

Comments

As an alternative to the standard comment delimiters (`/*` and `*/`) you can mark a single-line comment in a C++ program using the `//` character pair. All characters following the `//`, *through the end of the line*, are part of the comment and are ignored by the compiler.

```
void main ()  // this is a single-line comment
   {
```

```
/* you can use the traditional comment delimiters to mark a
   comment that encompasses more than one line ... */

// statements ...

}
```

Declaration Statements

In C, you must declare a local variable (that is, a variable defined within a function) at the beginning of a block, before any program statement. In C++, however, a declaration of a local variable is considered a normal program statement; you can therefore place it at any position where a statement can occur, provided that the declaration occurs before the variable is first referenced.

NOTE A *block* is a section of code that is delimited with the { and } characters. A variable defined within a given block can be referenced only within that block or within a nested block (unless it is hidden by an identically named variable within the nested block). That is, the block defines the *scope* of the variable.

Accordingly, in C++ you can make your code easier to read and maintain by placing the declaration for a variable immediately before the code that uses it, as in the following example:

```
void main ()
   {

   // other statements ...

   int Count = 0;
   while (++Count <= 100)
      {

      // loop statements ...

      }

   // other statements ...
```

```
    }
```

You can even declare a variable *within* a `for` statement:

```
// other statements ...

for (int i = 0; i < MAXLINES; ++i)
    {

    // other statements ...

    int Length = GetLineLength (i);
    if (Length == 0)
        break;

    // other statements ...

    }
if (i < MAXLINES)
    // then a 0 length line was encountered
```

In the above code, the declaration of the loop counter `i` occurs *outside* of the block that immediately follows the `for` statement; it can therefore be referenced after the `for` block. The variable `Length`, however, is declared *within* the `for` block, and can therefore be referenced only within this block.

If the declaration contains an initialization, the data item is initialized when the flow of program control reaches the declaration statement. Thus, in the example above, `i` is created and initialized once, whenever control reaches the `for` statement; `Length`, however, is created and initialized with each iteration of the `for` loop.

> **NOTE**   If a local variable is declared as `static`, it is created and initialized only once, the *first* time program control reaches the declaration statement.

Note that if a variable declaration contains an initialization, you must make sure that the declaration statement cannot be skipped. For example, the following `switch` construct generates an error:

```
switch (Code)
    {
```

```
case 1:
   // ...
   break;

case 2:
   int Count = 0;   // ERROR
   // ...
   break;

case 3:
   // ...
   break;
}
```

The compiler generates an error for the following reason: Count is initialized only if the case 2 branch of the switch statement receives control. If the case 3 branch received control and accessed Count, the variable would be uninitialized. (The case 3 branch has access to Count because the declaration precedes it within the same block. The compiler will generate an error even if the code in this branch does not actually reference Count; the fact that it *could* reference it is sufficient.) To eliminate this error, you could place the code for the case 2 branch within its own block, as follows:

```
case 2:
   {
   int Count = 0;
   // ...
   break;
   }
```

In this version of the switch statement, Count can be referenced only within the case 2 branch, after it has been initialized. Alternatively, you could eliminate the initialization from the declaration, and *assign* Count its initial value:

```
case 2:
   int Count;
   Count = 0;
   // ...
   break;
```

The Scope Resolution Operator

When you declare a variable in an inner scope that has the same name as a variable in an outer scope, the variable in the inner scope *hides* the one in the outer scope; that is, within the inner scope, the variable name refers to a different entity. For example, in the following code the int A declared within FuncB hides the double A declared outside of the function, causing the assignment within the function to change the value of the int variable rather than the double variable:

```
double A;

void main ()
   {
   int A;

   A = 5;    // assigns 5 to int A

   }
```

In C++, however, you can access a global variable (that is, one declared outside of any function), even if it is hidden by a local variable with the same name. To do this, you preface the variable name with the *scope resolution operator*, ::, as illustrated in the following code:

```
double A;  // global variable A

void main ()
   {
   int A;      // local variable A

   A = 5;      // assigns 5 to local int A
   ::A = 2.5  // assigns 2.5 to global double A

   }
```

Note that you can use the scope resolution operator to access only a global variable. You *cannot* use it to access a local variable declared within an enclosing block, as attempted in the following erroneous code:

```
void FuncX (int Code)
   {
   double A;

   if (Code == 1)
      {
```

```
    int A;

    // attempt to access double A in enclosing block:
    ::A = 2.5;   // ERROR: ::A specifies global A, which is an
                 // error if there is no variable A declared at
                 // global level
    // ...
    }
// ...
}
```

You can also use the scope resolution operator to access a global type or enumeration that is hidden by a local type or enumeration with the same name, as shown in the following example:

```
#include <iostream.h>

typedef int A;
enum {Red, White, Blue};

void main ()
    {
    typedef double A;
    enum {Blue, White, Red};

    cout << sizeof (A) << '\n';      // prints size of a double
    cout << sizeof (::A) << '\n';    // prints size of an int

    cout << (int)Blue << '\n';       // prints 0
    cout << (int)::Blue << '\n';     // prints 2
    }
```

NOTE   In the next two chapters, you will learn several additional uses of the scope resolution operator that pertain to C++ classes.

Inline Functions

If you declare a function using the `inline` keyword, such as the function

```
inline int FuncA (int X)
    {
```

```
// function code ...
}
```

the compiler will attempt to replace all calls to the function with the actual function code. Replacing a function call with a copy of the function code is known as *inline expansion* or *inlining*.

The definition of an inline function (that is, the declaration that includes the complete function code) must be present within every source file in which the function is called (the compiler must have immediate access to the code so that it can perform the inline expansion). To easiest way to ensure that an identical copy of the definition is available to each calling module is to define the function within a header file that you include within each source file. Unlike a non-inline function, if you change an inline function, all source files that call it must be recompiled.

> **NOTE**
>
> The `inline` directive does not guarantee that the function will be expanded inline. The compiler may need to generate a conventional function call in several situations—for example, if the function is recursive (that is, it calls itself), or if the function is called through a function pointer. Microsoft Visual C++ provides several compiler options that affect the handling of inline functions; to set these options, choose the Project... command on the Options menu, click the Compiler button..., and select the Optimizations item in the Category: list. Then choose the desired settings in the Inline Expansion of Functions: and Inline Function Size: lists; for information, click the Help button or press F1. You can also control inline expansion using the `auto_inline` pragma; for information o n this pragma, see the *C++ Language Reference* manual (Chapter 13, "Preprocessing") or the *C/C++ Language* online help files (the topic "auto_inline").

Making a function inline does not change its meaning; it merely affects the speed and size of the resulting code, generally increasing both. Accordingly, you might want to use the `inline` specifier when defining a *small* function that is called from relatively few places within your code, especially if it is called repeatedly within a loop.

An inline function is similar to a macro defined using the `#define` preprocessor directive. For example, the following inline function for returning the absolute value of an integer

```
inline int Abs (int N) {return N < 0 ? -N : N;}
```

is similar to the macro

```
#define ABS(N) ((N) < 0 ? -(N) : (N));
```

Calls to the inline function, however, are processed by the compiler, while calls to the macro are expanded by the preprocessor, which performs simple text substitution. Accordingly, the inline function has two important advantages over the macro. First, when the function is called, the compiler checks the type of the parameter it is passed (to make sure that it is an integer or a value that can be converted to an integer). Second, if an expression is passed to the function, it is evaluated only once. In contrast, if an expression is passed to the macro, it is evaluated twice, possibly causing unexpected side effects. For example, the following macro call would decrement I twice (probably not the expected or desired result!):

```
Abs (--I);
```

The macro does have an advantage over the inline function: You can pass it any appropriate data type and the macro will return the same type (for example, a `long`, `int`, or `double`). Although you can pass any numeric type to the function, the value will be converted to an `int` and the function will return an `int`, resulting in possible truncation or loss of precision. However, as you will see later in the chapter (under "Overloaded Functions"), in C++ you can overcome this limitation by defining several versions of the same function, one for each parameter type or set of types you want to pass to the function.

NOTE   See Chapter 4 for a description of inline member functions belonging to classes.

Default Function Parameters

In C++ you can save some programming effort by defining default parameter values when you declare a function. For example, the following declaration defines default values for the second and third parameters:

```
void ShowMessage (char *Text, int Length = -1, int Color = 0);
```

(In this hypothetical function, a Length value of −1 causes the function to calculate the length of the text, and a Color value of 0 displays the text in black letters.)

If you define a default value for a given parameter, you must define default values for all subsequent parameters (that is, all parameters to its right). For example, you could *not* declare a function as follows:

```
void ShowMessage (char *Text, int Length = -1, int Color);
// ERROR: missing default value for parameter 3
```

When you call a function, a default parameter works as follows: If you specify the parameter value, the compiler passes this value to the function; if you omit the parameter, the compiler passes the default parameter value. For example, when calling the ShowMessage function, you could specify either one, two, or three parameters:

```
ShowMessage ("Hello");      // same as ShowMessage ("Hello",-1, 0);
ShowMessage ("Hello", 5); // same as ShowMessage ("Hello", 5, 0);
ShowMessage ("Hello", 5, 8);
```

If you omit a default parameter when calling a function, you must also omit any parameters to its right (which will also have default values). For example, you could *not* call ShowMessage as follows:

```
ShowMessage ("Hello", ,8);  // ERROR: syntax error
```

When defining a default value, you can use an expression containing global variables or function calls (the expression may *not* contain local variables). For example, the following declaration is permissible (assuming that the code is placed *outside of* a function):

```
int Palette = 1;
int GetColor (int Pal);
void ShowMessage (char *Text, int Length = -1,
                  int Color = GetColor (Palette));
```

You can define default parameters within a function declaration or definition. However, once you have defined a default parameter, you cannot define it again in a subsequent function declaration or definition within the same scope. For example, the following code generates an error:

```
void ShowMessage (char *Text, int Length = -1, int Color = 0);

void main ()
   {

   // function code ...

   }

void ShowMessage (char *Text, int Length = -1, int Color = 0)
// ERROR: redefinition of default parameters 2 and 3

   {

   // function code ...

   }
```

You can, however, *add* one or more default parameters in a subsequent declaration or definition within the same scope, as in the following example:

```
void ShowMessage (char *Text, int Length = -1, int Color = 0);

// later in source file:

void ShowMessage (char *Text = "", int Length, int Color);
// OK: ADDS a default parameter value
```

Reference Types

A variable declared as a *reference* serves as an alias for another variable. You declare a reference using the & operator, as in the following example:

```
int Count = 0;
int &RefCount = Count;
```

In this example, `RefCount` is declared as a reference to an `int`, and is initialized so that it refers specifically to the `int` variable `Count`. This definition causes `RefCount` to become an alias for `Count`; that is, both `RefCount` and `Count` refer to the *same* memory location. The two variables will always have the same value, and an assignment made to one variable will affect the value of the other variable, as shown in the following code:

```
int Count = 0;
int &RefCount = Count;

// here, Count and RefCount both equal 0

RefCount = 1;

// here, Count and RefCount both equal 1

++Count;

// here, Count and RefCount both equal 2
```

> **NOTE** White space immediately before or after the & operator is not significant. Therefore, you could declare `RefCount` as `int& RefCount`, `int & RefCount`, `int &RefCount`, or even `int&RefCount` (although the last form is not very readable).

When you define a variable as a reference, you *must* initialize it, and you must initialize it with a variable of the declared type. Once you have performed this one-time initialization, you cannot make a reference variable refer to a different variable. Also, you cannot initialize a reference variable using a constant value (such as 5 or `'a'`), unless you have declared the variable as a reference to a `const` type (which will be explained in the section "Constant Types"):

```
int &RInt = 5;   // ERROR
```

> **NOTE** With a nonreference variable, an initialization in the variable definition is similar to a subsequent assignment expression that changes the value of the variable. With a reference variable, however, these two uses for the = operator are quite different. A reference initialization specifies the variable for which the reference will be an alias; in other words, the initialization specifies *which memory location* the reference variable will represent. A subsequent assignment expression *changes the value* of this memory location.

A reference variable is very different from a pointer. A pointer refers to a memory location that contains the address of the target memory location. A reference variable, however, refers directly to the target memory location (just like the variable that was used to initialize it). Figure 3.1 illustrates the differences between a variable, a reference to the variable, and a pointer to the variable; this figure assumes that the following declarations have been made:

```
int Count = 0;
int &RefCount = Count;
int *PtrCount = &Count;
```

Note that the pointer in the code above, PtrCount, could also be declared and initialized as follows:

```
int *PtrCount = &RefCount;   // equivalent to:
                             // int *PtrCount = &Count;
```

Because Count and RefCount refer to the same memory location, using the address operator (&) on either of them yields the same result. When in doubt about the behavior of a reference variable, remember that it almost always behaves exactly like the variable that was used to initialize it.

References and Functions

You can also declare functions parameters, as well as function return types, as references. For example, the following function has a parameter that is a reference to an int:

```
void FuncA (int &Parm);
```

When this function is called, it must be passed an int variable; this variable is used to initialize the reference parameter Parm. Within the function code, Parm is an alias

FIGURE 3.1:

A variable, a reference to a variable,
and a pointer to a variable

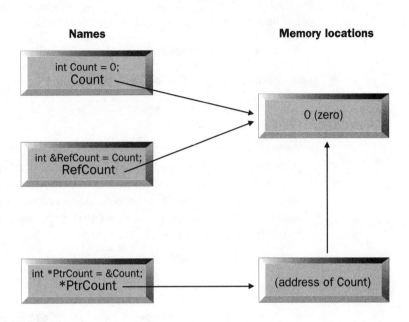

for the variable passed in the call, and any change made to Parm is also made to the
original passed variable. Thus, a reference parameter provides a way to pass a parameter to a function by reference rather than by value (in C and C++, nonreference
parameters are passed *by value*, meaning that the function receives a private *copy* of
the original variable). The following code shows the difference between a reference
parameter and a nonreference parameter:

```
void FuncA (int &Parm)   // reference parameter
   {
   ++Parm;
   }

void FuncB (int Parm)    // nonreference parameter
   {
   ++Parm;
   }

void main ()
   {
```

```
int N = 0;

FuncA (N);   // N passed by reference

// here, N equals 1

FuncB (N);   // N passed by value

// here, N still equals 1
}
```

As you can see in this example, both FuncA and FuncB increment the value of the parameter Parm. However, only FuncA, which receives the parameter as a reference, affects the value of the variable N that is passed from the calling function. Note that you cannot pass a constant (such as 5) to a reference parameter unless the parameter is declared as a reference to a const type, as will be explained in the section "Constants and Functions":

```
void FuncA (int &RInt);

void main ()
    {
    FuncA (5);   // ERROR: can't initialize reference using constant
                 // expression
    // ...
    }
```

If a large variable is passed to a function (for example, a big structure), using a reference parameter can make the function call more efficient. For a nonreference parameter, the entire contents of the variable is copied into the parameter; for a reference parameter, the parameter is merely initialized so that it refers directly to the original variable, and no separate copy of this variable is created.

As in C, you can use a pointer parameter to achieve the same basic advantages offered by a reference parameter (namely, the ability to alter the variable passed by the calling program, and the elimination of the copy operation). Reference parameters, however, can be manipulated using a simpler syntax, which is the same as that used for ordinary variables.

You can declare a function that *returns* a reference type by using the & operator, as in the following example:

```
int & GetIndex ();
```

This declaration means that a call to `GetIndex` produces a temporary alias for some existing integer variable (the particular variable depends upon how the function is implemented). Accordingly, you can place a call to `GetIndex` at any position within an expression where you could place an integer variable; the following are valid examples:

```
int N;

N = GetIndex ();   // copies value from the int variable
GetIndex () = 5;   // assigns 5 to the int variable
++GetIndex ();     // increments the int variable
```

The following code shows how `GetIndex` might be implemented and indicates the effects of calling the function:

```
int Index = 0;

int & GetIndex ()
    {
    return Index;
    }

void main ()
    {
    int N;

    // here Index equals 0

    N = GetIndex ();
    // here Index equals 0 and N equals 0

    GetIndex () = 5;
    // here Index equals 5

    ++GetIndex ();
    // here Index equals 6
    }
```

A function that has a reference return type must return a variable of the appropriate type (the function can return a constant, such as 5, only if it has been declared to return a reference to a `const`, as will be explained in the section "Constants and Functions"). The variable that is returned is used to initialize the temporary reference variable that is produced by the function call. In other words, assuming that Get-Index is defined as shown above, the function call and assignment

```
N = GetIndex ();
```

is equivalent to the code

```
int &Temp = Index;   // declare and initialize temporary reference
N = Temp;            // copy contents of temporary reference to N
```

Because a reference produced by a function call is used *after* the function has returned, the function should *not* return a variable that is destroyed when the function exits; specifically, it should not return an automatic variable or a parameter, as shown in the following dangerous code:

```
int &BadIdea1 ()
    {
    int i;

    return i;
    }

int &BadIdea2 (int Parm)
    {
    return Parm;
    }
```

This code does not generate compiler errors; however, the result of using the reference furnished by one of these functions is unpredictable. A function that has a reference return type can safely return a global variable, a static variable, or a dynamically allocated variable (dynamic variables will be explained in the section "The new and delete Operators").

In contrast, a function that returns a nonreference type can safely return an automatic variable or parameter, because the function call creates a *separate copy* of the variable's contents rather than merely generating a reference to the variable. For this same reason, however, a function that returns a nonreference type is less efficient than a function that returns a reference, especially if it returns a large data object.

NOTE   See Chapter 6 for further examples of passing and returning references from functions.

Constant Types

You can define a variable for storing a constant value, using the `const` keyword as in the following example:

```
const int MaxLines = 100;
```

NOTE   Because its value cannot be changed, a `const` object is sometimes called a *named constant* rather than a *constant variable*.

When you define a `const` variable, you must initialize it. This one-time initialization is your only opportunity to set the variable's value; you *cannot* change its value using an assignment. The following code illustrates legal and illegal operations with a `const` type:

```
const double CD = 2.5;
double D;

D = CD;     // OK to read const type

CD = 5.0;   // ERROR: cannot assign new value to const type

++CD;       // ERROR: cannot change value of const type
```

You can initialize a `const` variable using either a constant expression (such as 5 or `'a'`) or a variable. For example, the following `const` declarations are all valid (the first two initialize using constant expressions and the second two initialize using variables):

```
void Func (int Parm)
   {
   int I = 3;

   const int CI1 = 5;
   const int CI2 = 2 * sizeof (float);
```

```
const int CI3 = I;
const int CI4 = Parm;
}
```

If, however, you have initialized a const variable with an expression containing another variable, you *cannot* use the const to dimension an array. (This would be an invalid method for dynamically creating an array whose size is determined at runtime; see the last section in the chapter for a discussion on the correct method for allocating a dynamic array.) For example:

```
void Func (int Parm)
   {
   const int CI1 = 100;
   const int CI2 = Parm;

   char Buf1 [CI1];  // valid
   char Buf2 [CI2];  // ERROR: constant expression required
   }
```

You can use a const variable in the same way that a symbolic constant defined with the #define preprocessor directive is traditionally used in a C program. (Remember, however, that if you use a const variable where a constant expression is required, you must initialize the const variable with a constant expression.) Like a #define constant, a const variable can be defined within a header file that is included within one or more of the source files that compose a program. (Unlike a nonconstant variable, a constant variable is, by default, *local* to the file in which it is defined; it can therefore be defined within more than one source file without causing an error when the program is linked.)

NOTE   A const variable has the advantage over a #define constant that it can be referenced using a symbolic debugger.

Constants and Pointers

There are several ways that you can use the const keyword when declaring a pointer.

First, you can define a pointer to a constant type—for example, a pointer to a const int:

```
const int *PCInt;
```

You can freely change the value of such a pointer, but not the value of the variable that it points to—for example:

```
const int A = 1;
int B = 2;

const int *PCInt;   // no need to initialize; PCInt is not a const
PCInt = &A;

*PCInt = 5;         // ERROR: can't change variable pointed to

PCInt = &B;         // OK to change PCInt itself

*PCInt = 9;         // ERROR
```

Note that PCInt can be assigned the address of either a constant or nonconstant int variable. However, even if PCInt is assigned the address of a nonconstant variable, it cannot be used to change this variable. (In this case, the pointer serves as a read-only way to access a read-write variable.)

Second, you can define a constant pointer to a nonconstant variable, as in this example:

```
int N;
int *const CPInt = &N;
```

Since this pointer is a constant, it must be initialized when it is defined, and it cannot subsequently be assigned a different address. The pointer, however, can be used to change the value of the variable it points to, as demonstrated in the following code:

```
int A = 1;
int B = 2;

int *const CPInt = &A;   // must initialize CPInt

*CPInt = 5;              // OK to change variable pointed to

CPInt = &B;              // ERROR: can't change const pointer
```

Third, you can define a constant pointer to a constant object. In this case, you must initialize the pointer when defining it, and you can change neither the value of the pointer itself, nor the value of the variable that it points to.

Note, finally, that you *cannot* assign the address of a constant variable to a pointer to a nonconstant variable; doing so would provide a sneaky way of changing a constant variable, as shown in the following code:

```
const int N = 1;
int *PInt;

PInt = &N;  // ERROR: can't assign the address of a const int to
            // a pointer to a nonconst int

*PInt = 2;  // if assignment had been allowed, this statement
            // would change a constant variable!
```

Constants and References

You can also define a reference to a constant object. You can initialize this type of reference using a constant variable:

```
const int A = 1;
const int &RCIntA = A;
```

or you can initialize it using a nonconstant variable:

```
int B;
const int &RCIntB = B;
```

In either case, you *cannot* use the reference to change the value of the variable it refers to:

```
const int A = 1;
const int &RCIntA = A;

int B;
const int &RCIntB = B;

RCIntA = 5;   // ERROR: can't change value of reference to const
RCIntB = 10;  // ERROR: can't change value of reference to const
```

If you initialize a reference to a const type using a nonconstant variable, the reference serves as a read-only alias for that variable. (This is a rare case in which a reference behaves differently from the variable it refers to.)

You can also initialize a reference to a `const` using a constant expression (recalling that it is illegal to initialize a reference to a nonconstant variable with a constant expression)—for example:

```
const int &RCInt = 5;   // valid initialization
```

In this definition, the compiler (conceptually if not actually) creates a temporary `const int` variable containing the value 5, and then uses this variable to initialize `RCInt`.

Note that it is meaningless (although legal) to define a reference variable that is constant itself, since all reference variables are automatically constant:

```
int N;

int &const RCInt = N;   // legal but senseless
```

Finally, you cannot use a constant variable to initialize a reference to a nonconstant type, because doing so would provide an indirect way to change the constant variable:

```
const int CInt = 1;

int &RInt = CInt;   // ERROR

RInt = 5;             // this would change a const variable!
```

Constants and Functions

You can also declare function parameters, as well as function return types, using the `const` keyword.

Declaring a parameter as a `const` simply means that the function cannot change the value of its parameter; this information is probably not of much interest to the programmer calling the function because it is merely an implementation detail with no effect outside of the function:

```
void FuncA (const int N);   // FuncA can't change N; so what?
```

If a parameter is a *pointer* or *reference*, the function can normally change the value of the variable that is passed:

```
FuncA (int *PInt);
FuncB (int &RInt);
```

```
void main ()
   {
   int N = 1;

   FuncA (&N);   // FuncA can change value of N
   FuncB (N);    // FuncB can change value of N

   // ...
   }
```

If, however, a variable is a pointer or reference to a const type, the function *cannot* change the value of the variable that is passed; this information is usually of considerable interest to the programmer calling the function, because it guarantees that the function will not have the side effect of changing the value of a variable. For example:

```
FuncA (const int *PInt);
FuncB (const int &RInt);

void main ()
   {
   int N = 1;

   FuncA (&N);   // FuncA CANNOT change value of N
   FuncB (N);    // FuncB CANNOT change value of N

   // ...
   }
```

Furthermore, if a parameter is a pointer or reference to a const, you can pass the function a constant variable. (If the parameter is a pointer or reference to a nonconstant type, passing a constant is illegal because it would permit the constant to be changed.) For example, if N were declared as

```
const int N = 1;
```

you could legally pass the address of N to FuncA or pass N to FuncB, as in the code above.

Additionally, if a parameter is declared as a reference to a constant, you can pass the function a constant expression (recall that this is illegal for a parameter that is a reference to a nonconstant):

```
void FuncA (const int &RInt);

void main ()
```

```
{
FuncA (5);  // legal

// ...
}
```

If a function returns a fundamental type (such as `int` or `double`), adding `const` to the definition of the function return type does not have much significance, because you cannot *change* such a return value anyway (that is, it is not an *lvalue*). For example:

```
const int Func ();  // so what?
                    // return value can't be changed anyway
```

If, however, a function returns a pointer or reference to some type, adding the keyword `const` to the declaration means that the calling function cannot use the return value to alter the variable that is pointed to or referenced; for example:

```
const int *FuncA ()
    {
    static int Protected = 1;
    ++Protected;

    return &Protected;
    }

const int &FuncB ()
    {
    static int Safe = 100;
    --Safe;

    return Safe;
    }

void main (int Parm)
    {
    int N;

    N = *FuncA ();  // legal: N gets a copy of Protected
    N = FuncB ();   // legal: N gets a copy of Safe

    *FuncA () = 5;  // ERROR: attempt to change const type
    ++FuncB ();     // ERROR: attempt to change const type
    }
```

Note that both FuncA and FuncB change the value of an internal data item; however, because of the const keyword in the declarations, they prevent the calling function from changing the data items.

Overloaded Functions

In C++ you can define more than one function within a program using the *same name*, provided that each function differs from all other identically named functions in the number or type of parameters. For example, you could declare two different versions of the function Abs, one for obtaining the absolute value of an int and the other for obtaining the absolute value of a double, as follows:

```
int Abs (int N)
    {
    return N < 0 ? -N : N;
    }

double Abs (double N)
    {
    return N < 0.0 ? -N : N;
    }
```

When such identically named functions are declared within the same scope, they are known as *overloaded functions*. The compiler automatically calls the appropriate version of an overloaded function, based upon the type of the parameter or parameters passed in the actual function call, as shown in the following code:

```
int Abs (int N);          // both versions of Abs declared in file
double Abs (double N);  // scope

void main ()
    {
    int I;
    double D;

    I = Abs (5);      // calls 'int Abs (int N)'
    D = Abs (-2.5);  // calls 'double Abs (double N)'

    // ...

    }
```

Two overloaded functions must differ in one or both of the following ways:

- The functions have different numbers of parameters.

- The type of one or more parameters is different.

As you can see in the example above, overloaded functions can return different types. However, two overloaded functions may not differ *only* in their return types, as shown in the following erroneous code:

```
int Abs (int N)
   {
   return N < 0 ? -N : N;
   }

double Abs (int N)   // ERROR: an overloaded function that differs
                     // only by return type
   {
   return (double)(N < 0 ? -N : N);
   }
```

Also, if two parameters are identical except that only one of them is a `const` or a reference type, they are considered to be the same type when overloaded functions are defined. For example, you could *not* define overloaded functions as follows:

```
int Abs (int N);
int Abs (const int N);   // ERROR: parameter lists too similar
```

The compiler does not allow these overloaded functions because both `int` and `const int` are initialized using the same set of types; if you passed one of these types when calling the function, the compiler would be unable to determine which overloaded function to call. For the same reason, you cannot define overloaded functions like this:

```
int Abs (int N);
int Abs (int &N);   // ERROR: parameter lists too similar
```

If you pass an argument to an overloaded function that does not match the argument type defined by any of the function versions, the compiler will attempt to convert the argument to one of the defined types. The compiler will perform standard conversions (for example, `int` to `long`) as well as user-defined conversions (which are described in Chapter 6), as necessary. If the type cannot be converted, the compiler generates an error. Also, if the compiler is able to convert the parameters you pass so that they match the types defined for more than one overloaded function, it calls the function that matches most closely; if no single function matches most closely, it generates an error (the function call in this case being ambiguous). For details on the rather complex criteria that the compiler uses for comparing type matches, see the C++ *Language Reference Manual* (Chapter 12, "Overloading").

Default function parameters can also result in ambiguous overloaded function calls. Consider, for example, the following overloaded functions:

```
void Display (char *Buffer);
void Display (char *Buffer, int Length = 32);
```

The following call would generate an error, because the parameter list would match *both* overloaded functions:

```
Display ("Hello");   // ERROR: ambiguous call!
```

Note that the compiler does not generate an error when the above overloaded functions are defined (because it is *possible* to call the functions unambiguously). Rather, it flags an error only when an overloaded function is actually called ambiguously.

NOTE See Chapter 4 for information on overloading member functions of a C++ class (specifically, constructors), and Chapter 6 for a discussion on overloading standard C operators.

The new and delete Operators

You can use the C++ new and delete operators to allocate and release blocks of memory from the heap (in C++, the heap is also called the *free store*). When using new, you specify a data type; new then allocates a block of memory large enough to hold an object of the specified type, and it returns the address of the block as a pointer to the specified type. You can allocate a block of memory for storing an object of a built-in type such as an char, int, or double, as in the following code:

```
char *PChar;         // declare pointers
int *PInt;
double *PDouble;

PChar = new char;    // allocate memory objects
```

```
PInt = new int;
PDouble = new double;

*PChar = 'a';            // assign values
*PInt = 5;
*PDouble = 2.25;
```

More commonly, you use new to allocate memory for a user-defined type, such as a struct:

```
struct Node
   {
   char *String;
   int Value;
   Node *Next;
   };
```

```
// ...
```

```
Node *PNode;            // declare a pointer

PNode = new Node;       // allocate memory

PNode->Name = "hello";  // assign values
PNode->Value = 1;
PNode->Next = 0;
```

If the new operator is unable to allocate the requested memory, it returns the value 0. Therefore, you should check the pointer before using it:

```
PNode = new Node;
if (PNode == 0)
   // handle error condition ...
else
   // use PNode ...
```

When you have finished using a memory block allocated through the new operator, you can release the memory by using the delete operator on a pointer containing the address of the block. For example, the following statements would release the memory blocks allocated in the previous examples:

```
delete PChar;
delete PInt;
delete PDouble;
delete PNode;
```

Be sure not to invoke the `delete` operator more than once using the same address. Deleting a pointer containing 0, however, is always harmless. It is a good idea, therefore, to set a pointer variable to 0 immediately after using the `delete` operator on it.

The `new` and `delete` operators are useful for dynamically creating memory objects, especially when the number or size of the objects is unknown at compile time. Also, unlike a global or local named object that you have defined, you can precisely control the lifetime of an object created with `new`. A global defined object always lasts the entire duration of the program, and a local defined object always lasts until program control leaves the block in which it is defined; an object created with `new`, however, can be allocated at any point in the program, and it is not released until `delete` is invoked, or the program ends.

The `new` and `delete` operators are generally more useful than the traditional `malloc` family of memory allocation functions. Unlike `malloc`, the `new` operator automatically determines the correct size for the object and returns a pointer of the correct type. Also, as you will learn in Chapter 4, when it is used to allocate a class object, `new` automatically calls the class *constructor* (the class initialization function).

You can *overload* the `new` and `delete` operators to provide custom memory management for your program. For a general discussion on operator overloading, see Chapter 6. For information specifically on overloading `new` and `delete`, see the *C++ Tutorial* manual (Chapter 6, "More Features of Classes"), the *C++ Language Reference* manual (Chapter 11, "Special Member Functions"), the *Programming Techniques* manual (Chapter 3, "Managing Memory for 16-Bit C++ Programs"), or the *C/C++ Language* online help file (the topic "new operator, customizing").

Allocating Arrays with new

To allocate an array with `new`, you specify the base type (that is, the type of an array element) and indicate the number of elements within [ ] characters, as in the following examples:

```
void Func (int Size)
```

```
{
char *String = new char [25];    // array of 25 chars

int *ArrayInt = new int [Size]; // array of 'Size' ints

double *ArrayDouble;
ArrayDouble = new double [32];   // array of 32 doubles

// ...
}
```

When you allocate an array, new returns the address of the first array element. Notice that, unlike with a static array declaration, you can specify the number of elements in the array using a variable.

When you invoke delete to free an array, you must include a pair of empty [ ] characters to indicate that you are releasing an array rather than a single object of the base type. For example, the following statements would release the arrays allocated in the previous example:

```
delete [] String;
delete [] ArrayInt;
delete [] ArrayDouble;
```

Initializing Allocations

A memory block allocated with new is *not* automatically initialized to 0. However, when you use new to allocate memory object of a built-in type (such as a char), you can explicitly initialize the object with a constant of the appropriate type, using the following syntax:

```
char *PChar = new char ('a');  // initialize char with 'a'
int *PInt = new int (3);       // initialize int with 3
```

You can also initialize an object of a user-defined type (such as a struct) with an existing object of the same type:

```
struct Node
   {
   char *String;
   int Value;
   Node *Next;
   };
```

```
void Func ()
   {
   Node NodeA = {"hello", 1, 0};

   Node *PNode = new Node (NodeA);
   }
```

The contents of NodeA will be copied—field by field—into the new object allocated by the new operator.

> **NOTE** When using the new operator, you cannot initialize an array of a built-in type. As you will learn in Chapter 4, however, you can write a special function known as a *class constructor* for initializing an array of a user-defined type.

Summary

In this chapter, you learned how to translate your C programs to C++, and how to begin writing new programs in C++. The chapter also described many of the new features provided by C++ that do not depend upon classes. The following is a brief summary of the main topics:

- With only a few exceptions, C++ is a superset of the C language. You can therefore make the move to C++ by compiling your existing C programs—as well as the new programs you write—using the C++ compiler rather than the C compiler. You can then gradually add unique C++ features to your code.

- There are, however, several constructs that you may need to update when you port your C program to C++. Almost all of these constructs represent obsolete C programming practices and will be flagged by the C++ compiler.

- In C++, you can mark a single-line comment using the // characters.

- In C++, you can declare a local variable at any position in the code before it is referenced. You do *not* need to place all local declarations at the beginning of a block.

- You can reference a global variable that is hidden by an identically named local variable by prefacing the name of the global variable with the *scope resolution operator*, ::.

- If you declare a function using the *inline* keyword, the compiler will replace all calls to the function with a copy of the actual function code (whenever possible).

- When you declare or define a function, you can assign a default value to one or more of the parameters. If you omit a parameter with a default value when you call the function, the compiler will automatically pass the default value.

- You can use the & character to define a *reference* variable, which serves as an alias for another variable. You can also define function parameters and function return types as references.

- You can create a variable for storing a constant value by using the `const` keyword in the definition. A pointer or reference to a `const` type can be used as a read-only means of accessing a variable. A function parameter declared as a pointer or reference to `const` guarantees that the function cannot change the value of the variable that is passed.

- You can declare more than one function using the same name, provided that each function differs in the number or type of parameters. When such functions occur within the same scope, they are said to be *overloaded*. When you call an overloaded function, the compiler calls the function version that matches the number and types of the parameters that you pass.

- You can allocate and free blocks of memory from the free store (that is, the heap) using the C++ `new` and `delete` operators. These operators are well adapted to the needs of C++ programs, especially programs that use classes.

The next chapter introduces the central new feature of C++: classes.

CHAPTER

FOUR

Defining C++ Classes

4

- Defining a class and creating a class instance

- Accessing class members

- Encapsulation

- Constructors and destructors

- Inline member functions

- The this pointer

- Static class members

This chapter introduces C++ classes. When you define a class, you create a new data type, which can be used much like one of the built-in C++ data types. A class, however, contains code as well as data. A class allows you to encapsulate all of the code and data you need to manage a particular kind of program item, such as a window on the screen, a figure that the program draws, a device connected to a computer, or a task run by an operating system. This chapter describes the basic techniques needed to create and use individual classes. In the next chapter, you will learn how to define and use hierarchies of related classes.

Defining a Class

A C++ class is somewhat similar to a standard C structure, although the features of C++ classes go far beyond those provided by C structures. To understand C++ classes, it is useful to start by considering how structures are used in the C language.

A C structure allows you to group a set of related data items. As a simple example, if your C program draws a rectangle on the screen, you might find it convenient to store the coordinates of the rectangle within a structure defined as follows:

```
struct Rectangle
{
    int Left;
    int Top;
    int Right;
    int Bottom;
};
```

You could then define a function for drawing the rectangle, as in the following example:

```
void DrawRectangle (struct Rectangle *Rect)
    {
    Line (Rect->Left, Rect->Top, Rect->Right, Rect->Top);
    Line (Rect->Right, Rect->Top, Rect->Right, Rect->Bottom);
    Line (Rect->Right, Rect->Bottom, Rect->Left, Rect->Bottom);
    Line (Rect->Left, Rect->Bottom, Rect->Left, Rect->Top);
    }
```

In this example, Line is a hypothetical function that draws a line from the point given by the first two coordinates to the point given by the second two coordinates.

Such a function might be defined elsewhere in the program or obtained from a function library.

Finally, to draw a rectangle at a particular position, you would define and initialize a variable of type `Rectangle` and then pass this variable to the function `DrawRectangle`:

```
struct Rectangle Rect = {25, 25, 100, 100};

DrawRectangle (&Rect);
```

A C++ class, unlike a C structure, defines not only a collection of data items, but also the functions that operate upon these data items. Thus, in C++ you could combine both the coordinates of the rectangle *and* the function for drawing the rectangle within a single class definition, as in the following example:

```
class CRectangle
{
    int Left;
    int Top;
    int Right;
    int Bottom;

    void Draw (void)
        {
        Line (Left, Top, Right, Top);
        Line (Right, Top, Right, Bottom);
        Line (Right, Bottom, Left, Bottom);
        Line (Left, Bottom, Left, Top);
        }
};
```

Data items defined within a class are known as the *data members*, and functions defined within a class are known as *member functions*. In this class example, the data members are `Top`, `Left`, `Right`, and `Bottom`, and the member function is `Draw`. Notice that a member function can refer directly to any of the data members of the same class, without using any special syntax.

Creating a Class Instance

In C, providing a structure definition such as:

```
struct Rectangle
{
    int Left;
    int Top;
    int Right;
    int Bottom;
};
```

tells the compiler the form of the structure, but does not actually reserve memory or create a variable that you can use for storing data. To reserve memory and create a variable, you must provide a definition, such as the following:

```
struct Rectangle Rect;
```

In the same manner, defining a class, such as the class CRectangle shown in the previous sections, provides the compiler with a blueprint of the class, but does not actually reserve memory. As with a structure, you must define a data item, such as the following:

```
CRectangle Rect;
```

This definition creates an *instance* of the CRectangle class. An instance of a class is also known as an *object*; throughout the book, the terms *class instance* and *object* will be used synonymously. The class instance, Rect, occupies its own block of memory and can be used for storing data and performing operations on that data. As with a variable of a built-in type, an object will remain in existence until its definition goes out of scope. (For example, if it is defined within a function, it will be destroyed when the function returns.)

> **NOTE** Just as with C structures, the definition for a class must precede the definition and use of a class instance within the source file.

You can also create an instance of a class using the C++ new operator, as in the following statement:

```
CRectangle *PRect = new CRectangle;
```

This statement allocates a block of memory large enough to hold an instance of the class, and returns a pointer to this object. The object will remain allocated until you explicitly free it using the `delete` operator (as explained in Chapter 3 for built-in types):

```
delete PRectangle;
```

You can create any number of instances of a given class.

 **TIP**   In creating a class instance, you are not required to preface the name of the class with the word `class`. In C++, a class definition creates a new data type, which can be referred to using the class name alone.

Accessing Class Members

After you have created a class instance, you access the data members and member functions using a syntax similar to that used for C structures. However, with the current definition of the `Rectangle` class, the program would *not* be able to access any of its members. The reason is that—by default—all data members and member functions belonging to a class are *private*, meaning that they can be used only within the scope of the class itself. Thus, it is legal for the function `Draw` to access the data members `Top`, `Left`, `Right`, and `Bottom`, because `Draw` is a member function of the class. However, it would be illegal for the other parts of the program, such as the function `main`, to access the data members or call the member function `Draw`.

Fortunately, you can use the `public` *access specifier* to make one or more members *public*, rendering these members accessible to all other functions in the program (functions defined either within classes or outside of classes). For example, in the following version of the `Rectangle` class, all members are made public:

```
class CRectangle
{
public:
    int Left;
    int Top;
    int Right;
    int Bottom;
```

```
void Draw (void)
    {
    Line (Left, Top, Right, Top);
    Line (Right, Top, Right, Bottom);
    Line (Right, Bottom, Left, Bottom);
    Line (Left, Bottom, Left, Top);
    }
};
```

The access specifier applies to *all* members that come after it in the class definition (until another access specifier is encountered, as will be explained later).

Now that all members of Rectangle have been made public, they can be accessed using the dot operator (.), in the same way that fields of a C structure are accessed. For example:

```
CRectangle Rect;       // define a CRectangle object

Rect.Left = 5;         // assign values to the data members to
Rect.Top = 10;         // specify the rectangle coordinates
Rect.Right = 100;
Rect.Bottom = 150;

Rect.Draw ();          // draw the rectangle
```

Alternatively, you could dynamically create a class instance with the new operator, and then use a pointer to the instance to access the data members, as in the following code:

```
CRectangle *PRect = new CRectangle;

PRect->Left = 5;
PRect->Top = 10;
PRect->Right = 100;
PRect->Bottom = 150;

PRect->Draw ();
```

Encapsulation

According to the principle of *encapsulation*, the internal data structures used in - implementing a class should not be directly accessible to the user of the class (the advantages of encapsulation are discussed later). The current version of the Rectangle class, however, clearly violates this principle since the user can directly read or modify any of the data members.

To achieve greater encapsulation, CRectangle could be defined following the usual C++ custom of providing public access to the generally useful member functions (so far, only Draw), but denying access to the internal data members used by these functions (Left, Top, Right, and Bottom):

```cpp
class CRectangle
{
private:
    int Left;
    int Top;
    int Right;
    int Bottom;

public:
    void Draw (void)
        {
        Line (Left, Top, Right, Top);
        Line (Right, Top, Right, Bottom);
        Line (Right, Bottom, Left, Bottom);
        Line (Left, Bottom, Left, Top);
        }
};
```

The private access specifier makes the members that follow it private, so that they cannot be accessed except by member functions of the class. Like the public access specifier discussed previously, the private specifier affects all declarations that come after it, until another specifier is encountered. Therefore, this definition makes Top, Left, Right, and Bottom private, and it makes Draw public. (Note that the private specifier is not actually required at the beginning of the class definition, because class members are private by default; including the private specifier, however, makes this fact explicit to the reader of the program.)

NOTE
C++ provides a third access specifier, protected. The explanation of this specifier is postponed until Chapter 5, because it requires an understanding of inheritance.

The following code illustrates legal and illegal accesses to members of the current version of the CRectangle class:

```
void main ()
   {
   CRectangle Rect;      // define a CRectangle object

   Rect.Left = 5;        // ERROR: can't access private member
   Rect.Top = 10;        // ERROR
   Rect.Right = 100;     // ERROR
   Rect.Bottom = 150;    // ERROR

   Rect.Draw ();         // OK
   }
```

Now that the user of the class is denied direct access to the data members, the class must provide an alternative means for the user to specify the coordinates of the rectangle before the rectangle is drawn. A good way to do this is to provide a public member function that receives the desired coordinate values and uses these values to set the data members; the following is an example:

```
void SetCoord (int L, int T, int R, int B)
   {
   L = __min (__max (0,L), 80);
   T = __min (__max (0,T), 25);
   R = __min (__max (0,R), 80);
   B = __min (__max (0,B), 25);
   R = __max (R,L);
   B = __max (B,T);
   Left = L; Top = T; Right = R; Bottom = B;
   }
```

This function should be added to the public section of the CRectangle class definition, so that it can be called by any function in the program. Notice that before assigning the parameters to the data members of the class, SetCoord adjusts the parameters, if necessary, to make sure that they are within the ranges of valid values; it also makes sure that the right coordinate is greater than the left, and the bottom greater than the top. (The macros __max and __min are provided by the C run-time library; to use them in your program, you must include the STDLIB.H header file.)

You could now use the CRectangle class to draw a rectangle as follows:

```
void main ()
   {
   // ...

   CRectangle Rect;

   Rect.SetCoord (25,25,100,100);   // set rectangle coordinates
   Rect.Draw ();                    // draw the rectangle

   // ...
   };
```

Later in the chapter (in the section "Constructors"), you will learn how to initialize data members at the same time that you create an instance of the class.

You might also want to add a function that permits other parts of the program to *obtain* the current values of the rectangle coordinates. The following is an example of such a function:

```
void GetCoord (int *L, int *T, int *R, int *B)
   {
   *L = Left;
   *T = Top;
   *R = Right;
   *B = Bottom;
   }
```

This function should also be added to the public section of the class definition. The following is the complete CRectangle class definition, including both new member functions, SetCoord and GetCoord:

```
class CRectangle
{
private:
   int Left;
   int Top;
```

```
    int Right;
    int Bottom;
public:
   void Draw (void)
      {
      Line (Left, Top, Right, Top);
      Line (Right, Top, Right, Bottom);
      Line (Right, Bottom, Left, Bottom);
      Line (Left, Bottom, Left, Top);
      }
   void GetCoord (int *L, int *T, int *R, int *B)
      {
      *L = Left;
      *T = Top;
      *R = Right;
      *B = Bottom;
      }
  void SetCoord (int L, int T, int R, int B)
      {
      L = __min (__max (0,L), 80);
      T = __min (__max (0,T), 25);
      R = __min (__max (0,R), 80);
      B = __min (__max (0,B), 25);
      R = __max (R,L);
      B = __max (B,T);
      Left = L; Top = T; Right = R; Bottom = B;
      }
 };
```

By means of the SetCoord and GetCoord member functions, the CRectangle class now provides access to its private data members, but—in the spirit of encapsulation—only through a clearly defined interface that carefully checks the validity of the new assigned values.

The Benefits of Encapsulation

One obvious benefit of encapsulation is that it allows the designer of the class to check the validity of any value that is assigned to a data member, and thus helps prevent programming errors.

Another advantage of controlling access to internal data structures is that the author of the class can freely change the design of these data structures, without disturbing the other parts of the program that use the class (as long as the calling protocol of the public member functions remains the same). As a simple example, the author of the CRectangle class might decide to store the coordinates of the top and left of the rectangle, together with the width and height of the rectangle rather than the right and bottom coordinates. In this case, the data members might be defined as follows:

```
private:
    int Left;
    int Top;
    int Width;
    int Height;
```

As long as the calling protocols for the SetCoord and GetCoord functions remained the same, this internal change would not affect other portions of the program, or any other program that used the CRectangle class. (Of course, these two functions would have to be changed to convert between coordinate values and width and height values.) Encapsulation would thus prevent the user of the class from creating dependencies upon a specific internal data representation.

Constructors and Destructors

This section discusses two special types of member functions that you can define for a class: *constructors* and *destructors*.

Constructors

The current version of the CRectangle class allows you to initialize the data members by calling the SetCoord member function. As an alternative way of initializing data members, you can define a special member function known as a *constructor*. A constructor is called automatically whenever an instance of the class is created; it can initialize data members and perform any other initialization tasks required to prepare the class object for use.

A constructor has the same name as the class itself. When you define a constructor, you cannot specify a return value, not even void (a constructor never returns a value). A constructor may, however, take any number of parameters (zero or more).

For example, the following version of the CRectangle class has a constructor that takes four parameters, which are used to initialize the data members:

```
class CRectangle
{
private:
    int Left;
    int Top;
    int Right;
    int Bottom;

public:
    // constructor:
    CRectangle (int L, int T, int R, int B)
        {
        SetCoord (L, T, R, B);
        }

// definitions of other member functions ...

};
```

> **NOTE** If you want to be able to create instances of a class, you must make the constructor a *public* member function. (If you use the class only for deriving other classes, you can make the constructor a *protected* member, as explained in Chapter 5.)

Recall that the SetCoord member function checks the validity of its parameters and assigns the parameter values to the private data members that store the coordinates of the rectangle.

When you define an object, you pass the parameter values to the constructor using a syntax similar to a normal function call:

```
CRectangle Rect (25, 25, 100, 100);
```

This definition creates an instance of the CRectangle class and invokes the class's constructor, passing it the specified parameter values.

You also pass the parameter values to the constructor when you create a class instance using the new operator:

```
CRectangle *PRect = new CRectangle (25, 25, 100, 100);
```

The new operator automatically invokes the constructor for the object that it creates. (This is an important advantage of using new rather than other memory-allocation methods, such as the malloc function.)

With the constructor in place, you can create a CRectangle object and draw a rectangle in only two statements (rather than the three statements shown previously, in the section "Encapsulation"):

```
void main ()
   {
   CRectangle Rect (25,25,100,100); // create object and specify
                                    // rectangle dimensions
   Rect.Draw ();                    // draw the rectangle
   };
```

Default Constructors

A constructor that takes no parameters is known as a *default constructor*. A default constructor typically initializes data members by assigning them default values. For example, the following version of the CRectangle class has a default constructor that initializes all data members to 0:

```
class CRectangle
{
private:
   int Left;
   int Top;
   int Right;
   int Bottom;

public:
   CRectangle ()
      {
      Left = Top = Right = Bottom = 0;
      }

// definitions of other member functions ...

};
```

A constructor with one or more parameters, all of which have default values, is also considered to be a default constructor, because it *can* be invoked without passing parameters (see the section "Default Function Parameters" in Chapter 3).

If you do *not* define a constructor for a particular class, the compiler will generate a default constructor for you. Such a compiler-generated constructor will not assign initial values to the class's data members; therefore, if you want to explicitly initialize data members or perform any other initialization tasks, you must define your own constructor.

If a class has a default constructor (either explicitly defined or compiler-generated), you can define a class object without passing parameters; for example:

```
CRectangle Rect;
```

If you do not pass parameters to a constructor, however, *do not be tempted to include empty parentheses* in the object definition. Doing so will actually declare a function that returns a class type rather than defining an instance of a class:

```
CRectangle Rect ();   // declares a function that takes no
                      // parameters and returns a CRectangle
                      // object
```

(If you make this mistake, the compiler will not generate an error until you attempt to use Rect as if it were a class instance.)

See Chapter 6 for an explanation of the special properties of constructors that take a *single* parameter (in the section "Using Copy and Conversion Constructors").

Overloaded Constructors

Just as you can overload a global function (as explained in Chapter 3), you can also overload the class constructor or any other member function of a class except the destructor. (You cannot overload the destructor because it never takes parameters, as explained later.) In fact, overloaded constructors are quite common; they provide alternative ways to initialize a newly created class object. For example, the following definition of CRectangle provides overloaded constructors that allow you either to specify the initial values of the data members, or to simply accept default initial values:

```
class CRectangle
{
private:
    int Left;
    int Top;
    int Right;
    int Bottom;

public:
    // default constructor:
    CRectangle ()
        {
        Left = Top = Right = Bottom = 0;
        }

    // destructor with parms:
    CRectangle (int L, int T, int R, int B)
        {
        SetCoord (L, T, R, B);
        }

// definitions of other member functions ...

};
```

The following code demonstrates the use of the overloaded CRectangle constructors:

```
void main ()
    {
    // create an object with using default constructor:
    CRectangle Rect1;

    // create an object, specifying initial values:
    CRectangle Rect2 (25, 25, 100, 100);

    // ...

    }
```

If you define a constructor for a class, the compiler will *not* create a default constructor for you. If, therefore, you define one or more constructors, but do not include a default constructor among them, the class will *not have* a default constructor. As you will see later in the chapter, using a class that does not have a default constructor can cause errors in certain situations.

Member Initialization in Constructors

You are not permitted to initialize a data member of a class when you define it. Thus, the following class definition generates errors:

```
class C
{
private:
    int N = 0;              // ERROR
    const int CInt = 5;     // ERROR
    int &RInt = N;          // ERROR

// ...

};
```

It does not make sense to initialize a data member within a class definition, because the class definition merely indicates the *type* of each data member and does not actually reserve memory. Rather, you want to initialize the data members each time you create a specific *instance* of the class. The logical place to initialize data members, therefore, is within the class constructor. The example CRectangle class constructor initializes the data members by using *assignment* expressions. However, certain data types—specifically, constants and references—*cannot* be assigned values. To solve this problem, C++ provides a special constructor feature known as a *member initializer list* that allows you to *initialize* (rather than *assign* a value to) one or more data members.

A member initializer list is placed immediately after the parameter list in the constructor definition; it consists of a colon, followed by one or more *member initializers*, separated with commas. A member initializer consists of the name of a data member followed by the initial value in parentheses. For example, the constructor in the following class has a member initializer list that contains a member initializer for each data member:

```
class C
{
private:
    int N;
    const int CInt;
    int &RInt;
    // ...

public:
    C (int Parm) : N (Parm), CInt (5), RInt (N)
        {
        // constructor code ...
        }

    // ...
};
```

To illustrate the effect of this member initializer list, the following definition would create an object in which the data members N and CInt are initialized to 0 and 5, and the data member RInt is initialized so that it refers to N:

```
C CObject (0);
```

Initializing Member Objects   You can define a data member that is an object of another class; that is, you can embed an object of one class within an object of another class. Such a data member is known as a *member object*. You can initialize a member object by passing the required parameters to the object's constructor within the member initializer list of the constructor of the containing class. For example, the class C in the following code contains a member object of class CEmbedded, which is initialized within C's constructor:

```
class CEmbedded
{
    // ...

public:
    CEmbedded (int Parm1, int Parm2)
        {
        // ...
        }
```

```
    // ...

};

class CContainer
{
private:
    CEmbedded Embedded;

public:
    CContainer (int P1, int P2, int P3) : Embedded (P1, P2)
        {

        // constructor code ...

        }

    // ...
};
```

If you do *not* initialize a member object in the member initializer list of the constructor (or if the constructor is a compiler-generated default constructor), the compiler will automatically invoke the member object's default constructor, if one is available. (Recall that not every class has a default constructor; if a default constructor is not available, an error will result.)

NOTE   As you will see in Chapter 5, you can also use the member initializer list within a constructor of a derived class to pass values to a constructor belonging to a base class.

Destructors

You can also define a special member function known as a *destructor*, which is called automatically whenever a class object is destroyed. The name of the destructor is the same as the name of the class, prefaced with the ~ character. Like a constructor, the destructor must be defined with no return type (not even `void`); unlike a constructor, however, it cannot accept parameters. For example, if a class is named `CMessage`, its destructor would be defined as follows:

```
~CMessage ()
   {

   // destructor code ...

   }
```

A destructor can perform any tasks that are required before an object is destroyed. For example, the constructor for the following class (`CMessage`) allocates a block of memory for storing a message string; the destructor releases this memory immediately before a class instance is destroyed:

```
#include <string.h>

class CMessage
{
private:
   char *Buffer;  // stores message string

public:
   CMessage ()
      {
      Buffer = new char ('\0');   // initialize Buffer to
                                  // empty string
      }

   ~CMessage ()                    // class destructor
      {
      delete [] Buffer;           // free the memory
      }

   void Display ()
      {

      // code for displaying contents of Buffer ...

      }
   void Set (char *String)        // store a new message string
      {
      delete [] Buffer;
      Buffer = new char [strlen (String) + 1];
```

```
      strcpy (Buffer, String);
      }
};
```

When Constructors and Destructors Are Called

In general, a constructor is called when an object is created, and a destructor is called when an object is destroyed. The following list explains exactly when constructors and destructors are called for specific types of objects:

- For an object defined globally (that is, outside of any function), the constructor is called when the program first begins running, before main (or WinMain for a Windows program) receives control. The destructor is called when the program ends.

- For an object defined locally (that is, within a function), the constructor is called whenever the flow of control reaches the object definition, and the destructor is called when control passes out of the block in which the object is defined (that is, when the object goes out of scope).

- For an object defined locally using the static keyword, the constructor is called when control *first* reaches the object definition, and the destructor is called when the program ends.

- For an object created dynamically using the new operator, the constructor is called when the object is created and the destructor is called when the object is explicitly destroyed using the delete operator (if you do not explicitly destroy the object, the destructor will never be called.)

Arrays of Objects

You can define an array of objects, as in the following example:

CRectangle RectTable [10];

(CRectangle is the class shown in the previous examples.) You can also create an array of objects dynamically:

CRectangle *PRectTable = new CRectangle [10];

In either case, when the array is created, the compiler calls the default constructor for each element in the array, and when the array is destroyed, the compiler calls the destructor for each element (assuming that a destructor has been defined for the class). If the class does not have a default constructor, an error results.

If you *define* a named array of objects (as in the first example), you can initialize each element of the array by passing the desired values to a constructor; this technique is described in Chapter 6 (in the section "Initializing Arrays").

If, however, you have dynamically created an array using new, you cannot supply initializers for specific elements; rather, the compiler always calls the default constructor for each element. Also, for a dynamically created array, you must include the [ ] characters when destroying the array with the delete operator:

```
delete [] PRectTable;
```

If you omit the [ ] characters, the compiler will call the destructor only for the *first* array element.

NOTE The constructors for elements of an array are called in the order of increasing addresses. The destructors are called in the reverse order.

Inline Member Functions

In each of the example classes given so far in this chapter, the member functions are fully defined *within* the body of the class definition. As an alternative, you can *declare* a member function within the class, and *define* the function outside of the class. For instance, if the CRectangle member functions are defined outside of the class definition, the class could be defined as follows:

```
class CRectangle
{
private:
    int Left;
    int Top;
    int Right;
    int Bottom;

public:
    CRectangle ();
```

```
    CRectangle (int L, int T, int R, int B);
    void Draw (void);
    void GetCoord (int *L, int *T, int *R, int *B);
    void SetCoord (int L, int T, int R, int B);
};
```

When you define a member function outside of the class definition, you must preface the name of the function with the name of the class followed by the scope resolution operator (::). For example, the CRectangle member functions could be defined outside of the class definition as follows:

```
CRectangle::CRectangle ()
    {
    Left = Top = Right = Bottom = 0;
    }

CRectangle::CRectangle (int L, int T, int R, int B)
    {
    SetCoord (L,T,R,B);
    }

void CRectangle::Draw (void)
    {
    Line (Left, Top, Right, Top);
    Line (Right, Top, Right, Bottom);
    Line (Right, Bottom, Left, Bottom);
    Line (Left, Bottom, Left, Top);
    }

void CRectangle::GetCoord (int *L, int *T, int *R, int *B)
    {
    *L = Left;
    *T = Top;
    *R = Right;
    *B = Bottom;
    }

void CRectangle::SetCoord (int L, int T, int R, int B)
    {
    L = __min (__max (0,L), 80);
    T = __min (__max (0,T), 25);
    R = __min (__max (0,R), 80);
    B = __min (__max (0,B), 25);
    R = __max (R,L);
    B = __max (B,T);
```

```
    Left = L; Top = T; Right = R; Bottom = B;
    }
```

There is an important difference between a function defined within the body of the class and one defined outside of the class: A function that is defined within a class is treated as an inline function, while a function defined outside of the class is—by default—treated as a non-inline function (see the description of inline functions in Chapter 3). Accordingly, you might want to define very short functions within the body of the class and define longer functions outside of the class. For example, for the CRectangle class, the constructors and the GetCoord function (the shortest member functions) might be defined within the class as inline functions, and Draw and SetCoord (the two longest functions) might be defined outside the class as non-inline functions; see the complete CRectangle listing at the end of the next section.

You can *force* the compiler to treat a function defined outside of the class definition as inline, by using the inline keyword as explained in Chapter 3. For instance, you could make the function CRectangle::GetCoord inline by declaring it within the CRectangle class definition as follows,

```
void inline GetCoord (int *L, int *T, int *R, int *B);
```

and then defining it outside of the class definition, as follows:

```
void inline CRectangle::GetCoord (int *L, int *T, int *R, int *B)
    {
    *L = Left;
    *T = Top;
    *R = Right;
    *B = Bottom;
    }
```

Organizing the Source Files

If a program consists of more than one C++ source file, you generally place the class definition—together with the definitions of any inline member functions that are defined outside of the class—within a single header file (a .H file). You then include this header within any C++ source code file that uses the class. This arrangement ensures that the class definition, plus the code for any inline function, is available whenever the class is referenced or a member function is called. (Recall from Chapter 3 that the compiler must have access to the inline function code whenever it encounters a call to the function.)

Also, you generally place the definitions of any non-inline member functions within a separate C++ source code file, which is commonly known as the class *implementation* file. You must link the compiled version of the implementation file with your program (for example, by simply including the .CPP implementation file in the list of files in your Visual Workbench project.) Note that placing the definition of these functions within the header file rather than within a separate .CPP implementation file would result in a "symbol redefinition" LINK error if you included the header in more than one source file.

To illustrate, the following Listings 4.1 and 4.2 are the complete source code for the latest version of the CRectangle class. The definition of the CRectangle class is placed in a file named CRECT.H (the class header file), and the definitions of the non-inline member functions are placed in the file CRECT.CPP (the class implementation file).

Listing 4.1

```
// CRECT.H: CRectangle header file

class CRectangle
{
private:
    int Left;
    int Top;
    int Right;
    int Bottom;

public:
    CRectangle ()
        {
        Left = Top = Right = Bottom = 0;
        }
    CRectangle (int L, int T, int R, int B)
        {
        SetCoord (L, T, R, B);
        }
    void Draw (void);
    void GetCoord (int *L, int *T, int *R, int *B)
        {
        *L = Left;
        *T = Top;
        *R = Right;
        *B = Bottom;
```

```
        }
    void SetCoord (int L, int T, int R, int B);
};
```

Listing 4.2

```
// CRECT.CPP:  CRectangle implementation file

#include "crect.h"
#include <stdlib.h>

void Line (int X1, int Y1, int X2, int Y2);

void CRectangle::Draw (void)
    {
    Line (Left, Top, Right, Top);
    Line (Right, Top, Right, Bottom);
    Line (Right, Bottom, Left, Bottom);
    Line (Left, Bottom, Left, Top);
    }

void CRectangle::SetCoord (int L, int T, int R, int B)
    {
    L = __min (__max (0,L), 80);
    T = __min (__max (0,T), 25);
    R = __min (__max (0,R), 80);
    B = __min (__max (0,B), 25);
    R = __max (R,L);
    B = __max (B,T);
    Left = L; Top = T; Right = R; Bottom = B;
    }
```

(Recall that the CRectangle class assumes that the Line function is defined within another module.) CRECT.H must be included within any C++ file that references the CRectangle class (including CRECT.CPP!), and the compiled version of CRECT.CPP must be linked with the program.

The this Pointer

When you reference a data member of a class from code that is *outside* of the class, you always specify a particular instance of the class in the expression. The compiler therefore knows which copy of the data member to access. For example, the following code first prints the copy of the data member N belonging to the object Test1, and then prints the copy of N belonging to the object *PTest2:

```
CTest Test1;
CTest *PTest2 = new CTest;

// ...

cout << Test1.N << '\n';
cout << PTest2->N << '\n';
```

When you reference a data member *inside* a member function of a class, however, you do *not* specify a particular class instance:

```
class CTest
{
public:
    int N;

    int GetN ()
        {
        return N;   // N referenced without specifying an object
        }
}
```

Therefore, how does the compiler determine which copy of N is being referenced within a member function? To do this, the compiler actually passes to the member function a hidden pointer to the object that is referenced in the function call. The function implicitly uses this hidden pointer to access the correct copy of a data member. For instance, in the call:

```
Test.GetN ();
```

the compiler passes GetN a hidden pointer to the object Test. GetN implicitly uses this pointer to access the copy of N that belongs to the object Test.

You can directly access this hidden pointer using the C++ keyword this. In other words, within a member function, this is a predefined pointer that contains the address of the object referenced in the function call (the "current" object). Thus, GetN could be rewritten as follows:

```
int GetN ()
    {
```

```
    return this->N;   // equivalent to 'return N;'
    }
```

Prefacing the name of a data member with the expression this-> is valid but serves no purpose, because the use of the this pointer is implicit in a simple reference to the data member. Later in the book, however, you will see several practical uses for this.

If you need to access a global data item or function that has the same name as a data member or member function, you must preface the name with the scope resolution operator, ::. For example,

```
int N = 0;   // global N

class CTest
{
public:
    int N;   // data member N

    int Demo ()
      {
      cout << ::N << '\0';   // prints global N
      cout << N << '\0';      // accesses data member N using 'this'
      }
}
```

Static Class Members

Normally, each instance of a class has its own private copy of a data member that belongs to the class. If, however, you declare a data member using the static keyword, then a *single copy* of that data item will exist regardless of how many instances of the class have been created (even if *no* class instance has been created). For example, the following class defines the static data item Count:

```
class CTest
{
public:
    static int Count;

// remainder of class definition ...

}
```

No matter how many instances of CTest are created, there will be exactly one copy of Count.

In addition to declaring the static data member within the class, you must also define and initialize it *outside* of the class, as a global data item. Because the definition of a static data member occurs outside of the class, you must specify the class in which it is declared using the scope resolution operator (CTest::, in this example). For instance, you could define and initialize Count as follows:

```
int CTest::Count = 0;
```

Because a static data member exists independently of any class object, you can access it using the class name and the scope resolution operator without reference to a class instance, as shown in the following example:

```
void main ()
   {
   CTest::Count = 1;

   // ...
   }
```

You can think of a static data member as a hybrid between a global variable and a normal data member belonging to a class. Like a global variable, it is defined and initialized outside of a function, and it represents a single memory location that persists during the entire course of the program. Like a normal data member, however, it is declared within a class, its scope is limited to that class, and access to it can be controlled (that is, it can be made public, private, or protected).

You can also define a member function using the static keyword, as in the following example:

```
class CTest
{

// ...

static int GetCount ()
   {
   // function code ...
   }
```

```
// ...

}
```

A static member function has the following properties:

- Code outside of the class can call the function using the class name and the scope resolution operator, without reference to a class instance (a class instance need not even exist), as in the following example:

```
void main ()
    {
    int Count = CTest::GetCount ();

    // ...
    }
```

- A static member function can reference only static data members or static member functions that belong to its class. (Because it can be called without reference to a class instance, a static member function does not have a `this` pointer containing the address of an object. Therefore, if it attempted to access a nonstatic data member, the compiler would not be able to determine which object the data member belonged to.)

Static data members and member functions can be used to maintain a data item that applies to a class in general, or a data item shared by all instances of a class. The following program illustrates the use of static members to maintain a count of the current number of instances of a class:

```
#include <iostream.h>

class CTest
{
private:
    static int Count;

public:
    CTest ()
        {
        ++Count;
        }
    ~CTest ()
        {
```

```
        --Count;
        }
    static int GetCount ()
        {
        return Count;
        };
};

int CTest::Count = 0;

void main ()
    {
    cout << CTest::GetCount () << " objects exist\n";

    CTest Test1;
    CTest *PTest2 = new CTest;

    cout << CTest::GetCount () << " objects exist\n";

    delete PTest2;

    cout << CTest::GetCount () << " objects exist\n";
    }
```

This program prints the following:

```
0 objects exist
2 objects exist
1 objects exist
```

Summary

In this chapter, you learned how to define a class, how to create a class instance, and how to access the data and functions belonging to a class. You also learned about several special types of class members: constructors, destructors, inline member functions, and static members. The following are some of the specific concepts that were discussed:

- A class is somewhat similar to a structure in C. However, a class can contain both data items (known as *data members*) and functions (known as *member functions*) that operate upon the data items.

- A class definition creates a new type. To use the class, you must create an actual data item belonging to this type. Such a data item is known as an *instance* of the class or a class *object*.

- You can create a class object by defining it the same way you would define a variable of a built-in type. Alternatively, you can use the `new` and `delete` operators to dynamically create and destroy a class object.

- You access the members of a class using the `.` or `->` operators in the same way that you access the elements of a C structure. You can control access to class members by using the `public` or `private` *access specifiers* (by default, a member is private).

- According to the principle of *encapsulation*, you should use access specifiers to prevent the user from directly accessing data members used internally by the class. You can provide a member function that changes a data member, but only after it tests the validity of the value that the user supplies.

- A *constructor* is a special member function that is automatically called whenever you create an instance of the class. You typically use it to initialize data members or perform any other tasks required to prepare the class for use. A constructor can take any number of parameters; a *default constructor* is one that takes no parameters.

- A *destructor* is a special member function that is automatically called whenever a class object is destroyed. It can be used either to release memory allocated for the class object, or to perform other cleanup tasks.

- A member function can be defined within the body of the class, or it can merely be declared within the class and defined outside of the class.

- A member function defined within the class is automatically treated as an inline function. A member function defined outside of the class is treated as an inline function only if it is declared using the `inline` keyword.

- Within a member function, the C++ keyword *this* contains the address of the object referenced in the call to the function (that is, the particular object for which the member function was called).

- If a data member is defined using the `static` keyword, only a single copy of the data member exists, regardless of the number of instances of the class that are created. A static data member can be accessed using the class name and the scope resolution operator, without reference to a particular class instance.

- A member function defined using the `static` keyword can be called using the class name and the scope resolution operator, without reference to a specific object. It can access only static data members of the class.

In the next chapter, you will learn how to *derive* a new class from an existing one, so that you can adapt the class for managing new types of objects.

Deriving C++ Classes

5

- Deriving classes

- Creating hierarchies of classes

- Using virtual functions

In the previous chapter, you learned how to define independent classes. In this chapter, you will learn how to define classes that are derived from other classes. Deriving classes allows you to reuse the code and data structures belonging to existing classes, as well as to customize and extend existing classes for specific purposes.

You will also learn how to define and use *virtual* member functions. Virtual functions allow you to modify the behavior of existing classes and to write simple, elegant routines that can manage a variety of different program objects.

Deriving Classes

Suppose you have already written and tested the CRectangle class described in the previous chapter and are using this class in your program. You now decide that in addition to displaying open rectangles, you would like to display solid blocks (that is, rectangles filled with solid colors). To do this, you could define a new class, perhaps named CBlock. The CBlock class would contain most of the features of CRectangle, plus some additional facilities required for filling the rectangles once they have been drawn.

If you made CBlock an entirely new class, you would duplicate much of what you already wrote for the CRectangle class. Fortunately, C++ lets you avoid duplicating code and data by *deriving* a new class from an existing class. When you derive a new class, it *inherits* all of the data members and member functions belonging to the existing class.

For example, you could define the class CBlock as follows:

```
class CBlock : public CRectangle
{
};
```

The expression : public CRectangle causes the CBlock class to be derived from the CRectangle class. Because CBlock is derived from CRectangle, it inherits all of the data members and member functions belonging to CRectangle. In other words, although the CBlock class definition is empty, the CBlock class automatically possesses the GetCoord, SetCoord, and Draw member functions, as well as the Left, Top, Right, and Bottom data members that were defined for CRectangle. CRectangle is known as the *base* class, and CBlock as the *derived* class.

In general, you should include the keyword `public` in the first line of the derived class definition, as shown in the example. This keyword causes all members that are public in the base class to remain public in the derived class.

Once you have created a derived class, the next step is to add any new members that are required to meet the specific needs of the new class. For example, you might expand the `CBlock` definition as follows:

```
class CBlock : public CRectangle
{
private:
    int FillColor;   // stores the color used to fill the block

public:
    void Draw (void)
        {
        int L, T, R, B;

        CRectangle::Draw ();
        GetCoord (&L, &T, &R, &B);
        Fill ((L + R) / 2, (T + B) / 2, FillColor);
        }
    void SetColor (int Color)
        {
        FillColor = __max (0, Color);
        }
};
```

In addition to its inherited members, `CBlock` now has a new private data member, `FillColor` (which stores a code for the color used to fill the block), and a new public member function, `SetColor` (which assigns a color value to `FillColor`). `CBlock` also has a *new version* of the `Draw` member function, which draws a simple rectangle and then fills the inside of the rectangle with a solid color.

The `CBlock` class actually has *two* versions of the `Draw` function: one that it has inherited and one that it has explicitly defined. If you call `Draw` for a `CBlock` object, however, the version of the function defined within `CBlock` overrides the version defined within `Rectangle`, as shown in the following code:

```
CBlock Block;

// ...

Block.Draw ();   // calls the version of Draw defined within the
                 // CBlock class because Block is of type CBlock
```

> **NOTE**   Later in the chapter (in the section "Using Virtual Functions") you will learn a more powerful way to write an overriding member function.

The `CBlock` version of `Draw` begins by calling the `CRectangle` version of `Draw` to draw a simple rectangle:

```
CRectangle::Draw ();
```

The scope resolution expression (`CRectangle::`) preceding the call to `Draw` forces the compiler to call the version of the `Draw` function belonging to the `CRectangle` class. If the scope resolution expression were not included, the compiler would automatically call the version of `Draw` defined for the current class, `CBlock`. (Again, the version of the function defined within the current class overrides the inherited version.)

Next, the `Draw` function calls the inherited member function `GetCoord` to obtain the current values of the rectangle coordinates, and then it calls the function `Fill` to paint the inside of the rectangle with the current color value:

```
GetCoord (&L, &T, &R, &B);
Fill ((L + R) / 2, (T + B) / 2, FillColor);
```

`Fill` is a hypothetical function that fills a bordered area. The first two parameters give the coordinates of a point within the border, while the third parameter gives the value of the color to be used for painting the area. Such a function might be defined elsewhere in your program or obtained from a function library.

To illustrate the use of the `CBlock` class, the following code would draw a block:

```
CBlock Block;                        // create an instance of CBlock

Block.SetCoord (25,25,100,100);  // set coordinates of block
```

```
Block.SetColor (5);              // set color of block
Block.Draw ();                   // call version of Draw defined
                                 // for CBlock class
```

Providing Constructors for Derived Classes

Notice that the code for drawing a block using CBlock must call two member functions (SetCoord and SetColor) to set the values of the data members before calling Draw to draw the block. To make CBlock easier to use, you could add the following constructor, which would set the values of all data members when an instance of the class is created:

```
CBlock (int L, int T, int R, int B, int Color)
    : CRectangle (L, T, R, B)
    {
    SetColor (Color);
    }
```

The member initializer list in this constructor calls the constructor belonging to the base class (CRectangle), passing it the values that are to be assigned to the data members defined within the base class. (The member initializer list can be used to initialize a base class, as well as data members as described in Chapter 4 in the section "Member Initialization in Constructors".) The body of the CBlock constructor then calls SetColor to set the value of the FillColor data member. With this constructor in place, you could now create a CBlock object and draw a block with only two statements:

```
CBlock Block (25, 25, 100, 100, 5);
Block.Draw ();
```

You could also add the following default constructor, which would assign 0 to all data members:

```
CBlock ()
    {
    FillColor = 0;
    }
```

Because this constructor does *not* explicitly initialize the base class (the member initializer list is empty), the compiler *automatically* calls the base class's default constructor (CRectangle::CRectangle ()), which sets all of the data members defined within the base class to 0. (If the base class did not have a default constructor, an error would result.)

The `CBlock` default constructor allows you to create an object with all data members set to 0, without passing any values or calling any member functions:

```
CBlock Block;  // create a CBlock object with all data members
               // set to 0
```

See Listing 5.1, the complete listing for the `CBlock` class, including the two new constructors, at the end of the next section.

Order of Construction and Destruction

When you create an instance of a derived class, the compiler calls constructors in the following order:

1. The constructor of the base class.

2. The constructors for any member objects (that is, data members that are class objects). These constructors are called in the order in which the objects are defined.

3. The class's own constructor.

Destructors, where defined, are called in the exact opposite order.

Thus, when the body of a particular constructor is executed, you know that the base class and any member objects have already been initialized and may safely be used. Likewise, when the body of a particular destructor is executed, you know that the base class and any member objects have not yet been destroyed and may still be used.

Accessing Inherited Members

Even though `CBlock` has inherited the data members `Left`, `Top`, `Right`, and `Bottom` from its base class, it is *not* allowed to access them directly, because they are defined as private in the base class. Rather, it must use the public function, `GetCoord`, in the same manner as any other part of the program. This restriction leads to member function code that is somewhat awkward and inefficient. As an alternative, you could make the CRectangle data members *protected* rather than private by using the protected access specifier in place of the private specifier, as follows:

Listing 5.1

```
// CRECT1.H: CRectangle header file

class CRectangle
{
protected:
    int Left;
    int Top;
    int Right;
    int Bottom;

public:
    CRectangle ()
        {
        Left = Top = Right = Bottom = 0;
        }
    CRectangle (int L, int T, int R, int B)
        {
        SetCoord (L, T, R, B);
        }
    void Draw (void);
    void GetCoord (int *L, int *T, int *R, int *B)
        {
        *L = Left;
        *T = Top;
        *R = Right;
        *B = Bottom;
        }
    void SetCoord (int L, int T, int R, int B);
};
```

(Recall that this version of CRectangle assumes that the Draw and SetCoord member functions are defined outside of the class.) Like a private member, a protected member cannot be accessed from outside of the class; thus, the following type of access is still illegal:

```
void main ()
    {
    CRectangle Rect;
```

```
    Rect.Left = 10;   // ERROR: cannot access protected data member

}
```

However, unlike a private member, a protected member *can* be directly accessed from within a class that is *derived* from the class in which the member is defined. Thus, the CBlock class can now be rewritten to directly access the data members defined in CRectangle, as follows:

Listing 5.2

```
// CBLOCK.H: CBlock header file

#include "crect1.h"
#include <stdlib.h>

void Fill (int X, int Y, int Color);

class CBlock : public CRectangle
{
protected:
    int FillColor;

public:
    CBlock ()
        {
        FillColor = 0;
        }
    CBlock (int L, int T, int R, int B, int Color)
        : CRectangle (L, T, R, B)
        {
        SetColor (Color);
        }
    void Draw (void)
        {
        CRectangle::Draw ();
        Fill ((Left + Right) / 2, (Top + Bottom) / 2, FillColor);
        }
    void SetColor (int Color)
        {
        FillColor = __max (0, Color);
        }
};
```

Notice that CBlock makes the data member that it defines (FillColor) protected rather than private, so that it can be accessed from any class that is derived from CBlock (as discussed in the next section).

Public and Private Derivation

If you derive a class using the public keyword,

```
class CBlock : public CRectangle
{
// class definition ...
}
```

then all public members of the base class become public members of the derived class, and all protected members of the base class become protected members of the derived class.

If, however, you derive a class using the private keyword,

```
class CBlock : private CRectangle
{
// class definition ...
}
```

then all public and protected members of the base class become private members of the derived class. (If you specify neither the public nor the private keyword in the derivation, then the class is derived privately by default.)

With either type of derivation, private members in the base class are always inaccessible in the derived class (that is, although they are inherited by the derived class, and are therefore a part of any instance of the derived class, they cannot be directly accessed within the derived class code).

In C++, you almost always derive classes publicly; hence, you will see public derivations in all of the examples given in this book.

NOTE You can allow code within another class or within a global function to access the private or protected data members of your class by declaring the other class or function as a *friend* of your class. For an explanation of this technique, see the section "Overloading the Assignment Operator" in Chapter 6.

Creating Hierarchies of Classes

A derived class can serve as a base for yet another derived class. You can thus create hierarchies of related classes. For example, you might derive a class from CBlock, named CRoundBlock, for creating a rounded block (that is, a block with rounded corners), as follows:

```
class CRoundBlock : public CBlock
{
protected:
    int Radius;

public:
    CRoundBlock ()
        {
        int Radius = 0;
        }
    CRoundBlock (int L, int T, int R, int B, int Color, int Rad)
        : CBlock (L, T, R, B, Color)
        {
        SetRadius (Rad);
        }
    void Draw (void)
        {
        // draw a rounded, open rectangle (use Radius) ...

        // now fill the rectangle with color:
        Fill ((Left + Right) / 2, (Top + Bottom) / 2, FillColor);
        }
    void SetRadius (int Rad)
        {
        Radius = __max (0, Rad);
        }
};
```

NOTE The class CRoundBlock is said to be derived *directly* from CBlock, which is known as its *direct base*, and it is said to be derived *indirectly* from CRectangle, which is known as its *indirect base*.

CRoundBlock inherits all members of the CBlock class, including the members that CBlock inherits from CRectangle. CRoundBlock defines an additional data member, Radius, which stores the radius of the rounded corners, and it defines a new version of the Draw function, which draws a solid rectangle with rounded corners. CRoundBlock also provides a public member function, SetRadius, for setting the value of its data member Radius, and it provides both a default constructor that sets all data members to 0 and a constructor that initializes all data members with specific values.

The following code creates an instance of RoundBlock, initializing all data members, and then draws a rounded block:

```
CRoundBlock RoundBlock (10, 15, 50, 75, 5, 3);

RoundBlock.Draw ();
```

Figure 5.1 illustrates the hierarchy of example classes, while Figure 5.2 shows the figures drawn by each of these classes.

NOTE The CRoundBlock data member Radius is made protected so that it can be accessed by any class derived from CRoundBlock, but not by code outside of the class hierarchy.

Commercial class libraries, such as the Microsoft Foundation Classes and the Microsoft iostream class library, consist primarily of tree-like hierarchies of related classes. In such hierarchies, a single class often serves as the base for several derived classes (hence the tree-like structure). (Both of these class libraries are included with Microsoft Visual C++. The Microsoft Foundation Classes [MFC] are discussed in Part III of the book, and the iostream class library is discussed in Chapter 21.)

FIGURE 5.1:

The hierarchy of example classes

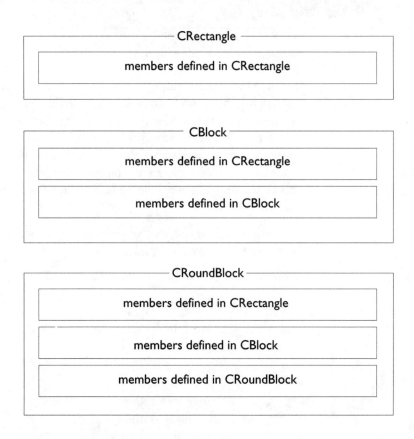

It is also possible for a class to be derived from more than one base class. This is known as *multiple inheritance,* and it is used in the iostream class library (discussed in Chapter 21).

The Advantages of Inheritance

As you can see from the simple examples that have been given, inheritance allows you to reuse code you have already written and data structures you have already designed. It thus prevents code and data duplication.

FIGURE 5.2:

The figures drawn by the example classes

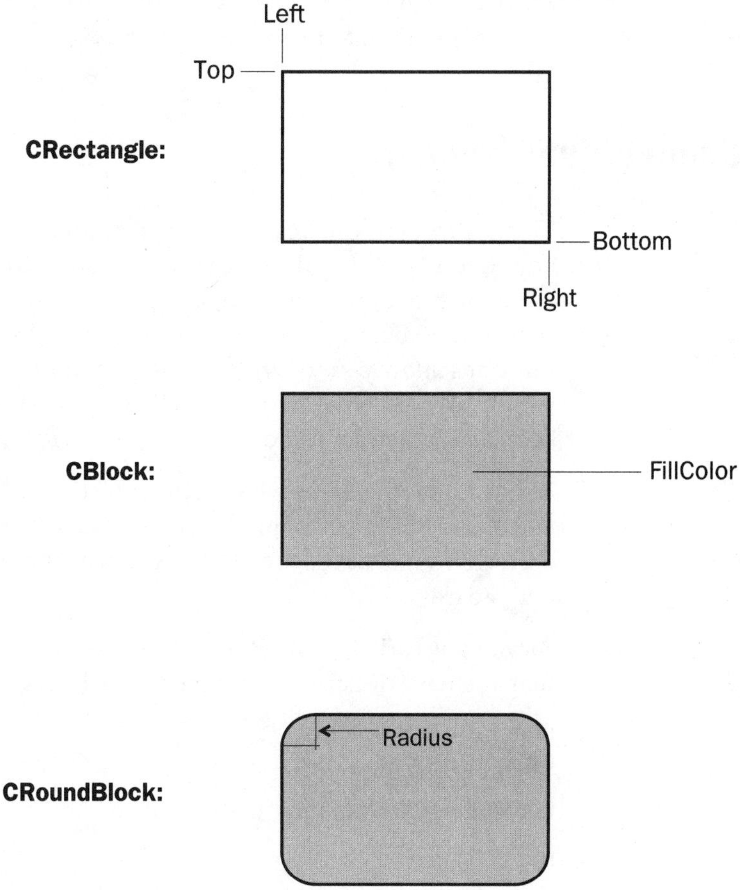

CRectangle:

CBlock:

CRoundBlock:

A related advantage of inheritance is that it can make your programs easier to maintain, since the code and data that handles a given task is generally contained within a single, easily located place in your code, and not scattered throughout the program.

Also, the hierarchies of classes you can define in C++ effectively model many real-world relationships. For example, deriving the CBlock class from the CRectangle class reflects the fact that a block is a *type of* rectangle (namely, one that is filled with color), and deriving the CRoundBlock class from CBlock reflects the fact that a rounded block is a type of block. As another example, the hierarchy of classes in the Microsoft Foundation Classes library closely models the relationships among the Windows items that these classes manage.

Using Virtual Functions

Virtual functions can be a bit difficult to understand at first. Learning about them, however, is well worth the effort. Not only do they form an important tool for object-oriented programming, but also they are used extensively in class libraries such as the Microsoft Foundation Classes. As you will learn in this section, virtual functions allow you to write simple, general-purpose routines for manipulating a variety of object types. They also allow you to easily modify the behavior of existing base classes, even if you do not have access to the source code for these classes.

To get a general idea of what virtual functions are, consider once more the `CRect-angle` and `CBlock` example classes that have been presented. Recall that `CBlock` is derived from `CRectangle`; that is, `CRectangle` is the base class, and `CBlock` is the derived class.

As you saw earlier, both of these classes define a member function named `Draw`. Say that you have declared an instance of each class:

```
CRectangle Rect;
CBlock Block;
```

Given these declarations, the statement

```
Rect.Draw ();
```

will clearly call the version of `Draw` defined within the `CRectangle` class, and the statement

```
Block.Draw ();
```

will clearly call the version of `Draw` defined within the `CBlock` class. In both statements, the compiler has no trouble determining which version of the function to call, since the call statement includes a reference to an instance of a specific class.

In C++, however, it is common to use a pointer to a base class to hold *either* the address of an instance of the base class *or* the address of an instance of a derived class. For example, consider the following CRectangle pointer:

```
CRectangle *PRect;
```

C++ allows you to assign this pointer the address of a CRectangle instance *or* an instance of a class derived (directly or indirectly) from CRectangle, without using a cast operation. For example, both of the assignment statements in the following code are legal:

```
CRectangle *PRect;  // declare a pointer to CRectangle

CRectangle Rect;    // create an instance of the CRectangle class
CBlock Block;       // create an instance of the CBlock class

PRect = &Rect;      // legal: assign address of CRectangle
                    // instance to pointer
PRect = &Block;     // also legal: assign address of CBlock
                    // instance to pointer
```

Assignments to Base Class Pointers

C++ allows you to freely assign the address of a derived class to a base class pointer because it is *safe* to use such a pointer. The base class pointer can be used to access only members that are defined within the base class. All of these members are also defined within the derived class (by inheritance); therefore, if the pointer contains the address of a derived class object, any member that can be referenced with the pointer will be defined.

Although you can force the compiler to assign the address of a base class to a derived class pointer by means of a cast operation, such a pointer is *not* safe because the pointer could be used to access members that are not actually defined in the object referenced (a base class does *not* always have all of the members defined in a derived class).

A problem arises, however, if you call the Draw member function using the PRect pointer. The compiler cannot know in advance which type of object PRect will point to when the program actually runs; therefore, it always generates a call to the version of Draw that is defined within the CRectangle class, since PRect is declared as a pointer to CRectangle.

For example, say that PRect points to Rect, which is an instance of the CRectangle class:

```
CRectangle *PRect;
CRectangle Rect;

// ...

PRect = &Rect;
```

In this case, using PRect to call the Draw member function will invoke the version of Draw defined within CRectangle, exactly as desired:

```
PRect->Draw ();
```

Assume, however, that PRect points to an instance of the CBlock class:

```
CRectangle *PRect;
CBlock Block;

// ...

PRect = &Block;
```

If you now use this pointer to call Draw,

```
PRect->Draw ();
```

the program will *still* call the version of Draw defined within CRectangle. The result is that the *wrong version* of the Draw member function is called, producing an open rectangle rather than the desired filled block.

The solution to this problem is to make Draw a *virtual* function. Defining Draw as virtual ensures that the correct version of the function will be called when the program is run, even if the function is called using a base class pointer. To make Draw a virtual function, you include the virtual keyword in the declaration of Draw within the base class, CRectangle, as follows:

```
class CRectangle
{
```

```
// other declarations ...

public:
    virtual void Draw (void);

// other declarations ...

}
```

Note that you cannot include the `virtual` keyword in the definition of `Draw`, which occurs outside of the class definition.

You can also include the `virtual` keyword in the declaration of `Draw` within the derived class `CBlock`, although it is not necessary to do so:

```
class CBlock : public CRectangle
{

// other declarations ...

public:
    virtual void Draw (void);

// other declarations ...

}
```

(If a function is declared as virtual in a base class, a function with the same name, return type, and parameters that is declared in a derived class is automatically considered to be virtual. You therefore do not need to repeat the `virtual` keyword in each derived class, although doing so might make the program easier to read and understand.)

If `Draw` is a defined as a virtual function and your program calls `Draw` using the `PRect` pointer,

```
CRectangle *PRect;

// ...

PRect->Draw ();
```

the compiler does *not* automatically generate a call to the version of `Draw` defined within `CRectangle`. Rather, it generates special code that calls the *correct* version of

Draw when the program is run. Thus, the following statements will result in calling the version of Draw defined within CRectangle:

```
CRectangle *PRect;
CRectangle Rect;

// ...

PRect = &Rect;
PRect->Draw ();
```

while the following statements will result in calling the version of Draw defined within CBlock:

```
CRectangle *PRect;
CBlock Block;

// ...

PRect = &Block;
PRect->Draw ();
```

Since the actual function address is not determined until the program is run, this calling mechanism is known as *late binding* or *dynamic binding*. The standard function-calling mechanism, in which the compiler knows in advance the exact target address of the call, is termed *early binding* or *static binding*.

> **TIP**
>
> For a virtual function, the program must store the address of the correct version of the function within each object. (More accurately, it stores the address of a *table* of virtual function addresses.) In addition to requiring additional storage, the virtual function-calling mechanism is less direct and therefore slightly slower than a standard function call. As a result, you should not make a member function virtual unless late binding is required.

The next two sections illustrate two different ways that you can use virtual functions in a program.

Polymorphism

Virtual functions support an important feature of object-oriented programming: *polymorphism.* Polymorphism is the ability to use a single instruction to perform one of a variety of different actions; the actual action that is performed depends upon the specific kind of object involved. As an example of how a virtual function supports polymorphism, if you have defined Draw as a virtual member function, you can use a *single* function call such as

```
PRect->Draw ();
```

to draw either a rectangle, a block, or a rounded block; the specific action performed depends upon the class of the object currently pointed to by PRect.

Using Virtual Functions to Handle Class Objects

Virtual functions allow you to write simple, general-purpose routines that can automatically handle a variety of different object types. For example, suppose that you are writing a drawing program that allows the user to draw rectangles, blocks, or rounded blocks. Each time the user draws one of these figures, the program invokes the new operator to dynamically create an object of the appropriate class (CRectangle, CBlock, or CRoundBlock) to manage the new figure. Because CBlock and CRoundBlock are both derived from CRectangle, you can conveniently store the pointers to all of the objects within a single array of CRectangle pointers, as in the following code:

```
const int MAXFIGS = 100;
CRectangle *PFigure [MAXFIGS];
int Count = 0;

// ...

// the user draws a block:
PFigure [Count++] = new CBlock (10, 15, 25, 30, 5);

// ...

// the user draws a rectangle:
```

```
PFigure [Count++] = new CRectangle (5, 8, 19, 23);

// ...

// the user draws a rounded block:
PFigure [Count++] = new CRoundBlock (27, 33, 43, 56, 10, 5);
```

Suppose now that you are writing a routine that redraws all the objects on the screen. If Draw were *not* a virtual function, for each element in the array you would somehow have to determine the type of the figure, and then call the appropriate version of Draw. For instance, you might add a data member named Type to the CRectangle class, which would store a code indicating the object's class:

```
class CRectangle
{
// other definitions ...

public:
    int Type;   // inherited by all derived classes; stores a code
                // indicating the object's class: RECT, BLOCK, or
                // ROUNDBLOCK
}
```

(This example assumes that the three constants RECT, BLOCK, and ROUNDBLOCK have been defined previously in the program.)

You could then use the Type member to determine the type of each figure in the array, and call the appropriate version of Draw:

```
for (int i = 0; i < Count; ++i)
    switch (PFigure [i]->Type)
        {
        case RECT:
            PFigure [i]->Draw ();
            break;

        case BLOCK:
            ((CBlock *)PFigure [i])->Draw ();
            break;

        case ROUNDBLOCK:
            ((CRoundBlock *)PFigure [i])->Draw ();
            break;
        }
```

Not only is this code cumbersome, but also it would require you to add a new `case` branch whenever you modify the program to support a new type of figure (by adding a new class to the hierarchy).

If, however, you declare the `Draw` function virtual (by adding the `virtual` keyword to its declaration in `CRectangle`), the program would *automatically* call the appropriate version of `Draw` for the current object type. Redrawing the figures could then be accomplished with the following code:

```
for (int i = 0; i < Count; ++i)
   PFigure [i]->Draw ();
```

This code is both much simpler and more elegant, plus it has the additional advantage that it will not require you to modify it if you add a class to the hierarchy to support another type of figure.

> **NOTE** An actual drawing program, of course, would probably support many more kinds of figures. You can use this same general approach, however, as long as all of the classes for managing specific figures are derived from a common base class.

Using Virtual Functions to Modify Base Classes

A virtual function can also be used to modify the behavior of a base class, without changing the base class code. For example, assume that you have been given the following class for displaying a message box (perhaps as part of a commercial class library):

```
class CMessageBox
{
protected:
   char *Message;

   virtual void DrawBackground (int L, int T, int R, int B);
   // paints a WHITE background in message box

public:
   CMessageBox ()
      {
      Message = new char ('\0');
      }
```

```
~CMessageBox ()
    {
    delete [] Message;
    }
void Display ()
    {
    DrawBackground (0, 0, 35, 25);

    // code for displaying Msg string ...

    }
void Set (char *Msg);
};
```

The public member function Set allows you to assign a message string, and the public member function Display displays the message within a box on the screen. Notice that Display erases the background by calling another member function, DrawBackground, passing it the dimensions of the message box; this function paints the background using a solid white color. DrawBackground is intended to be used internally by the class; it is *not* intended to be called from outside of the class, and it is therefore declared as a protected member.

DrawBackground is also declared as a virtual function. Accordingly, if you derive your own class from CMessageBox, which includes your own version of DrawBackground, your version of the function will override the version defined within CMessageBox, even when this function is called from within CMessageBox. For example, you could derive the following class from CMessageBox:

```
class CMyMessageBox : public CMessageBox
{
protected:
    virtual void DrawBackground (int L, int T, int R, int B)
        {
        // paint a BLUE background in message box ...
        }
};
```

Notice that the overriding version of DrawBackground draws a blue background rather than a white background. Thus, the following code would create an object and display a message box with a blue background:

```
CMyMessageBox MyMessageBox;

MyMessageBox.Set ("hello");
MyMessageBox.Display ();
```

By providing `DrawBackground` as a separate virtual function, the `CMessageBox` class allows you to change the behavior of the class (namely, the color or pattern that is drawn as the background within the box), *without* modifying the `CMessage-Box` source code (you do not even need to see the source code). As you will learn in Part III of this book, many of the classes defined in the MFC provide virtual functions that you can override in your derived classes, enabling you to easily modify the behavior of the MFC classes.

Summary

This chapter introduced the basic techniques for deriving new classes from existing classes, as well as for creating hierarchies of related classes. It also explained virtual functions and described several ways to use them. The following are the basic concepts and techniques that were presented:

- You can *derive* a new class from an existing class by specifying the name of the existing class in the definition of the new class. The existing class is known as the *base* class and the new class as the *derived* class.

- The derived class *inherits* all of the members of the base class. You can add new members to the derived class to adapt it for its purpose.

- A constructor for a derived class can explicitly initialize its base class by passing parameters to the base class constructor. If the derived class constructor does *not* explicitly initialize its base class, the compiler automatically calls the default constructor for the base class.

- If a data member in a base class is declared using the `protected` access specifier, the member can be accessed from within a derived class, but it *cannot* be accessed from other functions in the program.

- A derived class can serve as the base for another class, allowing you to create multilevel hierarchies of related classes.

- Inheritance (that is, the ability to derive one class from another) allows you to reuse code and data structures you have already written for a class. It can also make your program easier to maintain and at the same time help you model the relationships among the real-world items that your program manages.

- Each class in a hierarchy of derived classes can have its own version of a particular member function. If this function is declared as `virtual`, calling the function will automatically invoke the version of the function that is appropriate for the current object, even if the function is called through a pointer to the base class.

- Virtual functions support *polymorphism*, which is the ability to use a single instruction to perform one of a variety of different actions, the particular action depending upon the type of object involved.

- Virtual functions allow you to write simple, general-purpose routines that can handle a variety of different—but related—objects.

- Virtual functions also allow you to override the default behavior of a base class, without modifying the base class source code.

In the next chapter, you will learn about several additional C++ features that pertain to classes.

How Overriding Works

The chapter introduced virtual functions by explaining that if you call a virtual function using a pointer to a class object, the function call will be interpreted according to the actual type of the object rather than the type of the pointer. How does this property apply to a virtual function called from within a member function of a base class, as described in this section?

Recall from Chapter 4 that when a class member is referenced from within a member function, it is implicitly referenced using the `this` pointer. Thus, the `Display` member function of `CMessageBox` could be written in the following equivalent way:

```
class CMessageBox
{
```

```
// other declarations ...

public:
    void Display ()
        {
        this->DrawBackground (0, 0, 35, 25);

        // ...

        }

// other declarations ...

};
```

If DrawBackground were *not* virtual, the function call in Display would invoke the version of DrawBackground defined within CMessageBox (because within CMessageBox, this is a pointer to a CMessageBox object). However, if DrawBackground *is* virtual, the function call would invoke the version of DrawBackground defined within the current object's class. Thus, if Display is called for a CMyMessageBox object,

```
CMyMessageBox MyMessageBox;

// ...

MyMessageBox.Display ();
```

the overriding version of DrawBackground defined within CMyMessageBox would be called.

Overloading, Copying, and Converting

6

- Overloading operators

- Using copy and conversion constructors

This chapter describes several ways in which you can customize the behavior of the classes you create. Specifically, you will learn how to *overload* standard C++ operators to specify the way that they work with objects belonging to your class. You will also learn how to define special constructors that affect the way a class object is initialized with another object of the same type (a *copy constructor*) or the way another data type is converted to a class object (a *conversion constructor*).

Overloading Operators

The C++ operators work in predefined ways when used with the built-in data types. For example, when the + operator is used with two `int` variables, it performs an integer addition, and when + is used with two `double` variables, it performs a floating point addition operation. C++ also allows you to use standard operators with objects of classes, provided that you have defined the exact action that a given operator is to perform. Defining the way that an operator works with objects of a particular class is known as *overloading* the operator.

For example, suppose that you have defined the class `CCurrency` for storing and manipulating monetary amounts:

```
class CCurrency
{
private:
   long Dollars;
   int Cents;

public:
   CCurrency ()
      {
      Dollars = Cents = 0;
      }
   CCurrency (long Dol, int Cen)
      {
      SetAmount (Dol, Cen);
      }
   void GetAmount (long *PDol, int *PCen)
      {
      *PDol = Dollars;
      *PCen = Cents;
      }
```

```
void PrintAmount ()
   {
   cout.fill ('0');
   cout.width (1);
   cout << '$' << Dollars << '.';
   cout.width (2);
   cout << Cents << '\n';
   }
void SetAmount (long Dol, int Cen)
   {
   // adjust for cent amounts >= 100:
   Dollars = Dol + Cen / 100;
   Cents = Cen % 100;
   }
};
```

The CCurrency class stores monetary amounts as integer values, so that these amounts can be manipulated using fast, accurate integer operations. The class provides a default constructor that sets the dollar and cent values both to 0, and it provides a constructor that allows you to specify initial dollar and cent amounts. It also provides a separate member function (SetAmount) for setting the monetary amount, plus member functions for obtaining the amount (GetAmount) and printing the amount (PrintAmount). (The use of the cout members fill and width in PrintAmount will be explained in Chapter 23. Note that rather than storing the monetary amount in a single long integer as the total number of cents, it stores the number of dollars in a long member and the number of cents in a separate int member so that it can manage larger monetary amounts. As a result, it can handle a dollar value up to the maximum value of a long, which is 2,147,483,647.)

Instead of providing member functions for performing arithmetic operations on the monetary amounts, you can overload standard C++ operators so that you may perform arithmetic-using expressions just like those used with built-in data types. To overload an operator, you define a member function that is named by using the operator keyword, followed by the operator itself. For example, you could overload the + operator by adding the following member function to the CCurrency class definition:

```
class CCurrency
{

// other declarations ...

public:
```

```
CCurrency operator+ (CCurrency Curr)
    {
    CCurrency Temp (Dollars + Curr.Dollars,
                    Cents + Curr.Cents);
    return Temp;
    }

// other declarations ...

};
```

An operator function should be defined as *public* so that the operator can be used by other functions in the program. Once this function is defined, you can use the + operator as follows:

```
CCurrency Amount1 (12, 95);
CCurrency Amount2 (4, 38);
CCurrency Total;

Total = Amount1 + Amount2;
```

The C++ compiler interprets the expression `Amount1 + Amount2` as

```
Amount1.operator+ (Amount2);
```

The `operator+` function creates a temporary `CCurrency` object (`Temp`) containing the sum of the amounts stored in the two classes appearing in the addition expression. It then returns the temporary object. In the addition expression above, the returned object is assigned to the `CCurrency` object `Total`. (As you will see later in the chapter, this assignment causes the compiler to generate a member by member copy operation.)

Like the standard + operator, an expression containing more than one overloaded + operator is evaluated from left to right. For example, the following program uses the overloaded + operator to add the values stored in three `CCurrency` objects:

```
void main ()
    {
    CCurrency Advertising (235, 42);
    CCurrency Rent (823, 68);
    CCurrency Entertainment (1024, 32);
    CCurrency Overhead;

    Overhead = Advertising + Rent + Entertainment;
    Overhead.PrintAmount ();
```

```
        }
```

The `operator+` function could be simplified by replacing the explicit temporary `CCurrency` object with an implicit temporary object:

```
CCurrency operator+ (CCurrency Curr)
    {
    return CCurrency (Dollars + Curr.Dollars, Cents + Curr.Cents);
    }
```

When you call a class constructor within an expression, the compiler creates a temporary class object. The `operator+` function immediately returns the contents of this temporary object. (The section "Writing Copy Constructors," later in the chapter, explains how class objects are returned from functions.)

You could also make the `operator+` function more efficient by passing it a *reference* to a `CCurrency` object rather than an object itself. (As explained in Chapter 3, passing a reference eliminates the need to copy the object into a local parameter; this is especially important for large objects.) The following is the final version of the `operator+` function:

```
CCurrency operator+ (const CCurrency &Curr)
    {
    return CCurrency (Dollars + Curr.Dollars, Cents + Curr.Cents);
    }
```

(As was also explained in Chapter 3, using the `const` keyword when declaring the parameter guarantees that the function does not change the value of the parameter.)

Defining Additional Operator Functions

Like other functions in C++, operator functions can be overloaded to provide several ways to use the operator. For example, you might want to be able to use the + operator to add a `CCurrency` object to a constant `int` or `long` value. (With the operator function that has already been defined, both operands must be `CCurrency` objects.) To do this, you could add the following member function to the `CCurrency` class:

```
CCurrency operator+ (long Dol)
    {
    return CCurrency (Dollars + Dol, Cents);
    }
```

Adding this function would allow you to use the + operator as follows:

```
CCurrency Advertising (235, 42);
```

```
// ...
```

```
Advertising = Advertising + 100;
```

The compiler would interpret the expression `Advertising + 100` as

```
Advertising.operator+ (100)
```

and it would therefore call the newly defined version of `operator+`. You *cannot*, however, put the integer constant first, because the compiler would be forced to interpret the expression `100 + Advertising` as

```
100.operator+ (Advertising)   // nonsense!
```

To circumvent this limitation, you can write a *nonmember* operator function whose first parameter is a `long`:

```
// defined globally:
```

```
CCurrency operator+ (long Dol, const CCurrency &Curr)
    {
    return CCurrency (Dol + Curr.Dollars, Curr.Cents);
    }
```

Because this function is *not* a member of `CCurrency`, it cannot normally access the private data members of this class (namely, `Dollars` and `Cents`). To grant it access to the private members of `CCurrency`, you must make it a *friend* of the `CCurrency` class, by declaring it within the `CCurrency` class definition using the `friend` keyword:

```
class CCurrency
{
```

```
// other declarations ...
```

```
    friend CCurrency operator+ (long Dol, const CCurrency &Curr);
```

```
// other declarations ...
```

```
};
```

Even though a friend function is not a member of a class, it can access any of the private or protected members of the class that declares it a friend.

Once this new operator function has been defined, you could use the + operator as follows:

```
CCurrency Advertising (235, 42);

// ...

Advertising = 100 + Advertising;
```

The compiler would now interpret the expression 100 + Advertising as:

```
operator+ (100, Advertising)
```

and it would therefore call the *friend* version of the operator function.

Friend Classes

In a class definition, you can also declare another *class* as a friend, as in the following example:

```
class A
{
// ...

    friend class FriendOfA;

// ...
};
```

Because of this friend declaration, any member function of class FriendOfA can access the private and protected members of class A.

Note that you *could* have defined nonmember friend functions rather than member functions for the first two versions of operator+ (although there is no particular advantage in doing so):

```
friend CCurrency operator+ (const CCurrency &Curr1,
                            const CCurrency &Curr2);
friend CCurrency operator+ (const CCurrency &Curr, long Dol);
```

A nonmember function that overloads an operator must take at least one parameter that is a class object. (Thus, you cannot use an operator function to change the standard meaning of a C++ operator that occurs in an expression containing only built-in types.)

The following is the complete definition of the CCurrency class and the nonmember operator+ function:

```
#include <iostream.h>

class CCurrency
{
private:
    long Dollars;
    int Cents;

public:
    CCurrency ()
       {
       Dollars = Cents = 0;
       }
    CCurrency (long Dol, int Cen)
       {
       SetAmount (Dol, Cen);
       }
    void GetAmount (long *PDol, int *PCen)
       {
       *PDol = Dollars;
       *PCen = Cents;
       }
    void PrintAmount ()
       {
       cout.fill ('0');
       cout.width (1);
       cout << '$' << Dollars << '.';
       cout.width (2);
       cout << Cents << '\n';
       }
    void SetAmount (long Dol, int Cen)
       {
       // adjust for cent amounts >= 100:
       Dollars = Dol + Cen / 100;
       Cents = Cen % 100;
       }
```

```
     CCurrency operator+ (const CCurrency &Curr)
        {
       return CCurrency (Dollars + Curr.Dollars,
                         Cents + Curr.Cents);
        }
     CCurrency operator+ (long Dol)
        {
       return CCurrency (Dollars + Dol, Cents);
        }
     friend CCurrency operator+ (long Dol, const CCurrency &Curr);
};

CCurrency operator+ (long Dol, const CCurrency &Curr)
     {
     return CCurrency (Dol + Curr.Dollars, Curr.Cents);
     }
```

The following program demonstrates the use of all three of the operator functions that have been defined:

```
void main ()
     {
     CCurrency Advertising (235, 42);
     CCurrency Rent (823, 68);
     CCurrency Entertainment (1024, 32);
     CCurrency Overhead;

     Overhead = Advertising + Rent + Entertainment;
     Overhead.PrintAmount ();

     Overhead = Overhead + 100;
     Overhead.PrintAmount ();

     Overhead = 100 + Overhead;
     Overhead.PrintAmount ();

     }
```

This program would print the values:

```
$2083.42
$2183.42
$2283.42
```

In conclusion, defining three versions of the operator+ function makes it possible to use the + operator with two objects, with an object and a constant, or with a constant and an object. (The fourth possible combination, two constants, would cause the + operator to have its standard meaning.) Later in the chapter, in the section "Writing Conversion Constructors," you will learn how to write a special constructor that allows you to eliminate the two versions of the `operator+` function that are members of the `CCurrency` class.

Enhancing CCurrency

You could enhance the `CCurrency` class by adding support for negative monetary amounts (currently, the class behaves unpredictably if you assign a negative amount) and by overloading other operators. You could define operator functions for the − operator (for subtracting two objects, or an object and a constant), the * operator (for multiplying an object by a constant), and the / operator (for dividing an object by a constant).

When defining these operators, avoid the temptation to convert the dollar and cent values to a single `long int` value (storing the total number of cents). Doing so would simplify the arithmetic routines but would risk causing overflows (or it would reduce the maximum dollar amount the class can manage).

General Guidelines for Overloading Operators

You can overload almost any of the existing binary and unary C++ operators; the overloadable operators are listed below. When you overload an operator for a class, you define the *meaning* of the operator when it is used in an expression containing at least one class object. You cannot, however, change the *syntax* of the operator; specifically, you cannot change the operator's precedence, its associativity (the way it groups), or the number of operands that it takes. Also, you cannot redefine the standard meaning of an operator when it is used in an expression containing only built-in types.

```
+      -      *      /      %      ^      &      |      ~      !      =      <      >
+=     -=     *=     /=     %=     ^=     &=     |=     <<     >>     >>=    <<=    ==
!=     <=     >=     &&     ||     ++     --     ,      ->*    ->     ()     []
new    delete
```

You have already seen an example of overloading a binary operator. You can overload a unary operator using a member function that takes *no* parameters, such as

```
// defined within CCurrency class definition:
CCurrency operator- ()  // unary - (negation) operator
    {
    return CCurrency (-Dollars, Cents);
    }
```

or you can overload a unary operator using a nonmember friend function that takes one parameter,

```
// defined globally:
CCurrency operator- (CCurrency Curr)
    {
    return CCurrency (-Curr.Dollars, Curr.Cents);
    }
```

(These examples assume that the sign of the monetary amount is maintained in the Dollars member; for example, that -$5.75 would be stored as -5 in Dollars and +75 in Cents.)

The examples given here illustrate the general procedures for overloading an operator. However, when overloading certain operators (such as ++), you must observe special guidelines. The guidelines for overloading the assignment operator (=) are discussed in the next section. For a discussion of the procedures for overloading other specific operators, see the C++ *Language Reference* manual (Chapter 12, "Overloading"; there is no good discussion on this topic in the online help).

NOTE For a discussion on the operators overloaded by the iostream class library (such as <<, which you have seen many times), see Chapter 21. The operators overloaded by the Microsoft Foundation Classes are discussed in Part III of the book.

Overloading the Assignment Operator

C++ allows you to assign a class object to another object of the same class. By default, the compiler handles the assignment by generating a data-member by data-member copy operation. For example, if you made the following assignment,

```
CCurrency Money1 (12, 95);
CCurrency Money2;

Money2 = Money1;
```

the compiler would copy Money1.Dollars to Money2.Dollars, and then copy Money1.Cents to Money2.Cents (the same way that recent versions of C handle assignments of one struct to another). You can also create a temporary class object and assign it to a declared object, as a convenient way to reinitialize an existing object; for example:

```
CCurrency Money (85, 25);    // create an object

Money.PrintAmount ();        // display it

Money = CCurrency (24, 65);  // now create a temporary object and
                             // assign it to existing object
```

If the default assignment operation is not suitable for a class you have written, then you should overload the = operator, thereby specifying a custom assignment operation. For example, consider the following class, CMessage, which is designed for storing and displaying messages:

```
class CMessage
{
private:
   char *Buffer;  // stores message string

public:
   CMessage ()
      {
      Buffer = new char ('\0');   // initialize Buffer to
                                  // empty string
      }
   ~CMessage ()
      {
      delete [] Buffer;           // free the memory
      }
   void Display ()
```

```
        {
        cout << Buffer << '\n';    // display the message
        }
    void Set (char *String)        // store a new message string
        {
        delete [] Buffer;
        Buffer = new char [strlen (String) + 1];
        strcpy (Buffer, String);
        }
};
```

If you were to assign one CMessage object to another CMessage object, then the Buffer data member of *both* objects would point to the *same* block of memory. If you then called the Set member function to change the message stored by one object, this block of memory would be released, leaving the Buffer member of the other object pointing to unpredictable data. (The same thing would happen if one object were destroyed before the other object, because the destructor also releases the block of memory pointed to by Buffer.)

To provide a suitable routine for assigning one CMessage object to another, you could add the following operator function to the class definition:

```
class CMessage
{
// other declarations:

public:
    void operator= (const CMessage &Message)
        {
        delete [] Buffer;
        Buffer = new char [strlen (Message.Buffer) + 1];
        strcpy (Buffer, Message.Buffer);
        }

// other declarations:
}
```

Rather than simply copying the *address* of the memory block (stored in Buffer) from the source object to the destination object, the overloaded = operator creates an entirely new block of memory for the destination object, then copies the string into this memory. Thus, each object has its own copy of the string.

You could then safely assign one CMessage object to another, as in the following program:

```
void main ()
   {
   CMessage Message1;
   Message1.Set ("initial Message1 message");
   Message1.Display ();

   CMessage Message2;
   Message2.Set ("initial Message2 message");
   Message2.Display ();

   Message1 = Message2;
   Message1.Display ();
```

This program would print the following:

```
initial Message1 message
initial Message2 message
initial Message2 message
```

NOTE You must use a *member* function to overload the = operator. (You cannot use a nonmember friend function.)

The way the operator= function is written, you can include only a *single* assignment operator in an expression. If, however, the function returns a reference to the destination CMessage object, as follows

```
CMessage & operator= (const CMessage &Message)
   {
   delete [] Buffer;
   Buffer = new char [strlen (Message.Buffer) + 1];
   strcpy (Buffer, Message.Buffer);
   return *this;
   }
```

then you can string assignment operators together (as you can with the standard = operator); for example:

```
void main ()
   {
```

```
CMessage Message1;
CMessage Message2;
CMessage Message3;

Message1.Set ("hello");

Message1 = Message2 = Message3;
}
```

The compiler evaluates a series of assignments moving from right to left. In this example, it first invokes the `operator=` function to assign `Message3` to `Message2`. The operator function returns a reference to `Message2` (which now contains a copy of the string "hello"). The compiler then invokes the operator function to assign the `Message2` reference to `Message1`. The final result is that all three `CMessage` objects have separate copies of the string "hello".

As a final refinement, the `operator=` function should make sure that it has not inadvertently been called to assign an object to itself (doing so would cause the function to delete `Buffer` and then try to copy a string from it). If an object is being assigned to itself, the address of the source object (`&Message`) would be the same as the address of the current object (`this`). If the function detects a self assignment, it returns immediately since no copy operation is needed:

```
CMessage & operator= (const CMessage &Message)
    {
    if (&Message == this)
       return *this;
    delete [] Buffer;
    Buffer = new char [strlen (Message.Buffer) + 1];
    strcpy (Buffer, Message.Buffer);
    return *this;
    }
```

The following is the complete listing of the `CMessage` class, including the final version of the `operator=` function:

```
#include <string.h>
#include <iostream.h>

class CMessage
{
private:
    char *Buffer;  // stores message string
```

```
public:
   CMessage ()
      {
      Buffer = new char ('\0');   // initialize Buffer to
                                   // empty string
      }
   ~CMessage ()
      {
      delete [] Buffer;           // free the memory
      }
   void Display ()
      {
      cout << Buffer << '\n';     // display the message
      }
   void Set (char *String)        // store a new message string
      {
      delete [] Buffer;
      Buffer = new char [strlen (String) + 1];
      strcpy (Buffer, String);
      }
   CMessage & operator= (const CMessage &Message)
      {
      if (&Message == this)
         return *this;
      delete [] Buffer;
      Buffer = new char [strlen (Message.Buffer) + 1];
      strcpy (Buffer, Message.Buffer);
      return *this;
      }
};
```

Using Copy and Conversion Constructors

This section discusses the special properties of constructors that take a single parameter (including constructors that have additional parameters with default values and that therefore can be called with a single parameter). If the single (or first) parameter is the same type as the class, then the constructor is known as a *copy constructor*, and if the parameter is a different type, then the constructor is known as a *conversion constructor*.

The special features of each of these two types of constructors will be discussed separately. There is one important property, however, that they have in common: If a constructor takes a single parameter, you can initialize an object using an equals sign in the definition rather than the conventional constructor syntax. For example, if the class CTest has the constructor

```
CTest (int Parm)
    {
    // constructor code ...
    }
```

then you can create an object using the statement

```
CTest Test (5);
```

or the equivalent statement

```
CTest Test = 5;
```

The use of the equals sign is merely an alternative syntax for passing a single value to the constructor; it is an initialization, *not* an assignment. Because it is not an assignment, overloading the = operator has *no effect* on the operation.

Writing Copy Constructors

A copy constructor for a class is one that takes a single parameter that is a reference to the class type, as in the following example:

```
class CTest
{
// ...

public:
    CTest (const CTest &Test)
        {
        // use Test members to initialize new CTest object ...
        }

// ...
}
```

(Later in this section, you will see why the parameter must be a *reference* to an object rather than an actual object.)

If you do not define a copy constructor for a class, the compiler implicitly generates one for you. The compiler-generated constructor initializes the new object by performing a member-by-member copy operation from the existing object that is passed as a parameter. Accordingly, you can always initialize an object using an object of the same type, even if you have not defined a copy constructor for the class. For example, even though the CCurrency class presented earlier does not include a copy constructor, the following initializations are legal:

```
CCurrency Money1 (95, 34);

CCurrency Money2 (Money1);
CCurrency Money3 = Money1;
```

The initializations of Money2 and Money3 both invoke the compiler-generated copy constructor. As a result of these initializations, the objects Money2 and Money3 would both contain the same values as Money1 (that is, Dollars would equal 95, and Cents 34).

If the member-by-member copy operation performed by the compiler-generated copy constructor is unsuitable for a class you have written, and if you want to be able to initialize new objects with existing objects of the same type, you should define your own copy constructor. For example, the CMessage class presented earlier in the chapter should *not* be initialized using a simple memberwise copy operation (because it has a data member that is a pointer to a block of memory, as explained previously). You could add the following copy constructor to this class:

```
class CMessage
{
// ...

public:
    CMessage (const CMessage &Message)
        {
        Buffer = new char [strlen (Message.Buffer) + 1];
        strcpy (Buffer, Message.Buffer);
        }

//...
};
```

This copy constructor would allow you to safely initialize objects, as shown in the following code:

```
CMessage Message1;
Message1.Set ("hello");

CMessage Message2 (Message1);   // uses copy constructor
CMessage Message3 = Message1;   // uses copy constructor
```

The compiler also automatically invokes a class's copy constructor in the following two circumstances: when you pass a class object as a function parameter, and when a function returns a class object. Consider, for example, the following operator function:

```
CCurrency operator+ (CCurrency Curr)
    {
    return CCurrency (Dollars + Curr.Dollars, Cents + Curr.Cents);
    }
```

The parameter Curr is a CCurrency object; each time the function is called, Curr must be created and *initialized* using the object that is passed to the function. To initialize the parameter, the compiler invokes the copy constructor (either one you have defined, or a compiler-generated one).

NOTE Because the compiler invokes the copy constructor whenever you pass a class object to a function, you cannot pass a class object as the first parameter to the copy constructor function—rather, you must pass a *reference* to a class object. Passing an actual class object (assuming the compiler permitted it) would cause an infinite recursion.

Because the return type of the function is a CCurrency object, when you call the function, the compiler generates a temporary CCurrency object, and it uses the value specified in the return statement to initialize this temporary object. Again, the compiler invokes the copy constructor to perform the initialization.

Writing Conversion Constructors

A class conversion constructor is one that takes a single parameter of a type other than the class type. Such a constructor typically initializes a new object using data from an existing variable or object of another type. For example, you could add the following conversion constructor to the CCurrency class to permit initializing an object using a dollar and cent amount stored in a single floating-point number:

```
class CCurrency
{

// ...

public:
    // ...

    CCurrency (double DolAndCen)
        {
        Dollars = long (DolAndCen);
        Cents = int ((DolAndCen - Dollars) * 100.0 + 0.5);
        }

// ...
};
```

Notice that the constructor rounds the cent value stored in the DolAndCen parameter to the nearest whole number of cents. Notice, also, that the constructor explicitly converts values to standard types, using an alternative syntax that is permitted in C++, rather that the traditional *cast* notation. For example, it uses the expression long (DolAndCen) rather than the traditional notation (long)DolAndCen. (You can, of course, continue to use casts in C++, although the new syntax may be slightly easier to read for some expressions.)

This conversion constructor allows you to initialize CCurrency objects as follows:

```
CCurrency Bucks1 (29.63);
CCurrency Bucks2 = 43.247; // would be rounded to 43.25
```

```
CCurrency Bucks3 (2.0e9);   // close to max dollar value
CCurrency *Bucks = new CCurrency (534.85);
```

The CCurrency class definition given previously included the following constructor:

```
CCurrency (long Dol, int Cen)
    {
    SetAmount (Dol, Cen);
    }
```

This constructor could be changed to a conversion constructor by simply adding a default value to the second parameter:

```
CCurrency (long Dol, int Cen = 0)
    {
    SetAmount (Dol, Cen);
    }
```

Since this constructor can now accept a single parameter, you can use it to initialize CCurrency objects by specifying only the number of dollars:

```
// set Dollars to 25 and Cents to 0:
CCurrency Dough = 25L;
CCurrency *PDough = new CCurrency (25L);
```

An L is appended to each integer constant to make it a long value. If the L were not included, the constant would be considered an int, and the compiler would not know whether to convert the int to a double (so that it could call the constructor that takes a double) or whether to convert it to a long (so that it could call the constructor that takes a long). Such a situation is known as an *ambiguous call* to an overloaded function, and it generates a compiler error.

As another example, you could add the following conversion constructor to the CMessage class:

```
class CMessage
{
// ...

public:
    // ...

    CMessage (const char *String)
        {
```

```
        Buffer = new char [strlen (String) + 1];
        strcpy (Buffer, String);
        }

// ...
};
```

You could now initialize objects using a single string:

```
CMessage Note = "do it now";
CMessage *PNote = new CMessage ("remember!");
```

Implicit Use of Conversion Constructors

In addition to using a conversion constructor when you explicitly create a class object and initialize it with a single value of another type, the compiler also invokes an appropriate conversion constructor if it needs to convert a data item of another type to a class object. In other words, a class conversion constructor tells the compiler how to convert an object or variable of another type to an object of the class type. For example, the two CCurrency conversion constructors allow you to assign either a double value or a long value to an existing CCurrency object:

```
CCurrency Bucks;

Bucks = 29.95;
Bucks = 35L;
```

In both assignments, the compiler *first* converts the constant to a CCurrency object using the appropriate conversion constructor, and *then* assigns this object to the CCurrency object Bucks. (As explained earlier, the L is required in the second assignment to avoid an ambiguous call to the conversion constructor.)

As another example, assume that a function takes a CCurrency parameter,

```
void Insert (CCurrency Dinero);
```

Because of the two conversion constructors defined for CCurrency, you could pass this function either a double or a long value, as well as a CCurrency object. The compiler would call the appropriate conversion constructor to convert the value to a CCurrency object.

An important benefit of writing conversion constructors is that they can greatly extend the use of overloaded operators you have defined for the class, as well as free you from the need to write a separate operator function for each anticipated combination of operands. For example, the CCurrency class presently has three opera-tor+ functions:

```
class CCurrency
{
// ...

public:
    // ...

    CCurrency operator+ (const CCurrency &Curr)
        {
        return CCurrency (Dollars + Curr.Dollars,
                          Cents + Curr.Cents);
        }
    CCurrency operator+ (long Dol)
        {
        return CCurrency (Dollars + Dol, Cents);
        }
    friend CCurrency operator+ (long Dol, const CCurrency &Curr);

// ...
};
```

Given that CCurrency now has a conversion constructor that converts a long value to a class object (CCurrency (long Dol, int Cen = 0)), you could eliminate the two member operator+ functions and rewrite the nonmember function as follows:

```
class CCurrency
{
// ...

public:
    // ...

    friend CCurrency operator+ (const CCurrency &Curr1,
                                const CCurrency &Curr2);

// ...
};

CCurrency operator+ (const CCurrency &Curr1,
                     const CCurrency &Curr2)
    {
```

```
    return CCurrency (Curr1.Dollars + Curr2.Dollars,
                      Curr1.Cents + Curr2.Cents);
    }
```

This single operator function can handle the following + operations:

```
CCurrency Bucks1 (39, 95);
CCurrency Bucks2 (149, 85);
CCurrency Bucks3;

Bucks3 = Bucks1 + Bucks2;
Bucks3 = Bucks1 + 10L;
Bucks3 = 15L + Bucks1;
```

In the second two addition expressions, the compiler first converts the long constant to a CCurrency object (using the appropriate conversion constructor), and *then* invokes the operator+ friend function to add the two objects.

Furthermore, because CCurrency now has a conversion constructor that takes a *double* parameter, the single operator function can also handle floating-point values:

```
CCurrency Bucks1 (39, 95);
CCurrency Bucks2 (149, 85);
CCurrency Bucks3;

Bucks3 = Bucks1 + 29.51;
Bucks3 = 87.64 + Bucks1;
```

The following listings show the complete final versions of the CCurrency and CMessage classes, including the new copy and conversion constructors:

Listing 6.1

```
// CCURR.H: CCurrency header file

#include <string.h>
#include <iostream.h>

class CCurrency
{
private:
    long Dollars;
    int Cents;
```

```
public:
    CCurrency ()                          // default constructor
        {
        Dollars = Cents = 0;
        }
    CCurrency (long Dol, int Cen = 0)   // conversion constructor
        {
        SetAmount (Dol, Cen);
        }
    CCurrency (double DolAndCen)         // conversion constructor
        {
        Dollars = long (DolAndCen);
        Cents = int ((DolAndCen - Dollars) * 100.0 + 0.5);
        }
    void GetAmount (long *PDol, int *PCen)
        {
        *PDol = Dollars;
        *PCen = Cents;
        }
    void PrintAmount ()
        {
        cout.fill ('0');
        cout.width (1);
        cout << '$' << Dollars << '.';
        cout.width (2);
        cout << Cents << '\n';
        }
    void SetAmount (long Dol, int Cen)
        {
        Dollars = Dol + Cen / 100;
        Cents = Cen % 100;
        }
    friend CCurrency operator+ (const CCurrency &Curr1,
                                const CCurrency &Curr2);
};

CCurrency operator+ (const CCurrency &Curr1,
                     const CCurrency &Curr2)
    {
    return CCurrency (Curr1.Dollars + Curr2.Dollars,
                      Curr1.Cents + Curr2.Cents);
    }
```

Listing 6.2

```
// CMESS.H: CMessage header file

#include <string.h>
#include <iostream.h>

class CMessage
{
private:
   char *Buffer;

public:
   CMessage ()                            // default constructor
      {
      Buffer = new char ('\0');
      }
   CMessage (const CMessage &Message)  // copy constructor
      {
      Buffer = new char [strlen (Message.Buffer) + 1];
      strcpy (Buffer, Message.Buffer);
      }
   CMessage (const char *String)        // conversion constructor
      {
      Buffer = new char [strlen (String) + 1];
      strcpy (Buffer, String);
      }
   ~CMessage ()
      {
      delete [] Buffer;
      }
   void Display ()
      {
      cout << Buffer << '\n';
      }
   void Set (char *String)
      {
      delete [] Buffer;
      Buffer = new char [strlen (String) + 1];
      strcpy (Buffer, String);
      }
   CMessage & operator= (const CMessage &Message)
      {
```

```
        if (&Message == this)
           return *this;
        delete [] Buffer;
        Buffer = new char [strlen (Message.Buffer) + 1];
        strcpy (Buffer, Message.Buffer);
        return *this;
        }
};
```

> **NOTE** A class conversion constructor tells the compiler how to convert another data type to a class object. You can also write a *conversion function* that tells the compiler how to convert a class object to another data type. A conversion function is defined as a member function and is quite similar to an operator function used to overload a standard operator. Conversion functions are less common than conversion constructors, however, and must be defined judiciously to avoid introducing ambiguities. For information on defining them, see the *C++ Language Reference* manual (Chapter 11, "Special Member Functions").

Initializing Arrays

Arrays of objects were first described in Chapter 4. To initialize any type of array, you must use the standard array initialization syntax (inherited from the C language), as shown in the following example:

```
int Table [5] = {1, 2, 3, 4, 5};
```

A limitation of this syntax is that if you are initializing an array of objects, you can assign only a *single* value to each element—you *cannot* pass a series of values to a constructor. Copy constructors and conversion constructors, however, allow you to initialize objects using single values and are therefore useful for initializing arrays of objects. As an example, the following array of CCurrency objects is initialized using a variety of methods:

```
CCurrency Money (95, 34);

CCurrency MoneyTable [5] =
    {
    Money,
    CCurrency (15, 94),
```

```
10L,
12.23,
};
```

The first element (`MoneyTable [0]`) is initialized using an existing `CCurrency` object, by means of the copy constructor. The second element is initialized by invoking a constructor to create a temporary `CCurrency` object; this object is then used to initialize the array element, also by means of the copy constructor. The third element is initialized using a `long` constant, by means of the conversion constructor that takes a `long` parameter, and the fourth element is initialized using a `double` constant, by means of the other conversion constructor. The last array element is *not* explicitly initialized; therefore, the compiler calls the default constructor for this element.

As mentioned in Chapter 3, you *cannot* explicitly initialize an array of objects that is created dynamically using the `new` operator; rather, the compiler calls the default constructor for each element.

Summary

This chapter focused on the techniques for writing special functions that customize the behavior of class objects. It included the following points:

- An *operator function* allows you to *overload* a standard C++ operator; that is, it defines the way that the operator works with objects of a specific class.

- An operator function can be either a member function of a class, or a nonmember function. If it is a nonmember function, it is usually declared (within the class) as a *friend*, which permits it to directly access the private and protected data members of the class.

- A *copy constructor* for a class is one that takes a single parameter that is a reference to an existing class object. If you do not define a copy constructor, the compiler generates one for you, which initializes the new object by simply copying each data member from the existing object. If this behavior is not suitable for your class, you should define your own copy constructor.

- The compiler also calls the copy constructor when you pass a class object as a function parameter, or when a function returns a class object.

- A *conversion constructor* for a class is one that takes a single parameter of a type other than the class type. It can be used to initialize a new object using an existing variable or object of another type. The compiler also automatically calls the conversion constructor if it needs to convert a variable or object of the other type to a class object.

Many of the features of classes that have been described in this part of the book have a common purpose: to allow you to use class types in the same way that you use built-in types. In other words, C++ supports user-defined types (that is, classes) almost to the degree that it supports built-in types. To elaborate, you can do the following with classes:

- You can declare objects of a class in the same way that you declare variables of a built-in type. Furthermore, these objects obey the standard scope rules that apply to variables.
- Like variables of built-in types, you can initialize class objects when you define them.
- You can use standard C++ operators with class objects, as well as with variables of built-in types.
- The compiler will perform automatic conversions to and from class types, in the same way that it performs standard conversions among built-in types.

Because the compiler is unfamiliar with the details of a type that you define, to permit it to fully support this type, you must tell it the following:

- How to initialize the type (you specify this information by writing a copy constructor)
- How to use standard operators with objects of the type (by overloading operators)
- How to convert the type to or from other types (by writing conversion constructors and conversion functions)

PART III

Windows Programming with the MFC Library

In this part of the book, you will learn how to write Windows applications in C++, using the Microsoft Foundation Classes (MFC) library and the extensive set of development tools supplied with Microsoft Visual C++. Chapter 7 explains how to create a simple Windows program using the Microsoft AppWizard code-generating tool, and it describes how an MFC program works. In the remaining chapters, you will learn how to generate increasingly more sophisticated Windows programs using AppWizard, and how to add features to these programs using the other development tools as well as hand coding.

Chapters 8 through 12 present the basic techniques for implementing the two primary components of an MFC program: the *document* (the portion of the program that reads, writes, and stores data) and the *view* (the portion of the program that displays the data and processes user input). Chapters 13 and 14 explain the methods for designing elements of the user interface—specifically dialog boxes, tool bars, and status windows. Chapters 15 through 17 focus on techniques for reading and writing text and for displaying graphics. Chapters 18 and 19 discuss printing and exchanging data using the Clipboard and OLE (Object Linking and Embedding).

Generating a Windows Program

- Programming for Windows

- Creating and building the program

- The program classes and files

- How the program works

7

In this chapter, you will learn how to create a simple Windows program in C++, using the AppWizard application-generating tool and the Microsoft Foundation Classes library (the *MFC*). The chapter begins by describing various ways to write Windows programs with Microsoft Visual C++, and discusses the advantages of using AppWizard and the MFC. It then shows how to generate a basic program template using AppWizard and how to modify the generated code. Finally, it explains how the generated files are organized and how an MFC program works.

The remaining chapters in this part of the book demonstrate how to use the AppWizard and other development tools to create increasingly more advanced types of Windows applications. These chapters will build upon the basic skills and theoretical understanding that you gain here.

Programming for Windows

Microsoft Visual C++ provides several different pathways for writing Windows programs. First, you can write Windows programs in C or C++ by directly calling the functions provided by the Windows environment. These functions are known collectively as the Windows *application program interface* or *API*. Using this approach, you must write many lines of routine code before you can begin to focus on the tasks that are specific to your application.

Second, you can write Windows programs in C++ using the Microsoft Foundation Classes. The MFC provides a large collection of prewritten classes, as well as supporting code, which can handle many standard Windows programming tasks, such as creating windows and processing messages. You can also use the MFC to quickly add sophisticated features to your programs, such as tool bars, split window views, and OLE support. The MFC can thus simplify your Windows programs and make your programming tasks considerably easier.

Third, you can write Windows programs in C++ using both the MFC and the Microsoft Wizards. You can use the AppWizard to generate the basic source files for a variety of different types of Windows programs, and you can use the ClassWizard to generate much of the routine code required to derive classes, process messages, and handle dialog boxes. The code that is generated by the Wizards makes full use of the MFC. The AppWizard is not limited to generating simple program templates, but rather can be used to produce programs containing extensive collections of advanced features, including tool bars, status windows, context-sensitive online help, OLE support, and complete menus with functional commands for opening and saving files, printing, print previewing, and performing other tasks. Once you have used AppWizard to generate the basic source code, you can immediately begin adding code that is specific to the logic of your program.

Using this third approach, you benefit not only from the prewritten code in the MFC, but also from the generated source code that *uses* the MFC and handles many of the routine programming tasks. Employing the MFC and the Wizards is an especially beneficial way to generate Windows programs that fit one of the common application models (single document interface applications, multiple document interface applications, as well as "form" style programs that display collections of controls).

This book covers the third and highest-level pathway to writing Windows applications. Not only are the MFC and Wizards the most advanced and interesting Windows development tools included in Microsoft Visual C++, they are also the newest and least understood. It is indicative of the relative simplicity of using the MFC and Wizards that the book is able to explain how to program so many Windows features, for it would take a much larger volume to teach how to program this many features using the Windows API alone!

Creating and Building the Program

In this section you will create a program named WINGREET, which is an example of the simplest type of program that you can generate using the AppWizard. You will first generate the program source code, then make several modifications to the generated code, and finally build and run the program.

1. Generating the Source Code

The first step is to run the Visual Workbench and choose the AppWizard... command on the Project menu. (If a project is currently open, you do not have to close it; AppWizard will automatically create and open a new project for the application that it generates.) The MFC AppWizard dialog box will appear; you should now perform the following steps:

1. In the Directory: list box, select the name of the directory in which you want to store the program files. (If necessary, use the Drive: list box to select a different disk drive.)

2. If desired, you can have AppWizard create a new subdirectory for storing the program files. This subdirectory will be *within the directory you selected in step 1*. To do this, enter a name for the new subdirectory into the New Subdirectory: text box.

3. Enter the name of the program, WINGREET, into the Project Name: text box. The dialog box will now display the full path name for the program project file. The completed dialog box is illustrated in Figure 7.1. (In this figure, the project is stored in the C:\SAMPLES\WINGREET directory.)

FIGURE 7.1:

The completed MFC AppWizard dialog box

4. Click the Options... button within the MFC AppWizard dialog box. The Options dialog box will now appear. The Options dialog box allows you to choose the features of the program that AppWizard generates.

5. Remove the check marks from all options in the Options dialog box *except* the Generate Source Comments option. Removing these options will produce the simplest type of Windows program that AppWizard can generate. Leaving the comments, however, will help you understand the meaning of the source code for this program. The completed Options dialog box is shown in Figure 7.2.

FIGURE 7.2:

The completed Options dialog box

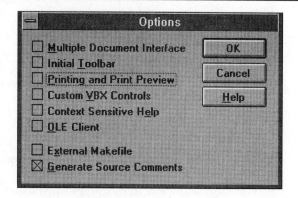

6. Click the OK button in the Options dialog box to remove it and return to the AppWizard dialog box.

7. You can click the Classes... button in the MFC AppWizard dialog box to change the names of the classes and source files that AppWizard creates. Click Classes... now if you want to view the names of these items, but do not make any changes, because the remainder of the exercise assumes that all items have their default names.

8. Click the OK button in the MFC AppWizard dialog box. AppWizard will now display the New Application Information dialog box, which shows the names of the classes and source files that will be created, as well as a list of the features you have selected. This dialog box is shown in Figure 7.3.

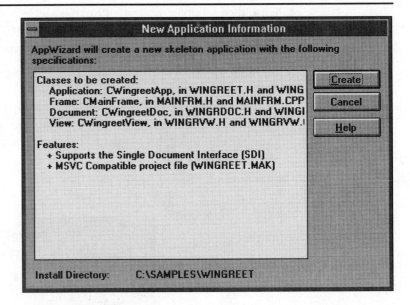

New Application Information

AppWizard will create a new skeleton application with the following specifications:

Classes to be created:
    Application: CWingreetApp, in WINGREET.H and WING
    Frame: CMainFrame, in MAINFRM.H and MAINFRM.CPP
    Document: CWingreetDoc, in WINGRDOC.H and WINGI
    View: CWingreetView, in WINGRVW.H and WINGRVW.I

Features:
    + Supports the Single Document Interface (SDI)
    + MSVC Compatible project file (WINGREET.MAK)

[Create]   [Cancel]   [Help]

Install Directory: C:\SAMPLES\WINGREET

9. Click the Create button in the New Application Information dialog box. AppWizard will now create the new directory (if you specified one), generate the program source files, and open a new project for the program.

Performing these steps causes AppWizard to create a large number of source files for the new program. These files will be explained later in the chapter (in the section "The Program Classes and Files"). AppWizard also creates and opens a Visual Workbench project for the program (projects were discussed in Chapter 2), so that you can immediately edit the source code, change build options, or build the program. If you close this project and later need to reopen it, choose the Open... command on the Project menu and select the project file WINGREET.MAK.

2. Modifying the Source Code

The source files generated by the AppWizard are sufficient to build a complete, working program. In other words, immediately after generating the files, you could build and run the program. Before building the program, however, you normally would use the various development tools to add features to the code that are specific to your application.

To provide you with some practice in working with the source files, this section describes how to add code that displays the string "Greetings!" centered within the program window. (If the generated code is unaltered, the program simply displays a blank window.) To do this, proceed as follows:

1. Open the source file WINGRDOC.H. The easiest way to open a source file belonging to the current program is to click the Open Project File button as shown below and then click the name of the desired file in the list. WINGRDOC.H is the header file for the program's *document class* (which is named `CWingreetDoc` and is derived from the MFC class `CDocument`). As you will see later in the chapter, the document class is responsible for reading, writing, and storing the program data. In this trivial example program, the document class simply stores the fixed message string ("Greetings!"), which constitutes the program data.

Open Project File

2. In the `CWingreetDoc` class definition you will add the protected data member `mMessage`, which stores a pointer to the message string, and you will add the public member function `GetMessage`, which returns a pointer to this string. To do this, enter the lines that are marked in bold within the following code:

```
class CWingreetDoc : public CDocument
{
protected: // create from serialization only
    CWingreetDoc();
    DECLARE_DYNCREATE(CWingreetDoc)

protected:
    char *mMessage;

public:
    char *GetMessage ()
        {
        return mMessage;
        }
```

```
// Attributes
public:

// remainder of CWingreetDoc definition ...
```

> **NOTE**
>
> In the example programs in this part of the book, the names of data members are prefaced with an m to distinguish them from parameters and other nonmember variables. (The names of data members defined by the MFC are prefaced with m_.)

This code excerpt shows the beginning of the CWingreetDoc class definition, and includes the code that was generated by AppWizard, as well as the lines of code that you manually add (which are marked in bold). In the instructions given in this book, all lines of code that you manually add or modify are marked in bold. Although you add or modify only the bold lines, the book typically shows a larger block of code to help you find the correct position within the generated source file to make your additions or modifications.

Listings 7.1 through 7.8, given later in the chapter, provide the full text of all of the main source files for the WINGREET program, including the code that you have added.

3. Open the file WINGRDOC.CPP, which is the implementation file for the program's document class (CWingreetDoc). Within the class constructor, add the statement marked in bold within the following code:

```
/////////////////////////////////////////////////////////////////////////////
// CWingreetDoc construction/destruction

CWingreetDoc::CWingreetDoc()
{
    // TODO: add one-time construction code here

    mMessage = "Greetings!";
}
```

As a result of adding this line, the data member mMessage will automatically be assigned the address of the string "Greetings!" when an instance of the CWingreetDoc class is created.

TIP. AppWizard inserts comments beginning with the word TODO at many (but not all) of the positions within the generated code where you would typically add code of your own.

4. Open the file WINGRVW.CPP, which is the implementation file for the program's *view* class (this class is named `CWingreetView` and is derived from the MFC class `CView`). As you will see later, the view class is responsible for processing input from the user and for managing the view window, which is used for displaying the program data.

5. In the file WINGRVW.CPP, add the statements marked in bold to the `OnDraw` member function:

```
/////////////////////////////////////////////////////////////////////////
// CWingreetView drawing

void CWingreetView::OnDraw(CDC* pDC)
{
    CWingreetDoc* pDoc = GetDocument();

    // TODO: add draw code here

    RECT ClientRect;
    GetClientRect (&ClientRect);
    pDC->DrawText
        (pDoc->GetMessage (),  // obtain the string
        -1,
        &ClientRect,
        DT_CENTER | DT_VCENTER | DT_SINGLELINE);
}
```

The MFC calls the `OnDraw` member function of the program's view class whenever the program window needs redrawing (for example, when the window is first created, when its size is changed, or when it is uncovered after being hidden by another window). The code you added to `OnDraw` displays the string that is stored in the document class ("Greetings!").

`OnDraw` obtains a pointer to the program's document class by calling the `CView` member function `GetDocument`. It then uses this pointer to call the `CWingreetDoc` member function `GetMessage` (which you added to the code in step 2) to obtain the message string. Although this is an elaborate method for getting a simple string, it is used here because it illustrates the typical way that the view class obtains program data from the document class, so that it can display this data.

OnDraw is passed a pointer to a *device context object* belonging to the MFC class CDC. A device context object is associated with a specific device (in WINGREET it is associated with the view window), and it provides a set of member functions for displaying output on that device. OnDraw uses the CDC member function DrawText to display the message string. To center the string within the view window, it calls the CWnd member function GetClientRect to obtain the current dimensions of the view window, and then supplies these dimensions (in a RECT structure) to Draw-Text, together with a set of flags that cause DrawText to center the string horizontally and vertically within the specified dimensions (DT_CENTER and DT_VCENTER). Device context objects and the DrawText function are discussed in Chapter 15.

In a more full-featured application, you would of course make many more changes to the source code generated by AppWizard, typically using a variety of tools, including the App Studio and the ClassWizard, which will be described in later chapters.

3. Building and Running the Program

To build the program, choose the Build WINGREET.EXE command on the Project menu, press Shift+F8, or click the Build button shown below. If the build process completes without error, you can run the program by choosing the Execute WINGREET.EXE command on the Project menu or by pressing Ctrl+F5. The WINGREET program window is shown in Figure 7.4.

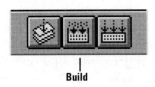

Build

FIGURE 7.4:

The WINGREET program window

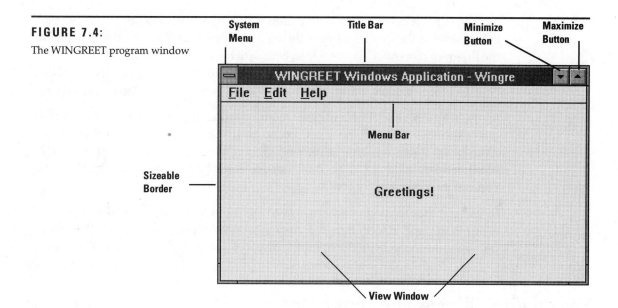

Notice that AppWizard has created code for displaying a complete menu. The Exit command on the File menu and the About command on the Help menu are fully functional; that is, AppWizard has generated all the code needed to implement these commands. The commands on the Edit menu are nonfunctional; that is, AppWizard has not supplied any of the code for implementing these commands, and therefore they are disabled. You will learn how to supply code to handle these commands in Chapters 8, 9, and 19.

The commands on the File menu (other than Exit) are partially functional. That is, AppWizard has generated some of the code needed to implement the commands. If you select the Open... command, the AppWizard-generated code displays a File Open dialog box that allows you to select a file to open. If you click OK, the name of the selected file is displayed in the window title bar, but the contents of the file are not actually read. Similarly, if you choose the Save As command (or the Save command for a new document), the AppWizard code displays the Save As dialog box, but does not actually write anything to a file. In Chapter 10, you will learn how to supply the code for performing the actual reading and writing operations.

Finally, when you select the New command (or when the program is first run), the AppWizard code displays the string "Wingre" in the title bar, rather than the name of a file (a file name is not available until you first save the document). This string is the name of the document *type*. By default, AppWizard derives this name from the program name; in Chapter 8, you will learn how to specify a different name (for example, "text" or "chart"). Also, the AppWizard code does not actually initialize a new document; in Chapter 9 you will learn how to supply code to perform this task.

If you "open" several files using the Open... command, you will notice that the File menu displays a list of the most recent files. When you quit the program, the AppWizard code saves this list in the program initialization file (WINGREET.INI, which it stores in the Windows directory), so that it can restore the list the next time you run the program.

In the next chapter, you will learn how to use the App Studio to remove unwanted menu items, and also to design a custom icon for a program. (Notice that if you minimize the WINGREET program, it displays a standard "AFX" icon.)

The Program Classes and Files

The WINGREET program is known as a *single document interface* (or *SDI*) application, meaning that it displays only one document at a time. When the AppWizard generates an SDI application, it derives four main classes:

- The document class
- The view class
- The main frame window class
- The application class

NOTE In Chapter 12 you will learn about the main classes and source files that AppWizard generates for multiple document interface (MDI) applications.

The primary program tasks are divided among these four main classes, and AppWizard creates separate source files for each class. By default, it derives the names of both the classes and the class source files from the name of the program (although, as mentioned previously, it allows you to specify other names).

The WINGREET document class is named `CWingreetDoc` and is derived from the MFC class `CDocument`. The `CWingreetDoc` header file is named WINGRDOC.H and the implementation file is named WINGRDOC.CPP (a general description of header and implementation files was given in the section "Organizing the Source Files" in Chapter 4). The document class is responsible for storing the program data and for reading and writing this data to disk files. The WINGREET document class stores only a single message string and does not perform disk I/O.

The WINGREET view class is named `CWingreetView` and is derived from the MFC class `CView`. The `CWingreetView` header file is named WINGRVW.H, and the implementation file is named WINGRVW.CPP. The view class is responsible for displaying the program data (on the screen, printer, or other device) and for processing input from the user. This class manages the *view window*, which is used for displaying program data on the screen. The WINGREET view class merely displays the message string within the view window.

The WINGREET main frame window class is named `CMainFrame` and is derived from the MFC class `CFrameWnd`. The `CMainFrame` header file is named MAINFRM.H, and the implementation file is named MAINFRM.CPP. The main frame window class manages the main program window, which serves to display a title bar, a menu bar, maximize and minimize buttons, borders, a system menu, and sometimes other user interface elements such as a tool bar or a status bar. Note that the view window—managed by the view class—occupies the empty portion of the main program window inside of these interface elements (which is known as the *client area* of the main program window). The view window has no visible elements except the text and graphics that the view class explicitly displays (such as the string "Greetings!" displayed by WINGREET). The view window is a *child* of the main program window, which means—among other things—that it is always displayed on top of and within the boundaries of the main program window.

Finally, the application class is named `CWingreetApp` and is derived from the MFC class `CWinApp`. The `CWinApp` header file is named WINGREET.H, and the implementation file is named WINGREET.CPP. The application class manages the program as a whole; that is, it performs general tasks that do not fall within the province of any of the other three classes, such as initializing the program and performing the final program cleanup. Every MFC Windows program must create exactly one instance of a class derived from `CWinApp`.

The four main classes communicate with each other and exchange data by calling each other's public member functions and by sending *messages* (messages will be

TABLE 7.1: The Main Program Classes and Source Files

Class	Class Name	Derived from	Header File	Implementation File	Primary Responsibilities
document	CWingreetDoc	CDocument	WINGRDOC.H	WINGRDOC.CPP	Storing program data; saving and loading program data from disk
view	CWingreetView	CView	WINGRVW.H	WINGRVW.CPP	Displaying program data; processing user input; managing view window
main frame window	CMainFrame	CFrameWnd	MAINFRM.H	MAINFRM.CPP	Managing main program window application
	CWingreetApp	CWinApp	WINGREET.H	WINGREET.CPP	General program tasks

explained in Chapter 8). Table 7.1 summarizes the features of the four main classes in the WINGREET program.

In addition to the source files for the four main classes, AppWizard generates several other files that are needed to build the program. The additional files are briefly described in Table 7.2. Note that AppWizard also creates a file named README.TXT, which describes all of the source files that it has generated for the program.

TABLE 7.2: Additional Source Files Generated by AppWizard

File	Purpose
RESOURCE.H	Contains constant definitions for program resources. This file is maintained by App Studio (you do not edit it directly), and it is included in all of the main .CPP files and in the main resource-definition file (WINGREET.RC).
STDAFX.CPP and STDAFX.H	Used for generating precompiled headers.
WINGREET.CLW	Stores information used by the ClassWizard tool (which is introduced in Chapter 8).
WINGREET.DEF	The program module-definition file, which furnishes information about the application that the Microsoft LINK program uses to prepare the executable application file. You normally do not need to edit this file, because it contains values that are suitable for most MFC Windows programs.
WINGREET.MAK	The program project file. To open the project, you choose the Open... command on the Visual Workbench Project menu and select this file.
WINGREET.RC	Contains definitions of program resources (resources include menus, dialog boxes, strings, keyboard accelerators, and icons). This file is maintained by the App Studio tool (you do not edit it directly), and it is processed by the Microsoft resource compiler (RC.EXE) when the program is built.
RES\WINGREET.ICO	Contains data for the program icon. Initially, this file contains the standard "AFX" icon; however, you can edit it using the App Studio. WINGREET.RC contains an ICON statement that causes the resource compiler to include this icon in the program's resources.
RES\WINGREET.RC2	Contains definitions of program resources that are *not* edited using App Studio. Initially, it contains version information resources. If you want to define any resources manually (rather than using App Studio), you can add them to this file. This file is included by the main resource file, WINGREET.RC.

The following listings, Listings 7.1 through 7.8, provide the complete text of the header and implementation files for the four main program classes. These listings contain the code that was generated by AppWizard, plus the manual code additions described in the exercise given previously in the chapter. The files you created in the exercise given in this section should match the files below; also, a complete set of these files is included in the \WINGREET subdirectory within the directory in which you installed the companion disk.

> **NOTE** For the example programs, the book lists only the C++ files that define and implement the main classes, because these are the files that you generally work with when you develop a program (that is, these are the files that you are most likely to directly edit). The STDAFX C++ files (STDAFX.H and STDAFX.CPP) and the other source files listed in Table 7.2 are seldom viewed or directly edited, but rather are created and maintained by various development tools; they are therefore not printed in the book.

Listing 7.1

```cpp
// wingreet.h : main header file for the WINGREET application
//

#ifndef __AFXWIN_H__
    #error include 'stdafx.h' before including this file for PCH
#endif

#include "resource.h"        // main symbols

/////////////////////////////////////////////////////////////////////////////
// CWingreetApp:
// See wingreet.cpp for the implementation of this class
//

class CWingreetApp : public CWinApp
{
public:
    CWingreetApp();

// Overrides
    virtual BOOL InitInstance();

// Implementation

    //{{AFX_MSG(CWingreetApp)
    afx_msg void OnAppAbout();
        // NOTE - the ClassWizard will add and remove member functions here.
        //    DO NOT EDIT what you see in these blocks of generated code !
    //}}AFX_MSG
    DECLARE_MESSAGE_MAP()
};
```

//

Listing 7.2

```cpp
// wingreet.cpp : Defines the class behaviors for the application.
//

#include "stdafx.h"
#include "wingreet.h"

#include "mainfrm.h"
#include "wingrdoc.h"
#include "wingrvw.h"

#ifdef _DEBUG
#undef THIS_FILE
static char BASED_CODE THIS_FILE[] = __FILE__;
#endif

////////////////////////////////////////////////////////////////////////
// CWingreetApp

BEGIN_MESSAGE_MAP(CWingreetApp, CWinApp)
    //{{AFX_MSG_MAP(CWingreetApp)
    ON_COMMAND(ID_APP_ABOUT, OnAppAbout)
        // NOTE - the ClassWizard will add and remove mapping macros here.
        //    DO NOT EDIT what you see in these blocks of generated code !
    //}}AFX_MSG_MAP
    // Standard file based document commands
    ON_COMMAND(ID_FILE_NEW, CWinApp::OnFileNew)
    ON_COMMAND(ID_FILE_OPEN, CWinApp::OnFileOpen)
END_MESSAGE_MAP()

////////////////////////////////////////////////////////////////////////
// CWingreetApp construction

CWingreetApp::CWingreetApp()
{
    // TODO: add construction code here,
    // Place all significant initialization in InitInstance
}

////////////////////////////////////////////////////////////////////////
// The one and only CWingreetApp object
```

```
CWingreetApp NEAR theApp;

/////////////////////////////////////////////////////////////////////////
// CWingreetApp initialization

BOOL CWingreetApp::InitInstance()
{
    // Standard initialization
    // If you are not using these features and wish to reduce the size
    //  of your final executable, you should remove from the following
    //  the specific initialization routines you do not need.

    SetDialogBkColor();          // set dialog background color to gray
    LoadStdProfileSettings();    // Load standard INI file options (including MRU)

    // Register the application's document templates.  Document templates
    //  serve as the connection between documents, frame windows and views.

    AddDocTemplate(new CSingleDocTemplate(IDR_MAINFRAME,
        RUNTIME_CLASS(CWingreetDoc),
        RUNTIME_CLASS(CMainFrame),      // main SDI frame window
        RUNTIME_CLASS(CWingreetView)));

    // create a new (empty) document
    OnFileNew();

    if (m_lpCmdLine[0] != '\0')
    {
        // TODO: add command line processing here
    }

    return TRUE;
}

/////////////////////////////////////////////////////////////////////////
// CAboutDlg dialog used for App About

class CAboutDlg : public CDialog
{
public:
    CAboutDlg();

// Dialog Data
    //{{AFX_DATA(CAboutDlg)
```

```
    enum { IDD = IDD_ABOUTBOX };
    //}}AFX_DATA

// Implementation
protected:
    virtual void DoDataExchange(CDataExchange* pDX);    // DDX/DDV support
    //{{AFX_MSG(CAboutDlg)
        // No message handlers
    //}}AFX_MSG
    DECLARE_MESSAGE_MAP()
};

CAboutDlg::CAboutDlg() : CDialog(CAboutDlg::IDD)
{
    //{{AFX_DATA_INIT(CAboutDlg)
    //}}AFX_DATA_INIT
}

void CAboutDlg::DoDataExchange(CDataExchange* pDX)
{
    CDialog::DoDataExchange(pDX);
    //{{AFX_DATA_MAP(CAboutDlg)
    //}}AFX_DATA_MAP
}

BEGIN_MESSAGE_MAP(CAboutDlg, CDialog)
    //{{AFX_MSG_MAP(CAboutDlg)
        // No message handlers
    //}}AFX_MSG_MAP
END_MESSAGE_MAP()

// App command to run the dialog
void CWingreetApp::OnAppAbout()
{
    CAboutDlg aboutDlg;
    aboutDlg.DoModal();
}

/////////////////////////////////////////////////////////////////////////////
// CWingreetApp commands
```

Listing 7.3

```
// wingrdoc.h : interface of the CWingreetDoc class
//
/////////////////////////////////////////////////////////////////////

class CWingreetDoc : public CDocument
{
protected: // create from serialization only
   CWingreetDoc();
   DECLARE_DYNCREATE(CWingreetDoc)

protected:
   char *mMessage;

public:
   char *GetMessage ()
      {
      return mMessage;
      }

// Attributes
public:

// Operations
public:

// Implementation
public:
   virtual ~CWingreetDoc();
   virtual void Serialize(CArchive& ar);  // overridden for document i/o
#ifdef _DEBUG
   virtual  void AssertValid() const;
   virtual  void Dump(CDumpContext& dc) const;
#endif
protected:
   virtual  BOOL  OnNewDocument();

// Generated message map functions
protected:
   //{{AFX_MSG(CWingreetDoc)
      // NOTE - the ClassWizard will add and remove member functions here.
      //    DO NOT EDIT what you see in these blocks of generated code !
   //}}AFX_MSG
   DECLARE_MESSAGE_MAP()
```

```
};

////////////////////////////////////////////////////////////////////////
```

Listing 7.4

```
// wingrdoc.cpp : implementation of the CWingreetDoc class
//

#include "stdafx.h"
#include "wingreet.h"

#include "wingrdoc.h"

#ifdef _DEBUG
#undef THIS_FILE
static char BASED_CODE THIS_FILE[] = __FILE__;
#endif

////////////////////////////////////////////////////////////////////////
// CWingreetDoc

IMPLEMENT_DYNCREATE(CWingreetDoc, CDocument)

BEGIN_MESSAGE_MAP(CWingreetDoc, CDocument)
    //{{AFX_MSG_MAP(CWingreetDoc)
        // NOTE - the ClassWizard will add and remove mapping macros here.
        //    DO NOT EDIT what you see in these blocks of generated code !
    //}}AFX_MSG_MAP
END_MESSAGE_MAP()

////////////////////////////////////////////////////////////////////////
// CWingreetDoc construction/destruction

CWingreetDoc::CWingreetDoc()
{
    // TODO: add one-time construction code here

    mMessage = "Greetings!";
}

CWingreetDoc::~CWingreetDoc()
{
}
```

```
BOOL CWingreetDoc::OnNewDocument()
{
    if (!CDocument::OnNewDocument())
        return FALSE;
    // TODO: add reinitialization code here
    // (SDI documents will reuse this document)
    return TRUE;
}

/////////////////////////////////////////////////////////////////////////
// CWingreetDoc serialization

void CWingreetDoc::Serialize(CArchive& ar)
{
    if (ar.IsStoring())
    {
        // TODO: add storing code here
    }
    else
    {
        // TODO: add loading code here
    }
}

/////////////////////////////////////////////////////////////////////////
// CWingreetDoc diagnostics

#ifdef _DEBUG
void CWingreetDoc::AssertValid() const
{
    CDocument::AssertValid();
}

void CWingreetDoc::Dump(CDumpContext& dc) const
{
    CDocument::Dump(dc);
}

#endif //_DEBUG

/////////////////////////////////////////////////////////////////////////
// CWingreetDoc commands
```

Listing 7.5

```
// mainfrm.h : interface of the CMainFrame class
//
/////////////////////////////////////////////////////////////////////////////

class CMainFrame : public CFrameWnd
{
protected: // create from serialization only
   CMainFrame();
   DECLARE_DYNCREATE(CMainFrame)

// Attributes
public:

// Operations
public:

// Implementation
public:
   virtual ~CMainFrame();
#ifdef _DEBUG
   virtual  void AssertValid() const;
   virtual  void Dump(CDumpContext& dc) const;
#endif


// Generated message map functions
protected:
   //{{AFX_MSG(CMainFrame)
      // NOTE - the ClassWizard will add and remove member functions here.
      //    DO NOT EDIT what you see in these blocks of generated code !
   //}}AFX_MSG
   DECLARE_MESSAGE_MAP()
};

/////////////////////////////////////////////////////////////////////////////
```

Listing 7.6

```
// mainfrm.cpp : implementation of the CMainFrame class
//

#include "stdafx.h"
#include "wingreet.h"
```

```
#include "mainfrm.h"

#ifdef _DEBUG
#undef THIS_FILE
static char BASED_CODE THIS_FILE[] = __FILE__;
#endif

/////////////////////////////////////////////////////////////////////////
// CMainFrame

IMPLEMENT_DYNCREATE(CMainFrame, CFrameWnd)

BEGIN_MESSAGE_MAP(CMainFrame, CFrameWnd)
    //{{AFX_MSG_MAP(CMainFrame)
        // NOTE - the ClassWizard will add and remove mapping macros here.
        //      DO NOT EDIT what you see in these blocks of generated code !
    //}}AFX_MSG_MAP
END_MESSAGE_MAP()

/////////////////////////////////////////////////////////////////////////
// CMainFrame construction/destruction

CMainFrame::CMainFrame()
{
    // TODO: add member initialization code here
}

CMainFrame::~CMainFrame()
{
}

/////////////////////////////////////////////////////////////////////////
// CMainFrame diagnostics

#ifdef _DEBUG
void CMainFrame::AssertValid() const
{
    CFrameWnd::AssertValid();
}

void CMainFrame::Dump(CDumpContext& dc) const
{
    CFrameWnd::Dump(dc);
}
```

```
#endif //_DEBUG

/////////////////////////////////////////////////////////////////////////
// CMainFrame message handlers
```

Listing 7.7

```
// wingrvw.h : interface of the CWingreetView class
//
/////////////////////////////////////////////////////////////////////////

class CWingreetView : public CView
{
protected: // create from serialization only
    CWingreetView();
    DECLARE_DYNCREATE(CWingreetView)

// Attributes
public:
    CWingreetDoc* GetDocument();

// Operations
public:

// Implementation
public:
    virtual ~CWingreetView();
    virtual void OnDraw(CDC* pDC);  // overridden to draw this view
#ifdef _DEBUG
    virtual void AssertValid() const;
    virtual void Dump(CDumpContext& dc) const;
#endif

// Generated message map functions
protected:
    //{{AFX_MSG(CWingreetView)
        // NOTE - the ClassWizard will add and remove member functions here.
        //    DO NOT EDIT what you see in these blocks of generated code !
    //}}AFX_MSG
    DECLARE_MESSAGE_MAP()
};
```

```
#ifndef _DEBUG // debug version in wingrvw.cpp
inline CWingreetDoc* CWingreetView::GetDocument()
   { return (CWingreetDoc*) m_pDocument; }
#endif
```

//

Listing 7.8

```
// wingrvw.cpp : implementation of the CWingreetView class
//

#include "stdafx.h"
#include "wingreet.h"

#include "wingrdoc.h"
#include "wingrvw.h"

#ifdef _DEBUG
#undef THIS_FILE
static char BASED_CODE THIS_FILE[] = __FILE__;
#endif

////////////////////////////////////////////////////////////////////////////////
// CWingreetView

IMPLEMENT_DYNCREATE(CWingreetView, CView)

BEGIN_MESSAGE_MAP(CWingreetView, CView)
   //{{AFX_MSG_MAP(CWingreetView)
      // NOTE - the ClassWizard will add and remove mapping macros here.
      //    DO NOT EDIT what you see in these blocks of generated code !
   //}}AFX_MSG_MAP
END_MESSAGE_MAP()

////////////////////////////////////////////////////////////////////////////////
// CWingreetView construction/destruction

CWingreetView::CWingreetView()
{
   // TODO: add construction code here
}

CWingreetView::~CWingreetView()
{
```

```
}

/////////////////////////////////////////////////////////////////////////
// CWingreetView drawing

void CWingreetView::OnDraw(CDC* pDC)
{
    CWingreetDoc* pDoc = GetDocument();

    // TODO: add draw code here

    RECT ClientRect;
    GetClientRect (&ClientRect);
    pDC->DrawText
        (pDoc->GetMessage (),   // obtain the string
        -1,
        &ClientRect,
        DT_CENTER | DT_VCENTER | DT_SINGLELINE);
}


/////////////////////////////////////////////////////////////////////////
// CWingreetView diagnostics

#ifdef _DEBUG
void CWingreetView::AssertValid() const
{
    CView::AssertValid();
}

void CWingreetView::Dump(CDumpContext& dc) const
{
    CView::Dump(dc);
}

CWingreetDoc* CWingreetView::GetDocument() // non-debug version is inline
{
    ASSERT(m_pDocument->IsKindOf(RUNTIME_CLASS(CWingreetDoc)));
    return (CWingreetDoc*) m_pDocument;
}

#endif //_DEBUG

/////////////////////////////////////////////////////////////////////////
// CWingreetView message handlers
```

How the Program Works

If you are accustomed to procedural programming for MS-DOS, or even if you are familiar with conventional Windows programming, you are probably wondering how the WINGREET program works—where it first receives control, what it does next, where it exits, and so on. This section briefly describes the overall flow of control of the program, and then discusses the tasks performed by the application initialization function, InitInstance. In subsequent chapters, you will learn how other portions of the code work (for example, Chapter 8 explains the parts of the code that handle messages, while Chapter 13 explains the code for displaying the About dialog box).

The Flow of Program Control

The following is a list of some of the significant events that occur when you run the WINGREET program. These five events were selected from the many program actions that take place, because they best help you understand how the WINGREET program works and illustrate the purpose of the different parts of the source code:

1. The CWinApp class constructor is called.

2. The program entry function, WinMain, receives control.

3. WinMain calls the program's InitInstance function.

4. WinMain enters a loop for processing messages.

5. WinMain exits and the program terminates.

Figure 7.5 illustrates this sequence of events, and the following sections describe each event in detail.

1. The CWinApp Constructor Is Called

As mentioned previously, an MFC application must define exactly one instance of its application class. The file WINGREET.CPP defines an instance of the WINGREET application class, CWingreetApp, in the following global definition:

```
CWingreetApp NEAR theApp;
```

FIGURE 7.5:

Significant events that occur when the GREET1 program is run

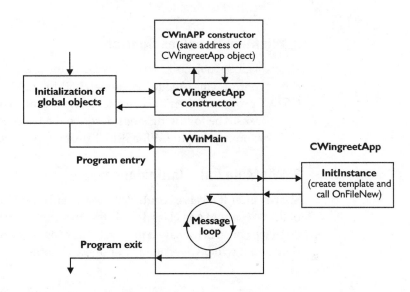

Because the `CWingreetApp` object is defined globally, the class constructor is called *before* the program entry function, `WinMain`, receives control. The `CWingreetApp` constructor generated by AppWizard does nothing:

```
CWingreetApp::CWingreetApp()
{
    // TODO: add construction code here,
    // Place all significant initialization in InitInstance
}
```

However, as you learned in Chapter 5, such a do-nothing constructor causes the compiler to invoke the default constructor of the base class, which is `CWinApp`. The `CWinApp` constructor (supplied by the MFC) performs the following two important tasks:

- It makes sure that the program declares only *one* application object (that is, only one object belonging to `CWinApp` or to a class derived from `CWinApp`).

- It saves the address of the program's `CWingreetApp` object in a global pointer declared by the MFC. It saves this address so that the MFC code can later call the `WingreetApp` member functions. Calling these member functions will be described under step 3.

2. WinMain Receives Control

After all global objects have been created, the program entry function, `WinMain`, receives control. This function is defined within the MFC code; it is linked to the WINGREET program when the executable file is built. The `WinMain` function performs many tasks. The following steps describe the tasks that are the most important for understanding how the WINGREET program works.

3. WinMain Calls InitInstance

Shortly after it receives control, `WinMain` calls the `InitInstance` member function of the `CWingreetApp` class. It calls this function by using the object address that the `CWinApp` constructor saved in step 1. `InitInstance` serves to initialize the application, and it will be described later in the chapter.

NOTE The MFC saves the address of the `WingreetApp` object in a `CWinApp` pointer, which it uses to call `InitInstance`. Because `InitInstance` is a virtual function (see Chapter 5), the overriding version of `InitInstance` defined within the `WinGreetApp` class receives control. `CWinApp` defines several other virtual functions that you can override. For example, you can override the `ExitInstance` function to perform final cleanup tasks immediately before your application terminates. For a description of the other overridable functions, see the documentation on the `CWinApp` class in the *Reference Volume I, Class Library Reference* manual or in the *Foundation Classes* online help file (the topic "CWinApp").

4. WinMain Processes Messages

After completing its initialization tasks, `WinMain` enters a loop that calls the Windows system to obtain and dispatch all *messages* that are sent to objects within the WINGREET program. Messages are explained in Chapter 8. Control remains within this loop during the remaining time that the application runs. However, calling the system to obtain and dispatch messages allows other portions of the program—as well as other Windows applications—to run.

> **NOTE** The message loop is actually contained in a member function named Run, which is called from `WinMain`.

5. WinMain Exits and the Program Terminates

When the user of the WINGREET program chooses the Exit command on the File menu, or the Close command on the system menu, the MFC code destroys the program window and calls the Windows API function `PostQuitMessage`, which causes the message loop to exit. The `WinMain` function subsequently returns, causing the application to terminate.

The InitInstance Function

`InitInstance` is a member function of the application class, `CWingreetApp`, and it is defined in the source file WINGREET.CPP. The MFC calls this function from `WinMain`, and its job is to initialize the application.

At the time `InitInstance` is called, a more traditional Windows application would simply create a main program window. Because of the new view-document programming model introduced by MFC version 2.0, however, the AppWizard code does something a bit more complex. It creates an object known as a *document template*. A document template stores information on the program's document class, its main frame window class, and its view class; it also stores the identifier of the program resources (the menu, icon, and so on). When the program opens a document, it uses the document template to create an object of the document class for storing the document, an object of the view class for creating a view window to display the document, and an object of the main frame window class to provide a main program window for framing the view window.

The following code creates the document template and stores it within the application object:

```
AddDocTemplate(new CSingleDocTemplate(IDR_MAINFRAME,
     RUNTIME_CLASS(CWingreetDoc),
```

```
RUNTIME_CLASS(CMainFrame),       // main SDI frame window
RUNTIME_CLASS(CWingreetView)));
```

This code works as follows:

- Each call to the RUNTIME_CLASS macro (which is defined by the MFC) returns information on the specified class, which enables the program to dynamically create an instance of this class. (Technically, RUNTIME_CLASS returns a pointer to a CRuntimeClass object.) The information for each class is passed to the CSingleDocTemplate constructor.

- The CSingleDocTemplate constructor is also passed (as the first parameter) the identifier of the program resources that are used when the document is displayed (namely, the identifier used for the strings, keyboard accelerators, menu, and icon; resources and their identifiers will be discussed in Chapter 8).

- The new operator creates an instance of the CSingleDocTemplate class. An instance of this class *is* a document template, which is suitable for a single document interface program.

- The address of the CSingleDocTemplate object is passed to the CWinApp member function AddDocTemplate. This function stores the document template within the application object so that the template will be available when a document is opened.

After creating the document template, InitInstance calls the CWinApp member function OnFileNew:

```
// create a new (empty) document
OnFileNew();
```

The OnFileNew function uses the document template to create a CWingreetDoc object, a CMainFrame object, a CWingreetView object, and the associated main program window and view window. The resources used for the main window (the menu, icon, and so on) are those identified by the resource identifier stored in the template. Because these objects and windows are created internally by OnFileNew, you do not see within the WINGREET code explicit definitions of the objects, nor do you see function calls for creating windows.

> **NOTE**
>
> The `OnFileNew` function is also called whenever the user subsequently chooses the New command on the File menu. On these subsequent calls, however, the function does not create new program objects or windows; rather, it reuses the existing objects and windows that it created the first time it was called.

If you need to perform any other application initialization tasks, the `InitInstance` function is the place to add the code.

Summary

This chapter introduced you to the Microsoft Foundation Classes library and the AppWizard application generation tool, by leading you through the steps for creating a simple Windows program. The following are some of the general techniques and concepts that were discussed:

- With Microsoft Visual C++, you can write a Windows program using one of three basic methods: hand coding and calling the Windows API functions, hand coding and using the MFC classes, or generating an MFC program using the Microsoft Wizards. The third approach is the easiest way to create conventional Windows programs, and it is the one discussed in this book.

- You can generate the basic source code files for a Windows program by running the AppWizard tool from the Visual Workbench and specifying the desired program features.

- Once you have generated the basic program template with AppWizard, you can add your application-specific features by directly editing the source code, or by using other Visual C++ tools such as the ClassWizard and the App Studio.

- An MFC Windows program generated using AppWizard has four main classes. The program tasks are apportioned among these classes, and each of these classes is defined in its own header file and is implemented in its own implementation file.

- The document class (derived from CDocument) is responsible for storing the program data, as well as for saving and loading this data from disk files.

- The view class (derived from CView) manages the view window. This class is responsible for processing user input and for displaying the document within the view window and on other devices.

- The main frame window class (derived from CFrameWnd) manages the main program window. This window displays user interface objects such a menu, borders, a title bar, maximize and minimize buttons, and sometimes a tool bar or a status bar. The view window is located in the blank area inside of these objects.

- The application class (derived from CWinApp) manages the application as a whole and performs such general tasks as initializing the application and doing the final application cleanup.

- The program entry function, WinMain, is defined within the MFC. Among its other actions, WinMain calls the InitInstance member function of your application class, and it processes messages.

- The InitInstance function initializes the program. This function creates and saves a document template, which stores information on the program's document, view, and main frame window classes. InitInstance then calls the CWinApp member function OnFileNew, which uses the document template both to create instances of these three classes and to create the main program window and view window.

CHAPTER

EIGHT

Implementing the View

-  The **MINIDRAW** program

- The **MINIEDIT** program

8

The *view* is the portion of a Microsoft Foundation Classes program that manages the view window, processes user input, and displays the document data within the view window and on other devices. As you saw in the previous chapter, when you generate a program using AppWizard, it derives a class from the MFC `CView` class specifically for managing the view. The view class derived by AppWizard does almost nothing itself, but rather serves as a template for you to add your own code. In the previous chapter, you added code to the WINGREET program's view class to display a simple string within the view window.

This chapter presents the first version of a simple drawing program named MINIDRAW. After generating the template for this program using AppWizard, you will add code to the view class to read mouse input from the user and to draw straight lines within the view window. You will use the ClassWizard tool to generate the functions for handling mouse input messages, and you will use App Studio for modifying the program menu and designing a program icon. In later chapters, you will create increasingly more complete versions of the MINIDRAW program.

The chapter also presents the first version of a simple text editing program, MINIEDIT. This program demonstrates how you can quickly create a fully functional text editor simply by deriving the program's view class from the MFC class `CEditView` rather than `CView`. In later chapters, you will also create more advanced versions of MINIEDIT.

The MINIDRAW Program

In this chapter, you will generate the first version of the MINIDRAW program and implement the basic features of the program's view class. The MINIDRAW program window is illustrated in Figure 8.1. MINIDRAW allows you to draw straight lines within the view window. To draw a line, you place the mouse cursor at one end of the line, press the left button, drag the cursor to the other end of the line, and release the button.

With this version of the program, all lines are erased whenever the window is redrawn (for example, when you change the window size or remove an overlapping window), or when you choose the New command on the File menu. In Chapter 9, you will implement the basic features of the document class, which will *save* the

FIGURE 8.1:

The MINIDRAW program window

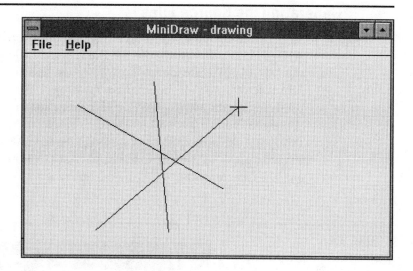

data for each line that is drawn, allowing the program to recreate the lines whenever the window is redrawn. In later chapters, you will add many other features to this program, such as commands for saving and loading drawings from disk, plus tools for drawing a variety of different shapes.

> **NOTE** Unlike the WINGREET program given in the previous chapter, MINIDRAW does *not* implement the OnDraw function for redrawing the window, because it does not store the data that would be required to redraw the lines. The version of the MINIDRAW program presented in Chapter 9, however, stores the data for the lines and implements an OnDraw function.

As with all the example programs given in this part of the book, you can either generate and modify the program source files yourself, following the step-by-step instructions given here, or simply load and examine the complete source files copied from the companion disk.

Generating the Source Files

To generate the program source files, use the AppWizard facility exactly as described in the previous chapter (in the section "1. Generating the Source Code"). In the MFC AppWizard dialog box, however, you should specify the project name MINIDRAW, and you should place the project files within a separate subdirectory used only for the MINIDRAW project. (You can have AppWizard create this subdirectory for you.) Figure 8.2 shows the completed MFC AppWizard dialog box; in this figure, the project files are stored in the C:\SAMPLES\MINIDRAW directory. As in the previous chapter, in the AppWizard Options dialog box, you should select *only* the Generate Source Comments option.

FIGURE 8.2:

The completed MFC AppWizard dialog box

When AppWizard finishes generating the source files, the MINIDRAW project will be opened in the Visual Workbench. Remember that you can later reopen this project, at any time you want to resume working on the program, by choosing the Open… command on the Project menu and selecting the file MINIDRAW.MAK.

Defining and Initializing View Class Data Members

You first need to add several members to the view class: the data members mClassName, mDragging, mHCross, mPointOld, and mPointOrigin, and the member function PreCreateWindow. To do this, open the file MINIDVW.H, and add the statements marked in bold to the beginning of the CMinidrawView class definition:

```
class CMinidrawView : public CView
{
protected: // create from serialization only
    CMinidrawView();
    DECLARE_DYNCREATE(CMinidrawView)

protected:
    CString mClassName;
    int mDragging;
    HCURSOR mHCross;
    CPoint mPointOld;
    CPoint mPointOrigin;

    virtual BOOL PreCreateWindow (CREATESTRUCT& cs);

// Attributes
public:
    CMinidrawDoc* GetDocument();

// remainder of CMinidrawView definition ...
```

You will see the purpose of these members in the discussions that follow.

Next, add initializations for the mDragging and mHCross data members to the CMinidrawView class constructor, which is in the file MINIDVW.CPP:

```
/////////////////////////////////////////////////////////////////////////////
// CMinidrawView construction/destruction

CMinidrawView::CMinidrawView()
{
    // TODO: add construction code here
```

```
    mDragging = 0;
    mHCross = AfxGetApp ()->LoadStandardCursor (IDC_CROSS);
}
```

mHCross stores a handle to the mouse cursor that the program displays when the cursor is within the view window. Calling AfxGetApp obtains a pointer to the program's application class object (the object of the class CMinidrawApp, which is derived from CWinApp). This pointer is used to call the CWinApp member function LoadStandardCursor, which is passed the identifier IDC_CROSS so that it returns a handle to the standard cross-shaped mouse cursor. Later, you will see how the MINIDRAW program displays this cursor within the view window (in the section "The OnMouseMove Function"). Table 8.1 lists additional values that you can pass to LoadStandardCursor to obtain handles to other standard cursors.

TABLE 8.1:   Values Identifying Standard Windows Cursors, Which You Can Pass to the LoadStandardCursor Function

Value	Cursor
IDC_ARROW	Standard arrow cursor
IDC_CROSS	Crosshairs cursor, used for selecting
IDC_IBEAM	I-beam cursor, used within text
IDC_ICON	Rectangular cursor, used when dragging a file
IDC_SIZE	Cursor consisting of a square with a smaller square inside, used when sizing an object
IDC_SIZENESW	Two-headed arrow cursor, with ends pointing northeast and southwest
IDC_SIZENS	Two-headed arrow cursor, with ends pointing north and south
IDC_SIZENWSE	Two-headed arrow cursor, with ends pointing northwest and southeast
IDC_SIZEWE	Two-headed arrow cursor, with ends pointing west and east
IDC_UPARROW	Vertical arrow cursor
IDC_WAIT	Hourglass cursor, used when the program is performing a lengthy task

Adding Message-Handling Functions

To allow the user to draw lines within the view window with the mouse, the program must respond to mouse events that occur within this window. To process this mouse input, you must add member functions to the view class that handle mouse *messages* that are sent to the view window. Before the chapter explains how to add the message-handling functions, however, the next section briefly introduces you to Windows messages.

Windows Messages

Every window in a Windows program has a function associated with it, known as a *window procedure*. When a significant event occurs that relates to the window, the Windows system calls this function, passing it an identifier for the event that occurred, as well as any associated data that is required to handle the event. This process is known as *sending a message to the window*.

When you create and manage a window using an MFC class, the MFC provides the window procedure for you. (All the windows in the example programs given in this part of the book are managed by MFC classes.) The window procedure provided by the MFC provides default handling for each type of message that can be sent. However, if you want to provide custom handling for a particular type of message, you can define a *message-handling function* that is a member of the class that manages the window. To define a message-handling function for a particular class, you can use the ClassWizard tool, as described in the next section.

For example, when the user presses the left mouse button while the mouse cursor is within the view window, the view window receives a message that has the identifier WM_LBUTTONDOWN. To provide your own processing for this message, you can use the ClassWizard to create a member function (of the program's view class) that handles this message.

Note that the MFC provides special handling for messages that are associated with user-interface objects, such as menus and tool bar buttons. (Menus are discussed in this chapter and in Chapter 9; other user-interface objects are discussed in Chapter 14.) These messages are known as *command messages*. Whenever the user chooses a user-interface object, or whenever one of these objects needs updating, the system sends a command message to the main program window. The MFC, however, immediately *reroutes* the message to the view window so that the message can be handled by the view class. If, however, the view class does not provide a handler, the MFC reroutes the message to the associated document class object. If the document class does not provide a handler, it reroutes the message to the main window. Finally, if the main window class does not provide a handler, it reroutes the message to the application class object. Thus, the MFC *extends* the basic Windows message mechanism so that command messages can be processed not only by objects that manage windows, but also by other objects; specifically, a command message can be sent to an object of any class that is derived from the MFC class CCmdTarget.

The important feature of the MFC command message routing mechanism is that the program can process a particular command at the most convenient and appropriate level. For instance, in a program generated by AppWizard, the Exit command on the File menu is handled by the application class, because this command affects the application as a whole. In contrast, the Save command on the File menu is handled by the document class, because this class has the responsibility for storing and saving the document data. Later in the book, you will learn how to add menu commands and other user-interface objects, how to choose the class that handles the command, and how to provide the message-handling function for the command.

NOTE   For a much more detailed explanation of the MFC message routing and handling mechanism, see the *Reference Volume I, Class Library Reference* manual (Chapter 3, "Working with Messages and Commands").

The OnLButtonDown Function

The next task is to define a message-handling function that processes the WM_LBUT-TONDOWN message. This message is sent whenever the user presses the left mouse button while the mouse cursor is within the view window. To define the function, perform the following steps:

1. Make sure that the MINIDRAW project is open in the Visual Workbench, and choose the ClassWizard... command on the Visual Workbench Project menu, or press Ctrl+W. The ClassWizard dialog box will appear.

2. Select the CMinidrawView class in the Class Name: list. You choose this class name because you want to add the message-handling function to the view class.

3. Select the CMinidrawView item in the Object IDs: list. Selecting this item allows you to provide a handler for any of the general notification messages that are sent to the view window. (The other items in the list are identifiers

for specific menu or accelerator commands; choosing one of these items allows you to provide a handler only for a message that originates from the selected command.)

4. Choose the WM_LBUTTONDOWN message in the Messages: list. This list displays the identifier of each type of notification message that can be sent to the view window. Notice that when you select a particular message, an explanation of that message appears at the bottom of the ClassWizard dialog box.

5. Click the Add Function button. ClassWizard now generates the basic code for the message-handling member function, which is named OnLButtonDown. Specifically, ClassWizard adds the function declaration to the CMinidrawView class definition within the file MINIDVW.H, it inserts a minimal function definition into the MINIDVW.CPP file, and it adds the function to the class *message map* (the message map is described in a sidebar given later in this section). Notice that a little hand now appears to the left of the WM_LBUTTONDOWN item in the Messages: list to indicate that the message is now handled, and that the name of the function and message are added to the Member Functions: list. The completed ClassWizard dialog box is shown in Figure 8.3.

6. Click the Edit Code button. The ClassWizard dialog box will be removed. ClassWizard will open the file MINIDVW.CPP (if it is not already open) and will place the insertion point within the OnLButtonDown function template that it just generated. ClassWizard delivers you to this function so that you can add your own code.

7. Add the statements marked in bold to the OnLButtonDown function:

```
/////////////////////////////////////////////////////////////////////////////
// CMinidrawView message handlers

void CMinidrawView::OnLButtonDown(UINT nFlags, CPoint point)
{
    // TODO: Add your message handler code here and/or call default

    mPointOrigin = point;
    mPointOld = point;
    SetCapture ();
    mDragging = 1;

    RECT Rect;
    GetClientRect (&Rect);
```

FIGURE 8.3:

The completed ClassWizard
dialog box

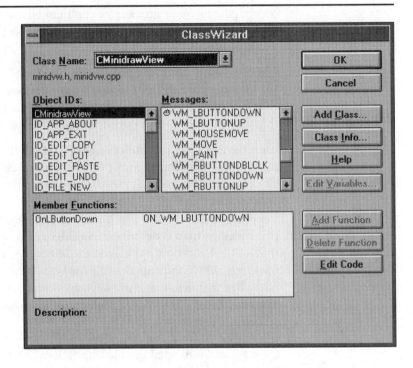

```
ClientToScreen (&Rect);
::ClipCursor (&Rect);

CView::OnLButtonDown(nFlags, point);
}
```

When the user presses the left mouse button while the cursor is over the view window, the OnLButtonDown function receives control, and the point parameter contains the current position of the mouse cursor. The code you added saves this position within the mPointOrigin and mPointOld data members. mPointOrigin stores the coordinates of the point where the left button was pressed, which will be the origin of the line that is to be drawn. mPointOld will be used by the other mouse message handlers to obtain the position of the mouse on the previous mouse message (as you will see shortly).

NOTE

The ClassWizard adds a line of code to the OnLButtonDown function that calls the version of OnLButtonDown defined within the base class. This is done so that the base class (or classes) can perform any required default message processing.

The call to the CWnd member function SetCapture *captures the mouse*, meaning that all subsequent mouse messages will be sent to the view window (until the capture is released, as explained later). Thus, the view window fully controls the mouse while the drag operation is taking place. Also, the data member mDragging is set to 1 to indicate to the other mouse message handlers that a drag operation is in progress.

NOTE

Because CMinidrawView is derived indirectly from CWnd, it inherits all of its many member functions (CMinidrawView is derived from CView, which in turn is derived from CWnd). To find out all the member functions available to a particular class, you must consult the class hierarchy that is given in the documentation on the class (in the *Reference Volume I, Class Library Reference* manual or in the online help). You can then view the documentation on each of the base classes for a description of the inherited functions. When the book refers to a particular member function, it generally indicates the class in which the function is actually defined; for example, the SetCapture function is described either as *the CWnd member function SetCapture* or simply as *CWnd::SetCapture* (using the scope resolution operator to indicate the class containing the function definition).

The remaining lines of code serve to confine the mouse cursor within the view window, so that the user does not try to draw a line outside of this window. The call to CWnd::GetClientRect obtains the current coordinates of the view window, and the call to CWnd::ClientToScreen converts these coordinates to *screen coordinates* (that is, coordinates with respect to the upper-left corner of the Windows screen). Finally, the call to ::ClipCursor confines the mouse cursor to the specified screen coordinates, thus keeping the cursor within the view window.

NOTE   ClipCursor is a function provided by the Windows application program interface (API); it is *not* defined within an MFC class. Because it is defined as a global function, its name is prefaced with the scope resolution operator (::). Using this operator is not actually necessary unless the API function name is hidden by a member function that has the same name. However, the book always prefaces the name of an API function with the scope resolution operator to clearly indicate that the function does not belong to the MFC.

The Message Map

When ClassWizard generates a message handler, in addition to declaring and defining the member function it also adds this function to an MFC contrivance known as a *message map*, which connects the function with the specific message it is intended to handle. The message map allows the MFC message mechanism to call the appropriate handler for each type of message. The AppWizard and ClassWizard tools generate all the code necessary to implement the message map. The message map is created using a set of MFC macros. In the MINIDRAW program, the following message map macros are added to the CMinidrawView class definition in MINIDVW.H,

```
// Generated message map functions
protected:
    //{{AFX_MSG(CMinidrawView)
    afx_msg void OnLButtonDown(UINT nFlags, CPoint point);
    afx_msg void OnMouseMove(UINT nFlags, CPoint point);
    afx_msg void OnLButtonUp(UINT nFlags, CPoint point);
    //}}AFX_MSG
    DECLARE_MESSAGE_MAP()
```

and the following macros are added to the view implementation file, MINIDVW.CPP:

```
BEGIN_MESSAGE_MAP(CMinidrawView, CView)
    //{{AFX_MSG_MAP(CMinidrawView)
    ON_WM_LBUTTONDOWN()
    ON_WM_MOUSEMOVE()
    ON_WM_LBUTTONUP()
    //}}AFX_MSG_MAP
END_MESSAGE_MAP()
```

When a message is sent to an object of a particular class, the MFC code consults the message map to determine whether the class has a handler for that message. If a handler is found, it receives control; if no handler is found, the MFC looks for a handler in the immediate base class. If it does not find a handler in the base class, the MFC continues to search up through the class hierarchy, calling the *first* handler that it finds. If it does not find any handler in the hierarchy, it provides default handling for the message (or, if it is a command message, it reroutes the message to the next target object in the sequence that was described previously).

The OnMouseMove Function

Next, you will define a function to handle the WM_MOUSEMOVE message. As the user moves the mouse cursor within the view window, this window receives a series of WM_MOUSEMOVE messages, each of which reports the current position of the cursor. To define a handler for this message, first use ClassWizard to generate the message-handling function template. Follow the numbered steps given in the previous section; in step 4, however, you should choose the WM_MOUSEMOVE message in the Messages: list rather than the WM_LBUTTONDOWN message. ClassWizard will generate a member function named OnMouseMove. The completed ClassWizard dialog box (just before you click the Edit Code button) is shown in Figure 8.4.

FIGURE 8.4:

The completed ClassWizard
dialog box for generating a
WM_MOUSEMOVE message
handler

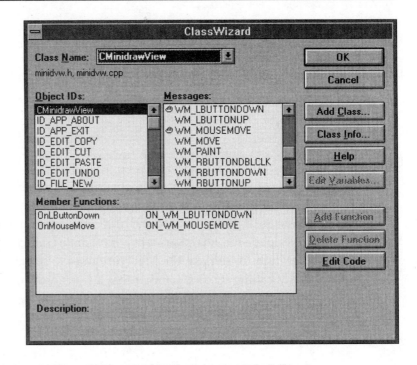

After you click the Edit Code button, enter the bold lines into the OnMouseMove
function:

```
void CMinidrawView::OnMouseMove(UINT nFlags, CPoint point)
{
    // TODO: Add your message handler code here and/or call default

    ::SetCursor (mHCross);

    if (mDragging)
        {
        CClientDC ClientDC (this);
        ClientDC.SetROP2 (R2_NOT);
        ClientDC.MoveTo (mPointOrigin);
        ClientDC.LineTo (mPointOld);
        ClientDC.MoveTo (mPointOrigin);
        ClientDC.LineTo (point);
```

```
    mPointOld = point;
    }

  CView::OnMouseMove(nFlags, point);
}
```

As the mouse cursor is moved within the view window, the OnMouseMove function is called at frequent intervals. The code that you added performs two main tasks. First, it calls the SetCursor Windows API function to display a cross-shaped cursor rather than the standard arrow cursor. (Recall that the handle to the cross-shaped cursor was obtained in the class constructor.) Note that later versions of the MINIDRAW program will display one of a variety of different cursors, depending upon which drawing tool is active. See the sidebar in this section for information on displaying the standard hourglass cursor.

Second, if a drag operation is in progress (that is, if mDragging is nonzero), the code you added performs the following steps:

1. It erases the line that was drawn on the previous WM_MOUSEMOVE message (if any).

2. It draws a new line from the origin of the line (that is, the point where the left button was pressed, stored in mPointOrigin) to the current position of the cursor (point).

3. It stores the current position of the cursor in the data member mPointOld.

To draw within the window, OnMouseMove first creates a device context object associated with the view window (device context objects were introduced in Chapter 7). It then calls the SetROP2 member function to create a drawing mode in which lines are drawn by *reversing* the current color on the screen. Under this mode, when a line is first drawn at a particular position, it is visible; however, when a line is drawn a second time at the same position, it becomes invisible. The mouse message handlers are thus able to easily draw and erase a series of temporary lines. The lines are drawn using the MoveTo function (which specifies the position of one end of the line) and the LineTo function (which specifies the position of the other end). Device context objects are explained in Chapter 15, and the SetROP2, MoveTo, and LineTo functions are described in Chapter 16.

Displaying the Hourglass

If you perform a lengthy task (such as reading a file) during the processing of a message, you should temporarily display the standard hourglass cursor to notify the user of the pause in normal message processing. To do this, you can place the following code within the function that performs the lengthy task:

```
// save the current cursor and display the hourglass:
HCURSOR HOldCursor = ::SetCursor (AfxGetApp ()->LoadStandardCursor (IDC_WAIT));
::ShowCursor (TRUE);

// code that performs a lengthy task ...

// restore the previous cursor:
::ShowCursor (FALSE);
::SetCursor (HOldCursor);
```

Notice that LoadStandardCursor returns the handle to the current mouse cursor, allowing the code to save this cursor and then restore if after the hourglass has been displayed. The calls to the Windows API function ShowCursor cause the hourglass cursor to appear even on a system that does not have a mouse installed. (On a system with a mouse, these calls are unnecessary but harmless.)

The overall result of the MouseMove function is that as the user drags the mouse cursor within the view window, a temporary line always connects the origin of the line with the current cursor position. (This line shows where the permanent line would be drawn if the user released the mouse button.)

The OnLButtonUp Function

Finally, you need to define a function to handle the WM_LBUTTONUP message, which is sent when the user releases the left mouse button. Use ClassWizard to create the basic function code in the same way you used it for the previous two messages; in the ClassWizard dialog box, however, be sure to choose the WM_LBUTTONUP identifier in the Messages: list. Then, add code as follows to the OnLButtonUp function:

```
void CMinidrawView::OnLButtonUp(UINT nFlags, CPoint point)
{
    // TODO: Add your message handler code here and/or call default

    if (mDragging)
        {
        mDragging = 0;
        ::ReleaseCapture ();
        ::ClipCursor (NULL);
        CClientDC ClientDC (this);
        ClientDC.SetROP2 (R2_NOT);
        ClientDC.MoveTo (mPointOrigin);
        ClientDC.LineTo (mPointOld);
        ClientDC.SetROP2 (R2_COPYPEN);
        ClientDC.MoveTo (mPointOrigin);
        ClientDC.LineTo (point);
        }

    CView::OnLButtonUp(nFlags, point);
}
```

If the user was dragging the mouse cursor (that is, mDragging is nonzero), the code that you added terminates the drag operation and draws a permanent line. Specifically, it performs the following steps:

1. It assigns 0 to mDragging to signal the other mouse message handlers that a drag operation is no longer in progress.

2. It calls the Windows API function ReleaseCapture to end the mouse capture; as a result, mouse messages will again be sent to any window that lies under the cursor.

3. It passes NULL to the Windows API function ClipCursor so the user can again move the mouse cursor anywhere on the screen.

4. It erases the temporary line drawn by the previous WM_MOUSEMOVE message handler.

5. It draws a permanent line from the line origin to the current position of the cursor.

WM_LBUTTONDOWN is the final mouse message that you need to handle in the MINIDRAW program. Table 8.2 provides a complete list of mouse notification messages. You might want to provide handlers for some of these messages in your other Windows programs.

TABLE 8.2: Mouse Notification Messages

Message	Mouse Event ·
WM_MOUSEMOVE	The user moved the mouse cursor to a new position within the client area.
WM_LBUTTONDOWN	The user pressed the left button.
WM_MBUTTONDOWN	The user pressed the middle button.
WM_RBUTTONDOWN	The user pressed the right button.
WM_LBUTTONUP	The user released the left button.
WM_MBUTTONUP	The user released the middle button.
WM_RBUTTONUP	The user released the right button.
WM_LBUTTONDBLCLK	The user double-clicked the left button.
WM_MBUTTONDBLCLK	The user double-clicked the middle button.
WM_RBUTTONDBLCLK	The user double-clicked the right button.

Designing the Program Resources

In this section, you will learn how to use the App Studio tool to customize the MINIDRAW program resources—specifically, the menu, one of the program's message strings, and the program icon. The easiest way to run App Studio, and to have it automatically open the MINIDRAW program resources, is to choose the App Studio command on the Visual Workbench Tools menu (the MINIDRAW project must be open). When App Studio begins running, it displays the resource dialog box

Mouse Message Parameters

The handlers for all mouse messages are passed two parameters: nFlags and point.

The nFlags parameter indicates the status of the mouse buttons, as well as the status of several keys on the keyboard, at the time the mouse event occurred. The status of each button or key is represented by a specific bit within nFlags. You can use the bit masks given in Table 8.3 to access the individual bits.

For example, the following code tests whether the shift key was down when the mouse was moved:

```
void CMinidrawView::OnMouseMove(UINT nFlags, CPoint point)
{
    if (nFlags & MK_SHIFT)
        // then Shift key was pressed when mouse was moved
```

The parameter point is a CPoint structure that supplies the coordinates of the mouse cursor at the time the event occurred. The x data member (point.x) contains the horizontal coordinate of the cursor, and the y data member (point.y) contains the vertical coordinate. The coordinates specify the position of the cursor with respect to the upper-left corner of the view window.

Stated more accurately, the point parameter supplies the coordinates of the *hot spot* within the mouse cursor. The hot spot is a single pixel within the cursor, which is designated when the cursor is designed. The hot spot for the standard arrow cursor is at the tip of the arrow, and the hot spot for the standard cross-shaped cursor is at the point where the lines intersect.

TABLE 8.3: Bit Masks for Accessing the Bits in the **nFlags** Parameter Passed to Mouse Message Handlers

Bit Mask	Meaning of Bit
MK_CONTROL	Set if Ctrl key is down
MK_LBUTTON	Set if left mouse button is down
MK_MBUTTON	Set if middle mouse button is down
MK_RBUTTON	Set if right mouse button is down
MK_SHIFT	Set if Shift key is down

(labeled "MINIDRAW.RC (MFC Resource Script)"), which permits you to choose each resource that you want to edit; this dialog box is shown in Figure 8.5.

To customize the MINIDRAW menu, do the following:

1. Select the Menu item in the Type: list within the resource dialog box.

2. Select the IDR_MAINFRAME menu identifier in the Resources: list.

3. Click the Open button. App Studio will now open the menu-designing window (labeled "IDR_MAINFRAME (Menu)"), which displays a visual representation of the MINIDRAW program menu as it was created by AppWizard.

4. Click on the File menu to open the drop-down menu, and delete all of the items on the menu *except* the New command, the Exit command, and the separator between these two commands. To delete a menu item (a command or separator), simply click on the item and press the Del key.

FIGURE 8.5:

The resource dialog box for choosing program resources in App Studio

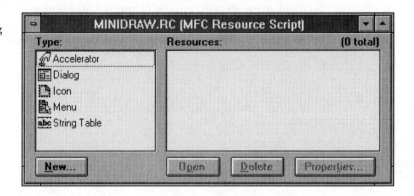

5. Click on the Edit menu and press Del to delete the entire Edit drop-down menu.

6. You have now deleted all unused menu items. Remove the menu-designing window by double-clicking its system menu (in the upper-left corner).

Next, customize the string that is used to display the program title and document type within the MINIDRAW window's title bar:

1. Select the String Table item in the Type: list within the resource dialog box.

2. Select the String Segment:0 item in the Resources: list.

3. Click the Open button. App Studio will now display the string table dialog box (labeled "(String Table)").

4. Select the first item in the list of string resources (the string with the `IDR_MAINFRAME` identifier) and click the Properties... button. App Studio will now open the string properties dialog box (labeled "String Editor: String Properties").

5. In the Caption: text box, edit the string so that it appears as follows:

`MiniDraw\ndrawing\nMINIDR Document`

The first part of this string ("MiniDraw") is used as the program name in the title bar, and the second part ("drawing") is used as the document type in the title bar, as shown in Figure 8.1. (You should specify no more than 8 characters for the document type name, because the MFC also uses it as the default file name when the user first saves the document.)

> **NOTE**
> The instructions given here are for specifying a document type within an existing program. Alternatively, when you first create an application using AppWizard, you can specify a document type by clicking the Classes... button in the MFC AppWizard dialog box, selecting the name of the document class in the New Application Classes: list, and entering a name for the document type into the Doc Type Name: text box.

6. Press Esc to remove the string properties dialog box, and then remove the string table dialog box by double-clicking its system menu.

Finally, if you want to design a custom program icon (to replace the standard AFX icon), do the following:

1. Select the Icon item in the Type: list within the MINIDRAW.RC dialog box.

2. Select the IDR_MAINFRAME identifier in the Resources: list.

3. Click the Open button. App Studio will open the icon-designing window (labeled "IDR_MAINFRAME (Icon)"), which allows you to edit the icon, together with a floating palette of drawing tools and colors. These two dialog boxes constitute the Graphics Editor tool provided by App Studio.

4. Edit the icon as desired. For information on using the commands and tools in the icon-designing window, see the *App Studio User's Guide* manual (Chapter 7, "Using the Graphics Editor"), or press F1 while working in the icon-designing window to view online help. The icon included with the MINIDRAW source files on the companion disk is shown in Figure 8.6.

FIGURE 8.6:

The MINIDRAW program icon

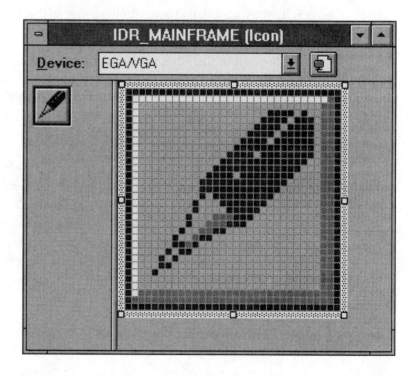

After you have made all desired changes to the program resources, save your modifications by choosing the Save command on the App Studio File menu. App Studio saves the primary resource information in the file MINIDRAW.RC (which is a text file known as a *resource script*), and it saves the icon data in the file MINIDRAW.ICO (which is a binary file stored in the \RES subdirectory; the main resource file, MINIDRAW.RC, contains an ICON statement that identifies this icon file). When the program is built, the Microsoft Resource Editor program (RC.EXE) processes the resource information in these files and adds the resource data to the executable program file.

NOTE With previous Windows development tools from Microsoft, you had to manually edit the resource script to define such items as menus. With Visual C++, however, the App Studio lets you create all types of resources, and it both generates and edits the resource script for you.

You can now quit the App Studio program and return to the Visual Workbench to continue working on the MINIDRAW program.

Customizing the Window

There are two problems with the MINIDRAW program as it is currently written. First, although the WM_MOUSEMOVE message handler that you wrote displays the desired cross-shaped cursor, Windows *also* attempts to display a standard arrow cursor, because the arrow cursor is assigned to the view window when it is created by the MFC. As a result, the cursor flickers back and forth between these two shapes as the user moves it within the view window.

The second problem is that if the user chooses a dark Window Background color using the Windows Control Panel, the lines drawn in the view window will be invisible or at least difficult to see. When the MFC creates the window, it assigns it a setting that causes the background to be painted using the current Window Background color. The program, however, always draws the lines in black.

The solution to both these problems is to customize the view window. To customize a window, you can override the CWnd virtual member function PreCreateWindow, which the MFC calls immediately before creating a window. To customize the view

221

window, you should add your own version of `PreCreateWindow` to the view class. You already added the declaration for this function to the `CMinidrawView` class definition (in the section "Define and Initialize View Class Data Members"). You should now add the function definition to the end of the MINIDVW.CPP file, as follows:

```
BOOL CMinidrawView::PreCreateWindow (CREATESTRUCT& cs)
   {
   mClassName = AfxRegisterWndClass
      (CS_HREDRAW | CS_VREDRAW,                // class styles
      0,                                       // no cursor
      (HBRUSH)::GetStockObject (WHITE_BRUSH),  // set white background brush
      0);                                      // no icon
   cs.lpszClass = mClassName;

   return CView::PreCreateWindow (cs);
   }
```

`PreCreateWindow` is passed a reference to a `CREATESTRUCT` structure; the fields of this structure store the window features that the MFC will specify when it creates the window, such as the window coordinates, the window styles, and so on. If you assign values to one or more of the fields of this structure, the MFC will use your values rather than its default ones.

One of the `CREATESTRUCT` fields (`lpszClass`) stores the name of the *Windows window class*. The Windows window class is *not* a C++ class; rather, it is a data structure maintained by the Windows system, which stores a set of general features that are used when the window is created. The code you just added calls `AfxRegisterWndClass` to create a new Windows window class, and then assigns the class name to the `lpszClass` `CREATESTRUCT` field, so that the view window will be created using the custom features stored within this Windows window class.

> **NOTE** `AfxRegisterWndClass` is a *global* function provided by the MFC; it is not a member of an MFC class.

The call to `AfxRegisterWndClass` specifies the following features:

- The first parameter specifies the class styles `CS_HREDRAW` and `CS_VREDRAW`. These styles cause the window to be redrawn whenever the user changes the size of the window (MFC view windows are normally created with these styles).

- The second parameter specifies the mouse cursor that Windows automatically displays within the window. This parameter is assigned 0 so that Windows will *not* attempt to display a cursor, because a cursor is explicitly displayed by the OnMouseMove function that you added. Thus, the flicker is eliminated.

- The third parameter supplies a standard white brush that will be used for painting the view window background (brushes are discussed in Chapter 16). As a result, the window background will always be white—and the black lines will always be visible—regardless of the Window Background color that the user has selected in the Control Panel.

- The last parameter specifies the window icon. Because the view window does not display an icon, it is assigned 0 (the program icon is assigned to the main frame window).

NOTE
The MINIDRAW program displays a custom cursor by assigning *no* cursor to the window class and then displaying the desired cursor from the OnMouseMove message-handling function. As an alternative method, you can simply assign the desired cursor to the window by passing its handle as the second parameter to AfxRegisterWndClass. This alternative method, however, does not allow you to easily *change* cursors as the program runs. (For example, later versions of the MINIDRAW program will change the cursor each time the user selects a new drawing tool.)

This section described the last of the changes to be made to the MINIDRAW program. You can now build and run the program.

The MINIDRAW Program Source Code

The C++ source code for the MINIDRAW program is given in the following listings, Listing 8.1 through 8.8. These listings contain the code that was generated by AppWizard, plus the manual code additions described previously in the chapter. If you followed the exercises given in this section, the files you created should be the same as these listings; a complete copy of these files is also included in the \MINIDRW1 subdirectory within the directory in which you installed the companion disk.

Listing 8.1

```
// minidraw.h : main header file for the MINIDRAW application
//

#ifndef __AFXWIN_H__
   #error include 'stdafx.h' before including this file for PCH
#endif

#include "resource.h"        // main symbols

/////////////////////////////////////////////////////////////////////////////
// CMinidrawApp:
// See minidraw.cpp for the implementation of this class
//

class CMinidrawApp : public CWinApp
{
public:
   CMinidrawApp();

// Overrides
   virtual BOOL InitInstance();

// Implementation

   //{{AFX_MSG(CMinidrawApp)
   afx_msg void OnAppAbout();
      // NOTE - the ClassWizard will add and remove member functions here.
      //    DO NOT EDIT what you see in these blocks of generated code !
   //}}AFX_MSG
   DECLARE_MESSAGE_MAP()
};

/////////////////////////////////////////////////////////////////////////////
```

Listing 8.2

```
// minidraw.cpp : Defines the class behaviors for the application.
//

#include "stdafx.h"
#include "minidraw.h"

#include "mainfrm.h"
#include "miniddoc.h"
#include "minidvw.h"

#ifdef _DEBUG
#undef THIS_FILE
static char BASED_CODE THIS_FILE[] = __FILE__;
#endif

/////////////////////////////////////////////////////////////////////////////
// CMinidrawApp

BEGIN_MESSAGE_MAP(CMinidrawApp, CWinApp)
    //{{AFX_MSG_MAP(CMinidrawApp)
    ON_COMMAND(ID_APP_ABOUT, OnAppAbout)
        // NOTE - the ClassWizard will add and remove mapping macros here.
        //      DO NOT EDIT what you see in these blocks of generated code !
    //}}AFX_MSG_MAP
    // Standard file based document commands
    ON_COMMAND(ID_FILE_NEW, CWinApp::OnFileNew)
    ON_COMMAND(ID_FILE_OPEN, CWinApp::OnFileOpen)
END_MESSAGE_MAP()

/////////////////////////////////////////////////////////////////////////////
// CMinidrawApp construction

CMinidrawApp::CMinidrawApp()
{
    // TODO: add construction code here,
    // Place all significant initialization in InitInstance
}

/////////////////////////////////////////////////////////////////////////////
// The one and only CMinidrawApp object

CMinidrawApp NEAR theApp;
```

```
/////////////////////////////////////////////////////////////////////////
// CMinidrawApp initialization

BOOL CMinidrawApp::InitInstance()
{
    // Standard initialization
    // If you are not using these features and wish to reduce the size
    //  of your final executable, you should remove from the following
    //  the specific initialization routines you do not need.

    SetDialogBkColor();         // set dialog background color to gray
    LoadStdProfileSettings();  // Load standard INI file options (including MRU)

    // Register the application's document templates.  Document templates
    //  serve as the connection between documents, frame windows and views.

    AddDocTemplate(new CSingleDocTemplate(IDR_MAINFRAME,
        RUNTIME_CLASS(CMinidrawDoc),
        RUNTIME_CLASS(CMainFrame),      // main SDI frame window
        RUNTIME_CLASS(CMinidrawView)));

    // create a new (empty) document
    OnFileNew();

    if (m_lpCmdLine[0] != '\0')
    {
        // TODO: add command line processing here
    }

    return TRUE;
}

/////////////////////////////////////////////////////////////////////////
// CAboutDlg dialog used for App About

class CAboutDlg : public CDialog
{
public:
    CAboutDlg();

// Dialog Data
    //{{AFX_DATA(CAboutDlg)
    enum { IDD = IDD_ABOUTBOX };
    //}}AFX_DATA
```

```
// Implementation
protected:
    virtual void DoDataExchange(CDataExchange* pDX);    // DDX/DDV support
    //{{AFX_MSG(CAboutDlg)
        // No message handlers
    //}}AFX_MSG
    DECLARE_MESSAGE_MAP()
};

CAboutDlg::CAboutDlg() : CDialog(CAboutDlg::IDD)
{
    //{{AFX_DATA_INIT(CAboutDlg)
    //}}AFX_DATA_INIT
}

void CAboutDlg::DoDataExchange(CDataExchange* pDX)
{
    CDialog::DoDataExchange(pDX);
    //{{AFX_DATA_MAP(CAboutDlg)
    //}}AFX_DATA_MAP
}

BEGIN_MESSAGE_MAP(CAboutDlg, CDialog)
    //{{AFX_MSG_MAP(CAboutDlg)
        // No message handlers
    //}}AFX_MSG_MAP
END_MESSAGE_MAP()

// App command to run the dialog
void CMinidrawApp::OnAppAbout()
{
    CAboutDlg aboutDlg;
    aboutDlg.DoModal();
}

/////////////////////////////////////////////////////////////////////////////
// CMinidrawApp commands
```

Listing 8.3

```
// miniddoc.h : interface of the CMinidrawDoc class
//
/////////////////////////////////////////////////////////////////////////////

class CMinidrawDoc : public CDocument
```

```
{
protected: // create from serialization only
    CMinidrawDoc();
    DECLARE_DYNCREATE(CMinidrawDoc)

// Attributes
public:

// Operations
public:

// Implementation
public:
    virtual ~CMinidrawDoc();
    virtual void Serialize(CArchive& ar);   // overridden for document i/o
#ifdef _DEBUG
    virtual  void AssertValid() const;
    virtual  void Dump(CDumpContext& dc) const;
#endif
protected:
    virtual  BOOL  OnNewDocument();

// Generated message map functions
protected:
    //{{AFX_MSG(CMinidrawDoc)
        // NOTE - the ClassWizard will add and remove member functions here.
        //    DO NOT EDIT what you see in these blocks of generated code !
    //}}AFX_MSG
    DECLARE_MESSAGE_MAP()
};
```

//

Listing 8.4

```
// miniddoc.cpp : implementation of the CMinidrawDoc class
//

#include "stdafx.h"
#include "minidraw.h"

#include "miniddoc.h"

#ifdef _DEBUG
#undef THIS_FILE
```

```
static char BASED_CODE THIS_FILE[] = __FILE__;
#endif

/////////////////////////////////////////////////////////////////////////
// CMinidrawDoc

IMPLEMENT_DYNCREATE(CMinidrawDoc, CDocument)

BEGIN_MESSAGE_MAP(CMinidrawDoc, CDocument)
    //{{AFX_MSG_MAP(CMinidrawDoc)
        // NOTE - the ClassWizard will add and remove mapping macros here.
        //    DO NOT EDIT what you see in these blocks of generated code !
    //}}AFX_MSG_MAP
END_MESSAGE_MAP()

/////////////////////////////////////////////////////////////////////////
// CMinidrawDoc construction/destruction

CMinidrawDoc::CMinidrawDoc()
{
    // TODO: add one-time construction code here
}

CMinidrawDoc::~CMinidrawDoc()
{
}

BOOL CMinidrawDoc::OnNewDocument()
{
    if (!CDocument::OnNewDocument())
        return FALSE;
    // TODO: add reinitialization code here
    // (SDI documents will reuse this document)
    return TRUE;
}

/////////////////////////////////////////////////////////////////////////
// CMinidrawDoc serialization

void CMinidrawDoc::Serialize(CArchive& ar)
{
    if (ar.IsStoring())
    {
        // TODO: add storing code here
    }
```

```
    else
    {
        // TODO: add loading code here
    }
}

/////////////////////////////////////////////////////////////////////////////
// CMinidrawDoc diagnostics

#ifdef _DEBUG
void CMinidrawDoc::AssertValid() const
{
    CDocument::AssertValid();
}

void CMinidrawDoc::Dump(CDumpContext& dc) const
{
    CDocument::Dump(dc);
}

#endif //_DEBUG

/////////////////////////////////////////////////////////////////////////////
// CMinidrawDoc commands
```

Listing 8.5

```
// mainfrm.h : interface of the CMainFrame class
//
/////////////////////////////////////////////////////////////////////////////

class CMainFrame : public CFrameWnd
{
protected: // create from serialization only
    CMainFrame();
    DECLARE_DYNCREATE(CMainFrame)

// Attributes
public:

// Operations
public:

// Implementation
public:
```

```
   virtual ~CMainFrame();
#ifdef _DEBUG
   virtual  void AssertValid() const;
   virtual  void Dump(CDumpContext& dc) const;
#endif


// Generated message map functions
protected:
   //{{AFX_MSG(CMainFrame)
      // NOTE - the ClassWizard will add and remove member functions here.
      //    DO NOT EDIT what you see in these blocks of generated code !
   //}}AFX_MSG
   DECLARE_MESSAGE_MAP()
};
```

//

Listing 8.6

```
// mainfrm.cpp : implementation of the CMainFrame class
//

#include "stdafx.h"
#include "minidraw.h"

#include "mainfrm.h"

#ifdef _DEBUG
#undef THIS_FILE
static char BASED_CODE THIS_FILE[] = __FILE__;
#endif

////////////////////////////////////////////////////////////////////////////
// CMainFrame

IMPLEMENT_DYNCREATE(CMainFrame, CFrameWnd)

BEGIN_MESSAGE_MAP(CMainFrame, CFrameWnd)
   //{{AFX_MSG_MAP(CMainFrame)
      // NOTE - the ClassWizard will add and remove mapping macros here.
      //    DO NOT EDIT what you see in these blocks of generated code !
   //}}AFX_MSG_MAP
END_MESSAGE_MAP()
```

```
/////////////////////////////////////////////////////////////////////////
// CMainFrame construction/destruction

CMainFrame::CMainFrame()
{
    // TODO: add member initialization code here
}

CMainFrame::~CMainFrame()
{
}


/////////////////////////////////////////////////////////////////////////
// CMainFrame diagnostics

#ifdef _DEBUG
void CMainFrame::AssertValid() const
{
    CFrameWnd::AssertValid();
}

void CMainFrame::Dump(CDumpContext& dc) const
{
    CFrameWnd::Dump(dc);
}

#endif //_DEBUG

/////////////////////////////////////////////////////////////////////////
// CMainFrame message handlers
```

Listing 8.7

```
// minidvw.h : interface of the CMinidrawView class
//
/////////////////////////////////////////////////////////////////////////

class CMinidrawView : public CView
{
protected: // create from serialization only
    CMinidrawView();
    DECLARE_DYNCREATE(CMinidrawView)

protected:
    CString mClassName;
```

```
      int mDragging;
      HCURSOR mHCross;
      CPoint mPointOld;
      CPoint mPointOrigin;

      virtual BOOL PreCreateWindow (CREATESTRUCT& cs);

// Attributes
public:
      CMinidrawDoc* GetDocument();

// Operations
public:

// Implementation
public:
      virtual ~CMinidrawView();
      virtual void OnDraw(CDC* pDC);   // overridden to draw this view
#ifdef _DEBUG
      virtual void AssertValid() const;
      virtual void Dump(CDumpContext& dc) const;
#endif

// Generated message map functions
protected:
      //{{AFX_MSG(CMinidrawView)
      afx_msg void OnLButtonDown(UINT nFlags, CPoint point);
      afx_msg void OnMouseMove(UINT nFlags, CPoint point);
      afx_msg void OnLButtonUp(UINT nFlags, CPoint point);
      //}}AFX_MSG
      DECLARE_MESSAGE_MAP()
};

#ifndef _DEBUG // debug version in minidvw.cpp
inline CMinidrawDoc* CMinidrawView::GetDocument()
      { return (CMinidrawDoc*) m_pDocument; }
#endif

/////////////////////////////////////////////////////////////////////////////
```

Listing 8.8

```cpp
// minidvw.cpp : implementation of the CMinidrawView class
//

#include "stdafx.h"
#include "minidraw.h"

#include "miniddoc.h"
#include "minidvw.h"

#ifdef _DEBUG
#undef THIS_FILE
static char BASED_CODE THIS_FILE[] = __FILE__;
#endif

/////////////////////////////////////////////////////////////////////////////
// CMinidrawView

IMPLEMENT_DYNCREATE(CMinidrawView, CView)

BEGIN_MESSAGE_MAP(CMinidrawView, CView)
    //{{AFX_MSG_MAP(CMinidrawView)
    ON_WM_LBUTTONDOWN()
    ON_WM_MOUSEMOVE()
    ON_WM_LBUTTONUP()
    //}}AFX_MSG_MAP
END_MESSAGE_MAP()

/////////////////////////////////////////////////////////////////////////////
// CMinidrawView construction/destruction

CMinidrawView::CMinidrawView()
{
    // TODO: add construction code here

    mDragging = 0;
    mHCross = AfxGetApp ()->LoadStandardCursor (IDC_CROSS);
}

CMinidrawView::~CMinidrawView()
{
}

/////////////////////////////////////////////////////////////////////////////
```

```
// CMinidrawView drawing

void CMinidrawView::OnDraw(CDC* pDC)
{
    CMinidrawDoc* pDoc = GetDocument();

    // TODO: add draw code here
}


/////////////////////////////////////////////////////////////////////////////
// CMinidrawView diagnostics

#ifdef _DEBUG
void CMinidrawView::AssertValid() const
{
    CView::AssertValid();
}

void CMinidrawView::Dump(CDumpContext& dc) const
{
    CView::Dump(dc);
}

CMinidrawDoc* CMinidrawView::GetDocument() // non-debug version is inline
{
    ASSERT(m_pDocument->IsKindOf(RUNTIME_CLASS(CMinidrawDoc)));
    return (CMinidrawDoc*) m_pDocument;
}

#endif //_DEBUG

/////////////////////////////////////////////////////////////////////////////
// CMinidrawView message handlers

void CMinidrawView::OnLButtonDown(UINT nFlags, CPoint point)
{
    // TODO: Add your message handler code here and/or call default

    mPointOrigin = point;
    mPointOld = point;
    SetCapture ();
    mDragging = 1;

    RECT Rect;
```

```
    GetClientRect (&Rect);
    ClientToScreen (&Rect);
    ::ClipCursor (&Rect);

    CView::OnLButtonDown(nFlags, point);
}

void CMinidrawView::OnMouseMove(UINT nFlags, CPoint point)
{
    // TODO: Add your message handler code here and/or call default

    ::SetCursor (mHCross);

    if (mDragging)
        {
        CClientDC ClientDC (this);
        ClientDC.SetROP2 (R2_NOT);
        ClientDC.MoveTo (mPointOrigin);
        ClientDC.LineTo (mPointOld);
        ClientDC.MoveTo (mPointOrigin);
        ClientDC.LineTo (point);
        mPointOld = point;
        }

    CView::OnMouseMove(nFlags, point);
}

void CMinidrawView::OnLButtonUp(UINT nFlags, CPoint point)
{
    // TODO: Add your message handler code here and/or call default

    if (mDragging)
        {
        mDragging = 0;
        ::ReleaseCapture ();
        ::ClipCursor (NULL);
        CClientDC ClientDC (this);
        ClientDC.SetROP2 (R2_NOT);
        ClientDC.MoveTo (mPointOrigin);
        ClientDC.LineTo (mPointOld);
        ClientDC.SetROP2 (R2_COPYPEN);
        ClientDC.MoveTo (mPointOrigin);
        ClientDC.LineTo (point);
        }
```

```
    CView::OnLButtonUp(nFlags, point);
}

BOOL CMinidrawView::PreCreateWindow (CREATESTRUCT& cs)
    {
    mClassName = AfxRegisterWndClass
        (CS_HREDRAW | CS_VREDRAW,                    // class styles
        0,                                           // no cursor
        (HBRUSH)::GetStockObject (WHITE_BRUSH),      // set white background brush
        0);                                          // no icon
    cs.lpszClass = mClassName;

    return CView::PreCreateWindow (cs);
    }
```

The MINIEDIT Program

You can easily create a full-featured text editor by deriving your view class from the MFC CEditView class, rather than from CView. A view class derived from CEditView allows the program user to enter and edit text within the view window, and contains support for a fairly complete collection of keyboard and menu editing commands; you do not need to implement these features yourself. In fact, CEditView supports almost all of the features of the Windows Notepad editor.

In this section, you will generate a program named MINIEDIT using the AppWizard. You will then modify the source code so that the view class is derived from CEditView rather than CView, thus creating an instant text editor within the view window. Next, you will use App Studio to add menu commands that allow the user to access some of the editor commands, as well as to modify several other program resources.

The MINIEDIT program window is shown in Figure 8.7. The program allows you to enter and edit text into the view window, and the view window displays scroll bars that permit you to scroll through the text if it does not all fit within the window. The program menu includes commands for printing the text; for undoing your last editing action; for cutting, copying, and pasting text; for selecting text; and for performing search and replace operations. Versions of MINIEDIT presented in subsequent chapters will add features such as commands for saving and loading text files from disk, plus a command for choosing fonts.

FIGURE 8.7:

The MINIEDIT program window

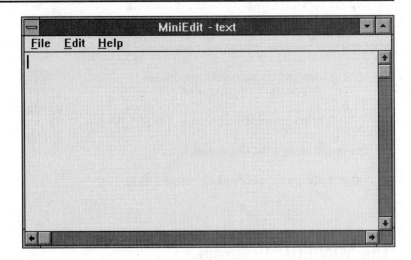

In later chapters you will learn about several other special-purpose view class provided by the MFC, which implement ready-to-use features. (Specifically, Chapter 11 explains CScrollView, which provides a scrolling view window, and Chapter 13 explains CFormView, which creates a scrolling view window that can be used to display a collection of controls.)

Creating the MINIEDIT Program

To create the MINIEDIT program, first use AppWizard to generate the source code files in the same way you used it for the previous example programs. In the MFC AppWizard dialog box, specify the project name MINIEDIT, and place the files in a separate subdirectory that is used exclusively for the MINIEDIT project. As before, in the AppWizard Options dialog box, select only the Generate Source Comments option.

After generating the source code, you should edit the two source files MINIEVW.H and MINIEVW.CPP in the Visual Workbench, and replace all occurrences of CView with CEditView. (There should be one occurrence of CView in MINIEVW.H and four occurrences in MINIEVW.CPP; see the complete listings given in the next section.) As a result, the program view class will be derived from CEditView rather than CView.

Next, run App Studio by choosing the App Studio command on the Visual Work-bench Tools menu, so that you can customize the program resources.

You will first modify the program menu, eliminating unused commands and add-ing new commands that invoke features provided by the CEditView class. To do this, select the Menu item in the Type: list, select the IDR_MAINFRAME identifier in the Resources: list, and click the Open button. When the menu-designing window opens, make the following changes:

1. Delete all items on the File menu, except the Exit command and the separa-tor above this command.

2. Double-click the empty square at the bottom of the Edit menu to add a new item. App Studio will open the menu item properties dialog box (labeled "Menu: Menu Item Properties"). Enter the identifier ID_FILE_PRINT into the ID: box, and enter the string &Print\tCtrl+P into the Caption: box. The new command will now appear on the File menu. (Notice that typing a & character before a character in the Caption: box causes the character to be un-derlined when it is displayed on the menu; the user can type the underlined character to choose the command.)

3. Using the mouse, drag the new command (Print Ctrl+P) from its current posi-tion at the bottom of the menu to the top of the menu. Figure 8.8 shows the completed File menu as it appears in the App Studio menu-designing window.

4. Use the technique described in step 2 to add four new commands to the Edit menu. Table 8.4 lists the identifier and caption for each of these commands,

TABLE 8.4: New Commands to Add to the Edit Menu

ID:	Caption:
ID_EDIT_SELECT_ALL	Select &All
ID_EDIT_FIND	&Find...
ID_EDIT_REPEAT	Find &Next\tF3
ID_EDIT_REPLACE	&Replace...

FIGURE 8.8:

The completed File menu in App Studio

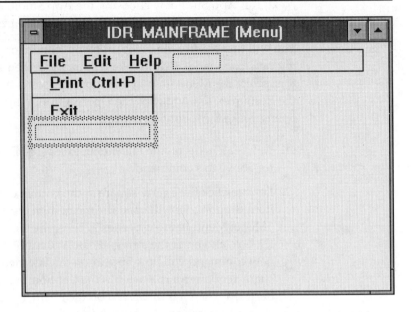

and Figure 8.9 shows the completed menu as it appears in App Studio. Note that after adding the Select All command, you should insert a separator. To insert a separator, simply select the Separator check box in the menu item properties dialog box, rather than entering an identifier and a caption.

5. You can now remove the menu-designing window by double-clicking its system menu.

Note that you must use the exact menu command identifiers that were given in the instructions, so that the message map defined within CEditView will route each command message to the appropriate message-handling function.

Notice that the captions for two of the commands you added (the Print command and the Find Next command) specify shortcut keys for executing the commands. Such shortcut keys are known as *keyboard accelerators* and must be defined using App Studio. To define these two keyboard accelerators, do the following:

1. Select the Accelerator item within the Type: list of the App Studio resource dialog box.

FIGURE 8.9:

The completed Edit menu
in App Studio

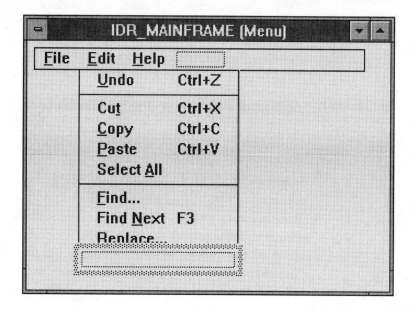

2. Select the `IDR_MAINFRAME` item within the Resources: list.

3. Click the Open button. App Studio will now open the accelerator dialog box (labeled "IDR_MAINFRAME (Accelerator)").

4. Click the New button in the accelerator dialog box. App Studio will now open the accelerator properties dialog box (labeled "Accel Table: Accel Properties").

5. Click the Next Key Typed button and then press the Ctrl+P keystroke. This will assign Ctrl+P as the accelerator keystroke.

6. Enter the identifier `ID_FILE_PRINT` into the ID: text box; this is the identifier you assigned to the Print command on the File menu. This will make Ctrl+P an accelerator keystroke for the Print command.

7. Click the New button again in the accelerator dialog box.

8. This time, specify the F3 keystroke and enter the `ID_EDIT_REPEAT` identifier in the accelerator properties dialog box. This will assign the F3 key as an accelerator keystroke for executing the Find Next command on the Edit menu.

9. You can now close the accelerator dialog box.

Next, update the message string used to display the program title and document type, which has the identifier IDR_MAINFRAME. Follow the procedure that was given previously for the MINIDRAW program (in the section "Designing the Program Resources"). This time, however, edit the caption so that it appears as follows:

`MiniEdit\ntext\nMINIED Document`

Finally, if desired, you can design a custom icon for the MINIEDIT program. Follow the instructions given previously for the MINIDRAW program (in the section "Designing the Program Resources"). The MINIEDIT icon that is provided on the companion disk is shown in Figure 8.10.

You can now build the MINIEDIT project, run the program, and experiment with its features. Notice that all of the menu commands are fully functional; most of these commands are handled by code provided by the CEditView class. Notice, also, that if you enter data into the view window and then exit MINIEDIT, the program asks if you want to save your data. If you answer yes and specify a file name, the program creates the file but does *not* actually write the text to the file; in Chapter 10, you will add code to save and load the data from disk files.

FIGURE 8.10:

The MINIEDIT program icon

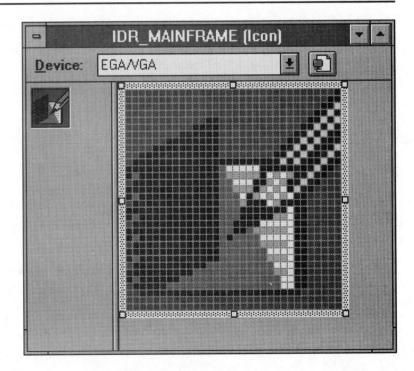

The MINIEDIT Program Source Code

The following listings, Listing 8.9 through 8.16, provide the C++ source code for the MINIEDIT program. The files below should match the files you created in the exercise; also, a complete set of these files is included in the \MINIEDT1 subdirectory within the directory in which you installed the companion disk.

Listing 8.9

```cpp
// miniedit.h : main header file for the MINIEDIT application
//

#ifndef __AFXWIN_H__
    #error include 'stdafx.h' before including this file for PCH
#endif

#include "resource.h"       // main symbols

/////////////////////////////////////////////////////////////////////////////
// CMinieditApp:
// See miniedit.cpp for the implementation of this class
//

class CMinieditApp : public CWinApp
{
public:
    CMinieditApp();

// Overrides
    virtual BOOL InitInstance();

// Implementation

    //{{AFX_MSG(CMinieditApp)
    afx_msg void OnAppAbout();
        // NOTE - the ClassWizard will add and remove member functions here.
        //    DO NOT EDIT what you see in these blocks of generated code !
    //}}AFX_MSG
```

```
    DECLARE_MESSAGE_MAP()
};

/////////////////////////////////////////////////////////////////////
```

Listing 8.10

```
// miniedit.cpp : Defines the class behaviors for the application.
//

#include "stdafx.h"
#include "miniedit.h"

#include "mainfrm.h"
#include "miniedoc.h"
#include "minievw.h"

#ifdef _DEBUG
#undef THIS_FILE
static char BASED_CODE THIS_FILE[] = __FILE__;
#endif

/////////////////////////////////////////////////////////////////////
// CMinieditApp

BEGIN_MESSAGE_MAP(CMinieditApp, CWinApp)
    //{{AFX_MSG_MAP(CMinieditApp)
    ON_COMMAND(ID_APP_ABOUT, OnAppAbout)
        // NOTE - the ClassWizard will add and remove mapping macros here.
        //      DO NOT EDIT what you see in these blocks of generated code !
    //}}AFX_MSG_MAP
    // Standard file based document commands
    ON_COMMAND(ID_FILE_NEW, CWinApp::OnFileNew)
    ON_COMMAND(ID_FILE_OPEN, CWinApp::OnFileOpen)
END_MESSAGE_MAP()

/////////////////////////////////////////////////////////////////////
// CMinieditApp construction

CMinieditApp::CMinieditApp()
{
    // TODO: add construction code here,
    // Place all significant initialization in InitInstance
}
```

```
//////////////////////////////////////////////////////////////////////
// The one and only CMinieditApp object

CMinieditApp NEAR theApp;

//////////////////////////////////////////////////////////////////////
// CMinieditApp initialization

BOOL CMinieditApp::InitInstance()
{
    // Standard initialization
    // If you are not using these features and wish to reduce the size
    //  of your final executable, you should remove from the following
    //  the specific initialization routines you do not need.

    SetDialogBkColor();         // set dialog background color to gray
    LoadStdProfileSettings();   // Load standard INI file options (including MRU)

    // Register the application's document templates.  Document templates
    //  serve as the connection between documents, frame windows and views.

    AddDocTemplate(new CSingleDocTemplate(IDR_MAINFRAME,
        RUNTIME_CLASS(CMinieditDoc),
        RUNTIME_CLASS(CMainFrame),      // main SDI frame window
        RUNTIME_CLASS(CMinieditView)));

    // create a new (empty) document
    OnFileNew();

    if (m_lpCmdLine[0] != '\0')
    {
        // TODO: add command line processing here
    }

    return TRUE;
}


//////////////////////////////////////////////////////////////////////
// CAboutDlg dialog used for App About

class CAboutDlg : public CDialog
{
public:
    CAboutDlg();
```

```
// Dialog Data
   //{{AFX_DATA(CAboutDlg)
   enum { IDD = IDD_ABOUTBOX };
   //}}AFX_DATA

// Implementation
protected:
   virtual void DoDataExchange(CDataExchange* pDX);    // DDX/DDV support
   //{{AFX_MSG(CAboutDlg)
      // No message handlers
   //}}AFX_MSG
   DECLARE_MESSAGE_MAP()
};

CAboutDlg::CAboutDlg() : CDialog(CAboutDlg::IDD)
{
   //{{AFX_DATA_INIT(CAboutDlg)
   //}}AFX_DATA_INIT
}

void CAboutDlg::DoDataExchange(CDataExchange* pDX)
{
   CDialog::DoDataExchange(pDX);
   //{{AFX_DATA_MAP(CAboutDlg)
   //}}AFX_DATA_MAP
}

BEGIN_MESSAGE_MAP(CAboutDlg, CDialog)
   //{{AFX_MSG_MAP(CAboutDlg)
      // No message handlers
   //}}AFX_MSG_MAP
END_MESSAGE_MAP()

// App command to run the dialog
void CMinieditApp::OnAppAbout()
{
   CAboutDlg aboutDlg;
   aboutDlg.DoModal();
}

/////////////////////////////////////////////////////////////////////////////
// CMinieditApp commands
```

Listing 8.11

```cpp
// miniedoc.h : interface of the CMinieditDoc class
//
///////////////////////////////////////////////////////////////////////

class CMinieditDoc : public CDocument
{
protected: // create from serialization only
   CMinieditDoc();
   DECLARE_DYNCREATE(CMinieditDoc)

// Attributes
public:

// Operations
public:

// Implementation
public:
   virtual ~CMinieditDoc();
   virtual void Serialize(CArchive& ar);  // overridden for document i/o
#ifdef _DEBUG
   virtual  void AssertValid() const;
   virtual  void Dump(CDumpContext& dc) const;
#endif
protected:
   virtual  BOOL  OnNewDocument();

// Generated message map functions
protected:
   //{{AFX_MSG(CMinieditDoc)
      // NOTE - the ClassWizard will add and remove member functions here.
      //    DO NOT EDIT what you see in these blocks of generated code !
   //}}AFX_MSG
   DECLARE_MESSAGE_MAP()
};


///////////////////////////////////////////////////////////////////////
```

Listing 8.12

```cpp
// miniedoc.cpp : implementation of the CMinieditDoc class
//
```

```
#include "stdafx.h"
#include "miniedit.h"

#include "miniedoc.h"

#ifdef _DEBUG
#undef THIS_FILE
static char BASED_CODE THIS_FILE[] = __FILE__;
#endif

/////////////////////////////////////////////////////////////////////////////
// CMinieditDoc

IMPLEMENT_DYNCREATE(CMinieditDoc, CDocument)

BEGIN_MESSAGE_MAP(CMinieditDoc, CDocument)
    //{{AFX_MSG_MAP(CMinieditDoc)
        // NOTE - the ClassWizard will add and remove mapping macros here.
        //    DO NOT EDIT what you see in these blocks of generated code !
    //}}AFX_MSG_MAP
END_MESSAGE_MAP()

/////////////////////////////////////////////////////////////////////////////
// CMinieditDoc construction/destruction

CMinieditDoc::CMinieditDoc()
{
    // TODO: add one-time construction code here
}

CMinieditDoc::~CMinieditDoc()
{
}

BOOL CMinieditDoc::OnNewDocument()
{
    if (!CDocument::OnNewDocument())
        return FALSE;
    // TODO: add reinitialization code here
    // (SDI documents will reuse this document)
    return TRUE;
}

/////////////////////////////////////////////////////////////////////////////
// CMinieditDoc serialization
```

```
void CMinieditDoc::Serialize(CArchive& ar)
{
    if (ar.IsStoring())
    {
        // TODO: add storing code here
    }
    else
    {
        // TODO: add loading code here
    }
}

/////////////////////////////////////////////////////////////////////////////
// CMinieditDoc diagnostics

#ifdef _DEBUG
void CMinieditDoc::AssertValid() const
{
    CDocument::AssertValid();
}

void CMinieditDoc::Dump(CDumpContext& dc) const
{
    CDocument::Dump(dc);
}

#endif //_DEBUG

/////////////////////////////////////////////////////////////////////////////
// CMinieditDoc commands
```

Listing 8.13

```
// mainfrm.h : interface of the CMainFrame class
//
/////////////////////////////////////////////////////////////////////////////

class CMainFrame : public CFrameWnd
{
protected: // create from serialization only
    CMainFrame();
    DECLARE_DYNCREATE(CMainFrame)
```

```
// Attributes
public:

// Operations
public:

// Implementation
public:
    virtual ~CMainFrame();
#ifdef _DEBUG
    virtual  void AssertValid() const;
    virtual  void Dump(CDumpContext& dc) const;
#endif


// Generated message map functions
protected:
    //{{AFX_MSG(CMainFrame)
        // NOTE - the ClassWizard will add and remove member functions here.
        //     DO NOT EDIT what you see in these blocks of generated code !
    //}}AFX_MSG
    DECLARE_MESSAGE_MAP()
};

//////////////////////////////////////////////////////////////////////////
```

Listing 8.14

```
// mainfrm.cpp : implementation of the CMainFrame class
//

#include "stdafx.h"
#include "miniedit.h"

#include "mainfrm.h"

#ifdef _DEBUG
#undef THIS_FILE
static char BASED_CODE THIS_FILE[] = __FILE__;
#endif

//////////////////////////////////////////////////////////////////////////
// CMainFrame

IMPLEMENT_DYNCREATE(CMainFrame, CFrameWnd)
```

```
BEGIN_MESSAGE_MAP(CMainFrame, CFrameWnd)
    //{{AFX_MSG_MAP(CMainFrame)
        // NOTE - the ClassWizard will add and remove mapping macros here.
        //     DO NOT EDIT what you see in these blocks of generated code !
    //}}AFX_MSG_MAP
END_MESSAGE_MAP()

/////////////////////////////////////////////////////////////////////////////
// CMainFrame construction/destruction

CMainFrame::CMainFrame()
{
    // TODO: add member initialization code here
}

CMainFrame::~CMainFrame()
{
}

/////////////////////////////////////////////////////////////////////////////
// CMainFrame diagnostics

#ifdef _DEBUG
void CMainFrame::AssertValid() const
{
    CFrameWnd::AssertValid();
}

void CMainFrame::Dump(CDumpContext& dc) const
{
    CFrameWnd::Dump(dc);
}

#endif //_DEBUG

/////////////////////////////////////////////////////////////////////////////
// CMainFrame message handlers
```

Listing 8.15

```
// minievw.h : interface of the CMinieditView class
//
/////////////////////////////////////////////////////////////////////////////
```

```
class CMinieditView : public CEditView
{
protected: // create from serialization only
    CMinieditView();
    DECLARE_DYNCREATE(CMinieditView)

// Attributes
public:
    CMinieditDoc* GetDocument();

// Operations
public:

// Implementation
public:
    virtual ~CMinieditView();
    virtual void OnDraw(CDC* pDC);  // overridden to draw this view
#ifdef _DEBUG
    virtual void AssertValid() const;
    virtual void Dump(CDumpContext& dc) const;
#endif

// Generated message map functions
protected:
    //{{AFX_MSG(CMinieditView)
        // NOTE - the ClassWizard will add and remove member functions here.
        //    DO NOT EDIT what you see in these blocks of generated code !
    //}}AFX_MSG
    DECLARE_MESSAGE_MAP()
};

#ifndef _DEBUG // debug version in minievw.cpp
inline CMinieditDoc* CMinieditView::GetDocument()
    { return (CMinieditDoc*) m_pDocument; }
#endif
```

///

Listing 8.16

```
// minievw.cpp : implementation of the CMinieditView class
//

#include "stdafx.h"
#include "miniedit.h"
```

```
#include "miniedoc.h"
#include "minievw.h"

#ifdef _DEBUG
#undef THIS_FILE
static char BASED_CODE THIS_FILE[] = __FILE__;
#endif

/////////////////////////////////////////////////////////////////////////
// CMinieditView

IMPLEMENT_DYNCREATE(CMinieditView, CEditView)

BEGIN_MESSAGE_MAP(CMinieditView, CEditView)
    //{{AFX_MSG_MAP(CMinieditView)
        // NOTE - the ClassWizard will add and remove mapping macros here.
        //    DO NOT EDIT what you see in these blocks of generated code !
    //}}AFX_MSG_MAP
END_MESSAGE_MAP()

/////////////////////////////////////////////////////////////////////////
// CMinieditView construction/destruction

CMinieditView::CMinieditView()
{
    // TODO: add construction code here
}

CMinieditView::~CMinieditView()
{
}

/////////////////////////////////////////////////////////////////////////
// CMinieditView drawing

void CMinieditView::OnDraw(CDC* pDC)
{
    CMinieditDoc* pDoc = GetDocument();

    // TODO: add draw code here
}
```

```
///////////////////////////////////////////////////////////////////////////
// CMinieditView diagnostics

#ifdef _DEBUG
void CMinieditView::AssertValid() const
{
    CEditView::AssertValid();
}

void CMinieditView::Dump(CDumpContext& dc) const
{
    CEditView::Dump(dc);
}

CMinieditDoc* CMinieditView::GetDocument() // non-debug version is inline
{
    ASSERT(m_pDocument->IsKindOf(RUNTIME_CLASS(CMinieditDoc)));
    return (CMinieditDoc*) m_pDocument;
}

#endif //_DEBUG

///////////////////////////////////////////////////////////////////////////
// CMinieditView message handlers
```

Summary

This chapter presented two example programs that showed you how to implement the view class of an MFC program. In the MINIDRAW example program, the view class was derived from the general-purpose CView class, and you had to add your own code to accept user input and display output in the view window. In the MINIEDIT program, however, the view class was derived from the special-purpose CEditView class, which implemented a full-featured text editor, without requiring you to add code to the view class. The following are some of the general concepts and techniques that were demonstrated:

- In an MFC program, a class object is sent *messages* to notify it of significant events. You can define a member function of a class that receives control whenever a particular type of message is sent. If you do not define a message-handling function for a particular type of message, the message will receive default processing.

- You can define a message-handling function using the ClassWizard tool, and then add your own code to the body of the function.

- Each type of message has an identifier. For example, when the user presses the left mouse button while the mouse cursor is within the view window, the view class object receives a message with the identifier WM_LBUTTONDOWN. If you want to respond to this event, you can use ClassWizard to define a WM_LBUTTONDOWN message handler as a member function of your view class.

- Windows program *resources* include menus, accelerator keystrokes, icons, and strings. AppWizard defines a default set of resources for a program that it generates. You can use App Studio to modify program resources or add new ones. An *accelerator keystroke* is a shortcut key combination that the user can press to immediately execute a menu command.

- You can customize the view window by defining a PreCreateWindow function as a member of your view class. Your version of this function overrides the PreCreateWindow virtual function defined within the MFC CWnd class, and is called immediately before the window is created. You assign any custom window features you want to the appropriate fields of the CREATE- STRUCT reference that the function is passed.

Implementing the Document

- Storing the graphic data

- Redrawing the window

- Adding menu commands

- Deleting the document data

- Implementing menu commands

- The MINIDRAW source code

9

As you have seen, the document class of an MFC program is responsible for storing the document data, and for saving and loading this data from disk files. Also, the document class must provide public member functions that allow other classes (specifically, the view class) to obtain or modify the data, so that the user can view and edit it, and it must handle menu commands that directly affect the document data.

In this chapter, you will build upon the MINIDRAW program you created in the previous chapter, by implementing the basic features of the document class. You will first add members to the document class for storing the coordinates of each line that the user draws. You will then modify the view class so that in addition to drawing each line, it also stores each line within the document class object. Next, you will implement the OnDraw member function of the view class, which will restore the lines whenever the window needs redrawing, using the data stored in the document object. (In the previous version of MINIDRAW, the lines were simply erased whenever the window was redrawn.)

Finally, you will add Undo and Delete All commands to the Edit menu. Both of these commands will be handled by the document class. The Undo command erases the most recently drawn line, and the Delete All command erases all lines in the drawing. In Chapter 10, you will add file I/O code to the document class, so that you will be able to save and load drawings from disk.

In this chapter, you will not use AppWizard to create a new set of source files; rather, you will use the MINIDRAW files you created in the previous chapter and add various features to these files. (If you did *not* create the files, you can obtain a copy of them from the \MINIDRW1 subdirectory of the directory in which you installed the companion disk.)

Storing the Graphic Data

In this section, you will make several additions to the MINIDRAW source code that will allow the program to store the graphic data. To open the MINIDRAW project, choose the Open... command on the Visual Workbench Project menu, select the directory in which you stored the MINIDRAW files, and select the project file MINIDRAW.MAK.

After opening the project, the first step is to define a new class to store the data for each line that the user draws. Add the following definition for the CLine class to the beginning of the document class header file, MINIDDOC.H:

```
// miniddoc.h : interface of the CMinidrawDoc class
//
/////////////////////////////////////////////////////////////////////////////

class CLine : public CObject
{
protected:
    int mX1, mY1, mX2, mY2;

public:
    CLine (int X1, int Y1, int X2, int Y2)
        {
        mX1 = X1;
        mY1 = Y1;
        mX2 = X2;
        mY2 = Y2;
        }
    void Draw (CDC *PDC);
};
```

The CLine data members mX1 and mY1 store the coordinates of one end of the line, and X2 and Y2 store the coordinates of the other end. CLine provides an inline constructor that initializes these data members. CLine also provides a member function, Draw, for drawing the line. You will see shortly why CLine is derived from CObject.

Next, add the required members to the CMinidrawDoc class by typing the statements marked in bold into the CMinidrawDoc class definition in MINIDDOC.H:

```
class CMinidrawDoc : public CDocument
{
protected: // create from serialization only
    CMinidrawDoc();
    DECLARE_DYNCREATE(CMinidrawDoc)

protected:
    CObArray mObArray;

public:
    void AddLine (int X1, int Y1, int X2, int Y2);
```

```
virtual void DeleteContents ();
CLine *GetLine (int Index);
int GetNumLines ();
```

```
// remainder of CWingreetDoc definition ...
```

The new data member mObArray is an instance of the MFC class CObArray. CObArray is one of the MFC *collection* classes, which are used for storing groups of variables or objects. A CObArray instance stores a set of pointers to CObject objects, in an array-like data structure. (CObject is the MFC class from which almost all other MFC classes are derived, directly or indirectly.) The data member mObArray is used to store a pointer to each CLine object that keeps information on a line. Because CLine is derived from CObject, the addresses of CLine objects can be stored within the CObject pointers maintained by the CObArray class.

The member functions AddLine, GetLine, and GetNumLines provide access to the line information stored in mObArray (which other classes cannot access directly, because it is protected). The DeleteContents member function is used for implementing several menu commands, and will be described later (in the section "Implementing Menu Commands").

Now type in the definition for the CLine::Draw function at the end of the document implementation file, MINIDDOC.CPP:

```
void CLine::Draw (CDC *PDC)
   {
   PDC->MoveTo (mX1, mY1);
   PDC->LineTo (mX2, mY2);
   }
```

Draw calls two CDC member functions, MoveTo and LineTo (which were introduced in Chapter 8), to draw the line at the coordinates stored in the current object.

Next, add the definitions for the AddLine, GetLine, and GetNumLines CMinidrawDoc member functions, also at the end of the MINIDDOC.CPP file:

```
void CMinidrawDoc::AddLine (int X1, int Y1, int X2, int Y2)
   {
   CLine *PLine = new CLine (X1, Y1, X2, Y2);
   mObArray.Add (PLine);
   }
```

```
CLine *CMinidrawDoc::GetLine (int Index)
   {
```

```
    if (Index < 0 || Index > mObArray.GetUpperBound ())
        return 0;
    return (CLine *)mObArray.GetAt (Index);
    }

int CMinidrawDoc::GetNumLines ()
    {
    return mObArray.GetSize ();
    }
```

AddLine creates a new CLine object and calls the CObArray member function Add to add the object pointer to the collection of CLine pointers stored by mObArray.

Note that the pointers stored by mObArray are indexed; the first pointer added has the index 0, the second pointer added has the index 1, and so on. The GetLine function returns the pointer that has the index specified by its parameter. GetLine first checks that the index is within the valid range. (The CObArray member function GetUpperBound returns the largest valid index; that is, the index of the last pointer that was added.) GetLine then returns the corresponding CLine pointer, which it obtains by calling the CObArray member function GetAt.

Finally, GetNumLines returns the number of CLine pointers currently stored by mObArray, which it obtains by calling the CObArray member function GetSize. As you will see, AddLine, GetLine, and GetNumLines are called by member functions of the view class.

The next step is to modify the OnLButtonUp member function of the view class, which is defined in the file MINIDVW.CPP. Recall from Chapter 8 that when the user releases the left mouse button after drawing a line, this function ends the drag operation and draws the line in its final position. Add calls to GetDocument and AddLine to store the new line:

```
void CMinidrawView::OnLButtonUp(UINT nFlags, CPoint point)
{
    // TODO: Add your message handler code here and/or call default

    if (mDragging)
        {
        mDragging = 0;
        ::ReleaseCapture ();
        ::ClipCursor (NULL);
        CClientDC ClientDC (this);
        ClientDC.SetROP2 (R2_NOT);
```

```
    ClientDC.MoveTo (mPointOrigin);
    ClientDC.LineTo (mPointOld);
    ClientDC.SetROP2 (R2_COPYPEN);
    ClientDC.MoveTo (mPointOrigin);
    ClientDC.LineTo (point);

    CMinidrawDoc* PDoc = GetDocument();
    PDoc->AddLine (mPointOrigin.x, mPointOrigin.y, point.x, point.y);
    }

  CView::OnLButtonUp(nFlags, point);
}
```

As this modification illustrates, in addition to displaying the document data, the view class needs to call member functions of the document class to update the data in response to editing actions of the user.

Redrawing the Window

Now that the program stores the data for the lines permanently within the document class object, the view class can use this data to restore the lines whenever the window is redrawn. Recall that whenever the view window needs redrawing, the system erases the window and then calls the OnDraw member function of the view class. You must add your own redrawing code to the minimal OnDraw function generated by AppWizard. To do this, add the lines marked in bold to the CMinidrawView::OnDraw function within the MINIDVW.CPP file:

```
void CMinidrawView::OnDraw(CDC* pDC)
{
    CMinidrawDoc* pDoc = GetDocument();

    // TODO: add draw code here

    int Index = pDoc->GetNumLines ();
    while (Index--)
        pDoc->GetLine (Index)->Draw (pDC);
}
```

> **NOTE**   The system actually erases only the portion of the view window that needs redrawing (for example, the portion that was covered by another window). In Chapter 11 you will learn how to increase the efficiency of the OnDraw function by redrawing only the erased portion.

The code you added simply calls the CMinidrawDoc::GetNumLines function to obtain the number of lines currently stored by the document object. For each line, it first calls the CMinidrawDoc::GetLine function to obtain a pointer to the corresponding CLine object, and it then uses this pointer to call the CLine::Draw function to draw the line.

Adding Menu Commands

Because the graphic data is stored within the document object, it is now possible to add commands to the Edit menu that allow the user to modify the data. In this chapter, you will add an Undo command for erasing the last line drawn, plus a Delete All command for erasing all lines in the drawing.

To add the Edit commands to the MINIDRAW program, run App Studio by choosing the App Studio command on the Visual Workbench Tools menu. In App Studio, select the Menu item in the Type: list, select the IDR_MAINFRAME identifier in the Resources: list, and click the Open button. App Studio will now open the menu-designing window (labeled "IDR_MAINFRAME (Menu)"), and you should do the following:

1. Double-click the empty box at the right end of the menu bar. App Studio will open the menu item properties dialog box (labeled "Menu: Menu Item Properties").

2. Into the Caption: text box, type &Edit. An Edit pop-up menu will now appear at the right end of the menu bar in the menu-designing window. (Note that you did not enter an identifier because you are defining a pop-up menu item; only menu commands are assigned identifiers.)

3. Using the mouse, drag the Edit pop-up menu to the left, so that it falls between the File menu and the Help menu.

4. Double-click the empty box contained within the Edit menu (below the Edit caption), to reopen the menu properties dialog box.

5. Into the ID: box enter ID_EDIT_UNDO, and into the Caption: text box enter &Undo\tCtrl+Z. An Undo command will now appear on the Edit menu.

6. Double-click the empty box at the bottom of the Edit menu (below the Undo command), and check the Separator option in the menu item properties dialog box. This will insert a separator under the Undo command.

7. Double-click the empty box at the bottom of the Edit menu, then enter ID_EDIT_CLEAR_ALL into the ID: box, and &Delete All into the Caption: box. This will add a Delete All command to the menu. The Edit menu is now complete and will appear as shown in Figure 9.1.

You do not need to define the Ctrl+Z accelerator for the Undo command, because AppWizard defined this accelerator when it first generated the program source code.

FIGURE 9.1:

The completed Edit menu in the App Studio menu-designing window

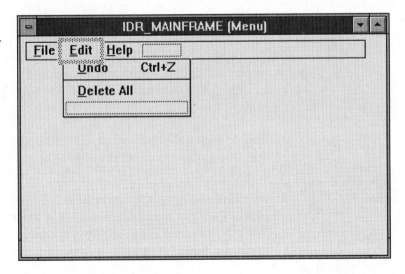

When designing a menu using the App Studio, you can create cascading menus, you can arrange menu commands into columns, and you can assign a variety of initial properties to menu items (for example, you can check or disable a menu command). For an explanation of the menu features you can create using App Studio, see the *App Studio User's Guide* (Chapter 4, "Using the Menu Editor"), or the online help accessed through the App Studio Help menu.

Deleting the Document Data

Whenever the user chooses the New command on the File menu, the MFC (specifically, the CWinApp member function OnFileNew) calls the virtual function CDocument::DeleteContents to delete the contents of the current document, prior to initializing a new document. You should write an overriding version of this function as a member of your document class to delete the data that is stored by this class. To do this for the MINIDRAW program, add the following DeleteContents function definition at the end of the MINIDDOC.CPP file:

```
void CMinidrawDoc::DeleteContents ()
   {
   int Index = mObArray.GetSize ();
   while (Index--)
      delete mObArray.GetAt (Index);
   mObArray.RemoveAll ();
   }
```

You already added the declaration for this function to the CMinidrawDoc class definition. DeleteContents first calls the CObArray member function GetSize to obtain the number of CLine pointers stored by the mObArray object. It then fetches each pointer by calling the CObArray::GetAt function and uses the delete operator to free each corresponding CLine object (recall that the CLine objects were created using the new operator). Finally, it calls the CObArray member function RemoveAll to delete all of the pointers currently stored by mObArray.

After calling DeleteContents, the MFC (indirectly) erases the view window and calls the OnDraw function of the view class. OnDraw, however, draws no lines because the lines have been deleted from the document class. The overall result is that the New command clears the view window, allowing the user to create a new drawing.

Implementing Menu Commands

You will now use ClassWizard to implement the code for the two commands you added to the Edit menu: Delete All and Undo.

Handling the Delete All Command

To define a message handler that receives control when the user chooses the Delete All command, perform the following steps:

1. Choose the ClassWizard... command on the Visual Workbench Browse menu or press Ctrl+W to open the ClassWizard dialog box.

2. In the Class Name: list, choose CMinidrawDoc so that the Delete All message-handling function will be made a member of the document class. Recall from Chapter 8 that a command message can be handled by any of the four main program classes (the view, document, frame window, or application class). The document class is selected to handle the Delete All command, because this command directly affects the document data (it erases it), and therefore falls within the province of the document class.

3. In the Object IDs: list, select the identifier ID_EDIT_CLEAR_ALL; recall that this is the identifier you assigned to the Delete All menu command when you designed the menu in App Studio. As soon as you select this identifier, the Messages: list displays identifiers for the two types of messages that this menu command can send to the document class: COMMAND and UPDATE_COM-MAND_UI. The COMMAND identifier refers to the message that is sent when the user *chooses* the menu item; the UPDATE_COMMAND_UI identifier refers the message that is sent when the user first opens the pop-up menu that contains the command.

4. Select the COMMAND message in the Messages: list.

5. Click the Add Function button to generate the message-handling function. When ClassWizard displays the Add Member Function message box, click the OK button to proceed with the function generation. ClassWizard now declares the message-handling function, OnEditClearAll, within the CMinidrawDoc class definition in MINIDDOC.H; adds a minimal function definition to MINIDDOC.CPP; and generates the code necessary to insert the

function into the document class message map. The completed ClassWizard dialog box is shown in Figure 9.2.

6. Click the Edit Code button in the ClassWizard dialog box. ClassWizard will open the MINIDDOC.CPP file (if necessary) and place the caret within the `OnEditClearAll` function so that you can enter your own code for this message handler.

7. Add code as follows to the `OnEditClearAll` function:

```
void CMinidrawDoc::OnEditClearAll()
{
    // TODO: Add your command handler code here

    DeleteContents ();
    UpdateAllViews (0);
}
```

FIGURE 9.2:

The ClassWizard dialog box for generating a **COMMAND** message handler for the Delete All menu command

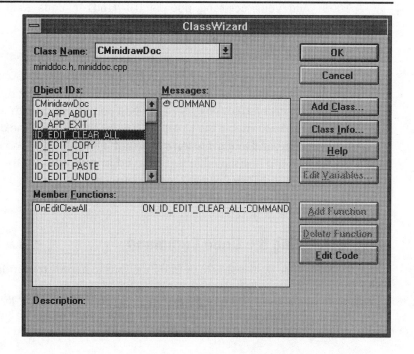

The call to `DeleteContents` (which you just defined) deletes the contents of the document. The call to the `CDocument` member function `UpdateAllViews` then erases the current contents of the view window. (`UpdateAllViews` actually does more than this, as Chapter 11 will explain.)

The next step is to define a message-handling function for the `UPDATE_COMMAND_UI` message that is sent when the user first opens the pop-up menu containing the Delete All command (that is, the Edit menu). Because this message is sent *before* the pop-up menu becomes visible, the handler can be used to initialize the command according to the current state of the program. You will add a handler that enables the Delete All command if the document contains one or more lines, but disables it if the document contains no lines. To do this, follow the steps just described; in step 4, however, select the `UPDATE_COMMAND_UI` identifier in the Messages: list. ClassWizard will generate a function named `OnUpdateEditClearAll`. After clicking the Edit Code button, add code to this function as follows :

```
void CMinidrawDoc::OnUpdateEditClearAll(CCmdUI* pCmdUI)
{
    // TODO: Add your command update UI handler code here

    pCmdUI->Enable (mObArray.GetSize ());
}
```

`OnUpdateEditClearAll` is passed a pointer to a `CCmdUI` object. `CCmdUI` is an MFC class that provides member functions for initializing menu commands (and other user-interface objects). The code you added calls the `CCmdUI` member function `Enable` to enable the Delete All menu command if the document contains at least one line, and to disable the command if the document contains no lines. When the command is disabled, it is displayed in gray text and the user cannot choose it. Consequently, the `OnEditClearAll` function will never be called when the document is empty.

Handling the Undo Command

The final task is to define functions to handle the Undo command on the Edit menu.

First, define a function that receives control when the user chooses the Undo command. To do this, use ClassWizard, following the steps given in the previous section. In step 3, however, choose the `ID_EDIT_UNDO` identifier in the Object IDs: list.

Initializing Menu Commands

A message-handling function that processes an UPDATE_COMMAND_UI message for a menu command is passed a pointer to a CCmdUI object, which is attached to the menu command. CCmdUI provides four member functions that you can use to initialize the menu command: Enable, SetCheck, SetRadio, and SetText.

You can pass Enable TRUE to enable the command, or FALSE to disable it:

```
virtual void Enable (BOOL bOn = TRUE);
```

You can pass SetCheck 1 to check the menu item, or 0 to uncheck it:

```
virtual void SetCheck (int nCheck = 1);
```

Normally, a menu command representing a program option is checked if the option is currently selected.

You can pass SetRadio TRUE to check the menu item using a bullet, or FALSE to remove the bullet:

```
virtual void SetRadio (BOOL bOn = TRUE);
```

Usually, a bullet is used rather than a standard check mark to indicate which option is selected within a group of mutually exclusive options (for example, three menu options for choosing left, right, or centered text justification). Finally, you can call SetText to change the menu command caption:

```
virtual void SetText (LPCSTR lpszText);
```

where lpszText is a pointer to the new menu text. For example, if the previous editing action was to delete text, you might call SetText to set the text for the Undo command to "Undo Delete".

As you will see in Chapter 14, you can define UPDATE_COMMAND_UI message handlers for other user interface objects, such as tool bar buttons, and use these same four CCmdUI member functions to update these other objects. The specific action of each of these functions depends upon the type of user-interface object that is being acted upon.

ClassWizard will define a function named OnEditUndo. Add code to this function, as follows:

```
void CMinidrawDoc::OnEditUndo()
{
    // TODO: Add your command handler code here

    int Index = mObArray.GetUpperBound ();
    if (Index > -1)
        {
        delete mObArray.GetAt (Index);
        mObArray.RemoveAt (Index);
        }
    UpdateAllViews (0);
}
```

The code you added first calls the CObArray member function GetUpperBound to obtain the index of the last line added to the document. It then calls CObArray:: GetAt to obtain the pointer to the CLine object for the last line, and it uses the delete operator to delete this object. Finally, it calls UpdateAllViews, which results in erasing the view window and calling the CMinidrawView::OnDraw function; OnDraw then redraws the lines that remain in the document. Note that if the user repeatedly chooses the Undo command, OnEditUndo keeps erasing lines, until all lines are gone.

Second, define a function to initialize the Undo menu command. To do this, use ClassWizard according to the steps given in the previous section. In step 3, however, select the ID_EDIT_UNDO identifier in the Object IDs: list, and in step 4, select the UPDATE_COMMAND_UI message identifier in the Message: list. ClassWizard will create a function named OnUpdateEditUndo. Add code to this function, as follows:

```
void CMinidrawDoc::OnUpdateEditUndo(CCmdUI* pCmdUI)
{
    // TODO: Add your command update UI handler code here

    pCmdUI->Enable (mObArray.GetSize ());
}
```

This function works exactly like the OnUpdateEditClearAll function described previously. Namely, it enables the Undo command only if there is at least one line to erase.

Recall that an accelerator keystroke, Ctrl+Z, was assigned to the Undo menu command; that is, both the Undo menu command and the Ctrl+Z keyboard accelerator have the same identifier, ID_EDIT_UNDO. When the user presses the accelerator keystroke, the system first calls OnUpdateEditUndo. If OnUpdateEditUndo enables the menu command, the system then calls OnEditUndo, so that the accelerator keystroke receives the same processing as the menu command. If, however, OnUpdateEditUndo disables the menu command, the system does *not* call OnEditUndo. Thus, if OnUpdateEditUndo disables the menu command, the accelerator keystroke is also disabled, and OnEditUndo will never be called unless there is at least one line in the document.

This is the last change to make to the current version of MINIDRAW. You can now build and run the program.

The MINIDRAW Source Code

The following listings, Listings 9.1 through 9.8, are the C++ source files for the version of the MINIDRAW program presented in this chapter. These files contain the code generated by AppWizard plus all the modifications and additions you made in this chapter as well as in the previous chapter. Note that a complete copy of these files—in addition to the other MINIDRAW source files—is contained in the \MINIDRW2 subdirectory within the directory in which you installed the companion disk.

Listing 9.1

```
// minidraw.h : main header file for the MINIDRAW application
//

#ifndef __AFXWIN_H__
    #error include 'stdafx.h' before including this file for PCH
#endif

#include "resource.h"       // main symbols

/////////////////////////////////////////////////////////////////////////////
// CMinidrawApp:
// See minidraw.cpp for the implementation of this class
//

class CMinidrawApp : public CWinApp
{
```

```
public:
    CMinidrawApp();

// Overrides
    virtual BOOL InitInstance();

// Implementation

    //{{AFX_MSG(CMinidrawApp)
    afx_msg void OnAppAbout();
        // NOTE - the ClassWizard will add and remove member functions here.
        //    DO NOT EDIT what you see in these blocks of generated code !
    //}}AFX_MSG
    DECLARE_MESSAGE_MAP()
};
```

///

Listing 9.2

```
// minidraw.cpp : Defines the class behaviors for the application.
//

#include "stdafx.h"
#include "minidraw.h"

#include "mainfrm.h"
#include "miniddoc.h"
#include "minidvw.h"

#ifdef _DEBUG
#undef THIS_FILE
static char BASED_CODE THIS_FILE[] = __FILE__;
#endif

///////////////////////////////////////////////////////////////////////
// CMinidrawApp

BEGIN_MESSAGE_MAP(CMinidrawApp, CWinApp)
    //{{AFX_MSG_MAP(CMinidrawApp)
    ON_COMMAND(ID_APP_ABOUT, OnAppAbout)
        // NOTE - the ClassWizard will add and remove mapping macros here.
        //    DO NOT EDIT what you see in these blocks of generated code !
    //}}AFX_MSG_MAP
```

```
   // Standard file based document commands
   ON_COMMAND(ID_FILE_NEW, CWinApp::OnFileNew)
   ON_COMMAND(ID_FILE_OPEN, CWinApp::OnFileOpen)
END_MESSAGE_MAP()

/////////////////////////////////////////////////////////////////////////////
// CMinidrawApp construction

CMinidrawApp::CMinidrawApp()
{
   // TODO: add construction code here,
   // Place all significant initialization in InitInstance
}

/////////////////////////////////////////////////////////////////////////////
// The one and only CMinidrawApp object

CMinidrawApp NEAR theApp;

/////////////////////////////////////////////////////////////////////////////
// CMinidrawApp initialization

BOOL CMinidrawApp::InitInstance()
{
   // Standard initialization
   // If you are not using these features and wish to reduce the size
   //  of your final executable, you should remove from the following
   //  the specific initialization routines you do not need.

   SetDialogBkColor();         // set dialog background color to gray
   LoadStdProfileSettings();   // Load standard INI file options (including MRU)

   // Register the application's document templates.  Document templates
   //  serve as the connection between documents, frame windows and views.

   AddDocTemplate(new CSingleDocTemplate(IDR_MAINFRAME,
         RUNTIME_CLASS(CMinidrawDoc),
         RUNTIME_CLASS(CMainFrame),       // main SDI frame window
         RUNTIME_CLASS(CMinidrawView)));

   // create a new (empty) document
   OnFileNew();

   if (m_lpCmdLine[0] != '\0')
   {
```

```
        // TODO: add command line processing here
    }

    return TRUE;
}

/////////////////////////////////////////////////////////////////////////////
// CAboutDlg dialog used for App About

class CAboutDlg : public CDialog
{
public:
    CAboutDlg();

// Dialog Data
    //{{AFX_DATA(CAboutDlg)
    enum { IDD = IDD_ABOUTBOX };
    //}}AFX_DATA

// Implementation
protected:
    virtual void DoDataExchange(CDataExchange* pDX);    // DDX/DDV support
    //{{AFX_MSG(CAboutDlg)
        // No message handlers
    //}}AFX_MSG
    DECLARE_MESSAGE_MAP()
};

CAboutDlg::CAboutDlg() : CDialog(CAboutDlg::IDD)
{
    //{{AFX_DATA_INIT(CAboutDlg)
    //}}AFX_DATA_INIT
}

void CAboutDlg::DoDataExchange(CDataExchange* pDX)
{
    CDialog::DoDataExchange(pDX);
    //{{AFX_DATA_MAP(CAboutDlg)
    //}}AFX_DATA_MAP
}

BEGIN_MESSAGE_MAP(CAboutDlg, CDialog)
    //{{AFX_MSG_MAP(CAboutDlg)
        // No message handlers
```

```
    //}}AFX_MSG_MAP
END_MESSAGE_MAP()

// App command to run the dialog
void CMinidrawApp::OnAppAbout()
{
    CAboutDlg aboutDlg;
    aboutDlg.DoModal();
}

/////////////////////////////////////////////////////////////////////////////
// CMinidrawApp commands
```

Listing 9.3

```
// miniddoc.h : interface of the CMinidrawDoc class
//
/////////////////////////////////////////////////////////////////////////////

class CLine : public CObject
{
protected:
    int mX1, mY1, mX2, mY2;

public:
    CLine (int X1, int Y1, int X2, int Y2)
        {
        mX1 = X1;
        mY1 = Y1;
        mX2 = X2;
        mY2 = Y2;
        }
    void Draw (CDC *PDC);
};

class CMinidrawDoc : public CDocument
{
protected: // create from serialization only
    CMinidrawDoc();
    DECLARE_DYNCREATE(CMinidrawDoc)

protected:
    CObArray mObArray;
```

```
public:
    void AddLine (int X1, int Y1, int X2, int Y2);
    virtual void DeleteContents ();
    CLine *GetLine (int Index);
    int GetNumLines ();

// Attributes
public:

// Operations
public:

// Implementation
public:
    virtual ~CMinidrawDoc();
    virtual void Serialize(CArchive& ar);   // overridden for document i/o
#ifdef _DEBUG
    virtual  void AssertValid() const;
    virtual  void Dump(CDumpContext& dc) const;
#endif
protected:
    virtual  BOOL  OnNewDocument();

// Generated message map functions
protected:
    //{{AFX_MSG(CMinidrawDoc)
    afx_msg void OnEditClearAll();
    afx_msg void OnUpdateEditClearAll(CCmdUI* pCmdUI);
    afx_msg void OnEditUndo();
    afx_msg void OnUpdateEditUndo(CCmdUI* pCmdUI);
    //}}AFX_MSG
    DECLARE_MESSAGE_MAP()
};
```

`////////////////////////////////////////////////////////////////////////`

Listing 9.4

```
// miniddoc.cpp : implementation of the CMinidrawDoc class
//

#include "stdafx.h"
#include "minidraw.h"
```

```
#include "miniddoc.h"

#ifdef _DEBUG
#undef THIS_FILE
static char BASED_CODE THIS_FILE[] = __FILE__;
#endif

/////////////////////////////////////////////////////////////////////////////
// CMinidrawDoc

IMPLEMENT_DYNCREATE(CMinidrawDoc, CDocument)

BEGIN_MESSAGE_MAP(CMinidrawDoc, CDocument)
    //{{AFX_MSG_MAP(CMinidrawDoc)
    ON_COMMAND(ID_EDIT_CLEAR_ALL, OnEditClearAll)
    ON_UPDATE_COMMAND_UI(ID_EDIT_CLEAR_ALL, OnUpdateEditClearAll)
    ON_COMMAND(ID_EDIT_UNDO, OnEditUndo)
    ON_UPDATE_COMMAND_UI(ID_EDIT_UNDO, OnUpdateEditUndo)
    //}}AFX_MSG_MAP
END_MESSAGE_MAP()

/////////////////////////////////////////////////////////////////////////////
// CMinidrawDoc construction/destruction

CMinidrawDoc::CMinidrawDoc()
{
    // TODO: add one-time construction code here
}

CMinidrawDoc::~CMinidrawDoc()
{
}

BOOL CMinidrawDoc::OnNewDocument()
{
    if (!CDocument::OnNewDocument())
        return FALSE;
    // TODO: add reinitialization code here
    // (SDI documents will reuse this document)
    return TRUE;
}

/////////////////////////////////////////////////////////////////////////////
// CMinidrawDoc serialization
```

```
void CMinidrawDoc::Serialize(CArchive& ar)
{
   if (ar.IsStoring())
   {
      // TODO: add storing code here
   }
   else
   {
      // TODO: add loading code here
   }
}

/////////////////////////////////////////////////////////////////////////////
// CMinidrawDoc diagnostics

#ifdef _DEBUG
void CMinidrawDoc::AssertValid() const
{
   CDocument::AssertValid();
}

void CMinidrawDoc::Dump(CDumpContext& dc) const
{
   CDocument::Dump(dc);
}

#endif //_DEBUG

/////////////////////////////////////////////////////////////////////////////
// CMinidrawDoc commands

void CLine::Draw (CDC *PDC)
   {
   PDC->MoveTo (mX1, mY1);
   PDC->LineTo (mX2, mY2);
   }

void CMinidrawDoc::AddLine (int X1, int Y1, int X2, int Y2)
   {
   CLine *PLine = new CLine (X1, Y1, X2, Y2);
   mObArray.Add (PLine);
   }

CLine *CMinidrawDoc::GetLine (int Index)
   {
```

```
    if (Index < 0 || Index > mObArray.GetUpperBound ())
        return 0;
    return (CLine *)mObArray.GetAt (Index);
    }

int CMinidrawDoc::GetNumLines ()
    {
    return mObArray.GetSize ();
    }

void CMinidrawDoc::DeleteContents ()
    {
    int Index = mObArray.GetSize ();
    while (Index--)
        delete mObArray.GetAt (Index);
    mObArray.RemoveAll ();
    }

void CMinidrawDoc::OnEditClearAll()
{
    // TODO: Add your command handler code here

    DeleteContents ();
    UpdateAllViews (0);
}

void CMinidrawDoc::OnUpdateEditClearAll(CCmdUI* pCmdUI)
{
    // TODO: Add your command update UI handler code here

    pCmdUI->Enable (mObArray.GetSize ());
}

void CMinidrawDoc::OnEditUndo()
{
    // TODO: Add your command handler code here

    int Index = mObArray.GetUpperBound ();
    if (Index > -1)
        {
        delete mObArray.GetAt (Index);
        mObArray.RemoveAt (Index);
        }
    UpdateAllViews (0);
}
```

```
void CMinidrawDoc::OnUpdateEditUndo(CCmdUI* pCmdUI)
{
    // TODO: Add your command update UI handler code here

    pCmdUI->Enable (mObArray.GetSize ());
}
```

Listing 9.5

```
// mainfrm.h : interface of the CMainFrame class
//
/////////////////////////////////////////////////////////////////////////

class CMainFrame : public CFrameWnd
{
protected: // create from serialization only
    CMainFrame();
    DECLARE_DYNCREATE(CMainFrame)

// Attributes
public:

// Operations
public:

// Implementation
public:
    virtual ~CMainFrame();
#ifdef _DEBUG
    virtual  void AssertValid() const;
    virtual  void Dump(CDumpContext& dc) const;
#endif


// Generated message map functions
protected:
    //{{AFX_MSG(CMainFrame)
        // NOTE - the ClassWizard will add and remove member functions here.
        //    DO NOT EDIT what you see in these blocks of generated code !
    //}}AFX_MSG
    DECLARE_MESSAGE_MAP()
};


/////////////////////////////////////////////////////////////////////////
```

Listing 9.6

```cpp
// mainfrm.cpp : implementation of the CMainFrame class
//

#include "stdafx.h"
#include "minidraw.h"

#include "mainfrm.h"

#ifdef _DEBUG
#undef THIS_FILE
static char BASED_CODE THIS_FILE[] = __FILE__;
#endif

/////////////////////////////////////////////////////////////////////////////
// CMainFrame

IMPLEMENT_DYNCREATE(CMainFrame, CFrameWnd)

BEGIN_MESSAGE_MAP(CMainFrame, CFrameWnd)
    //{{AFX_MSG_MAP(CMainFrame)
        // NOTE - the ClassWizard will add and remove mapping macros here.
        //     DO NOT EDIT what you see in these blocks of generated code !
    //}}AFX_MSG_MAP
END_MESSAGE_MAP()

/////////////////////////////////////////////////////////////////////////////
// CMainFrame construction/destruction

CMainFrame::CMainFrame()
{
    // TODO: add member initialization code here
}

CMainFrame::~CMainFrame()
{
}

/////////////////////////////////////////////////////////////////////////////
// CMainFrame diagnostics

#ifdef _DEBUG
void CMainFrame::AssertValid() const
{
```

```
    CFrameWnd::AssertValid();
}

void CMainFrame::Dump(CDumpContext& dc) const
{
    CFrameWnd::Dump(dc);
}

#endif //_DEBUG

/////////////////////////////////////////////////////////////////////////////
// CMainFrame message handlers
```

Listing 9.7

```
// minidvw.h : interface of the CMinidrawView class
//
/////////////////////////////////////////////////////////////////////////////

class CMinidrawView : public CView
{
protected: // create from serialization only
    CMinidrawView();
    DECLARE_DYNCREATE(CMinidrawView)

protected:
    CString mClassName;
    int mDragging;
    HCURSOR mHCross;
    CPoint mPointOld;
    CPoint mPointOrigin;

    virtual BOOL PreCreateWindow (CREATESTRUCT& cs);

// Attributes
public:
    CMinidrawDoc* GetDocument();

// Operations
public:

// Implementation
public:
    virtual ~CMinidrawView();
    virtual void OnDraw(CDC* pDC);  // overridden to draw this view
```

```
#ifdef _DEBUG
   virtual void AssertValid() const;
   virtual void Dump(CDumpContext& dc) const;
#endif

// Generated message map functions
protected:
   //{{AFX_MSG(CMinidrawView)
   afx_msg void OnLButtonDown(UINT nFlags, CPoint point);
   afx_msg void OnMouseMove(UINT nFlags, CPoint point);
   afx_msg void OnLButtonUp(UINT nFlags, CPoint point);
   //}}AFX_MSG
   DECLARE_MESSAGE_MAP()
};

#ifndef _DEBUG // debug version in minidvw.cpp
inline CMinidrawDoc* CMinidrawView::GetDocument()
   { return (CMinidrawDoc*) m_pDocument; }
#endif
```

//

Listing 9.8

```
// minidvw.cpp : implementation of the CMinidrawView class
//

#include "stdafx.h"
#include "minidraw.h"

#include "miniddoc.h"
#include "minidvw.h"

#ifdef _DEBUG
#undef THIS_FILE
static char BASED_CODE THIS_FILE[] = __FILE__;
#endif

////////////////////////////////////////////////////////////////////////
// CMinidrawView

IMPLEMENT_DYNCREATE(CMinidrawView, CView)

BEGIN_MESSAGE_MAP(CMinidrawView, CView)
   //{{AFX_MSG_MAP(CMinidrawView)
```

```
    ON_WM_LBUTTONDOWN()
    ON_WM_MOUSEMOVE()
    ON_WM_LBUTTONUP()
    //}}AFX_MSG_MAP
END_MESSAGE_MAP()

/////////////////////////////////////////////////////////////////////////
// CMinidrawView construction/destruction

CMinidrawView::CMinidrawView()
{
    // TODO: add construction code here

    mDragging = 0;
    mHCross = AfxGetApp ()->LoadStandardCursor (IDC_CROSS);
}


CMinidrawView::~CMinidrawView()
{
}

/////////////////////////////////////////////////////////////////////////
// CMinidrawView drawing

void CMinidrawView::OnDraw(CDC* pDC)
{
    CMinidrawDoc* pDoc = GetDocument();

    // TODO: add draw code here

    int Index = pDoc->GetNumLines ();
    while (Index--)
        pDoc->GetLine (Index)->Draw (pDC);
}



/////////////////////////////////////////////////////////////////////////
// CMinidrawView diagnostics

#ifdef _DEBUG
void CMinidrawView::AssertValid() const
{
    CView::AssertValid();
}
```

```
void CMinidrawView::Dump(CDumpContext& dc) const
{
    CView::Dump(dc);
}

CMinidrawDoc* CMinidrawView::GetDocument() // non-debug version is inline
{
    ASSERT(m_pDocument->IsKindOf(RUNTIME_CLASS(CMinidrawDoc)));
    return (CMinidrawDoc*) m_pDocument;
}

#endif //_DEBUG

/////////////////////////////////////////////////////////////////////////////
// CMinidrawView message handlers

void CMinidrawView::OnLButtonDown(UINT nFlags, CPoint point)
{
    // TODO: Add your message handler code here and/or call default

    mPointOrigin = point;
    mPointOld = point;
    SetCapture ();
    mDragging = 1;

    RECT Rect;
    GetClientRect (&Rect);
    ClientToScreen (&Rect);
    ::ClipCursor (&Rect);

    CView::OnLButtonDown(nFlags, point);
}

void CMinidrawView::OnMouseMove(UINT nFlags, CPoint point)
{
    // TODO: Add your message handler code here and/or call default

    ::SetCursor (mHCross);

    if (mDragging)
        {
        CClientDC ClientDC (this);
        ClientDC.SetROP2 (R2_NOT);
        ClientDC.MoveTo (mPointOrigin);
        ClientDC.LineTo (mPointOld);
```

```
        ClientDC.MoveTo (mPointOrigin);
        ClientDC.LineTo (point);
        mPointOld = point;
        }

    CView::OnMouseMove(nFlags, point);
}

void CMinidrawView::OnLButtonUp(UINT nFlags, CPoint point)
{
    // TODO: Add your message handler code here and/or call default

    if (mDragging)
        {
        mDragging = 0;
        ::ReleaseCapture ();
        ::ClipCursor (NULL);
        CClientDC ClientDC (this);
        ClientDC.SetROP2 (R2_NOT);
        ClientDC.MoveTo (mPointOrigin);
        ClientDC.LineTo (mPointOld);
        ClientDC.SetROP2 (R2_COPYPEN);
        ClientDC.MoveTo (mPointOrigin);
        ClientDC.LineTo (point);

        CMinidrawDoc* PDoc = GetDocument();
        PDoc->AddLine (mPointOrigin.x, mPointOrigin.y, point.x, point.y);
        }

    CView::OnLButtonUp(nFlags, point);
}

BOOL CMinidrawView::PreCreateWindow (CREATESTRUCT& cs)
    {
    mClassName = AfxRegisterWndClass
        (CS_HREDRAW | CS_VREDRAW,             // class styles
        0,                                    // no cursor
        (HBRUSH)::GetStockObject (WHITE_BRUSH), // set white background brush
        0);                                   // no icon
    cs.lpszClass = mClassName;

    return CView::PreCreateWindow (cs);
    }
```

Summary

In this chapter, you learned how to write code to perform the main duties of the document class: storing the program data, providing access to the data through public member functions, and handling menu commands that directly affect the document data. The following are some of the general techniques and concepts that were explored:

- If the document consists of discrete data items, such as graphic figures, you should define a class for storing, displaying, and performing other operations on these items.

- The document class can conveniently store groups of variables or class objects by using one of the MFC collection classes. For example, an instance of the MFC `CObArray` class can store a collection of pointers to class objects, in an array-like data structure. The objects that you store must belong to a class derived from the MFC `CObject` class.

- The document class should provide public member functions that allow the view class to obtain or modify the document data. For example, the `OnDraw` function of the view class needs to obtain the document data so that it can redraw this data in the view window. Also, the view class must be able to change or add data to the document, in response to editing actions of the user.

- Menu commands that directly alter the document data, such as an Undo or Delete All command on the Edit menu, should be handled by the document class. You can add a handler for a menu command message to the document class using the ClassWizard.

- You can define handlers for two types of menu command messages: a `COMMAND_UPDATE_UI` message, which is sent when the pop-up menu containing the command is first opened, and a `COMMAND` message, which is sent whenever the user chooses the menu command.

- A `COMMAND_UPDATE_UI` message handler initializes the menu item, using member functions of the `CCmdUI` object that it is passed. If this function disables the menu item, any accelerator keystroke assigned to the menu command will also be disabled.

- A `COMMAND` message handler carries out the menu command.

CHAPTER

TEN

Storing Documents

- Adding file I/O to MINIDRAW

- Adding file I/O to MINIEDIT

In this chapter, you will learn how to write the code to perform an additional important task of the document class: saving and loading the document data to and from disk files. To demonstrate the basic MFC file I/O techniques, the chapter shows you how to add code for supporting the File menu commands (New, Open, Save, and Save As) to both the MINIDRAW and the MINIEDIT example programs that you created previously. You will also learn how to add the drag-drop feature to these programs, which allows the user to open files by dragging them from the Windows File Manager and dropping them in the program window.

Adding File I/O to MINIDRAW

In this section you will add Open, Save, and Save As commands to the MINIDRAW program, as well as the code necessary to support these commands. You should add all features to the MINIDRAW source files you created in Chapter 9. (If you did not create these files, you can obtain a copy of them from the \MINIDRW2 subdirectory within the directory in which you installed the companion disk.)

Adding the File Menu Commands

After you open the MINIDRAW project in the Visual Workbench, run App Studio by choosing the App Studio command on the Tools menu. To modify the program menu, select the Menu item in the Type: list, select the IDR_MAINFRAME identifier in the Resources: list, and click the Open button; App Studio will open the menu-designing window. Immediately below the existing New command on the File menu, you should now add Open, Save, and Save As commands; a separator; and a Recent File command. Use the techniques described in the previous chapters. For each new command, Table 10.1 lists the identifier, the caption, and any other feature that you should select in the menu item properties dialog box. Figure 10.1 shows the completed File menu as it appears in App Studio.

You can now close the menu-designing window. You do not need to define the keyboard accelerators for these commands, because AppWizard defined them for you

TABLE 10.1: The Properties of the MINIDRAW New File Menu Items

ID:	Caption:	Other Features
ID_FILE_OPEN	&Open...\tCtrl+O	none
ID_FILE_SAVE	&Save\tCtrl+S	none
ID_FILE_SAVE_AS	Save &As...	none
none	none	Separator
ID_FILE_MRU_FILE1	Recent File	Grayed

FIGURE 10.1:

The completed File menu for the MINIDRAW program

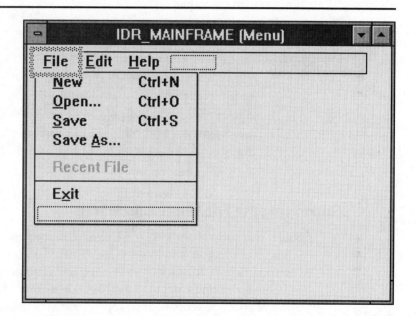

when you first generated the application. (Recall that the menu generated by AppWizard included each of the commands listed in Table 10.1; in Chapter 8, however, you deleted them because they were not needed for the first two versions of MINIDRAW.)

The next step is to modify the `IDR_MAINFRAME` resource string. In the resource dialog box, select the String Table item in the IDs: list, select the String Segment:0 item in the Resources: list, and click the Open button. In the string properties dialog box, select the first string (with the `IDR_MAINFRAME` identifier), and click the Properties... button. You should now edit the string in the Captions: text box so that it matches the following:

```
MiniDraw\ndrawing\nMINIDR Document\nMiniDraw Files (*.drw)\n.drw
```

The text you added to the end of the string ("\nMiniDraw Files (*.drw)\n.drw") specifies the *default file extension* that the MFC code uses when it displays the Open or Save As dialog box. As a result, if the user does *not* specify a file extension when opening or saving a file, the Open dialog box will display a list of all files with the .DRW extension, and the Save As dialog box will add the .DRW extension to the specified file name.

> **NOTE** The instructions given here are for adding a default file extension to an existing program. Alternatively, when you first create an application using AppWizard, you can specify a default file extension by clicking the Classes... button in the MFC AppWizard dialog box, selecting the name of the document class in the New Application Classes: list, and entering the desired extension (one to three characters, *not* including the dot) into the File Extension: text box.

Supporting the File Menu Commands

When you added the Undo and Delete All commands to the Edit menu (in the previous chapter), you had to use ClassWizard to define message handlers for these commands. You do not, however, need to define handlers for the Open, Save, and Save As commands, because the MFC classes provide handlers for you. You do, however, need to write code to *support* the MFC message handlers.

The Open menu command is handled by the `OnFileOpen` member function of the `CWinApp` class (the MFC class from which the MINIDRAW application class is derived). `OnFileOpen` displays the standard Windows File Open dialog box, which is shown in Figure 10.2. If the user selects a file and clicks the OK button, `OnFileOpen` proceeds to open the file for reading and then calls the `Serialize` member function of the document class (`CMinidrawDoc::Serialize`). The `Serialize` function must perform the actual read operation. `OnFileOpen` also stores the full file path of the loaded file and displays the file name in the title bar of the main window.

FIGURE 10.2:

The standard File Open dialog box

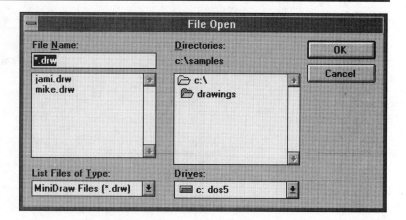

The Save command is handled by the `OnFileSave` member function of the `CDocument` class (the MFC class from which the MINIDRAW document class is derived), and the Save As command is handled by the `OnFileSaveAs` member function of `CDocument`. `OnFileSaveAs`—as well as `OnFileSave` if the document is being saved for the first time—first displays the File Save As dialog box shown in Figure 10.3, to allow the user to specify the file name. Both `OnFileSave` and `OnFileSaveAs` open the file for writing, and then call `CMinidrawDoc::Serialize` to perform the actual write operation. These functions also store the full file path and display the file name in the title bar.

 NOTE If the file has not yet been saved, the File Save As dialog box displays a default file name in the File Name: text box. This name is created by adding the default file extension (".drw" for MINIDRAW) to the document type name ("drawing" for MINIDRAW, which you specified in Chapter 8).

The MFC also automatically maintains a list of recent files on the File menu. The user can select any of these file names to immediately open the file. The MFC code even saves this file list in the program's initialization file (MINIDRAW.INI), so that it can preserve the list when the user quits and restarts the program.

FIGURE 10.3:

The standard File Save As dialog box

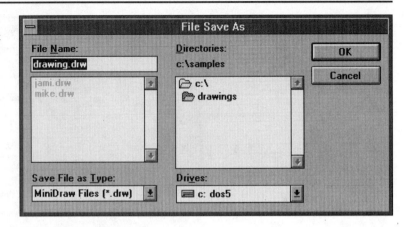

Serializing the Document Data

When AppWizard generated the MINIDRAW program, it defined the following minimal `Serialize` function as a member of the document class (in the file MINIDDOC.CPP):

```
///////////////////////////////////////////////////////////////////////////
// CMinidrawDoc serialization

void CMinidrawDoc::Serialize(CArchive& ar)
{
    if (ar.IsStoring())
    {
        // TODO: add storing code here
    }
    else
    {
        // TODO: add loading code here
    }
}
```

You must add your own code to this minimal definition for reading or writing the document data. To help you do this, the MFC passes `Serialize` a reference to an instance of the MFC class `CArchive`. The `CArchive` object is attached to the open file, and it provides a set of member functions that allow you to easily read data from this file, or write data to it.

The CArchive member function IsStoring returns TRUE if the file has been opened for writing (that is, if the user chose the Save or Save As command), and IsStoring returns FALSE if the file has been opened for reading (that is, if the user chose the Open command). Consequently, you should place the output code within the if block and the input code within the else block.

In MINIDRAW, the document class stores only a single data member, mObArray, which manages a set of CLine objects. Fortunately, the CObArray class provides a Serialize member function, which manages the reading or writing of all of the objects stored by the CObArray object. As a result, you need only add two calls to CObArray::Serialize to the CMinidrawDoc::Serialize function, as follows:

```
/////////////////////////////////////////////////////////////////////////////
// CMinidrawDoc serialization

void CMinidrawDoc::Serialize(CArchive& ar)
{
   if (ar.IsStoring())
   {
      // TODO: add storing code here

      mObArray.Serialize (ar);
   }
   else
   {
      // TODO: add loading code here

      mObArray.Serialize (ar);
   }
}
```

If the data is being *written* to the file, CObArray::Serialize performs two main steps for each CLine object that it stores within the file.

1. It writes information on the object's class.

2. It calls the object's Serialize member function, which writes the object's data to the file.

If the data is being *read* from the file, `CObArray::Serialize` performs the following two steps for each `CLine` object:

1. It reads the class information, dynamically creates an object of the appropriate class (that is, `CLine`), and saves the pointer to the object.

2. It calls the object's `Serialize` member function, which reads the data from the file into the object.

NOTE
`CObArray::Serialize` performs these steps by calling member functions of the `CArchive` object (`WriteObject` and `ReadObject`), which do the actual work.

You must provide code that supports the serialization of the `CLine` objects. To do this you must first include two MFC macros, `DECLARE_SERIAL` and `IMPLEMENT_SE-RIAL`, in the definition of the `CLine` class, and you must define a default class constructor. These macros and the default constructor allow `CObArray::Serialize` first to store the class information in the file, and later to use this class information to dynamically create objects of the correct class (that is, the macros and constructor allow `CObArray::Serialize` to perform step 1 in both of the lists above).

Add the `DECLARE_SERIAL` macro and the default constructor to the `CLine` class definition within MINIDDOC.H:

```
class CLine : public CObject
{
protected:
    int mX1, mY1, mX2, mY2;

    CLine ()
        {}
    DECLARE_SERIAL (CLine)

public:

// remainder of CLine definition ...
```

The parameter passed to `DECLARE_SERIAL` is simply the name of the class.

Insert the IMPLEMENT_SERIAL macro just above the CLine::Draw function definition within MINIDDOC.CPP:

```
IMPLEMENT_SERIAL (CLine, CObject, 1)

void CLine::Draw (CDC *PDC)
    {
    PDC->MoveTo (mX1, mY1);
    PDC->LineTo (mX2, mY2);
    }
```

The first parameter passed to IMPLEMENT_SERIAL is the name of the class, and the second parameter is the name of the base class. The third parameter is a number that identifies the particular version of the program. This number is stored within the file, and only a program that has specified this same number can read the file. Version numbers thus prevent one version of a program from trying to read the data saved by another version, which may have a different format. The current version of the MINIDRAW program is assigned a version number of 1; in later versions of the program, this number will be incremented whenever the format of the data changes.

Second, you need to add a Serialize member function to the CLine class, which will be called by CObArray::Serialize to read or write the data for each line. Add the Serialize declaration to the public section of the CLine class definition, in MINIDDOC.H:

```
public:
    CLine (int X1, int Y1, int X2, int Y2)
        {
        mX1 = X1;
        mY1 = Y1;
        mX2 = X2;
        mY2 = Y2;
        }
    void Draw (CDC *PDC);
    virtual void Serialize (CArchive& ar);
```

Then, add the following Serialize definition to the MINIDDOC.CPP file, immediately following the definition of Draw:

```
void CLine::Serialize (CArchive& ar)
    {
    if (ar.IsStoring())
        ar << (WORD)mX1 << (WORD)mY1 << (WORD)mX2 << (WORD)mY2;
```

```
else
   ar >> (WORD &)mX1 >> (WORD &)mY1 >> (WORD &)mX2 >> (WORD &)mY2;
}
```

> **NOTE**   A class whose objects are to be serialized, such as CLine, must be derived—directly or indirectly—from the MFC CObject class, which provides the basic serialization support.

The CLine::Serialize function performs the actual reading and writing operations, rather than simply calling the Serialize member function of another class. Serialize uses the overloaded << operator to write the CLine data members to the file, and it uses the overloaded >> operator to read the values of the data members from the file. Both of these overloaded operators are defined by the CArchive class, and can be used for reading and writing a variety of data types. The supported data types, however, do not include int; therefore, each of the data members is converted (using a type cast) from an int to the supported type WORD. (WORD is a typedef for unsigned short; it is defined in the Windows API header file, WINDOWS.H.)

> **NOTE**   You can read or write the following fundamental types using the << or >> overloaded operators and a CArchive object: BYTE (unsigned char), WORD (unsigned short), LONG (signed long), DWORD (unsigned long), float, and double.

Conclusion   As you can see from the file I/O code you added to MINIDRAW, a class object is normally responsible for writing or reading its own data to or from disk; that is, it must provide a Serialize member function that writes or reads its data members to or from permanent storage on disk. For a data member that is *not* an object, the Serialize function can use the overloaded << and >> operators provided by CArchive to directly write or read the data member. For a data member that *is* an object, it can call the object's Serialize member to have the object write or read its own data.

Setting the Modified Flag

The CDocument class maintains a *modified flag*, which indicates whether the document currently contains unsaved data. Before the MFC calls the DeleteContents member function of the program's document class to delete the document data, it checks this flag. (It calls DeleteContents before creating a new document, opening an existing document, or exiting the program.) If the modified flag is TRUE, indicating that the document contains unsaved data, it displays a message and allows the user to save the data.

CDocument sets the modified flag to FALSE whenever a document is first opened, and when it is saved. Your responsibility is to call the CDocument::SetModified-Flag function to set the flag to TRUE whenever the document data is altered. To maintain the modified flag for the MINIDRAW program, first add a call to Set-Modified to the AddLine function in MINIDDOC.CPP:

```
void CMinidrawDoc::AddLine (int X1, int Y1, int X2, int Y2)
    {
    CLine *PLine = new CLine (X1, Y1, X2, Y2);
    mObArray.Add (PLine);
    SetModifiedFlag ();
    }
```

Now add a call to SetModified to the OnEditClearAll function, also in MINIDDOC.CPP:

```
void CMinidrawDoc::OnEditClearAll()
{
    // TODO: Add your command handler code here

    DeleteContents ();
    UpdateAllViews (0);
    SetModifiedFlag ();
}
```

Finally, add a SetModified call to OnEditUndo in MINIDDOC.CPP:

```
void CMinidrawDoc::OnEditUndo()
{
    // TODO: Add your command handler code here

    int Index = mObArray.GetUpperBound ();
    if (Index > -1)
```

```
      {
      delete mObArray.GetAt (Index);
      mObArray.RemoveAt (Index);
      }
   UpdateAllViews (0);
   SetModifiedFlag ();
}
```

You can set the modified flag to FALSE, by passing FALSE to the SetModified function, although you do not normally need to do this since CDocument handles this task for you.

Supporting Drag-Drop

If a program provides support for the drag-drop feature of Windows (available beginning with version 3.1), the user can open a file by dragging it from the File Manager and dropping it on the program window.

To support the drag-drop feature in the MINIDRAW function, you need only add a call to the DragAcceptFiles member function of the main window object (which it inherits from the CWnd class). You should add this call to the InitInstance function in MINIDRAW.CPP, as follows:

```
BOOL CMinidrawApp::InitInstance()
{
   // other statements ...

   // create a new (empty) document
   OnFileNew();

   m_pMainWnd->DragAcceptFiles ();

   // other statements ...
}
```

The program application object contains a data member, m_pMainWnd (defined in CWinApp), which is a pointer that stores the address of the main window object. InitInstance uses this pointer to call DragAcceptFiles. The call to DragAcceptFiles must be placed *after* the call to OnFileNew (which creates the main window object, among other tasks), so that the m_pMainWnd pointer will contain a valid address.

As a result of calling `DragAcceptFiles`, whenever the user drops a file on the program window, the MFC automatically opens the file, creates a `CArchive` object, and calls the document object's `Serialize` function, just as if the user had chosen the Open... menu command and had selected the file. You therefore do not need to write any additional code to support the drag-drop feature.

The MINIDRAW Source Code

The following listings, Listings 10.1 through 10.8, are the C++ source files for the latest version of the MINIDRAW program. A complete copy of these files is contained in the \MINIDRW3 subdirectory within the directory storing the companion disk files.

Listing 10.1

```
// minidraw.h : main header file for the MINIDRAW application
//

#ifndef __AFXWIN_H__
    #error include 'stdafx.h' before including this file for PCH
#endif

#include "resource.h"       // main symbols

/////////////////////////////////////////////////////////////////////////////
// CMinidrawApp:
// See minidraw.cpp for the implementation of this class
//

class CMinidrawApp : public CWinApp
{
public:
    CMinidrawApp();

// Overrides
    virtual BOOL InitInstance();

// Implementation

    //{{AFX_MSG(CMinidrawApp)
    afx_msg void OnAppAbout();
```

```
    // NOTE - the ClassWizard will add and remove member functions here.
    //      DO NOT EDIT what you see in these blocks of generated code !
  //}}AFX_MSG
  DECLARE_MESSAGE_MAP()
};
```

///

Listing 10.2

```
// minidraw.cpp : Defines the class behaviors for the application.
//

#include "stdafx.h"
#include "minidraw.h"

#include "mainfrm.h"
#include "miniddoc.h"
#include "minidvw.h"

#ifdef _DEBUG
#undef THIS_FILE
static char BASED_CODE THIS_FILE[] = __FILE__;
#endif

/////////////////////////////////////////////////////////////////////
// CMinidrawApp

BEGIN_MESSAGE_MAP(CMinidrawApp, CWinApp)
    //{{AFX_MSG_MAP(CMinidrawApp)
    ON_COMMAND(ID_APP_ABOUT, OnAppAbout)
        // NOTE - the ClassWizard will add and remove mapping macros here.
        //      DO NOT EDIT what you see in these blocks of generated code !
    //}}AFX_MSG_MAP
    // Standard file based document commands
    ON_COMMAND(ID_FILE_NEW, CWinApp::OnFileNew)
    ON_COMMAND(ID_FILE_OPEN, CWinApp::OnFileOpen)
END_MESSAGE_MAP()
```

```
/////////////////////////////////////////////////////////////////////
// CMinidrawApp construction

CMinidrawApp::CMinidrawApp()
{
    // TODO: add construction code here,
    // Place all significant initialization in InitInstance
}


/////////////////////////////////////////////////////////////////////
// The one and only CMinidrawApp object

CMinidrawApp NEAR theApp;

/////////////////////////////////////////////////////////////////////
// CMinidrawApp initialization

BOOL CMinidrawApp::InitInstance()
{
    // Standard initialization
    // If you are not using these features and wish to reduce the size
    //  of your final executable, you should remove from the following
    //  the specific initialization routines you do not need.

    SetDialogBkColor();         // set dialog background color to gray
    LoadStdProfileSettings();   // Load standard INI file options (including MRU)

    // Register the application's document templates.  Document templates
    //  serve as the connection between documents, frame windows and views.

    AddDocTemplate(new CSingleDocTemplate(IDR_MAINFRAME,
        RUNTIME_CLASS(CMinidrawDoc),
        RUNTIME_CLASS(CMainFrame),      // main SDI frame window
        RUNTIME_CLASS(CMinidrawView)));

    // create a new (empty) document
    OnFileNew();

    m_pMainWnd->DragAcceptFiles ();

    if (m_lpCmdLine[0] != '\0')
    {
        // TODO: add command line processing here
    }
```

```
    return TRUE;
}

////////////////////////////////////////////////////////////////////////////
// CAboutDlg dialog used for App About

class CAboutDlg : public CDialog
{
public:
    CAboutDlg();

// Dialog Data
    //{{AFX_DATA(CAboutDlg)
    enum { IDD = IDD_ABOUTBOX };
    //}}AFX_DATA

// Implementation
protected:
    virtual void DoDataExchange(CDataExchange* pDX);    // DDX/DDV support
    //{{AFX_MSG(CAboutDlg)
        // No message handlers
    //}}AFX_MSG
    DECLARE_MESSAGE_MAP()
};

CAboutDlg::CAboutDlg() : CDialog(CAboutDlg::IDD)
{
    //{{AFX_DATA_INIT(CAboutDlg)
    //}}AFX_DATA_INIT
}

void CAboutDlg::DoDataExchange(CDataExchange* pDX)
{
    CDialog::DoDataExchange(pDX);
    //{{AFX_DATA_MAP(CAboutDlg)
    //}}AFX_DATA_MAP
}

BEGIN_MESSAGE_MAP(CAboutDlg, CDialog)
    //{{AFX_MSG_MAP(CAboutDlg)
        // No message handlers
    //}}AFX_MSG_MAP
END_MESSAGE_MAP()
```

```
// App command to run the dialog
void CMinidrawApp::OnAppAbout()
{
   CAboutDlg aboutDlg;
   aboutDlg.DoModal();
}


/////////////////////////////////////////////////////////////////////////////
// CMinidrawApp commands
```

Listing 10.3

```
// miniddoc.h : interface of the CMinidrawDoc class
//
/////////////////////////////////////////////////////////////////////////////

class CLine : public CObject
{
protected:
   int mX1, mY1, mX2, mY2;

   CLine ()
      {}
   DECLARE_SERIAL (CLine)

public:
   CLine (int X1, int Y1, int X2, int Y2)
      {
      mX1 = X1;
      mY1 = Y1;
      mX2 = X2;
      mY2 = Y2;
      }
   void Draw (CDC *PDC);
   virtual void Serialize (CArchive& ar);
};

class CMinidrawDoc : public CDocument
{
protected: // create from serialization only
   CMinidrawDoc();
   DECLARE_DYNCREATE(CMinidrawDoc)

protected:
   CObArray mObArray;
```

```
public:
    void AddLine (int X1, int Y1, int X2, int Y2);
    virtual void DeleteContents ();
    CLine *GetLine (int Index);
    int GetNumLines ();

// Attributes
public:

// Operations
public:

// Implementation
public:
    virtual ~CMinidrawDoc();
    virtual void Serialize(CArchive& ar);   // overridden for document i/o
#ifdef _DEBUG
    virtual  void AssertValid() const;
    virtual  void Dump(CDumpContext& dc) const;
#endif
protected:
    virtual  BOOL  OnNewDocument();

// Generated message map functions
protected:
    //{{AFX_MSG(CMinidrawDoc)
    afx_msg void OnEditClearAll();
    afx_msg void OnUpdateEditClearAll(CCmdUI* pCmdUI);
    afx_msg void OnEditUndo();
    afx_msg void OnUpdateEditUndo(CCmdUI* pCmdUI);
    //}}AFX_MSG
    DECLARE_MESSAGE_MAP()
};
```

//

Listing 10.4

```
// miniddoc.cpp : implementation of the CMinidrawDoc class
//

#include "stdafx.h"
#include "minidraw.h"
```

```
#include "miniddoc.h"

#ifdef _DEBUG
#undef THIS_FILE
static char BASED_CODE THIS_FILE[] = __FILE__;
#endif

/////////////////////////////////////////////////////////////////////////////
// CMinidrawDoc

IMPLEMENT_DYNCREATE(CMinidrawDoc, CDocument)

BEGIN_MESSAGE_MAP(CMinidrawDoc, CDocument)
    //{{AFX_MSG_MAP(CMinidrawDoc)
    ON_COMMAND(ID_EDIT_CLEAR_ALL, OnEditClearAll)
    ON_UPDATE_COMMAND_UI(ID_EDIT_CLEAR_ALL, OnUpdateEditClearAll)
    ON_COMMAND(ID_EDIT_UNDO, OnEditUndo)
    ON_UPDATE_COMMAND_UI(ID_EDIT_UNDO, OnUpdateEditUndo)
    //}}AFX_MSG_MAP
END_MESSAGE_MAP()

/////////////////////////////////////////////////////////////////////////////
// CMinidrawDoc construction/destruction

CMinidrawDoc::CMinidrawDoc()
{
    // TODO: add one-time construction code here
}

CMinidrawDoc::~CMinidrawDoc()
{
}

BOOL CMinidrawDoc::OnNewDocument()
{
    if (!CDocument::OnNewDocument())
        return FALSE;
    // TODO: add reinitialization code here
    // (SDI documents will reuse this document)
    return TRUE;
}
```

```
/////////////////////////////////////////////////////////////////////////
// CMinidrawDoc serialization

void CMinidrawDoc::Serialize(CArchive& ar)
{
   if (ar.IsStoring())
   {
      // TODO: add storing code here

   mObArray.Serialize (ar);
   }
   else
   {
      // TODO: add loading code here

   mObArray.Serialize (ar);
   }
}

/////////////////////////////////////////////////////////////////////////
// CMinidrawDoc diagnostics

#ifdef _DEBUG
void CMinidrawDoc::AssertValid() const
{
   CDocument::AssertValid();
}

void CMinidrawDoc::Dump(CDumpContext& dc) const
{
   CDocument::Dump(dc);
}

#endif //_DEBUG

/////////////////////////////////////////////////////////////////////////
// CMinidrawDoc commands

IMPLEMENT_SERIAL (CLine, CObject, 1)

void CLine::Draw (CDC *PDC)
```

```
   {
   PDC->MoveTo (mX1, mY1);
   PDC->LineTo (mX2, mY2);
   }

void CLine::Serialize (CArchive& ar)
   {
   if (ar.IsStoring())
      ar << (WORD)mX1 << (WORD)mY1 << (WORD)mX2 << (WORD)mY2;
   else
      ar >> (WORD &)mX1 >> (WORD &)mY1 >> (WORD &)mX2 >> (WORD &)mY2;
   }

void CMinidrawDoc::AddLine (int X1, int Y1, int X2, int Y2)
   {
   CLine *PLine = new CLine (X1, Y1, X2, Y2);
   mObArray.Add (PLine);
   SetModifiedFlag ();
   }

CLine *CMinidrawDoc::GetLine (int Index)
   {
   if (Index < 0 || Index > mObArray.GetUpperBound ())
      return 0;
   return (CLine *)mObArray.GetAt (Index);
   }

int CMinidrawDoc::GetNumLines ()
   {
   return mObArray.GetSize ();
   }

void CMinidrawDoc::DeleteContents ()
   {
   int Index = mObArray.GetSize ();
   while (Index--)
      delete mObArray.GetAt (Index);
   mObArray.RemoveAll ();
   }
// :end addition

void CMinidrawDoc::OnEditClearAll()
{
   // TODO: Add your command handler code here
```

```
    DeleteContents ();
    UpdateAllViews (0);
    SetModifiedFlag ();
}

void CMinidrawDoc::OnUpdateEditClearAll(CCmdUI* pCmdUI)
{
    // TODO: Add your command update UI handler code here

    pCmdUI->Enable (mObArray.GetSize ());
}

void CMinidrawDoc::OnEditUndo()
{
    // TODO: Add your command handler code here

    int Index = mObArray.GetUpperBound ();
    if (Index > -1)
        {
        delete mObArray.GetAt (Index);
        mObArray.RemoveAt (Index);
        }
    UpdateAllViews (0);
    SetModifiedFlag ();
}

void CMinidrawDoc::OnUpdateEditUndo(CCmdUI* pCmdUI)
{
    // TODO: Add your command update UI handler code here

    pCmdUI->Enable (mObArray.GetSize ());
}
```

Listing 10.5

```
// mainfrm.h : interface of the CMainFrame class
//
/////////////////////////////////////////////////////////////////////////

class CMainFrame : public CFrameWnd
{
protected: // create from serialization only
    CMainFrame();
    DECLARE_DYNCREATE(CMainFrame)
```

```
// Attributes
public:

// Operations
public:

// Implementation
public:
    virtual ~CMainFrame();
#ifdef _DEBUG
    virtual  void AssertValid() const;
    virtual  void Dump(CDumpContext& dc) const;
#endif


// Generated message map functions
protected:
    //{{AFX_MSG(CMainFrame)
        // NOTE - the ClassWizard will add and remove member functions here.
        //     DO NOT EDIT what you see in these blocks of generated code !
    //}}AFX_MSG
    DECLARE_MESSAGE_MAP()
};
```

///

Listing 10.6

```
// mainfrm.cpp : implementation of the CMainFrame class
//

#include "stdafx.h"
#include "minidraw.h"

#include "mainfrm.h"

#ifdef _DEBUG
#undef THIS_FILE
static char BASED_CODE THIS_FILE[] = __FILE__;
#endif

/////////////////////////////////////////////////////////////////////////////
// CMainFrame

IMPLEMENT_DYNCREATE(CMainFrame, CFrameWnd)
```

```
BEGIN_MESSAGE_MAP(CMainFrame, CFrameWnd)
    //{{AFX_MSG_MAP(CMainFrame)
        // NOTE - the ClassWizard will add and remove mapping macros here.
        //      DO NOT EDIT what you see in these blocks of generated code !
    //}}AFX_MSG_MAP
END_MESSAGE_MAP()

/////////////////////////////////////////////////////////////////////////////
// CMainFrame construction/destruction

CMainFrame::CMainFrame()
{
    // TODO: add member initialization code here
}

CMainFrame::~CMainFrame()
{
}

/////////////////////////////////////////////////////////////////////////////
// CMainFrame diagnostics

#ifdef _DEBUG
void CMainFrame::AssertValid() const
{
    CFrameWnd::AssertValid();
}

void CMainFrame::Dump(CDumpContext& dc) const
{
    CFrameWnd::Dump(dc);
}

#endif //_DEBUG

/////////////////////////////////////////////////////////////////////////////
// CMainFrame message handlers
```

Listing 10.7

```
// minidvw.h : interface of the CMinidrawView class
//
/////////////////////////////////////////////////////////////////////////////
```

```
class CMinidrawView : public CView
{
protected: // create from serialization only
    CMinidrawView();
    DECLARE_DYNCREATE(CMinidrawView)

protected:
    CString mClassName;
    int mDragging;
    HCURSOR mHCross;
    CPoint mPointOld;
    CPoint mPointOrigin;

    virtual BOOL PreCreateWindow (CREATESTRUCT& cs);

// Attributes
public:
    CMinidrawDoc* GetDocument();

// Operations
public:

// Implementation
public:
    virtual ~CMinidrawView();
    virtual void OnDraw(CDC* pDC);   // overridden to draw this view
#ifdef _DEBUG
    virtual void AssertValid() const;
    virtual void Dump(CDumpContext& dc) const;
#endif

// Generated message map functions
protected:
    //{{AFX_MSG(CMinidrawView)
    afx_msg void OnLButtonDown(UINT nFlags, CPoint point);
    afx_msg void OnMouseMove(UINT nFlags, CPoint point);
    afx_msg void OnLButtonUp(UINT nFlags, CPoint point);
    //}}AFX_MSG
    DECLARE_MESSAGE_MAP()
};

#ifndef _DEBUG // debug version in minidvw.cpp
inline CMinidrawDoc* CMinidrawView::GetDocument()
    { return (CMinidrawDoc*) m_pDocument; }
#endif
```

///

Listing 10.8

```cpp
// minidvw.cpp : implementation of the CMinidrawView class
//

#include "stdafx.h"
#include "minidraw.h"

#include "miniddoc.h"
#include "minidvw.h"

#ifdef _DEBUG
#undef THIS_FILE
static char BASED_CODE THIS_FILE[] = __FILE__;
#endif

///////////////////////////////////////////////////////////////////////////////
// CMinidrawView

IMPLEMENT_DYNCREATE(CMinidrawView, CView)

BEGIN_MESSAGE_MAP(CMinidrawView, CView)
    //{{AFX_MSG_MAP(CMinidrawView)
    ON_WM_LBUTTONDOWN()
    ON_WM_MOUSEMOVE()
    ON_WM_LBUTTONUP()
    //}}AFX_MSG_MAP
END_MESSAGE_MAP()

///////////////////////////////////////////////////////////////////////////////
// CMinidrawView construction/destruction

CMinidrawView::CMinidrawView()
{
    // TODO: add construction code here

    mDragging = 0;
    mHCross = AfxGetApp ()->LoadStandardCursor (IDC_CROSS);
```

```
}

CMinidrawView::~CMinidrawView()
{
}

//////////////////////////////////////////////////////////////////////////
// CMinidrawView drawing

void CMinidrawView::OnDraw(CDC* pDC)
{
    CMinidrawDoc* pDoc = GetDocument();

    // TODO: add draw code here

    int Index = pDoc->GetNumLines ();
    while (Index--)
        pDoc->GetLine (Index)->Draw (pDC);
}


//////////////////////////////////////////////////////////////////////////
// CMinidrawView diagnostics

#ifdef _DEBUG
void CMinidrawView::AssertValid() const
{
    CView::AssertValid();
}

void CMinidrawView::Dump(CDumpContext& dc) const
{
    CView::Dump(dc);
}

CMinidrawDoc* CMinidrawView::GetDocument() // non-debug version is inline
{
    ASSERT(m_pDocument->IsKindOf(RUNTIME_CLASS(CMinidrawDoc)));
    return (CMinidrawDoc*) m_pDocument;
}

#endif //_DEBUG
```

```
////////////////////////////////////////////////////////////////////////////
// CMinidrawView message handlers

void CMinidrawView::OnLButtonDown(UINT nFlags, CPoint point)
{
    // TODO: Add your message handler code here and/or call default

    mPointOrigin = point;
    mPointOld = point;
    SetCapture ();
    mDragging = 1;

    RECT Rect;
    GetClientRect (&Rect);
    ClientToScreen (&Rect);
    ::ClipCursor (&Rect);

    CView::OnLButtonDown(nFlags, point);
}

void CMinidrawView::OnMouseMove(UINT nFlags, CPoint point)
{
    // TODO: Add your message handler code here and/or call default

    ::SetCursor (mHCross);

    if (mDragging)
        {
        CClientDC ClientDC (this);
        ClientDC.SetROP2 (R2_NOT);
        ClientDC.MoveTo (mPointOrigin);
        ClientDC.LineTo (mPointOld);
        ClientDC.MoveTo (mPointOrigin);
        ClientDC.LineTo (point);
        mPointOld = point;
        }

    CView::OnMouseMove(nFlags, point);
}

void CMinidrawView::OnLButtonUp(UINT nFlags, CPoint point)
{
    // TODO: Add your message handler code here and/or call default
```

```
   if (mDragging)
      {
      mDragging = 0;
      ::ReleaseCapture ();
      ::ClipCursor (NULL);
      CClientDC ClientDC (this);
      ClientDC.SetROP2 (R2_NOT);
      ClientDC.MoveTo (mPointOrigin);
      ClientDC.LineTo (mPointOld);
      ClientDC.SetROP2 (R2_COPYPEN);
      ClientDC.MoveTo (mPointOrigin);
      ClientDC.LineTo (point);

      CMinidrawDoc* PDoc = GetDocument();
      PDoc->AddLine (mPointOrigin.x, mPointOrigin.y, point.x, point.y);
      }

   CView::OnLButtonUp(nFlags, point);
}

BOOL CMinidrawView::PreCreateWindow (CREATESTRUCT& cs)
   {
   mClassName = AfxRegisterWndClass
      (CS_HREDRAW | CS_VREDRAW,                  // class styles
      0,                                         // no cursor
      (HBRUSH)::GetStockObject (WHITE_BRUSH),    // set white background brush
      0);                                        // no icon
   cs.lpszClass = mClassName;

   return CView::PreCreateWindow (cs);
   }
```

Adding File I/O to MINIEDIT

In this section, you will add support for file I/O to the MINIEDIT program. Specifically, you will add New, Open, Save, Save As, and Recent File commands to the File menu, and you will write the code necessary to support these commands.

You should make your modifications to the source files you created in Chapter 8. (If you did not create these files, you can obtain a copy of them from the \MINIEDT1 subdirectory within the directory containing your companion disk files.)

Defining the Resources

After opening the MINIEDIT project in the Visual Workbench, run the App Studio program to modify the program menu and the IDR_RESOURCE string.

In App Studio, first open the menu-designing window using the technique described previously. *Above* the existing Print command, add New, Open, Save, and Save As commands. Then, *below* the Print command, add a separator and a Recent File command. Table 10.2 lists the identifier, caption, and other feature for each of the menu items that you need to add, while Figure 10.4 shows the completed File menu as it appears in App Studio.

Next, open the string table dialog box, and edit the IDR_MAINFRAME string so that it reads as follows:

`MiniEdit\ntext\nMINIED Document\nMiniEdit Files (*.txt)\n.txt`

The text at the end of this string ("\nMiniEdit Files (*.txt)\n.txt") specifies .TXT as the default file extension.

TABLE 10.2: The Properties of the MINIEDIT New File Menu Items

ID:	Caption:	Other Features
ID_FILE_NEW	&New\tCtrl+N	none
ID_FILE_OPEN	&Open...\tCtrl+O	none
ID_FILE_SAVE	&Save\tCtrl+S	none
ID_FILE_SAVE_AS	Save &As...	none
none	none	Separator
ID_FILE_MRU_FILE1	Recent File	Grayed

FIGURE 10.4:

The completed File menu for the MINIEDIT program

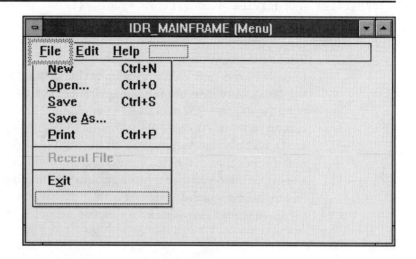

Adding Supporting Code

To support the menu commands, you must first define an overriding version of the DeleteContents virtual function as a member of the document class. As you have seen, the MFC calls this function before creating a new document (in response to the New command) or opening an existing document (in response to the Open command), and its duty is to delete the document data. Add the following declaration to the CMinieditDoc class definition in MINIEDOC.H:

```
class CMinieditDoc : public CDocument
{
protected: // create from serialization only
   CMinieditDoc();
   DECLARE_DYNCREATE(CMinieditDoc)

   virtual void DeleteContents ();

// remainder of CMinieditDoc definition ...
```

And add the following function definition to the end of the MINIEDOC.CPP file:

```
void CMinieditDoc::DeleteContents ()
   {
   POSITION Pos = GetFirstViewPosition ();
```

```
CEditView *PCEditView = (CEditView *)GetNextView (Pos);
PCEditView->SetWindowText ("");
}
```

Because the view class is derived from CEditView, the document text is stored internally by the view window itself. To change this text, DeleteContents first calls the CDocument member functions GetFirstViewPosition and GetNextView to obtain a pointer to the document's view class. These two functions allow you to access all views in a document that has more than a single view attached to it. (Chapter 11 will discuss documents that have several views.) GetFirstViewPosition obtains the index of the first view object (or, in the case of MINIEDIT, the *only* view object). GetNewView then returns a pointer to this object and updates the parameter Pos to the index of the next view in the list, or it assigns 0 to Pos if there are no more views. (GetNextView can change Pos because it is a reference parameter.)

> **NOTE**
>
> The CEditView class assigns the "EDIT" predefined Windows window class to the view window. A window belonging to this Windows window class is known as an *edit control*. The Windows code that supports an edit control not only stores the text displayed in the control, but also provides a large set of editing features.

Once DeleteContents has obtained the address of the view object, it uses it to call the CWnd::SetWindowText function to set the window text to the empty string, thereby deleting the document text.

> **NOTE**
>
> The size of the buffer that the CEditView window uses to store text is limited to approximately 40KB (the exact limit depending upon the amount of free space available in the program's heap). If you try to open a file that is larger than this, the CEditView code displays a warning and does not read in the file. If you try to type in more than this amount of text, the view window stops accepting characters (without issuing a warning).

Next, you must add code to the document's Serialize function to read and write the text when the user opens or saves a document. Fortunately, the CEditView class provides a member function named `SerializeRaw` that does all the work for you. Therefore, you should delete the existing code from the `CMinieditDoc::Serialize` function in the MINIEDOC.CPP file (that is, the `if` and `else` statements) and add the following statements:

```
void CMinieditDoc::Serialize(CArchive& ar)
{
    POSITION Pos = GetFirstViewPosition ();
    CEditView *PCEditView = (CEditView *)GetNextView (Pos);
    PCEditView->SerializeRaw (ar);
}
```

As in `DeleteContents`, the `GetFirstViewPosition` and `GetNextView` function calls obtain a pointer to the program's view object. The `SerializeRaw` function reads and writes the file as pure text (without storing class information in the file).

Finally, to implement the drag-drop file opening feature, include a call to `DragAcceptFiles` within the `InitInstance` function in MINIEDIT.CPP:

```
BOOL CMinieditApp::InitInstance()
{
    // other statements ...

    // create a new (empty) document
    OnFileNew();

    m_pMainWnd->DragAcceptFiles ();

    // other statements ...
}
```

For the MINIEDIT program, you do not need to set the modified flag (as described in the previous section), because the `CEditView` class handles this task for you.

The MINIEDIT Source Code

The following listings, Listings 10.9 through 10.16, provide the C++ source code for the version of MINIEDIT you created in this chapter. A complete copy of these files is included in the \MINIEDT2 subdirectory within the directory in which you installed the companion disk.

The CArchive Read and Write Functions

In this chapter, you learned how to read or write a data member that is a fundamental type using the CArchive overloaded << and >> operators. You also learned how to read or write a member object by calling the object's Serialize member function. CArchive also provides Read and Write functions that allow you to read or write arbitrary blocks of data. You might need to use these functions, for example, to store a structure or a text buffer.

The Read function has the following form:

```
UINT Read (void FAR* lpBuf, UINT nMax);
```

where lpBuf is the address of the memory location that is to receive the data, and nMax is the number of bytes to read.

The Write function has the following form:

```
void Write (const void FAR* lpBuf, UINT nMax);
```

where lpBuf is the address of the block of data you want to write, and nMax is the number of bytes to write. The Write function writes only the raw bytes from the specified location; it does not format the data or add class information.

Listing 10.9

```
// miniedit.h : main header file for the MINIEDIT application
//

#ifndef __AFXWIN_H__
    #error include 'stdafx.h' before including this file for PCH
#endif

#include "resource.h"       // main symbols
```

```
//////////////////////////////////////////////////////////////////////////////
// CMinieditApp:
// See miniedit.cpp for the implementation of this class
//

class CMinieditApp : public CWinApp
{
public:
    CMinieditApp();

// Overrides
    virtual BOOL InitInstance();

// Implementation

    //{{AFX_MSG(CMinieditApp)
    afx_msg void OnAppAbout();
        // NOTE - the ClassWizard will add and remove member functions here.
        //      DO NOT EDIT what you see in these blocks of generated code !
    //}}AFX_MSG
    DECLARE_MESSAGE_MAP()
};

//////////////////////////////////////////////////////////////////////////////
```

Listing 10.10

```
// miniedit.cpp : Defines the class behaviors for the application.
//

#include "stdafx.h"
#include "miniedit.h"

#include "mainfrm.h"
#include "miniedoc.h"
#include "minievw.h"

#ifdef _DEBUG
#undef THIS_FILE
static char BASED_CODE THIS_FILE[] = __FILE__;
#endif
```

```
////////////////////////////////////////////////////////////////////////
// CMinieditApp

BEGIN_MESSAGE_MAP(CMinieditApp, CWinApp)
    //{{AFX_MSG_MAP(CMinieditApp)
    ON_COMMAND(ID_APP_ABOUT, OnAppAbout)
        // NOTE - the ClassWizard will add and remove mapping macros here.
        //    DO NOT EDIT what you see in these blocks of generated code !
    //}}AFX_MSG_MAP
    // Standard file based document commands
    ON_COMMAND(ID_FILE_NEW, CWinApp::OnFileNew)
    ON_COMMAND(ID_FILE_OPEN, CWinApp::OnFileOpen)
END_MESSAGE_MAP()

////////////////////////////////////////////////////////////////////////
// CMinieditApp construction

CMinieditApp::CMinieditApp()
{
    // TODO: add construction code here,
    // Place all significant initialization in InitInstance
}

////////////////////////////////////////////////////////////////////////
// The one and only CMinieditApp object

CMinieditApp NEAR theApp;

////////////////////////////////////////////////////////////////////////
// CMinieditApp initialization

BOOL CMinieditApp::InitInstance()
{
    // Standard initialization
    // If you are not using these features and wish to reduce the size
    //  of your final executable, you should remove from the following
    //  the specific initialization routines you do not need.

    SetDialogBkColor();        // set dialog background color to gray
    LoadStdProfileSettings();  // Load standard INI file options (including MRU)

    // Register the application's document templates.  Document templates
    //  serve as the connection between documents, frame windows and views.
```

```cpp
    AddDocTemplate(new CSingleDocTemplate(IDR_MAINFRAME,
        RUNTIME_CLASS(CMinieditDoc),
        RUNTIME_CLASS(CMainFrame),       // main SDI frame window
        RUNTIME_CLASS(CMinieditView)));

    // create a new (empty) document
    OnFileNew();

    m_pMainWnd->DragAcceptFiles ();

    if (m_lpCmdLine[0] != '\0')
    {
        // TODO: add command line processing here
    }

    return TRUE;
}


/////////////////////////////////////////////////////////////////////////////
// CAboutDlg dialog used for App About

class CAboutDlg : public CDialog
{
public:
    CAboutDlg();

// Dialog Data
    //{{AFX_DATA(CAboutDlg)
    enum { IDD = IDD_ABOUTBOX };
    //}}AFX_DATA

// Implementation
protected:
    virtual void DoDataExchange(CDataExchange* pDX);    // DDX/DDV support
    //{{AFX_MSG(CAboutDlg)
        // No message handlers
    //}}AFX_MSG
    DECLARE_MESSAGE_MAP()
};

CAboutDlg::CAboutDlg() : CDialog(CAboutDlg::IDD)
{
    //{{AFX_DATA_INIT(CAboutDlg)
    //}}AFX_DATA_INIT
}
```

```
void CAboutDlg::DoDataExchange(CDataExchange* pDX)
{
   CDialog::DoDataExchange(pDX);
   //{{AFX_DATA_MAP(CAboutDlg)
   //}}AFX_DATA_MAP
}

BEGIN_MESSAGE_MAP(CAboutDlg, CDialog)
   //{{AFX_MSG_MAP(CAboutDlg)
      // No message handlers
   //}}AFX_MSG_MAP
END_MESSAGE_MAP()

// App command to run the dialog
void CMinieditApp::OnAppAbout()
{
   CAboutDlg aboutDlg;
   aboutDlg.DoModal();
}

////////////////////////////////////////////////////////////////////
// CMinieditApp commands
```

Listing 10.11

```
// miniedoc.h : interface of the CMinieditDoc class
//
////////////////////////////////////////////////////////////////////

class CMinieditDoc : public CDocument
{
protected: // create from serialization only
   CMinieditDoc();
   DECLARE_DYNCREATE(CMinieditDoc)

   virtual void DeleteContents ();

// Attributes
public:

// Operations
public:
```

```
// Implementation
public:
   virtual ~CMinieditDoc();
   virtual void Serialize(CArchive& ar);   // overridden for document i/o
#ifdef _DEBUG
   virtual  void AssertValid() const;
   virtual  void Dump(CDumpContext& dc) const;
#endif
protected:
   virtual  BOOL  OnNewDocument();

// Generated message map functions
protected:
   //{{AFX_MSG(CMinieditDoc)
      // NOTE - the ClassWizard will add and remove member functions here.
      //    DO NOT EDIT what you see in these blocks of generated code !
   //}}AFX_MSG
   DECLARE_MESSAGE_MAP()
};

///////////////////////////////////////////////////////////////////////////
```

Listing 10.12

```
// miniedoc.cpp : implementation of the CMinieditDoc class
//

#include "stdafx.h"
#include "miniedit.h"

#include "miniedoc.h"

#ifdef _DEBUG
#undef THIS_FILE
static char BASED_CODE THIS_FILE[] = __FILE__;
#endif

///////////////////////////////////////////////////////////////////////////
// CMinieditDoc

IMPLEMENT_DYNCREATE(CMinieditDoc, CDocument)

BEGIN_MESSAGE_MAP(CMinieditDoc, CDocument)
   //{{AFX_MSG_MAP(CMinieditDoc)
```

```
      // NOTE - the ClassWizard will add and remove mapping macros here.
      //    DO NOT EDIT what you see in these blocks of generated code !
   //}}AFX_MSG_MAP
END_MESSAGE_MAP()

/////////////////////////////////////////////////////////////////////////////
// CMinieditDoc construction/destruction

CMinieditDoc::CMinieditDoc()
{
   // TODO: add one-time construction code here
}

CMinieditDoc::~CMinieditDoc()
{
}

BOOL CMinieditDoc::OnNewDocument()
{
   if (!CDocument::OnNewDocument())
      return FALSE;
   // TODO: add reinitialization code here
   // (SDI documents will reuse this document)
   return TRUE;
}


/////////////////////////////////////////////////////////////////////////////
// CMinieditDoc serialization

void CMinieditDoc::Serialize(CArchive& ar)
{
   POSITION Pos = GetFirstViewPosition ();
   CEditView *PCEditView = (CEditView *)GetNextView (Pos);
   PCEditView->SerializeRaw (ar);
}


/////////////////////////////////////////////////////////////////////////////
// CMinieditDoc diagnostics

#ifdef _DEBUG
void CMinieditDoc::AssertValid() const
{
   CDocument::AssertValid();
}
```

```
void CMinieditDoc::Dump(CDumpContext& dc) const
{
   CDocument::Dump(dc);
}

#endif //_DEBUG

/////////////////////////////////////////////////////////////////////////////
// CMinieditDoc commands

void CMinieditDoc::DeleteContents ()
   {
   POSITION Pos = GetFirstViewPosition ();
   CEditView *PCEditView = (CEditView *)GetNextView (Pos);
   PCEditView->SetWindowText ("");
   }
```

Listing 10.13

```
// mainfrm.h : interface of the CMainFrame class
//
/////////////////////////////////////////////////////////////////////////////

class CMainFrame : public CFrameWnd
{
protected: // create from serialization only
   CMainFrame();
   DECLARE_DYNCREATE(CMainFrame)

// Attributes
public:

// Operations
public:

// Implementation
public:
   virtual ~CMainFrame();
#ifdef _DEBUG
   virtual  void AssertValid() const;
   virtual  void Dump(CDumpContext& dc) const;
#endif
```

```
// Generated message map functions
protected:
    //{{AFX_MSG(CMainFrame)
        // NOTE - the ClassWizard will add and remove member functions here.
        //      DO NOT EDIT what you see in these blocks of generated code !
    //}}AFX_MSG
    DECLARE_MESSAGE_MAP()
};
```

///

Listing 10.14

```
// mainfrm.cpp : implementation of the CMainFrame class
//

#include "stdafx.h"
#include "miniedit.h"

#include "mainfrm.h"

#ifdef _DEBUG
#undef THIS_FILE
static char BASED_CODE THIS_FILE[] = __FILE__;
#endif

/////////////////////////////////////////////////////////////////////////////
// CMainFrame

IMPLEMENT_DYNCREATE(CMainFrame, CFrameWnd)

BEGIN_MESSAGE_MAP(CMainFrame, CFrameWnd)
    //{{AFX_MSG_MAP(CMainFrame)
        // NOTE - the ClassWizard will add and remove mapping macros here.
        //      DO NOT EDIT what you see in these blocks of generated code !
    //}}AFX_MSG_MAP
END_MESSAGE_MAP()

/////////////////////////////////////////////////////////////////////////////
// CMainFrame construction/destruction

CMainFrame::CMainFrame()
{
    // TODO: add member initialization code here
}
```

```
CMainFrame::~CMainFrame()
{
}

//////////////////////////////////////////////////////////////////////
// CMainFrame diagnostics

#ifdef _DEBUG
void CMainFrame::AssertValid() const
{
    CFrameWnd::AssertValid();
}

void CMainFrame::Dump(CDumpContext& dc) const
{
    CFrameWnd::Dump(dc);
}

#endif //_DEBUG

//////////////////////////////////////////////////////////////////////
// CMainFrame message handlers
```

Listing 10.15

```
// minievw.h : interface of the CMinieditView class
//
//////////////////////////////////////////////////////////////////////

class CMinieditView : public CEditView
{
protected: // create from serialization only
    CMinieditView();
    DECLARE_DYNCREATE(CMinieditView)

// Attributes
public:
    CMinieditDoc* GetDocument();

// Operations
public:
```

```
// Implementation
public:
    virtual ~CMinieditView();
    virtual void OnDraw(CDC* pDC);   // overridden to draw this view
#ifdef _DEBUG
    virtual void AssertValid() const;
    virtual void Dump(CDumpContext& dc) const;
#endif

// Generated message map functions
protected:
    //{{AFX_MSG(CMinieditView)
        // NOTE - the ClassWizard will add and remove member functions here.
        //     DO NOT EDIT what you see in these blocks of generated code !
    //}}AFX_MSG
    DECLARE_MESSAGE_MAP()
};

#ifndef _DEBUG // debug version in minievw.cpp
inline CMinieditDoc* CMinieditView::GetDocument()
    { return (CMinieditDoc*) m_pDocument; }
#endif
```

///

Listing 10.16

```
// minievw.cpp : implementation of the CMinieditView class
//

#include "stdafx.h"
#include "miniedit.h"

#include "miniedoc.h"
#include "minievw.h"

#ifdef _DEBUG
#undef THIS_FILE
static char BASED_CODE THIS_FILE[] = __FILE__;
#endif

///////////////////////////////////////////////////////////////////////////
// CMinieditView
```

```
IMPLEMENT_DYNCREATE(CMinieditView, CEditView)

BEGIN_MESSAGE_MAP(CMinieditView, CEditView)
    //{{AFX_MSG_MAP(CMinieditView)
        // NOTE - the ClassWizard will add and remove mapping macros here.
        //    DO NOT EDIT what you see in these blocks of generated code !
    //}}AFX_MSG_MAP
END_MESSAGE_MAP()

/////////////////////////////////////////////////////////////////////////////
// CMinieditView construction/destruction

CMinieditView::CMinieditView()
{
    // TODO: add construction code here
}


CMinieditView::~CMinieditView()
{
}

/////////////////////////////////////////////////////////////////////////////
// CMinieditView drawing

void CMinieditView::OnDraw(CDC* pDC)
{
    CMinieditDoc* pDoc = GetDocument();

    // TODO: add draw code here
}


/////////////////////////////////////////////////////////////////////////////
// CMinieditView diagnostics

#ifdef _DEBUG
void CMinieditView::AssertValid() const
{
    CEditView::AssertValid();
}

void CMinieditView::Dump(CDumpContext& dc) const
{
    CEditView::Dump(dc);
}
```

```
CMinieditDoc* CMinieditView::GetDocument() // non-debug version is inline
{
    ASSERT(m_pDocument->IsKindOf(RUNTIME_CLASS(CMinieditDoc)));
    return (CMinieditDoc*) m_pDocument;
}

#endif //_DEBUG

/////////////////////////////////////////////////////////////////////////////
// CMinieditView message handlers
```

Summary

In this chapter, you learned how to add file I/O capability to the program's document class. The example programs given in this chapter illustrated the following general techniques and concepts:

- The MFC classes provide message handlers for the New, Open, Save, and Save As commands on the File menu. You therefore do not need to use ClassWizard to define handlers for these commands. You do, however, need to write code to support the MFC message handlers.

- The MFC classes also automatically maintain a list on the File menu of the most recently opened files. The user can choose one of these items to quickly reopen a file.

- The MFC handlers for the Open and Save As commands display the standard File Open and File Save As dialog boxes for obtaining the file name from the user.

- You can edit the IDR_MAINFRAME string resource in App Studio to specify the default file extension that is used by the File Open and File Save As dialog boxes.

- Before opening the document, the MFC handlers for the New and Open commands call the DeleteContents member function of the document class. You should write an overriding version of this function that deletes the document data.

- The MFC handlers for the Open, Save, and Save As commands open the file and then call the `Serialize` member function of your document class to perform the actual reading or writing of data.

- AppWizard defines a minimal `Serialize` function within your document class. You should add code to this function to read or write the data stored by the document class.

- The `Serialize` function is passed a reference to a `CArchive` object that is attached to the open file, and provides member functions for reading or writing data to this file.

- The `Serialize` function can read or write a data member that is a fundamental type by using the overloaded << and >> operators with the `CArchive` object.

- The `Serialize` function can read or write a member object by calling the object's own `Serialize` function. If the member object belongs to a class you have defined, you must add a `Serialize` function to that class, which reads or writes the object's data.

- If the view class is derived from `CEditView`, you can quickly store or load the text displayed in the view window by calling the `CEditView` member function `SerializeRaw`.

- You can read or write arbitrary blocks of data by calling the `CArchive` member functions `Read` or `Write`.

- Whenever the program data has been changed, the document class should call the `CDocument` member function `SetModifiedFlag`. Calling this function notifies the MFC that the document has changed; the MFC will subsequently give the user an opportunity to save the data before the data is deleted.

- You can provide support for the Windows drag-drop feature by placing a call to the `DragAcceptFiles` member function of the main window class within the `InitInstance` function.

Scrolling and Splitting Views

Adding scrolling capability

Adding splitting capability

Updating the views

The MINIDRAW source code

11

In this chapter, you will learn how to add scrolling and splitting capabilities to the view window of an MFC program. The scrolling capability allows the user to view and edit any portion of a document that is larger than the view window. The splitting capability allows the user to create more than one view of a single document, and to scroll each view independently. You will discover that these two features are relatively easy to add to a program; almost all of the work is done by the special-purpose MFC classes that support the features.

To illustrate the programming techniques, the chapter shows you how to add scrolling and splitting to the MINIDRAW program. You should add the features to the MINIDRAW source files you created in the previous chapter. (If you did not create theses files, you can obtain a copy of them from the \MINIDRW3 subdirectory of the directory containing the companion disk files.)

Adding Scrolling Capability

In the previous version of MINIDRAW, if a drawing was larger than the current size of the view window, the user could view and edit only the portion of the drawing that fit within the window. You will now add vertical and horizontal scroll bars to the view window, as well as the code necessary to support scrolling, so that the user can view or edit any portion of a drawing that is larger than the window. The MINIDRAW scroll bars that you will implement are shown in Figure 11.1.

The first step is to derive the MINIDRAW view class from CScrollView *rather than* CView. Like the CEditView class (which you used in the MINIEDIT program to create an edit window), CScrollView is a special-purpose view class derived from the general purpose CView class. The hierarchy of MFC view classes is illustrated in Figure 11.2 (CFormView will be discussed in Chapter 13). Simply deriving the view class from CScrollView automatically adds scroll bars to the view window, and provides most of the code for supporting scrolling operations. You will, however, have to add some supporting code of your own.

To derive the view class from CScrollView, simply replace all occurrences of the class name CView with the class name CScrollView, within the MINIDVW.H and MINIDVW.CPP source files. (If your files match the ones listed in the book, you will find one occurrence of CView in MINIDVW.H and eight occurrences in MINIDVW.CPP.)

FIGURE 11.1:

The MINIDRAW scroll bars

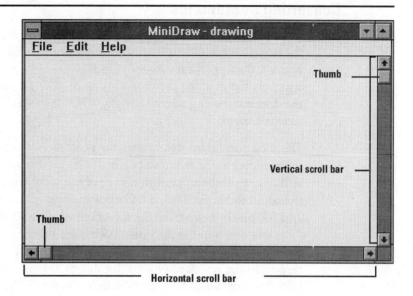

FIGURE 11.2:

The hierarchy of the view classes

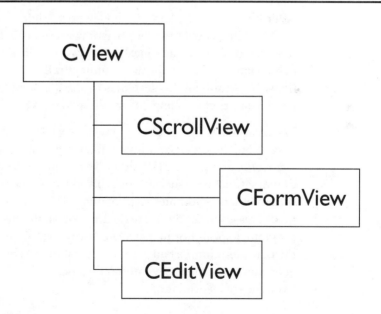

Converting Coordinates

Before you make the next change to the code, you should understand a little about the way that the CScrollView code supports scrolling. When a document is first opened, the upper-left corner of the drawing appears at the upper-left corner of the window, just as in the previous version of MINIDRAW. If, however, the user scrolls the document using a scroll bar, the MFC adjusts a drawing attribute known as the *viewport origin*.

The viewport origin determines the position of the text or graphics that you draw with respect to the window. Normally, if you draw a dot at the coordinates (0, 0), it will appear at the upper-left corner of the view window, and if you draw a dot at the coordinates (50, 100), it will appear 50 pixels from the left edge of the window and 100 pixels down from the top of the window. If, however, the user has scrolled 75 pixels down in the document using the vertical scroll bar, the MFC will adjust the viewport origin so that both of these dots will appear at *higher* positions with respect to the window. Now, a dot that is drawn at (0, 0) will no longer be visible (all output drawn outside of the window is simply ignored), and a dot drawn at (50, 100) will appear 25 pixels down from the top of the window. Figure 11.3 illustrates the view window before and after scrolling.

After the MFC has adjusted the viewport origin in response to a scrolling action, the MINIDRAW OnDraw function redraws the lines in the view window, specifying the same coordinates for each line that it always specifies. However, because of the change in the viewport origin, the lines automatically appear at their proper scrolled positions. The beauty of this system is that the OnDraw function does not need to be altered to support scrolling; the scrolling logic is handled invisibly by the MFC.

The coordinates that you specify when you draw an object are known as the *logical coordinates*; the actual coordinates of an object within the window are known as *device coordinates*. Figure 11.4 shows the difference. All coordinates passed to MFC drawing functions (such as MoveTo and LineTo) are logical coordinates. However, certain other coordinates used by the MFC (such as the cursor position passed to mouse message handlers) are device coordinates. Before scrolling was added to the program, logical coordinates were always equal to device coordinates and the distinction was unimportant. Now that scrolling has been added to the program, however, you must make several modifications to the code to convert between these two types of coordinates.

A view window before and after
scrolling

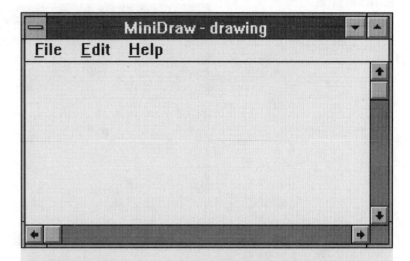

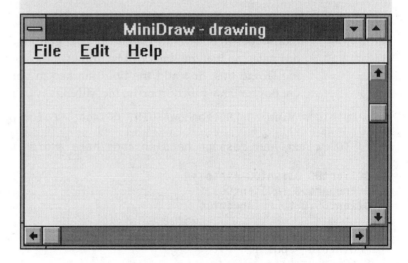

FIGURE 11.4:

Logical coordinates vs. device coordinates; in this figure, the user has scrolled down 75 pixels

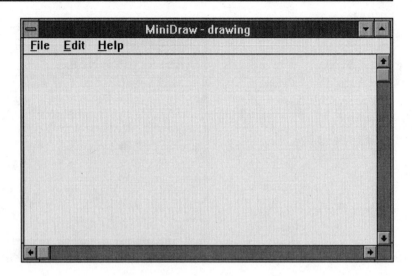

Specifically, you must convert the position of the mouse pointer that is passed to the mouse message-handling functions (point) from device coordinates to logical coordinates, so that the lines will be drawn at the correct positions within the drawing. To do this, first add the lines marked in bold in the following code to the OnLButtonDown function in the file MINIDVW.CPP:

```
void CMinidrawView::OnLButtonDown(UINT nFlags, CPoint point)
{
    // TODO: Add your message handler code here and/or call default

    CClientDC ClientDC (this);
    OnPrepareDC (&ClientDC);
    ClientDC.DPtoLP (&point);

    mPointOrigin = point;
    mPointOld = point;
    SetCapture ();
    mDragging = 1;

    // other statements ...

}
```

To convert device coordinates to logical coordinates for a particular device, you must use a device context object that is associated with that device. Recall that a device context object manages output to a device; it stores drawing attributes and provides member functions for displaying text or graphics. The first added statement creates a device context object associated with the view window. The second statement is a call to the CScrollView member function OnPrepareDC, which adjusts the viewpoint origin for the device context object based upon the current scrolled position of the drawing. (The viewpoint origin is one of the drawing attributes stored by a device context object.) Finally, the third statement is a call to the CDC member function DPtoLP, which converts the cursor position stored in point from device coordinates to logical coordinates, using the new viewpoint origin that was just set. Once point has been converted to logical coordinates, the coordinates it contains can be used for drawing the line.

NOTE The device context object that is passed to the OnDraw function has *already* had its viewpoint origin properly adjusted for the current scrolled position of the drawing. However, whenever you create your own device context object, you must pass it to the OnPrepareDC function to adjust the viewpoint origin, before you use it.

You should now add the same three statements to the OnMouseMove and OnLButtonUp mouse-handling functions in MINIDVW.CPP. The following code shows the position of the statements you should add to OnMouseMove:

```
void CMinidrawView::OnMouseMove(UINT nFlags, CPoint point)
{
    // TODO: Add your message handler code here and/or call default

    CClientDC ClientDC (this);
    OnPrepareDC (&ClientDC);
    ClientDC.DPtoLP (&point);

    ::SetCursor (mHCross);

    // other statements ...

}
```

and the following shows the position of the statements within OnLButtonUp:

```
void CMinidrawView::OnLButtonUp(UINT nFlags, CPoint point)
{
    // TODO: Add your message handler code here and/or call default

    if (mDragging)
        {
        mDragging = 0;
        ::ReleaseCapture ();
        ::ClipCursor (NULL);

        CClientDC ClientDC (this);
        OnPrepareDC (&ClientDC);
        ClientDC.DPtoLP (&point);

        ClientDC.SetROP2 (R2_NOT);

    // other statements ...

}
```

Limiting the Drawing Size

When the user moves a scroll bar thumb (see Figure 11.1) to a particular position within the scroll bar, the MFC code in CScrollView must scroll to the corresponding position in the drawing. For example, if the user drags the thumb to the bottom of the vertical scroll bar, the MFC must scroll to the bottom of the drawing; similarly, when the user drags the thumb to the right end of the horizontal scroll bar, the MFC must scroll to the right edge of the drawing. Consequently, the MFC must know the overall *size* of the drawing.

To report the size of the drawing for the MINIDRAW program, you should override the OnInitialUpdate virtual function, by adding the following declaration to the protected section of the CMinidrawView class definition in MINIDVW.H,

```
protected:
    CString mClassName;
    int mDragging;
    HCURSOR mHCross;
    CPoint mPointOld;
    CPoint mPointOrigin;
```

```
virtual void OnInitialUpdate ();
virtual BOOL PreCreateWindow (CREATESTRUCT& cs);
```

and by adding the following function definition to the end of the MINIDVW.CPP file:

```
void CMinidrawView::OnInitialUpdate ()
    {
    SIZE Size = {640, 480};
    SetScrollSizes (MM_TEXT, Size);
    CScrollView::OnInitialUpdate ();
    }
```

The MFC calls the OnInitialUpdate member function of the view class immediately before a new drawing is first displayed (when the program begins running, and in response to the New and Open menu commands).

The call to the CScrollView member function SetScrollSizes tells the MFC the size of the drawing. The horizontal and vertical dimensions of the drawing are assigned to a SIZE structure, which is passed as the second parameter. In the current version of the MINIDRAW program, the drawing is simply set to a constant size: 640 pixels wide and 480 pixels high. (These dimensions were chosen to make the drawing the same size as the full Windows screen in standard VGA mode.)

TIP

A full-featured drawing program would probably allow the user to set the size of each new drawing. This would be especially important if the program prints drawings, so that the user can create drawings that are the appropriate size for the printed page. After the user specifies the size, the size should be stored by the document class, and when the drawing is saved in a file, the size should be saved along with the other drawing data.

> **NOTE**
>
> In the MINIDRAW program, the document has a fixed size, and therefore the size needs to be specified only once. If your application allows the document size to change as the user enters or deletes data, you must call `SetScrollSizes` each time the size changes; this is best done within an `OnUpdate` member function of the view class, which will be explained later in the chapter (in the section "Redrawing Efficiently").

The first parameter passed to `SetScrollSizes` indicates the *mapping mode* that you are using. Like the viewport origin, the mapping mode is a drawing attribute maintained by the device context object. The mapping mode specifies the units and coordinate system used to draw text and graphics. The MINIDRAW program (as well as all of the other example programs in the book) uses the `MM_TEXT` mapping mode. In the `MM_TEXT` mapping mode, all units are in pixels, horizontal coordinates increase as you go to the right, and vertical coordinates increase as you go down (see Figure 11.5). Chapter 16 briefly describes the alternative mapping modes.

FIGURE 11.5:

The MM_TEXT mapping mode

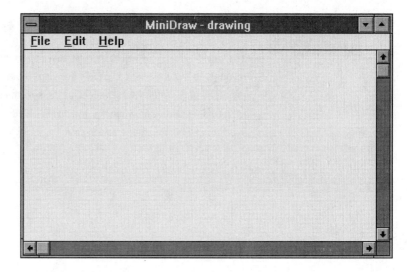

Because a MINIDRAW drawing has a specified size, you must add features to the program that prevent the user from drawing lines *outside* of the drawing area. (As the program is currently written, if the view window is larger than the drawing, the user could draw lines outside of the drawing; scrolling would not work properly with these extraneous lines.) The first step is to add code to the OnDraw function to draw a border at the right and bottom of the drawing area whenever the view window is redrawn; these borders would show the program user the boundaries of the drawing. To do this, add the bold lines to the OnDraw function in the MINIDVW.CPP file:

```
void CMinidrawView::OnDraw(CDC* pDC)
{
    CMinidrawDoc* pDoc = GetDocument();

    // TODO: add draw code here

    CSize ScrollSize = GetTotalSize ();
    pDC->MoveTo (ScrollSize.cx, 0);
    pDC->LineTo (ScrollSize.cx, ScrollSize.cy);
    pDC->LineTo (0, ScrollSize.cy);

    int Index = pDoc->GetNumLines ();
    while (Index--)
        pDoc->GetLine (Index)->Draw (pDC);
}
```

The new code first calls the CScrollView member function GetTotalSize, which returns a CSize object containing the size of the drawing (that is, the drawing size you set through the call to the SetScrollSizes function). The code then uses the dimensions contained in the CSize object to draw lines at the right and bottom edges of the drawing.

Next, you need to add code to the OnLButtonDown message handler to prevent the user from placing lines outside of the drawing area. To do this, rewrite the OnLButtonDown in the MINIDVW.CPP file, so that it is as follows (the new or changed lines are marked in bold):

```
void CMinidrawView::OnLButtonDown(UINT nFlags, CPoint point)
{
    // TODO: Add your message handler code here and/or call default
```

```
CClientDC ClientDC (this);
OnPrepareDC (&ClientDC);
ClientDC.DPtoLP (&point);

// test whether cursor is within drawing area of view window:
CSize ScrollSize = GetTotalSize ();
CRect ScrollRect (0, 0, ScrollSize.cx, ScrollSize.cy);
if (!ScrollRect.PtInRect (point))
    return;

// save cursor position, capture mouse, & set dragging flag:
mPointOrigin = point;
mPointOld = point;
SetCapture ();
mDragging = 1;

// clip mouse cursor:
ClientDC.LPtoDP (&ScrollRect);
CRect ViewRect;
GetClientRect (&ViewRect);
CRect IntRect;
IntRect.IntersectRect (&ScrollRect, &ViewRect);
ClientToScreen (&IntRect);
::ClipCursor (&IntRect);

CScrollView::OnLButtonDown(nFlags, point);
}
```

Because the view class received a mouse message, the mouse cursor must be within the view window; the cursor, however, may be outside the area of the drawing. To test whether the cursor is within the drawing, the added code defines an object of the MFC CRect class (named ScrollRect) and assigns this object the dimensions of the drawing (obtained by calling GetTotalSize). The code then passes the coordinates of the cursor to the CRect member function PtInRect, which returns TRUE only if the cursor coordinates fall within the rectangular area stored in ScrollRect. If the cursor is found to be outside the drawing, the function returns immediately so that the user cannot start drawing a line outside of the drawing.

In addition to preventing the user from *initiating* a line outside of the drawing area, the function must also prevent the user from *extending* a line beyond the drawing area. Accordingly, the code you added must confine the cursor to the portion of the view window that is within the drawing; in other words, it must restrict the cursor to the *intersection* of the drawing and the view window. (Recall that in the previous version of MINIDRAW, the cursor was confined so that it could be moved *anywhere* within the view window.) To do this, the added code first calls the CDC member function LPtoDP to convert the coordinates of the drawing stored in ScrollRect from logical coordinates to device coordinates. It then defines a CRect object, View-Rect, assigning it the device coordinates of the view window (obtained by calling GetClientRect). Next, it defines another CRect object, IntRect, and calls the CRect member function IntersectRect to assign IntRect the coordinates of the *intersection* of the drawing area and the view window area. Finally, it calls the CWnd::ClientToScreen function to convert IntRect to screen coordinates, and it passes IntRect to ::ClipCursor to confine the cursor to the intersection area. These rectangular areas are illustrated in Figure 11.6.

FIGURE 11.6a:

The areas in which the mouse cursor is confined for a drawing that is smaller than the view window, and for a drawing that is larger than the view window; in both cases, the cursor is confined within the intersection of the view window and the drawing

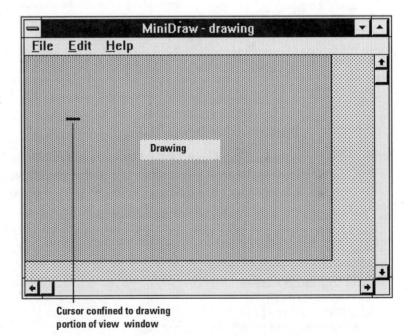

Cursor confined to drawing
portion of view window

FIGURE 11.6b:

The areas in which the mouse cursor is confined for a drawing that is smaller than the view window, and for a drawing that is larger than the view window; in both cases, the cursor is confined within the intersection of the view window and the drawing

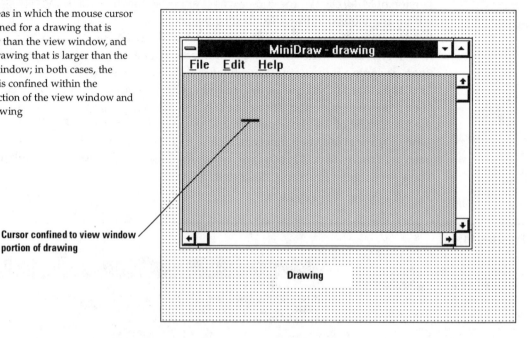

Cursor confined to view window portion of drawing

Drawing

Changing the Mouse Cursor

As a final refinement, you will now modify the program so that the mouse cursor is set to the cross shape when it is within the drawing area of the view window (to indicate that a line can be drawn) and to the standard arrow shape when the cursor is outside of the drawing area (to indicate that a line cannot be drawn). To do this, add the mHArrow data member to the CMinidrawView class definition in MINIDVW.H,

```
protected:
    CString mClassName;
    int mDragging;
    HCURSOR mHArrow;
    HCURSOR mHCross;
    CPoint mPointOld;
    CPoint mPointOrigin;
```

and initialize `mHArrow` within the `CMinidrawView` constructor in MINIDVW.CPP, as follows:

```
CMinidrawView::CMinidrawView()
{
    // TODO: add construction code here

    mDragging = 0;
    mHArrow = AfxGetApp ()->LoadStandardCursor (IDC_ARROW);
    mHCross = AfxGetApp ()->LoadStandardCursor (IDC_CROSS);
}
```

This initialization assigns `mHArrow` a handle for the standard arrow-shaped mouse cursor.

Next, modify the `OnMouseMove` function in MINIDVW.CPP so that it is as follows:

```
void CMinidrawView::OnMouseMove(UINT nFlags, CPoint point)
{
    // TODO: Add your message handler code here and/or call default

    CClientDC ClientDC (this);
    OnPrepareDC (&ClientDC);
    ClientDC.DPtoLP (&point);

    CSize ScrollSize = GetTotalSize ();
    CRect ScrollRect (0, 0, ScrollSize.cx, ScrollSize.cy);
    if (ScrollRect.PtInRect (point))
        ::SetCursor (mHCross);
    else
        ::SetCursor (mHArrow);

    if (mDragging)
        {
        ClientDC.SetROP2 (R2_NOT);
        ClientDC.MoveTo (mPointOrigin);
        ClientDC.LineTo (mPointOld);
        ClientDC.MoveTo (mPointOrigin);
        ClientDC.LineTo (point);
        mPointOld = point;
        }

    CScrollView::OnMouseMove(nFlags, point);
}
```

Rather than always displaying the cross-shaped cursor, the new version of On-MouseMove displays the cross-shaped cursor when the cursor is within the drawing area (ScrollRect), and it displays the arrow-shaped cursor when the cursor is outside of the drawing area. Figure 11.7 illustrates the MINIDRAW program when the drawing is smaller than the view window, showing the line that marks the edges of the drawing. In this figure, notice that because the drawing fits entirely within the view window, the MFC code has hidden the scroll bars. (The scroll bars will reappear if the window size is reduced so that the drawing no longer fits completely within the window.)

FIGURE 11.7:

The MINIDRAW program with a drawing that is smaller than the view window

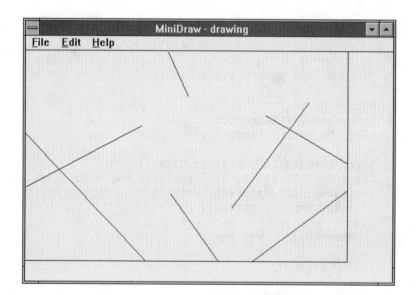

Adding Splitting Capability

In this section, you will add a split box to the MINIDRAW program window, which will allow the user to divide the window into two separate view windows, also known as *panes*. The border between the two panes is known as the *split bar*. The two view windows display the same drawing; however, each can be scrolled independently to display different parts of this drawing. To divide the window, the user can double-click the split box (to divide it into two equal views) or drag the split box to the desired position. When the window is split, a single vertical scroll bar scrolls both view windows simultaneously; however, each view has its own horizontal scroll bar so that the views can be scrolled independently in the horizontal direction. These features are illustrated in Figure 11.8.

To add splitting capability to the program, you must modify the main frame window class. First, add declarations for mSplitterWnd and OnCreateClient to the CMainFrame class definition in MAINFRM.H:

```
class CMainFrame : public CFrameWnd
{
protected: // create from serialization only
    CMainFrame();
    DECLARE_DYNCREATE(CMainFrame)

protected:
    CSplitterWnd mSplitterWnd;
    virtual BOOL OnCreateClient (LPCREATESTRUCT lpcs, CCreateContext* pContext);

// remainder of CMainFrame definition ...

}
```

FIGURE 11.8a:

The MINIDRAW program before the view window is split, immediately after it is split, and after the right pane has been scrolled horizontally

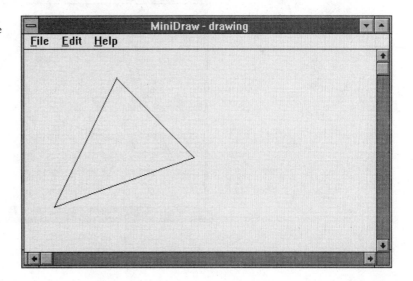

FIGURE 11.8b:

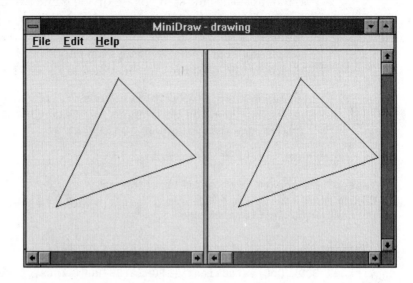

FIGURE 11.8c:

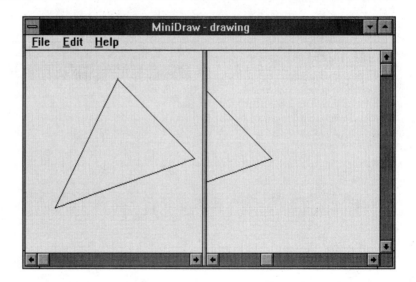

Next, add the following OnCreateClient definition to the end of the MAIN-FRM.CPP file:

```
BOOL CMainFrame::OnCreateClient (LPCREATESTRUCT lpcs, CCreateContext* pContext)
   {
   return mSplitterWnd.Create
      (this,             // parent of splitter window
      1,                 // maximum rows
      2,                 // maximum columns
      CSize (15, 15),    // minimum view window size
      pContext);         // pass on context information
   }
```

The new member object mSplitterWnd is an instance of the MFC class CSplitterWnd (which is derived from CWnd). This object serves to create and manage a splitter window, which is a window that contains one or more view windows.

The MFC calls the virtual function OnCreateClient when the main frame window is first created. The default version of this function creates a single view window that fills the client area of the main frame window. The overriding version of this function that you just defined calls CSplitterWnd::Create to create a splitter window *rather than* creating a view window. The splitter window itself initially creates a single view window; if the user later double-clicks the split box, the splitter window then creates another view window to provide a second view of the drawing.

The first parameter passed to Create specifies the parent of the splitter window; passing this makes the splitter window a child of the main frame window.

NOTE The splitter window is a child of the main frame window. In turn, each view window is a child of the splitter window.

The second parameter specifies the maximum number of views in the vertical direction; passing 1 means that the user *cannot* divide the window with a horizontal split bar (hence, no horizontal split box appears in the window). Similarly, the third parameter specifies the maximum number of views in the horizontal direction; passing 2 means that the user can divide the window into a left and right view, as shown in Figure 11.8. You can assign only 1 or 2 to the second or third parameter; if you assigned 2 to both of these parameters, the user could divide the window into four views (try it!).

The fourth parameter sets the minimum horizontal and vertical sizes of a view; the user is not permitted to move the split bar to a position that would create a view that has a smaller horizontal or vertical dimension. The fifth parameter passes on context information that was passed to the `OnCreateClient` function.

Updating the Views

Each view window created by the splitter window is managed by an object of the `CMinidrawView` class (the same class that managed the single view window in the previous version of MINIDRAW). The MFC automatically calls the `CMinidraw-View::OnDraw` function (which you defined previously) to redraw a view window whenever some external event has invalidated the window data (for example, the user has enlarged the window or removed an overlapping window).

When the user draws a line in one view window, the other view window needs to be redrawn so that the line will appear in *both* views (provided that the second view is scrolled to an area of the drawing containing the line). The MFC, however, does *not* automatically call the `OnDraw` function of the second view. Rather, after drawing a line in one view, the program must explicitly call the `UpdateAllViews` member function of the document class to force the MFC to call the `OnDraw` function of the other view. Accordingly, you should add the following call to `UpdateAllViews` to the end of the routine that draws the line in the `OnLButtonUp` function in MINIDVW.CPP:

```
void CMinidrawView::OnLButtonUp(UINT nFlags, CPoint point)
{
    // TODO: Add your message handler code here and/or call default

    if (mDragging)
        {
        mDragging = 0;
        ::ReleaseCapture ();
        ::ClipCursor (NULL);
        CClientDC ClientDC (this);
        ClientDC.SetROP2 (R2_NOT);
        ClientDC.MoveTo (mPointOrigin);
        ClientDC.LineTo (mPointOld);
        ClientDC.SetROP2 (R2_COPYPEN);
        ClientDC.MoveTo (mPointOrigin);
        ClientDC.LineTo (point);
```

```
    CMinidrawDoc* PDoc = GetDocument();
    PDoc->AddLine (mPointOrigin.x, mPointOrigin.y, point.x, point.y);
    PDoc->UpdateAllViews (this);
    }

  CView::OnLButtonUp(nFlags, point);
}
```

The UpdateAllViews function (defined in CDocument) forces the OnDraw function to be called for all views associated with the document, *except* the one indicated by the first parameter. In MINIDRAW, passing this to UpdateAllViews results in calling the OnDraw function for the other view only. (The current view does not need redrawing because it already displays the new line.) As a result of this addition, when the user completes drawing a line in one view, it quickly appears in the other view.

> **NOTE**   If you pass 0 to UpdateAllViews *all* views will be redrawn. The MINIDRAW program can have at most two views. If both a horizontal and a vertical split box were included, a single document interface program could have as many as four views of a single document. As you will see in Chapter 12, in a multiple document interface program, there can be more than four views of a single document.

Redrawing Efficiently

A problem with the technique given in the previous section is that when the user draws a single line in one view, the other view is forced to recreate the entire drawing, even portions of the drawing that are not currently visible in the view window. In this section, you will modify the MINIDRAW program so that when the user draws a line in one view, the second view redraws *only the affected portion* of the drawing, increasing the efficiency of updating the views.

The first step is to provide a member function of the CLine class, GetDimRect, which supplies the dimensions of the rectangle that bounds the line stored in the object; this rectangle represents the portion of the window that is affected when the line is drawn. Add the following GetDimRect declaration to the public section of the CLine definition in MINIDDOC.H,

```
public:
    CLine (int X1, int Y1, int X2, int Y2)
        {
        mX1 = X1;
        mY1 = Y1;
        mX2 = X2;
        mY2 = Y2;
        }
    void Draw (CDC *PDC);
    CRect GetDimRect ();
    virtual void Serialize (CArchive& ar);
```

and add the following function definition to the end of the MINIDDOC.CPP implementation file:

```
CRect CLine::GetDimRect ()
    {
    return CRect
      (min (mX1, mX2),
       min (mY1, mY2),
       max (mX1, mX2) + 1,
       max (mY1, mY2) + 1);
    }
```

GetDimRect returns a CRect object containing the dimensions of the bounding rectangle; the min and max macros (defined in WINDOWS.H) are used to make sure that the left field is smaller than the right field, and that the top field is smaller than the bottom field (otherwise, some of the functions that will be called will interpret the rectangle as empty).

The next step is to modify the AddLine member function of the document class so that it returns a pointer to the CLine object that stores the newly added line. Change the AddLine declaration (which appears in the public section of the CMinidrawDoc definition in MINIDDOC.H) so that it reads as follows:

```
CLine *AddLine (int X1, int Y1, int X2, int Y2);
```

Now change the AddLine definition in MINIDDOC.CPP as follows:

```
CLine *CMinidrawDoc::AddLine (int X1, int Y1, int X2, int Y2)
    {
    CLine *PLine = new CLine (X1, Y1, X2, Y2);
```

```
    mObArray.Add (PLine);
    SetModifiedFlag ();
    return PLine;
    }
```

Next, you should change the call to UpdateAllViews in the OnLButtonUp function (in MINIDVW.CPP) to the following:

```
void CMinidrawView::OnLButtonUp(UINT nFlags, CPoint point)
{
    // TODO: Add your message handler code here and/or call default

    if (mDragging)
        {
        mDragging = 0;
        ::ReleaseCapture ();
        ::ClipCursor (NULL);

        CClientDC ClientDC (this);
        OnPrepareDC (&ClientDC);
        ClientDC.DPtoLP (&point);

        ClientDC.SetROP2 (R2_NOT);
        ClientDC.MoveTo (mPointOrigin);
        ClientDC.LineTo (mPointOld);
        ClientDC.SetROP2 (R2_COPYPEN);
        ClientDC.MoveTo (mPointOrigin);
        ClientDC.LineTo (point);

        CMinidrawDoc* PDoc = GetDocument();
        CLine *PCLine;
        PCLine = PDoc->AddLine (mPointOrigin.x, mPointOrigin.y, point.x, point.y);
        PDoc->UpdateAllViews (this, 0, PCLine);
        }

    CScrollView::OnLButtonUp(nFlags, point);
}
```

The new code saves the pointer to the new CLine object that is returned by Add-Line, and then passes this pointer as the third parameter to UpdateAllViews. UpdateAllViews has the following format:

```
void UpdateAllViews (CView* pSender, LPARAM lHint = 0L, CObject* pHint = NULL);
```

The second and third parameters (which are optional) supply information ("hints") about the modification that has been made to the document. You will now see how this information can be used to increase the efficiency of redrawing the view windows.

The CDocument::UpdateAllViews function calls the OnUpdate virtual member function of each view object, passing OnUpdate the values of the two hint parameters (lHint and pHint). The default implementation of OnUpdate (defined in CView) ignores the hint values and always causes the *entire view window* to be redrawn. To increase the efficiency of redrawing, you should define an overriding version of OnUpdate, which uses the hint information to cause only the affected area of the view window to be redrawn. To do this for the MINIDRAW program, add the following declaration to the protected section of the CMinidrawView class definition in MINIDVW.H,

```
virtual void OnUpdate (CView* pSender, LPARAM lHint, CObject* pHint);
```

and add the following definition to the end of the MINIDVW.CPP file:

```
void CMinidrawView::OnUpdate (CView* pSender, LPARAM lHint, CObject* pHint)
    {
    if (pHint != 0)
        {
        CRect InvalidRect = ((CLine *)pHint)->GetDimRect ();
        CClientDC ClientDC (this);
        OnPrepareDC (&ClientDC);
        ClientDC.LPtoDP (&InvalidRect);
        InvalidateRect (&InvalidRect);
        }
    else
        CScrollView::OnUpdate (pSender, lHint, pHint);
    }
```

If OnUpdate has been called by UpdateAllViews, the pHint parameter will contain a pointer to a CLine object. OnUpdate, however, is also called by the default implementation of the OnInitialUpdate function (which receives control when a new drawing is first displayed, as explained earlier in the chapter); in this case, the pHint parameter will be set to 0. OnUpdate therefore begins by testing the value of pHint.

If pHint parameter contains a pointer to a CLine object (that is, it is nonzero), OnUpdate performs the following steps:

1. It uses the CLine pointer to call the CLine::GetDimRect function to obtain the bounding rectangle of the newly added line, which it stores in InvalidRect.

2. It creates a device context object, ClientDC, and calls CScrollView::On-PrepareDC to adjust the object for the current scrolled position of the drawing.

3. It calls CDC::LPtoDP to convert the coordinates in InvalidRect from logical coordinates to device coordinates.

4. It passes InvalidRect to the CWnd member function InvalidateRect. This function call marks the specified rectangular area for redrawing, and causes the view class's OnDraw function to be called. The coordinates passed to InvalidateRect must be device coordinates.

> **NOTE** The total portion of the view window marked for redrawing is known as the *update region*. Calling InvalidateRect adds the specified rectangular area to the current update region; this process is known as *invalidating* the rectangular area.

If, however, pHint does not contain a CLine pointer (that is, it is zero), OnUpdate calls the default implementation of OnUpdate, which marks the *entire* view window for redrawing and causes OnDraw to be called.

The current version of the OnDraw function always redraws the entire drawing, even if only a portion of the drawing is marked for redrawing. You will now rewrite OnDraw so that it redraws only the marked area, thus increasing its efficiency. The following is the new version of OnDraw:

```
void CMinidrawView::OnDraw(CDC* pDC)
{
    CMinidrawDoc* pDoc = GetDocument();

    // TODO: add draw code here

    CSize ScrollSize = GetTotalSize ();
    pDC->MoveTo (ScrollSize.cx, 0);
    pDC->LineTo (ScrollSize.cx, ScrollSize.cy);
    pDC->LineTo (0, ScrollSize.cy);

    CRect ClipRect;
    CRect DimRect;
    CRect IntRect;
```

```
CLine *PLine;
pDC->GetClipBox (&ClipRect);

int Index = pDoc->GetNumLines ();
while (Index--)
    {
    PLine = pDoc->GetLine (Index);
    DimRect = PLine->GetDimRect ();
    if (IntRect.IntersectRect (DimRect, ClipRect))
        PLine->Draw (pDC);
    }
}
```

The new version of OnDraw calls the CDC::GetClipBox function to obtain the dimensions of the area that is marked for repainting. Before drawing each line, it calls CLine::GetDimRect to obtain the bounding rectangle of the line, and it then calls CRect::IntersectRect to determine whether the bounding rectangle of the line falls within the area marked for repainting. (IntersectRect returns TRUE only if the two rectangles passed to it have a nonempty intersection; that is, if they overlap.) It draws the line *only* if the line's bounding rectangle is within the marked area.

NOTE If you attempt to draw outside the area marked for repainting (the update region), the output is clipped (that is, ignored). In MINIDRAW, it would probably be just as efficient to simply redraw all of the lines, because drawing lines is fast. However, a full-featured drawing or CAD program typically draws much more complex figures; in such a program, the added efficiency of redrawing only those figures that fall within the update region can be significant.

The workings of the code you added in this section can be briefly summarized as follows: When the user draws a line in one view window, the view class calls CDocument::UpdateAllViews, passing it a pointer to the CLine object holding the new line. UpdateAllViews then calls the OnUpdate function for the other view, passing it the CLine pointer. OnUpdate invalidates the portion of the window bounding the new line, causing OnDraw to be called. Finally, OnDraw redraws only those lines that fall within the invalidated area (that is, the new line plus any other lines in that area).

Note that when the view window needs repainting due to an external event (such as the user removing an overlapping window), Windows also invalidates only the area of the window that needs redrawing. The new version of OnDraw then draws only the lines that fall within this area. Thus, the new OnDraw version is more efficient, whether it is called in response to a newly drawn line or in response to an external event.

The MINIDRAW Source Code

The following are the C++ source files for the version of MINIDRAW presented in this chapter. A complete copy of these files is contained in the \MINIDRW4 companion disk file subdirectory.

Listing 11.1

```
// minidraw.h : main header file for the MINIDRAW application
//

#ifndef __AFXWIN_H__
    #error include 'stdafx.h' before including this file for PCH
#endif

#include "resource.h"        // main symbols

/////////////////////////////////////////////////////////////////////////////
// CMinidrawApp:
// See minidraw.cpp for the implementation of this class
//

class CMinidrawApp : public CWinApp
{
public:
    CMinidrawApp();

// Overrides
    virtual BOOL InitInstance();

// Implementation

    //{{AFX_MSG(CMinidrawApp)
    afx_msg void OnAppAbout();
```

```
    // NOTE - the ClassWizard will add and remove member functions here.
    //     DO NOT EDIT what you see in these blocks of generated code !
  //}}AFX_MSG
  DECLARE_MESSAGE_MAP()
};
```

///

Listing 11.2

```
// minidraw.cpp : Defines the class behaviors for the application.
//

#include "stdafx.h"
#include "minidraw.h"

#include "mainfrm.h"
#include "miniddoc.h"
#include "minidvw.h"

#ifdef _DEBUG
#undef THIS_FILE
static char BASED_CODE THIS_FILE[] = __FILE__;
#endif

/////////////////////////////////////////////////////////////////////////////
// CMinidrawApp

BEGIN_MESSAGE_MAP(CMinidrawApp, CWinApp)
    //{{AFX_MSG_MAP(CMinidrawApp)
    ON_COMMAND(ID_APP_ABOUT, OnAppAbout)
        // NOTE - the ClassWizard will add and remove mapping macros here.
        //     DO NOT EDIT what you see in these blocks of generated code !
    //}}AFX_MSG_MAP
    // Standard file based document commands
    ON_COMMAND(ID_FILE_NEW, CWinApp::OnFileNew)
    ON_COMMAND(ID_FILE_OPEN, CWinApp::OnFileOpen)
END_MESSAGE_MAP()

/////////////////////////////////////////////////////////////////////////////
// CMinidrawApp construction

CMinidrawApp::CMinidrawApp()
{
```

```
   // TODO: add construction code here,
   // Place all significant initialization in InitInstance
}

/////////////////////////////////////////////////////////////////////////////
// The one and only CMinidrawApp object

CMinidrawApp NEAR theApp;

/////////////////////////////////////////////////////////////////////////////
// CMinidrawApp initialization

BOOL CMinidrawApp::InitInstance()
{
   // Standard initialization
   // If you are not using these features and wish to reduce the size
   //  of your final executable, you should remove from the following
   //  the specific initialization routines you do not need.

   SetDialogBkColor();          // set dialog background color to gray
   LoadStdProfileSettings();    // Load standard INI file options (including MRU)

   // Register the application's document templates.  Document templates
   //  serve as the connection between documents, frame windows and views.

   AddDocTemplate(new CSingleDocTemplate(IDR_MAINFRAME,
         RUNTIME_CLASS(CMinidrawDoc),
         RUNTIME_CLASS(CMainFrame),       // main SDI frame window
         RUNTIME_CLASS(CMinidrawView)));

   // create a new (empty) document
   OnFileNew();

   m_pMainWnd->DragAcceptFiles ();

   if (m_lpCmdLine[0] != '\0')
   {
      // TODO: add command line processing here
   }

   return TRUE;
}
```

```
////////////////////////////////////////////////////////////////////////
// CAboutDlg dialog used for App About

class CAboutDlg : public CDialog
{
public:
   CAboutDlg();

// Dialog Data
   //{{AFX_DATA(CAboutDlg)
   enum { IDD = IDD_ABOUTBOX };
   //}}AFX_DATA

// Implementation
protected:
   virtual void DoDataExchange(CDataExchange* pDX);    // DDX/DDV support
   //{{AFX_MSG(CAboutDlg)
      // No message handlers
   //}}AFX_MSG
   DECLARE_MESSAGE_MAP()
};

CAboutDlg::CAboutDlg() : CDialog(CAboutDlg::IDD)
{
   //{{AFX_DATA_INIT(CAboutDlg)
   //}}AFX_DATA_INIT
}

void CAboutDlg::DoDataExchange(CDataExchange* pDX)
{
   CDialog::DoDataExchange(pDX);
   //{{AFX_DATA_MAP(CAboutDlg)
   //}}AFX_DATA_MAP
}

BEGIN_MESSAGE_MAP(CAboutDlg, CDialog)
   //{{AFX_MSG_MAP(CAboutDlg)
      // No message handlers
   //}}AFX_MSG_MAP
END_MESSAGE_MAP()

// App command to run the dialog
void CMinidrawApp::OnAppAbout()
```

```
{
   CAboutDlg aboutDlg;
   aboutDlg.DoModal ();
}

/////////////////////////////////////////////////////////////////////////////
// CMinidrawApp commands
```

Listing 11.3

```
// miniddoc.h : interface of the CMinidrawDoc class
//
/////////////////////////////////////////////////////////////////////////////

class CLine : public CObject
{
protected:
   int mX1, mY1, mX2, mY2;

   CLine ()
       {}
   DECLARE_SERIAL (CLine)

public:
   CLine (int X1, int Y1, int X2, int Y2)
       {
       mX1 = X1;
       mY1 = Y1;
       mX2 = X2;
       mY2 = Y2;
       }
   void Draw (CDC *PDC);
   CRect GetDimRect ();
   virtual void Serialize (CArchive& ar);
};

class CMinidrawDoc : public CDocument
{
protected: // create from serialization only
   CMinidrawDoc();
   DECLARE_DYNCREATE(CMinidrawDoc)

protected:
   CObArray mObArray;
```

```
public:
   CLine *AddLine (int X1, int Y1, int X2, int Y2);
   virtual void DeleteContents ();
   CLine *GetLine (int Index);
   int GetNumLines ();

// Attributes
public:

// Operations
public:

// Implementation
public:
   virtual ~CMinidrawDoc();
   virtual void Serialize(CArchive& ar);   // overridden for document i/o
#ifdef _DEBUG
   virtual  void AssertValid() const;
   virtual  void Dump(CDumpContext& dc) const;
#endif
protected:
   virtual  BOOL  OnNewDocument();

// Generated message map functions
protected:
   //{{AFX_MSG(CMinidrawDoc)
   afx_msg void OnEditClearAll();
   afx_msg void OnUpdateEditClearAll(CCmdUI* pCmdUI);
   afx_msg void OnEditUndo();
   afx_msg void OnUpdateEditUndo(CCmdUI* pCmdUI);
   //}}AFX_MSG
   DECLARE_MESSAGE_MAP()
};
```

//

Listing 11.4

```
// miniddoc.cpp : implementation of the CMinidrawDoc class
//

#include "stdafx.h"
#include "minidraw.h"

#include "miniddoc.h"
```

```
#ifdef _DEBUG
#undef THIS_FILE
static char BASED_CODE THIS_FILE[] = __FILE__;
#endif

/////////////////////////////////////////////////////////////////////////////
// CMinidrawDoc

IMPLEMENT_DYNCREATE(CMinidrawDoc, CDocument)

BEGIN_MESSAGE_MAP(CMinidrawDoc, CDocument)
    //{{AFX_MSG_MAP(CMinidrawDoc)
    ON_COMMAND(ID_EDIT_CLEAR_ALL, OnEditClearAll)
    ON_UPDATE_COMMAND_UI(ID_EDIT_CLEAR_ALL, OnUpdateEditClearAll)
    ON_COMMAND(ID_EDIT_UNDO, OnEditUndo)
    ON_UPDATE_COMMAND_UI(ID_EDIT_UNDO, OnUpdateEditUndo)
    //}}AFX_MSG_MAP
END_MESSAGE_MAP()

/////////////////////////////////////////////////////////////////////////////
// CMinidrawDoc construction/destruction

CMinidrawDoc::CMinidrawDoc()
{
    // TODO: add one-time construction code here
}

CMinidrawDoc::~CMinidrawDoc()
{
}

BOOL CMinidrawDoc::OnNewDocument()
{
    if (!CDocument::OnNewDocument())
        return FALSE;
    // TODO: add reinitialization code here
    // (SDI documents will reuse this document)
    return TRUE;
}

/////////////////////////////////////////////////////////////////////////////
// CMinidrawDoc serialization
```

```
void CMinidrawDoc::Serialize(CArchive& ar)
{
    if (ar.IsStoring())
    {
        // TODO: add storing code here

    mObArray.Serialize (ar);
    }
    else
    {
        // TODO: add loading code here

    mObArray.Serialize (ar);
    }
}

/////////////////////////////////////////////////////////////////////////////
// CMinidrawDoc diagnostics

#ifdef _DEBUG
void CMinidrawDoc::AssertValid() const
{
    CDocument::AssertValid();
}

void CMinidrawDoc::Dump(CDumpContext& dc) const
{
    CDocument::Dump(dc);
}

#endif //_DEBUG

/////////////////////////////////////////////////////////////////////////////
// CMinidrawDoc commands

IMPLEMENT_SERIAL (CLine, CObject, 1)

void CLine::Draw (CDC *PDC)
    {
    PDC->MoveTo (mX1, mY1);
    PDC->LineTo (mX2, mY2);
    }

CRect CLine::GetDimRect ()
    {
```

```
      return CRect
        (min (mX1, mX2),
         min (mY1, mY2),
         max (mX1, mX2) + 1,
         max (mY1, mY2) + 1);
      }

void CLine::Serialize (CArchive& ar)
    {
    if (ar.IsStoring())
        ar << (WORD)mX1 << (WORD)mY1 << (WORD)mX2 << (WORD)mY2;
    else
        ar >> (WORD &)mX1 >> (WORD &)mY1 >> (WORD &)mX2 >> (WORD &)mY2;
    }

CLine *CMinidrawDoc::AddLine (int X1, int Y1, int X2, int Y2)
    {
    CLine *PLine = new CLine (X1, Y1, X2, Y2);
    mObArray.Add (PLine);
    SetModifiedFlag ();
    return PLine;
    }

CLine *CMinidrawDoc::GetLine (int Index)
    {
    if (Index < 0 || Index > mObArray.GetUpperBound ())
        return 0;
    return (CLine *)mObArray.GetAt (Index);
    }

int CMinidrawDoc::GetNumLines ()
    {
    return mObArray.GetSize ();
    }

void CMinidrawDoc::DeleteContents ()
    {
    int Index = mObArray.GetSize ();
    while (Index--)
        delete mObArray.GetAt (Index);
    mObArray.RemoveAll ();
    }

void CMinidrawDoc::OnEditClearAll()
{
```

```
    // TODO: Add your command handler code here

    DeleteContents ();
    UpdateAllViews (0);
    SetModifiedFlag ();
}

void CMinidrawDoc::OnUpdateEditClearAll(CCmdUI* pCmdUI)
{
    // TODO: Add your command update UI handler code here

    pCmdUI->Enable (mObArray.GetSize ());
}

void CMinidrawDoc::OnEditUndo()
{
    // TODO: Add your command handler code here

    int Index = mObArray.GetUpperBound ();
    if (Index > -1)
        {
        delete mObArray.GetAt (Index);
        mObArray.RemoveAt (Index);
        }
    UpdateAllViews (0);
    SetModifiedFlag ();
}

void CMinidrawDoc::OnUpdateEditUndo(CCmdUI* pCmdUI)
{
    // TODO: Add your command update UI handler code here

    pCmdUI->Enable (mObArray.GetSize ());
}
```

Listing 11.5

```
// mainfrm.h : interface of the CMainFrame class
//
/////////////////////////////////////////////////////////////////////

class CMainFrame : public CFrameWnd
{
protected: // create from serialization only
    CMainFrame();
```

```
    DECLARE_DYNCREATE(CMainFrame)

protected:
    CSplitterWnd mSplitterWnd;
    virtual BOOL OnCreateClient (LPCREATESTRUCT lpcs, CCreateContext* pContext);

// Attributes
public:

// Operations
public:

// Implementation
public:
    virtual ~CMainFrame();
#ifdef _DEBUG
    virtual  void AssertValid() const;
    virtual  void Dump(CDumpContext& dc) const;
#endif


// Generated message map functions
protected:
    //{{AFX_MSG(CMainFrame)
        // NOTE - the ClassWizard will add and remove member functions here.
        //      DO NOT EDIT what you see in these blocks of generated code !
    //}}AFX_MSG
    DECLARE_MESSAGE_MAP()
};

/////////////////////////////////////////////////////////////////////////////
```

Listing 11.6

```
// mainfrm.cpp : implementation of the CMainFrame class
//

#include "stdafx.h"
#include "minidraw.h"

#include "mainfrm.h"

#ifdef _DEBUG
#undef THIS_FILE
```

```
static char BASED_CODE THIS_FILE[] = __FILE__;
#endif

/////////////////////////////////////////////////////////////////////////////
// CMainFrame

IMPLEMENT_DYNCREATE(CMainFrame, CFrameWnd)

BEGIN_MESSAGE_MAP(CMainFrame, CFrameWnd)
    //{{AFX_MSG_MAP(CMainFrame)
        // NOTE - the ClassWizard will add and remove mapping macros here.
        //     DO NOT EDIT what you see in these blocks of generated code !
    //}}AFX_MSG_MAP
END_MESSAGE_MAP()

/////////////////////////////////////////////////////////////////////////////
// CMainFrame construction/destruction

CMainFrame::CMainFrame()
{
    // TODO: add member initialization code here
}

CMainFrame::~CMainFrame()
{
}

/////////////////////////////////////////////////////////////////////////////
// CMainFrame diagnostics

#ifdef _DEBUG
void CMainFrame::AssertValid() const
{
    CFrameWnd::AssertValid();
}

void CMainFrame::Dump(CDumpContext& dc) const
{
    CFrameWnd::Dump(dc);
}

#endif //_DEBUG

/////////////////////////////////////////////////////////////////////////////
// CMainFrame message handlers
```

```
BOOL CMainFrame::OnCreateClient (LPCREATESTRUCT lpcs, CCreateContext* pContext)
   {
   return mSplitterWnd.Create
      (this,             // parent of splitter window
      1,                 // maximum rows
      2,                 // maximum columns
      CSize (15, 15),    // minimum pane size
      pContext);         // pass on context information
   }
```

Listing 11.7

```
// minidvw.h : interface of the CMinidrawView class
//
/////////////////////////////////////////////////////////////////////////////

class CMinidrawView : public CScrollView
{
protected: // create from serialization only
   CMinidrawView();
   DECLARE_DYNCREATE(CMinidrawView)

protected:
   CString mClassName;
   int mDragging;
   HCURSOR mHArrow;
   HCURSOR mHCross;
   CPoint mPointOld;
   CPoint mPointOrigin;

   virtual void OnInitialUpdate ();
   virtual void OnUpdate (CView* pSender, LPARAM lHint, CObject* pHint);
   virtual BOOL PreCreateWindow (CREATESTRUCT& cs);

// Attributes
public:
   CMinidrawDoc* GetDocument();

// Operations
public:

// Implementation
public:
   virtual ~CMinidrawView();
```

```
    virtual void OnDraw(CDC* pDC);   // overridden to draw this view
#ifdef _DEBUG
    virtual void AssertValid() const;
    virtual void Dump(CDumpContext& dc) const;
#endif

// Generated message map functions
protected:
    //{{AFX_MSG(CMinidrawView)
    afx_msg void OnLButtonDown(UINT nFlags, CPoint point);
    afx_msg void OnMouseMove(UINT nFlags, CPoint point);
    afx_msg void OnLButtonUp(UINT nFlags, CPoint point);
    //}}AFX_MSG
    DECLARE_MESSAGE_MAP()
};

#ifndef _DEBUG // debug version in minidvw.cpp
inline CMinidrawDoc* CMinidrawView::GetDocument()
    { return (CMinidrawDoc*) m_pDocument; }
#endif

/////////////////////////////////////////////////////////////////////////
```

Listing 11.8

```
// minidvw.cpp : implementation of the CMinidrawView class
//

#include "stdafx.h"
#include "minidraw.h"

#include "miniddoc.h"
#include "minidvw.h"

#ifdef _DEBUG
#undef THIS_FILE
static char BASED_CODE THIS_FILE[] = __FILE__;
#endif

/////////////////////////////////////////////////////////////////////////
// CMinidrawView

IMPLEMENT_DYNCREATE(CMinidrawView, CScrollView)
```

```
BEGIN_MESSAGE_MAP(CMinidrawView, CScrollView)
    //{{AFX_MSG_MAP(CMinidrawView)
    ON_WM_LBUTTONDOWN()
    ON_WM_MOUSEMOVE()
    ON_WM_LBUTTONUP()
    ON_WM_KEYDOWN()
    //}}AFX_MSG_MAP
END_MESSAGE_MAP()

/////////////////////////////////////////////////////////////////////////////
// CMinidrawView construction/destruction

CMinidrawView::CMinidrawView()
{
    // TODO: add construction code here

    mDragging = 0;
    mHArrow = AfxGetApp ()->LoadStandardCursor (IDC_ARROW);
    mHCross = AfxGetApp ()->LoadStandardCursor (IDC_CROSS);
}


CMinidrawView::~CMinidrawView()
{
}

/////////////////////////////////////////////////////////////////////////////
// CMinidrawView drawing

void CMinidrawView::OnDraw(CDC* pDC)
{
    CMinidrawDoc* pDoc = GetDocument();

    // TODO: add draw code here

    CSize ScrollSize = GetTotalSize ();
    pDC->MoveTo (ScrollSize.cx, 0);
    pDC->LineTo (ScrollSize.cx, ScrollSize.cy);
    pDC->LineTo (0, ScrollSize.cy);

    CRect ClipRect;
    CRect DimRect;
    CRect IntRect;
    CLine *PLine;
    pDC->GetClipBox (&ClipRect);
```

```
        int Index = pDoc->GetNumLines ();
        while (Index--)
            {
            PLine = pDoc->GetLine (Index);
            DimRect = PLine->GetDimRect ();
            if (IntRect.IntersectRect (DimRect, ClipRect))
                PLine->Draw (pDC);
            }
}

/////////////////////////////////////////////////////////////////////////////
// CMinidrawView diagnostics

#ifdef _DEBUG
void CMinidrawView::AssertValid() const
{
    CScrollView::AssertValid();
}

void CMinidrawView::Dump(CDumpContext& dc) const
{
    CScrollView::Dump(dc);
}

CMinidrawDoc* CMinidrawView::GetDocument() // non-debug version is inline
{
    ASSERT(m_pDocument->IsKindOf(RUNTIME_CLASS(CMinidrawDoc)));
    return (CMinidrawDoc*) m_pDocument;
}

#endif //_DEBUG

/////////////////////////////////////////////////////////////////////////////
// CMinidrawView message handlers

void CMinidrawView::OnLButtonDown(UINT nFlags, CPoint point)
{
    // TODO: Add your message handler code here and/or call default

    CClientDC ClientDC (this);
    OnPrepareDC (&ClientDC);
    ClientDC.DPtoLP (&point);

    // test whether cursor is within drawing area of view window:
    CSize ScrollSize = GetTotalSize ();
```

```
    CRect ScrollRect (0, 0, ScrollSize.cx, ScrollSize.cy);
    if (!ScrollRect.PtInRect (point))
        return;

    // save cursor position, capture mouse, & set dragging flag:
    mPointOrigin = point;
    mPointOld = point;
    SetCapture ();
    mDragging = 1;

    // clip mouse cursor:
    ClientDC.LPtoDP (&ScrollRect);
    CRect ViewRect;
    GetClientRect (&ViewRect);
    CRect IntRect;
    IntRect.IntersectRect (&ScrollRect, &ViewRect);
    ClientToScreen (&IntRect);
    ::ClipCursor (&IntRect);

    CScrollView::OnLButtonDown(nFlags, point);
}

void CMinidrawView::OnMouseMove(UINT nFlags, CPoint point)
{
    // TODO: Add your message handler code here and/or call default

    CClientDC ClientDC (this);
    OnPrepareDC (&ClientDC);
    ClientDC.DPtoLP (&point);

    CSize ScrollSize = GetTotalSize ();
    CRect ScrollRect (0, 0, ScrollSize.cx, ScrollSize.cy);
    if (ScrollRect.PtInRect (point))
        ::SetCursor (mHCross);
    else
        ::SetCursor (mHArrow);

    if (mDragging)
        {
        ClientDC.SetROP2 (R2_NOT);
        ClientDC.MoveTo (mPointOrigin);
        ClientDC.LineTo (mPointOld);
        ClientDC.MoveTo (mPointOrigin);
        ClientDC.LineTo (point);
```

```
        mPointOld = point;
        }

    CScrollView::OnMouseMove(nFlags, point);
}

void CMinidrawView::OnLButtonUp(UINT nFlags, CPoint point)
{
    // TODO: Add your message handler code here and/or call default

    if (mDragging)
        {
        mDragging = 0;
        ::ReleaseCapture ();
        ::ClipCursor (NULL);

        CClientDC ClientDC (this);
        OnPrepareDC (&ClientDC);
        ClientDC.DPtoLP (&point);

        ClientDC.SetROP2 (R2_NOT);
        ClientDC.MoveTo (mPointOrigin);
        ClientDC.LineTo (mPointOld);
        ClientDC.SetROP2 (R2_COPYPEN);
        ClientDC.MoveTo (mPointOrigin);
        ClientDC.LineTo (point);

        CMinidrawDoc* PDoc = GetDocument();
        CLine *PCLine;
        PCLine = PDoc->AddLine (mPointOrigin.x, mPointOrigin.y, point.x, point.y);
        PDoc->UpdateAllViews (this, 0, PCLine);
        }

    CScrollView::OnLButtonUp(nFlags, point);
}

BOOL CMinidrawView::PreCreateWindow (CREATESTRUCT& cs)
    {
    mClassName = AfxRegisterWndClass
        (CS_HREDRAW | CS_VREDRAW,                   // class styles
        0,                                          // no cursor
        (HBRUSH)::GetStockObject (WHITE_BRUSH),     // set white background brush
        0);                                         // no icon
    cs.lpszClass = mClassName;
```

```
    return CScrollView::PreCreateWindow (cs);
    }

void CMinidrawView::OnInitialUpdate ()
    {
    SIZE Size = {640, 480};
    SetScrollSizes (MM_TEXT, Size);
    CScrollView::OnInitialUpdate ();
    }

void CMinidrawView::OnUpdate (CView* pSender, LPARAM lHint, CObject* pHint)
    {
    if (pHint != 0)
        {
        CRect InvalidRect = ((CLine *)pHint)->GetDimRect ();
        CClientDC ClientDC (this);
        OnPrepareDC (&ClientDC);
        ClientDC.LPtoDP (&InvalidRect);
        InvalidateRect (&InvalidRect);
        }
    else
        CScrollView::OnUpdate (pSender, lHint, pHint);
    }
```

Summary

In this chapter, you added scrolling and splitting capabilities to the MINIDRAW program window. The following is a brief summary of the general techniques for adding scrolling:

- If you derive your view class from the MFC class CScrollView, rather than from CView, the view window will display horizontal and vertical scroll bars, and the MFC code will handle most of the logic of scrolling the document displayed in the view window. You must, however, add some supporting code of your own.

- When the user scrolls the document, the MFC adjusts the *viewport origin*, which determines the position of the text or graphics you draw with respect to the view window.

- You do *not* need to modify the OnDraw function to support scrolling. The viewport origin of the device context object passed to OnDraw has already been adjusted. You simply display text or graphics at the correct position within the document. The adjusted viewport origin automatically makes the output appear at the appropriate position with respect to the window.

- If, however, you create your own device context object, you must pass it to the CScrollView::OnPrepareDC function to adjust its viewport origin for the current scrolled position of the document, before you use the device context object.

- The coordinates you specify when you draw an object are known as *logical coordinates*; the actual coordinates of an object with respect to the window are known as *device coordinates*. Once the document has been scrolled, these two types of coordinates are no longer the same.

- The MFC sometimes uses logical coordinates (for example, when you call a drawing function), and it sometimes uses device coordinates (for example, when it reports the position of the mouse cursor to a message handler). You can convert device coordinates to logical coordinates by calling CDC::DPtoLP, and you can convert logical coordinates to device coordinates by calling CDC::LPtoDP.

- You must call the CScrollView::SetScrollSizes function to specify the *size* of the document that is being scrolled. You typically call SetScroll-Sizes from an overriding version of the OnInitialUpdate function, defined as a member of your view class. OnInitialUpdate is called before a new drawing is first displayed.

- If a document has a fixed size, you may need to change the logic of your program to prevent the user from attempting to add text of graphics outside of the document boundaries.

The following is a summary of the general techniques for adding splitting capability:

- Within the main frame window class, add a data member that is an object of the CSplitterWnd MFC class.

- Within the main frame window class, define an overriding version of the virtual function OnCreateClient, which is called when the main frame window is first created.

- From the `OnCreateClient` function, call the `Create` member function of the `CSplitterWnd` object to create a *splitter window*.

- The splitter window displays a horizontal split box, a vertical split box, or both types of split boxes. A split box allows the user to divide the program window into separate view windows, or *panes*.

When a document has more than a single view, a view object must update the other views whenever the user edits the data that it displays. The following are the main steps for doing this efficiently:

- When the user changes the data in a view, the view object calls the `Update-AllViews` member function of the document class, passing it "hint" information, which describes the modification that was made.

- `UpdateAllViews` calls the virtual `OnUpdate` member function of each view object, passing it the hint information. You should define an overriding version of this function that calls the `CWnd::InvalidateRect` function to invalidate the affected area of the view window; this area can be calculated from the hint information.

- `InvalidateRect` causes the `OnDraw` function of the view class to be called. `OnDraw` should call `GetClipBox` to obtain the dimensions of the invalidated area and redraw only the text and graphics that fall within this area.

Writing MDI Applications

- The multiple document interface

- Generating the program

- Modifying the code

- Customizing the resources

- The MINIEDIT source code

12

In the previous chapters in this part of the book, you learned how to write *single document interface*, or *SDI*, Windows programs. An SDI program allows the user to view and edit only one document at a time. In this chapter, you will learn how to write *multiple document interface*, or *MDI*, programs. An MDI program allows the user to open several documents at a time; each document is viewed and edited within a separate child window that is contained within the application workspace of the main program window.

Although managing several open documents might seem to be a difficult task, Windows and the MFC provide code that does most of the work for you. If your application can be written within the strictures of the standard MDI program model, you can take advantage of this code and save a great amount of programming effort. To illustrate the techniques for writing MDI programs, the chapter explains how to write an MDI version of the MINIEDIT editing program.

The Multiple Document Interface

When you first run the MDI version of MINIEDIT, which you will create in this chapter, the program opens a new, empty document in a child window (see Figure 12.1). If you then choose the New or Open... command on the File menu to create a new document or read an existing one, the newly opened document is displayed within a *separate child window* rather than replacing the original document.

You can use the Open... and New commands to open as many documents as you wish. Figure 12.2 shows the program after several documents have been opened. To work on a particular document, you must activate its child window. You can activate a window by clicking in it, or by pressing—repeatedly if necessary—the Ctrl+Tab or Ctrl+F6 key, which activates the *next* child window. You can also activate a specific child window by choosing its title from the Window menu.

You can close the document in the active window by choosing the Close command on the File menu or by double-clicking the system menu in the document's window. The Save, Save As..., and Print commands on the File menu, as well as all of the commands on the Edit menu, affect the document in the active window.

You can click the maximize button in a child window to make that window fill the entire application workspace of the main program window. You can also click the

FIGURE 12.1:

The MDI version of MINIEDIT when the program first starts running

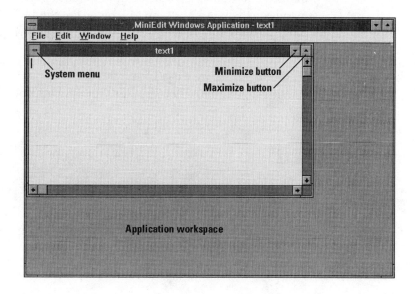

FIGURE 12.2:

The MDI version of MINIEDIT after several documents have been opened

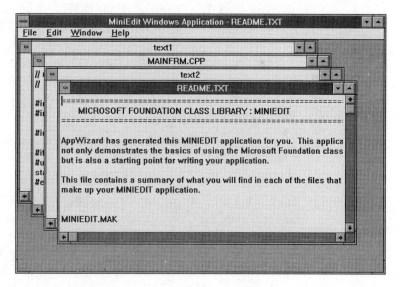

minimize button in a child window to reduce it to an icon. You can choose commands on the Window menu to arrange the child windows in a cascaded (overlapping) or tiled (nonoverlapping) pattern, or to arrange the icons for any child windows that have been minimized.

If all documents are closed, only the File and Help menus are displayed, and the File menu displays only commands for opening new or existing documents.

NOTE   If you use the Open... command to open a document that is already displayed in a child window, the program will simply activate the exisiting child window rather than creating a new window. Thus, a given document can be viewed through only one child window. As you will see later in the chapter, however, some MDI programs allow the user to open two or more child windows on the same document.

Generating the Program

To create the MDI version of MINIEDIT, begin by running AppWizard to generate a new set of source files. First choose the AppWizard... command on the Visual Workbench Project menu. In the MFC AppWizard dialog box select an empty directory that you reserve exclusively for the new program files you are going to create (if you want AppWizard to create a new project directory for you, enter a subdirectory name into the New Subdirectory: list box), and enter the name of the program, MINIEDIT, into the Project Name: text box.

Next, click the Options... button. In the Options dialog box, choose *only* the Multiple Document Interface option and the Generate Source Comments options, as shown in Figure 12.3, and click the OK button.

Back in the MFC AppWizard dialog box, click the Classes... button, and AppWizard will open the Classes dialog box. In the New Application Classes: list, choose the class name `CMinieditDoc` (the program's document class). Into the File Extension: text box, enter `txt` to specify the default file extension, and into the Doc Type Name: text box enter `text`, to specify the default file name. The completed dialog box is shown in Figure 12.4. Click OK when you are done. As a result of specifying

FIGURE 12.3:

The completed Options dialog box for generating the MDI version of the MINIEDIT program

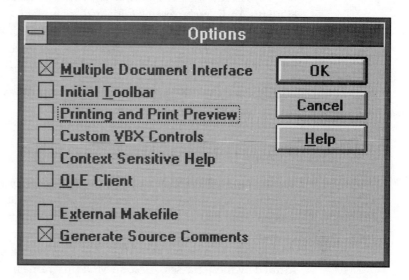

FIGURE 12.4:

The completed Classes dialog box

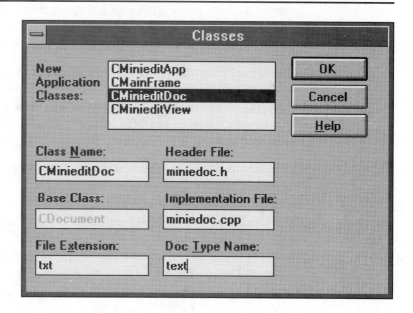

the .txt default file extension, when you later run the program, the File Open and File Save As dialog boxes will initially display all files with the .TXT extension, and the File Save As dialog box will append the .TXT extension if you do not type one. As a result of specifying the text default file name, the new documents you create in MINIEDIT will be assigned the default file names TEXT1, TEXT2, and so on.

Finally, click the OK button in the MFC AppWizard dialog box to generate the source files and to open the new project.

The Program Classes and Files

The classes and files that AppWizard generates for an MDI program are similar to the classes and files it generates for an SDI program (which were described in the section "The Program Classes and Files" in Chapter 7). Like an SDI program, an MDI program contains an application class, a document class, a main frame window class, and a view class. There are, however, some differences in the tasks performed by these classes. Also, an MDI program employs an additional class: a *child frame window class*.

An MDI program's application class, like that of an SDI program, manages the program as a whole and includes an InitInstance member function for initializing the program. In MINIEDIT, the application class is named CMinieditApp; its header file is MINIEDIT.H and its implementation file is MINIEDIT.CPP.

Also like an SDI program, an MDI program's document class stores the document data and performs file I/O. An MDI program, however, creates a separate instance of this class for each open document, rather than reusing a single instance. In MINIEDIT, the document class is named CMinieditDoc; its header file is MINIEDOC.H and its implementation file is MINIEDOC.CPP.

An MDI program's main frame window class, like that of an SDI program, manages the main program window. However, rather than being derived directly from the CFrameWnd MFC class, it is derived from CMDIFrameWnd (which is derived from CFrameWnd). Also, in an MDI program, the main frame window does *not* contain a single view window; rather, it contains the general application workspace. Within the application workspace is a separate *child frame window* for each open document; as you will see, each child frame window contains a separate view window.

Because the main frame window is not associated with a specific open document, its class is *not* included in the program template. (Recall from Chapter 7 that the template stores information on the classes used for storing and displaying a specific document.) Because the main frame window is not automatically created when the first document is opened (as in an SDI program), the InitInstance function must explicitly create it using the following code:

```
// create main MDI Frame window
CMainFrame* pMainFrame = new CMainFrame;
if (!pMainFrame->LoadFrame(IDR_MAINFRAME))
    return FALSE;
pMainFrame->ShowWindow(m_nCmdShow);
pMainFrame->UpdateWindow();
m_pMainWnd = pMainFrame;
```

The first statement creates an instance of the main frame window class, CMain-Frame. The call to the CFrameWnd member function LoadFrame creates the main frame window itself, using the resources that have the IDR_MAINFRAME identifier; these are the resources (the menu, string, and icon) that are associated with the main frame window. The call to CWnd::ShowWindow makes the window visible, and the call to CWnd::UpdateWindow causes the client area of the window to be drawn. Finally, the window handle is stored in the CWinApp data member m_pMainWnd.

In MINIEDIT, the main frame window class header file is MAINFRM.H and its implementation file is MAINFRM.CPP.

In an MDI program, the child frame window class manages the child frame windows. Each child frame window contains a view window for displaying an open document. A child frame window class is not used in an SDI program. Figure 12.5 illustrates the child frame window, as well as the other windows created in an MDI program.

Rather than deriving a custom class to handle the child frame windows, AppWizard uses the predefined MFC class CMDIChildWnd; consequently, the program does not have a header or implementation file for this class. CMDIChildWnd is derived from the general frame window class, CFrameWnd. The hierarchy of the MFC classes used for managing MDI programs is shown in Figure 12.6.

FIGURE 12.5:

The windows in an MDI program; in this figure, there is only a single open document

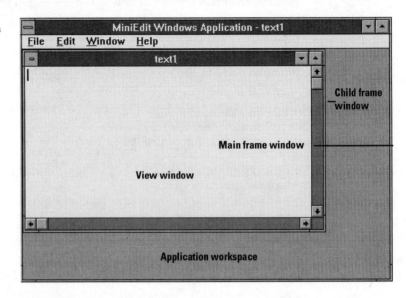

FIGURE 12.6:

The MFC classes used for managing MDI program windows

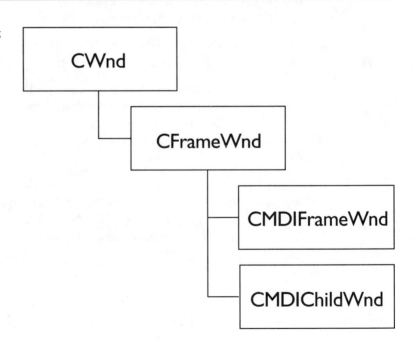

Because the `CMDIChildWnd` class is used for creating and managing the child frame window that frames each document that is opened, the `InitInstance` function includes it in the program's document template (rather than including the main frame window class, as in an SDI program):

```
AddDocTemplate(new CMultiDocTemplate(IDR_TEXTTYPE,
    RUNTIME_CLASS(CMinieditDoc),
    RUNTIME_CLASS(CMDIChildWnd),        // standard MDI child frame
    RUNTIME_CLASS(CMinieditView)));
```

Notice that the template belongs to the class `CMultiDocTemplate`, which is suitable for MDI programs, rather than the class `CSingleDocTemplate`, which was used in the previous version of MINIEDIT. Notice also that the template is assigned the resources with the `IDR_TEXTTYPE` identifier; these are the resources (the menu, string, and icon) associated with the child frame windows.

Finally, the view class in an MDI program is used for creating and managing the view window that displays each open document. The view window for each document occupies the client area of the document's child frame window. In MINIEDIT, the view class is named `CMinieditView`; its header file is MINIEVW.H and its implementation file is MINIEVW.CPP.

Modifying the Code

You will now modify the MINIEDIT source code to provide editing features for each view window and to perform file I/O. As explained in Chapter 8, to provide editing features, you must derive the view class from `CEditView` rather than from `CView`. To do this, change every occurrence of the class name `CView` to `CEditView` within the MINIEVW.H and MINIEVW.CPP source files. (There should be one occurrence of `CView` in MINIEVW.H and four occurrences in MINIEVW.CPP.)

To add support for file I/O, add code as follows to the `Serialize` function in the MINIEDOC.CPP file:

```
//////////////////////////////////////////////////////////////////////////////
// CMinieditDoc serialization

void CMinieditDoc::Serialize(CArchive& ar)
{
```

```
POSITION Pos = GetFirstViewPosition ();
CEditView *PCEditView = (CEditView *)GetNextView (Pos);
PCEditView->SerializeRaw (ar);
}
```

These statements were explained in Chapter 10 (in the section "Adding Supporting Code").

Note that for the MDI version of MINIEDIT you do *not* need to add a DeleteContents function. As explained in Chapter 10, in the SDI version, DeleteContents removes the text from the view window in response to the New command on the

Planning Ahead

In this chapter you spend quite a bit of time adding features to the MDI version of MINIEDIT that are already included in the SDI version. This is necessary because you had to generate an entirely new set of source files to create an MDI program. It is *not* possible to use AppWizard to convert an existing SDI program to an MDI program.

In general, AppWizard cannot be used to add features directly to an existing program. For example, one of the features that AppWizard supports is a program tool bar. If you generate a program without a tool bar, you *cannot* run AppWizard again at a later time to add a tool bar directly to the program. To add a tool bar with AppWizard, you would have to generate an entirely new program, and then either copy the code for the tool bar into your existing program, or copy all features you have added to your existing program into the newly generated source files.

To simplify the code listings and discussions, the exercises in this book use only those AppWizard features that are required for the current version of the example program. Later exercises sometimes have you *add* AppWizard features to create more advanced program versions. For your own applications, however, you can save much programming effort by planning ahead! When you generate an AppWizard program, you should try to include *every* feature that you anticipate needing.

File menu. In the MDI version, however, the New command creates a *new* view window rather than reusing an existing view window; thus, text does not need to be removed. Also, unlike the SDI version, you do not need to add a call to the Drag-AcceptFiles function to support the drag-drop feature in an MDI program, because AppWizard has already added this statement for you.

Customizing the Resources

In this section you will customize the MINIEDIT program resources. You will modify the menu, add accelerator keystrokes, edit one of the program strings, and provide a custom icon. To begin, make sure that the MINIEDIT project is opened, and choose the App Studio command on the Visual Workbench Project menu.

To modify the menu, choose the Menu item in the Type: list box within the App Studio resource dialog box. Notice that because MINIEDIT is now an MDI program, *two* menu identifiers appear in the Resources: list, IDR_MAINFRAME and IDR_TEXTTYPE. IDR_MAINFRAME is the identifier of the menu that is displayed when *no* documents are open; you do not need to modify this menu. IDR_TEXTTYPE is the identifier of the menu displayed when at least one document is open. (The name of this identifier is derived from the "text" default file name you specified when generating the program with AppWizard.) Select the IDR_TEXTTYPE identifier and click the Open button.

In the menu-designing window, first open the File menu. Immediately under the existing Save As… command, add a separator and then a Print command. Table 12.1 shows the properties of the added menu items, and Figure 12.7 shows the completed File menu.

TABLE 12.1: New Items to Add to the File Menu

ID:	Caption:	Other Features
none	none	Separator
ID_FILE_PRINT	&Print\tCtrl+P	none

FIGURE 12.7:

The completed File menu

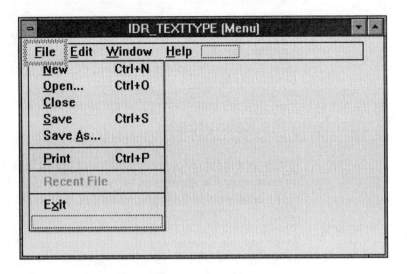

Next, open the Edit menu and, immediately under the existing Paste command, add a Select All command, a separator, and Find..., Find Next, and Replace... commands. These menu items are described in Table 12.2, while the completed Edit menu is shown in Figure 12.8.

TABLE 12.2: New Items to Add to the Edit Menu

ID:	Caption:	Other Features
ID_EDIT_SELECT_ALL	Select &All	none
none	none	Separator
ID_EDIT_FIND	&Find...	none
ID_EDIT_REPEAT	Find &Next\tF3	none
ID_EDIT_REPLACE	&Replace...	none

FIGURE 12.8:

The completed Edit menu

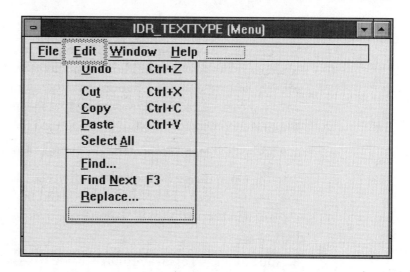

To finish customizing the MINIEDIT menu, open the Window menu, click on the New Window command, and press the Del key to delete the command.

The next step is to add accelerator keystrokes for the Print and Find Next menu commands. To do this, use the procedure that was described in Chapter 8 (in the section "Create the MINIEDIT Program"). Table 12.3 summarizes the properties of the two accelerator keystrokes that are to be defined.

TABLE 12.3: Properties of the Accelerators Keystrokes to Add to the MINIEDIT

ID:	Key:
ID_FILE_PRINT	Ctrl+P
ID_EDIT_REPEAT	F3

Copying Menu Items

You can copy menu items from one program to another. Accordingly, you could copy the new File and Edit menu items from the previous version of MINIEDIT (presented in Chapter 10) rather than redefining these items within the current version. Assuming that the menu-designing window for the current version of MINIEDIT is open, do the following:

1. Choose the Open… command on the App Studio File menu.

2. In the Open dialog box select the MINIEDIT.RC resource file belonging to the *previous version* of MINIEDIT (if you did not create the file, you can find a copy of it in the \MINIEDT2 companion disk subdirectory), and click the OK button.

3. App Studio will open a resource dialog box—labeled "MINIEDIT.RC (MFC Resource Script)"—for the previous version of MINIEDIT. There will now be two resource dialog boxes open in App Studio.

4. In the resource dialog box for the previous MINIEDIT version, select the Menu item in the Type: list, select the `IDR_MAINFRAME` identifier in the Resources: list, and click the Open button. App Studio will now open a menu-designing window for the previous version of MINIEDIT.

5. Copy the desired items from the newly opened menu-designing window to the menu-designing window for the current program version. To copy a menu item from one menu-designing window to the other, press the Ctrl key and then use the mouse to drag the item from the source menu to the target menu (if you drag without pressing Ctrl, the item will be *moved* rather than copied).

The New Window Command

All of the code required to implement the commands on the Window menu is provided by Windows and the MFC. The New Window command on this menu creates an additional child frame window and view window for displaying the document in the currently active child window. The purpose of this command is to allow the user to view and edit a single document within more than one view window.

For the MINIEDIT program, however, the New Window command is deleted for the following reason: A view window derived from `CEditView` stores the document text internally. If the program created more than one view window displaying a single document, it would be difficult to efficiently update other views each time the user makes a change in one view.

In a more conventional MDI program, the document data is stored centrally within the document class object. In such a program, you can allow the user to create multiple document views (through the New Window command or by using a split bar). Whenever the user makes a change in one view, the view class object can call the `UpdateAllViews` member function of the document class to update all the other views, using the techniques described in Chapter 11 (in the section "Updating the Views").

TIP

Rather than defining new accelerator keystrokes, you can copy them from the previous version of MINIEDIT, using the same basic procedure that was described earlier in this section for copying menu items.

Next, you need to edit the IDR_MAINFRAME string resource to modify the program name that is displayed in the main frame window. To do this, select the String Table item in the Type: list within the resource dialog box. Then select the String Segment:0 item in the Resources: list and click the Open button. In the string properties dialog box, select the string with the identifier `IDR_MAINFRAME` (the first string) and click the Properties... button. Now edit the string so that it reads as follows:

```
MiniEdit Windows Application
```

Finally, if you want to customize one or both of the program icons, select the Icon item in the Type: list of the resource dialog box. Notice that the Resources: list displays identifiers for *two* icons. The `IDR_MAINFRAME` icon is displayed when the main frame window is minimized. (It is also displayed in the Windows Program Manager if the program is added to a Program Manager group.) The `IDR_TEXTTYPE` icon is displayed within the application workspace when a child frame window is minimized. To customize one of these icons, select its identifier, click the Open button to open the icon-designing window, and use the commands and tools provided by the App Studio Graphics Editor to create the desired pattern.

Copying an Icon

Once you have opened the icon-designing window, rather that designing a new icon, you can copy an icon from another program. For example, if you created an icon for the previous version of MINIEDIT, you could copy it to the current version. Do the following:

1. Choose the Open... command on the App Studio File menu to open the resource file for the program containing the icon you want to copy (the source icon).

2. Open the icon-designing window for the source icon. Click in the window containing the source icon to make sure it is active.

3. Choose the Copy... command on the App Studio Edit menu, or press Ctrl+C, to copy the source icon into the Clipboard.

4. Click in the icon-designing window for the target icon.

5. Choose the Paste command on the App Studio Edit menu, or press Ctrl+V.

The MINIEDIT Source Code

The following listings, Listings 12.1 through 12.8, are the C++ source code listings for the MDI version of MINIEDIT that you created in this chapter. A complete copy of these files is included in the \MINIEDT3 subdirectory within the directory in which you installed the companion disk.

Listing 12.1

```
// miniedit.h : main header file for the MINIEDIT application
//

#ifndef __AFXWIN_H__
    #error include 'stdafx.h' before including this file for PCH
#endif

#include "resource.h"        // main symbols

/////////////////////////////////////////////////////////////////////////////
// CMinieditApp:
// See miniedit.cpp for the implementation of this class
//

class CMinieditApp : public CWinApp
{
public:
    CMinieditApp();

// Overrides
    virtual BOOL InitInstance();

// Implementation

    //{{AFX_MSG(CMinieditApp)
    afx_msg void OnAppAbout();
        // NOTE - the ClassWizard will add and remove member functions here.
        //    DO NOT EDIT what you see in these blocks of generated code !
    //}}AFX_MSG
    DECLARE_MESSAGE_MAP()
};

/////////////////////////////////////////////////////////////////////////////
```

Listing 12.2

```
// miniedit.cpp : Defines the class behaviors for the application.
//

#include "stdafx.h"
#include "miniedit.h"

#include "mainfrm.h"
#include "miniedoc.h"
#include "minievw.h"

#ifdef _DEBUG
#undef THIS_FILE
static char BASED_CODE THIS_FILE[] = __FILE__;
#endif

/////////////////////////////////////////////////////////////////////////////
// CMinieditApp

BEGIN_MESSAGE_MAP(CMinieditApp, CWinApp)
    //{{AFX_MSG_MAP(CMinieditApp)
    ON_COMMAND(ID_APP_ABOUT, OnAppAbout)
        // NOTE - the ClassWizard will add and remove mapping macros here.
        //     DO NOT EDIT what you see in these blocks of generated code !
    //}}AFX_MSG_MAP
    // Standard file based document commands
    ON_COMMAND(ID_FILE_NEW, CWinApp::OnFileNew)
    ON_COMMAND(ID_FILE_OPEN, CWinApp::OnFileOpen)
END_MESSAGE_MAP()

/////////////////////////////////////////////////////////////////////////////
// CMinieditApp construction

CMinieditApp::CMinieditApp()
{
    // TODO: add construction code here,
    // Place all significant initialization in InitInstance
}

/////////////////////////////////////////////////////////////////////////////
// The one and only CMinieditApp object

CMinieditApp NEAR theApp;
```

```
/////////////////////////////////////////////////////////////////////////////
// CMinieditApp initialization

BOOL CMinieditApp::InitInstance()
{
    // Standard initialization
    // If you are not using these features and wish to reduce the size
    //  of your final executable, you should remove from the following
    //  the specific initialization routines you do not need.

    SetDialogBkColor();           // set dialog background color to gray
    LoadStdProfileSettings();  // Load standard INI file options (including MRU)

    // Register the application's document templates.  Document templates
    //  serve as the connection between documents, frame windows and views.

    AddDocTemplate(new CMultiDocTemplate(IDR_TEXTTYPE,
        RUNTIME_CLASS(CMinieditDoc),
        RUNTIME_CLASS(CMDIChildWnd),          // standard MDI child frame
        RUNTIME_CLASS(CMinieditView)));

    // create main MDI Frame window
    CMainFrame* pMainFrame = new CMainFrame;
    if (!pMainFrame->LoadFrame(IDR_MAINFRAME))
        return FALSE;
    pMainFrame->ShowWindow(m_nCmdShow);
    pMainFrame->UpdateWindow();
    m_pMainWnd = pMainFrame;

    // enable file manager drag/drop and DDE Execute open
    m_pMainWnd->DragAcceptFiles();
    EnableShellOpen();
    RegisterShellFileTypes();

    // simple command line parsing
    if (m_lpCmdLine[0] == '\0')
    {
        // create a new (empty) document
        OnFileNew();
    }
    else if ((m_lpCmdLine[0] == '-' || m_lpCmdLine[0] == '/') &&
        (m_lpCmdLine[1] == 'e' || m_lpCmdLine[1] == 'E'))
    {
        // program launched embedded - wait for DDE or OLE open
    }
```

```
   else
   {
      // open an existing document
      OpenDocumentFile(m_lpCmdLine);
   }

   return TRUE;
}

//////////////////////////////////////////////////////////////////////
// CAboutDlg dialog used for App About

class CAboutDlg : public CDialog
{
public:
   CAboutDlg();

// Dialog Data
   //{{AFX_DATA(CAboutDlg)
   enum { IDD = IDD_ABOUTBOX };
   //}}AFX_DATA

// Implementation
protected:
   virtual void DoDataExchange(CDataExchange* pDX);    // DDX/DDV support
   //{{AFX_MSG(CAboutDlg)
      // No message handlers
   //}}AFX_MSG
   DECLARE_MESSAGE_MAP()
};

CAboutDlg::CAboutDlg() : CDialog(CAboutDlg::IDD)
{
   //{{AFX_DATA_INIT(CAboutDlg)
   //}}AFX_DATA_INIT
}

void CAboutDlg::DoDataExchange(CDataExchange* pDX)
{
   CDialog::DoDataExchange(pDX);
   //{{AFX_DATA_MAP(CAboutDlg)
   //}}AFX_DATA_MAP
}
```

```
BEGIN_MESSAGE_MAP(CAboutDlg, CDialog)
   //{{AFX_MSG_MAP(CAboutDlg)
      // No message handlers
   //}}AFX_MSG_MAP
END_MESSAGE_MAP()

// App command to run the dialog
void CMinieditApp::OnAppAbout()
{
   CAboutDlg aboutDlg;
   aboutDlg.DoModal();
}

/////////////////////////////////////////////////////////////////////////////
// CMinieditApp commands
```

Listing 12.3

```
// miniedoc.h : interface of the CMinieditDoc class
//
/////////////////////////////////////////////////////////////////////////////

class CMinieditDoc : public CDocument
{
protected: // create from serialization only
   CMinieditDoc();
   DECLARE_DYNCREATE(CMinieditDoc)

// Attributes
public:

// Operations
public:

// Implementation
public:
   virtual ~CMinieditDoc();
   virtual void Serialize(CArchive& ar);  // overridden for document i/o
#ifdef _DEBUG
   virtual  void AssertValid() const;
   virtual  void Dump(CDumpContext& dc) const;
#endif
protected:
   virtual  BOOL  OnNewDocument();
```

```
// Generated message map functions
protected:
    //{{AFX_MSG(CMinieditDoc)
        // NOTE - the ClassWizard will add and remove member functions here.
        //     DO NOT EDIT what you see in these blocks of generated code !
    //}}AFX_MSG
    DECLARE_MESSAGE_MAP()
};
```

///

Listing 12.4

```
// miniedoc.cpp : implementation of the CMinieditDoc class
//

#include "stdafx.h"
#include "miniedit.h"

#include "miniedoc.h"

#ifdef _DEBUG
#undef THIS_FILE
static char BASED_CODE THIS_FILE[] = __FILE__;
#endif

/////////////////////////////////////////////////////////////////////////
// CMinieditDoc

IMPLEMENT_DYNCREATE(CMinieditDoc, CDocument)

BEGIN_MESSAGE_MAP(CMinieditDoc, CDocument)
    //{{AFX_MSG_MAP(CMinieditDoc)
        // NOTE - the ClassWizard will add and remove mapping macros here.
        //     DO NOT EDIT what you see in these blocks of generated code !
    //}}AFX_MSG_MAP
END_MESSAGE_MAP()

/////////////////////////////////////////////////////////////////////////
// CMinieditDoc construction/destruction

CMinieditDoc::CMinieditDoc()
{
```

```
    // TODO: add one-time construction code here
}

CMinieditDoc::~CMinieditDoc()
{
}

BOOL CMinieditDoc::OnNewDocument()
{
    if (!CDocument::OnNewDocument())
        return FALSE;
    // TODO: add reinitialization code here
    // (SDI documents will reuse this document)
    return TRUE;
}

/////////////////////////////////////////////////////////////////////////////
// CMinieditDoc serialization

void CMinieditDoc::Serialize(CArchive& ar)
{
    POSITION Pos = GetFirstViewPosition ();
    CEditView *PCEditView = (CEditView *)GetNextView (Pos);
    PCEditView->SerializeRaw (ar);
}

/////////////////////////////////////////////////////////////////////////////
// CMinieditDoc diagnostics

#ifdef _DEBUG
void CMinieditDoc::AssertValid() const
{
    CDocument::AssertValid();
}

void CMinieditDoc::Dump(CDumpContext& dc) const
{
    CDocument::Dump(dc);
}

#endif //_DEBUG

/////////////////////////////////////////////////////////////////////////////
// CMinieditDoc commands
```

Listing 12.5

```
// mainfrm.h : interface of the CMainFrame class
//
///////////////////////////////////////////////////////////////////////////

class CMainFrame : public CMDIFrameWnd
{
    DECLARE_DYNAMIC(CMainFrame)
public:
    CMainFrame();

// Attributes
public:

// Operations
public:

// Implementation
public:
    virtual ~CMainFrame();
#ifdef _DEBUG
    virtual  void AssertValid() const;
    virtual  void Dump(CDumpContext& dc) const;
#endif


// Generated message map functions
protected:
    //{{AFX_MSG(CMainFrame)
        // NOTE - the ClassWizard will add and remove member functions here.
        //    DO NOT EDIT what you see in these blocks of generated code !
    //}}AFX_MSG
    DECLARE_MESSAGE_MAP()
};

///////////////////////////////////////////////////////////////////////////
```

Listing 12.6

```
// mainfrm.cpp : implementation of the CMainFrame class
//

#include "stdafx.h"
#include "miniedit.h"
```

```
#include "mainfrm.h"

#ifdef _DEBUG
#undef THIS_FILE
static char BASED_CODE THIS_FILE[] = __FILE__;
#endif

/////////////////////////////////////////////////////////////////////////////
// CMainFrame

IMPLEMENT_DYNAMIC(CMainFrame, CMDIFrameWnd)

BEGIN_MESSAGE_MAP(CMainFrame, CMDIFrameWnd)
    //{{AFX_MSG_MAP(CMainFrame)
        // NOTE - the ClassWizard will add and remove mapping macros here.
        //    DO NOT EDIT what you see in these blocks of generated code !
    //}}AFX_MSG_MAP
END_MESSAGE_MAP()

/////////////////////////////////////////////////////////////////////////////
// CMainFrame construction/destruction

CMainFrame::CMainFrame()
{
    // TODO: add member initialization code here
}

CMainFrame::~CMainFrame()
{
}

/////////////////////////////////////////////////////////////////////////////
// CMainFrame diagnostics

#ifdef _DEBUG
void CMainFrame::AssertValid() const
{
    CMDIFrameWnd::AssertValid();
}

void CMainFrame::Dump(CDumpContext& dc) const
{
    CMDIFrameWnd::Dump(dc);
}
```

```
#endif //_DEBUG

////////////////////////////////////////////////////////////////////////
// CMainFrame message handlers
```

Listing 12.7

```
// minievw.h : interface of the CMinieditView class
//
////////////////////////////////////////////////////////////////////////

class CMinieditView : public CEditView
{
protected: // create from serialization only
    CMinieditView();
    DECLARE_DYNCREATE(CMinieditView)

// Attributes
public:
    CMinieditDoc* GetDocument();

// Operations
public:

// Implementation
public:
    virtual ~CMinieditView();
    virtual void OnDraw(CDC* pDC);  // overridden to draw this view
#ifdef _DEBUG
    virtual void AssertValid() const;
    virtual void Dump(CDumpContext& dc) const;
#endif

// Generated message map functions
protected:
    //{{AFX_MSG(CMinieditView)
        // NOTE - the ClassWizard will add and remove member functions here.
        //     DO NOT EDIT what you see in these blocks of generated code !
    //}}AFX_MSG
    DECLARE_MESSAGE_MAP()
};
```

```
#ifndef _DEBUG // debug version in minievw.cpp
inline CMinieditDoc* CMinieditView::GetDocument()
   { return (CMinieditDoc*) m_pDocument; }
#endif
```

//

Listing 12.8

```
// minievw.cpp : implementation of the CMinieditView class
//

#include "stdafx.h"
#include "miniedit.h"

#include "miniedoc.h"
#include "minievw.h"

#ifdef _DEBUG
#undef THIS_FILE
static char BASED_CODE THIS_FILE[] = __FILE__;
#endif

////////////////////////////////////////////////////////////////////////
// CMinieditView

IMPLEMENT_DYNCREATE(CMinieditView, CEditView)

BEGIN_MESSAGE_MAP(CMinieditView, CEditView)
   //{{AFX_MSG_MAP(CMinieditView)
      // NOTE - the ClassWizard will add and remove mapping macros here.
      //    DO NOT EDIT what you see in these blocks of generated code !
   //}}AFX_MSG_MAP
END_MESSAGE_MAP()

////////////////////////////////////////////////////////////////////////
// CMinieditView construction/destruction

CMinieditView::CMinieditView()
{
   // TODO: add construction code here
}
```

```
CMinieditView::~CMinieditView()
{
}

////////////////////////////////////////////////////////////////////////////
// CMinieditView drawing

void CMinieditView::OnDraw(CDC* pDC)
{
    CMinieditDoc* pDoc = GetDocument();

    // TODO: add draw code here
}



////////////////////////////////////////////////////////////////////////////
// CMinieditView diagnostics

#ifdef _DEBUG
void CMinieditView::AssertValid() const
{
    CEditView::AssertValid();
}

void CMinieditView::Dump(CDumpContext& dc) const
{
    CEditView::Dump(dc);
}

CMinieditDoc* CMinieditView::GetDocument() // non-debug version is inline
{
    ASSERT(m_pDocument->IsKindOf(RUNTIME_CLASS(CMinieditDoc)));
    return (CMinieditDoc*) m_pDocument;
}

#endif //_DEBUG

////////////////////////////////////////////////////////////////////////////
// CMinieditView message handlers
```

Summary

In this chapter, you learned how to write programs that conform to the multiple document interface application model. The following are the general techniques and concepts that were explained:

- The programs presented in previous chapters are known as single document interface, or SDI, applications. They permit the user to open only a single document at a time.

- Multiple document interface, or MDI, programs allow the user to open several documents at once, and to view and edit each document in a separate child window.

- Windows and the MFC provide most of the code for supporting the MDI interface.

- To generate an MDI program using AppWizard, simply choose the multiple document interface option in the AppWizard Options dialog box. AppWizard will create all required classes and source files.

- In an MDI program, the application, document, and view classes perform the same basic roles as in an SDI program.

- As in an SDI program, the main frame window class of an MDI program manages the main program window. In an MDI program, however, the main window does *not* contain a single view window for viewing a document; rather, it contains the application workspace. The main frame window class is thus not associated with a particular document and is therefore not included in the document template.

- In addition to the four classes used in an SDI program, an MDI program employs a *child frame window* class. This class manages the child frame window that is created for each open document. Each child frame window is displayed within the application workspace and contains a view window for displaying the document.

- Rather than deriving a new class, an MDI program generated by AppWizard uses the MFC `CMDIChildWnd` class as the child frame window class. Because an object of this class is created each time a document is opened, it is included in the program's document template.

- When generating a program using AppWizard, you should specify *all* features that may be required, because it is difficult to use AppWizard to "retrofit" features in an existing program.

- An MDI program has a set of resources (a menu, a string, an icon, and an accelerator) that have the identifier IDR_MAINFRAME and that are associated with the main frame window. The menu is displayed when *no* documents are open, and the icon is displayed when the main window is minimized.

- An MDI program has another set of resources (a menu, a string, and an icon) that are associated with each child frame window used to display a document. (All these resources have the same identifier; the name of this identifier is based upon the name of the program, or upon the document type name if you specify one when you generate the program.) The menu is displayed when a document is open, and the icon is displayed when a child frame window is minimized.

Creating Custom Dialog Boxes

- Creating a modal dialog box

- Other types of dialog boxes

13

In Windows programs, dialog boxes are one of the most important devices for displaying and obtaining information from the user. In the programs you have created so far, AppWizard has generated the resources and code necessary for displaying a simple dialog box in response to the "About" command on the Help menu. In this chapter, you will learn how to create dialog boxes of your own design and how to display them from your programs.

The chapter provides detailed instructions for designing and displaying a conventional modal dialog box, which is one that is displayed temporarily over the main program window and is removed as soon as the user has read or entered the required information. These techniques are illustrated through an example program that displays a dialog box for formatting text. The last section of the chapter then discusses several other types of dialog boxes: modeless dialog boxes (which can be left open while the user continues to work in the main program window), form views (view windows based upon dialog templates), and common dialog boxes (prewritten, standard dialog boxes).

Creating a Modal Dialog Box

In this section, you will learn how to create and display a modal dialog box by writing an example program, FONTDEMO. FONTDEMO displays several lines of text within its view window, using the Windows System font (see Figure 13.1). If you choose the Format command on the Text menu, or press the Ctrl+F accelerator keystroke, FONTDEMO displays the Format dialog box, which allows you to change the way the lines of text in the view window are formatted (see Figure 13.2).

The Format dialog box allows you to specify the style of the characters (bold, italic, underlined, or any combination of these features), the line justification (left, center, or right), the pitch of the characters (variable or fixed), and the line spacing (you can enter 1, 2, or 3 for single-, double-, or triple-spaced lines). As soon as you change any feature in the Format dialog box, the text in the Sample area of this dialog box is immediately reformatted to show the currently selected combination of features. If you click the OK button, the dialog box is closed and the selected formatting features are applied to the text in the main window. If you click the Cancel button,

FIGURE 13.1:

The FONTDEMO program window

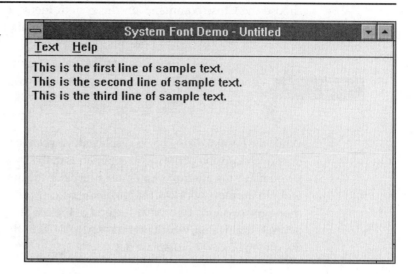

FIGURE 13.2:

The Format dialog box

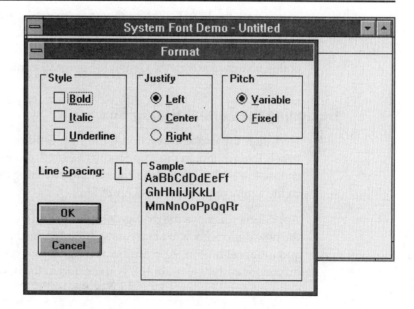

choose the Close command on the system menu, or press Esc, the dialog box is closed but the text in the main window is left unaltered.

While the Format dialog box is displayed, you cannot activate the main program window or choose any of the menu commands in the main window. (The program beeps if you make the attempt.) You must first close the dialog box before you can resume work in the main window. Such a dialog box is known as *modal* and is the most common type of dialog box. Near the end of the chapter, you will learn how to create a *modeless* dialog box, which permits you to work in the main program window while the dialog box is still displayed.

Generating the Program

To generate the FONTDEMO program, choose the AppWizard... command on the Project menu and enter the project name FONTDEMO. As usual, place the project files within a subdirectory reserved exclusively for these files, and in the Options dialog box choose *only* the Generate Source Comments option.

Designing the Format Dialog Box

To design the dialog box, choose the App Studio command on the Visual Workbench Tools menu. In the App Studio resources dialog box, click the New... button, choose the Dialog item in the New Resource dialog box, and click the OK button to create a new dialog box (see Figure 13.3).

App Studio displays the dialog-designing window, containing a full-size replica of the new dialog box you are creating. Initially, the dialog box has only an OK button and a Cancel button. App Studio also displays a control palette, which contains a button for each type of control you can add to the dialog box. Figure 13.4 shows the

FIGURE 13.3:

The New Resource Dialog box

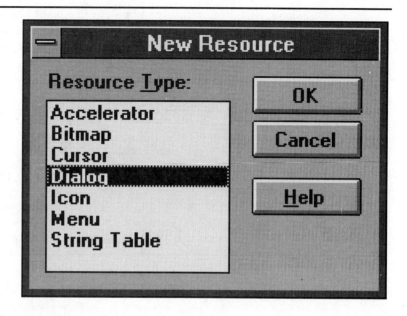

FIGURE 13.4:

A new dialog box and control palette in App Studio

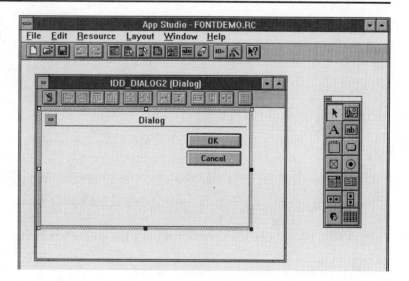

dialog-designing window and palette in App Studio; Figure 13.5 shows the palette, indicating the type of control that corresponds to each button (if the palette is not visible, press F2). All of the controls on this palette are explained in a sidebar given later in this section.

FIGURE 13.5:

The control palette, showing the type of control that can be added using each of the buttons

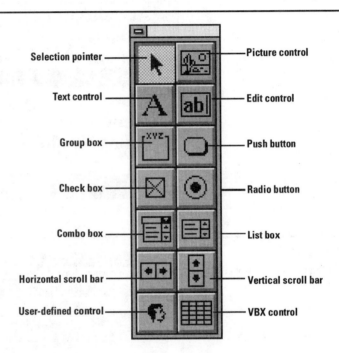

Selection pointer

Picture control

Text control

Edit control

Group box

Push button

Check box

Radio button

Combo box

List box

Horizontal scroll bar

Vertical scroll bar

User-defined control

VBX control

Figure 13.6 shows the Format dialog box as it should appear when you have completed designing it in App Studio, and Table 13.1 lists the properties of the dialog box itself as well as the properties of each control that you will add.

To begin, select the dialog box by clicking the selection pointer in the upper-left corner of the control palette, and then clicking within the dialog box (but *not* within a control). You can then enlarge the dialog box by dragging the lower-right corner to the desired position. Next, set the dialog box properties by double-clicking within the

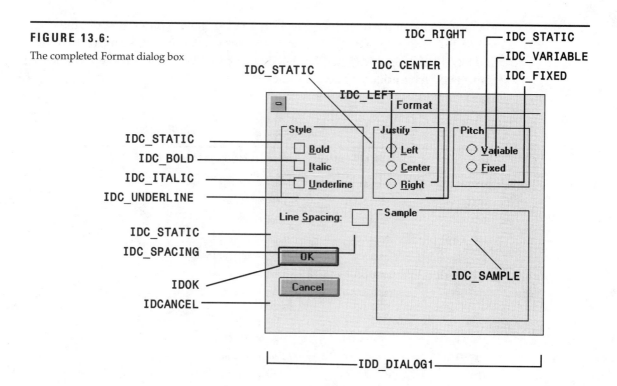

FIGURE 13.6:

The completed Format dialog box

dialog box (but *not* within a control) to open the dialog properties window (labeled "Dialog Properties"). Within this window, enter the title Format into the Caption: text box. Do not change any of the other properties; the default values are acceptable. Note that Table 13.1 lists only the properties that you *change* from their default values.

You should now add the dialog box controls and set their properties. To add a particular type of control, click the appropriate button within the palette (see Figure 13.5), and then click the desired target location within the dialog box; the control will initially be inserted at that position. You can then use the mouse to move or change the size of the control. To set the control's properties, double-click within the control to open the properties window, and enter the control identifier and any other properties listed for that control in Table 13.1. If you need to delete a control you have added, select it by clicking within it and press the Del key.

TABLE 13.1: Properties of the Format Dialog Box and Its Controls

ID:	Type of Control	Nondefault Properties
IDD_DIALOG1	Dialog box	Caption: Format
IDC_STATIC	Group box	Caption: Style
IDD_BOLD	Check box	Caption: &Bold
IDC_ITALIC	Check box	Caption: &Italic
IDC_UNDERLINE	Check box	Caption: &Underline
IDC_STATIC	Group box	Caption: Justify
IDC_LEFT	Radio button	Caption: &Left Group Tabstop
IDC_CENTER	Radio button	Caption: &Center
IDC_RIGHT	Radio button	Caption: &Right
IDC_STATIC	Group box	Caption: Pitch
IDC_VARIABLE	Radio button	Caption: &Variable Group Tabstop
IDC_FIXED	Radio button	Caption: &Fixed
IDC_STATIC	Text control	Caption: Line &Spacing:
IDC_SPACING	Edit control (text box)	none
IDC_SAMPLE	Group box	Caption: Sample
IDOK	Push button	Caption: OK Default Button
IDCANCEL	Push button	Caption: Cancel

The position and size of the selected object (dialog box or control) are displayed in the lower-right corner of the App Studio window. These measurements are not in absolute units (such as pixels); rather, they are *in dialog box units*, which are scaled according to the size of fhe font used to display text in the dialog box controls. (You can choose the font by clicking the Font... button in the dialog properties window.) Thus, if you design a dialog box and then change the font to a larger size, the dialog box and all the controls it contains will automatically be enlarged to accommodate the new size of the text.

Note that the & character within a control's caption causes the following character to be underlined. When the dialog box is displayed, the user can activate the control by pressing the Alt key in conjunction with the underlined character. If the control is a check box or radio button, pressing the Alt key combination will check the button. If the control is a push button, pressing the key combination will activate the button command, as if the button had been clicked. If the control is a text control, pressing the key combination will place the insertion point within the following edit control (that is, the edit control occurring next in the tab order; the tab order will be explained in the next section).

As you can see in Table 13.1, most of the controls are assigned a unique, descriptive identifier; this identifier is used to reference the control within the program. However, controls that are *not* referenced within the program do not need unique identifiers, and are left with the default identifiers provided by App Studio (specifically, the controls with the `IDC_STATIC` identifier).

Assigning a control the Tabstop property allows the user to access the control by pressing the Tab and Shift+Tab keystrokes, which move the focus from one control to the next; the next section explains how to set the order in which controls receive the focus. The Group property will also be explained in the next section.

Finally, assigning the OK push button the Default Button property causes the button to be displayed with a thick border, and allows the user to activate the button (thereby closing the dialog box) by simply pressing Enter.

Using Controls

Figure 13.5 showed each type of control you can add to a dialog box.

A picture control displays an empty rectangular frame, a solid rectangular block, or an icon. You specify which object is displayed by setting the control's properties. A text control displays a text string. It is ordinarily used to label an edit control or other type of control. A group box is a labeled border that can be used to group a set of related controls. Picture controls, text controls, and group boxes do not accept user input.

An edit control allows the user to enter text and provides complete editing facilities, such as backspacing, deleting, cutting, and pasting. If you specify the Multiline style (through the Styles option of the properties dialog box), the user can enter multiple lines, allowing the edit control to serve as a small text editor.

A push button is typically used to execute some task immediately. Normally, a check box is used to enable or disable an option that can be turned on or off independently, and a radio button is used to select one of a group of mutually exclusive options.

A list box displays a list of items, such as file names or fonts, and allows the user to scroll through the list and select the desired item.

A combo box combines a list box with either an edit control or a text control. A *simple* combo box consists of an edit control and a list box that is permanently displayed below it. A *drop-down* combo box consists of an edit control and a list box that appears only when the user clicks the down arrow displayed above the list. A *drop-list* combo box consists of a text control and a list box that appears only when the user clicks the down arrow. You specify the type of combo box through the Styles option of the properties dialog box.

The two scroll bar controls are used for displaying horizontal or vertical scroll bars anywhere within the dialog box. These controls allow the user to adjust some quantity that varies continuously—for example, the height of a font, the intensity of a color, or the tracking speed of the mouse.

A user-defined control is a custom control that you (or a third-party supplier) have designed and programmed. With the user-defined control button on the control palette you can set the position and size of a user-defined control. The control, however, will be displayed as a simple rectangle; its actual appearance and behavior will not be manifested until the program is run. Creating custom controls is discussed in the *Microsoft Windows Software Development Kit Guide to Programming* manual (Chapter 20, "Dynamic-Link Libraries"), which is not included with Visual C++ but may be obtained from Microsoft.

A VBX control is a special type of user-defined control that conforms to the VBX format (which is also used for controls in Microsoft Visual Basic). App Studio provides extensive support for VBX controls, allowing you to set their properties, view their actual appearance, and test their behavior. For information on using them, see the *Class Libraries User's Guide* manual (Chapter 17, "Programming with VBX Controls"), the *App Studio User's Guide* (Chapter 3, "Using the Dialog Editor"), or the *App Studio* help file (accessed through the App Studio Help menu; the topic "VBX controls").

Setting the Tab Order

Your next task is to set the *tab order* for the controls. In setting the tab order, you assign a sequential number to each control (that is, you assign 1 to one control, 2 to another control, and so on). The tab order has the following effects:

- The tab order governs the order in which controls that have been assigned the Tabstop property are activated as the user presses the Tab or Shift+Tab keystroke. Pressing Tab activates the *next* control with the Tabstop property in the tab order, while pressing Shift+Tab activates the *previous* Tabstop control in the tab order.

- The tab order is used to define *groups* of controls. If a control has the Group property, that control as well as all controls that follow it in the tab order belong to a single group; if, however, a following control also has the Group property, it does *not* belong to the same group, but rather starts a new group. If a collection of radio buttons belong to the same group, whenever the user clicks a button, Windows automatically removes the check from the previously checked button within the group (the buttons must have the Auto property). Also, the user can use an arrow key to move the check mark from radio button to radio button within a single group.

- If a text control has an underlined character (that is, a character preceded with an &), pressing the Alt key in conjunction with this character activates the next edit control that follows it in the tab order. Therefore, a text control used as a label should immediately precede the associated edit control in the tab order.

To set the tab order, choose the Set Tab Order command on the App Studio Layout menu, or press Ctrl+D. App Studio will place a number on each control. To set the tab order, click the first control in the desired order, then click the second control, then the third, and so on. When you are done, the controls should have the numbers shown in Figure 13.7. Press Esc to remove the numbers.

NOTE For more information on using App Studio to design a dialog box, see the *App StudioUser's Guide* manual (Chapter 3, "Using the Dialog Editor") or the *App Studio* help file (accessed through the App Studio Help menu; the topic "dialog editor").

You have now finished designing the dialog box. You can save your work by choosing the Save command on the App Studio File menu; however, leave App Studio running and the dialog-designing window open, so that you can generate a class to manage the dialog box as explained in the next section.

FIGURE 13.7:

The tab order for the Format dialog box

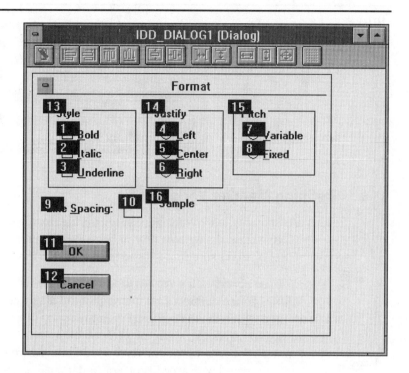

Creating a Class to Manage the Dialog Box

The next step is to generate a class for managing the Format dialog box that you just designed. While the dialog-designing window is open, choose the ClassWizard... command on the App Studio Resource menu, or press Ctrl+W, to run the Class-Wizard tool. ClassWizard will recognize that you have not yet defined a class for the Format dialog box; it will therefore display the Add Class dialog box. Enter the class name CFormat into the Class Name: text box; ClassWizard will then automatically enter the file name FORMAT.H into the Header File: text box, as well as enter the file name FORMAT.CPP into the Implementation File: text box. The completed Add Class dialog box is shown in Figure 13.8. Click the Create Class button to generate the header and implementation files.

FIGURE 13.8:

The completed Add Class dialog box

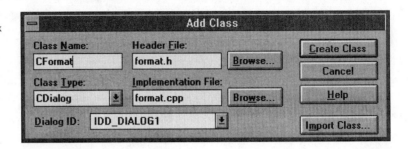

Defining Member Variables

As soon as ClassWizard has created the files for the CFormat class, it opens the main ClassWizard dialog box. (If you have closed this dialog box, reopen it by pressing Ctrl+W; make sure that CFormat is selected in the Class Name: list.)

You can now use ClassWizard to add data members to the CFormat class. ClassWizard allows you to define a data member of the dialog class for each control that is contained within the dialog box. When the dialog box is displayed, the MFC automatically transfers the value of each of these data members to the corresponding control. For example, if you have used ClassWizard to define an integer data member associated with an edit control, and if the data member is set to 1 when the dialog box is first displayed, a 1 will appear in the edit control. Also, when the user dismisses the dialog box by clicking the OK button, the value contained within each control is transferred back to the corresponding data member. (If the user closes the dialog box by clicking the Cancel button, pressing Escape, or choosing the Close system menu command, the control values are *not* transferred to the data members.) The type of the data member (or members) that you can define for a particular control, and the way that the exchange mechanism works, depends upon the type of the control (several types of controls will be described shortly).

> **TIP**
>
> The MFC automatically transfers data both when the dialog box is first opened and when it is closed. You can force the MFC to transfer the control data to or from the data members at any time the dialog box is displayed by calling the CWnd::UpdateData function from a member function of the dialog class.

To define data members for FONTDEMO, click the Edit Variables... button in the ClassWizard dialog box. ClassWizard will now open the Edit Member Variables dialog box, which is shown in Figure 13.9. In this dialog box, the Control IDs: list displays the identifier of each control that can be assigned a data member. Begin by selecting the IDC_BOLD identifier to define a data member for the Bold check box.

FIGURE 13.9:

The Edit Member Variables dialog box, before defining data members

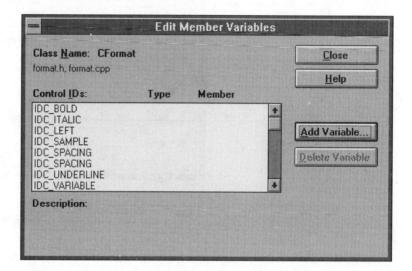

Then click the Add Variable... button to display the Add Member Variable dialog box. Into the Member Variable Name: text box, enter mBold as the data member name. Leave the default selections in the Property: and Variable Type: lists. The completed Add Member Variable dialog box is shown in Figure 13.10. Click the OK button when you are done.

The default selection in the Property: list, Value, creates a data member of a fundamental type rather than a member object. (Defining member objects will be discussed later.) The default selection in the Variable Type: list, BOOL, creates a data member that can be assigned TRUE or FALSE.

Using the same method, define a data member for the Italic check box (IDC_ITALIC) named mItalic, as well as data member for the Underline check box (IDC_UNDERLINE) named mUnderline.

The completed Add Member Variable dialog box, for defining a data member associated with the Bold check box (IDC_BOLD)

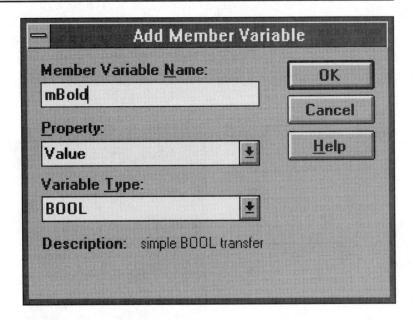

The next step is to assign data members for the radio buttons. Rather than assigning a data member for each radio button, you assign a single data member for each *group* of radio buttons. Before the dialog box is displayed, the data member should be assigned the number of the radio button within the group that is to be initially checked; the number 0 indicates the *first* radio button in the group (in the tab order), the number 1 indicates the second, and so on. When the dialog box is first opened, the MFC will then check the indicated radio button (if you assign the data member −1, *no* button in the group will be checked). Likewise, when the user clicks OK, the MFC assigns the data member the number of the radio button in the group that is currently checked (or the value −1 if *no* button is checked).

Accordingly, the Edit Member Variables dialog box shows only the identifier of the *first* radio button in each of the two groups, IDC_LEFT (for the group starting with the Left button) and IDC_VARIABLE (for the group starting with the Variable button). First, assign a member variable for the IDC_LEFT radio button group; in the Add Member Variable dialog box, enter the variable name mJustify and leave the default selections in the two lists. (Notice that the Variable Type: list contains the type int; the data member is made an int so that it can store the number of the checked radio button.) Using the same method, assign a data member named mPitch for the IDC_VARIABLE radio button group.

Next, assign a data member for the edit control (IDC_SPACING) named mSpacing. This time, in the Add Member Variable dialog box, select int in the Variable Type: list rather than accepting the default selection (CString), so that the number displayed in the edit control will be converted from and to an integer. Also, when you return to the Edit Member Variables dialog box, two new text boxes will be displayed at the bottom of the dialog box, as shown in Figure 13.11. These text boxes allow you to enter the range of valid values for the selected data member. If you enter values into these text boxes, when the user clicks the OK button to dismiss the dialog box, the MFC will make sure that the value that the user has entered is within the specified range (if the value is *not* in this range, the MFC displays a warning and keeps the dialog box open). For the IDC_SPACING control, enter 1 into the Minimum Value: box and 3 into the Maximum Value box: (so that the user can specify only single-, double-, or triple-line spacing).

FIGURE 13.11:

The completed Edit Member Variables dialog box

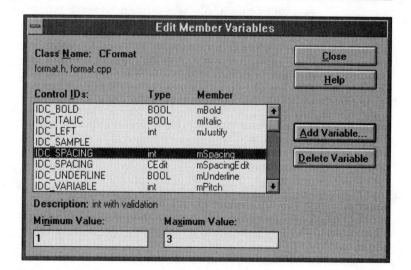

431

Your final task is to define a member object for managing the edit control. To do this, select the IDC_SPACING identifier in the Control IDs: list and click the Add Variable... button (yes, you can define two data members for a single control, provided that they have different properties). Into the Member Variable Name: text box, enter the name mSpacingEdit. In the Property: list, select the Control item; this will cause the data member to be an object of the MFC CEdit class (rather than a fundamental type). CEdit provides a set of member functions that can be used to manage an edit control; as you will see later, the dialog class uses one of these functions.

You have now finished defining the data members for the dialog controls. The Edit Member Variables dialog box should appear as shown in Figure 13.11. Click the Close button to close this dialog box, and then click the OK button in the main ClassWizard dialog box. ClassWizard will write the code for defining all of the data members you have specified directly to the header and implementation files for the dialog class (FORMAT.H and FORMAT.CPP). You can now save your work in App Studio, temporarily quit the program (if desired), and return to the Visual Workbench.

Defining Message Handlers

Like any window, a dialog box receives a variety of messages to inform it of significant events, and you must add message-handling functions to the dialog class if you want to handle any of these events. For the FONTDEMO program, you need to add functions for handling the messages that are sent when the dialog box is first opened, when the dialog box needs repainting, and when the user clicks a check box or radio button.

To define the required message-handling functions, run ClassWizard from within the Visual Workbench (the FONTDEMO project must be open). In the ClassWizard dialog box, make sure that CFormat is selected in the Class Name: list.

To define the first two message handlers, select CFormat in the Object IDs: list. The Messages: list will now display the identifiers of the general notification messages that can be sent to the dialog box. (This list does not include messages sent from controls.) First, select WM_INITDIALOG, and click the Add Function button to define a handler for this message; ClassWizard will create a function named OnInitDialog. The WM_INITDIALOG message is sent when the dialog box is first created, just before it is displayed. Then, select WM_PAINT in the Messages: list, and click the Add Function; ClassWizard will create a message-handling function named OnPaint. The WM_PAINT message is sent whenever the dialog box needs painting or repainting.

You now need to provide a message handler for each check box or radio button, which receives control whenever the user clicks the button (to check it or uncheck it). To define a message handler for the Bold check box, select IDC_BOLD in the Object IDs: list, select BN_CLICKED in the Messages: list, and click the Add Function... button. In the Add Member Function dialog box, simply click OK to accept the default function name, OnClickedBold. Use this same procedure to define functions for each of the other check boxes and radio buttons; in all cases, accept the default function name. Table 13.2 lists the identifier of each check box and radio button, plus the name of the message-handling function that processes the BN_CLICKED message sent by the button.

TABLE 13.2: Handlers for the BN_CLICKED Messages Sent by the Check Boxes and Radio Buttons in the Format Dialog Box

Object ID:	Name of Message Handler
IDC_BOLD	OnClickedBold
IDC_CENTER	OnClickedCenter
IDC_FIXED	OnClickedFixed
IDC_ITALIC	OnClickedItalic
IDC_LEFT	OnClickedLeft
IDC_RIGHT	OnClickedRight
IDC_UNDERLINE	OnClickedUnderline
IDC_VARIABLE	OnClickedVariable

Finally, you need to define a function that receives control whenever the user changes the contents of the IDC_SPACING edit control. To do this, select IDC_SPAC-ING in the Object IDs: list. The Messages: list will now display all of the different messages that the edit control can send to the dialog box; select the EN_CHANGE message, which is sent whenever the user changes the text in the edit control. Then click the Add Function... button and accept the default function name, OnChangeSpac-ing. Figure 13.12 shows the ClassWizard dialog box after all member functions have been added.

FIGURE 13.12:

The completed ClassWizard dialog box, after all message-handling functions have been defined for the CFormat dialog class

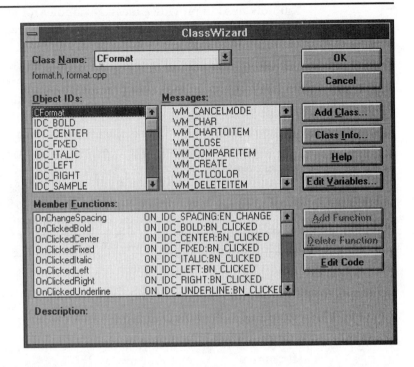

Modifying the CFormat Code

In this section, you will complete the coding of the CFormat class. To begin, open the file FORMAT.H and add the following two enumerated type definitions to the beginning of the file:

```
// format.h : header file
//

enum {JUSTIFY_LEFT, JUSTIFY_CENTER, JUSTIFY_RIGHT};
enum {PITCH_VARIABLE, PITCH_FIXED};
```

The enumerators in these definitions will be used to refer to the radio buttons. The enumerators in the first definition (which have the values 0, 1, and 2) refer to the numbers of the radio buttons in the Justify group of the Format dialog box, and the enumerators in the second group refer to the numbers of the radio buttons in the Pitch group.

Next, add the following definition for the mRectSample data member to the end of the CFormat class definition:

```
// added member:
protected:
   RECT mRectSample;
```

Now open the file FORMAT.CPP and add code as follows to the OnInitDialog member function:

```
BOOL CFormat::OnInitDialog()
{
   CDialog::OnInitDialog();

   // TODO: Add extra initialization here

   GetDlgItem (IDC_SAMPLE)->GetWindowRect (&mRectSample);
   ScreenToClient (&mRectSample);

   mSpacingEdit.LimitText (1);

   return TRUE;  // return TRUE  unless you set the focus to a control
}
```

As mentioned, the OnInitDialog function receives control when the Format dialog box is opened, immediately before it becomes visible. The first added statement stores the screen coordinates of the Sample group box in the data member mRectSample. The second statement then converts the screen coordinates to client coordinates (that is, coordinates with respect to the upper-left corner of the inside of the dialog box). mRectSample will be used for displaying the sample text within the group box.

The third statement you added uses the CEdit member object, mSpacingEdit, to call the CEdit member function LimitText. Passing LimitText a value of 1 prevents the user from entering more than one character into the IDC_SPACING edit control.

MFC Control Classes

The MFC provides a class for managing each major type of control. These classes are listed in Table 13.3. You can use their member functions to obtain information or perform operations on the controls within a dialog box. For example, the FONTDEMO program used the CEdit member function Limit-Text to limit the number of characters that can be entered into an edit control. For a complete list of the member functions for a particular control class, see the documentation on that class in the *Reference Volume I, Class Library Reference* manual, or in the *Foundation Classes* online help file.

To use one of these member functions to manage a control within a dialog box, you must create an object of the control class, which is attached to the control. There are two simple ways to do this. First, you can use the ClassWizard Edit Member Variables dialog box to create a member object, such as the mSpacingEdit member object that you defined for the FONTDEMO program. (In the Add Member Variable dialog box, select the Control item in the Property: list.) ClassWizard will create an object of the class that is appropriate for the type of the control (for example, it will define a CEdit object for an edit control).

Second, you can call the CWnd member function GetDlgItem to obtain a pointer to a temporary control object. For example, in the FONTDEMO program, rather than creating a permanent member object for managing the edit control, you could call GetDlgItem to obtain a temporary object, and use this object to call LimitText, as in the following code:

```
((CEdit *)GetDlgItem (IDC_SPACING))->LimitText (1);
```

TABLE 13.3: The MFC Classes for Managing Controls

MFC Class	Type of Control
CButton	Buttons: push buttons, check boxes, radio buttons, and group boxes
CBitmapButton	Buttons that display bitmaps you design yourself
CComboBox	Combo boxes
CEdit	Edit controls
CListBox	List boxes
CScrollBar	Scroll bars: vertical or horizontal
CStatic	Text controls, empty rectangular frames, and solid rectangular blocks
CVBControl	VBX controls

The next step is to complete the coding of the message-handling functions that receive control whenever the user clicks a check box. First, complete the function for the Bold check box as follows:

```
void CFormat::OnClickedBold()
{
    // TODO: Add your control notification handler code here
    mBold = !mBold;
    InvalidateRect (&mRectSample);
    UpdateWindow ();
}
```

The first statement toggles the value of the mBold data member between TRUE and FALSE. Thus, if the box is *not* checked (and mBold is FALSE), clicking the control will check it and cause OnClickedBold to set mBold to TRUE. If the box is already checked, clicking it will remove the check mark and cause OnClickedBold to set mBold to FALSE.

The second added statement invalidates (that is, marks for repainting) the portion of the dialog box occupied by the Sample group box, and the third statement causes the OnPaint member function of the dialog class to be called immediately; OnPaint then displays the text using the new format.

Now complete the functions for the Italic and Underline check boxes as follows:

```
void CFormat::OnClickedItalic()
{
```

```
    // TODO: Add your control notification handler code here
    mItalic = !mItalic;
    InvalidateRect (&mRectSample);
    UpdateWindow ();
}

void CFormat::OnClickedUnderline()
{
    // TODO: Add your control notification handler code here
    mUnderline = !mUnderline;
    InvalidateRect (&mRectSample);
    UpdateWindow ();
}
```

Complete the message-handling functions for the radio buttons, as follows:

```
void CFormat::OnClickedCenter()
{
    // TODO: Add your control notification handler code here
    if (IsDlgButtonChecked (IDC_CENTER))
        {
        mJustify = JUSTIFY_CENTER;
        InvalidateRect (&mRectSample);
        UpdateWindow ();
        }
}

void CFormat::OnClickedFixed()
{
    // TODO: Add your control notification handler code here
    if (IsDlgButtonChecked (IDC_FIXED))
        {
        mPitch = PITCH_FIXED;
        InvalidateRect (&mRectSample);
        UpdateWindow ();
        }
}

void CFormat::OnClickedLeft()
{
    // TODO: Add your control notification handler code here
    if (IsDlgButtonChecked (IDC_LEFT))
        {
        mJustify = JUSTIFY_LEFT;
```

```
        InvalidateRect (&mRectSample);
        UpdateWindow ();
        }
}

void CFormat::OnClickedRight()
{
    // TODO: Add your control notification handler code here
    if (IsDlgButtonChecked (IDC_RIGHT))
        {
        mJustify = JUSTIFY_RIGHT;
        InvalidateRect (&mRectSample);
        UpdateWindow ();
        }
}

void CFormat::OnClickedVariable()
{
    // TODO: Add your control notification handler code here
    if (IsDlgButtonChecked (IDC_VARIABLE))
        {
        mPitch = PITCH_VARIABLE;
        InvalidateRect (&mRectSample);
        UpdateWindow ();
        }
}
```

Each of these functions first calls `CWnd::IsDlgButtonChecked` to make sure that the radio button has been checked. (The message-handling function is called whenever the user clicks and thereby checks the radio button; it is also sometimes called when the user moves the focus to the button with the Tab key, *without* checking the button.) If the button is checked, the function assigns the number of the radio button to the appropriate data member (`mJustify` or `mPitch`). Later, you will see how these data members are used.

MFC Functions for Managing Dialog Boxes

A dialog class is derived from the MFC CDialog class, which in turn is derived from CWnd. Both CDialog and CWnd provide member functions for managing dialog boxes, which you can call from your dialog class. Some of these functions affect individual controls contained in the dialog box, others affect groups of controls, and still others affect the dialog box itself. You normally call these functions from the message-handling functions of your dialog class, which receive control while the dialog box is displayed. The CWnd functions are listed in Table 13.4 and the CDialog functions are listed in Table 13.5. See the documentation on each of these functions for details (in the *Reference Volume I, Class Library Reference* manual or in the *Foundation Classes* online help file).

TABLE 13.4: CWnd Member Functions for Managing Dialog Box Controls

Function	Purpose
CheckDlgButton	Checks or unchecks a button control
CheckRadioButton	Checks a specified radio button and unchecks all other radio buttons within a designated group
DlgDirList	Adds a list of files, directories, or drives to a list box
DlgDirListComboBox	Adds a list of files, directories, or drives to the list box within a combo box
DlgDirSelect	Obtains the currently selected file, directory, or drive from a list box
DlgDirSelectComboBox	Obtains the currently selected file, directory, or drive from the list box within a combo box
GetCheckedRadioButton	Returns the identifier of the checked radio button within a designated group of radio buttons
GetDlgItem	Returns a pointer to a temporary object for a specified control
GetDlgItemInt	Returns the numeric value represented by the text in a specified control
GetDlgItemText	Obtains the text displayed within a control
GetNextDlgGroupItem	Returns a pointer to a temporary object for the next (or previous) control within a group of controls

TABLE 13.4: `CWnd` Member Functions for Managing Dialog Box Controls (continued)

Function	Purpose
GetNextDlgTabItem	Returns a pointer to a temporary object for the next control that is assigned a tab stop
IsDlgButtonChecked	Returns the checked status of a button control
SendDlgItemMessage	Sends a message to a control
SetDlgItemInt	Converts an integer to text, and assigns this text to a control
SetDlgItemText	Sets the text that is displayed by a control

TABLE 13.5: `CDialog` Member Functions for Managing Dialog Boxes and Controls

Function	Purpose
EndDialog	Closes a modal dialog box
GetDefID	Returns the identifier of the current default push button within the dialog box
GotoDlgCtrl	Assigns the input focus to a specified control within the dialog box
MapDialogRect	Converts the coordinates of a control in dialog units to screen units
NextDlgCtrl	Assigns the input focus to the next control in the dialog box tab order
PrevDlgCtrl	Assigns the input focus to the previous control in the dialog box tab order
SetDefID	Converts the specified push button control into the default push button

Next, add code as follows to the `OnChangeSpacing` function, which receives control whenever the user changes the contents of the edit control:

```
void CFormat::OnChangeSpacing()
{
    // TODO: Add your control notification handler code here
    int Temp;
    Temp = (int)GetDlgItemInt (IDC_SPACING);
    if (Temp > 0 && Temp < 4)
        {
        mSpacing = Temp;
        InvalidateRect (&mRectSample);
        UpdateWindow ();
        }
}
```

OnChangeSpacing first calls CWnd::GetDlgItemInt to obtain the contents of the edit control as an integer value. If the value is valid, it then saves it in the mSpacing data member and forces the sample text to be redrawn.

Finally, you should add the following code to the OnPaint function, which is called whenever the dialog box needs repainting:

```
void CFormat::OnPaint()
{
   CPaintDC dc(this); // device context for painting

   // TODO: Add your message handler code here

   // Do not call CDialog::OnPaint() for painting messages
   CFont Font;
   LOGFONT LF;
   int LineHeight;
   CFont *PtrOldFont;
   int X, Y;

   // fill LF with the features of a standard system font:
   CFont TempFont;
   if (mPitch == PITCH_VARIABLE)
      TempFont.CreateStockObject (SYSTEM_FONT);
   else
      TempFont.CreateStockObject (SYSTEM_FIXED_FONT);
   TempFont.GetObject (sizeof (LOGFONT), &LF);

   // now customize lfWeight, lfItalic, and lfUnderline fields:
   if (mBold)
      LF.lfWeight = FW_BOLD;
   if (mItalic)
      LF.lfItalic = 1;
   if (mUnderline)
      LF.lfUnderline = 1;

   // create and select font:
   Font.CreateFontIndirect (&LF);
   PtrOldFont = dc.SelectObject (&Font);

   // set justification:
   switch (mJustify)
      {
```

```
     case JUSTIFY_LEFT:
        dc.SetTextAlign (TA_LEFT);
        X = mRectSample.left + 5;
        break;
     case JUSTIFY_CENTER:
        dc.SetTextAlign (TA_CENTER);
        X = (mRectSample.left + mRectSample.right) / 2;
        break;
     case JUSTIFY_RIGHT:
        dc.SetTextAlign (TA_RIGHT);
        X = mRectSample.right - 5;
        break;
     }

// draw lines:
LineHeight = LF.lfHeight * mSpacing;
Y = mRectSample.top + 15;
dc.TextOut (X, Y, "AaBbCdDdEeFf");
Y += LineHeight;
dc.TextOut (X, Y, "GhHhIiJjKkLl");
Y += LineHeight;
dc.TextOut (X, Y, "MmNnOoPpQqRr");

// unselect font:
dc.SelectObject (PtrOldFont);
}
```

The OnPaint function serves only to redraw the three lines of sample text within the Sample group box; it does *not* need to redraw the controls, because the controls redraw themselves. An explanation of the different techniques used in drawing the lines of text will be given in Chapter 15; the following is a brief summary of the steps that OnPaint performs:

- It obtains the properties of the Windows System font (the fixed-pitch or variable-pitch System font, depending upon the setting of mPitch).

- It modifies the font properties according to the values of the mBold, mItalic, and mUnderline data members, and creates a new font with the modified properties, which will be used to draw the text.

- It sets the text justification according to the value of mJustify.

- It uses the CDC::TextOut function to draw the text, using the member variable mSpacing to calculate the space between each line.

> **NOTE**
>
> If a window class is derived from `CView`, the `CView` class provides an `OnPaint` message-handling function, which prepares a device context object and then calls the `OnDraw` member function of the view window class. However, because a dialog class is not derived from `CView`, it must provide an `OnPaint` function itself if it needs to repaint the dialog box window. Note, also, that an `OnPaint` function must create a device context object belonging to the `CPaintDC` MFC class (rather than the `CClientDC` class, which is used for creating device context objects within other types of functions). ClassWizard adds the code to the `OnPaint` function to create the device context object for you.

Displaying the Dialog Box

You have now completed coding the `CFormat` class, which contains the code that manages the Format dialog box once it has been displayed. The next phase is to provide the code that creates the dialog class object and displays the dialog box.

Defining the Resources

The first step is to provide a menu command that allows the user to open the Format dialog box. To do this, run App Studio again by choosing the App Studio command on the Visual Workbench Tools menu (the FONTDEMO project must be open). In App Studio, open the menu-designing window for the IDR_MAINFRAME menu and perform the following tasks:

1. Delete the File drop-down menu.

2. Delete the Edit drop-down menu.

3. Insert a Text drop-down menu before the Help menu.

4. Add a Format command, a separator, and an Exit command to the new Text menu. The properties of the Text menu and each of the items you add to

Closing the Dialog Box

The MFC class `CDialog` provides default message handlers that receive control when the user closes the dialog box. When the user clicks the OK button, the `CDialog::OnOK` function receives control; this function calls `CWnd::UpdateData` to transfer the data from the dialog box controls to the associated data members, and then it calls `CDialog::EndDialog` to close the dialog box. If the user clicks the Cancel button, presses Esc, or chooses the Close command on the system menu, the `CDialog::OnCancel` function receives control, which simply calls `CDialog::EndDialog` to close the dialog box.

If your program needs to perform any final tasks before the dialog box is closed, you can use ClassWizard to define your own versions of these message-handling functions. To define your own version of `OnOK`, select the `IDOK` object identifier and select the `BN_CLICKED` message. To define your own version of `OnCancel`, select the `IDCANCEL` object identifier and select the `BN_CLICKED` message. The following is the `OnOK` function definition generated by ClassWizard:

```
void CFormat::OnOK()
{
    // TODO: Add extra validation here

    CDialog::OnOK();
}
```

Notice that ClassWizard includes a call to the `CDialog` version of the function, which performs the required default processing. In either an `OnOK` or `OnCancel` function generated by ClassWizard, you should add your statements *before* the call to `CDialog::OnOK`.

it are listed in Table 13.6, while the completed Text menu is shown in Figure 13.13.

Next, define the keyboard accelerator for the Format command. Use the method described previously, specifying the identifier of the Format command, ID_TEXT_FORMAT, and the Ctrl+F keystroke.

TABLE 13.6:   The Properties of the Text Menu Items

ID:	Caption:	Other Features
none	&Text	Popup
ID_TEXT_FORMAT	&Format...\tCtrl+F	none
none	none	Separator
ID_APP_EXIT	E&xit	none

FIGURE 13.13:

The completed Text menu

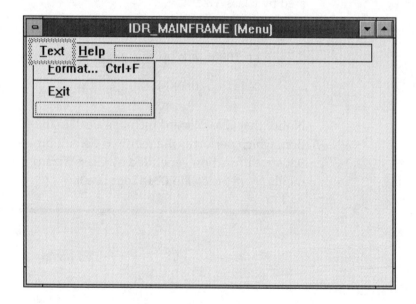

446

Finally, open the string table dialog box and edit the IDR_MAINFRAME string. Change this string from

```
FONTDEMO Windows Application\nFontde\nFONTDE Document
```

to

```
System Font Demo\n\nFONTDE Document
```

This modification will cause the MFC to display the caption "System Font Demo - Untitled" in the main program window, without including a document type name. You can now save your work, quit App Studio, and return to the Visual Workbench.

Adding a Menu Message Handler

Once you have returned to the Visual Workbench, your first task is to define a message-handling function that receives control when the user chooses the Format menu command (or presses the Ctrl+F accelerator keystroke). To do this, run ClassWizard and choose the CFontdemoDoc class name in the Class Name: list box. This selection will cause the message-handling function to be added to the program's document class. In the FONTDEMO program, the choice of class to handle the Format menu command is somewhat arbitrary. In an actual word processing application, however, the Format command would directly affect the document itself (rather than a specific *view* of the document or the application as a whole), and therefore the Format command would best be handled by the document class.

Next, select the identifier for the Format command, ID_TEXT_FORMAT, in the Object IDs: list; select the COMMAND message in the Messages: list; and click the Add Function... button to define the message-handling function. Accept the default function name, OnTextFormat.

Modifying the Source Code

In this section, you will make the required code additions to the document and view classes. First, add the following six data member definitions to the end of the CFontdemoDoc class definition in the file FONTDDOC.H:

```
// added data members:
public:
    BOOL mBold;
    BOOL mItalic;
    int mJustify;
```

```
int mPitch;
int mSpacing;
BOOL mUnderline;
```

These data members store the formatting features of the document; they correspond to the similarly named data members of the dialog class. Next, add code to initialize these data members to the CFontdemoDoc constructor in the file FONTDDOC.CPP:

```
CFontdemoDoc::CFontdemoDoc()
{
    // TODO: add one-time construction code here

    mBold = FALSE;
    mItalic = FALSE;
    mJustify = JUSTIFY_LEFT;
    mPitch = PITCH_VARIABLE;
    mSpacing = 1;
    mUnderline = FALSE;
}
```

These initializations will cause the text to be displayed without the bold, italic, or underlined style; in a variable-pitch font; left-justified; and with single-line spacing.

The next step is to add the code for displaying the Format dialog box to the FONTDDOC.CPP file. At the beginning of this file, add an include statement for the FORMAT.H header file, so that the dialog class definition is available within FONTDDOC.CPP:

```
// fontddoc.cpp : implementation of the CFontdemoDoc class
//

#include "stdafx.h"
#include "fontdemo.h"

#include "fontddoc.h"
#include "format.h"
```

Then add code as follows to the OnTextFormat function that you generated using ClassWizard:

```
void CFontdemoDoc::OnTextFormat()
{
    // TODO: Add your command handler code here

    // declare a dialog class object:
    CFormat FormatDlg;
```

```
// initialize dialog class data members:
FormatDlg.mBold = mBold;
FormatDlg.mItalic = mItalic;
FormatDlg.mJustify = mJustify;
FormatDlg.mPitch = mPitch;
FormatDlg.mSpacing = mSpacing;
FormatDlg.mUnderline = mUnderline;

// display dialog box:
if (FormatDlg.DoModal () == IDOK)
    {
    // save values set in dialog box:
    mBold = FormatDlg.mBold;
    mItalic = FormatDlg.mItalic;
    mJustify = FormatDlg.mJustify;
    mPitch = FormatDlg.mPitch;
    mSpacing = FormatDlg.mSpacing;
    mUnderline = FormatDlg.mUnderline;

    // redraw the text:
    UpdateAllViews (NULL);
    }
}
```

The added code first creates an instance of the dialog class. An instance of a dialog class for a modal dialog box is normally defined as a local variable (which is destroyed as soon as the function in which it is defined returns), because a modal dialog box is displayed only temporarily and is closed before the function returns.

The added code next transfers the values of the document class data members that store the formatting information to the corresponding data members of the dialog class, so that these values will be displayed when the dialog box is first opened.

Next, the code calls the CDialog member function DoModal, which displays the dialog box. DoModal does not return until the user closes the dialog box. If the user closes the dialog box by clicking the OK button, DoModal returns the value IDOK. In this case, OnTextFormat transfers the new values of the dialog class data members back to the document class data members, and then calls UpdateAllViews, which forces the view window to be erased and the OnDraw member function of the view class to receive control. (If the user cancels the dialog box, the document class data members and view window are left unchanged.)

When OnDraw receives control, it redraws the lines of text in the view window, using the new formatting values stored in the document class data members. You should now open the file FONTDVW.CPP and add the code required to perform this task. First, insert an include statement for FORMAT.H at the beginning of the file, so that the enumerators referring to the radio buttons and corresponding styles can be used within FONTDVW.CPP:

```
// fontdvw.cpp : implementation of the CFontdemoView class
//

#include "stdafx.h"
#include "fontdemo.h"

#include "fontddoc.h"
#include "fontdvw.h"

#include "format.h"
```

Then add the code for redrawing the lines to the OnDraw function definition, as follows:

```
void CFontdemoView::OnDraw(CDC* pDC)
{
    CFontdemoDoc* pDoc = GetDocument();

    // TODO: add draw code here

    RECT ClientRect;
    CFont Font;
    LOGFONT LF;
    int LineHeight;
    CFont *PtrOldFont;
    int X, Y;

    // fill LF with the features of a standard system font:
    CFont TempFont;
    if (pDoc->mPitch == PITCH_VARIABLE)
        TempFont.CreateStockObject (SYSTEM_FONT);
    else
        TempFont.CreateStockObject (SYSTEM_FIXED_FONT);
    TempFont.GetObject (sizeof (LOGFONT), &LF);
```

```
// now customize lfWeight, lfItalic, and lfUnderline fields:
if (pDoc->mBold)
   LF.lfWeight = FW_BOLD;
if (pDoc->mItalic)
   LF.lfItalic = 1;
if (pDoc->mUnderline)
   LF.lfUnderline = 1;

// create and select font:
Font.CreateFontIndirect (&LF);
PtrOldFont = pDC->SelectObject (&Font);

// set justification:
GetClientRect (&ClientRect);
switch (pDoc->mJustify)
   {
   case JUSTIFY_LEFT:
      pDC->SetTextAlign (TA_LEFT);
      X = ClientRect.left + 5;
      break;
   case JUSTIFY_CENTER:
      pDC->SetTextAlign (TA_CENTER);
      X = ClientRect.right / 2;
      break;
   case JUSTIFY_RIGHT:
      pDC->SetTextAlign (TA_RIGHT);
      X = ClientRect.right - 5;
      break;
   }

// set text color and background mode:
pDC->SetTextColor (::GetSysColor (COLOR_WINDOWTEXT));
pDC->SetBkMode (TRANSPARENT);

// draw lines:
LineHeight = LF.lfHeight * pDoc->mSpacing;
Y = 5;
pDC->TextOut (X, Y, "This is the first line of sample text.");
Y += LineHeight;
pDC->TextOut (X, Y, "This is the second line of sample text.");
Y += LineHeight;
pDC->TextOut (X, Y, "This is the third line of sample text.");
```

```
// unselect font:
pDC->SelectObject (PtrOldFont);
}
```

This code is similar to the code you added to the `OnPaint` function of the dialog class. The techniques will be explained in Chapter 15.

Setting the Colors

The code you added to the `OnDraw` function of the view class included the following statement:

```
pDC->SetTextColor (::GetSysColor (COLOR_WINDOWTEXT));
```

This statement obtains the current Window Text color that the user has set through the Windows Control Panel, and then assigns this value as the color used to display the text in the view window. Also, the MFC erases the window, using the Window Background color set through the Control Panel. Consequently, the view window conforms to the current Control Panel color scheme.

In contrast, the Format dialog box is displayed using fixed colors. The text is displayed in black (which is the default color if you do not call `SetTextColor` to specify another color). By default, a program generated by AppWizard sets the dialog box background color to gray. To make the text in the dialog box more readable, you can change the background color to white by modifying the call to `SetDialogBkColor` within the `InitInstance` function in FONTDEMO.CPP from:

```
SetDialogBkColor();          // set dialog background color to gray
```

to the following:

```
SetDialogBkColor (RGB (255, 255, 255)); // set dialog b/g color to white
```

Calling `SetDialogBkColor` without passing a parameter sets the dialog background color to gray because the default value of the parameter is

```
RGB (192, 192, 192)
```

which specifies a light gray color. Note that calling `SetDialogBkColor` changes the color of *all* dialog boxes that the program subsequently displays.

The DIALOG1 Source Code

The following listings, Listings 13.1 through 13.8, are the C++ source code listings for the FONTDEMO program you created in this chapter. Note that a copy of these files is included in the \FONTDEMO subdirectory of the companion disk directory.

Listing 13.1

```cpp
// fontdemo.h : main header file for the FONTDEMO application
//

#ifndef __AFXWIN_H__
    #error include 'stdafx.h' before including this file for PCH
#endif

#include "resource.h"        // main symbols

/////////////////////////////////////////////////////////////////////////////
// CFontdemoApp:
// See fontdemo.cpp for the implementation of this class
//

class CFontdemoApp : public CWinApp
{
public:
    CFontdemoApp();

// Overrides
    virtual BOOL InitInstance();

// Implementation

    //{{AFX_MSG(CFontdemoApp)
    afx_msg void OnAppAbout();
        // NOTE - the ClassWizard will add and remove member functions here.
        //    DO NOT EDIT what you see in these blocks of generated code !
    //}}AFX_MSG
    DECLARE_MESSAGE_MAP()
};

/////////////////////////////////////////////////////////////////////////////
```

Listing 13.2

```cpp
// fontdemo.cpp : Defines the class behaviors for the application.
//

#include "stdafx.h"
#include "fontdemo.h"

#include "mainfrm.h"
#include "fontddoc.h"
#include "fontdvw.h"

#ifdef _DEBUG
#undef THIS_FILE
static char BASED_CODE THIS_FILE[] = __FILE__;
#endif

/////////////////////////////////////////////////////////////////////////////
// CFontdemoApp

BEGIN_MESSAGE_MAP(CFontdemoApp, CWinApp)
    //{{AFX_MSG_MAP(CFontdemoApp)
    ON_COMMAND(ID_APP_ABOUT, OnAppAbout)
        // NOTE - the ClassWizard will add and remove mapping macros here.
        //    DO NOT EDIT what you see in these blocks of generated code !
    //}}AFX_MSG_MAP
    // Standard file based document commands
    ON_COMMAND(ID_FILE_NEW, CWinApp::OnFileNew)
    ON_COMMAND(ID_FILE_OPEN, CWinApp::OnFileOpen)
END_MESSAGE_MAP()

/////////////////////////////////////////////////////////////////////////////
// CFontdemoApp construction

CFontdemoApp::CFontdemoApp()
{
    // TODO: add construction code here,
    // Place all significant initialization in InitInstance
}

/////////////////////////////////////////////////////////////////////////////
```

```
// The one and only CFontdemoApp object

CFontdemoApp NEAR theApp;

///////////////////////////////////////////////////////////////////////////
// CFontdemoApp initialization

BOOL CFontdemoApp::InitInstance()
{
    // Standard initialization
    // If you are not using these features and wish to reduce the size
    //  of your final executable, you should remove from the following
    //  the specific initialization routines you do not need.

    SetDialogBkColor (RGB (255, 255, 255)); // set dialog b/g color to white
    LoadStdProfileSettings();  // Load standard INI file options (including MRU)

    // Register the application's document templates.  Document templates
    //  serve as the connection between documents, frame windows and views.

    AddDocTemplate(new CSingleDocTemplate(IDR_MAINFRAME,
        RUNTIME_CLASS(CFontdemoDoc),
        RUNTIME_CLASS(CMainFrame),      // main SDI frame window
        RUNTIME_CLASS(CFontdemoView)));

    // create a new (empty) document
    OnFileNew();

    if (m_lpCmdLine[0] != '\0')
    {
        // TODO: add command line processing here
    }

    return TRUE;
}


///////////////////////////////////////////////////////////////////////////
// CAboutDlg dialog used for App About

class CAboutDlg : public CDialog
{
public:
    CAboutDlg();
```

```
// Dialog Data
    //{{AFX_DATA(CAboutDlg)
    enum { IDD = IDD_ABOUTBOX };
    //}}AFX_DATA

// Implementation
protected:
    virtual void DoDataExchange(CDataExchange* pDX);    // DDX/DDV support
    //{{AFX_MSG(CAboutDlg)
        // No message handlers
    //}}AFX_MSG
    DECLARE_MESSAGE_MAP()
};

CAboutDlg::CAboutDlg() : CDialog(CAboutDlg::IDD)
{
    //{{AFX_DATA_INIT(CAboutDlg)
    //}}AFX_DATA_INIT
}

void CAboutDlg::DoDataExchange(CDataExchange* pDX)
{
    CDialog::DoDataExchange(pDX);
    //{{AFX_DATA_MAP(CAboutDlg)
    //}}AFX_DATA_MAP
}

BEGIN_MESSAGE_MAP(CAboutDlg, CDialog)
    //{{AFX_MSG_MAP(CAboutDlg)
        // No message handlers
    //}}AFX_MSG_MAP
END_MESSAGE_MAP()

// App command to run the dialog
void CFontdemoApp::OnAppAbout()
{
    CAboutDlg aboutDlg;
    aboutDlg.DoModal();
}

/////////////////////////////////////////////////////////////////////////////
// CFontdemoApp commands
```

Listing 13.3

```cpp
// fontddoc.h : interface of the CFontdemoDoc class
//
/////////////////////////////////////////////////////////////////////

class CFontdemoDoc : public CDocument
{
protected: // create from serialization only
    CFontdemoDoc();
    DECLARE_DYNCREATE(CFontdemoDoc)

// Attributes
public:

// Operations
public:

// Implementation
public:
    virtual ~CFontdemoDoc();
    virtual void Serialize(CArchive& ar);   // overridden for document i/o
#ifdef _DEBUG
    virtual  void AssertValid() const;
    virtual  void Dump(CDumpContext& dc) const;
#endif
protected:
    virtual  BOOL  OnNewDocument();

// Generated message map functions
protected:
    //{{AFX_MSG(CFontdemoDoc)
    afx_msg void OnTextFormat();
    //}}AFX_MSG
    DECLARE_MESSAGE_MAP()

// added data members:
public:
    BOOL mBold;
    BOOL mItalic;
    int mJustify;
    int mPitch;
    int mSpacing;
```

```
    BOOL mUnderline;
};
```

//

Listing 13.4

```
// fontddoc.cpp : implementation of the CFontdemoDoc class
//

#include "stdafx.h"
#include "fontdemo.h"

#include "fontddoc.h"
#include "format.h"

#ifdef _DEBUG
#undef THIS_FILE
static char BASED_CODE THIS_FILE[] = __FILE__;
#endif

/////////////////////////////////////////////////////////////////////////////
// CFontdemoDoc

IMPLEMENT_DYNCREATE(CFontdemoDoc, CDocument)

BEGIN_MESSAGE_MAP(CFontdemoDoc, CDocument)
    //{{AFX_MSG_MAP(CFontdemoDoc)
    ON_COMMAND(ID_TEXT_FORMAT, OnTextFormat)
    //}}AFX_MSG_MAP
END_MESSAGE_MAP()

/////////////////////////////////////////////////////////////////////////////
// CFontdemoDoc construction/destruction

CFontdemoDoc::CFontdemoDoc()
{
    // TODO: add one-time construction code here

    mBold = FALSE;
    mItalic = FALSE;
    mJustify = JUSTIFY_LEFT;
    mPitch = PITCH_VARIABLE;
```

```
    mSpacing = 1;
    mUnderline = FALSE;
}

CFontdemoDoc::~CFontdemoDoc()
{
}

BOOL CFontdemoDoc::OnNewDocument()
{
    if (!CDocument::OnNewDocument())
        return FALSE;
    // TODO: add reinitialization code here
    // (SDI documents will reuse this document)
    return TRUE;
}

/////////////////////////////////////////////////////////////////////////////
// CFontdemoDoc serialization

void CFontdemoDoc::Serialize(CArchive& ar)
{
    if (ar.IsStoring())
    {
        // TODO: add storing code here
    }
    else
    {
        // TODO: add loading code here
    }
}

/////////////////////////////////////////////////////////////////////////////
// CFontdemoDoc diagnostics

#ifdef _DEBUG
void CFontdemoDoc::AssertValid() const
{
    CDocument::AssertValid();
}

void CFontdemoDoc::Dump(CDumpContext& dc) const
{
    CDocument::Dump(dc);
}
```

```
#endif //_DEBUG

//////////////////////////////////////////////////////////////////////
// CFontdemoDoc commands

void CFontdemoDoc::OnTextFormat()
{
   // TODO: Add your command handler code here

   // declare a dialog class object:
   CFormat FormatDlg;

   // initialize dialog class data members:
   FormatDlg.mBold = mBold;
   FormatDlg.mItalic = mItalic;
   FormatDlg.mJustify = mJustify;
   FormatDlg.mPitch = mPitch;
   FormatDlg.mSpacing = mSpacing;
   FormatDlg.mUnderline = mUnderline;

   // display dialog box:
   if (FormatDlg.DoModal () == IDOK)
      {
      // save values set in dialog box:
      mBold = FormatDlg.mBold;
      mItalic = FormatDlg.mItalic;
      mJustify = FormatDlg.mJustify;
      mPitch = FormatDlg.mPitch;
      mSpacing = FormatDlg.mSpacing;
      mUnderline = FormatDlg.mUnderline;

      // redraw the text:
      UpdateAllViews (NULL);
      }
}
```

Listing 13.5

```
// mainfrm.h : interface of the CMainFrame class
//
//////////////////////////////////////////////////////////////////////

class CMainFrame : public CFrameWnd
{
```

```
protected: // create from serialization only
    CMainFrame();
    DECLARE_DYNCREATE(CMainFrame)

// Attributes
public:

// Operations
public:

// Implementation
public:
    virtual ~CMainFrame();
#ifdef _DEBUG
    virtual  void AssertValid() const;
    virtual  void Dump(CDumpContext& dc) const;
#endif


// Generated message map functions
protected:
    //{{AFX_MSG(CMainFrame)
        // NOTE - the ClassWizard will add and remove member functions here.
        //    DO NOT EDIT what you see in these blocks of generated code !
    //}}AFX_MSG
    DECLARE_MESSAGE_MAP()
};
```

//

Listing 13.6

```
// mainfrm.cpp : implementation of the CMainFrame class
//

#include "stdafx.h"
#include "fontdemo.h"

#include "mainfrm.h"

#ifdef _DEBUG
#undef THIS_FILE
static char BASED_CODE THIS_FILE[] = __FILE__;
#endif
```

```
/////////////////////////////////////////////////////////////////////
// CMainFrame

IMPLEMENT_DYNCREATE(CMainFrame, CFrameWnd)

BEGIN_MESSAGE_MAP(CMainFrame, CFrameWnd)
    //{{AFX_MSG_MAP(CMainFrame)
        // NOTE - the ClassWizard will add and remove mapping macros here.
        //     DO NOT EDIT what you see in these blocks of generated code !
    //}}AFX_MSG_MAP
END_MESSAGE_MAP()

/////////////////////////////////////////////////////////////////////
// CMainFrame construction/destruction

CMainFrame::CMainFrame()
{
    // TODO: add member initialization code here
}

CMainFrame::~CMainFrame()
{
}

/////////////////////////////////////////////////////////////////////
// CMainFrame diagnostics

#ifdef _DEBUG
void CMainFrame::AssertValid() const
{
    CFrameWnd::AssertValid();
}

void CMainFrame::Dump(CDumpContext& dc) const
{
    CFrameWnd::Dump(dc);
}

#endif //_DEBUG

/////////////////////////////////////////////////////////////////////
// CMainFrame message handlers
```

Listing 13.7

```
// fontdvw.h : interface of the CFontdemoView class
//
/////////////////////////////////////////////////////////////////////////////

class CFontdemoView : public CView
{
protected: // create from serialization only
    CFontdemoView();
    DECLARE_DYNCREATE(CFontdemoView)

// Attributes
public:
    CFontdemoDoc* GetDocument();

// Operations
public:

// Implementation
public:
    virtual ~CFontdemoView();
    virtual void OnDraw(CDC* pDC);  // overridden to draw this view
#ifdef _DEBUG
    virtual void AssertValid() const;
    virtual void Dump(CDumpContext& dc) const;
#endif

// Generated message map functions
protected:
    //{{AFX_MSG(CFontdemoView)
        // NOTE - the ClassWizard will add and remove member functions here.
        //    DO NOT EDIT what you see in these blocks of generated code !
    //}}AFX_MSG
    DECLARE_MESSAGE_MAP()
};

#ifndef _DEBUG // debug version in fontdvw.cpp
inline CFontdemoDoc* CFontdemoView::GetDocument()
    { return (CFontdemoDoc*) m_pDocument; }
#endif

/////////////////////////////////////////////////////////////////////////////
```

Listing 13.8

```
// fontdvw.cpp : implementation of the CFontdemoView class
//

#include "stdafx.h"
#include "fontdemo.h"

#include "fontddoc.h"
#include "fontdvw.h"

#include "format.h"

#ifdef _DEBUG
#undef THIS_FILE
static char BASED_CODE THIS_FILE[] = __FILE__;
#endif

/////////////////////////////////////////////////////////////////////////
// CFontdemoView

IMPLEMENT_DYNCREATE(CFontdemoView, CView)

BEGIN_MESSAGE_MAP(CFontdemoView, CView)
    //{{AFX_MSG_MAP(CFontdemoView)
        // NOTE - the ClassWizard will add and remove mapping macros here.
        //     DO NOT EDIT what you see in these blocks of generated code !
    //}}AFX_MSG_MAP
END_MESSAGE_MAP()

/////////////////////////////////////////////////////////////////////////
// CFontdemoView construction/destruction

CFontdemoView::CFontdemoView()
{
    // TODO: add construction code here
}

CFontdemoView::~CFontdemoView()
{
}

/////////////////////////////////////////////////////////////////////////
// CFontdemoView drawing
```

```
void CFontdemoView::OnDraw(CDC* pDC)
{
    CFontdemoDoc* pDoc = GetDocument();

    // TODO: add draw code here

    RECT ClientRect;
    CFont Font;
    LOGFONT LF;
    int LineHeight;
    CFont *PtrOldFont;
    int X, Y;

    // fill LF with the features of a standard system font:
    CFont TempFont;
    if (pDoc->mPitch == PITCH_VARIABLE)
        TempFont.CreateStockObject (SYSTEM_FONT);
    else
        TempFont.CreateStockObject (SYSTEM_FIXED_FONT);
    TempFont.GetObject (sizeof (LOGFONT), &LF);

    // now customize lfWeight, lfItalic, and lfUnderline fields:
    if (pDoc->mBold)
        LF.lfWeight = FW_BOLD;
    if (pDoc->mItalic)
        LF.lfItalic = 1;
    if (pDoc->mUnderline)
        LF.lfUnderline = 1;

    // create and select font:
    Font.CreateFontIndirect (&LF);
    PtrOldFont = pDC->SelectObject (&Font);

    // set justification:
    GetClientRect (&ClientRect);
    switch (pDoc->mJustify)
        {
        case JUSTIFY_LEFT:
            pDC->SetTextAlign (TA_LEFT);
            X = ClientRect.left + 5;
            break;
```

```
        case JUSTIFY_CENTER:
            pDC->SetTextAlign (TA_CENTER);
            X = ClientRect.right / 2;
            break;
        case JUSTIFY_RIGHT:
            pDC->SetTextAlign (TA_RIGHT);
            X = ClientRect.right - 5;
            break;
    }

    // set text color and background mode:
    pDC->SetTextColor (::GetSysColor (COLOR_WINDOWTEXT));
    pDC->SetBkMode (TRANSPARENT);

    // draw lines:
    LineHeight = LF.lfHeight * pDoc->mSpacing;
    Y = 5;
    pDC->TextOut (X, Y, "This is the first line of sample text.");
    Y += LineHeight;
    pDC->TextOut (X, Y, "This is the second line of sample text.");
    Y += LineHeight;
    pDC->TextOut (X, Y, "This is the third line of sample text.");

    // unselect font:
    pDC->SelectObject (PtrOldFont);
}


/////////////////////////////////////////////////////////////////////////
// CFontdemoView diagnostics

#ifdef _DEBUG
void CFontdemoView::AssertValid() const
{
    CView::AssertValid();
}

void CFontdemoView::Dump(CDumpContext& dc) const
{
    CView::Dump(dc);
}
```

```
CFontdemoDoc* CFontdemoView::GetDocument() // non-debug version is inline
{
    ASSERT(m_pDocument->IsKindOf(RUNTIME_CLASS(CFontdemoDoc)));
    return (CFontdemoDoc*) m_pDocument;
}

#endif //_DEBUG

///////////////////////////////////////////////////////////////////////////
// CFontdemoView message handlers
```

Other Types of Dialog Boxes

The modal dialog box, which was discussed in detail in this chapter, is the most commonly used type of dialog box. This section briefly introduces you to three other types of dialog boxes that you can use in your MFC programs: modeless dialog boxes, form views, and common dialog boxes.

Modeless Dialog Boxes

While a modal dialog box is displayed, the main program window is disabled; the user must therefore close the dialog box before continuing to work in the main window. When you display a *modeless dialog box*, however, the main program window is *not* disabled. As a result, the user can continue working within the main window while the dialog box remains displayed, and the user can switch the focus back and forth between the main window and the dialog box. A modeless dialog box is useful for providing a secondary window that the user can employ in conjunction with the main window. For example, a spell-checking command for a word processor typically displays a modeless dialog box so that the user can make a correction in the document and then resume the spelling check, without having to close and reopen the dialog box.

As with a modal dialog box, you can design a modeless dialog box using App Studio. Typically, however, you assign a modeless dialog box a thin border rather than the default thick border. To do this, double-click the dialog box in App Studio, select the Styles item from the list in the upper-right corner of the dialog properties window, and select the Thin item from the Border: list. Similarly, as with a modal dialog box, you can use ClassWizard to derive a class from `CDialog` to manage a modeless dialog box, and to define data members and message-handling functions.

The following are several differences in the way you display a modeless dialog box:

- You should declare the instance of the dialog class as a global object, or create it using the `new` operator, *rather* than making it a local object. This is necessary because a modeless dialog box remains opened after the function that displays it returns, and the object that manages the dialog box must not be destroyed when this function returns. If you create the object using `new`, be sure to use `delete` to delete the object when you are done with it.

- You display a modeless dialog box by calling `CDialog::Create` rather than `CDialog::DoModal`. Unlike `DoModal`, the `Create` function returns immediately, leaving the dialog box displayed.

- The dialog class must close a modeless dialog box by calling `DestroyWindow` rather than `EndDialog`. You should define your own version of the `OnCancel` function (explained previously), which closes the dialog box by calling `DestroyWindow`; the default version of this function is unsuitable for a modeless dialog box because it calls `EndDialog`.

Form Views

A *form view* is a special type of view window that is based upon a dialog template. Rather than providing an empty surface in which the program can display text or graphics (as a standard view window), a form view displays a collection of predefined controls. A form view is thus a hybrid between a standard view window and a dialog box; like a standard view window, it permanently fills the main program window (or child window in an MDI program), and the user can scroll it if its contents are not completely visible. Like a dialog box, it displays and receives messages from a collection of controls, and it can be designed using the dialog-editing facilities of App Studio. A form view is useful for creating utilities, data entry programs, and other types of applications in which the main window consists primarily of a collection of controls, such as check boxes, edit controls, text controls, and push buttons.

A view class that manages a form view is derived from the MFC `CFormView` class rather than from `CView`. For complete instructions on creating a form view, see the *App Studio User's Guide* manual (Chapter 3, "Using the Dialog Editor," under the heading "Creating a Form View"). See also the *Reference Volume I, Class Library*

Reference manual (the documentation on the `CFormView` class), or the *Foundation Classes* online help file (the topic "CFormView").

Common Dialog Boxes

A *common dialog box* is one that is designed and written by Windows to perform a specific task, such as opening a file or choosing a color. The MFC provides a class for managing each type of common dialog box; these classes are summarized in Table 13.7

TABLE 13.7: Windows Common Dialog Boxes

MFC Class	Dialog Box(es) Managed
CColorDialog	Color (for choosing a color)
CFileDialog	Open (for opening a file), Save As (for saving a file under a specified file name)
CFindReplaceDialog	Find (for finding text), Replace (for replacing text)
CFontDialog	Font (for choosing a text font)
CPrintDialog	Print (for printing a file), Print Setup (for specifying printer settings)

The MFC uses several of these dialog boxes. The MFC code for processing the Open and Save As commands on the File menu uses the `CFileDialog` common dialog box, and the code for processing the Print and Print Setup commands (described in Chapter 18) uses the `CPrintDialog` common dialog box. Also, the `CEditView` MFC class uses the `CFindReplaceDialog` dialog box for implementing the Find and Replace commands on the Edit menu (as described in Chapter 8).

You can display these dialog boxes from your own code to save a great amount of programming effort. You can also customize the appearance and behavior of a common dialog box when you display it. You will learn how to use the `CFontDialog` class in Chapter 15 and the `CColorDialog` class in Chapter 16.

Summary

In this chapter, you learned how to design, display, and manage modal dialog boxes, and you were briefly introduced to several types of special-purpose dialog boxes. The following are the general concepts and techniques that were discussed:

- A modal dialog box is a temporary window that is opened over the main program window to display and obtain information from the user. The user must close a modal dialog box before resuming work in the main window.

- After generating the program with AppWizard, you can design a dialog box by running App Studio and opening the dialog-designing window. App Studio displays a full-sized replica of the dialog box you are creating and provides a palette that allows you to add controls to the dialog box.

- You can use the mouse to change the size or position of the dialog box or any of the controls contained within it. You can set the properties of the dialog box or any control by double-clicking the object and entering the desired values into the properties window. The standard controls you can add by using the palette are shown in Figure 13.5.

- A picture control displays an empty rectangular frame, a solid rectangular block, or an icon.

- A text control displays a text string.

- A group box is a labeled border that can be used to group a set of related controls.

- An edit control allows the user to enter text and provides complete editing facilities.

- A push button is typically used to execute some task immediately.

- A check box is used to enable or disable an option that can be turned on or off independently.

- A radio button is used to select one of a group of mutually exclusive options.

- A list box displays a list of items, such as file names or fonts, and allows the user to scroll through the list and select the desired item.

- A combo box combines a list box with either an edit control or a text control.

- Scroll bar controls are used for displaying horizontal or vertical scroll bars anywhere within the dialog box.

- You can use ClassWizard to create a class (derived from `CDialog`) to manage the dialog box.

- You can also use ClassWizard to define data members of the dialog class. Each of these data members is associated with a particular control, and the MFC automatically transfers data between the data member and the control when the dialog box is displayed.

- Finally, you can use ClassWizard to define message-handling functions for the dialog class.

- You display a modal dialog box by calling the `CDialog::DoModal` function. Control does not return from this call until the user has closed the dialog box.

- You can specify the background color used for dialog boxes by calling the `SetDialogBkColor` function from the `InitInstance` member function of the application class.

- A modeless dialog box is one that can be left open while the user continues to work in the main program window.

- A form view is a special type of view window that displays a collection of controls and that can be designed in App Studio.

- Windows provides a set of predefined common dialog boxes for performing standard tasks, such as opening files or choosing fonts.

Including Tool Bars and Status Bars

- Adding a tool bar and status bar to a new program

- Adding a tool bar to MINIDRAW

- Adding a status bar to MINIDRAW

- The MINIDRAW source code

In this chapter, you will learn how to create two sophisticated user-interface elements that are supported by the Microsoft Foundation Classes: tool bars and status bars. A tool bar consists of a row of buttons, normally displayed at the top of the main program window; the user can click one of these buttons to immediately execute a command or choose an option. A status bar is usually displayed at the bottom of the main window, and is used for printing messages and showing the status of keys or program modes (for example, the Caps Lock key or the overwrite mode in a word processor).

You will learn how to use AppWizard to create a new program that includes a preliminary tool bar and status bar, as well as how to modify these elements to suit the needs of your application. You will also learn how to add a custom tool bar and status bar to an existing MFC program; in the exercises, you will add these features to the MINIDRAW program that you created in previous chapters.

Adding a Tool Bar and Status Bar to a New Program

When you generate a new application using AppWizard, you can include a preliminary tool bar and status bar in the main program window by simply selecting the Initial Toolbar option in the AppWizard Options dialog box. To see what these features look like, generate a basic AppWizard program, naming the program TEST and selecting only the Initial Toolbar feature in the Options dialog box, as shown in Figure 14.1. When you have produced the source files, build and run the program. Figure 14.2 shows the window of the resulting application.

Each of the buttons displayed on the initial tool bar of the TEST program—except the Print button—corresponds to a command on the program menu. Specifically, there is a button for each of the following commands: the New, Open…, and Save commands on the File menu; the Cut, Copy, and Paste commands on the Edit menu; and the About command on the Help menu. Notice that the Cut, Copy, Paste, and Print buttons are *disabled* (that is, they are displayed in light colors and do not respond to the mouse). These buttons are disabled because the program does not initially have message-handling functions for them (the corresponding menu items are also disabled for the same reason); you must provide the handlers yourself using the techniques that will be presented later in the chapter.

FIGURE 14.1:

The AppWizard Options dialog box for generating the TEST program with an initial tool bar and status bar

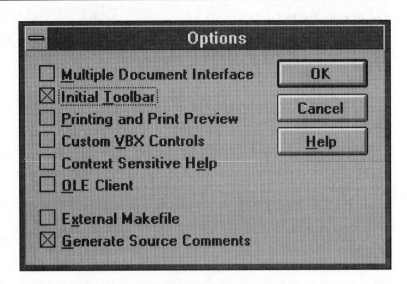

FIGURE 14.2:

The TEST program window

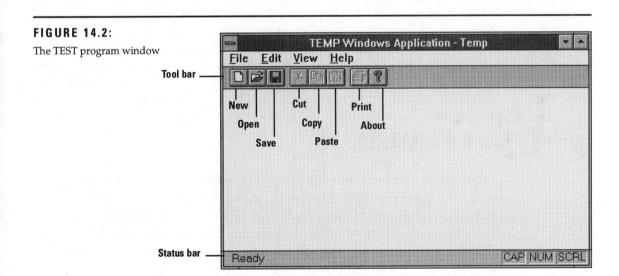

When the user highlights a menu command, or presses the mouse button while the cursor is on a button, the program displays a description of the command within the left *indicator* of the status bar. (Each section of the status bar is known as an indicator.) The three indicators on the right are used to display the current status of the Caps Lock, Num Lock, and Scroll Lock keys. Later in the chapter, you will learn how to specify the description that is displayed for a particular tool bar button or menu command.

The tool bar and status bar generated by AppWizard are termed *initial* because you will probably need to modify them to suit your particular application. You may want to remove some of the buttons on the tool bar, or add new buttons. For example, if you remove a menu command, you will probably want to remove the corresponding button on the tool bar; and if you add a menu command, you may want to add a matching button. You can also include a button for a command that is *not* on the program menu.

Additionally, you might want to modify the status bar. For example, you might add an indicator to display the current status of a program mode, such as the overwrite mode in an editor, or the "record" mode that is active while the program records a macro. The remaining sections in this chapter show you how to add a tool bar and a status bar to an existing MFC program (a program that was initially generated without the Initial Toolbar option). The techniques presented in these sections, however, will also allow you to modify an initial tool bar or status bar generated by AppWizard.

Adding a Tool Bar to MINIDRAW

In this section, you will add a tool bar to the latest version of the MINIDRAW program, which you created in Chapter 11. (If you did not create this version of the program, you can obtain a complete set of the source files in the \MINIDRW4 subdirectory of your directory containing the companion disk files.) The MINIDRAW program, sporting the new tool bar that you will create, is shown in Figure 14.3.

The tool bar contains ten buttons. The first seven buttons allow the user to select a tool for drawing a particular shape; the last three buttons allow the user to choose the thickness of the lines used to draw the figures. (Note that you can choose only one of the first seven buttons, and only one of the last three buttons.) You will not,

FIGURE 14.3:

The MINIDRAW program with its
new tool bar

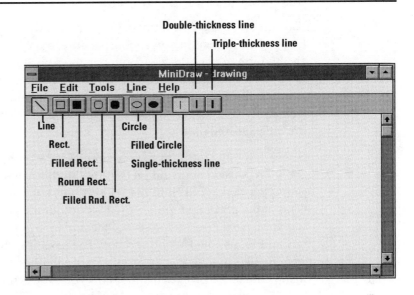

however, add the code for drawing the different figures or using the different line thicknesses until Chapter 16. (The program in this chapter always draws simple lines, regardless of the tool that is selected.)

In this chapter, you will also add menu commands that correspond to the buttons, so that the user can select a drawing tool or line thickness using either a button or a menu command.

Defining the Resources

The first phase of the project is to use App Studio to define the resources for the new version of MINIDRAW. To begin, open the MINIDRAW.MAK project in the Visual Workbench, and choose the App Studio command on the Tools menu to run App Studio.

Designing the Tool Bar Buttons

You will first design the bitmap that is used for displaying the tool bar. The images for all of the buttons in a given tool bar are contained within a single bitmap. To create this bitmap, click the New button in the App Studio resource dialog box, choose the Bitmap item in the Resource Type: list that appears, and click the OK button. App Studio will open the bitmap-designing window—labeled "IDB_BITMAP1 (Bitmap)"—and display a palette of drawing tools and colors that you can use to draw the desired pattern.

Before designing the bitmap, you should set the bitmap properties by choosing the Show Properties command on the App Studio Window menu to open the bitmap properties dialog box. Into the ID: text box, enter the identifier IDR_MAINFRAME. (This is the general identifier used for resources associated with the main frame window.) Next, specify the size of the bitmap by entering 160 into the Width: text box and 15 into the Height: text box. The resulting bitmap will be 160 pixels wide and 15 pixels high. The standard width of a tool bar button is 16 pixels; the total bitmap width of 160 pixels will thus allow you to design 10 buttons. The bitmap height is set to the standard height of a tool bar button, 15 pixels. The completed bitmap properties dialog box is shown in Figure 14.4.

You should also have App Studio display grid lines to help you design the individual tool bar buttons. To do this, choose the Grid Settings... command on the Image menu. Then, select the Pixel Grid option so that App Studio draws grid lines showing the location of each pixel, and select the Tile Grid option so that it draws grid

FIGURE 14.4:

The completed bitmap properties dialog box

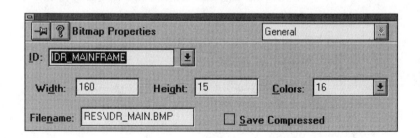

lines around the position of each button. Into the Width: text box, enter the width of a button, 16 pixels, and into the Height: text box, enter the height of a button, 15 pixels. The completed Grid Settings dialog box is shown in Figure 14.5.

FIGURE 14.5:

The completed Grid Settings dialog box

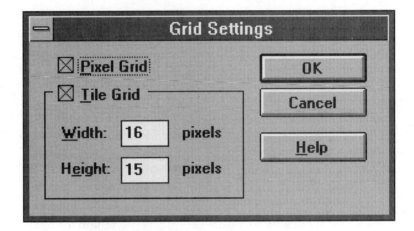

The bitmap-designing window, shown in Figure 14.6, is divided into two panes. The left pane shows the bitmap in its actual size. The right pane displays an enlarged view of the bitmap in which you design the desired pattern. Notice that the individual tool bar buttons are marked with the grid lines that you specified.

NOTE You design only a *single* image for a given button. The MFC automatically changes the button's appearance when the button is "pressed" (that is, when the user presses the mouse button while the cursor is over the button), when it is selected, when it is in the "indeterminate" state, or when it is disabled. These states are described later in the chapter.

You should now use the App Studio drawing tools to design each button. For a complete description of these tools, see the *App Studio User's Guide* (Chapter 7, "Using the Graphics Editor"), or press F1 while working in the bitmap-designing window to view the online help. You should design the buttons in the same order

The bitmap-designing window
(maximized) before creating the
bitmap for the tool bar buttons

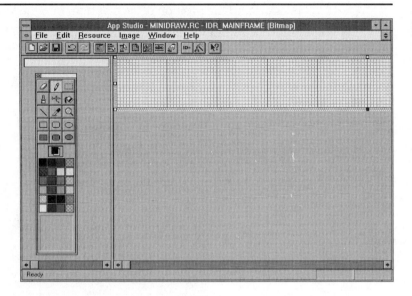

in which they are to be displayed within the program window. Include only the design you want to appear within the central area of each button; do not include borders around individual buttons or gaps between buttons, because the MFC adds these features automatically when it displays the tool bar.

NOTE   After the MFC adds borders to the pattern you have designed for a bitmap button, the final button is 24 pixels wide by 22 pixels high.

Figure 14.7 shows the first five buttons within the completed bitmap for the MINIDRAW program, and Figure 14.8 shows the second five buttons. In this bitmap, the background color is light gray and the foreground color is black. You can draw your own variations on these patterns, but keep in mind the commands that the buttons represent, which are labeled in Figure 14.3.

FIGURE 14.7:

The first five tool bar buttons in the bitmap-designing window

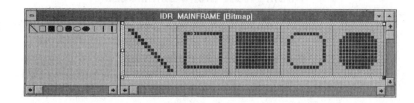

FIGURE 14.8:

The second five tool bar buttons in the bitmap-designing window

TIP

Although you might want to be more creative in your use of color, in general, the most effective colors for tool bar buttons are black, dark gray, light gray, and white. When a button is selected, disabled, or displayed in the indeterminate state, the MFC manipulates the button colors to indicate the button state. These manipulations—as well as the three-dimensional appearance of the button— are most effective when you design the button using shades of gray.

TIP

If you generated an initial tool bar using AppWizard (rather than adding one by hand as described in this section), you can modify the buttons by opening the bitmap-designing window for the IDR_MAINFRAME bitmap and following the general procedures that were given here. If you want to add or remove buttons, you can quickly change the width of the bitmap by dragging the selection handles that are displayed at the right end of the bitmap.

Adding New Menu Commands

You will now use App Studio to add a menu command corresponding to each tool bar button. To do this, open the menu-designing window for the IDR_MAINFRAME menu. To the right of the existing Edit menu, insert a Tools pop-up menu, and add to this menu the items that are shown in Table 14.1. Notice that for each menu command, the table includes a command description that you should enter into the Prompt: text box of the menu item properties dialog box. The MFC automatically displays this description within the status bar (which you will create later in the chapter) whenever the user highlights the menu item or presses the mouse button while the cursor is over the button.

TABLE 14.1: Properties of the Tools Menu Items

ID:	Caption:	Prompt:	Other Features
none	&Tools	none	Popup
ID_TOOLS_LINE	&Line	Select tool to draw straight lines	none
ID_TOOLS_RECTANGLE	&Rectangle	Select tool to draw open rectangles	none
ID_TOOLS_RECTFILL	R&ect Fill	Select tool to draw filled rectangles	none
ID_TOOLS_RECTROUND	Re&ct Round	Select tool to draw open rectangles with rounded corners	none
ID_TOOLS_RECTROUNDFILL	Rec&t Round Fill	Select tool to draw filled rectangles with rounded corners	none
ID_TOOLS_CIRCLE	C&ircle	Select tool to draw open circles or ellipses	none
ID_TOOLS_CIRCLEFILL	Circle &Fill	Select tool to draw filled circles or ellipses	none

The completed Tools menu is shown in Figure 14.9. The commands on this menu correspond to the first seven tool bar buttons and allow the user to choose the current drawing tool.

FIGURE 14.9:

The completed Tools menu

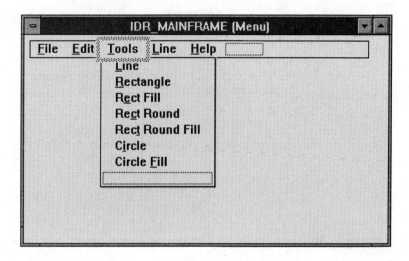

Next, to the right of the Tools menu, insert a Line pop-up menu, containing the items described in Table 14.2. The completed Line menu is shown in Figure 14.10. The commands on this menu correspond to the last three tool bar buttons and allow the user to choose the thickness of the lines used to draw the figures.

TABLE 14.2: Properties of the Line Menu Items

ID:	Caption:	Prompt:	Other Features
none	&Line	none	Popup
ID_LINE_SINGLE	&Single	Draw using single-thickness lines	none
ID_LINE_DOUBLE	&Double	Draw using double-thickness lines	none
ID_LINE_TRIPLE	&Triple	Draw using triple-thickness lines	none

FIGURE 14.10:

The completed Line menu

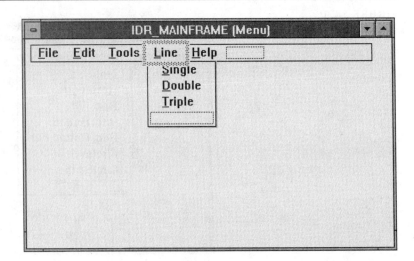

> **TIP**
>
> If you have generated an initial tool bar using AppWizard, and have added one or more buttons to the tool bar bitmap, you might want to add corresponding commands to the program menu. You are not required, however, to have a menu command that corresponds to each tool bar button.

When you have completed defining the new menu items, you can save your work, temporarily quit App Studio, and return to the Visual Workbench.

Modifying the Code

In this section, you will modify the MINIDRAW code to support the tool bar you just designed. The first step is to define a message-handling function within the main frame window class for the WM_CREATE message, which is sent when this window has just been created, immediately before it becomes visible. In this function, you will create the tool bar.

To define the message handler, invoke ClassWizard from within the Visual Workbench (the MINIDRAW project must be open). In the Class Name: list, select the main frame window class, CMainFrame. Then select CMainFrame in the Object IDs: list, select the WM_CREATE identifier in the Messages: list, and click the Add Function button. ClassWizard will immediately add a message-handling function named OnCreate to the CMainFrame class definition.

Before adding code to the OnCreate function, you need to define two data objects. First, open the MAINFRM.H header file and define mToolBar as a protected data member of the CMainFrame class:

```
class CMainFrame : public CFrameWnd
{
protected: // create from serialization only
    CMainFrame();
    DECLARE_DYNCREATE(CMainFrame)

protected:
    CSplitterWnd mSplitterWnd;
    CToolBar mToolBar;

// remainder of CMainFrame definition ...

}
```

CToolBar is the MFC class for managing tool bars. Figure 14.11 illustrates the hierarchy of MFC classes for managing tool bars, as well as status bars and dialog bars (discussed later in the chapter).

Now open the MAINFRM.CPP file and define the ButtonIDs array, which will be used in creating the tool bar:

```
///////////////////////////////////////////////////////////////////////
// CMainFrame

IMPLEMENT_DYNCREATE(CMainFrame, CFrameWnd)

BEGIN_MESSAGE_MAP(CMainFrame, CFrameWnd)
    //{{AFX_MSG_MAP(CMainFrame)
    ON_WM_CREATE()
    //}}AFX_MSG_MAP
END_MESSAGE_MAP()

// IDs for tool bar buttons:
static UINT ButtonIDs [] =
    {
    ID_TOOLS_LINE,
    ID_SEPARATOR,
```

```
ID_TOOLS_RECTANGLE,
ID_TOOLS_RECTFILL,
ID_SEPARATOR,
ID_TOOLS_RECTROUND,
ID_TOOLS_RECTROUNDFILL,
ID_SEPARATOR,
ID_TOOLS_CIRCLE,
ID_TOOLS_CIRCLEFILL,
ID_SEPARATOR,
ID_SEPARATOR,
ID_LINE_SINGLE,
ID_LINE_DOUBLE,
ID_LINE_TRIPLE
};
```

FIGURE 14.11:

The hierarchy of MFC classes for managing tool bars, status bars, and dialog bars

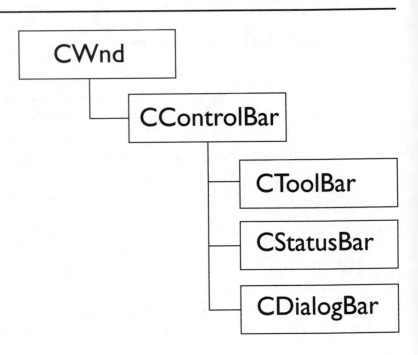

This array will be used to assign an identifier to each button within the bitmap that you designed. Notice that each button is assigned the *same* identifier as the corresponding menu command. As you will see, this allows you to process both the tool bar button and the menu command using a single message-handling function. The special identifier ID_SEPARATOR, is *not* assigned to a tool bar button; rather, it causes the MFC to display a space between two adjoining buttons. Thus, the ButtonIDs array would assign the ID_TOOLS_LINE identifier to the first button in the bitmap, ID_TOOLS_RECTANGLE to the second button, ID_TOOLS_RECTFILL to the third button, ID_TOOLS_RECTROUND to the fourth button, and so on. There would be a space between the first and second buttons, between the third and fourth buttons, and between the fifth and sixth buttons, and there would be a double-width space between the seventh and eighth buttons.

Also in the MAINFRM.CPP file, add code as follows to the OnCreate function that was defined by ClassWizard:

```
int CMainFrame::OnCreate(LPCREATESTRUCT lpCreateStruct)
{
    if (CFrameWnd::OnCreate(lpCreateStruct) == -1)
        return -1;

    // TODO: Add your specialized creation code here

    if (!mToolBar.Create (this) ||
        !mToolBar.LoadBitmap (IDR_MAINFRAME) ||
        !mToolBar.SetButtons (ButtonIDs, sizeof (ButtonIDs) / sizeof (UINT)))
        return -1;

    return 0;
}
```

The call to CToolBar::Create creates the tool bar; passing this specifies that the main frame window is to be the parent (the tool bar is a child window). The call to LoadBitmap loads the bitmap that you created in App Studio. Finally, passing the ButtonIDs array to SetButtons assigns an identifier to each button in the bitmap and specifies spaces between buttons, as explained previously. If any of these functions returns zero, indicating an error, OnCreate returns a value of −1, which signifies that an error has occurred and causes the window to be destroyed.

Before continuing on to the next step, you might want to build the MINIDRAW program to see the results of your work. If you run the program, the tool bar will be displayed; the buttons, however, will be disabled (that is, they will be displayed in light colors and will not respond to the mouse), because you have not yet defined handlers to process the button messages. For the same reason, the corresponding menu items will also be disabled.

> **NOTE**
>
> If you generated an initial tool bar using AppWizard, a `CToolBar` object will already be defined (named `m_wndToolBar`) and the `OnCreate` function will already be fully implemented. If, however, you added or removed one or more buttons from the bitmap, you must update the array containing the button identifiers, which is named `buttons` and is located near the top of the `MAINFRM.CPP` file.

Writing Handlers for the Button Messages

You now need to define and implement the message-handling functions that process the tool bar buttons and the corresponding menu commands.

To define the handlers, run ClassWizard from within the Visual Workbench. Select the `CMinidrawApp` class within the Class Name: list so that the *application* class will handle the messages from the tool bar buttons and the newly added menu commands. (The application class was chosen because the current drawing tool and line thickness affect the operation of the application as a whole, rather than affecting a particular document or view.)

Now select the `ID_LINE_DOUBLE` identifier in the Object IDs: list, select the COMMAND message in the Messages: list, click the Add Function... button, and accept the default function name, `OnLineDouble`. The `OnLineDouble` function will receive control when the user *either* clicks the double-line button *or* chooses the Double command on the Line menu. Later, you will see how a single function is able to process both events.

Next, while the `ID_LINE_DOUBLE` identifier is still selected in the Object IDs: list, select the `UPDATE_COMMAND_UI` message in the Messages: list, click the Add Function... button, and again accept the default function name, `OnUpdateLineDouble`.

OnUpdateLineDouble receives control at regular intervals, whenever the system is idle, so that it can update the double-line button. OnUpdateLineDouble also receives control whenever the user opens the Line drop-down menu, so that it can initialize the Double menu command (as explained in Chapter 9).

Before adding code to the OnLineDouble and OnUpdateLineDouble functions, proceed to use ClassWizard to generate the message-handling functions for the remaining tool bar buttons (and their matching menu commands). To do this, consult Table 14.3, which describes each message-handling function that you need to define. Note that in all cases you should accept the default function name proposed by ClassWizard.

TABLE 14.3: Message-Handling Functions for the MINIDRAW Tool Bar Buttons

Button/ Menu-Command Identifier	Message Identifier	Message-handling Function
ID_LINE_DOUBLE	COMMAND	OnLineDouble
ID_LINE_DOUBLE	UPDATE_COMMAND_UI	OnUpdateLineDouble
ID_LINE_SINGLE	COMMAND	OnLineSingle
ID_LINE_SINGLE	UPDATE_COMMAND_UI	OnUpdateLineSingle
ID_LINE_TRIPLE	COMMAND	OnLineTriple
ID_LINE_TRIPLE	UPDATE_COMMAND_UI	OnUpdateLineTriple
ID_TOOLS_CIRCLE	COMMAND	OnToolsCircle
ID_TOOLS_CIRCLE	UPDATE_COMMAND_UI	OnUpdateToolsCircle
ID_TOOLS_CIRCLEFILL	COMMAND	OnToolsCirclefill
ID_TOOLS_CIRCLEFILL	UPDATE_COMMAND_UI	OnUpdateToolsCirclefill
ID_TOOLS_LINE	COMMAND	OnToolsLine
ID_TOOLS_LINE	UPDATE_COMMAND_UI	OnUpdateToolsLine
ID_TOOLS_RECTANGLE	COMMAND	OnToolsRectangle
ID_TOOLS_RECTANGLE	UPDATE_COMMAND_UI	OnUpdateToolsRectangle
ID_TOOLS_RECTFILL	COMMAND	OnToolsRectfill
ID_TOOLS_RECTFILL	UPDATE_COMMAND_UI	OnUpdateToolsRectfill
ID_TOOLS_RECTROUND	COMMAND	OnToolsRectround
ID_TOOLS_RECTROUND	UPDATE_COMMAND_UI	OnUpdateToolsRectround
ID_TOOLS_RECTROUNDFILL	COMMAND	OnToolsRectroundfill
ID_TOOLS_RECTROUNDFILL	UPDATE_COMMAND_UI	OnUpdateToolsRectroundfill

Before implementing the newly defined message handlers, you need to define and initialize two new data members of the application class: mCurrentThickness, which stores the current line thickness (1, 2, or 3), and mCurrentTool, which stores the identifier of the currently selected tool button. Add the definitions to the end of the CMinidrawApp class definition in MINIDRAW.H:

```
// added data members:
public:
    int mCurrentThickness;
    UINT mCurrentTool;
```

Add the initializations to the CMinidrawApp constructor in MINIDRAW.CPP:

```
CMinidrawApp::CMinidrawApp()
{
    // TODO: add construction code here,
    // Place all significant initialization in InitInstance

    mCurrentThickness = 1;
    mCurrentTool = ID_TOOLS_LINE;
}
```

The version of MINIDRAW presented in Chapter 16 will use mCurrentTool to determine the type of figure to generate when the user begins drawing with the mouse, and it will use mCurrentThickness to determine the thickness of the lines to employ when generating a figure. The initializations you added will cause the program to draw simple lines, which are one pixel thick, until the user chooses another drawing tool or line thickness.

The final step is to add code to the 20 message-handling functions defined by ClassWizard. You need add only a single statement to each function, as follows:

```
/////////////////////////////////////////////////////////////////////////
// CMinidrawApp commands

void CMinidrawApp::OnLineDouble()
{
    // TODO: Add your command handler code here
    mCurrentThickness = 2;
}

void CMinidrawApp::OnUpdateLineDouble(CCmdUI* pCmdUI)
{
    // TODO: Add your command update UI handler code here
```

```
    pCmdUI->SetCheck (mCurrentThickness == 2 ? 1 : 0);
}

void CMinidrawApp::OnLineSingle()
{
    // TODO: Add your command handler code here
    mCurrentThickness = 1;
}

void CMinidrawApp::OnUpdateLineSingle(CCmdUI* pCmdUI)
{
    // TODO: Add your command update UI handler code here
    pCmdUI->SetCheck (mCurrentThickness == 1 ? 1 : 0);
}

void CMinidrawApp::OnLineTriple()
{
    // TODO: Add your command handler code here
    mCurrentThickness = 3;
}

void CMinidrawApp::OnUpdateLineTriple(CCmdUI* pCmdUI)
{
    // TODO: Add your command update UI handler code here
    pCmdUI->SetCheck (mCurrentThickness == 3 ? 1 : 0);
}

void CMinidrawApp::OnUpdateToolsCircle(CCmdUI* pCmdUI)
{
    // TODO: Add your command update UI handler code here
    pCmdUI->SetCheck (mCurrentTool == ID_TOOLS_CIRCLE ? 1 : 0);
}

void CMinidrawApp::OnToolsCircle()
{
    // TODO: Add your command handler code here
    mCurrentTool = ID_TOOLS_CIRCLE;
}

void CMinidrawApp::OnToolsCirclefill()
{
    // TODO: Add your command handler code here
    mCurrentTool = ID_TOOLS_CIRCLEFILL;
}
```

```
void CMinidrawApp::OnUpdateToolsCirclefill(CCmdUI* pCmdUI)
{
    // TODO: Add your command update UI handler code here
    pCmdUI->SetCheck (mCurrentTool == ID_TOOLS_CIRCLEFILL ? 1 : 0);
}

void CMinidrawApp::OnUpdateToolsLine(CCmdUI* pCmdUI)
{
    // TODO: Add your command update UI handler code here
    pCmdUI->SetCheck (mCurrentTool == ID_TOOLS_LINE ? 1 : 0);
}

void CMinidrawApp::OnToolsLine()
{
    // TODO: Add your command handler code here
    mCurrentTool = ID_TOOLS_LINE;
}

void CMinidrawApp::OnToolsRectangle()
{
    // TODO: Add your command handler code here
    mCurrentTool = ID_TOOLS_RECTANGLE;
}

void CMinidrawApp::OnUpdateToolsRectangle(CCmdUI* pCmdUI)
{
    // TODO: Add your command update UI handler code here
    pCmdUI->SetCheck (mCurrentTool == ID_TOOLS_RECTANGLE ? 1 : 0);
}

void CMinidrawApp::OnUpdateToolsRectfill(CCmdUI* pCmdUI)
{
    // TODO: Add your command update UI handler code here
    pCmdUI->SetCheck (mCurrentTool == ID_TOOLS_RECTFILL ? 1 : 0);
}

void CMinidrawApp::OnToolsRectfill()
{
    // TODO: Add your command handler code here
    mCurrentTool = ID_TOOLS_RECTFILL;
}

void CMinidrawApp::OnToolsRectround()
{
    // TODO: Add your command handler code here
```

```
        mCurrentTool = ID_TOOLS_RECTROUND;
}

void CMinidrawApp::OnUpdateToolsRectround(CCmdUI* pCmdUI)
{
    // TODO: Add your command update UI handler code here
    pCmdUI->SetCheck (mCurrentTool == ID_TOOLS_RECTROUND ? 1 : 0);
}

void CMinidrawApp::OnUpdateToolsRectroundfill(CCmdUI* pCmdUI)
{
    // TODO: Add your command update UI handler code here
    pCmdUI->SetCheck (mCurrentTool == ID_TOOLS_RECTROUNDFILL ? 1 : 0);
}

void CMinidrawApp::OnToolsRectroundfill()
{
    // TODO: Add your command handler code here
    mCurrentTool = ID_TOOLS_RECTROUNDFILL;
}
```

To understand how these functions work, first consider OnLineDouble. This function receives control whenever the user either clicks the double-line button on the tool bar or chooses the Double command on the Line menu. In either case, it simply sets the value of the mCurrentThickness data member to 2.

After the mCurrentThickness data member has been set to 2, the double-line button on the tool bar should be selected and the Double menu command should be checked, so that the user can easily see which line thickness is being used. This task is performed by OnUpdateLineDouble. OnUpdateLineDouble is called as soon as the program becomes idle, *and* it is called the next time the user opens the Line popup menu. In either case, OnUpdateLineDouble is passed a pointer to a CCmdUI object, and it simply calls the CCmdUI member function SetCheck, passing it a nonzero value (a nonzero value is passed because mCurrentThickness has been set to 2). If OnUpdateLineDouble is called at idle time, the CCmdUI object is associated with the tool bar button, and calling SetCheck selects this button. If OnUpdateLineDouble is called in response to the user's opening the Line menu, the CCmdUI object is associated with the menu command, and calling SetCheck checks this command. Thus, SetCheck performs the appropriate action depending upon the type of the user-interface object. The selected button and the checked menu item are illustrated below.

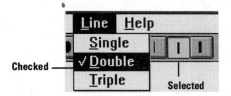

Checked —

Selected

The OnUpdateLineSingle and OnUpdateLineTriple functions are also called at idle-time and the next time the user opens the Line menu. As you can see in the code above, each of these functions passes 0 to SetCheck, thereby *unselecting* the button (if it is selected) or *unchecking* the menu command (if it is checked). Thus, the selection or check mark moves from the previously selected item to the currently selected one.

In general, whenever the user selects a particular line thickness using either the tool bar or the Line menu, the three functions, OnUpdateLineDouble, OnUpdate-LineSingle, and OnUpdateLineTriple, ensure that the corresponding button is selected and that the other two line-thickness buttons are unselected. Likewise, they ensure that only the corresponding menu command is checked on the Line menu.

The functions that handle the seven tool buttons, and the corresponding commands on the Tools menu, work in an exactly analogous way to set the value of the mCurrentTool data member, and to select the current button or check the current menu item.

> **NOTE**   If you generated an initial tool bar using AppWizard, you must write message handlers for any of the nonimplemented commands.

CCmdUI Member Functions

The CCmdUI class provides four member functions that you can use to manage either a tool bar button or a menu command: Enable, SetCheck, SetRadio, and SetText. Each of these functions performs the appropriate action, depending upon whether the CCmdUI object is associated with a tool bar button or menu command.

If you pass FALSE to Enable, it disables either a tool bar button or a menu command, by displaying the object in faint colors and preventing it from being clicked or chosen. If you pass TRUE to Enable, it restores the button or menu command to its normal state.

As you have seen, if you pass 1 to SetCheck it selects a tool bar button or checks a menu command, and if you pass 0 to SetCheck, it unselects a tool bar button or removes the check mark from a menu command. Also, if you pass 2 to SetCheck, it sets a tool bar button to the *indeterminate* state (or simply checks a menu command). Below, you can see a normal, a disabled, a selected, and an indeterminate tool bar button.

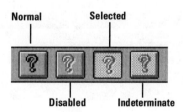

If you pass TRUE to SetRadio, it checks a menu command using a bullet rather than a check mark, or it selects a tool bar button (just like SetCheck). If you pass FALSE to SetRadio, it removes the bullet from a menu command or unselects a button.

Finally, you can call SetText to set the caption for a menu command; this function is not used for tool bar buttons.

You can also use the CCmdUI functions for several additional types of user-interface objects: status-bar indicators, dialog-bar buttons, and other dialog-bar controls. In each case, the function performs the appropriate action (if any) for the particular type of object. For complete details on these member functions, see the documentation on the CCmdUI class in the *Reference Volume I, Class Library Reference* manual, or in the *Foundation Classes* online help file.

Adding a Status Bar to MINIDRAW

To add a status bar to an MFC program, you need only define an object of the CStatusBar class as a member of the main frame window class, define an array storing the identifiers of the desired status-bar indicators, and then call two CStatusBar member functions from the OnCreate member function of the main frame window class (Create and SetIndicators). The MINIDRAW program, with the new status bar that you will add, is shown in Figure 14.12.

FIGURE 14.12:

The MINIDRAW program, complete with new status bar

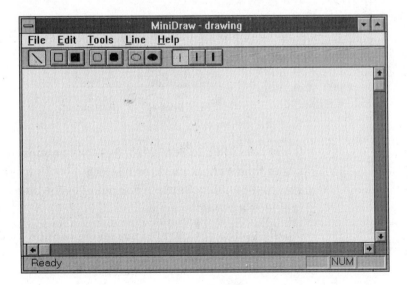

To add the status bar, begin by opening the MAINFRM.H file and defining a CStatusBar object within the CMainFrame class definition, as follows:

```
class CMainFrame : public CFrameWnd
{
protected: // create from serialization only
    CMainFrame();
    DECLARE_DYNCREATE(CMainFrame)

protected:
    CSplitterWnd mSplitterWnd;
    CStatusBar mStatusBar;
    CToolBar mToolBar;

    virtual BOOL OnCreateClient (LPCREATESTRUCT lpcs, CCreateContext* pContext);

// remainder of CMainFrame definition ...

}
```

Next, open the MAINFRM.CPP file, and define the IndicatorIDs array as follows (place this array immediately after the ButtonIDs array that you defined previously):

```
// IDs for status bar indicators:
static UINT IndicatorIDs [] =
    {
    ID_SEPARATOR,
    ID_INDICATOR_CAPS,
    ID_INDICATOR_NUM,
    ID_INDICATOR_SCRL,
    };
```

IndicatorIDs stores the identifier of each indicator that is to be displayed in the status bar. The identifier ID_SEPARATOR creates a blank space; because this identifier is placed first in the array, the resulting status bar will have a blank indicator at its left end. The first indicator in a status bar should be blank because the MFC automatically displays command descriptions within this indicator.

The three remaining identifiers assigned to IndicatorIDs are defined by the MFC. The MFC provides message-handling functions for indicators that have these identifiers; these functions display the current status of the Caps Lock, Num Lock, and Scroll Lock keyboard keys. Note that the first indicator in the array is aligned at the left edge of the status bar, and the remaining indicators are aligned at the right edge.

Finally, add the code for creating the status bar to the OnCreate function within the MAINFRM.CPP file:

```
int CMainFrame::OnCreate(LPCREATESTRUCT lpCreateStruct)
{
    if (CFrameWnd::OnCreate(lpCreateStruct) == -1)
        return -1;

    // TODO: Add your specialized creation code here

    if (!mToolBar.Create (this) ||
        !mToolBar.LoadBitmap (IDR_MAINFRAME) ||
        !mToolBar.SetButtons (ButtonIDs, sizeof (ButtonIDs) / sizeof (UINT)))
        return -1;

    if (!mStatusBar.Create (this) ||
        !mStatusBar.SetIndicators (IndicatorIDs,
        sizeof (IndicatorIDs) / sizeof (UINT)))
        return -1;

    return 0;
}
```

The added code begins with a call to CStatusBar::Create, which creates the status bar. Passing the IndicatorIDs array to CStatusBar::SetIndicators then specifies the identifier of each indicator within the status bar.

Because the MFC provides all of the message-handling functions necessary for displaying information within the status bar, your programming job is over. You can now build and run the program.

The MFC will automatically display command descriptions within the first indicator. As explained previously, when the user highlights a menu item, or presses the mouse button while the cursor is over a button, the MFC displays the command's description. You can specify the description that is displayed for a particular menu command—or a tool bar button that has the same identifier as the menu command—by entering the desired text into the Prompt: text box when setting the menu item properties in App Studio. The description is stored as a string resource that has the same identifier as the menu command. If you want to specify a description for a tool bar button that has no corresponding menu command, define a new string resource that has the same identifier as the button.

The MFC also automatically displays the status of the Caps Lock, Num Lock, and Scroll Lock keys in the second, third, and fourth indicators.

The Idle Prompt

When no menu command is highlighted, and no tool bar button is pressed, the MFC displays the *idle prompt* in the first indicator of the status bar. By default, the idle prompt is "Ready". If you want to specify a different idle prompt, run App Studio, open the string table dialog box, and edit the string with the identifier AFX_IDS_IDLEMESSAGE. Change this string from "Ready" to whatever prompt you want.

NOTE If you specify the Initial Toolbar option when generating a program with AppWizard, all code necessary to display the status bar described in this section will be included in your source files. If you want to change either the indicators that are included or the arrangement of the indicators, you can edit the array containing the indicator identifiers, which is named indicators, and is defined near the beginning of the MAINFRM.CPP file.

The MINIDRAW Source Code

The following listings, Listings 14.1 through 14.8, are the C++ source code listings for the version of the MINIDRAW program you created in this chapter; these files include the code for creating both the tool bar and the status bar. You will find a complete copy of these files in the \MINIDRW5 companion disk subdirectory.

Listing 14.1

```
// minidraw.h : main header file for the MINIDRAW application
//

#ifndef __AFXWIN_H__
```

Dialog Bars

The MFC supports an additional user-interface element known as a *dialog bar* (although this feature is not automatically generated by AppWizard). A dialog bar is managed by the MFC CDialogBar class. Unlike a tool bar managed by the CToolBar class, a dialog bar is based upon a dialog box template. Accordingly, you can design the bar within the dialog-designing window of App Studio, and you can include any type of control that is available for a dialog box.

A dialog bar can be placed at the top or bottom of the main frame window, or along the left or right side of this window. As in a dialog box, the user can press the Tab and Shift+Tab keys to move among the controls.

Creating a dialog bar is similar to creating a form view (described in Chapter 13). For complete information, see the documentation on the CDialogBar class in the *Reference Volume I, Class Library Reference* manual, or in the *Foundation Classes* online help file.

```
    #error include 'stdafx.h' before including this file for PCH
#endif

#include "resource.h"       // main symbols

/////////////////////////////////////////////////////////////////////////////
// CMinidrawApp:
// See minidraw.cpp for the implementation of this class
//

class CMinidrawApp : public CWinApp
{
public:
    CMinidrawApp();

// Overrides
    virtual BOOL InitInstance();
```

```
// Implementation

    //{{AFX_MSG(CMinidrawApp)
    afx_msg void OnAppAbout();
    afx_msg void OnLineDouble();
    afx_msg void OnUpdateLineDouble(CCmdUI* pCmdUI);
    afx_msg void OnLineSingle();
    afx_msg void OnUpdateLineSingle(CCmdUI* pCmdUI);
    afx_msg void OnLineTriple();
    afx_msg void OnUpdateLineTriple(CCmdUI* pCmdUI);
    afx_msg void OnUpdateToolsCircle(CCmdUI* pCmdUI);
    afx_msg void OnToolsCircle();
    afx_msg void OnToolsCirclefill();
    afx_msg void OnUpdateToolsCirclefill(CCmdUI* pCmdUI);
    afx_msg void OnUpdateToolsLine(CCmdUI* pCmdUI);
    afx_msg void OnToolsLine();
    afx_msg void OnToolsRectangle();
    afx_msg void OnUpdateToolsRectangle(CCmdUI* pCmdUI);
    afx_msg void OnUpdateToolsRectfill(CCmdUI* pCmdUI);
    afx_msg void OnToolsRectfill();
    afx_msg void OnToolsRectround();
    afx_msg void OnUpdateToolsRectround(CCmdUI* pCmdUI);
    afx_msg void OnUpdateToolsRectroundfill(CCmdUI* pCmdUI);
    afx_msg void OnToolsRectroundfill();
    //}}AFX_MSG
    DECLARE_MESSAGE_MAP()

// added data members:
public:
    int mCurrentThickness;
    UINT mCurrentTool;
};
```

//

Listing 14.2

```
// minidraw.cpp : Defines the class behaviors for the application.
//

#include "stdafx.h"
#include "minidraw.h"

#include "mainfrm.h"
#include "miniddoc.h"
```

```
#include "minidvw.h"

#ifdef _DEBUG
#undef THIS_FILE
static char BASED_CODE THIS_FILE[] = __FILE__;
#endif

/////////////////////////////////////////////////////////////////////////////
// CMinidrawApp

BEGIN_MESSAGE_MAP(CMinidrawApp, CWinApp)
    //{{AFX_MSG_MAP(CMinidrawApp)
    ON_COMMAND(ID_APP_ABOUT, OnAppAbout)
    ON_COMMAND(ID_LINE_DOUBLE, OnLineDouble)
    ON_UPDATE_COMMAND_UI(ID_LINE_DOUBLE, OnUpdateLineDouble)
    ON_COMMAND(ID_LINE_SINGLE, OnLineSingle)
    ON_UPDATE_COMMAND_UI(ID_LINE_SINGLE, OnUpdateLineSingle)
    ON_COMMAND(ID_LINE_TRIPLE, OnLineTriple)
    ON_UPDATE_COMMAND_UI(ID_LINE_TRIPLE, OnUpdateLineTriple)
    ON_UPDATE_COMMAND_UI(ID_TOOLS_CIRCLE, OnUpdateToolsCircle)
    ON_COMMAND(ID_TOOLS_CIRCLE, OnToolsCircle)
    ON_COMMAND(ID_TOOLS_CIRCLEFILL, OnToolsCirclefill)
    ON_UPDATE_COMMAND_UI(ID_TOOLS_CIRCLEFILL, OnUpdateToolsCirclefill)
    ON_UPDATE_COMMAND_UI(ID_TOOLS_LINE, OnUpdateToolsLine)
    ON_COMMAND(ID_TOOLS_LINE, OnToolsLine)
    ON_COMMAND(ID_TOOLS_RECTANGLE, OnToolsRectangle)
    ON_UPDATE_COMMAND_UI(ID_TOOLS_RECTANGLE, OnUpdateToolsRectangle)
    ON_UPDATE_COMMAND_UI(ID_TOOLS_RECTFILL, OnUpdateToolsRectfill)
    ON_COMMAND(ID_TOOLS_RECTFILL, OnToolsRectfill)
    ON_COMMAND(ID_TOOLS_RECTROUND, OnToolsRectround)
    ON_UPDATE_COMMAND_UI(ID_TOOLS_RECTROUND, OnUpdateToolsRectround)
    ON_UPDATE_COMMAND_UI(ID_TOOLS_RECTROUNDFILL, OnUpdateToolsRectroundfill)
    ON_COMMAND(ID_TOOLS_RECTROUNDFILL, OnToolsRectroundfill)
    //}}AFX_MSG_MAP
    // Standard file based document commands
    ON_COMMAND(ID_FILE_NEW, CWinApp::OnFileNew)
    ON_COMMAND(ID_FILE_OPEN, CWinApp::OnFileOpen)
END_MESSAGE_MAP()

/////////////////////////////////////////////////////////////////////////////
// CMinidrawApp construction

CMinidrawApp::CMinidrawApp()
{
    // TODO: add construction code here,
```

```
      // Place all significant initialization in InitInstance

      mCurrentThickness = 1;
      mCurrentTool = ID_TOOLS_LINE;
}


/////////////////////////////////////////////////////////////////////////////
// The one and only CMinidrawApp object

CMinidrawApp NEAR theApp;

/////////////////////////////////////////////////////////////////////////////
// CMinidrawApp initialization

BOOL CMinidrawApp::InitInstance()
{
      // Standard initialization
      // If you are not using these features and wish to reduce the size
      //  of your final executable, you should remove from the following
      //  the specific initialization routines you do not need.

      SetDialogBkColor();          // set dialog background color to gray
      LoadStdProfileSettings();    // Load standard INI file options (including MRU)

      // Register the application's document templates.  Document templates
      //  serve as the connection between documents, frame windows and views.

      AddDocTemplate(new CSingleDocTemplate(IDR_MAINFRAME,
            RUNTIME_CLASS(CMinidrawDoc),
            RUNTIME_CLASS(CMainFrame),      // main SDI frame window
            RUNTIME_CLASS(CMinidrawView)));

      // create a new (empty) document
      OnFileNew();

      m_pMainWnd->DragAcceptFiles ();

      if (m_lpCmdLine[0] != '\0')
      {
         // TODO: add command line processing here
      }

      return TRUE;
}
```

```
/////////////////////////////////////////////////////////////////////////////
// CAboutDlg dialog used for App About

class CAboutDlg : public CDialog
{
public:
   CAboutDlg();

// Dialog Data
   //{{AFX_DATA(CAboutDlg)
   enum { IDD = IDD_ABOUTBOX };
   //}}AFX_DATA

// Implementation
protected:
   virtual void DoDataExchange(CDataExchange* pDX);    // DDX/DDV support
   //{{AFX_MSG(CAboutDlg)
      // No message handlers
   //}}AFX_MSG
   DECLARE_MESSAGE_MAP()
};

CAboutDlg::CAboutDlg() : CDialog(CAboutDlg::IDD)
{
   //{{AFX_DATA_INIT(CAboutDlg)
   //}}AFX_DATA_INIT
}

void CAboutDlg::DoDataExchange(CDataExchange* pDX)
{
   CDialog::DoDataExchange(pDX);
   //{{AFX_DATA_MAP(CAboutDlg)
   //}}AFX_DATA_MAP
}

BEGIN_MESSAGE_MAP(CAboutDlg, CDialog)
   //{{AFX_MSG_MAP(CAboutDlg)
      // No message handlers
   //}}AFX_MSG_MAP
END_MESSAGE_MAP()

// App command to run the dialog
void CMinidrawApp::OnAppAbout()
{
   CAboutDlg aboutDlg;
```

```
    aboutDlg.DoModal();
}

//////////////////////////////////////////////////////////////////////
// CMinidrawApp commands

void CMinidrawApp::OnLineDouble()
{
    // TODO: Add your command handler code here
    mCurrentThickness = 2;
}

void CMinidrawApp::OnUpdateLineDouble(CCmdUI* pCmdUI)
{
    // TODO: Add your command update UI handler code here
    pCmdUI->SetCheck (mCurrentThickness == 2 ? 1 : 0);
}

void CMinidrawApp::OnLineSingle()
{
    // TODO: Add your command handler code here
    mCurrentThickness = 1;
}

void CMinidrawApp::OnUpdateLineSingle(CCmdUI* pCmdUI)
{
    // TODO: Add your command update UI handler code here
    pCmdUI->SetCheck (mCurrentThickness == 1 ? 1 : 0);
}

void CMinidrawApp::OnLineTriple()
{
    // TODO: Add your command handler code here
    mCurrentThickness = 3;
}

void CMinidrawApp::OnUpdateLineTriple(CCmdUI* pCmdUI)
{
    // TODO: Add your command update UI handler code here
    pCmdUI->SetCheck (mCurrentThickness == 3 ? 1 : 0);
}

void CMinidrawApp::OnUpdateToolsCircle(CCmdUI* pCmdUI)
{
    // TODO: Add your command update UI handler code here
```

```
    pCmdUI->SetCheck (mCurrentTool == ID_TOOLS_CIRCLE ? 1 : 0);
}

void CMinidrawApp::OnToolsCircle()
{
    // TODO: Add your command handler code here
    mCurrentTool = ID_TOOLS_CIRCLE;
}

void CMinidrawApp::OnToolsCirclefill()
{
    // TODO: Add your command handler code here
    mCurrentTool = ID_TOOLS_CIRCLEFILL;
}

void CMinidrawApp::OnUpdateToolsCirclefill(CCmdUI* pCmdUI)
{
    // TODO: Add your command update UI handler code here
    pCmdUI->SetCheck (mCurrentTool == ID_TOOLS_CIRCLEFILL ? 1 : 0);
}

void CMinidrawApp::OnUpdateToolsLine(CCmdUI* pCmdUI)
{
    // TODO: Add your command update UI handler code here
    pCmdUI->SetCheck (mCurrentTool == ID_TOOLS_LINE ? 1 : 0);
}

void CMinidrawApp::OnToolsLine()
{
    // TODO: Add your command handler code here
    mCurrentTool = ID_TOOLS_LINE;
}

void CMinidrawApp::OnToolsRectangle()
{
    // TODO: Add your command handler code here
    mCurrentTool = ID_TOOLS_RECTANGLE;
}

void CMinidrawApp::OnUpdateToolsRectangle(CCmdUI* pCmdUI)
{
    // TODO: Add your command update UI handler code here
    pCmdUI->SetCheck (mCurrentTool == ID_TOOLS_RECTANGLE ? 1 : 0);
}
```

```
void CMinidrawApp::OnUpdateToolsRectfill(CCmdUI* pCmdUI)
{
    // TODO: Add your command update UI handler code here
    pCmdUI->SetCheck (mCurrentTool == ID_TOOLS_RECTFILL ? 1 : 0);
}

void CMinidrawApp::OnToolsRectfill()
{
    // TODO: Add your command handler code here
    mCurrentTool = ID_TOOLS_RECTFILL;
}

void CMinidrawApp::OnToolsRectround()
{
    // TODO: Add your command handler code here
    mCurrentTool = ID_TOOLS_RECTROUND;
}

void CMinidrawApp::OnUpdateToolsRectround(CCmdUI* pCmdUI)
{
    // TODO: Add your command update UI handler code here
    pCmdUI->SetCheck (mCurrentTool == ID_TOOLS_RECTROUND ? 1 : 0);
}

void CMinidrawApp::OnUpdateToolsRectroundfill(CCmdUI* pCmdUI)
{
    // TODO: Add your command update UI handler code here
    pCmdUI->SetCheck (mCurrentTool == ID_TOOLS_RECTROUNDFILL ? 1 : 0);
}

void CMinidrawApp::OnToolsRectroundfill()
{
    // TODO: Add your command handler code here
    mCurrentTool = ID_TOOLS_RECTROUNDFILL;
}
```

Listing 14.3

```
// miniddoc.h : interface of the CMinidrawDoc class
//
/////////////////////////////////////////////////////////////////////////////

class CLine : public CObject
{
protected:
```

```
   int mX1, mY1, mX2, mY2;

   CLine ()
      {}
   DECLARE_SERIAL (CLine)
public:
   CLine (int X1, int Y1, int X2, int Y2)
      {
      mX1 = X1;
      mY1 = Y1;
      mX2 = X2;
      mY2 = Y2;
      }
   void Draw (CDC *PDC);
   CRect GetDimRect ();
   virtual void Serialize (CArchive& ar);
};

class CMinidrawDoc : public CDocument
{
protected: // create from serialization only
   CMinidrawDoc();
   DECLARE_DYNCREATE(CMinidrawDoc)

protected:
   CObArray mObArray;

public:
   CLine *AddLine (int X1, int Y1, int X2, int Y2);
   virtual void DeleteContents ();
   CLine *GetLine (int Index);
   int GetNumLines ();

// Attributes
public:

// Operations
public:

// Implementation
public:
   virtual ~CMinidrawDoc();
   virtual void Serialize(CArchive& ar);   // overridden for document i/o
#ifdef _DEBUG
```

```
   virtual  void AssertValid() const;
   virtual  void Dump(CDumpContext& dc) const;
#endif
protected:
   virtual  BOOL  OnNewDocument();

// Generated message map functions
protected:
   //{{AFX_MSG(CMinidrawDoc)
   afx_msg void OnEditClearAll();
   afx_msg void OnUpdateEditClearAll(CCmdUI* pCmdUI);
   afx_msg void OnEditUndo();
   afx_msg void OnUpdateEditUndo(CCmdUI* pCmdUI);
   //}}AFX_MSG
   DECLARE_MESSAGE_MAP()
};

/////////////////////////////////////////////////////////////////////////////
```

Listing 14.4

```
// miniddoc.cpp : implementation of the CMinidrawDoc class
//

#include "stdafx.h"
#include "minidraw.h"

#include "miniddoc.h"

#ifdef _DEBUG
#undef THIS_FILE
static char BASED_CODE THIS_FILE[] = __FILE__;
#endif

/////////////////////////////////////////////////////////////////////////////
// CMinidrawDoc

IMPLEMENT_DYNCREATE(CMinidrawDoc, CDocument)

BEGIN_MESSAGE_MAP(CMinidrawDoc, CDocument)
   //{{AFX_MSG_MAP(CMinidrawDoc)
   ON_COMMAND(ID_EDIT_CLEAR_ALL, OnEditClearAll)
   ON_UPDATE_COMMAND_UI(ID_EDIT_CLEAR_ALL, OnUpdateEditClearAll)
   ON_COMMAND(ID_EDIT_UNDO, OnEditUndo)
   ON_UPDATE_COMMAND_UI(ID_EDIT_UNDO, OnUpdateEditUndo)
```

```
    //}}AFX_MSG_MAP
END_MESSAGE_MAP()

/////////////////////////////////////////////////////////////////////////
// CMinidrawDoc construction/destruction

CMinidrawDoc::CMinidrawDoc()
{
    // TODO: add one-time construction code here
}

CMinidrawDoc::~CMinidrawDoc()
{
}

BOOL CMinidrawDoc::OnNewDocument()
{
    if (!CDocument::OnNewDocument())
        return FALSE;
    // TODO: add reinitialization code here
    // (SDI documents will reuse this document)
    return TRUE;
}


/////////////////////////////////////////////////////////////////////////
// CMinidrawDoc serialization

void CMinidrawDoc::Serialize(CArchive& ar)
{
    if (ar.IsStoring())
    {
        // TODO: add storing code here

    mObArray.Serialize (ar);
    }
    else
    {
        // TODO: add loading code here

    mObArray.Serialize (ar);
    }
}


/////////////////////////////////////////////////////////////////////////
```

```
// CMinidrawDoc diagnostics

#ifdef _DEBUG
void CMinidrawDoc::AssertValid() const
{
    CDocument::AssertValid();
}

void CMinidrawDoc::Dump(CDumpContext& dc) const
{
    CDocument::Dump(dc);
}

#endif //_DEBUG

/////////////////////////////////////////////////////////////////////////////
// CMinidrawDoc commands

IMPLEMENT_SERIAL (CLine, CObject, 1)

void CLine::Draw (CDC *PDC)
    {
    PDC->MoveTo (mX1, mY1);
    PDC->LineTo (mX2, mY2);
    }

CRect CLine::GetDimRect ()
    {
    return CRect
      (min (mX1, mX2),
       min (mY1, mY2),
       max (mX1, mX2) + 1,
       max (mY1, mY2) + 1);
    }

void CLine::Serialize (CArchive& ar)
    {
    if (ar.IsStoring())
       ar << (WORD)mX1 << (WORD)mY1 << (WORD)mX2 << (WORD)mY2;
    else
       ar >> (WORD &)mX1 >> (WORD &)mY1 >> (WORD &)mX2 >> (WORD &)mY2;
    }

CLine *CMinidrawDoc::AddLine (int X1, int Y1, int X2, int Y2)
```

```
   {
   CLine *PLine = new CLine (X1, Y1, X2, Y2);
   mObArray.Add (PLine);
   SetModifiedFlag ();
   return PLine;
   }

CLine *CMinidrawDoc::GetLine (int Index)
   {
   if (Index < 0 || Index > mObArray.GetUpperBound ())
      return 0;
   return (CLine *)mObArray.GetAt (Index);
   }

int CMinidrawDoc::GetNumLines ()
   {
   return mObArray.GetSize ();
   }

void CMinidrawDoc::DeleteContents ()
   {
   int Index = mObArray.GetSize ();
   while (Index--)
      delete mObArray.GetAt (Index);
   mObArray.RemoveAll ();
   }

void CMinidrawDoc::OnEditClearAll()
{
   // TODO: Add your command handler code here

   DeleteContents ();
   UpdateAllViews (0);
   SetModifiedFlag ();
}

void CMinidrawDoc::OnUpdateEditClearAll(CCmdUI* pCmdUI)
{
   // TODO: Add your command update UI handler code here

   pCmdUI->Enable (mObArray.GetSize ());
}
```

```
void CMinidrawDoc::OnEditUndo()
{
    // TODO: Add your command handler code here

    int Index = mObArray.GetUpperBound ();
    if (Index > -1)
        {
        delete mObArray.GetAt (Index);
        mObArray.RemoveAt (Index);
        }
    UpdateAllViews (0);
    SetModifiedFlag ();
}

void CMinidrawDoc::OnUpdateEditUndo(CCmdUI* pCmdUI)
{
    // TODO: Add your command update UI handler code here

    pCmdUI->Enable (mObArray.GetSize ());
}
```

Listing 14.5

```
// mainfrm.h : interface of the CMainFrame class
//
/////////////////////////////////////////////////////////////////////////////

class CMainFrame : public CFrameWnd
{
protected: // create from serialization only
    CMainFrame();
    DECLARE_DYNCREATE(CMainFrame)

protected:
    CSplitterWnd mSplitterWnd;
    CStatusBar mStatusBar;
    CToolBar mToolBar;

    virtual BOOL OnCreateClient (LPCREATESTRUCT lpcs, CCreateContext* pContext);

// Attributes
public:

// Operations
```

```
public:

// Implementation
public:
    virtual ~CMainFrame();
#ifdef _DEBUG
    virtual  void AssertValid() const;
    virtual  void Dump(CDumpContext& dc) const;
#endif


// Generated message map functions
protected:
    //{{AFX_MSG(CMainFrame)
    afx_msg int OnCreate(LPCREATESTRUCT lpCreateStruct);
    //}}AFX_MSG
    DECLARE_MESSAGE_MAP()
};
```

///

Listing 14.6

```
// mainfrm.cpp : implementation of the CMainFrame class
//

#include "stdafx.h"
#include "minidraw.h"

#include "mainfrm.h"

#ifdef _DEBUG
#undef THIS_FILE
static char BASED_CODE THIS_FILE[] = __FILE__;
#endif

///////////////////////////////////////////////////////////////////////
// CMainFrame

IMPLEMENT_DYNCREATE(CMainFrame, CFrameWnd)

BEGIN_MESSAGE_MAP(CMainFrame, CFrameWnd)
    //{{AFX_MSG_MAP(CMainFrame)
    ON_WM_CREATE()
    //}}AFX_MSG_MAP
```

```
END_MESSAGE_MAP()

// IDs for tool bar buttons:
static UINT ButtonIDs [] =
    {
    ID_TOOLS_LINE,
    ID_SEPARATOR,
    ID_TOOLS_RECTANGLE,
    ID_TOOLS_RECTFILL,
    ID_SEPARATOR,
    ID_TOOLS_RECTROUND,
    ID_TOOLS_RECTROUNDFILL,
    ID_SEPARATOR,
    ID_TOOLS_CIRCLE,
    ID_TOOLS_CIRCLEFILL,
    ID_SEPARATOR,
    ID_SEPARATOR,
    ID_LINE_SINGLE,
    ID_LINE_DOUBLE,
    ID_LINE_TRIPLE
    };

// IDs for status bar indicators:
static UINT IndicatorIDs [] =
    {
    ID_SEPARATOR,
    ID_INDICATOR_CAPS,
    ID_INDICATOR_NUM,
    ID_INDICATOR_SCRL
    };

/////////////////////////////////////////////////////////////////////////////
// CMainFrame construction/destruction

CMainFrame::CMainFrame()
{
    // TODO: add member initialization code here
}

CMainFrame::~CMainFrame()
{
}
```

```
////////////////////////////////////////////////////////////////////////
// CMainFrame diagnostics

#ifdef _DEBUG
void CMainFrame::AssertValid() const
{
    CFrameWnd::AssertValid();
}

void CMainFrame::Dump(CDumpContext& dc) const
{
    CFrameWnd::Dump(dc);
}

#endif //_DEBUG

////////////////////////////////////////////////////////////////////////
// CMainFrame message handlers

BOOL CMainFrame::OnCreateClient (LPCREATESTRUCT lpcs, CCreateContext* pContext)
    {
    return mSplitterWnd.Create
        (this,                // parent of splitter window
        1,                    // maximum rows
        2,                    // maximum columns
        CSize (15, 15),       // minimum pane size
        pContext);            // pass on context information
    }

int CMainFrame::OnCreate(LPCREATESTRUCT lpCreateStruct)
{
    if (CFrameWnd::OnCreate(lpCreateStruct) == -1)
        return -1;

    // TODO: Add your specialized creation code here

    if (!mToolBar.Create (this) ||
        !mToolBar.LoadBitmap (IDR_MAINFRAME) ||
        !mToolBar.SetButtons (ButtonIDs, sizeof (ButtonIDs) / sizeof (UINT)))
        return -1;

    if (!mStatusBar.Create (this) ||
        !mStatusBar.SetIndicators (IndicatorIDs,
        sizeof (IndicatorIDs) / sizeof (UINT)))
```

```
        return -1;

    return 0;
}
```

Listing 14.7

```
// minidvw.h : interface of the CMinidrawView class
//
/////////////////////////////////////////////////////////////////////////////

class CMinidrawView : public CScrollView
{
protected: // create from serialization only
    CMinidrawView();
    DECLARE_DYNCREATE(CMinidrawView)

protected:
    CString mClassName;
    int mDragging;
    HCURSOR mHArrow;
    HCURSOR mHCross;
    CPoint mPointOld;
    CPoint mPointOrigin;

    virtual void OnInitialUpdate ();
    virtual void OnUpdate (CView* pSender, LPARAM lHint, CObject* pHint);
    virtual BOOL PreCreateWindow (CREATESTRUCT& cs);

// Attributes
public:
    CMinidrawDoc* GetDocument();

// Operations
public:

// Implementation
public:
    virtual ~CMinidrawView();
    virtual void OnDraw(CDC* pDC);   // overridden to draw this view
#ifdef _DEBUG
```

```
    virtual void AssertValid() const;
    virtual void Dump(CDumpContext& dc) const;
#endif

// Generated message map functions
protected:
    //{{AFX_MSG(CMinidrawView)
    afx_msg void OnLButtonDown(UINT nFlags, CPoint point);
    afx_msg void OnMouseMove(UINT nFlags, CPoint point);
    afx_msg void OnLButtonUp(UINT nFlags, CPoint point);
    //}}AFX_MSG
    DECLARE_MESSAGE_MAP()
};

#ifndef _DEBUG // debug version in minidvw.cpp
inline CMinidrawDoc* CMinidrawView::GetDocument()
    { return (CMinidrawDoc*) m_pDocument; }
#endif
```

///

Listing 14.8

```
// minidvw.cpp : implementation of the CMinidrawView class
//

#include "stdafx.h"
#include "minidraw.h"

#include "miniddoc.h"
#include "minidvw.h"

#ifdef _DEBUG
#undef THIS_FILE
static char BASED_CODE THIS_FILE[] = __FILE__;
#endif

/////////////////////////////////////////////////////////////////////////////
// CMinidrawView

IMPLEMENT_DYNCREATE(CMinidrawView, CScrollView)

BEGIN_MESSAGE_MAP(CMinidrawView, CScrollView)
    //{{AFX_MSG_MAP(CMinidrawView)
    ON_WM_LBUTTONDOWN()
```

```
    ON_WM_MOUSEMOVE()
    ON_WM_LBUTTONUP()
    ON_WM_KEYDOWN()
    //}}AFX_MSG_MAP
END_MESSAGE_MAP()

/////////////////////////////////////////////////////////////////////////
// CMinidrawView construction/destruction

CMinidrawView::CMinidrawView()
{
    // TODO: add construction code here

    mDragging = 0;
    mHArrow = AfxGetApp ()->LoadStandardCursor (IDC_ARROW);
    mHCross = AfxGetApp ()->LoadStandardCursor (IDC_CROSS);
}

CMinidrawView::~CMinidrawView()
{
}

/////////////////////////////////////////////////////////////////////////
// CMinidrawView drawing

void CMinidrawView::OnDraw(CDC* pDC)
{
    CMinidrawDoc* pDoc = GetDocument();

    // TODO: add draw code here

    CSize ScrollSize = GetTotalSize ();
    pDC->MoveTo (ScrollSize.cx, 0);
    pDC->LineTo (ScrollSize.cx, ScrollSize.cy);
    pDC->LineTo (0, ScrollSize.cy);

    CRect ClipRect;
    CRect DimRect;
    CRect IntRect;
    CLine *PLine;
    pDC->GetClipBox (&ClipRect);

    int Index = pDoc->GetNumLines ();
    while (Index--)
        {
```

```
      PLine = pDoc->GetLine (Index);
      DimRect = PLine->GetDimRect ();
      if (IntRect.IntersectRect (DimRect, ClipRect))
         PLine->Draw (pDC);
      }
}


/////////////////////////////////////////////////////////////////////////
// CMinidrawView diagnostics

#ifdef _DEBUG
void CMinidrawView::AssertValid() const
{
   CScrollView::AssertValid();
}

void CMinidrawView::Dump(CDumpContext& dc) const
{
   CScrollView::Dump(dc);
}

CMinidrawDoc* CMinidrawView::GetDocument() // non-debug version is inline
{
   ASSERT(m_pDocument->IsKindOf(RUNTIME_CLASS(CMinidrawDoc)));
   return (CMinidrawDoc*) m_pDocument;
}

#endif //_DEBUG


/////////////////////////////////////////////////////////////////////////
// CMinidrawView message handlers

void CMinidrawView::OnLButtonDown(UINT nFlags, CPoint point)
{
   // TODO: Add your message handler code here and/or call default

   CClientDC ClientDC (this);
   OnPrepareDC (&ClientDC);
   ClientDC.DPtoLP (&point);

   // test whether cursor is within drawing area of view window:
   CSize ScrollSize = GetTotalSize ();
   CRect ScrollRect (0, 0, ScrollSize.cx, ScrollSize.cy);
   if (!ScrollRect.PtInRect (point))
```

```
        return;

    // save cursor position, capture mouse, & set dragging flag:
    mPointOrigin = point;
    mPointOld = point;
    SetCapture ();
    mDragging = 1;

    // clip mouse cursor:
    ClientDC.LPtoDP (&ScrollRect);
    CRect ViewRect;
    GetClientRect (&ViewRect);
    CRect IntRect;
    IntRect.IntersectRect (&ScrollRect, &ViewRect);
    ClientToScreen (&IntRect);
    ::ClipCursor (&IntRect);

    CScrollView::OnLButtonDown(nFlags, point);
}

void CMinidrawView::OnMouseMove(UINT nFlags, CPoint point)
{
    // TODO: Add your message handler code here and/or call default

    CClientDC ClientDC (this);
    OnPrepareDC (&ClientDC);
    ClientDC.DPtoLP (&point);

    CSize ScrollSize = GetTotalSize ();
    CRect ScrollRect (0, 0, ScrollSize.cx, ScrollSize.cy);
    if (ScrollRect.PtInRect (point))
        ::SetCursor (mHCross);
    else
        ::SetCursor (mHArrow);

    if (mDragging)
        {
        ClientDC.SetROP2 (R2_NOT);
        ClientDC.MoveTo (mPointOrigin);
        ClientDC.LineTo (mPointOld);
        ClientDC.MoveTo (mPointOrigin);
        ClientDC.LineTo (point);
        mPointOld = point;
        }
```

```
    CScrollView::OnMouseMove(nFlags, point);
}

void CMinidrawView::OnLButtonUp(UINT nFlags, CPoint point)
{
    // TODO: Add your message handler code here and/or call default

    if (mDragging)
        {
        mDragging = 0;
        ::ReleaseCapture ();
        ::ClipCursor (NULL);

        CClientDC ClientDC (this);
        OnPrepareDC (&ClientDC);
        ClientDC.DPtoLP (&point);

        ClientDC.SetROP2 (R2_NOT);
        ClientDC.MoveTo (mPointOrigin);
        ClientDC.LineTo (mPointOld);
        ClientDC.SetROP2 (R2_COPYPEN);
        ClientDC.MoveTo (mPointOrigin);
        ClientDC.LineTo (point);

        CMinidrawDoc* PDoc = GetDocument();
        CLine *PCLine;
        PCLine = PDoc->AddLine (mPointOrigin.x, mPointOrigin.y, point.x, point.y);
        PDoc->UpdateAllViews (this, 0, PCLine);
        }

    CScrollView::OnLButtonUp(nFlags, point);
}

BOOL CMinidrawView::PreCreateWindow (CREATESTRUCT& cs)
    {
    mClassName = AfxRegisterWndClass
        (CS_HREDRAW | CS_VREDRAW,            // class styles
        0,                                   // no cursor
        (HBRUSH)::GetStockObject (WHITE_BRUSH),   // set white background brush
        0);                                  // no icon
    cs.lpszClass = mClassName;

    return CScrollView::PreCreateWindow (cs);
    }
```

```
void CMinidrawView::OnInitialUpdate ()
   {
   SIZE Size = {640, 480};
   SetScrollSizes (MM_TEXT, Size);
   CScrollView::OnInitialUpdate ();
   }

void CMinidrawView::OnUpdate (CView* pSender, LPARAM lHint, CObject* pHint)
   {
   if (pHint != 0)
      {
      CRect InvalidRect = ((CLine *)pHint)->GetDimRect ();
      CClientDC ClientDC (this);
      OnPrepareDC (&ClientDC);
      ClientDC.LPtoDP (&InvalidRect);
      InvalidateRect (&InvalidRect);
      }
   else
      CScrollView::OnUpdate (pSender, lHint, pHint);
   }
```

Summary

This chapter described the techniques for adding custom tool bars and status bars to your MFC programs. The following are the general points that were discussed:

- If you are generating a program using AppWizard, you can include a preliminary tool bar and status bar by specifying the Initial Toolbar option. The initial tool bar contains buttons that allow the user to quickly execute many of the program's menu commands. The initial status bar displays descriptions of the menu and tool bar commands, as well as the status of several keys.

- You will probably need to modify the initial tool bar to make it more suitable for your particular application.

- To add a custom tool bar to an existing MFC program, the first step is to use App Studio to create a single bitmap that contains an image for each button to be displayed in the tool bar.

- If desired, you can define menu commands corresponding to one or more of your tool bar buttons, to provide the user with an alternative way to execute the command.

- To add a tool bar, you must also define an object of the MFC `CToolBar` class as a member of your main frame window class, and then create the tool bar by calling several `CToolBar` member functions (`Create`, `LoadBitmap`, and `SetButtons`). These functions should be called from a `WM_CREATE` message-handling function within the main frame window class; you can define this message handler using ClassWizard.

- You define message-handling functions that process the tool bar commands in the same way that you define message handlers for menu commands. In fact, a single function can handle messages from either a tool bar button or a corresponding menu command.

- You can add a status bar to an existing MFC program by defining an instance of the `CStatusBar` class as a member of your main frame window class, and then calling the `CStatusBar` member functions `Create` and `SetIndicators` from the `WM_CREATE` message handler of the main frame window class.

FIFTEEN

Performing Character I/O

- Displaying text

- Reading the keyboard

- Managing the caret

- The TEXTDEMO source code

- The ECHO source code

The programs given in previous chapters have relied primarily on standard Windows interface elements—such as title bars, menus, edit controls, text controls, and status bars—for displaying information and obtaining input from the user. When you use these elements, Windows and the MFC provide the code for drawing text and for reading character input. In this chapter, you will learn how to do the work yourself. Specifically, you will learn how to display text directly within a view window, how to read individual characters that the user types, and how to manage the blinking *caret* that marks the position in a document where characters are inserted.

Displaying Text

In this section, you will create an example program named TEXTDEMO, which demonstrates the main steps for displaying lines of text within a view window. The TEXTDEMO program allows you to select a font by choosing the Font... command on the Options menu, which opens the Font dialog box. In the Font dialog box, you can select the font name (for example, Courier), the style (for example, bold), the font size, one or more font effects (strikeout or underline), as well as the text color. Once you have selected all desired font features and have closed the Font dialog box, the program displays complete information on the font; additionally, the lines of text containing this information are displayed *using* the specified font. Figure 15.1 shows the Font dialog box after the user has chosen a set of features, and Figure 15.2 shows the resulting TEXTDEMO program window after the user has clicked OK to close the dialog box.

NOTE

As you will discover in Chapter 18, the techniques you learn here can also be used to display text on a printed page.

FIGURE 15.1:

The Font dialog box, specifying the features of a font

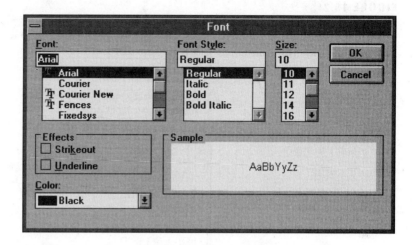

Generating the Program

To generate the TEXTDEMO source files, run AppWizard from the Visual Work-bench. In AppWizard, name the project TEXTDEMO, specify a project subdirectory that is reserved exclusively for the TEXTDEMO project, and select only the Generate Source Comments item in the Options dialog box.

Writing Code to Display the Lines

The first step is to write the code for displaying the lines of text in the view window. As usual, this text is stored by the document class (later you will see how it is generated) and it is displayed by the OnDraw member function of the view class.

Before adding code to OnDraw, open the TEXTDVW.H file and enter the following definition for the constant MARGIN, which stores the width of the margin between the top and left edge of the view window and the text:

```
// textdvw.h : interface of the CTextdemoView class
//
/////////////////////////////////////////////////////////////////////////////

const int MARGIN = 10;      // margin displayed at top and left of view window
```

FIGURE 15.2:

The resulting TEXTDEMO program window, after clicking OK in the Font dialog box shown in Figure 15.1

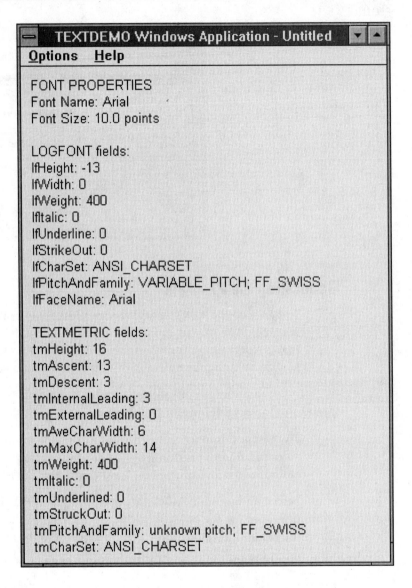

```
TEXTDEMO Windows Application - Untitled

Options   Help

FONT PROPERTIES
Font Name: Arial
Font Size: 10.0 points

LOGFONT fields:
lfHeight: -13
lfWidth: 0
lfWeight: 400
lfItalic: 0
lfUnderline: 0
lfStrikeOut: 0
lfCharSet: ANSI_CHARSET
lfPitchAndFamily: VARIABLE_PITCH; FF_SWISS
lfFaceName: Arial

TEXTMETRIC fields:
tmHeight: 16
tmAscent: 13
tmDescent: 3
tmInternalLeading: 3
tmExternalLeading: 0
tmAveCharWidth: 6
tmMaxCharWidth: 14
tmWeight: 400
tmItalic: 0
tmUnderlined: 0
tmStruckOut: 0
tmPitchAndFamily: unknown pitch; FF_SWISS
tmCharSet: ANSI_CHARSET
```

Now open TEXTDVW.CPP and add the code for displaying the lines of text to the OnDraw function:

```
void CTextdemoView::OnDraw(CDC* pDC)
{
    CTextdemoDoc* pDoc = GetDocument();

    // TODO: add draw code here

    // return if font has not yet been created:
    if (pDoc->mFont.m_hObject == NULL)
        return;

    RECT ClipRect;
    int LineHeight;
    TEXTMETRIC TM;
    int Y = MARGIN;

    // select font into device context object:
    pDC->SelectObject (&pDoc->mFont);

    // obtain text metrics:
    pDC->GetTextMetrics (&TM);
    LineHeight = TM.tmHeight + TM.tmExternalLeading;

    // set other text attributes:
    pDC->SetTextColor (pDoc->mColor);
    pDC->SetBkMode (TRANSPARENT);

    // obtain coordinates of update region:
    pDC->GetClipBox (&ClipRect);

    // display title line:
    pDC->TextOut (MARGIN, Y, "FONT PROPERTIES");

    // display text lines:
    for (int Line = 0; Line < NUMLINES; ++Line)
        {
        Y += LineHeight;
        if (Y + LineHeight >= ClipRect.top && Y <= ClipRect.bottom)
            pDC->TextOut (MARGIN, Y, pDoc->mLineTable [Line]);
        }
}
```

The code you added to OnDraw illustrates the basic steps for displaying text within a view window, which can be summarized as follows:

1. Obtain a device context object.

2. Select a text font.

3. Obtain text measurements.

4. Set other text attributes.

5. Obtain the dimensions of the update region (that is, the portion of the view window marked for repainting).

6. Display the text lines that fall within the update region.

If the user has not yet chosen the Font... menu command to select a font, OnDraw returns immediately, because no text is yet available. (The text describes a font and is generated immediately after the user selects a font, as will be described later in the chapter.)

OnDraw does not do anything to accomplish step 1, because it is passed a handle to a device context object that has already been created. Recall that to display text or graphics, you must have a device context object. A device context object is associated with a specific device (such as a window on the screen or a printer); it stores information on the font and other display attributes, and provides member functions for drawing text and graphics on the associated device. If a program displays output from a function other than the OnDraw member function of the view class, it must create its own device context object. (This technique is demonstrated by the CEchoView::OnChar function in the ECHO program presented later in the chapter.)

To specify the font that is used to display the text (step 2), OnDraw calls the CDC member function SelectObject:

```
pDC->SelectObject (&pDoc->mFont);
```

SelectObject is passed the address of a font object. This object contains a complete description of the desired font. As you will see later in the chapter, the document class initializes the font object with a font description whenever the user chooses a new font. Once the font object is selected into the device context object, all subsequent text output generated through that device context is displayed using the font that matches the description stored in the font object (or using the closest matching font if the device does not have a font that matches the description exactly). Note that if you do not select a font, text is displayed in the default System font.

> **NOTE** As you will see in Chapter 16, the CDC::SelectObject function can be used not only to select a font, but also to select various other types of objects that affect the drawing of graphics.

Once it has selected the font, OnDraw obtains the dimensions of the font characters (step 3) by calling the CDC member function GetTextMetrics:

```
TEXTMETRIC TM;

// ...

pDC->GetTextMetrics (&TM);
LineHeight = TM.tmHeight + TM.tmExternalLeading;
```

GetTextMetrics provides a complete description of the actual font that is used to display text on the device. This information is stored within a TEXTMETRIC structure. (As you will see later, the TEXTDEMO program prints the values of the fields of this structure for each font that the user chooses.) To calculate the total height of a line of text, OnDraw adds the tmHeight field of the TEXTMETRIC structure (which contains the height of the tallest letter) to the tmExternalLeading field (which contains the recommended amount of vertical space to leave between lines); it stores the result in LineHeight, which will be used to calculate the starting position of each line. Figure 15.3 shows some of the other TEXTMETRIC fields that contain character dimensions.

OnDraw next sets two other text attributes (step 4):

```
pDC->SetTextColor (pDoc->mColor);
pDC->SetBkMode (TRANSPARENT);
```

The call to SetTextColor sets the text to the color that the user selected when choosing the font, which is stored in the mColor data member of the document class. If you do not specify a text color, text is displayed in black.

FIGURE 15.3:

Text measurements provided by the
CDC member function
GetTextMetrics

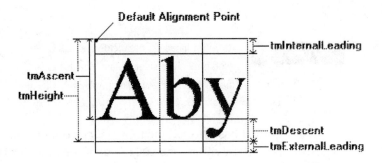

The call to SetBkMode sets the text background mode. The text *background* refers to the spaces surrounding the characters within the character cells. Passing TRANS-PARENT to SetBkMode causes the characters to be drawn directly on top of the existing window colors, without painting the background. If you pass SetBkMode the value OPAQUE, a text background will be drawn when the characters are displayed, overwriting the existing underlying colors within the window (this is the default background mode). The default background color used in the OPAQUE mode is white; you can set a different color by calling SetBkColor. OnDraw specifies the TRANSPARENT mode so that it does not have to worry about setting the text background color; the characters are displayed directly on top of the view window background color (which conforms to the "Window Background" color that the user sets through the Windows Control Panel).

Table 15.1 summarizes the CDC functions for setting text attributes, and Table 15.2 summarizes the CDC functions for obtaining the current setting of each attribute. Note that the SetMapMode and GetMapMode functions listed in these tables set and

TABLE 15.1: CDC Functions for Setting Text Attributes

Function	Purpose
SetBkColor	Specifies the color used to paint the text background (the *background* refers to the areas within the character cells surrounding the letters)
SetBkMode	Enables or disables the painting of text background
SetMapMode	Sets the current mapping mode, which specifies the coordinate system and the units used to position text or graphics
SetTextAlign	Specifies the way text is aligned
SetTextCharacterExtra	Adjusts the horizontal spacing between characters to create expanded or condensed text
SetTextColor	Specifies the color used to draw the text (the letters, not the background)

TABLE 15.2: CDC Functions for Obtaining the Settings of Text Attributes

Function	Purpose
GetBkColor	Gets the text background color
GetBkMode	Gets the text background mode
SetMapMode	Gets the current mapping mode
SetTextAlign	Gets the text alignment style
SetTextCharacterExtra	Gets the amount of extra intercharacter spacing
SetTextColor	Gets the text color

obtain the current mapping mode, which affects the output of both text and graphics; the mapping mode will be discussed in Chapter 16 (in the section "The Mapping Mode"). For complete information on these functions, see the documentation on the CDC class in the *Reference Volume I, Class Library Reference* manual, or in the *Foundation Classes* online help file.

OnDraw next obtains the dimensions of the update region (step 5) by calling the CDC member function GetClipBox:

```
pDC->GetClipBox (&ClipRect);
```

<blockquote>
NOTE Stated more precisely, GetClipBox returns the coordinates of the smallest rectangle that *bounds* the update region. The update region is not necessarily rectangular.
</blockquote>

Finally, OnDraw displays the lines of text (step 6) using the CDC member function TextOut:

```
// display title line:
pDC->TextOut (MARGIN, Y, "FONT PROPERTIES");

// display text lines:
for (int Line = 0; Line < NUMLINES; ++Line)
   {
   Y += LineHeight;
   if (Y + LineHeight >= ClipRect.top && Y <= ClipRect.bottom)
      pDC->TextOut (MARGIN, Y, pDoc->mLineTable [Line]);
   }
```

The first two parameters passed to TextOut specify the coordinates of the upper-left corner of the first character in the string to be displayed (that is, the *alignment point* within this character, as shown in Figure 15.3; note that you can change the position of the alignment point by calling CDC::SetTextAlign). The LineHeight variable is used to provide the proper vertical space between each line.

The third parameter passed to TextOut is the string that is to be displayed (or a CString object containing the string). The text for each line of text—other than the first line—is stored in the mLineTable member of the document class; in the next section, you will see how this text is generated.

TextOut is the simplest and most general-purpose function for displaying text. The CDC class provides several other text output functions that provide additional features. These functions are summarized in Table 15.3.

TABLE 15.3: **CDC** Member Functions for Displaying Text

Function	Purpose
DrawText	Draws text that is formatted within a specified rectangle—you can have this function expand tabs; align text at the left, center, or right of the formatting rectangle; and break lines between words to fit within the rectangle
ExtTextOut	Draws text within a specified rectangle—you can have this function clip text that falls outside of the rectangle, fill the rectangle with the text background color, and alter the spacing between characters
TabbedTextOut	Displays text like TextOut, but expands tab characters using the specified tab stops
TextOut	Displays a string at a specified starting position

Creating the Font Object and Storing the Text

In this section, you will add code to the TEXTDEMO document class for displaying the Font dialog box (in response to the Font... menu command), for initializing the font object according to the user's selections in the Font dialog box, and for generating the text displayed in the view window.

To create the menu command for opening the Font dialog box, run App Studio and open the menu-designing window for the IDR_MAINFRAME menu. First, delete the File and Edit drop-down menus, and then insert a new Options drop-down menu to the left of the Help menu. Table 15.4 lists the properties of the items in this menu, and Figure 15.4 shows the completed Options menu.

TABLE 15.4: The Properties of the **TEXTDEMO** Options Menu Items

ID:	Caption:	Other Features
none	&Options	Popup
ID_OPTIONS_FONT	&Font...	none
none	none	Separator
ID_APP_EXIT	E&xit	none

FIGURE 15.4:

The completed Options menu

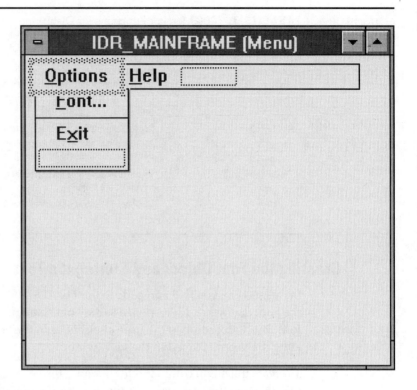

While running App Studio, you can also modify the IDR_MAINFRAME string resource, so that it matches the following:

TEXTDEMO Windows Application\n\nTEXTDE Document

This modification will prevent the MFC from displaying the document type in the program's title bar.

If you wish, you can modify the program's icon at this time by editing the IDR_MAINFRAME icon resource. The icon belonging to the TEXTDEMO program provided on the companion disk is shown in Figure 15.5.

You can now save your work, quit App Studio, and return to the Visual Workbench. In the Visual Workbench, run ClassWizard to create a handler for the Font command that you added to the TEXTDEMO menu. In the ClassWizard dialog box, select the CTextdemoDoc class in the Class Name: list, and select the ID_OPTIONS_FONT

FIGURE 15.5:

The TEXTDEMO program icon
provided on the companion disk, as
it appears in App Studio

FIGURE 15.5:

The TEXTDEMO program icon
provided on the companion disk, as
it appears in App Studio

item in the Object IDs: list (the identifier of the Font menu command). Then, select
the COMMAND message in the Messages: list, click the Add Function... button, and accept the default function name OnOptionsFont.

Before implementing the OnOptionsFont function, you need to open the
TEXTDDOC.H header file and define several new variables. At the beginning of the
file, define the constant NUMLINES, which contains the number of lines of text that
will be displayed (not including the title line):

```
// textddoc.h : interface of the CTextdemoDoc class
//
/////////////////////////////////////////////////////////////////////////

const int NUMLINES = 28;     // number of lines stored in document &
                             // displayed in view window
```

Then add the following new data member definitions to the end of the CText-demoDoc class definition:

```
// added data members:
public:
    COLORREF mColor;
    CString mLineTable [NUMLINES];
    CFont mFont;
```

The mColor data member stores the text color that the user selects in the Format dialog box. mLineTable is an array of CString objects, which is used to store the lines of text displayed in the view window. mFont is a member of the MFC CFont class and is the font object that is used for setting the font.

Now open the TEXTDDOC.CPP file and add code as follows to the OnOptionsFont function:

```
void CTextdemoDoc::OnOptionsFont()
{
    // TODO: Add your command handler code here

    // display Font dialog box:
    CFontDialog FontDialog;
    if (FontDialog.DoModal () != IDOK)
        return;

    // set mColor:
    mColor = FontDialog.GetColor ();  // get color chosen by user

    // initialize font object:
    mFont.DeleteObject ();
    mFont.CreateFontIndirect (&FontDialog.m_lf);

    // store values in mLineTable:

    // store values chosen by user:
    int Num = 0;

    mLineTable [Num++] = "Font Name: " + FontDialog.GetFaceName ();

    mLineTable [Num] =   "Font Size: ";
    char NumBuf [18];
    sprintf
        (NumBuf,"%d.%d points",
        FontDialog.GetSize () / 10,
```

```
    FontDialog.GetSize () % 10);
mLineTable [Num++] += NumBuf;

mLineTable [Num++] = "";

// store LOGFONT values:

mLineTable [Num++] = "LOGFONT fields:";

mLineTable [Num] =    "lfHeight: ";
sprintf (NumBuf,"%d",FontDialog.m_lf.lfHeight);
mLineTable [Num++] += NumBuf;

mLineTable [Num] =    "lfWidth: ";
sprintf (NumBuf,"%d",FontDialog.m_lf.lfWidth);
mLineTable [Num++] += NumBuf;

mLineTable [Num] =    "lfWeight: ";
sprintf (NumBuf,"%d",FontDialog.m_lf.lfWeight);
mLineTable [Num++] += NumBuf;

mLineTable [Num] =    "lfItalic: ";
sprintf (NumBuf,"%d",FontDialog.m_lf.lfItalic);
mLineTable [Num++] += NumBuf;

mLineTable [Num] =    "lfUnderline: ";
sprintf (NumBuf,"%d",FontDialog.m_lf.lfUnderline);
mLineTable [Num++] += NumBuf;

mLineTable [Num] =    "lfStrikeOut: ";
sprintf (NumBuf,"%d",FontDialog.m_lf.lfStrikeOut);
mLineTable [Num++] += NumBuf;

mLineTable [Num] = "lfCharSet: ";
switch (FontDialog.m_lf.lfCharSet)
   {
   case ANSI_CHARSET:
      mLineTable [Num++] += "ANSI_CHARSET";
      break;

   case DEFAULT_CHARSET:
      mLineTable [Num++] += "DEFAULT_CHARSET";
      break;
```

```
    case SYMBOL_CHARSET:
       mLineTable [Num++] += "SYMBOL_CHARSET";
       break;

    case SHIFTJIS_CHARSET:
       mLineTable [Num++] += "SHIFTJIS_CHARSET";
       break;

    case OEM_CHARSET:
       mLineTable [Num++] += "OEM_CHARSET";
       break;

    default:
       mLineTable [Num++] += "unknown character set";
       break;
    }

mLineTable [Num] = "lfPitchAndFamily: ";
switch (FontDialog.m_lf.lfPitchAndFamily & 0x0003)
    {
    case DEFAULT_PITCH:
       mLineTable [Num] += "DEFAULT_PITCH; ";
       break;

    case FIXED_PITCH:
       mLineTable [Num] += "FIXED_PITCH; ";
       break;

    case VARIABLE_PITCH:
       mLineTable [Num] += "VARIABLE_PITCH; ";
       break;

    default:
       mLineTable [Num] += "unknown pitch; ";
       break;
    }
switch (FontDialog.m_lf.lfPitchAndFamily & 0x00F0)
    {
    case FF_DECORATIVE:
       mLineTable [Num++] += "FF_DECORATIVE";
       break;

    case FF_DONTCARE:
       mLineTable [Num++] += "FF_DONTCARE";
       break;
```

```
      case FF_MODERN:
         mLineTable [Num++] += "FF_MODERN";
         break;

      case FF_ROMAN:
         mLineTable [Num++] += "FF_ROMAN";
         break;

      case FF_SCRIPT:
         mLineTable [Num++] += "FF_SCRIPT";
         break;

      case FF_SWISS:
         mLineTable [Num++] += "FF_SWISS";
         break;

      default:
         mLineTable [Num++] += "unknown family";
         break;
   }

mLineTable [Num] = "lfFaceName: ";
mLineTable [Num++] += FontDialog.m_lf.lfFaceName;

mLineTable [Num++] = "";

// store TEXTMETRIC values:

// create a device context object associated with the view window:
POSITION Pos = GetFirstViewPosition ();
CView *PView = GetNextView (Pos);
CClientDC ClientDC (PView);

// select new font into device context object:
ClientDC.SelectObject (&mFont);
TEXTMETRIC TM;
ClientDC.GetTextMetrics (&TM);

mLineTable [Num++] = "TEXTMETRIC fields:";

mLineTable [Num] = "tmHeight: ";
sprintf (NumBuf,"%d", TM.tmHeight);
mLineTable [Num++] += NumBuf;
```

```
mLineTable [Num] = "tmAscent: ";
sprintf (NumBuf,"%d", TM.tmAscent);
mLineTable [Num++] += NumBuf;

mLineTable [Num] = "tmDescent: ";
sprintf (NumBuf,"%d", TM.tmDescent);
mLineTable [Num++] += NumBuf;

mLineTable [Num] = "tmInternalLeading: ";
sprintf (NumBuf,"%d", TM.tmInternalLeading);
mLineTable [Num++] += NumBuf;

mLineTable [Num] = "tmExternalLeading: ";
sprintf (NumBuf,"%d", TM.tmExternalLeading);
mLineTable [Num++] += NumBuf;

mLineTable [Num] = "tmAveCharWidth: ";
sprintf (NumBuf,"%d", TM.tmAveCharWidth);
mLineTable [Num++] += NumBuf;

mLineTable [Num] = "tmMaxCharWidth: ";
sprintf (NumBuf,"%d", TM.tmMaxCharWidth);
mLineTable [Num++] += NumBuf;

mLineTable [Num] = "tmWeight: ";
sprintf (NumBuf,"%d", TM.tmWeight);
mLineTable [Num++] += NumBuf;

mLineTable [Num] = "tmItalic: ";
sprintf (NumBuf,"%d", TM.tmItalic);
mLineTable [Num++] += NumBuf;

mLineTable [Num] = "tmUnderlined: ";
sprintf (NumBuf,"%d", TM.tmUnderlined);
mLineTable [Num++] += NumBuf;

mLineTable [Num] = "tmStruckOut: ";
sprintf (NumBuf,"%d", TM.tmStruckOut);
mLineTable [Num++] += NumBuf;

mLineTable [Num] = "tmPitchAndFamily: ";
switch (TM.tmPitchAndFamily & 0x0003)
    {
    case DEFAULT_PITCH:
```

```
      mLineTable [Num] += "DEFAULT_PITCH; ";
      break;

   case FIXED_PITCH:
      mLineTable [Num] += "FIXED_PITCH; ";
      break;

   case VARIABLE_PITCH:
      mLineTable [Num] += "VARIABLE_PITCH; ";
      break;

   default:
      mLineTable [Num] += "unknown pitch; ";
      break;
   }
switch (TM.tmPitchAndFamily & 0x00F0)
   {
   case FF_DECORATIVE:
      mLineTable [Num++] += "FF_DECORATIVE";
      break;

   case FF_DONTCARE:
      mLineTable [Num++] += "FF_DONTCARE";
      break;

   case FF_MODERN:
      mLineTable [Num++] += "FF_MODERN";
      break;

   case FF_ROMAN:
      mLineTable [Num++] += "FF_ROMAN";
      break;

   case FF_SCRIPT:
      mLineTable [Num++] += "FF_SCRIPT";
      break;

   case FF_SWISS:
      mLineTable [Num++] += "FF_SWISS";
      break;

   default:
      mLineTable [Num++] += "unknown family";
      break;
   }
```

```
mLineTable [Num] = "tmCharSet: ";
switch (TM.tmCharSet)
    {
    case ANSI_CHARSET:
        mLineTable [Num++] += "ANSI_CHARSET";
        break;

    case DEFAULT_CHARSET:
        mLineTable [Num++] += "DEFAULT_CHARSET";
        break;

    case SYMBOL_CHARSET:
        mLineTable [Num++] += "SYMBOL_CHARSET";
        break;

    case SHIFTJIS_CHARSET:
        mLineTable [Num++] += "SHIFTJIS_CHARSET";
        break;

    case OEM_CHARSET:
        mLineTable [Num++] += "OEM_CHARSET";
        break;

    default:
        mLineTable [Num++] += "unknown character set";
        break;
    }

// force redrawing of view window:
UpdateAllViews (NULL);
}
```

As explained, OnOptionsFont receives control whenever the user chooses the Font... command on the Options menu. The code you added to OnOptionsFont performs the following main steps:

1. It displays the Font dialog box.

2. It passes a font description—based upon the information that the user entered into the Font dialog box—to the CFont::CreateFontIndirect function to initialize the font object (mFont).

3. It also writes the font description to a series of strings, which are stored in mLineTable.

4. It creates a device context object and selects the font object into the device context object.

5. It calls the GetTextMetrics member function of the device context object to obtain the features of the actual device font.

6. It writes these font features to a series of strings, which are also stored in mLineTable.

7. It calls UpdateAllViews to force the OnDraw function of the view class to display the lines of text contained in mLineTable (using the new font).

The Font dialog box is one of the common dialog boxes provided by windows (which were introduced in Chapter 13). The dialog box is displayed by creating a local object of the MFC CFontDialog class and then calling the OnModal member function. If the user closes the dialog box by clicking OK (that is, OnModal returns IDOK), OnOptionsFont continues; otherwise, it returns immediately:

```
// display Font dialog box:
CFontDialog FontDialog;
if (FontDialog.DoModal () != IDOK)
    return;
```

NOTE The Font dialog box displayed by TEXTDEMO allows the user to choose any of the fonts available for the Windows *screen*.

After the Font dialog box is closed (that is, after the call to DoModal returns), the OnOptionsFont function calls CFontDialog member functions and accesses public CFontDialog data members to obtain information on the font that the user selected. Specifically, it calls CFontDialog::GetColor to obtain the value of the text color that the user chose (it saves this value in CTextdemoDoc::mColor, which OnDraw uses to set the text color):

```
mColor = FontDialog.GetColor ();  // get color chosen by user
```

<table>
<tr><td>NOTE</td><td>Although it is selected in the Font dialog box, the text color is *not* a feature of a font. Rather, it is a text attribute that must be assigned to a device context object by calling the CDC::SetTextColor function.</td></tr>
</table>

Also, OnOptionsFont calls CFontDialog::GetFaceName to obtain the font name that the user selected in the Font: list of the Font dialog box (for example, Arial), and it calls CFongDialog::GetSize to obtain the font size that the user selected in the Size: list. It writes both of these values to strings in mLineTable so that they will be displayed in the view window:

```
mLineTable [Num++] = "Font Name: " + FontDialog.GetFaceName ();

mLineTable [Num] =    "Font Size: ";
char NumBuf [18];
sprintf
    (NumBuf,"%d.%d points",
    FontDialog.GetSize () / 10,
    FontDialog.GetSize () % 10);
mLineTable [Num++] += NumBuf;
```

Most importantly, OnOptionsFont obtains a complete description of the selected font from the CFontDialog::m_lf data member, which is a LOGFONT structure (a standard Windows structure). It first uses the LOGFONT structure to initialize the mFont font object, using the following two statements:

```
mFont.DeleteObject ();
mFont.CreateFontIndirect (&FontDialog.m_lf);
```

The call to CFont::DeleteObject removes the existing font information from the font object in case this object was previously initialized (by a prior call to On-OptionsFont). If the font object was *not* previously initialized, calling DeleteObject is unnecessary but harmless. Passing the LOGFONT structure to CFont::Create-FontIndirect initializes or reinitializes the font object with a description of the newly chosen font. After the call to CreateFontIndirect, the font information is stored within the font object, and the font object is ready to be selected into a device context object so that text can be displayed using this font.

OnOptionsFont also writes the value of each field of the TEXTMETRIC structure to a string within mLineTable, so that these fields will be displayed within the view window:

```
mLineTable [Num++] = "LOGFONT fields:";

mLineTable [Num] =   "lfHeight: ";
sprintf (NumBuf,"%d",FontDialog.m_lf.lfHeight);
mLineTable [Num++] += NumBuf;

mLineTable [Num] =   "lfWidth: ";
sprintf (NumBuf,"%d",FontDialog.m_lf.lfWidth);
mLineTable [Num++] += NumBuf;

// and so on ...
```

OnOptionsFont next creates a device context object associated with the view window, selects the newly initialized font object into this device context object, and then calls CDC::GetTextMetrics to obtain information on the actual font that will be used to display text in the window:

```
POSITION Pos = GetFirstViewPosition ();
CView *PView = GetNextView (Pos);
CClientDC ClientDC (PView);

// select new font into device context object:
ClientDC.SelectObject (&mFont);
TEXTMETRIC TM;
ClientDC.GetTextMetrics (&TM);
```

As explained previously, OnDraw selects the font object into the device context object so that it can display the text using this font. OnOptionsFont, however, selects the font object merely to obtain *information* on the font (by calling GetTextMetrics). OnOptionsFont then writes the contents of each field of the TEXTMETRIC structure to mLineTable.

You may have noticed that the LOGFONT and TEXTMETRIC structures are similar and have a number of fields that store the same information. There is an important theoretical difference between these two structures, however. A LOGFONT structure is used to initialize a font object and stores a description of the *desired* font; there is no guarantee that a font matching this description is actually available for any particular output device. When you select a font object into a device context, text is displayed using the actual physical font that matches the description most closely.

Using Stock Fonts

Displaying the Font dialog and using a font object allows the user to choose *any* of the fonts that are available for the screen. As an alternative, you can quickly select a *stock font*, without displaying the Font dialog box or using a font object. A stock font is one of a small set of standard Windows fonts commonly used to display information on the screen. To use one of the stock fonts, you need only call the CDC member function SelectStockObject:

```
CGdiObject* SelectStockObject (int nIndex);
```

The parameter nIndex is the index of the desired font; you can assign it one of the values described in Table 15.5. The fonts corresponding to these values are illustrated in Figure 15.6.

As an example, the following OnDraw function selects the fixed-pitch system font before displaying text in a window:

```
void CTextdemoView::OnDraw(CDC* pDC)
{
    CTextdemoDoc* pDoc = GetDocument();

    // TODO: add draw code here

    pDC->SelectStockObject (SYSTEM_FIXED_FONT);

    // set other text attributes ...

    // display the text in the view window ...
}
```

As you will learn in Chapter 16, you can use the SelectStockObject function to choose other stock objects, such as the brushes and pens employed in drawing graphics.

The values that GetTextMetrics assigns the TEXTMETRIC structure describe the *actual* available font used to display text. (Because the Font dialog box allows the user to select only fonts that are actually available for the screen, the LOGFONT and TEXTMETRIC structures displayed by TEXTDEMO always match. In general, however, these two structures do not necessarily match.)

You can now build and run the TEXTDEMO program.

TABLE 15.5: The Font Values You Can Assign the nIndex Parameter of the SelectStockObject Function

nIndex Value	Font Chosen
SYSTEM_FONT	Variable-pitch system font. This is the font that Windows uses to draw text on title bars, menus, and other window components. This is the default font that is used for displaying text on the screen if you do *not* select a font into a device context object.
SYSTEM_FIXED_FONT	Fixed-pitch system font. This highly legible font is the one used to draw window text in the Windows Notepad, Cardfile, and Terminal programs.
ANSI_VAR_FONT	A variable-pitch font that is smaller than the one specified by the SYSTEM_FONT value.
ANSI_FIXED_FONT	A fixed-pitch font that is smaller than the one specified by the SYSTEM_FIXED_FONT value.
DEVICE_DEFAULT_FONT	The default font for the device.
OEM_FIXED_FONT	A fixed-pitch font that matches the character set used by the underlying hardware. This font, sometimes known as Terminal, is used for displaying windowed DOS applications.

FIGURE 15.6:

The stock fonts

This is the SYSTEM_FONT stock font.

This is the SYSTEM_FIXED_FONT stock font.

This is the ANSI_VAR_FONT stock font.

This is the ANSI_FIXED_FONT stock font.

This is the DEVICE_DEFAULT_FONT stock font.

This is the OEM_FIXED_FONT stock font.

Supporting Scrolling

The problem with the TEXTDEMO program is that the lines of text may not fit completely within the view window (especially if the user selects a large font). Therefore, in this section you will add scrolling to the view window. Since you already learned the techniques for supporting scrolling in Chapter 11, the instructions given in this section will be brief.

First, open the TEXTDVW.H source file and change the single occurrence of CView to CScrollView. Then, add the following definition for the OnUpdate function to the end of the CTextdemoView class definition:

```
// added member function:
protected:
    virtual void OnUpdate (CView* pSender, LPARAM lHint, CObject* pHint);
```

Next, open the TEXTDVW.CPP file and change all occurrences of CView to CScrollView (you should find four occurrences). Add the following OnUpdate function implementation to the end of this file:

```
void CTextdemoView::OnUpdate (CView* pSender, LPARAM lHint, CObject* pHint)
    {
    CTextdemoDoc* PDoc = GetDocument();

    if (PDoc->mFont.m_hObject == NULL)  // font not yet created
        SetScrollSizes (MM_TEXT, CSize (0,0));
    else                                // font created
        {
        CClientDC ClientDC (this);
        int LineWidth = 0;
        SIZE Size;
        TEXTMETRIC TM;

        ClientDC.SelectObject (&PDoc->mFont);
        ClientDC.GetTextMetrics (&TM);

        for (int Line = 0; Line < NUMLINES; ++Line)
            {
            Size = ClientDC.GetTextExtent
                (PDoc->mLineTable [Line],
                 PDoc->mLineTable [Line].GetLength ());
```

```
        if (Size.cx > LineWidth)
            LineWidth = Size.cx;
        }

    Size.cx = LineWidth + MARGIN;
    Size.cy = (TM.tmHeight + TM.tmExternalLeading) * (NUMLINES + 1) + MARGIN;

    SetScrollSizes (MM_TEXT, Size);
    ScrollToPosition (CPoint (0, 0));
    }

CScrollView::OnUpdate (pSender, lHint, pHint);
}
```

The OnUpdate virtual function is called when the view window is first created, and also whenever the CTextdemoDoc::OnOptionsFont function calls CDocument::‑ UpdateAllViews after the user chooses a new font (OnUpdate was explained in Chapter 11). OnUpdate sets the document scroll size (that is, the size of the body of text), based upon the size of the new font.

To set the new document size, OnUpdate calls CScrollView::SetScrollSizes. If a font has not yet been selected, it specifies a zero document size to hide the scroll bars, because no text is displayed. If a font has been selected, OnUpdate must determine the total height and width of the text.

To calculate the height of the text, it creates a device context object for the view window, selects the font object into this device context object, and calls GetTextMetrics to obtain the measurements of the characters. The total height of the text is the height of a single line times the number of lines, plus the top margin:

```
Size.cy = (TM.tmHeight + TM.tmExternalLeading) * (NUMLINES + 1) + MARGIN;
```

To calculate the width of the text, it calls CDC::GetLength to obtain the width of each line. It sets the text width to the width of the widest line (which it saves in LineWidth) plus the margin:

```
Size.cx = LineWidth + MARGIN;
```

Note that the GetTextMetrics function reports the *average* width of a character (in the tmAveCharWidth TEXTMETRIC field). For a variable-pitch font, you cannot use this information to obtain the width of a given character or string of characters, because the widths of the characters vary. The GetLength function, however, returns the actual width of a specific string of characters.

After setting the document size, `OnUpdate` calls `CScrollView::ScrollToPosition` to scroll the view window to the beginning of the text:

```
SetScrollSizes (MM_TEXT, Size);
ScrollToPosition (CPoint (0, 0));
```

Finally, `OnUpdate` calls the `CScrollView` version of the `OnUpdate` function so that it can perform its default processing (namely, invalidating the entire view window so that it will be redrawn):

```
CScrollView::OnUpdate (pSender, lHint, pHint);
```

You can now build and run the TEXTDEMO program, and use the new scroll bars to scroll through the text it displays. Leave the TEXTDEMO project open in the Visual Workbench, however, because you will be adding features to the program in the next section.

Reading the Keyboard

You will now learn how to read the keys that the user types while the program window is active. Like reading mouse input (described in Chapter 8), reading the keyboard is accomplished by providing an appropriate message handler in the program's view class. You will first learn how to provide a handler for the WM_KEY-DOWN message, which is sent when *any* key is pressed. You will then learn how to provide a handler for the WM_CHAR message, sent when a character key is typed.

Reading Keys with a WM_KEYDOWN Message Handler

Whenever the user presses a key, the system sends a WM_KEYDOWN message to the window that currently has the *input focus*. The input focus belongs either to the current *active window* or to a child window belonging to the active window. (The active window is the one with a highlighted title bar, or a highlighted border if it is a dialog box.) Providing a WM_KEYDOWN message handler is especially useful for processing keys that do not enter printable characters—for example, the arrow and function keys.

NOTE If the user presses a *system key*, the focus window is sent a WM_SYSKEYDown message rather than a WM_KEYDOWN message. The system keys are PrtSc, Alt, or any key pressed simultaneously with Alt. The system keys are normally processed by Windows, rather than by an application program.

To learn how to process WM_KEYDOWN messages, you will now add a keyboard interface to the TEXTDEMO program, which will allow the user to scroll through the text using keystrokes as well as the scroll bars. To begin, make sure that the TEXTDEMO project is open in the Visual Workbench, and activate the ClassWizard tool. In the ClassWizard dialog box, select CTextdemoView in the Class Name: list so that the keystrokes will be processed by the view class. Select CTextdemoView in the Object IDs: list, select the WM_KEYDOWN identifier in the Messages: list, and click the Add Function button. ClassWizard will add a message handler named OnKeyDown to the program's view class.

Now open the TEXTDVW.CPP file and add code as follows to the OnKeyDown function:

```
void CTextdemoView::OnKeyDown(UINT nChar, UINT nRepCnt, UINT nFlags)
{
    // TODO: Add your message handler code here and/or call default

    CSize DocSize = GetTotalSize ();
    RECT ClientRect;
    GetClientRect (&ClientRect);

    switch (nChar)
        {
        case VK_LEFT:      // left arrow
            if (ClientRect.right < DocSize.cx)
                SendMessage (WM_HSCROLL, SB_LINEUP);
            break;

        case VK_RIGHT:     // right arrow
            if (ClientRect.right < DocSize.cx)
                SendMessage (WM_HSCROLL, SB_LINEDOWN);
            break;
```

```
    case VK_UP:        // up arrow
       if (ClientRect.bottom < DocSize.cy)
          SendMessage (WM_VSCROLL, SB_LINEUP);
       break;

    case VK_DOWN:      // down arrow
       if (ClientRect.bottom < DocSize.cy)
          SendMessage (WM_VSCROLL, SB_LINEDOWN);
       break;

    case VK_HOME:      // Home key
       if (::GetKeyState (VK_CONTROL) & 0x8000)  // Ctrl pressed
          {
          if (ClientRect.bottom < DocSize.cy)
             SendMessage (WM_VSCROLL, SB_TOP);
          }
       else                                      // Home key alone
          {
          if (ClientRect.right < DocSize.cx)
             SendMessage (WM_HSCROLL, SB_TOP);
          }
       break;

    case VK_END:       // End key
       if (::GetKeyState (VK_CONTROL) & 0x8000)  // Ctrl pressed
          {
          if (ClientRect.bottom < DocSize.cy)
             SendMessage (WM_VSCROLL, SB_BOTTOM);
          }
       else                                      // End key alone
          {
          if (ClientRect.right < DocSize.cx)
             SendMessage (WM_HSCROLL, SB_BOTTOM);
          }
       break;

    case VK_PRIOR:     // PgUp key
       if (ClientRect.bottom < DocSize.cy)
          SendMessage (WM_VSCROLL, SB_PAGEUP);
       break;
```

```
case VK_NEXT:        // PgDn key
    if (ClientRect.bottom < DocSize.cy)
        SendMessage (WM_VSCROLL, SB_PAGEDOWN);
    break;
    }
}
```

The first parameter passed to OnKeyDown, nChar, contains a value known as a *virtual key code*, which indicates the key that was pressed. OnKeyDown uses this code to branch to the appropriate routine. Table 15.6 lists the virtual key codes for the keys that do not generate WM_CHAR messages. (Keys that generate WM_CHAR messages are not included because, as you will learn in the next section, they are more easily processed in a WM_CHAR message handler, where they are identified by character code.)

TABLE 15.6:   Virtual Key Codes for Keys that Do Not Generate WM_CHAR Messages

Value (decimal)	Symbolic Constant	Key
12	VK_CLEAR	Numeric keypad with 5 NumLock off
16	VK_SHIFT	Shift
17	VK_CONTROL	Control
19	VK_PAUSE	Pause
20	VK_CAPITAL	Caps Lock
33	VK_PRIOR	Page Up
34	VK_NEXT	Page Down
35	VK_END	End
36	VK_HOME	Home
37	VK_LEFT	Left Arrow
38	VK_UP	Up Arrow
39	VK_RIGHT	Right Arrow
40	VK_DOWN	Down Arrow
45	VK_INSERT	Insert
46	VK_DELETE	Delete
112	VK_F1	F1
113	VK_F2	F2
114	VK_F3	F3

TABLE 15.6: Virtual Key Codes for Keys that Do Not Generate **WM_CHAR** Messages (continued)

Value (decimal)	Symbolic Constant	Key
115	VK_F4	F4
116	VK_F5	F5
117	VK_F6	F6
118	VK_F7	F7
119	VK_F8	F8
120	VK_F9	F9
121	VK_F10	F10
122	VK_F11	F11
123	VK_F12	F12
144	VK_NUMLOCK	Num Lock
145	VK_SCROLL	Scroll Lock

If the user pressed the Home key or the End key, OnKeyDown calls the Windows API function GetKeyState to determine whether the Control key was pressed simultaneously; for example:

```
case VK_HOME:      // Home key
   if (::GetKeyState (VK_CONTROL) & 0x8000)
      {
      // then Control key was pressed simultaneously with the Home key;
      // process Ctrl+Home keystroke
      }
   else
      {
      // then Control key was not pressed;
      // process Home key
      }
```

When calling GetKeyState, you assign the parameter the virtual code of the key you want to test. (You can obtain this code from Table 15.6.) GetKeyState returns a value indicating the state of the specified key at the time the WM_KEYDOWN message was generated. If the key was pressed, the high-order bit of the GetKeyState return value will be set to 1; this can be tested as in the following example:

```
if (::GetKeyState (VK_SHIFT) & 0x8000)
   // then Shift key was pressed
```

Also, if the key was toggled at the time the WM_KEYDOWN message was generated, then the low-order bit of the GetKeyState return value will be set. A key is *toggled* if it has been pressed an odd number of times since the system was started. The following example indicates how you can test whether a key is toggled:

```
if (::GetKeyState (VK_CAPITAL) & 0x0001)
   // then Caps Lock is toggled on
```

Testing the toggled state is generally most useful for keys used to turn some state on or off, such as Caps Lock, Num Lock, Scroll Lock, and Insert. Note that GetKeyState indicates whether a key was pressed or toggled on *at the time the key that generated the WM_KEYDOWN message was pressed*. It does *not* return the current status of the key (which might have changed by the time the message is processed). To obtain the *current* status of a key, you can call the GetAsyncKeyState Windows API function.

OnKeyDown processes each keystroke by sending one of the messages that is normally sent by a scroll bar when the user performs some action on the scroll bar with the mouse. The message is sent to the view window itself by calling the CWnd::SendMessage function. The CScrollView class provides a handler for each of these messages, which scrolls the window and adjusts the position of the scroll bar thumb, just as if the user had clicked on the scroll bar.

For example, if the user has pressed the down-arrow key, OnKeyDown sends the *same* message that the vertical scroll bar sends when the user clicks within the bar below the thumb. This message has the identifier WM_VSCROLL (indicating that it originates from the vertical scroll bar) and is sent with the code SB_LINEDOWN (indicating the specific scroll bar action):

```
case VK_DOWN:      // down arrow
   if (ClientRect.bottom < DocSize.cy)
     SendMessage (WM_VSCROLL, SB_LINEDOWN);
   break;
```

When the WM_VSCROLL message handler provided by CScrollView processes this message, it scrolls the text one line down.

Each scroll bar message is accompanied with an SB_ code indicating the specific scrolling action that occurred. Figure 15.7 shows the SB_ codes that are sent when the user clicks on various positions within the vertical or horizontal scroll bar.

FIGURE 15.7:

The SB_ codes sent with scroll bar messages when the user clicks on various positions within the vertical or horizontal scroll bar

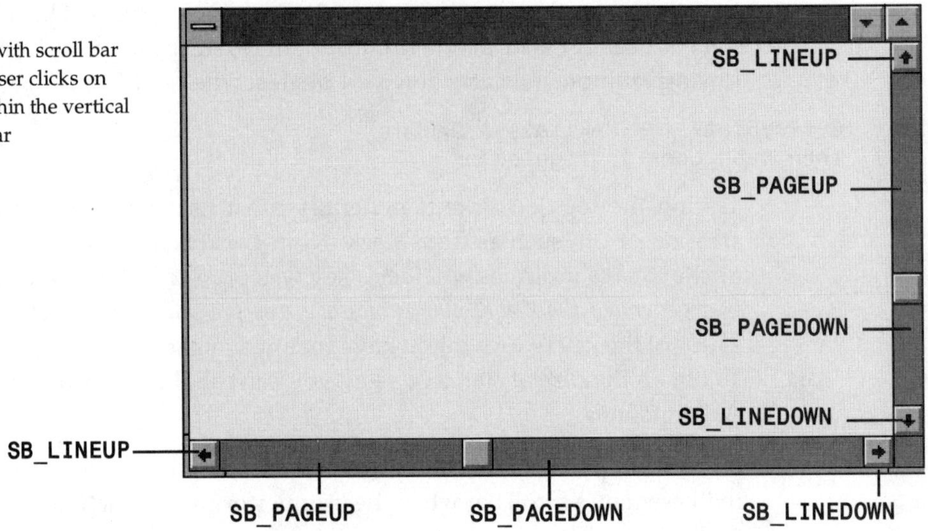

Table 15.7 lists each of the keystrokes that is processed by the OnKeyDown function, indicating the action that is performed in response to the keystroke and the scroll bar message that OnKeyDown sends to the view window in order to generate this action. (In this table, the term *page* refers to the amount of text that fits within the window).

Note, finally, that before sending a scroll bar message, the OnKeyDown function makes sure that the corresponding scroll bar is visible. (The CScrollView code does not expect to receive messages from a scroll bar that is hidden, the code does not work properly if such messages are sent.) The MFC hides the horizontal scroll bar if the view window is as wide as or wider than the text, and it hides the vertical scroll bar if the view window is as high as or higher than the text. To obtain the sizes

TABLE 15.7: Scrolling Keystrokes Processed by the **OnKeyDown** Function of the TEXTDEMO Program

Keystroke	Action	Equivalent Message
Left Arrow	Scroll one character left	WM_HSCROLL, SB_LINEUP
Right Arrow	Scroll one character right	WM_HSCROLL, SB_LINEDOWN
Up Arrow	Scroll one line up	WM_VSCROLL, SB_LINEUP
Down Arrow	Scroll one line down	WM_VSCROLL, SB_LINEDOWN
Home	Scroll left as far as possible	WM_HSCROLL, SB_TOP
Ctrl+Home	Scroll up as far as possible	WM_VSCROLL, SB_TOP
End	Scroll right as far as possible	WM_HSCROLL, SB_BOTTOM
Ctrl+End	Scroll down as far as possible	WM_VSCROLL, SB_BOTTOM
Page Up	Scroll one page up	WM_VSCROLL, SB_PAGEUP
Page Down	Scroll one page down	WM_VSCROLL, SB_PAGEDOWN

of the text, OnView calls CScrollView::GetTotalSize, and to obtain the size of the view window, it calls GetClientRect:

```
CSize DocSize = GetTotalSize ();
RECT ClientRect;
GetClientRect (&ClientRect);
```

Before sending a horizontal scroll bar message, it checks the text width as follows:

```
if (ClientRect.right < DocSize.cx)
   // then horizontal scroll bar is visible;;
   // therefore send message ...
```

Likewise, before sending a vertical scroll bar message, it checks the text height as follows:

```
if (ClientRect.bottom < DocSize.cy)
   // then vertical scroll bar is visible;
   // therefore send message ...
```

This section completes the changes to TEXTDEMO; you can now build and run the program. The C++ source code for TEXTDEMO is given near the end of the chapter.

Reading Keys with a WM_CHAR Message Handler

For most of the keys on the keyboard, when the user types the key, Windows sends a WM_CHAR message to the window with the input focus.(The keys that do *not* send WM_CHAR messages are listed in Table 15.6.) When a program allows the user to type in text, it is easiest to read the keystrokes by providing a WM_CHAR message handler. A WM_CHAR message handler is more convenient than a WM_KEYDOWN message handler because it is passed the standard ANSI code for the character typed, rather than a virtual key code that must be translated into a character code. The character code passed to a WM_CHAR handler can be immediately inserted into a character string for storing the text, and it can be directly displayed in a window or on another device using a function such as TextOut.

When the user types text into a program, the program typically echoes these characters within the program window. To illustrate the basic techniques required for reading text and echoing characters, this section presents the ECHO program. The ECHO program reads characters typed by the user and displays these characters at the top of the program window. When the line reaches the right window border, the user can continue typing; the characters, however, will no longer be visible. The user can choose the Clear command on the Edit menu to erase the line, and begin typing another one. Figure 15.8 illustrates the program window after the user has typed several characters.

Generating the Source Code

Use AppWizard to generate the program source code, assigning the project name ECHO and choosing only the Generate Source Comments option in the Options dialog box.

Modifying the Resources

Run App Studio and open the menu-designing window for the IDR_MAINFRAME menu. First delete the entire File menu. Then delete all items on the Edit menu, but leave the empty Edit menu in place. Add the items described in Table 15.8 to the Edit menu; the completed Edit menu will appear as shown in Figure 15.9.

FIGURE 15.8:

The ECHO program window after the user has entered some text

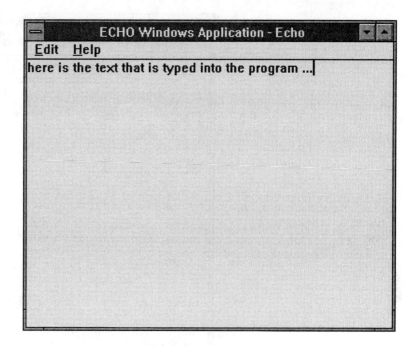

TABLE 15.8: The Properties of the Edit Menu Items

ID:	Caption	Other Features
none	&Edit	Popup
ID_EDIT_CLEAR	&Clear	none
none	none	Separator
ID_APP_EXIT	E&xit	none

FIGURE 15.9:

The completed Edit menu

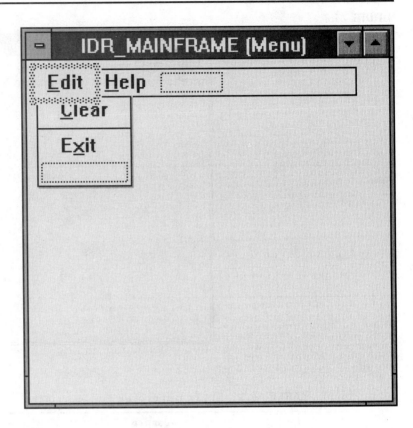

While you are running App Studio, you might also want to open the icon-designing window for the IDR_MAINFRAME icon and design a custom program icon. The icon provided with the ECHO program on the companion disk is shown in Figure 15.10.

Defining the Message Handlers

You will now define functions to handle the WM_CHAR message sent whenever the user types a character, as well as the menu message sent whenever the user chooses the Clear command on the Edit menu.

To define the message handlers, return to the Visual Workbench and run the ClassWizard tool. Then, in the ClassWizard dialog box, select the CEchoView class in the Class Name: list so that the messages will be handled by the program view class.

FIGURE 15.10:

The ECHO program icon provided on the companion disk, as it appears in App Studio

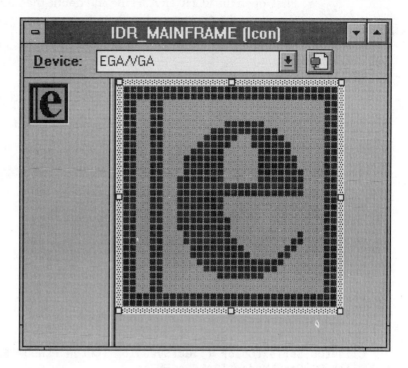

Next, select the CEchoView class in the Object IDs: list, select the WM_CHAR item in the Messages: list, and click the Add Function button; ClassWizard will generate a WM_CHAR message handler named OnChar. Then choose the ID_EDIT_CLEAR item (the identifier of the Clear command) in the Object IDs: list, select the COMMAND item in the Messages list, and click the Add Function... button. Accept the default name for the menu command handler, OnEditClear.

Adding Code

You will now add a data member to store the line of text, you will implement the message-handling functions you just generated, and you will add code to the OnDraw function of the view class.

First, open the ECHODOC.H file and define the public data member mTextLine at the end of the CEchoDoc class definition:

```
// added data member:
public:
    CString mTextLine;
```

This data member will be used to store the characters that the user types.

Next, open ECHOVIEW.CPP and add code as follows to the OnChar function:

```
void CEchoView::OnChar(UINT nChar, UINT nRepCnt, UINT nFlags)
{
    // TODO: Add your message handler code here and/or call default

    if (nChar < 32)
        {
        ::MessageBeep (-1);
        return;
        }

    CEchoDoc* PDoc = GetDocument();
    PDoc->mTextLine += nChar;

    CClientDC ClientDC (this);
    ClientDC.SetTextColor (::GetSysColor (COLOR_WINDOWTEXT));
    ClientDC.SetBkMode (TRANSPARENT);
    ClientDC.TextOut (0, 0, PDoc->mTextLine);
}
```

OnChar receives control whenever the user types a character key, and the nChar parameter contains the ANSI code for the character.

Notice that if the user has typed a keystroke that generates a character code value *below* 32, OnChar beeps and exits. Character code values less than 32 are generated by control keystrokes, such as Ctrl+A, Enter, or Tab, rather than by keys for printable characters. In general, a program either ignores control keystrokes or uses them to trigger some control action. For example, in response to the Backspace key (character code 8), a program might erase the previous character, and in response to the Enter key (character code 13), a program might generate a new line. Some of the commonly used control keystrokes are described in Table 15.9. If you pass a character code for a control keystroke to a function such as TextOut, Windows will print a rectangle, indicating that the code does not correspond to a printable character.

TABLE 15.9: Common Control Keystrokes

Keystroke	Meaning	nChar Value (Decimal)
↵	Backspace	8
Tab	Tab	9
Ctrl+↵	Line feed	10
↵	Carriage return	13
Esc	Escape	27

OnChar next adds the new character to the end of the string containing the text, using the overloaded CString += operator:

```
CEchoDoc* PDoc = GetDocument();
PDoc->mTextLine += nChar;
```

Finally, OnChar creates a device context object for the view window and uses it to display the complete string, including the new character at the end. Even though only the character at the end is being added to the window, it is easier to redisplay the entire string, than to figure out the position of the end character and printing only that character. (Determining the exact position of a character within a string is difficult for variable-pitch and italicized fonts.)

Notice that rather than setting the text to a specific color, OnChar assigns it the "Window Text" color that the user has set through the Control Panel, which it obtains by passing the value COLOR_WINDOWTEXT to the Windows API function GetSysColor:

```
ClientDC.SetTextColor (::GetSysColor (COLOR_WINDOWTEXT));
```

> **WARNING** Recall from Chapter 11 that if the view window supports scrolling (that is, if it is derived from CScrollView), you must pass a CClientDC device context object that you create to the CView::OnPrepareDC function *before* displaying text or graphics. OnPrepareDC adjusts the device context object for the current scrolled position of the document, so that the output will appear at the correct positions. (You do not need to call OnPrepareDC for advice context object passed to an OnDraw function, because it has *already* been adjusted.)

Although `OnDraw` displays the updated character string whenever the user types a character, the program must also redisplay the characters whenever the window needs redrawing. To do this, add code as follows to the `OnDraw` function, also in the ECHOVIEW.CPP file:

```
void CEchoView::OnDraw(CDC* pDC)
{
    CEchoDoc* pDoc = GetDocument();

    // TODO: add draw code here

    pDC->SetTextColor (::GetSysColor (COLOR_WINDOWTEXT));
    pDC->SetBkMode (TRANSPARENT);
    pDC->TextOut (0, 0, pDoc->mTextLine);
}
```

Note that rather than drawing the text itself, the `OnChar` function *could* call the `CDocument::UpdateAllViews` function to force `OnDraw` to display the text. However, displaying the text directly from `OnChar` not only is more efficient, but also avoids the flicker that would occur each time the view window is repainted by `OnDraw`. (Flicker occurs because the update region of the window is erased immediately before `OnDraw` is called.)

Finally, add code as follows to the `OnEditClear` function:

```
void CEchoView::OnEditClear()
{
    // TODO: Add your command handler code here

    CEchoDoc* PDoc = GetDocument();
    PDoc->mTextLine.Empty ();
    PDoc->UpdateAllViews (NULL);
}
```

The added code calls the `CString` member function `Empty` to erase the characters stored in `mTextLine`, setting the length of the string to zero. It then calls `UpdateAllViews` to cause the view window to be erased.

You can now build and run the ECHO program, and try typing in a line of text. Leave the ECHO project open in the Visual Workbench, however, because you are not done with this program.

Managing the Caret

When you ran the ECHO program, you probably noticed that it lacked something important: the familiar blinking caret marking the insertion point within the text. In this section, you will add a caret.

To manage the caret, you must first define several new message-handling functions. The purpose of each of these functions will be explained when you add the function code. Begin by running ClassWizard from within the Visual Workbench. In the ClassWizard dialog box, select the CEchoView class in the Class Name: list, and select the CEditView item in the Object IDs: list.

You will define handlers for three of the notification messages that are sent to the view window. First, select the WM_CREATE message in the Messages: list and click the Add Function button to create a message handler named OnCreate. Then define handlers for the WM_KILLFOCUS and WM_SETFOCUS messages, which will be named OnKillFocus and OnSetFocus.

Before implementing the new message handlers, open the ECHOVIEW.H header file and add the following data member definitions to the end of the CEchoView class definition:

```
// added data members:
private:
    POINT mCaretPos;
    int mXCaret, mYCaret;
```

The data member mCaretPos stores the current position of the caret, mXCaret stores the width of the caret, and mYCaret stores the height of the caret.

Now open the ECHOVIEW.CPP file and add the following initializations to the CEchoView constructor:

```
CEchoView::CEchoView()
{
    // TODO: add construction code here
    mCaretPos.x = mCaretPos.y = 0;
}
```

These initializations will cause the caret to appear initially at the upper-left corner of the view window.

In this same file, add the following code to the OnCreate function:

```
int CEchoView::OnCreate(LPCREATESTRUCT lpCreateStruct)
{
    if (CView::OnCreate(lpCreateStruct) == -1)
        return -1;

    // TODO: Add your specialized creation code here
    CClientDC ClientDC (this);
    TEXTMETRIC TM;

    mXCaret = ::GetSystemMetrics (SM_CXBORDER) * 2;
    ClientDC.GetTextMetrics (&TM);
    mYCaret = TM.tmHeight + TM.tmExternalLeading;

    return 0;
}
```

The OnCreate function is called after the view window is first created, before it becomes visible. The code you added calculates and stores the size of the caret that will be displayed. Rather than setting the caret to some arbitrary width, OnCreate bases the width upon the current width of a window border, so that the caret will have an appropriate width regardless of the video mode (that is, the caret width will be scaled according to the size of other standard window elements). It obtains the width of a window border by passing SM_CXBORDER to the Windows API function GetSystemMetrics. OnCreate makes the caret height the same as the height of the characters, which it obtains by creating a device context object and calling the familiar GetTextMetrics function.

Next, implement the OnSetFocus function (also in ECHOVIEW.CPP), as follows:

```
void CEchoView::OnSetFocus(CWnd* pOldWnd)
{
    CView::OnSetFocus(pOldWnd);

    // TODO: Add your message handler code here
    CreateSolidCaret (mXCaret, mYCaret);
    SetCaretPos (mCaretPos);
    ShowCaret ();
}
```

OnSetFocus is called whenever the view window receives the input focus—specifically, when the view window is first created and whenever the user switches to the ECHO program after working in another program. OnSetFocus calls the CWnd member function `CreateSolidCaret` to create the caret, passing this function the caret width and height. It then calls `CWnd::SetCaretPos` to place the caret at the correct position. Because a newly created caret is initially invisible, it must also call `CWnd::ShowCaret` to make the caret appear.

Note that when the view window is created, `OnSetFocus` is called *after* `OnCreate`. Therefore, it can use the caret dimensions set by `OnCreate`. It is easy to understand why you must create the caret before the view window is first created; however, why do you need to create it *every time* the view window receives the focus? The reason is that the caret is *destroyed* whenever the view window loses the focus, through the following statement, which you should add to the `OnKillFocus` function:

```
void CEchoView::OnKillFocus(CWnd* pNewWnd)
{
    CView::OnKillFocus(pNewWnd);

    // TODO: Add your message handler code here
    ::DestroyCaret ();
}
```

The function `OnKillFocus` is called whenever the view window loses the input focus. The caret is a shared Windows resource; only *one* caret may be displayed on the Windows desktop at a given time, and it should be displayed within the window that currently has the input focus to show the user where text is being inserted. Therefore, the caret must be destroyed when the view window loses the focus, so that the next window that receives the focus is free to display it.

To maintain the caret, you must also modify the `OnChar` and `OnEditClear` functions. First, add the statements marked in bold to the `OnChar` function:

```
void CEchoView::OnChar(UINT nChar, UINT nRepCnt, UINT nFlags)
{
    // TODO: Add your message handler code here and/or call default

    if (nChar < 32)
        {
        ::MessageBeep (-1);
        return;
        }

    CEchoDoc* PDoc = GetDocument();
    PDoc->mTextLine += nChar;
```

```
    CClientDC ClientDC (this);
    ClientDC.SetTextColor (::GetSysColor (COLOR_WINDOWTEXT));
    ClientDC.SetBkMode (TRANSPARENT);
    HideCaret ();
    ClientDC.TextOut (0, 0, PDoc->mTextLine);
    CSize Size = ClientDC.GetTextExtent
        (TextLine,
        TextLine.GetLength ());
    CaretPos.x = Size.cx;
    SetCaretPos (CaretPos);
    ShowCaret ();
}
```

After the new character has been inserted at the end of the line, the added code calls GetTextExtent to determine the new length of the line, and then calls SetCaretPos to move the caret to the end of the line (where the next character will be inserted).

Also, before drawing the text, the added code calls CWnd::HideCaret to make the caret invisible; after drawing the text and moving the caret, it calls CWnd::Show-Caret to make the caret visible again. This is done because writing to the window while the caret is visible can cause screen corruption at the position of the caret. Note that you do *not* need to hide the caret when drawing from the OnDraw function, because Windows automatically hides the caret before this function is called and restores the caret after the function returns. (For the same reason, you do not need to hide the caret within an OnPaint function, such as the OnPaint function used to redraw text in the dialog box, which was presented in Chapter 13.) Therefore, you do not need to modify OnDraw.

NOTE Calling HideCaret is cumulative; that is, if you call HideCaret more than once without calling ShowCaret, you must then call ShowCaret the same number of times to make the caret visible again.

Finally, you need to add two statements to the end of the OnEditClear function:

```
void CEchoView::OnEditClear()
{
    // TODO: Add your command handler code here

    CEchoDoc* PDoc = GetDocument();
    PDoc->mTextLine.Empty ();
```

```
    PDoc->UpdateAllViews (NULL);
    CaretPos.x = 0;
    SetCaretPos (CaretPos);
}
```

The added statements reposition the caret at the left edge of the window after the text has been deleted in response to the Clear command on the Edit menu.

You have now completed modifying ECHO, and you can build and run the program. The C++ source code is given at the end of the chapter (following the source code for the TEXTDEMO program).

The TEXTDEMO Source Code

The following listings, Listings 15.1 through 15.8, provide the C++ source code for the TEXTDEMO program that you created in this chapter. You will find a copy of each of these files, as well as the other source files for the program, in the \TEXTDEMO companion disk subdirectory.

Listing 15.1

```
// textdemo.h : main header file for the TEXTDEMO application
//

#ifndef __AFXWIN_H__
    #error include 'stdafx.h' before including this file for PCH
#endif

#include "resource.h"       // main symbols

/////////////////////////////////////////////////////////////////////////////
// CTextdemoApp:
// See textdemo.cpp for the implementation of this class
//

class CTextdemoApp : public CWinApp
{
public:
    CTextdemoApp();
```

```
// Overrides
    virtual BOOL InitInstance();

// Implementation

    //{{AFX_MSG(CTextdemoApp)
    afx_msg void OnAppAbout();
        // NOTE - the ClassWizard will add and remove member functions here.
        //    DO NOT EDIT what you see in these blocks of generated code !
    //}}AFX_MSG
    DECLARE_MESSAGE_MAP()
};
```

//

Listing 15.2

```
// textdemo.cpp : Defines the class behaviors for the application.
//

#include "stdafx.h"
#include "textdemo.h"

#include "mainfrm.h"
#include "textddoc.h"
#include "textdvw.h"

#ifdef _DEBUG
#undef THIS_FILE
static char BASED_CODE THIS_FILE[] = __FILE__;
#endif

////////////////////////////////////////////////////////////////////////////
// CTextdemoApp

BEGIN_MESSAGE_MAP(CTextdemoApp, CWinApp)
    //{{AFX_MSG_MAP(CTextdemoApp)
    ON_COMMAND(ID_APP_ABOUT, OnAppAbout)
        // NOTE - the ClassWizard will add and remove mapping macros here.
        //    DO NOT EDIT what you see in these blocks of generated code !
    //}}AFX_MSG_MAP
    // Standard file based document commands
```

```
    ON_COMMAND(ID_FILE_NEW, CWinApp::OnFileNew)
    ON_COMMAND(ID_FILE_OPEN, CWinApp::OnFileOpen)
END_MESSAGE_MAP()

/////////////////////////////////////////////////////////////////////////
// CTextdemoApp construction

CTextdemoApp::CTextdemoApp()
{
    // TODO: add construction code here,
    // Place all significant initialization in InitInstance
}

/////////////////////////////////////////////////////////////////////////
// The one and only CTextdemoApp object

CTextdemoApp NEAR theApp;

/////////////////////////////////////////////////////////////////////////
// CTextdemoApp initialization

BOOL CTextdemoApp::InitInstance()
{
    // Standard initialization
    // If you are not using these features and wish to reduce the size
    //  of your final executable, you should remove from the following
    //  the specific initialization routines you do not need.

    SetDialogBkColor();        // set dialog background color to gray
    LoadStdProfileSettings();  // Load standard INI file options (including MRU)

    // Register the application's document templates.  Document templates
    //  serve as the connection between documents, frame windows and views.

    AddDocTemplate(new CSingleDocTemplate(IDR_MAINFRAME,
        RUNTIME_CLASS(CTextdemoDoc),
        RUNTIME_CLASS(CMainFrame),       // main SDI frame window
        RUNTIME_CLASS(CTextdemoView)));

    // create a new (empty) document
    OnFileNew();

    if (m_lpCmdLine[0] != '\0')
    {
```

```
        // TODO: add command line processing here
    }

    return TRUE;
}

//////////////////////////////////////////////////////////////////////////
// CAboutDlg dialog used for App About

class CAboutDlg : public CDialog
{
public:
    CAboutDlg();

// Dialog Data
    //{{AFX_DATA(CAboutDlg)
    enum { IDD = IDD_ABOUTBOX };
    //}}AFX_DATA

// Implementation
protected:
    virtual void DoDataExchange(CDataExchange* pDX);    // DDX/DDV support
    //{{AFX_MSG(CAboutDlg)
        // No message handlers
    //}}AFX_MSG
    DECLARE_MESSAGE_MAP()
};

CAboutDlg::CAboutDlg() : CDialog(CAboutDlg::IDD)
{
    //{{AFX_DATA_INIT(CAboutDlg)
    //}}AFX_DATA_INIT
}

void CAboutDlg::DoDataExchange(CDataExchange* pDX)
{
    CDialog::DoDataExchange(pDX);
    //{{AFX_DATA_MAP(CAboutDlg)
    //}}AFX_DATA_MAP
}

BEGIN_MESSAGE_MAP(CAboutDlg, CDialog)
    //{{AFX_MSG_MAP(CAboutDlg)
        // No message handlers
```

```
   //}}AFX_MSG_MAP
END_MESSAGE_MAP()

// App command to run the dialog
void CTextdemoApp::OnAppAbout()
{
   CAboutDlg aboutDlg;
   aboutDlg.DoModal();
}

////////////////////////////////////////////////////////////////////////////
// CTextdemoApp commands
```

Listing 15.3

```
// textddoc.h : interface of the CTextdemoDoc class
//
////////////////////////////////////////////////////////////////////////////

const int NUMLINES = 28;    // number of lines stored in document &
                            // displayed in view window

class CTextdemoDoc : public CDocument
{
protected: // create from serialization only
   CTextdemoDoc();
   DECLARE_DYNCREATE(CTextdemoDoc)

// Attributes
public:

// Operations
public:

// Implementation
public:
   virtual ~CTextdemoDoc();
   virtual void Serialize(CArchive& ar);  // overridden for document i/o
#ifdef _DEBUG
   virtual  void AssertValid() const;
   virtual  void Dump(CDumpContext& dc) const;
#endif
protected:
   virtual  BOOL  OnNewDocument();
```

```
// Generated message map functions
protected:
    //{{AFX_MSG(CTextdemoDoc)
    afx_msg void OnOptionsFont();
    //}}AFX_MSG
    DECLARE_MESSAGE_MAP()

// added data members:
public:
    COLORREF mColor;
    CString mLineTable [NUMLINES];
    CFont mFont;
};
```

///

Listing 15.4

```
// textddoc.cpp : implementation of the CTextdemoDoc class
//

#include "stdafx.h"
#include "textdemo.h"

#include "textddoc.h"

#ifdef _DEBUG
#undef THIS_FILE
static char BASED_CODE THIS_FILE[] = __FILE__;
#endif

/////////////////////////////////////////////////////////////////////////
// CTextdemoDoc

IMPLEMENT_DYNCREATE(CTextdemoDoc, CDocument)

BEGIN_MESSAGE_MAP(CTextdemoDoc, CDocument)
    //{{AFX_MSG_MAP(CTextdemoDoc)
    ON_COMMAND(ID_OPTIONS_FONT, OnOptionsFont)
    //}}AFX_MSG_MAP
END_MESSAGE_MAP()

/////////////////////////////////////////////////////////////////////////
// CTextdemoDoc construction/destruction
```

```
CTextdemoDoc::CTextdemoDoc()
{
    // TODO: add one-time construction code here
}

CTextdemoDoc::~CTextdemoDoc()
{
}

BOOL CTextdemoDoc::OnNewDocument()
{
    if (!CDocument::OnNewDocument())
        return FALSE;
    // TODO: add reinitialization code here
    // (SDI documents will reuse this document)
    return TRUE;
}

/////////////////////////////////////////////////////////////////////////////
// CTextdemoDoc serialization

void CTextdemoDoc::Serialize(CArchive& ar)
{
    if (ar.IsStoring())
    {
        // TODO: add storing code here
    }
    else
    {
        // TODO: add loading code here
    }
}

/////////////////////////////////////////////////////////////////////////////
// CTextdemoDoc diagnostics

#ifdef _DEBUG
void CTextdemoDoc::AssertValid() const
{
    CDocument::AssertValid();
}
```

```
void CTextdemoDoc::Dump(CDumpContext& dc) const
{
    CDocument::Dump(dc);
}

#endif //_DEBUG

/////////////////////////////////////////////////////////////////////////
// CTextdemoDoc commands

void CTextdemoDoc::OnOptionsFont()
{
    // TODO: Add your command handler code here

    // display Font dialog box:
    CFontDialog FontDialog;
    if (FontDialog.DoModal () != IDOK)
        return;

    // set mColor:
    mColor = FontDialog.GetColor ();  // get color chosen by user

    // initialize font object:
    mFont.DeleteObject ();
    mFont.CreateFontIndirect (&FontDialog.m_lf);

    // store values in mLineTable:

    // store values chosen by user:
    int Num = 0;

    mLineTable [Num++] = "Font Name: " + FontDialog.GetFaceName ();

    mLineTable [Num] =    "Font Size: ";
    char NumBuf [18];
    sprintf
        (NumBuf,"%d.%d points",
        FontDialog.GetSize () / 10,
        FontDialog.GetSize () % 10);
    mLineTable [Num++] += NumBuf;

    mLineTable [Num++] = "";

    // store LOGFONT values:
```

```
mLineTable [Num++] = "LOGFONT fields:";

mLineTable [Num] =    "lfHeight: ";
sprintf (NumBuf,"%d",FontDialog.m_lf.lfHeight);
mLineTable [Num++] += NumBuf;

mLineTable [Num] =    "lfWidth: ";
sprintf (NumBuf,"%d",FontDialog.m_lf.lfWidth);
mLineTable [Num++] += NumBuf;

mLineTable [Num] =    "lfWeight: ";
sprintf (NumBuf,"%d",FontDialog.m_lf.lfWeight);
mLineTable [Num++] += NumBuf;

mLineTable [Num] =    "lfItalic: ";
sprintf (NumBuf,"%d",FontDialog.m_lf.lfItalic);
mLineTable [Num++] += NumBuf;

mLineTable [Num] =    "lfUnderline: ";
sprintf (NumBuf,"%d",FontDialog.m_lf.lfUnderline);
mLineTable [Num++] += NumBuf;

mLineTable [Num] =    "lfStrikeOut: ";
sprintf (NumBuf,"%d",FontDialog.m_lf.lfStrikeOut);
mLineTable [Num++] += NumBuf;

mLineTable [Num] = "lfCharSet: ";
switch (FontDialog.m_lf.lfCharSet)
   {
   case ANSI_CHARSET:
      mLineTable [Num++] += "ANSI_CHARSET";
      break;

   case DEFAULT_CHARSET:
      mLineTable [Num++] += "DEFAULT_CHARSET";
      break;

   case SYMBOL_CHARSET:
      mLineTable [Num++] += "SYMBOL_CHARSET";
      break;

   case SHIFTJIS_CHARSET:
      mLineTable [Num++] += "SHIFTJIS_CHARSET";
      break;
```

```
     case OEM_CHARSET:
        mLineTable [Num++] += "OEM_CHARSET";
        break;

     default:
        mLineTable [Num++] += "unknown character set";
        break;
     }

mLineTable [Num] = "lfPitchAndFamily: ";
switch (FontDialog.m_lf.lfPitchAndFamily & 0x0003)
     {
     case DEFAULT_PITCH:
        mLineTable [Num] += "DEFAULT_PITCH; ";
        break;

     case FIXED_PITCH:
        mLineTable [Num] += "FIXED_PITCH; ";
        break;

     case VARIABLE_PITCH:
        mLineTable [Num] += "VARIABLE_PITCH; ";
        break;

     default:
        mLineTable [Num] += "unknown pitch; ";
        break;
     }
switch (FontDialog.m_lf.lfPitchAndFamily & 0x00F0)
     {
     case FF_DECORATIVE:
        mLineTable [Num++] += "FF_DECORATIVE";
        break;

     case FF_DONTCARE:
        mLineTable [Num++] += "FF_DONTCARE";
        break;

     case FF_MODERN:
        mLineTable [Num++] += "FF_MODERN";
        break;

     case FF_ROMAN:
        mLineTable [Num++] += "FF_ROMAN";
        break;
```

```
    case FF_SCRIPT:
       mLineTable [Num++] += "FF_SCRIPT";
       break;

    case FF_SWISS:
       mLineTable [Num++] += "FF_SWISS";
       break;

    default:
       mLineTable [Num++] += "unknown family";
       break;
    }

mLineTable [Num] = "lfFaceName: ";
mLineTable [Num++] += FontDialog.m_lf.lfFaceName;

mLineTable [Num++] = "";

// store TEXTMETRIC values:

// create a device context object associated with the view window:
POSITION Pos = GetFirstViewPosition ();
CView *PView = GetNextView (Pos);
CClientDC ClientDC (PView);

// select new font into device context object:
ClientDC.SelectObject (&mFont);
TEXTMETRIC TM;
ClientDC.GetTextMetrics (&TM);

mLineTable [Num++] = "TEXTMETRIC fields:";

mLineTable [Num] = "tmHeight: ";
sprintf (NumBuf,"%d", TM.tmHeight);
mLineTable [Num++] += NumBuf;

mLineTable [Num] = "tmAscent: ";
sprintf (NumBuf,"%d", TM.tmAscent);
mLineTable [Num++] += NumBuf;

mLineTable [Num] = "tmDescent: ";
sprintf (NumBuf,"%d", TM.tmDescent);
mLineTable [Num++] += NumBuf;
```

```
mLineTable [Num] = "tmInternalLeading: ";
sprintf (NumBuf,"%d", TM.tmInternalLeading);
mLineTable [Num++] += NumBuf;

mLineTable [Num] = "tmExternalLeading: ";
sprintf (NumBuf,"%d", TM.tmExternalLeading);
mLineTable [Num++] += NumBuf;

mLineTable [Num] = "tmAveCharWidth: ";
sprintf (NumBuf,"%d", TM.tmAveCharWidth);
mLineTable [Num++] += NumBuf;

mLineTable [Num] = "tmMaxCharWidth: ";
sprintf (NumBuf,"%d", TM.tmMaxCharWidth);
mLineTable [Num++] += NumBuf;

mLineTable [Num] = "tmWeight: ";
sprintf (NumBuf,"%d", TM.tmWeight);
mLineTable [Num++] += NumBuf;

mLineTable [Num] = "tmItalic: ";
sprintf (NumBuf,"%d", TM.tmItalic);
mLineTable [Num++] += NumBuf;

mLineTable [Num] = "tmUnderlined: ";
sprintf (NumBuf,"%d", TM.tmUnderlined);
mLineTable [Num++] += NumBuf;

mLineTable [Num] = "tmStruckOut: ";
sprintf (NumBuf,"%d", TM.tmStruckOut);
mLineTable [Num++] += NumBuf;

mLineTable [Num] = "tmPitchAndFamily: ";
switch (TM.tmPitchAndFamily & 0x0003)
    {
    case DEFAULT_PITCH:
       mLineTable [Num] += "DEFAULT_PITCH; ";
       break;

    case FIXED_PITCH:
       mLineTable [Num] += "FIXED_PITCH; ";
       break;
```

```
   case VARIABLE_PITCH:
      mLineTable [Num] += "VARIABLE_PITCH; ";
      break;

   default:
      mLineTable [Num] += "unknown pitch; ";
      break;
   }
switch (TM.tmPitchAndFamily & 0x00F0)
   {
   case FF_DECORATIVE:
      mLineTable [Num++] += "FF_DECORATIVE";
      break;

   case FF_DONTCARE:
      mLineTable [Num++] += "FF_DONTCARE";
      break;

   case FF_MODERN:
      mLineTable [Num++] += "FF_MODERN";
      break;

   case FF_ROMAN:
      mLineTable [Num++] += "FF_ROMAN";
      break;

   case FF_SCRIPT:
      mLineTable [Num++] += "FF_SCRIPT";
      break;

   case FF_SWISS:
      mLineTable [Num++] += "FF_SWISS";
      break;

   default:
      mLineTable [Num++] += "unknown family";
      break;
   }

mLineTable [Num] = "tmCharSet: ";
switch (TM.tmCharSet)
   {
   case ANSI_CHARSET:
      mLineTable [Num++] += "ANSI_CHARSET";
      break;
```

```
        case DEFAULT_CHARSET:
            mLineTable [Num++] += "DEFAULT_CHARSET";
            break;

        case SYMBOL_CHARSET:
            mLineTable [Num++] += "SYMBOL_CHARSET";
            break;

        case SHIFTJIS_CHARSET:
            mLineTable [Num++] += "SHIFTJIS_CHARSET";
            break;

        case OEM_CHARSET:
            mLineTable [Num++] += "OEM_CHARSET";
            break;

        default:
            mLineTable [Num++] += "unknown character set";
            break;
        }

    // force redrawing of view window:
    UpdateAllViews (NULL);
}
```

Listing 15.5

```
// mainfrm.h : interface of the CMainFrame class
//
/////////////////////////////////////////////////////////////////////////

class CMainFrame : public CFrameWnd
{
protected: // create from serialization only
    CMainFrame();
    DECLARE_DYNCREATE(CMainFrame)

// Attributes
public:

// Operations
public:
```

```
// Implementation
public:
    virtual ~CMainFrame();
#ifdef _DEBUG
    virtual  void AssertValid() const;
    virtual  void Dump(CDumpContext& dc) const;
#endif


// Generated message map functions
protected:
    //{{AFX_MSG(CMainFrame)
        // NOTE - the ClassWizard will add and remove member functions here.
        //      DO NOT EDIT what you see in these blocks of generated code !
    //}}AFX_MSG
    DECLARE_MESSAGE_MAP()
};

////////////////////////////////////////////////////////////////////////
```

Listing 15.6

```
// mainfrm.cpp : implementation of the CMainFrame class
//

#include "stdafx.h"
#include "textdemo.h"

#include "mainfrm.h"

#ifdef _DEBUG
#undef THIS_FILE
static char BASED_CODE THIS_FILE[] = __FILE__;
#endif

////////////////////////////////////////////////////////////////////////
// CMainFrame

IMPLEMENT_DYNCREATE(CMainFrame, CFrameWnd)

BEGIN_MESSAGE_MAP(CMainFrame, CFrameWnd)
    //{{AFX_MSG_MAP(CMainFrame)
        // NOTE - the ClassWizard will add and remove mapping macros here.
```

```
    //    DO NOT EDIT what you see in these blocks of generated code !
   //}}AFX_MSG_MAP
END_MESSAGE_MAP()

/////////////////////////////////////////////////////////////////////
// CMainFrame construction/destruction

CMainFrame::CMainFrame()
{
    // TODO: add member initialization code here
}

CMainFrame::~CMainFrame()
{
}

/////////////////////////////////////////////////////////////////////
// CMainFrame diagnostics

#ifdef _DEBUG
void CMainFrame::AssertValid() const
{
    CFrameWnd::AssertValid();
}

void CMainFrame::Dump(CDumpContext& dc) const
{
    CFrameWnd::Dump(dc);
}

#endif //_DEBUG

/////////////////////////////////////////////////////////////////////
// CMainFrame message handlers
```

Listing 15.7

```
// textdvw.h : interface of the CTextdemoView class
//
/////////////////////////////////////////////////////////////////////

const int MARGIN = 10;      // margin displayed at top and left of view window

class CTextdemoView : public CScrollView
{
```

```
protected: // create from serialization only
   CTextdemoView();
   DECLARE_DYNCREATE(CTextdemoView)

// Attributes
public:
   CTextdemoDoc* GetDocument();

// Operations
public:

// Implementation
public:
   virtual ~CTextdemoView();
   virtual void OnDraw(CDC* pDC);  // overridden to draw this view
#ifdef _DEBUG
   virtual void AssertValid() const;
   virtual void Dump(CDumpContext& dc) const;
#endif

// Generated message map functions
protected:
   //{{AFX_MSG(CTextdemoView)
   afx_msg void OnKeyDown(UINT nChar, UINT nRepCnt, UINT nFlags);
   //}}AFX_MSG
   DECLARE_MESSAGE_MAP()

// added member function:
protected:
   virtual void OnUpdate (CView* pSender, LPARAM lHint, CObject* pHint);
};

#ifndef _DEBUG // debug version in textdvw.cpp
inline CTextdemoDoc* CTextdemoView::GetDocument()
   { return (CTextdemoDoc*) m_pDocument; }
#endif

/////////////////////////////////////////////////////////////////////////
```

Listing 15.8

```
// textdvw.cpp : implementation of the CTextdemoView class
//
```

```
#include "stdafx.h"
#include "textdemo.h"

#include "textddoc.h"
#include "textdvw.h"

#ifdef _DEBUG
#undef THIS_FILE
static char BASED_CODE THIS_FILE[] = __FILE__;
#endif

/////////////////////////////////////////////////////////////////////////////
// CTextdemoView

IMPLEMENT_DYNCREATE(CTextdemoView, CScrollView)

BEGIN_MESSAGE_MAP(CTextdemoView, CScrollView)
    //{{AFX_MSG_MAP(CTextdemoView)
    ON_WM_KEYDOWN()
    //}}AFX_MSG_MAP
END_MESSAGE_MAP()

/////////////////////////////////////////////////////////////////////////////
// CTextdemoView construction/destruction

CTextdemoView::CTextdemoView()
{
    // TODO: add construction code here

}

CTextdemoView::~CTextdemoView()
{
}

/////////////////////////////////////////////////////////////////////////////
// CTextdemoView drawing

void CTextdemoView::OnDraw(CDC* pDC)
{
    CTextdemoDoc* pDoc = GetDocument();

    // TODO: add draw code here
```

```
    // return if font has not yet been created:
    if (pDoc->mFont.m_hObject == NULL)
        return;

    RECT ClipRect;
    int LineHeight;
    TEXTMETRIC TM;
    int Y = MARGIN;

    // select font into device context object:
    pDC->SelectObject (&pDoc->mFont);

    // obtain text metrics:
    pDC->GetTextMetrics (&TM);
    LineHeight = TM.tmHeight + TM.tmExternalLeading;

    // set other text attributes:
    pDC->SetTextColor (pDoc->mColor);
    pDC->SetBkMode (TRANSPARENT);

    // obtain coordinates of update region:
    pDC->GetClipBox (&ClipRect);

    // display title line:
    pDC->TextOut (MARGIN, Y, "FONT PROPERTIES");

    // display text lines:
    for (int Line = 0; Line < NUMLINES; ++Line)
        {
        Y += LineHeight;
        if (Y + LineHeight >= ClipRect.top && Y <= ClipRect.bottom)
            pDC->TextOut (MARGIN, Y, pDoc->mLineTable [Line]);
        }
}

/////////////////////////////////////////////////////////////////////////////
// CTextdemoView diagnostics

#ifdef _DEBUG
void CTextdemoView::AssertValid() const
{
    CScrollView::AssertValid();
}
```

```
void CTextdemoView::Dump(CDumpContext& dc) const
{
    CScrollView::Dump(dc);
}

CTextdemoDoc* CTextdemoView::GetDocument() // non-debug version is inline
{
    ASSERT(m_pDocument->IsKindOf(RUNTIME_CLASS(CTextdemoDoc)));
    return (CTextdemoDoc*) m_pDocument;
}

#endif //_DEBUG

/////////////////////////////////////////////////////////////////////////////
// CTextdemoView message handlers

void CTextdemoView::OnUpdate (CView* pSender, LPARAM lHint, CObject* pHint)
    {
    CTextdemoDoc* PDoc = GetDocument();

    if (PDoc->mFont.m_hObject == NULL)  // font not yet created
        SetScrollSizes (MM_TEXT, CSize (0,0));
    else                                // font created
        {
        CClientDC ClientDC (this);
        int LineWidth = 0;
        SIZE Size;
        TEXTMETRIC TM;

        ClientDC.SelectObject (&PDoc->mFont);
        ClientDC.GetTextMetrics (&TM);

        for (int Line = 0; Line < NUMLINES; ++Line)
            {
            Size = ClientDC.GetTextExtent
                (PDoc->mLineTable [Line],
                 PDoc->mLineTable [Line].GetLength ());
            if (Size.cx > LineWidth)
                LineWidth = Size.cx;
            }

        Size.cx = LineWidth + MARGIN;
        Size.cy = (TM.tmHeight + TM.tmExternalLeading) * (NUMLINES + 1) + MARGIN;
```

```
        SetScrollSizes (MM_TEXT, Size);
        ScrollToPosition (CPoint (0, 0));
        }

    CScrollView::OnUpdate (pSender, lHint, pHint);
    }


void CTextdemoView::OnKeyDown(UINT nChar, UINT nRepCnt, UINT nFlags)
{
    // TODO: Add your message handler code here and/or call default

    CSize DocSize = GetTotalSize ();
    RECT ClientRect;
    GetClientRect (&ClientRect);

    switch (nChar)
        {
        case VK_LEFT:       // left arrow
            if (ClientRect.right < DocSize.cx)
                SendMessage (WM_HSCROLL, SB_LINEUP);
            break;

        case VK_RIGHT:      // right arrow
            if (ClientRect.right < DocSize.cx)
                SendMessage (WM_HSCROLL, SB_LINEDOWN);
            break;

        case VK_UP:         // up arrow
            if (ClientRect.bottom < DocSize.cy)
                SendMessage (WM_VSCROLL, SB_LINEUP);
            break;

        case VK_DOWN:       // down arrow
            if (ClientRect.bottom < DocSize.cy)
                SendMessage (WM_VSCROLL, SB_LINEDOWN);
            break;

        case VK_HOME:       // Home key
            if (::GetKeyState (VK_CONTROL) & 0x8000)  // Ctrl pressed
                {
                if (ClientRect.bottom < DocSize.cy)
                    SendMessage (WM_VSCROLL, SB_TOP);
                }
            else                                        // Home key alone
```

```
        {
        if (ClientRect.right < DocSize.cx)
            SendMessage (WM_HSCROLL, SB_TOP);
        }
    break;

case VK_END:        // End key
    if (::GetKeyState (VK_CONTROL) & 0x8000)   // Ctrl pressed
        {
        if (ClientRect.bottom < DocSize.cy)
            SendMessage (WM_VSCROLL, SB_BOTTOM);
        }
    else                                       // End key alone
        {
        if (ClientRect.right < DocSize.cx)
            SendMessage (WM_HSCROLL, SB_BOTTOM);
        }
    break;

case VK_PRIOR:      // PgUp key
    if (ClientRect.bottom < DocSize.cy)
        SendMessage (WM_VSCROLL, SB_PAGEUP);
    break;

case VK_NEXT:       // PgDn key
    if (ClientRect.bottom < DocSize.cy)
        SendMessage (WM_VSCROLL, SB_PAGEDOWN);
    break;
    }
}
```

The ECHO Source Code

The following listings, Listings 15.9 through 15.16, contain the C++ source code for the ECHO program given in this chapter. A set of these files is contained in the \ECHO subdirectory of the directory in which you installed the companion disk files.

Listing 15.9

```
// echo.h : main header file for the ECHO application
//

#ifndef __AFXWIN_H__
    #error include 'stdafx.h' before including this file for PCH
#endif

#include "resource.h"        // main symbols

/////////////////////////////////////////////////////////////////////////////
// CEchoApp:
// See echo.cpp for the implementation of this class
//

class CEchoApp : public CWinApp
{
public:
    CEchoApp();

// Overrides
    virtual BOOL InitInstance();

// Implementation

    //{{AFX_MSG(CEchoApp)
    afx_msg void OnAppAbout();
        // NOTE - the ClassWizard will add and remove member functions here.
        //     DO NOT EDIT what you see in these blocks of generated code !
    //}}AFX_MSG
    DECLARE_MESSAGE_MAP()
};


/////////////////////////////////////////////////////////////////////////////
```

Listing 15.10

```
// echo.cpp : Defines the class behaviors for the application.
//

#include "stdafx.h"
#include "echo.h"
```

```
#include "mainfrm.h"
#include "echodoc.h"
#include "echoview.h"

#ifdef _DEBUG
#undef THIS_FILE
static char BASED_CODE THIS_FILE[] = __FILE__;
#endif

/////////////////////////////////////////////////////////////////////////////
// CEchoApp

BEGIN_MESSAGE_MAP(CEchoApp, CWinApp)
    //{{AFX_MSG_MAP(CEchoApp)
    ON_COMMAND(ID_APP_ABOUT, OnAppAbout)
        // NOTE - the ClassWizard will add and remove mapping macros here.
        //    DO NOT EDIT what you see in these blocks of generated code !
    //}}AFX_MSG_MAP
    // Standard file based document commands
    ON_COMMAND(ID_FILE_NEW, CWinApp::OnFileNew)
    ON_COMMAND(ID_FILE_OPEN, CWinApp::OnFileOpen)
END_MESSAGE_MAP()

/////////////////////////////////////////////////////////////////////////////
// CEchoApp construction

CEchoApp::CEchoApp()
{
    // TODO: add construction code here,
    // Place all significant initialization in InitInstance
}

/////////////////////////////////////////////////////////////////////////////
// The one and only CEchoApp object

CEchoApp NEAR theApp;

/////////////////////////////////////////////////////////////////////////////
// CEchoApp initialization

BOOL CEchoApp::InitInstance()
{
    // Standard initialization
    // If you are not using these features and wish to reduce the size
```

```
//   of your final executable, you should remove from the following
//   the specific initialization routines you do not need.

SetDialogBkColor();          // set dialog background color to gray
LoadStdProfileSettings();   // Load standard INI file options (including MRU)

// Register the application's document templates.  Document templates
//   serve as the connection between documents, frame windows and views.

AddDocTemplate(new CSingleDocTemplate(IDR_MAINFRAME,
     RUNTIME_CLASS(CEchoDoc),
     RUNTIME_CLASS(CMainFrame),      // main SDI frame window
     RUNTIME_CLASS(CEchoView)));

// create a new (empty) document
OnFileNew();

if (m_lpCmdLine[0] != '\0')
{
    // TODO: add command line processing here
}

return TRUE;
}

/////////////////////////////////////////////////////////////////////////////
// CAboutDlg dialog used for App About

class CAboutDlg : public CDialog
{
public:
    CAboutDlg();

// Dialog Data
    //{{AFX_DATA(CAboutDlg)
    enum { IDD = IDD_ABOUTBOX };
    //}}AFX_DATA

// Implementation
protected:
    virtual void DoDataExchange(CDataExchange* pDX);   // DDX/DDV support
    //{{AFX_MSG(CAboutDlg)
        // No message handlers
```

```
    //}}AFX_MSG
    DECLARE_MESSAGE_MAP()
};

CAboutDlg::CAboutDlg() : CDialog(CAboutDlg::IDD)
{
    //{{AFX_DATA_INIT(CAboutDlg)
    //}}AFX_DATA_INIT
}

void CAboutDlg::DoDataExchange(CDataExchange* pDX)
{
    CDialog::DoDataExchange(pDX);
    //{{AFX_DATA_MAP(CAboutDlg)
    //}}AFX_DATA_MAP
}

BEGIN_MESSAGE_MAP(CAboutDlg, CDialog)
    //{{AFX_MSG_MAP(CAboutDlg)
        // No message handlers
    //}}AFX_MSG_MAP
END_MESSAGE_MAP()

// App command to run the dialog
void CEchoApp::OnAppAbout()
{
    CAboutDlg aboutDlg;
    aboutDlg.DoModal();
}


/////////////////////////////////////////////////////////////////////////////
// CEchoApp commands
```

Listing 15.11

```
// echodoc.h : interface of the CEchoDoc class
//
/////////////////////////////////////////////////////////////////////////////

class CEchoDoc : public CDocument
{
protected: // create from serialization only
    CEchoDoc();
    DECLARE_DYNCREATE(CEchoDoc)
```

```
// Attributes
public:

// Operations
public:

// Implementation
public:
    virtual ~CEchoDoc();
    virtual void Serialize(CArchive& ar);   // overridden for document i/o
#ifdef _DEBUG
    virtual  void AssertValid() const;
    virtual  void Dump(CDumpContext& dc) const;
#endif
protected:
    virtual  BOOL  OnNewDocument();

// Generated message map functions
protected:
    //{{AFX_MSG(CEchoDoc)
    //}}AFX_MSG
    DECLARE_MESSAGE_MAP()

// added data member:
public:
    CString mTextLine;
};

//////////////////////////////////////////////////////////////////////////////
```

Listing 15.12

```
// echodoc.cpp : implementation of the CEchoDoc class
//

#include "stdafx.h"
#include "echo.h"

#include "echodoc.h"

#ifdef _DEBUG
#undef THIS_FILE
static char BASED_CODE THIS_FILE[] = __FILE__;
#endif
```

```
//////////////////////////////////////////////////////////////
// CEchoDoc

IMPLEMENT_DYNCREATE(CEchoDoc, CDocument)

BEGIN_MESSAGE_MAP(CEchoDoc, CDocument)
    //{{AFX_MSG_MAP(CEchoDoc)
    //}}AFX_MSG_MAP
END_MESSAGE_MAP()

//////////////////////////////////////////////////////////////
// CEchoDoc construction/destruction

CEchoDoc::CEchoDoc()
{
    // TODO: add one-time construction code here
}

CEchoDoc::~CEchoDoc()
{
}

BOOL CEchoDoc::OnNewDocument()
{
    if (!CDocument::OnNewDocument())
        return FALSE;
    // TODO: add reinitialization code here
    // (SDI documents will reuse this document)
    return TRUE;
}

//////////////////////////////////////////////////////////////
// CEchoDoc serialization

void CEchoDoc::Serialize(CArchive& ar)
{
    if (ar.IsStoring())
    {
        // TODO: add storing code here
    }
    else
    {
        // TODO: add loading code here
    }
}
```

```
////////////////////////////////////////////////////////////////////////
// CEchoDoc diagnostics

#ifdef _DEBUG
void CEchoDoc::AssertValid() const
{
    CDocument::AssertValid();
}

void CEchoDoc::Dump(CDumpContext& dc) const
{
    CDocument::Dump(dc);
}

#endif //_DEBUG

////////////////////////////////////////////////////////////////////////
// CEchoDoc commands
```

Listing 15.13

```
// mainfrm.h : interface of the CMainFrame class
//
////////////////////////////////////////////////////////////////////////

class CMainFrame : public CFrameWnd
{
protected: // create from serialization only
    CMainFrame();
    DECLARE_DYNCREATE(CMainFrame)

// Attributes
public:

// Operations
public:

// Implementation
public:
    virtual ~CMainFrame();
#ifdef _DEBUG
    virtual  void AssertValid() const;
    virtual  void Dump(CDumpContext& dc) const;
#endif
```

```
// Generated message map functions
protected:
    //{{AFX_MSG(CMainFrame)
        // NOTE - the ClassWizard will add and remove member functions here.
        //      DO NOT EDIT what you see in these blocks of generated code !
    //}}AFX_MSG
    DECLARE_MESSAGE_MAP()
};
```

///

Listing 15.14

```
// mainfrm.cpp : implementation of the CMainFrame class
//

#include "stdafx.h"
#include "echo.h"

#include "mainfrm.h"

#ifdef _DEBUG
#undef THIS_FILE
static char BASED_CODE THIS_FILE[] = __FILE__;
#endif

/////////////////////////////////////////////////////////////////////////////
// CMainFrame

IMPLEMENT_DYNCREATE(CMainFrame, CFrameWnd)

BEGIN_MESSAGE_MAP(CMainFrame, CFrameWnd)
    //{{AFX_MSG_MAP(CMainFrame)
        // NOTE - the ClassWizard will add and remove mapping macros here.
        //      DO NOT EDIT what you see in these blocks of generated code !
    //}}AFX_MSG_MAP
END_MESSAGE_MAP()

/////////////////////////////////////////////////////////////////////////////
// CMainFrame construction/destruction

CMainFrame::CMainFrame()
{
```

```
    // TODO: add member initialization code here
}

CMainFrame::~CMainFrame()
{
}

/////////////////////////////////////////////////////////////////////////////
// CMainFrame diagnostics

#ifdef _DEBUG
void CMainFrame::AssertValid() const
{
    CFrameWnd::AssertValid();
}

void CMainFrame::Dump(CDumpContext& dc) const
{
    CFrameWnd::Dump(dc);
}

#endif //_DEBUG

/////////////////////////////////////////////////////////////////////////////
// CMainFrame message handlers
```

Listing 15.15

```
// echoview.h : interface of the CEchoView class
//
/////////////////////////////////////////////////////////////////////////////

class CEchoView : public CView
{
protected: // create from serialization only
    CEchoView();
    DECLARE_DYNCREATE(CEchoView)

// Attributes
public:
    CEchoDoc* GetDocument();

// Operations
public:
```

```
// Implementation
public:
    virtual ~CEchoView();
    virtual void OnDraw(CDC* pDC);   // overridden to draw this view
#ifdef _DEBUG
    virtual void AssertValid() const;
    virtual void Dump(CDumpContext& dc) const;
#endif

// Generated message map functions
protected:
    //{{AFX_MSG(CEchoView)
    afx_msg void OnChar(UINT nChar, UINT nRepCnt, UINT nFlags);
    afx_msg void OnEditClear();
    afx_msg void OnKillFocus(CWnd* pNewWnd);
    afx_msg void OnSetFocus(CWnd* pOldWnd);
    afx_msg int OnCreate(LPCREATESTRUCT lpCreateStruct);
    //}}AFX_MSG
    DECLARE_MESSAGE_MAP()

// added data members:
private:
    POINT mCaretPos;
    int mXCaret, mYCaret;
};

#ifndef _DEBUG // debug version in echoview.cpp
inline CEchoDoc* CEchoView::GetDocument()
    { return (CEchoDoc*) m_pDocument; }
#endif
```

//

Listing 15.16

```
// echoview.cpp : implementation of the CEchoView class
//

#include "stdafx.h"
#include "echo.h"

#include "echodoc.h"
#include "echoview.h"
```

```
#ifdef _DEBUG
#undef THIS_FILE
static char BASED_CODE THIS_FILE[] = __FILE__;
#endif

/////////////////////////////////////////////////////////////////////////
// CEchoView

IMPLEMENT_DYNCREATE(CEchoView, CView)

BEGIN_MESSAGE_MAP(CEchoView, CView)
    //{{AFX_MSG_MAP(CEchoView)
    ON_WM_CHAR()
    ON_COMMAND(ID_EDIT_CLEAR, OnEditClear)
    ON_WM_KILLFOCUS()
    ON_WM_SETFOCUS()
    ON_WM_CREATE()
    //}}AFX_MSG_MAP
END_MESSAGE_MAP()

/////////////////////////////////////////////////////////////////////////
// CEchoView construction/destruction

CEchoView::CEchoView()
{
    // TODO: add construction code here
        mCaretPos.x = mCaretPos.y = 0;
}

CEchoView::~CEchoView()
{
}

/////////////////////////////////////////////////////////////////////////
// CEchoView drawing

void CEchoView::OnDraw(CDC* pDC)
{
    CEchoDoc* pDoc = GetDocument();

    // TODO: add draw code here
```

```
    pDC->SetTextColor (::GetSysColor (COLOR_WINDOWTEXT));
    pDC->SetBkMode (TRANSPARENT);
    pDC->TextOut (0, 0, pDoc->mTextLine);
}


/////////////////////////////////////////////////////////////////////////////
// CEchoView diagnostics

#ifdef _DEBUG
void CEchoView::AssertValid() const
{
    CView::AssertValid();
}

void CEchoView::Dump(CDumpContext& dc) const
{
    CView::Dump(dc);
}

CEchoDoc* CEchoView::GetDocument() // non-debug version is inline
{
    ASSERT(m_pDocument->IsKindOf(RUNTIME_CLASS(CEchoDoc)));
    return (CEchoDoc*) m_pDocument;
}

#endif //_DEBUG

/////////////////////////////////////////////////////////////////////////////
// CEchoView message handlers

void CEchoView::OnChar(UINT nChar, UINT nRepCnt, UINT nFlags)
{
    // TODO: Add your message handler code here and/or call default

    if (nChar < 32)
        {
        ::MessageBeep (-1);
        return;
        }

    CEchoDoc* PDoc = GetDocument();
    PDoc->mTextLine += nChar;
```

```
    CClientDC ClientDC (this);
    ClientDC.SetTextColor (::GetSysColor (COLOR_WINDOWTEXT));
    ClientDC.SetBkMode (TRANSPARENT);
    HideCaret ();
    ClientDC.TextOut (0, 0, PDoc->mTextLine);
    CSize Size = ClientDC.GetTextExtent
        (PDoc->mTextLine,
        PDoc->mTextLine.GetLength ());
    mCaretPos.x = Size.cx;
    SetCaretPos (mCaretPos);
    ShowCaret ();
}

void CEchoView::OnEditClear()
{
    // TODO: Add your command handler code here

    CEchoDoc* PDoc = GetDocument();
    PDoc->mTextLine.Empty ();
    PDoc->UpdateAllViews (NULL);
    mCaretPos.x = 0;
    SetCaretPos (mCaretPos);
}

int CEchoView::OnCreate(LPCREATESTRUCT lpCreateStruct)
{
    if (CView::OnCreate(lpCreateStruct) == -1)
        return -1;

    // TODO: Add your specialized creation code here
    CClientDC ClientDC (this);
    TEXTMETRIC TM;

    mXCaret = ::GetSystemMetrics (SM_CXBORDER) * 2;
    ClientDC.GetTextMetrics (&TM);
    mYCaret = TM.tmHeight + TM.tmExternalLeading;

    return 0;
}

void CEchoView::OnKillFocus(CWnd* pNewWnd)
{
    CView::OnKillFocus(pNewWnd);
```

```
    // TODO: Add your message handler code here
    ::DestroyCaret ();
}

void CEchoView::OnSetFocus(CWnd* pOldWnd)
{
    CView::OnSetFocus(pOldWnd);

    // TODO: Add your message handler code here
    CreateSolidCaret (mXCaret, mYCaret);
    SetCaretPos (mCaretPos);
    ShowCaret ();
}
```

Summary

In this chapter, you learned how to display lines of text in the view window, how to read character and noncharacter keys from the keyboard, and how to display and manage a caret for marking the text insertion point. The following are some of the general facts and techniques that were covered:

- The first step in displaying text in a window is to obtain a device context object. If you are displaying text from an OnDraw function, you can use the device context object whose address is passed to the function.

- If you do not want to display text using the default System font, the second step in displaying text is to select an alternative font by calling CDC::SelectObject (to select a font matching your description) or CDC::SelectStockObject (to select a stock font).

- The third step is to call CDC::GetTextMetrics if you need to obtain the size or other features of the characters in the selected font.

- The fourth step is to set any text attributes you would like to change from their default values. To do this, you call CDC member functions, such as SetTextColor for setting the text color or SetTextCharacterExtra for changing the character spacing.

- The fifth step is to call CDC::GetClipBox to obtain the dimensions of the update region, so that you can increase the program's efficiency by displaying text only within the area of the window that needs redrawing.

- The sixth and final step is to display the text within the update region, using a `CDC` function such as `TextOut` or `DrawText`.

- You can have the user choose a font by displaying the Font common dialog box. To display this dialog box, you create an object of the MFC `CFontDialog` class and then call the `DoModal` member function. After `DoModal` returns, you can obtain a complete description of the selected font by accessing data members and calling member functions of the `CFontDialog` object.

- You can use the font information supplied by the `CFontDialog` object to initialize a font object (which is an instance of `CFont`). The font object can then be selected into a device context object to begin displaying text using the font.

- You can read the keyboard by providing a handler for the `WM_KEYDOWN` message, which is sent when any key (except a system key) is pressed. The handler is passed a virtual key code identifying the key. A `WM_KEYDOWN` message handler is especially suitable for processing noncharacter keys, such as Home, End, or a function key.

- The most convenient way to read character keys (that is, keys corresponding to printable characters) is to provide a `WM_CHAR` message handler, which is passed the actual ANSI code for the character typed.

- To display a caret, you should call `CWnd::CreateSolidCaret` and `CWnd::-ShowCaret` to create and show the caret within a `WM_SETFOCUS` message handler, which receives control whenever the window obtains the input focus.

- You should call `::DestroyCaret` to destroy the caret within a `WM_KILLFOCUS` message handler, which is sent whenever the window loses the input focus. Destroying the caret allows the next window that receives the focus to display the caret. (Only one caret may be displayed at a given time.)

- You can move the caret to the desired position by calling `CWnd::SetCaretPos`.

- Before drawing in a window—from a function other than `OnDraw` or `On-Paint`—you must first call `CWnd::HideCaret` to hide the caret, and then call `CWnd::ShowCaret` to restore the caret after the drawing is completed.

SIXTEEN

16

Using Drawing Functions

- Creating the device context object

- Selecting drawing tools

- Setting drawing attributes

- Drawing the graphics

- The MINIDRAW program

In this chapter and in the following chapter (Chapter 17), you will learn how to create and manipulate graphic images using two different approaches. In this chapter, you will learn how to call Windows' drawing functions to create graphic images at program run-time; these functions are well suited for generating drawings that are composed of individual geometric shapes, such as lines, arcs, and rectangles. In Chapter 17, you will learn how to create and display bitmaps, which store the actual pixels used to produce an image on a device; bitmaps are well suited for creating more complex drawings, which are not easily divided into separate geometric shapes. The techniques presented in these two chapters are closely related. As you will learn, you can use drawing functions to change the pattern of pixels within a bitmap, and you can use bit operations to manipulate images created with drawing functions (for example, moving or stretching an image).

This chapter explains how to use the graphics-drawing functions provided by Windows and the MFC. These functions, used in conjunction with the bitmap techniques that will be given in Chapter 17, provide a complete set of tools for creating graphic images within a view window or on another device such as a printer. The first four sections in the chapter explain the basic steps that you follow when you create a drawing. In the final section, you will develop a version of the MINIDRAW program that draws a variety of different figures and illustrates many of the techniques explained in the chapter.

Creating the Device Context Object

As you have seen, to display text or graphics you must have a device context object that is associated with the window or device that is to receive the output. When creating graphics, the device context object stores the set of drawing tools and attributes that you select, and provides a collection of member functions for drawing points, lines, rectangles, and other figures.

To display graphics from the OnDraw member function of the view class, you can simply use the device context object whose address is passed to the function, as in the following example:

```
void CMyView::OnDraw(CDC* pDC)
    {
```

```
// display graphics using 'pDC->'

}
```

The `OnDraw` function is called whenever the view window needs redrawing, and, if the view class supports scrolling (that is, the view class is derived from `CScrollView`), the device context object that is passed to it has already been adjusted for the current scrolled position of the document.

To display graphics from another function, you must explicitly create a device context object that is a member of the MFC `CClientDC` class, and, if the view class supports scrolling, you must call the `CScrollView::OnPrepareDC` function to adjust the device context object for the current scrolled position of the document. The following is an example:

```
void CMyView::OtherFunction ()
    {
    CClientDC ClientDC (this);

    // IF VIEW CLASS SUPPORTS SCROLLING:
    OnPrepareDC (&ClientDC);

    // display graphics using 'ClientDC.'
    }
```

Graphics within the *view window* are generally repainted by the `OnDraw` member function of the view class. Occasionally, however, you might need to repaint graphics within another type of window, such as a dialog box. Repainting of a nonview window is done from a `WM_PAINT` message handler, which is named `OnPaint`. When you create a device context object within an `OnPaint` function, you must derive it from `CPaintDC` *rather than* from `CClientDC`, as shown in the following example:

```
void CMyDialog::OnPaint()
    {
    CPaintDC PaintDC (this);

    // display graphics using 'PaintDC.'
    }
```

For an example of an `OnPaint` function that repaints a dialog box, see the section "Modifying the CFormat Code" in Chapter 13.

The drawing functions discussed in this chapter are defined within the CDC class; because CDC is the base class for all of the other MFC device context classes, these functions can be called using any type of device context object.

This chapter focuses on drawing graphics within a window (primarily a view window). However, the functions and techniques that it presents are largely device-independent and can be used to display graphics on other types of devices, such as printers or plotters. Chapter 18 explains the techniques for printing text or graphics.

Selecting Drawing Tools

Windows provides two tools that affect the way the drawing functions work: the *pen* and the *brush*. The current pen affects the way that lines are drawn; it affects straight or curved lines (created using the LineTo or Arc function), as well as the borders drawn around closed figures (such as rectangles and ellipses). As you will see, a closed figure consists of two separate elements: a border and an interior. The current brush affects the way that the interiors of closed figures are drawn.

When you first create a device context, it has a default pen and brush. The default pen draws a solid black line that has a width of one pixel, regardless of the current mapping mode (mapping modes are explained later in the chapter). The default brush fills the interior of closed figures with solid white. For each of these two tools, Table 16.1 lists the drawing functions that are affected by the tool and gives the identifier of the tool that is selected by default. (This is the identifier that you would pass to the SelectStockObject function if you wanted to select the tool, as described in the next section.)

To change the current pen or brush, either you can select a stock pen or brush, or you can create a custom pen or brush and then select it into the device context object.

Selecting Stock Drawing Tools

To select a stock pen or brush, you can simply call the CDC member function SelectStockObject:

```
CGdiObject* SelectStockObject (int nIndex);
```

The parameter nIndex is a code for the particular stock object you want to select into the device context object. The nIndex values for selecting stock pens and

TABLE 16.1: The Drawing Tools

Drawing Tool	Default Tool Selected	Drawing Functions Affected
Pen	BLACK_PEN	Arc
		Chord
		Ellipse
		LineTo
		Pie
		Polygon
		PolyLine
		PolyPolygon
		Rectangle
		RoundRect
Brush	WHITE_BRUSH	Chord
		Ellipse
		ExtFloodFill
		FloodFill
		Pie
		Polygon
		PolyPolygon
		Rectangle
		RoundRect

brushes are listed in Table 16.2. (As explained in Chapter 15, you can also call SelectStockObject to select a stock font.)

For example, the following code would select a white pen and a gray brush:

```
void CMyView::OnDraw(CDC* pDC)
    {
    pDC->SelectStockObject (WHITE_PEN);
    pDC->SelectStockObject (GRAY_BRUSH);

    // call other graphics functions and draw graphics ...
    // (lines and borders will be white, interiors of closed
    // figures will be gray)
    }
```

TABLE 16.2: Values Passed to `SelectStockObject` for Selecting Stock Pens and Brushes

Value	Stock Object
BLACK_BRUSH	Black brush
DKGRAY_BRUSH	Dark gray brush
GRAY_BRUSH	Gray brush
LTGRAY_BRUSH	Light gray brush
NULL_BRUSH	Null brush (interior not filled)
WHITE_BRUSH	White brush
BLACK_PEN	Black pen
NULL_PEN	Null pen (no line or border drawn)
WHITE_PEN	White pen

If you select the NULL_PEN stock pen, *no* line will be drawn; this choice is not very useful. Likewise, if you select the NULL_BRUSH stock brush, the interior of a closed figure will not be filled; this tool is useful for drawing a figure such as a rectangle that consists of only a border, leaving the existing graphics on the inside of the border unchanged. The MINIDRAW program given at the end of the chapter selects NULL_BRUSH when drawing an open figure.

NOTE All stock pens draw lines that are exactly 1 pixel wide, regardless of the current mapping mode.

Creating Custom Drawing Tools

You can create a custom pen or brush by performing the following steps:

1. Create an instance of the CPen class for a pen, or the CBrush class for a brush.

2. Call the appropriate member function to initialize the pen or brush.

3. Select the pen or brush object into the device context object, saving the pointer to the former pen or brush object.

4. Call drawing functions to produce the graphic output.

5. Select the old pen or brush back into the device context object.

To create a temporary pen or brush, you can declare the instance of the CPen or CBrush class as a local object within the function that generates the graphics output. (This method is demonstrated by the example code at the end of this section.) If, however, you are going to use a given pen or brush repeatedly throughout the course of the program, it would be more efficient to declare the object as a data member of the view class.

To initialize a pen, you can call the CPen member function CreatePen:

```
BOOL CreatePen (int nPenStyle, int nWidth, DWORD crColor);
```

The nPenStyle parameter specifies the style of line that the pen will draw; the values you can assign nPenStyle—and the resulting lines—are shown in Figure 16.1. Assigning the PS_NULL style creates a pen that is the same as the NULL_PEN stock pen. The PS_INSIDEFRAME style causes the pen to draw a border around a closed figure entirely within the figure's bounding rectangle. (The bounding rectangle and the effect of the PS_INSIDEFRAME style are explained later.) The styles PS_DASH, PS_DOT, PS_DASHDOT, and PS_DASHDOTDOT can be used only if the pen has a width of 1.

The nWidth parameter specifies the width of the line that the pen draws, in logical units. If you assign a width value of 0, the line will be exactly 1 pixel wide regardless of the current mapping mode. (This is the same line width generated by the stock pens.)

The crColor parameter specifies the color of the line. It is easiest to specify a color using the RGB macro:

```
COLORREF RGB(cRed, cGreen, cBlue)
```

The cRed, cGreen, and cBlue parameters indicate the relative intensities of red, green, and blue; each parameter may be assigned a value in the range from 0 to 255.

Note that a line can be assigned only a *pure* color. A pure color is one of the solid colors that are available under the current video mode (in standard VGA mode, there are 16 pure colors). If you assign a color value that does not correspond to one of the pure colors, the line will be drawn using the closest pure color. There is, however, one exception to this rule: If the pen has the PS_INSIDEFRAME style and a width greater than 1, Windows will use a *dithered* color if the color value you assign does not correspond to a pure color. A dithered color is one that is generated by

FIGURE 16.1:

Values you can assign the
nPenStyle parameter

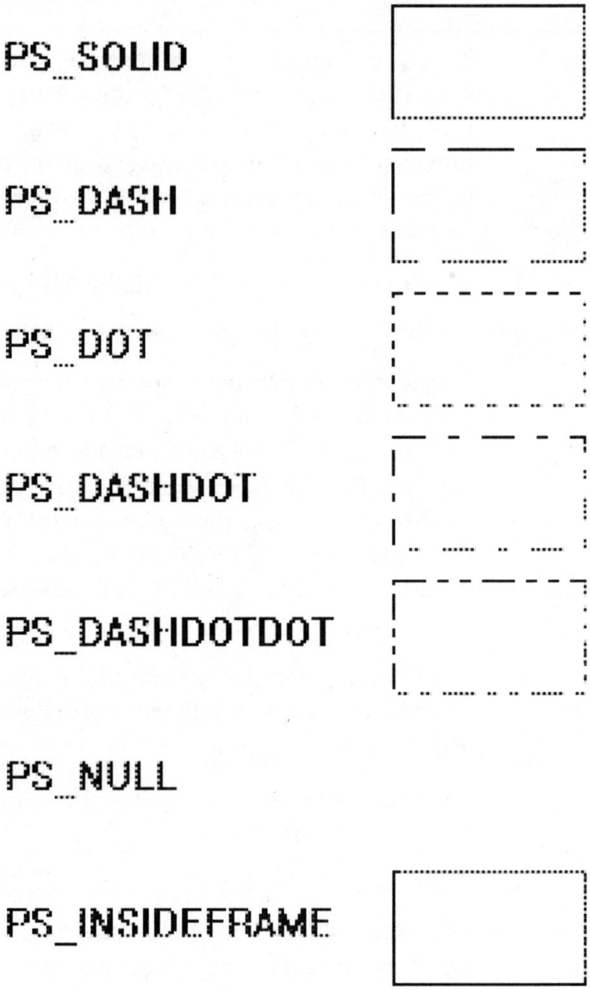

PS_SOLID

PS_DASH

PS_DOT

PS_DASHDOT

PS_DASHDOTDOT

PS_NULL

PS_INSIDEFRAME

combining different colored pixels in a uniform pattern. For example, a light red dithered color is created by displaying a pattern consisting of pure red and pure white pixels (the proportion of white to red pixels determines the lightness of the resulting color).

You can initialize a brush so that it fills the inside of figures with a solid color by calling the CBrush member function CreateSolidBrush,

```
BOOL CreateSolidBrush (DWORD crColor);
```

where the crColor parameter specifies the fill color. You can specify any color value; if the value you assign does not correspond to a pure color, Windows will generate a dithered color.

Alternatively, you can initialize a brush to fill the inside of figures with a hatched pattern by calling the CBrush member function CreateHatchBrush:

```
BOOL CreateHatchBrush (int nIndex, DWORD crColor);
```

The parameter nIndex specifies the desired pattern; the values you can assign nIndex—and the resulting patterns—are shown in Figure 16.2. The crColor parameter specifies the color of the hatch lines.

FIGURE 16.2:

Values you can assign the nIndex parameter

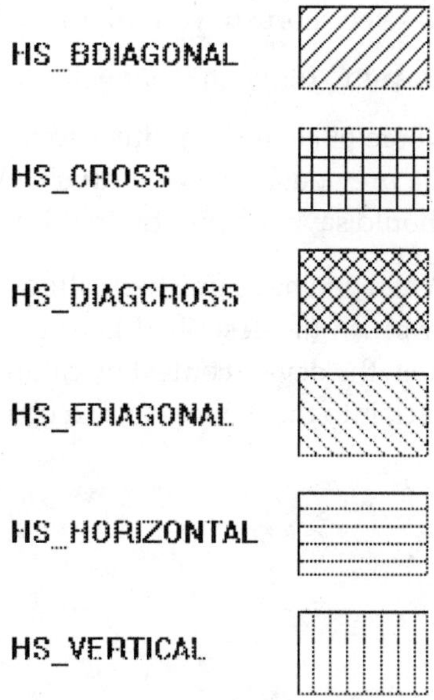

HS_BDIAGONAL

HS_CROSS

HS_DIAGCROSS

HS_FDIAGONAL

HS_HORIZONTAL

HS_VERTICAL

Finally, you can initialize a brush that fills figures with a custom pattern by calling the CBrush member function CreatePatternBrush:

BOOL CreatePatternBrush (CBitmap* pBitmap);

The pBitmap parameter is a pointer to a bitmap object. When a figure is drawn using the brush, the interior is completely filled with copies of the bitmap, placed side-by-side. You can create the bitmap using one of the methods explained in Chapter 17; you should give it a size of 8 pixels by 8 pixels. (If the bitmap is monochrome, Windows will draw it using the current text and background colors.)

Once you have initialized the pen or brush, you must select it into the device context object using the CDC member function SelectObject. To select a pen, you call the following version of SelectObject,

CPen* SelectObject (CPen* pPen);

where pPen is a pointer to the pen object. SelectObject returns a pointer to the *previous* pen object selected into the device context object. (If you have not previously selected a pen, this will be the default pen.)

To select a brush, you call the following version of SelectObject,

CBrush* SelectObject (CBrush* pBrush);

where pBrush is a pointer to the brush object. SelectObject returns a pointer to the previously selected brush. When calling either version of SelectObject, you should save the pointer that is returned.

When you have finished calling graphics functions to display output using the pen or brush (as described later in the chapter), you should *remove* the pen or brush from the device context by calling SelectObject again to select the previous object back into the device context object.

You should remove the pen or brush from the device context object so that the device context object is not left with an invalid handle after the pen or brush object is destroyed. (When you initialize a pen or brush, Windows supplies a handle that is stored within the pen or brush object; when you select the pen or brush object, the device context object also stores this handle.) You do not need to perform this step, however, if you are certain that the device context object will be destroyed *before* the pen or brush object is destroyed.

The following example OnDraw function illustrates the steps that have been explained in this section:

```
void CMyView::OnDraw(CDC* pDC)
   {
   CBrush Brush;            // declare brush object
   CPen Pen;               // declare pen object
   CBrush *PtrOldBrush;    // stores pointer to previous brush
   CPen *PtrOldPen;        // stores pointer to previous pen

   // initialize solid, 3-pixel wide, blue pen:
   Pen.CreatePen (PS_SOLID, 3, RGB (0, 0, 255));

   // initialize solid, yellow brush:
   Brush.CreateSolidBrush (RGB (255, 255, 0));

   // select pen into device context object:
   PtrOldPen = pDC->SelectObject (&Pen);

   // select brush into device context object:
   PtrOldBrush = pDC->SelectObject (&Brush);

   // set any required drawing attributes ...
   // call drawing functions to create graphics output ...
   // (lines and borders will be blue, interiors of closed
   // figures will be yellow)

   // remove new pen and brush from device context object:
   pDC->SelectObject (PtrOldPen);
   pDC->SelectObject (PtrOldBrush);
   }
```

Setting Drawing Attributes

When you first create a device context object, it has a default set of attributes that affect the way the graphics-drawing functions work. The CDC class provides member functions for changing these attributes. These functions are listed in Table 16.3.

TABLE 16.3: Drawing Attributes

Drawing Attribute	Default Value	Function(s) Used to Set	Drawing Function(s) Affected
Background color	White	SetBkColor	LineTo
Background mode	OPAQUE	SetBkMode	LineTo
Brush origin	0, 0 (screen coordinates)	SetBrushOrg	Chord
		UnRealizeObject	Ellipse
			Pie
			Polygon
			PolyPolygon
			Rectangle
			RoundRect
Current position	0, 0 (client coordinates)	MoveTo	LineTo
Drawing mode	R2_COPYPEN	SetROP2	Arc
			Chord
			Ellipse
			LineTo
			Pie
			Polygon
			PolyLine
			PolyPolygon
			Rectangle
			RoundRect
Mapping mode	MM_TEXT	SetMapMode	All drawing functions
Polygon-filling mode	ALTERNATE	SetPolyFillMode	Polygon
			PolyPolygon

The first column in Table 16.3 gives the attribute, while the second column gives the default value of this attribute in a newly created device context object. The third column gives the CDC member function that you call to change the setting of the attribute, and the fourth column lists the drawing function or functions that are affected by the attribute. This table lists all attributes that affect the graphics-drawing functions; the attributes that affect only the display of text were described in Chapter 15 (in the section "Writing Code to Display the Lines").

The mapping mode attribute is explained in the next section, and each of the other attributes is explained in the discussion on the function or functions that it affects, later in the chapter.

The Mapping Mode

The current mapping mode affects all of the graphics-drawing functions. The mapping mode defines the units and the coordinate system used to display graphics and text; it determines the way that Windows interprets all measurement and co-ordinate values that you pass to graphics output functions as well as all other functions that accept *logical coordinates*. The current mapping mode, however, does *not* affect functions that are passed *device coordinates*. The basic distinction between logical coordinates and device coordinates was explained in Chapter 11 (in the section "Converting Coordinates").

Device coordinates specify the position of an object in terms of the horizontal and vertical distance of the object *in pixels* (also known as *device units*) from the upper-left corner of the window (or the upper-left corner of the printable area of a page). Horizontal measurements increase as you move right, and vertical measurements increase as you move down. For device coordinates, the *origin* (that is, the point 0, 0) is always at the upper-left corner.

Under the default mapping mode (which has the identifier MM_TEXT), logical coordinates are also in pixels, with horizontal measurements increasing as you move right and vertical measurements increasing as you move down (see Figure 16.3). As you saw in Chapter 11, the *origin* of the MM_TEXT logical coordinate system (that is, the point 0, 0) is initially at the upper-left corner of the window; however, if a view window supports scrolling, the MFC will adjust the relative position of the origin as the user scrolls the document (by changing an attribute known as the *viewport origin*).

FIGURE 16.3:

The coordinate system for the default mapping mode (MM_TEXT)

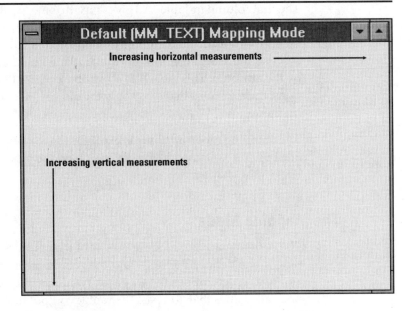

Creating an alternative mapping mode changes both the logical coordinate units and the directions of increasing logical coordinate measurements. To designate an alternative mapping mode, you call the CDC member function SetMapMode,

```
int SetMapMode (int nMapMode);
```

where nMapMode is an index that specifies the new mapping mode. Table 16.4 lists each of the values you can assign nMapMode, and for each value it gives the size of a logical unit in the resulting mapping mode. The MM_TEXT value specifies the default mapping mode.

For the MM_HIENGLISH, MM_HIMETRIC, MM_LOENGLISH, MM_LOMETRIC, and MM_TWIPS mapping modes, horizontal measurements increase as you move right, and vertical measurements increase *as you move up* (unlike the default mapping mode). Because positive vertical measurements indicate points above the top of the view window, to display an object within the view window, you must assign it a negative vertical coordinate.

TABLE 16.4: The Alternative Mapping Modes

Value Assigned nMapMode Parameter	Size of Logical Unit
MM_ANISOTROPIC	(you define)
MM_HIENGLISH	0.001 inch
MM_HIMETRIC	0.01 millimeter
MM_ISOTROPIC	(you define)
MM_LOWENGLISH	0.01 inch
MM_LOMETRIC	0.1 millimeter
MM_TEXT (default mapping mode)	1 device unit (pixel)
MM_TWIPS	$1/1440$ inch ($1/20$ point)

Figure 16.3 illustrates the coordinate system for the default mapping mode (MM_TEXT), and Figure 16.4 illustrates the coordinate systems for the alternative mapping modes (MM_HIENGLISH, MM_HIMETRIC, MM_LOENGLISH, MM_LOMETRIC, and MM_TWIPS).

FIGURE 16.4:

The coordinate systems for the nondefault mapping modes (MM_HIENGLISH, MM_HIMETRIC, MM_LOENGLISH, MM_LOMETRIC, and MM_TWIPS)

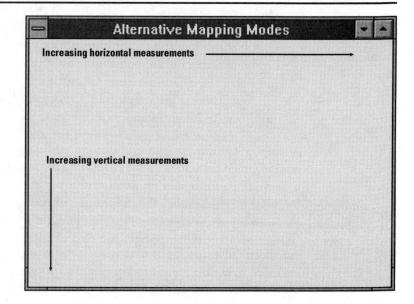

Alternative Mapping Modes

Increasing horizontal measurements

Increasing vertical measurements

Note that the MM_ANISOMETRIC and MM_ISOMETRIC mapping modes allow you to specify the orientation of the axes and to designate logical units of any size, thereby creating a custom mapping mode. (For the MM_ISOMETRIC mode, the vertical and horizontal units must be the same size, but for the MM_ANISOMETRIC mode, they can be different sizes.) To specify these values, you use the CDC member functions Set-WindowExt and SetViewportExt. For information on defining and using alternative mapping modes, see the documentation on the CDC member functions SetMapMode, SetWindowExt, and SetViewportExt in the *Reference Volume I, Class Library Reference* manual, or in the *Foundation Classes* online help file.

TIP

You must supply logical coordinates when calling any of the text display functions given in Chapter 15, the graphics-drawing functions given in this chapter, or the bit-operation functions (such as BitBlt) given in Chapter 17. However, many Windows functions and notification messages use device coordinates; for example, WM_MOUSEMOVE, WM_SIZE, GetClientRect, MoveWindow, ScrollWindow, and ShowWindow. If you are using the default mapping mode and your view window does *not* support scrolling, you need not be concerned about the type of units used by a particular function or message, because logical coordinates will be the same as device coordinates. If, however, your view class supports scrolling or you are using an alternative mapping mode, you must pay attention to the type of units that are employed (which should be indicated in the documentation on the function or message). Recall from Chapter 11 that you can convert logical coordinates to device coordinates by calling the CDC member function LPtoDP, and you can convert device coordinates to logical coordinates by calling the CDC member function DPtoLP.

An important advantage of using one of the alternative mapping modes (that is, a mapping mode other than MM_TEXT) is that the size of an image you draw is not dependent upon the device on which you draw it. (With the default mapping mode, the image size depends upon the device resolution.) Accordingly, alternative mapping modes are useful for programs that conform to the WYSIWYG principle (What You See Is What You Get; that is, programs in which the size of an object on the screen is the same as its size on any printer or other output device). For the sake of clarity, however, the example programs given in the remainder of the book continue to use the default MM_TEXT mapping mode.

Drawing the Graphics

After you have created the device context and have selected all desired drawing tools and attributes, you are finally ready to start drawing graphics. The CDC class provides member functions for drawing points, lines, and closed figures.

For all of these functions, the position of the figure is specified in logical coordinates. Also, whenever a pair of coordinates specifying a point is passed to a function, *the horizontal coordinate is always passed before the vertical coordinate.* The horizontal coordinate is often referred to as the x coordinate, and the vertical coordinate as the y coordinate.

Drawing Points

You can color a single pixel by calling the CDC member function SetPixel, as in the following example:

```
pDC->SetPixel (10, 15, RGB (255, 0, 0));
```

> **NOTE**   The SetPixel example, as well as the example calls in the following sections, assumes that pDC is a pointer to a valid device context—either one passed to an OnDraw function or one that you have explicitly defined.

The first two parameters specify the horizontal and vertical coordinates of the pixel in logical units, and the third parameter specifies the pixel color. If the color you specify does not match one of the pure colors that are currently available, SetPixel will use the closest pure color. (Obviously, it cannot use a dithered color for a single pixel!)

The MFC provides alternative versions of most of the drawing functions, which allow you to specify coordinates by passing appropriate structures, rather than by passing individual horizontal and vertical coordinates. For example, you can pass a single POINT structure to the SetPixel function in place of the first two parameters. For the syntax of these alternative function versions, see the *Reference Volume I, Class Library Reference* manual or the *Foundation Classes* online help file.

The MANDEL Program

The MANDEL program demonstrates the use of the SetPixel function, as well as several other drawing techniques. When you run this program, it immediately begins drawing a fractal pattern (specifically, the Mandelbrot set), which completely fills the client area. If you change the size of the window, or if you remove an overlapping window, MANDEL erases its client area and begins redrawing the pattern. If you want to see the completed image (which can take quite a while to generate), be careful that you do not cause the program to erase its window. Figure 16.5 shows the program window after a complete fractal pattern has been drawn.

FIGURE 16.5:

The MANDEL program with a complete fractal pattern

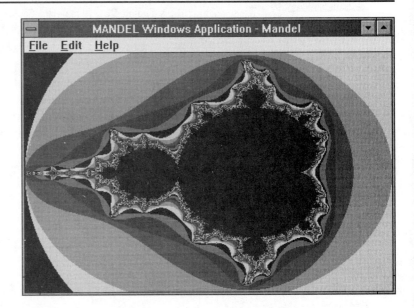

Use AppWizard to generate the MANDEL program, choosing only the Generate Source Comments option in the Options dialog box. When you have produced the source files, begin by opening the MANDEL.H file and declaring the virtual member function OnIdle at the end of the CMandelApp class definition:

```
// added member function;
public:
    virtual BOOL OnIdle (LONG lCount);
```

Then, open the MANDEL.CPP file and enter the following definition for the OnIdle function at the end of the file:

```
BOOL CMandelApp::OnIdle (LONG lCount)
{
    CWinApp::OnIdle (lCount);

    CMandelView *PView =
        (CMandelView *)((CFrameWnd *)m_pMainWnd)->GetActiveView ();
    PView->DrawCol ();

    return (TRUE);
}
```

The OnIdle function is called periodically whenever the system is idle—that is, whenever there are no messages to be processed. The code you added to OnIdle first calls the base class version of this virtual function to perform any required default idle-time processing. It then calls the CFrameWnd::GetActiveView function to obtain a pointer to the view class. (The address of the main frame window class that is used to call this function is obtained from the m_pMainWnd data member of the application class.) Next, it calls the DrawCol member function of the view class (which you will define later) to draw a single column of the fractal pattern. Finally, it returns the value TRUE, which causes the MFC to continue calling OnIdle while waiting for the next message.

Because drawing the fractal pattern can take a long time (more that an hour for a large pattern), the MANDEL program does *not* draw the complete figure from the OnDraw function. Doing so would block message processing during the entire time the pattern is being drawn, preventing the user from exiting the program, switching to another program, or performing any other tasks in Windows. (A message-handling function, such as OnDraw, must return control before the next message can be processed.) Rather, MANDEL draws only a *single column* of pixels within the pattern each time the OnIdle function is called. After drawing this column, OnIdle returns, allowing any pending messages to be dispatched. The next time OnIdle receives control, it draws the next column. This process continues until the pattern is complete.

> **TIP**
>
> Even drawing a single column can take a long time, resulting in a significant delay in processing messages (although a much smaller delay than if the entire pattern were drawn while processing a single message!). To make the system more responsive while the pattern is being drawn, you could modify the program so that it draws only a *portion* of a column each time OnIdle is called.

Before modifying more code, you need to define a message handler for the WM_SIZE message, which will be explained later. To do this, run ClassWizard and select the CMandelView class in the Class Name: list; then select CMandelView in the Object IDs: list, select WM_SIZE in the Messages: list, and click the Add Function button to create a handler named OnSize.

Next, open the MANDEVW.H file and add the following member declarations to the end of the CMandelView class definition:

```
// added members:
private:
    int Col;
    int ColMax;
    float CR;
    float DCI;
    float DCR;
    int RowMax;

public:
    void DrawCol ();
```

Col is used to store the number of the next column of pixels within the fractal pattern that is to be drawn. ColMax and RowMax store the numbers of the last row and column. (These values depend upon the size of the view window; later, you will see how they are set.) CR, DCI, and DCR are variables used in generating the fractal pattern, and DrawCol is the function that draws each column of the pattern.

Now open MANDEVW.CPP and add the definitions marked in bold type to the beginning of the file:

```
// mandevw.cpp : implementation of the CMandelView class
//

#include "stdafx.h"
#include "mandel.h"

#include "mandedoc.h"
#include "mandevw.h"

#ifdef _DEBUG
#undef THIS_FILE
static char BASED_CODE THIS_FILE[] = __FILE__;
#endif

// define Mandelbrot set constants:
#define CIMAX 1.2
#define CIMIN -1.2
#define CRMAX 1.0
#define CRMIN -2.0
#define NMAX 128

// colors used to create Mandelbrot pattern:
DWORD ColorTable [6] =
   {0x0000ff,  // red
    0x00ff00,  // green
    0xff0000,  // blue
    0x00ffff,  // yellow
    0xffff00,  // cyan
    0xff00ff}; // magenta
```

The constants and the ColorTable array are used in generating the fractal pattern. Leave the MANDEVW.CPP file open, because the remaining modifications will be made within this same file.

Add the following initialization to the CMandelView constructor,

```
CMandelView::CMandelView()
{
```

```
    // TODO: add construction code here
    Col = 0;
}
```

and enter the following definition of the DrawCol function at the end of the file:

```
void CMandelView::DrawCol ()
{
    CClientDC ClientDC (this);
    float CI;
    int ColorVal;
    float I;
    float ISqr;
    float R;
    int Row;
    float RSqr;

    if (Col > ColMax || GetParentFrame ()->IsIconic ())
        return;

    CI = CIMAX;
    for (Row = 0; Row <= RowMax; ++Row)
        {
        R = 0.0;
        I = 0.0;
        RSqr = 0.0;
        ISqr = 0.0;
        ColorVal = 0;
        while (ColorVal < NMAX && RSqr + ISqr < 4)
            {
            ++ColorVal;
            RSqr = R * R;
            ISqr = I * I;
            I *= R;
            I += I + CI;
            R = RSqr - ISqr + CR;
            }
        ClientDC.SetPixel (Col, Row, ColorTable [ColorVal % 6]);
        CI -= DCI;
        }
    Col++;
    CR += DCR;
}
```

Each time `DrawCol` is called, it draws the next column of pixels within the fractal pattern, moving from left to right. `DrawCol` creates a `CClientDC` device context object, and then uses the Mandelbrot equation to calculate a color value for each pixel in the current column. To color each pixel, it calls the `CDC` member function `SetPixel`. A description of the method for calculating the color value of each pixel is beyond the scope of current discussion; for an explanation, see one of the many books and articles on fractals. Notice that `DrawCol` returns immediately without drawing a column if the main frame window has been reduced to an icon—that is, if `CWnd::IsIconic` returns `TRUE` (the address of the main frame window object used to call this function is obtained by calling `CWnd::GetParentFrame`).

Note that the fractal pattern fills the entire view window; accordingly, the values of several of the data members used in its creation depend upon the current view window size. These members must be set in response to the `WM_SIZE` message, which is sent when the window is first created and whenever it changes in size. To set the data members, add the following code to the handler for this message, `OnSize`:

```
void CMandelView::OnSize(UINT nType, int cx, int cy)
{
    CView::OnSize(nType, cx, cy);

    // TODO: Add your message handler code here
    if (cx == 0 || cy == 0)
        return;

    ColMax = cx;
    RowMax = cy;

    DCR = (float)((CRMAX - CRMIN) / ColMax);
    DCI = (float)((CIMAX - CIMIN) / RowMax);
}
```

After `OnSize` is called, the view window is erased, and then the `OnDraw` function is called to repaint the window. `OnDraw` is also called when the view window needs redrawing for any other reason (such as the user's removing an overlapping window). `OnDraw` does not draw the image itself; rather, it simply resets the column back to 0 so that `DrawCol` begins redrawing the fractal pattern—a column at a time—starting with the first column. Complete the `OnDraw` definition as follows:

```
void CMandelView::OnDraw(CDC* pDC)
{
    CMandelDoc* pDoc = GetDocument();
```

```
    // TODO: add draw code here
    Col = 0;
    CR = CRMIN;
}
```

You can now build and run the MANDEL program.

The MANDEL Program Source Code   The following listings, Listing 16.1 through Listing 16.8, provide the C++ source code for the MANDEL program. A copy of these files is contained in the \MANDEL companion disk subdirectory.

Listing 16.1

```
// mandel.h : main header file for the MANDEL application
//

#ifndef __AFXWIN_H__
    #error include 'stdafx.h' before including this file for PCH
#endif

#include "resource.h"        // main symbols


/////////////////////////////////////////////////////////////////////////////
// CMandelApp:
// See mandel.cpp for the implementation of this class
//

class CMandelApp : public CWinApp
{
public:
    CMandelApp();

// Overrides
    virtual BOOL InitInstance();

// Implementation

    //{{AFX_MSG(CMandelApp)
    afx_msg void OnAppAbout();
        // NOTE - the ClassWizard will add and remove member functions here.
        //    DO NOT EDIT what you see in these blocks of generated code !
    //}}AFX_MSG
    DECLARE_MESSAGE_MAP()
```

```
// added member function;
public:
    virtual BOOL OnIdle (LONG lCount);

};
```

//

Listing 16.2

```
// mandel.cpp : Defines the class behaviors for the application.
//

#include "stdafx.h"
#include "mandel.h"

#include "mainfrm.h"
#include "mandedoc.h"
#include "mandevw.h"

#ifdef _DEBUG
#undef THIS_FILE
static char BASED_CODE THIS_FILE[] = __FILE__;
#endif

////////////////////////////////////////////////////////////////////////////
// CMandelApp

BEGIN_MESSAGE_MAP(CMandelApp, CWinApp)
    //{{AFX_MSG_MAP(CMandelApp)
    ON_COMMAND(ID_APP_ABOUT, OnAppAbout)
        // NOTE - the ClassWizard will add and remove mapping macros here.
        //    DO NOT EDIT what you see in these blocks of generated code !
    //}}AFX_MSG_MAP
    // Standard file based document commands
    ON_COMMAND(ID_FILE_NEW, CWinApp::OnFileNew)
    ON_COMMAND(ID_FILE_OPEN, CWinApp::OnFileOpen)
END_MESSAGE_MAP()

////////////////////////////////////////////////////////////////////////////
// CMandelApp construction

CMandelApp::CMandelApp()
{
```

```
    // TODO: add construction code here,
    // Place all significant initialization in InitInstance
}

/////////////////////////////////////////////////////////////////////////
// The one and only CMandelApp object

CMandelApp NEAR theApp;

/////////////////////////////////////////////////////////////////////////
// CMandelApp initialization

BOOL CMandelApp::InitInstance()
{
    // Standard initialization
    // If you are not using these features and wish to reduce the size
    //  of your final executable, you should remove from the following
    //  the specific initialization routines you do not need.

    SetDialogBkColor();         // set dialog background color to gray
    LoadStdProfileSettings();   // Load standard INI file options (including MRU)

    // Register the application's document templates.  Document templates
    //  serve as the connection between documents, frame windows and views.

    AddDocTemplate(new CSingleDocTemplate(IDR_MAINFRAME,
            RUNTIME_CLASS(CMandelDoc),
            RUNTIME_CLASS(CMainFrame),      // main SDI frame window
            RUNTIME_CLASS(CMandelView)));

    // create a new (empty) document
    OnFileNew();

    if (m_lpCmdLine[0] != '\0')
    {
        // TODO: add command line processing here
    }

    return TRUE;
}

/////////////////////////////////////////////////////////////////////////
// CAboutDlg dialog used for App About
```

```
class CAboutDlg : public CDialog
{
public:
    CAboutDlg();

// Dialog Data
    //{{AFX_DATA(CAboutDlg)
    enum { IDD = IDD_ABOUTBOX };
    //}}AFX_DATA

// Implementation
protected:
    virtual void DoDataExchange(CDataExchange* pDX);    // DDX/DDV support
    //{{AFX_MSG(CAboutDlg)
        // No message handlers
    //}}AFX_MSG
    DECLARE_MESSAGE_MAP()
};

CAboutDlg::CAboutDlg() : CDialog(CAboutDlg::IDD)
{
    //{{AFX_DATA_INIT(CAboutDlg)
    //}}AFX_DATA_INIT
}

void CAboutDlg::DoDataExchange(CDataExchange* pDX)
{
    CDialog::DoDataExchange(pDX);
    //{{AFX_DATA_MAP(CAboutDlg)
    //}}AFX_DATA_MAP
}

BEGIN_MESSAGE_MAP(CAboutDlg, CDialog)
    //{{AFX_MSG_MAP(CAboutDlg)
        // No message handlers
    //}}AFX_MSG_MAP
END_MESSAGE_MAP()

// App command to run the dialog
void CMandelApp::OnAppAbout()
{
    CAboutDlg aboutDlg;
    aboutDlg.DoModal();
}
```

```
/////////////////////////////////////////////////////////////////////
// CMandelApp commands

BOOL CMandelApp::OnIdle (LONG lCount)
{
   CWinApp::OnIdle (lCount);

   CMandelView *PView =
      (CMandelView *)((CFrameWnd *)m_pMainWnd)->GetActiveView ();
   PView->DrawCol ();

   return (TRUE);
}
```

Listing 16.3

```
// mandedoc.h : interface of the CMandelDoc class
//
/////////////////////////////////////////////////////////////////////

class CMandelDoc : public CDocument
{
protected: // create from serialization only
   CMandelDoc();
   DECLARE_DYNCREATE(CMandelDoc)

// Attributes
public:

// Operations
public:

// Implementation
public:
   virtual ~CMandelDoc();
   virtual void Serialize(CArchive& ar);   // overridden for document i/o
#ifdef _DEBUG
   virtual  void AssertValid() const;
   virtual  void Dump(CDumpContext& dc) const;
#endif
protected:
   virtual  BOOL  OnNewDocument();
```

```
// Generated message map functions
protected:
    //{{AFX_MSG(CMandelDoc)
        // NOTE - the ClassWizard will add and remove member functions here.
        //      DO NOT EDIT what you see in these blocks of generated code !
    //}}AFX_MSG
    DECLARE_MESSAGE_MAP()
};
```

///

Listing 16.4

```
// mandedoc.cpp : implementation of the CMandelDoc class
//

#include "stdafx.h"
#include "mandel.h"

#include "mandedoc.h"

#ifdef _DEBUG
#undef THIS_FILE
static char BASED_CODE THIS_FILE[] = __FILE__;
#endif

///////////////////////////////////////////////////////////////////////////
// CMandelDoc

IMPLEMENT_DYNCREATE(CMandelDoc, CDocument)

BEGIN_MESSAGE_MAP(CMandelDoc, CDocument)
    //{{AFX_MSG_MAP(CMandelDoc)
        // NOTE - the ClassWizard will add and remove mapping macros here.
        //      DO NOT EDIT what you see in these blocks of generated code !
    //}}AFX_MSG_MAP
END_MESSAGE_MAP()

///////////////////////////////////////////////////////////////////////////
// CMandelDoc construction/destruction

CMandelDoc::CMandelDoc()
{
    // TODO: add one-time construction code here
}
```

```
CMandelDoc::~CMandelDoc()
{
}

BOOL CMandelDoc::OnNewDocument()
{
    if (!CDocument::OnNewDocument())
        return FALSE;
    // TODO: add reinitialization code here
    // (SDI documents will reuse this document)
    return TRUE;
}

/////////////////////////////////////////////////////////////////////////
// CMandelDoc serialization

void CMandelDoc::Serialize(CArchive& ar)
{
    if (ar.IsStoring())
    {
        // TODO: add storing code here
    }
    else
    {
        // TODO: add loading code here
    }
}


/////////////////////////////////////////////////////////////////////////
// CMandelDoc diagnostics

#ifdef _DEBUG
void CMandelDoc::AssertValid() const
{
    CDocument::AssertValid();
}

void CMandelDoc::Dump(CDumpContext& dc) const
{
    CDocument::Dump(dc);
}

#endif //_DEBUG
```

```
/////////////////////////////////////////////////////////////////////////
// CMandelDoc commands
```

Listing 16.5

```
// mainfrm.h : interface of the CMainFrame class
//
/////////////////////////////////////////////////////////////////////////

class CMainFrame : public CFrameWnd
{
protected: // create from serialization only
   CMainFrame();
   DECLARE_DYNCREATE(CMainFrame)

// Attributes
public:

// Operations
public:

// Implementation
public:
   virtual ~CMainFrame();
#ifdef _DEBUG
   virtual  void AssertValid() const;
   virtual  void Dump(CDumpContext& dc) const;
#endif


// Generated message map functions
protected:
   //{{AFX_MSG(CMainFrame)
      // NOTE - the ClassWizard will add and remove member functions here.
      //    DO NOT EDIT what you see in these blocks of generated code !
   //}}AFX_MSG
   DECLARE_MESSAGE_MAP()
};


/////////////////////////////////////////////////////////////////////////
```

Listing 16.6

```
// mainfrm.cpp : implementation of the CMainFrame class
//

#include "stdafx.h"
#include "mandel.h"

#include "mainfrm.h"

#ifdef _DEBUG
#undef THIS_FILE
static char BASED_CODE THIS_FILE[] = __FILE__;
#endif

/////////////////////////////////////////////////////////////////////////////
// CMainFrame

IMPLEMENT_DYNCREATE(CMainFrame, CFrameWnd)

BEGIN_MESSAGE_MAP(CMainFrame, CFrameWnd)
    //{{AFX_MSG_MAP(CMainFrame)
        // NOTE - the ClassWizard will add and remove mapping macros here.
        //      DO NOT EDIT what you see in these blocks of generated code !
    //}}AFX_MSG_MAP
END_MESSAGE_MAP()


/////////////////////////////////////////////////////////////////////////////
// CMainFrame construction/destruction

CMainFrame::CMainFrame()
{
    // TODO: add member initialization code here
}

CMainFrame::~CMainFrame()
{
}

/////////////////////////////////////////////////////////////////////////////
// CMainFrame diagnostics
```

```
#ifdef _DEBUG
void CMainFrame::AssertValid() const
{
   CFrameWnd::AssertValid();
}

void CMainFrame::Dump(CDumpContext& dc) const
{
   CFrameWnd::Dump(dc);
}

#endif //_DEBUG

/////////////////////////////////////////////////////////////////////////////
// CMainFrame message handlers
```

Listing 16.7

```
// mandevw.h : interface of the CMandelView class
//
/////////////////////////////////////////////////////////////////////////////

class CMandelView : public CView
{
protected: // create from serialization only
   CMandelView();
   DECLARE_DYNCREATE(CMandelView)

// Attributes
public:
   CMandelDoc* GetDocument();

// Operations
public:

// Implementation
public:
   virtual ~CMandelView();
   virtual void OnDraw(CDC* pDC);  // overridden to draw this view
#ifdef _DEBUG
   virtual void AssertValid() const;
   virtual void Dump(CDumpContext& dc) const;
#endif
```

```
// Generated message map functions
protected:
    //{{AFX_MSG(CMandelView)
    afx_msg void OnSize(UINT nType, int cx, int cy);
    //}}AFX_MSG
    DECLARE_MESSAGE_MAP()

// added members:
private:
    int Col;
    int ColMax;
    float CR;
    float DCI;
    float DCR;
    int RowMax;

public:
    void DrawCol ();
};

#ifndef _DEBUG // debug version in mandevw.cpp
inline CMandelDoc* CMandelView::GetDocument()
    { return (CMandelDoc*) m_pDocument; }
#endif
```

///

Listing 16.8

```
// mandevw.cpp : implementation of the CMandelView class
//

#include "stdafx.h"
#include "mandel.h"

#include "mandedoc.h"
#include "mandevw.h"

#ifdef _DEBUG
#undef THIS_FILE
static char BASED_CODE THIS_FILE[] = __FILE__;
#endif

// define Mandelbrot set constants:
#define CIMAX 1.2
```

```
#define CIMIN -1.2
#define CRMAX 1.0
#define CRMIN -2.0
#define NMAX 128          .

// colors used to create Mandelbrot pattern:
DWORD ColorTable [6] =
    {0x0000ff,  // red
     0x00ff00,  // green
     0xff0000,  // blue
     0x00ffff,  // yellow
     0xffff00,  // cyan
     0xff00ff}; // magenta

////////////////////////////////////////////////////////////////////////
// CMandelView

IMPLEMENT_DYNCREATE(CMandelView, CView)

BEGIN_MESSAGE_MAP(CMandelView, CView)
    //{{AFX_MSG_MAP(CMandelView)
    ON_WM_SIZE()
    //}}AFX_MSG_MAP
END_MESSAGE_MAP()

////////////////////////////////////////////////////////////////////////
// CMandelView construction/destruction

CMandelView::CMandelView()
{
    // TODO: add construction code here
    Col = 0;
}

CMandelView::~CMandelView()
{
}

////////////////////////////////////////////////////////////////////////
// CMandelView drawing

void CMandelView::OnDraw(CDC* pDC)
{
    CMandelDoc* pDoc = GetDocument();
```

```
    // TODO: add draw code here
    Col = 0;
    CR = CRMIN;
}


////////////////////////////////////////////////////////////////////////////
// CMandelView diagnostics

#ifdef _DEBUG
void CMandelView::AssertValid() const
{
    CView::AssertValid();
}


void CMandelView::Dump(CDumpContext& dc) const
{
    CView::Dump(dc);
}


CMandelDoc* CMandelView::GetDocument() // non-debug version is inline
{
    ASSERT(m_pDocument->IsKindOf(RUNTIME_CLASS(CMandelDoc)));
    return (CMandelDoc*) m_pDocument;
}


#endif //_DEBUG

////////////////////////////////////////////////////////////////////////////
// CMandelView message handlers

void CMandelView::OnSize(UINT nType, int cx, int cy)
{
    CView::OnSize(nType, cx, cy);

    // TODO: Add your message handler code here
    if (cx == 0 ¦¦ cy == 0)
        return;

    ColMax = cx;
    RowMax = cy;

    DCR = (float)((CRMAX - CRMIN) / ColMax);
    DCI = (float)((CIMAX - CIMIN) / RowMax);
}
```

```
void CMandelView::DrawCol ()
{
    CClientDC ClientDC (this);
    float CI;
    int ColorVal;
    float I;
    float ISqr;
    float R;
    int Row;
    float RSqr;

    if (Col > ColMax || GetParentFrame ()->IsIconic ())
        return;

    CI = CIMAX;
    for (Row = 0; Row <= RowMax; ++Row)
        {
        R = 0.0;
        I = 0.0;
        RSqr = 0.0;
        ISqr = 0.0;
        ColorVal = 0;
        while (ColorVal < NMAX && RSqr + ISqr < 4)
            {
            ++ColorVal;
            RSqr = R * R;
            ISqr = I * I;
            I *= R;
            I += I + CI;
            R = RSqr - ISqr + CR;
            }
        ClientDC.SetPixel (Col, Row, ColorTable [ColorVal % 6]);
        CI -= DCI;
        }
    Col++;
    CR += DCR;
}
```

Figure 16.6 shows the icon for the MANDEL program that is included in the version of this program provided on the companion disk.

FIGURE 16.6:

MANDEL.ICO, the MANDEL program icon, as it appears in App Studio

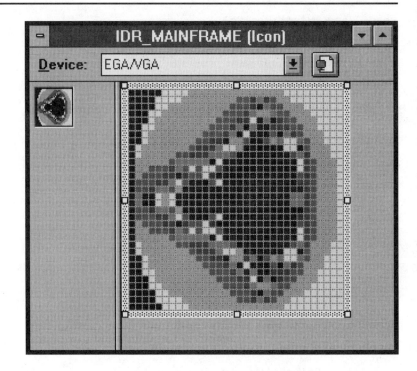

Drawing Lines

To draw a straight line, you first call MoveTo to specify the starting point of the line, and then call LineTo to specify the ending point and to generate the line. For example, the following code draws a line from the point (5, 15) to the point (25, 40):

```
pDC->MoveTo (5, 15);
pDC->LineTo (25, 40);
```

The parameters you pass to the MoveTo function specify the horizontal and vertical coordinates of the new *current point*. The LineTo function draws a line from the current point to the end point specified by the parameters you pass it. LineTo also resets the current point to the specified end point. Consequently, if you are drawing a series of connected lines, you need to call MoveTo only before the first call to

LineTo. For example, the following code draws a connected series of lines that form a "W":

```
pDC->MoveTo (50, 50);
pDC->LineTo (100, 150);
pDC->LineTo (150, 100);
pDC->LineTo (200, 150);
pDC->LineTo (250, 50);
```

NOTE When a device context is first created, the current point is at the logical coordinates (0, 0).

Alternatively, you can draw a series of connected lines by calling the PolyLine function. For example, the following code draws the same series of connected lines as the previous example:

```
POINT Points [5];

Points [0].x = 50;
Points [0].y = 50;
Points [1].x = 100;
Points [1].y = 150;
Points [2].x = 150;
Points [2].y = 100;
Points [3].x = 200;
Points [3].y = 150;
Points [4].x = 250;
Points [4].y = 50;

pDC->PolyLine (&Points, 5);
```

The first parameter passed to PolyLine is a pointer to an array of POINT structures giving the points to be connected, and the second parameter indicates the total number of points.

NOTE   The `Polyline` function neither uses nor resets the current point.

You can draw a curved line that is a segment of an ellipse by calling the `Arc` function, which has the following form:

```
BOOL Arc
   (int x1, int y1,    // u-l corner of bounding rectangle
    int x2, int y2,    // l-r corner of bounding rectangle
    int x3, int y3,    // starting point for arc
    int x4, int y4 );  // ending point for arc
```

Notice that `Arc` is passed four pairs of coordinates. The first pair of coordinates specifies the upper-left corner of the rectangle that bounds the ellipse (the arc is a segment of this ellipse), while the second pair of coordinates specifies the lower-right corner of the bounding rectangle. The third pair of coordinates indicates the starting point of the arc, and the fourth pair of coordinates gives the ending point of the arc. The arc extends from the starting point in a counterclockwise direction to the ending point. Note that the starting and ending points do not actually have to be on the ellipse; rather, they can be anywhere along a line that originates at the center of the bounding rectangle and passes through the desired starting or ending point on the ellipse. These coordinates—and the resulting arc—are illustrated in Figure 16.7.

The style, thickness, and color of lines drawn using any of the functions described in this section are determined by the pen that is currently selected into the device context object. The line is also affected by the current *drawing mode*. The drawing mode specifies the way that Windows combines the color of the pen with the current colors on the display device. The final color of each pixel within the line depends upon the current color of the pixel, the color of the pen, and the drawing mode. Under the default drawing mode, Windows simply copies the pen color to the display; thus, if the pen is red, each pixel within the resulting line will always be colored red regardless of its current color. You can change the drawing mode by calling the `CDC` member function `SetRop2`:

```
int SetROP2 (int nDrawMode);
```

The `nDrawMode` parameter specifies the desired drawing mode. There are 16 possible drawing modes; the most common ones are listed in Table 16.5. (See the documentation on this function for a description of the more esoteric drawing modes.)

The coordinates passed to the Arc
function

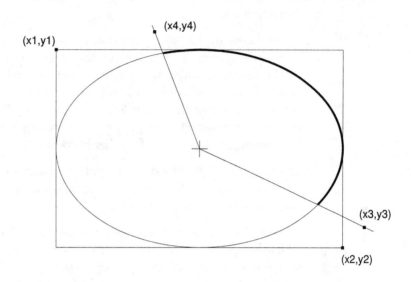

TABLE 16.5: Useful Drawing Modes

dDrawMode Value	Effect
RC_COPYPEN	The pixel is the pen color (the default mode)
RC_NOTCOPYPEN	The pixel is the inverse of the pen color
R2_NOT	The pixel is the inverse of its former color
R2_BLACK	The pixel is always black
R2_WHITE	The pixel is always white
R2_NOP	The pixel is unchanged

For each drawing mode, the table describes the resulting color of each pixel in a line that is drawn using the mode. Note that the value R2_COPY specifies the default drawing mode.

If you choose the R2_NOT drawing mode, a line will be drawn by inverting the existing screen colors. This method of drawing has several advantages. First, the line will be visible over almost any screen color; you can thus use the R2_NOT mode to draw a visible line within an area containing mixed colors. Also, if you draw the same line a second time, the line will automatically be erased and the existing screen colors restored; thus, you can use this mode for drawing selection rectangles, for creating animation, and for other purposes.

Choosing the R2_NOP mode is equivalent to selecting both a NULL pen and a NULL brush (yes, as you will see in the next section, the drawing mode also affects the colors painted by the current brush).

Note, finally, that when you draw a nonsolid line (that is, a line drawn using a pen with the PS_DASH, PS_DOT, PS_DASHDOT, or PS_DASHDOTDOT style), the color used to fill the gaps in the line depends upon the current background mode and background color. (These attributes also affect the spaces between characters when drawing text, and were explained in Chapter 15.) Recall that you set the background mode by calling SetBkMode:

```
int SetBkMode (int nBkMode);
```

If you assign nBkMode the value OPAQUE (the default value), the gaps will be filled with the current background color. If you assign it the value TRANSPARENT, the gaps will not be filled (the existing display colors will remain). As you learned, you set the background color by calling SetBkColor:

```
DWORD SetBkColor (DWORD crColor);
```

Drawing Closed Figures

The CDC class also provides a set of functions for drawing closed figures—that is, figures that completely enclose one or more areas. The following is a list of these functions:

- Rectangle
- RoundRect

- Ellipse

- Chord

- Pie

- Polygon

- PolyPolygon

To draw a simple rectangle, call the Rectangle function, as in the following example:

```
pDC->Rectangle (25, 50, 175, 225);
```

The upper-left corner of the rectangle drawn by this call would be at the position (25, 50), and the lower-right corner would be at (175, 225).

You can draw a rectangle with rounded corners by calling the RoundRect function:

```
BOOL RoundRect
    (int x1, int y1,     // u-l corner of rectangle
     int x2, int y2,     // l-r corner of rectangle
     int x3, int y3);    // dimensions of rectangle bounding corner ellipse
```

The first pair of coordinates passed to RoundRect specifies the position of the upper-left corner of the rectangle, and the second pair of coordinates specifies the position of the lower-right corner. The third pair of coordinates gives the width and height of the rectangle bounding the ellipse used to draw the rounded corners. These parameters are illustrated in Figure 16.8.

To draw a circle or ellipse, call the Ellipse function:

```
BOOL Ellipse
    (int x1, int y1,     // u-l corner of bounding rectangle
     int x2, int y2 );   // l-r corner of bounding rectangle
```

The first pair of coordinates specifies the position of the upper-left corner of the rectangle bounding the ellipse, and the second pair specifies the position of the lower-right corner of the bounding rectangle. See Figure 16.9.

You can draw a chord by calling the Chord function:

```
BOOL Chord
    (int x1, int y1,     // u-l corner of bounding rectangle
     int x2, int y2,     // l-r corner of bounding rectangle
     int x3, int y3,     // starting point for chord
     int x4, int y4 );   // ending point for chord
```

FIGURE 16.8:

The coordinates passed to the
RoundRect function

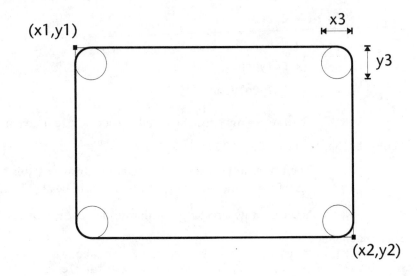

FIGURE 16.9:

The coordinates passed to the
Ellipse function

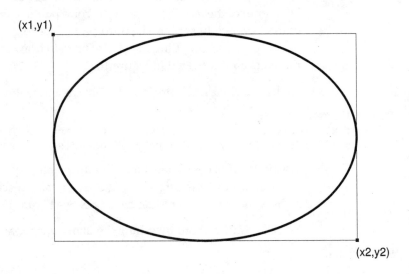

A chord consists of the area bounded by the intersection of an ellipse and a line segment. The first two pairs of coordinates you pass to Chord specify the rectangle bounding the ellipse. The third pair of coordinates specifies the starting point of the chord on the ellipse, and the fourth pair of coordinates specifies the ending point of the chord. As with the Arc function, the chord is drawn from the starting point in a counterclockwise direction to the ending point, and the specified starting and ending points do not need to be on the ellipse. These coordinates are illustrated in Figure 16.10.

To draw a pie-shaped figure, you can call the Pie function:

```
BOOL Pie
    (int x1, int y1,      // u-l corner of bounding rectangle
     int x2, int y2,      // l-r corner of bounding rectangle
     int x3, int y3,      // starting point for pie
     int x4, int y4 );    // ending point for pie
```

FIGURE 16.10:

The coordinates passed to the Chord function

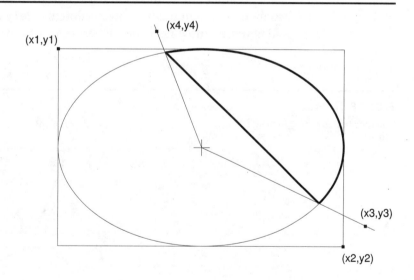

653

The coordinates passed to the `Pie` function work the same way as those passed to the `Arc` and `Chord` functions. They are illustrated in Figure 16.11.

The `Polygon` function draws a polygon, which consists of two or more vertices connected by lines. For example, the following code draws a triangle:

```
POINT Points [3];

Points [0].x = 20;
Points [0].y = 10;
Points [1].x = 30;
Points [1].y = 30;
Points [2].x = 10;
Points [2].y = 30;

DC.Polygon (&Points, 3);
```

The first parameter passed to `Polygon` is a pointer to an array of POINT structures; the members of this array specify the coordinates of the vertices. The second parameter specifies the number of vertices to be connected. Unlike the `PolyLine` function discussed in the previous section, the `Polygon` function always creates a closed figure, by drawing a line—if necessary—from the last vertex specified to the

FIGURE 16.11:

The coordinates passed to the `Pie` function

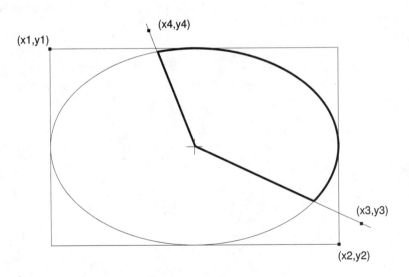

first vertex. In the above example, Polygon would connect the first point (Points [0]) to the second point, the second point to the third point, and the third point to the first point, making a closed triangle. In contrast, PolyLine would connect only the first point to the second point and the second point to the third point.

You can draw an entire series of polygons by calling the CDC member function PolyPolygon. You can also call the SetPolyFillMode function to change the polygon filling mode, which affects the way complex polygons are filled. For details, see the documentation on these two functions in the *Reference Volume I, Class Library Reference* manual or in the *Foundation Classes* online help file.

For each of the closed figures discussed in this section, the borders are drawn using the current pen, and the interiors are filled using the current brush. Note that if you draw a closed figure with a pen that has been assigned the PS_INSIDEFRAME style, the border is drawn entirely within the bounding rectangle. Note, also, that if you want to draw a closed figure *without* filling the interior (that is, you want to leave the current graphics inside the border undisturbed), you can call SelectStockObject to select the NULL_BRUSH stock object before drawing the figure.

The current drawing mode—set by calling SetROP2—affects the way that both the border and the interior of a closed figure are drawn, in the same way that it affects the drawing of lines, which was described previously.

> **NOTE** If you are using a patterned brush (that is, one created by calling CreateHatchBrush or CreatePatternBrush), you can use the CDC member functions UnrealizeObject and SetBrushOrg to adjust the alignment of the fill pattern. Also, the background mode and color (set by calling CDC::SetBkMode and CDC::SetBkColor) affect the way Windows paints the spaces between the hatch lines drawn with a hatched brush, in the same way that these attributes affect text and nonsolid lines.

Other Drawing Functions

Table 16.6 lists several additional drawing functions that you might find useful.

TABLE 16.6: Some Additional Drawing Functions

Function	Purpose
DrawFocusRect	Draws a rectangular border using a dotted line, without filling the interior; the border is drawn by inverting the existing screen colors, so that calling this function a second time with the same coordinates erases the border
ExtFloodFill	Fills an area on the display surface that is bounded by a given color, using the current brush; you can optionally fill an area that consists of a specified color
FillRect	Fills a rectangular area using the specified brush, without drawing a border
FloodFill	Fills an area on the display surface that is bounded by a given color, using the current brush
FrameRect	Draws a rectangular border using the specified brush, without filling the interior
InvertRect	Inverts the existing colors within a rectangular area on the display

The MINIDRAW Program

This section presents a new version of the MINIDRAW program, which adds the following features (see Figure 16.12):

- The user can draw a variety of different shapes, the particular shape depending upon the drawing tool that is selected. A drawing tool is selected by clicking a button on the tool bar, or by choosing a command on the Tools menu.

- The user can specify the thickness of the lines used for drawing figures (single, double, or triple) by clicking a tool bar button, or by choosing a command on the Options menu.

- The user can select the color of the figures that are drawn by choosing a command on the Options menu.

The code that you will add to the MINIDRAW program demonstrates not only many of the techniques for drawing graphics that were presented in this chapter, but also several of the techniques for designing class hierarchies and using polymorphism that were explained in Chapter 5.

You will make all changes to the MINIDRAW source files that you created in Chapter 14. (If necessary, you can obtain a copy of these files from the \MINIDRW5 companion disk subdirectory.) To begin, open the MINIDRAW.MAK project in the Visual Workbench, and run App Studio. In App Studio, open the menu-designing

FIGURE 16.12:

The MINIDRAW program window

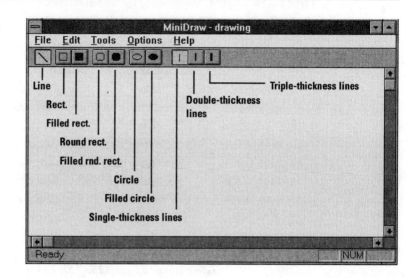

window for the `IDR_MAINFRAME` menu. Now delete the Line pop-up menu, and replace it with an Options pop-up menu, which contains two cascading pop-up menus. Table 16.7 lists the properties of the new menu items, and Figure 16.13 shows the finished result.

TABLE 16.7: The Properties of the MINIDRAW Options Menu Items

The Options pop-up menu and the items it contains:		
ID:	**Caption:**	**Other Features**
none	&Options	Popup
none	&Color	Popup
none	&Line Thickness	Popup

TABLE 16.7: The Properties of the MINIDRAW Options Menu Items (continued)

The items on the Color pop-up menu:

ID:	Caption:	Prompt:	Other Features
ID_COLOR_BLACK	&Black	Draw using black	none
ID_COLOR_WHITE	&White	Draw using white	none
ID_COLOR_RED	&Red	Draw using red	none
ID_COLOR_GREEN	&Green	Draw using green	none
ID_COLOR_BLUE	B&lue	Draw using blue	none
ID_COLOR_YELLOW	&Yellow	Draw using yellow	none
ID_COLOR_CYAN	&Cyan	Draw using cyan	none
ID_COLOR_MAGENTA	&Magenta	Draw using magenta	none
ID_COLOR_CUSTOM	C&ustom	Select a custom drawing color	none

The items on the Line Thickness pop-up menu:

ID:	Caption:	Prompt:	Other Features
ID_LINE_SINGLE	&Single	Draw using single-thickness lines	none
ID_LINE_DOUBLE	&Double	Draw using double-thickness lines	none
ID_LINE_TRIPLE	&Triple	Draw using triple-thickness lines	none

You should now return to the Visual Workbench and run the ClassWizard tool to define handlers for the new menu commands you added. In the ClassWizard dialog box, select the CMinidrawApp class in the Class Name: list. You will now define both a COMMAND message handler and an UPDATE_COMMAND_UI message handler for each of the commands on the Color pop-up menu. In all cases, accept the default

FIGURE 16.13:

The completed Options menu in App Studio

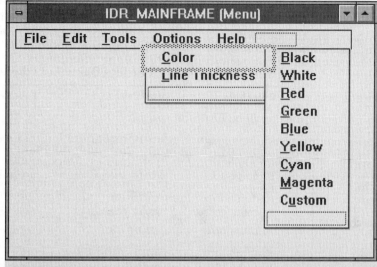

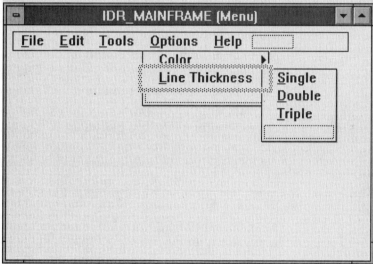

function name. For each of these message handlers, Table 16.8 lists the command identifier (which you select in the Object IDs: list), the message identifier (which you select in the Messages: list), and the default name of the message-handling function.

TABLE 16.8: Message-Handling Functions for the Color Menu Commands

Object ID:	Message:	Function Name
ID_COLOR_BLACK	COMMAND	OnColorBlack
ID_COLOR_BLACK	UPDATE_COMMAND_UI	OnUpdateColorBlack
ID_COLOR_BLUE	COMMAND	OnColorBlue
ID_COLOR_BLUE	UPDATE_COMMAND_UI	OnUpdateColorBlue
ID_COLOR_CUSTOM	COMMAND	OnColorCustom
ID_COLOR_CUSTOM	UPDATE_COMMAND_UI	OnUpdateColorCustom
ID_COLOR_CYAN	COMMAND	OnColorCyan
ID_COLOR_CYAN	UPDATE_COMMAND_UI	OnUpdateColorCyan
ID_COLOR_GREEN	COMMAND	OnColorGreen
ID_COLOR_GREEN	UPDATE_COMMAND_UI	OnUpdateColorGreen
ID_COLOR_MAGENTA	COMMAND	OnColorMagenta
ID_COLOR_CUSTOM	UPDATE_COMMAND_UI	OnUpdateColorMagenta
ID_COLOR_RED	COMMAND	OnColorRed
ID_COLOR_RED	UPDATE_COMMAND_UI	OnUpdateColorRed
ID_COLOR_WHITE	COMMAND	OnColorWhite
ID_COLOR_WHITE	UPDATE_COMMAND_UI	OnUpdateColorWhite
ID_COLOR_YELLOW	COMMAND	OnColorYellow
ID_COLOR_YELLOW	UPDATE_COMMAND_UI	OnUpdateColorYellow

Next, open the MINIDRAW.H file and add definitions for two new data members to the end of the CMinidrawApp class definition:

```
// added data members:
public:
    COLORREF mCurrentColor;
    int mCurrentThickness;
    UINT mCurrentTool;
    UINT mIdxColorCmd;
```

mCurrentColor stores the value of the color that is currently used to draw figures, and mIdxColorCmd stores the identifier of the command on the Color menu that was chosen to obtain that color. To initialize these data members, open the MINIDRAW.CPP file and add the statements marked in bold to the CMinidrawApp constructor:

```
CMinidrawApp::CMinidrawApp()
{
    // TODO: add construction code here,
    // Place all significant initialization in InitInstance

    mCurrentColor = RGB (0,0,0);
    mCurrentThickness = 1;
    mCurrentTool = ID_TOOLS_LINE;
    mIdxColorCmd = ID_COLOR_BLACK;
}
```

Also in MINIDRAW.CPP, implement the handlers for the new menu items, as follows:

```
void CMinidrawApp::OnColorBlack()
{
    // TODO: Add your command handler code here
    mCurrentColor = RGB (0,0,0);
    mIdxColorCmd = ID_COLOR_BLACK;
}

void CMinidrawApp::OnUpdateColorBlack(CCmdUI* pCmdUI)
{
    // TODO: Add your command update UI handler code here
    pCmdUI->SetCheck (mIdxColorCmd == ID_COLOR_BLACK ? 1 : 0);
}

void CMinidrawApp::OnColorBlue()
{
    // TODO: Add your command handler code here
    mCurrentColor = RGB (0,0,255);
    mIdxColorCmd = ID_COLOR_BLUE;
}

void CMinidrawApp::OnUpdateColorBlue(CCmdUI* pCmdUI)
{
    // TODO: Add your command update UI handler code here
    pCmdUI->SetCheck (mIdxColorCmd == ID_COLOR_BLUE ? 1 : 0);
}
```

```cpp
void CMinidrawApp::OnColorCustom()
{
    // TODO: Add your command handler code here
    CColorDialog ColorDialog;

    if (ColorDialog.DoModal () == IDOK)
        {
        mCurrentColor = ColorDialog.GetColor ();
        mIdxColorCmd = ID_COLOR_CUSTOM;
        }
}

void CMinidrawApp::OnUpdateColorCustom(CCmdUI* pCmdUI)
{
    // TODO: Add your command update UI handler code here
    pCmdUI->SetCheck (mIdxColorCmd == ID_COLOR_CUSTOM ? 1 : 0);
}

void CMinidrawApp::OnColorCyan()
{
    // TODO: Add your command handler code here
    mCurrentColor = RGB (0,255,255);
    mIdxColorCmd = ID_COLOR_CYAN;
}

void CMinidrawApp::OnUpdateColorCyan(CCmdUI* pCmdUI)
{
    // TODO: Add your command update UI handler code here
    pCmdUI->SetCheck (mIdxColorCmd == ID_COLOR_CYAN ? 1 : 0);
}

void CMinidrawApp::OnColorGreen()
{
    // TODO: Add your command handler code here
    mCurrentColor = RGB (0,255,0);
    mIdxColorCmd = ID_COLOR_GREEN;
}

void CMinidrawApp::OnUpdateColorGreen(CCmdUI* pCmdUI)
{
    // TODO: Add your command update UI handler code here
    pCmdUI->SetCheck (mIdxColorCmd == ID_COLOR_GREEN ? 1 : 0);
}
```

```
void CMinidrawApp::OnColorMagenta()
{
    // TODO: Add your command handler code here
    mCurrentColor = RGB (255,0,255);
    mIdxColorCmd = ID_COLOR_MAGENTA;
}

void CMinidrawApp::OnUpdateColorMagenta(CCmdUI* pCmdUI)
{
    // TODO: Add your command update UI handler code here
    pCmdUI->SetCheck (mIdxColorCmd == ID_COLOR_MAGENTA ? 1 : 0);
}

void CMinidrawApp::OnColorRed()
{
    // TODO: Add your command handler code here
    mCurrentColor = RGB (255,0,0);
    mIdxColorCmd = ID_COLOR_RED;
}

void CMinidrawApp::OnUpdateColorRed(CCmdUI* pCmdUI)
{
    // TODO: Add your command update UI handler code here
    pCmdUI->SetCheck (mIdxColorCmd == ID_COLOR_RED ? 1 : 0);
}

void CMinidrawApp::OnColorWhite()
{
    // TODO: Add your command handler code here
    mCurrentColor = RGB (255,255,255);
    mIdxColorCmd = ID_COLOR_WHITE;
}

void CMinidrawApp::OnUpdateColorWhite(CCmdUI* pCmdUI)
{
    // TODO: Add your command update UI handler code here
    pCmdUI->SetCheck (mIdxColorCmd == ID_COLOR_WHITE ? 1 : 0);
}

void CMinidrawApp::OnColorYellow()
{
    // TODO: Add your command handler code here
    mCurrentColor = RGB (255,255,0);
    mIdxColorCmd = ID_COLOR_YELLOW;
}
```

```
void CMinidrawApp::OnUpdateColorYellow(CCmdUI* pCmdUI)
{
    // TODO: Add your command update UI handler code here
    pCmdUI->SetCheck (mIdxColorCmd == ID_COLOR_YELLOW ? 1 : 0);
}
```

These menu message handlers work exactly like the ones you added to the program in Chapter 14; for an explanation, see the section "Writing Handlers for the Button Messages" in Chapter 14. Notice that the OnColorCustom function, which receives control when the user chooses the Custom command on the Color menu, displays the Color common dialog box, which allows the user to select a custom color. This dialog box is shown in Figure 16.14. The technique for displaying a common dialog box was discussed in Chapter 15, in the section "Creating the Font Object and Storing the Text."

Defining Classes for the Figures

Your next task is to open the MINIDDOC.H header file for the document class and *replace* the CLine class definition with the following class definitions:

```
// class hierarchy for figures:

class CFigure : public CObject
{
protected:
    COLORREF mColor;
    int mX1, mY1, mX2, mY2;

    virtual void Serialize (CArchive& ar);
    DECLARE_SERIAL (CFigure)

public:
    virtual void Draw (CDC *PDC) {}
    CRect GetDimRect ();
};

class CLine : public CFigure
{
protected:
    int mThickness;
```

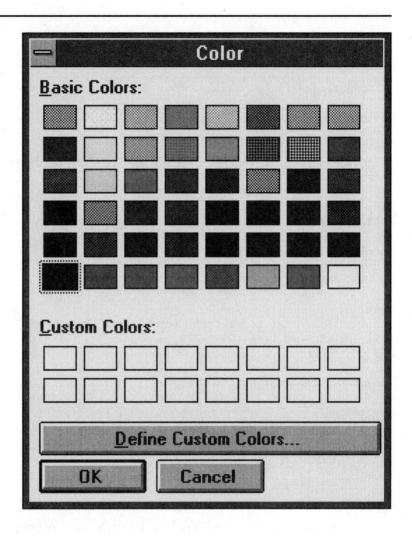

```
    CLine () {}
    virtual void Serialize (CArchive& ar);
    DECLARE_SERIAL (CLine)

public:
    CLine (int X1, int Y1, int X2, int Y2, COLORREF Color, int Thickness);
    virtual void Draw (CDC *PDC);
};
```

```
class CRectangle : public CFigure
{
protected:
    int mThickness;

    CRectangle () {}
    virtual void Serialize (CArchive& ar);
    DECLARE_SERIAL (CRectangle)

public:
    CRectangle (int X1, int Y1, int X2, int Y2, COLORREF Color, int Thickness);
    virtual void Draw (CDC *PDC);
};

class CRectFill : public CFigure
{
protected:
    CRectFill () {}
    DECLARE_SERIAL (CRectFill)

public:
    CRectFill (int X1, int Y1, int X2, int Y2, COLORREF Color);
    virtual void Draw (CDC *PDC);
};

class CRectRound : public CFigure
{
protected:
    int mThickness;

    CRectRound () {}
    virtual void Serialize (CArchive& ar);
    DECLARE_SERIAL (CRectRound)

public:
    CRectRound (int X1, int Y1, int X2, int Y2, COLORREF Color, int Thickness);
    virtual void Draw (CDC *PDC);
};

class CRectRoundFill : public CFigure
{
protected:
    CRectRoundFill () {}
    DECLARE_SERIAL (CRectRoundFill)
```

```
public:
    CRectRoundFill (int X1, int Y1, int X2, int Y2, COLORREF Color);
    virtual void Draw (CDC *PDC);
};

class CCircle : public CFigure
{
protected:
    int mThickness;

    CCircle () {}
    virtual void Serialize (CArchive& ar);
    DECLARE_SERIAL (CCircle)

public:
    CCircle (int X1, int Y1, int X2, int Y2, COLORREF Color, int Thickness);
    virtual void Draw (CDC *PDC);
};

class CCircleFill : public CFigure
{
protected:
    CCircleFill () {}
    DECLARE_SERIAL (CCircleFill)

public:
    CCircleFill (int X1, int Y1, int X2, int Y2, COLORREF Color);
    virtual void Draw (CDC *PDC);
};
```

Notice that in the hierarchy of classes you just defined, there is a single base class, CFigure (derived from CObject), plus a class derived from CFigure for each type of figure that the program can draw. This hierarchy is shown in Figure 16.15. In general, CFigure provides data members and member functions that are used for *all* types of figures, and the derived class for each figure provides members used specifically for that type of figure.

Specifically, CFigure contains the data member for storing the figure color (mColor) because all types of figures have a color. Likewise, CFigure contains four data members for storing coordinates (mX1, mY1, mX2, mY2) because the position and size of all types of figures are specified using four coordinates. In contrast, only lines

FIGURE 16.15:

The hierarchy of classes for drawing
and storing figures

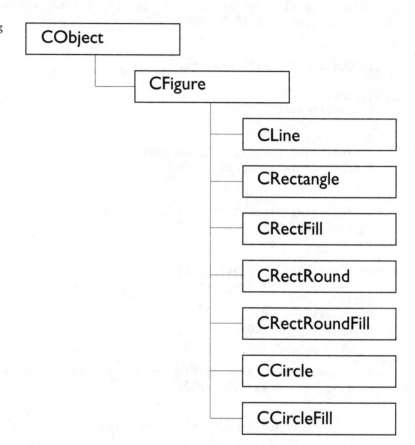

and open figures have a line thickness (solid figures do not); therefore, a data member for storing the thickness (mThickness) is provided only within the classes for open figures and lines. Each derived class provides its own constructor for initializing the data members.

CFigure also provides a member function that calculates the dimensions of the rectangle that bounds the figure (GetDimRect), because a single routine works for any type of figure. Additionally, CFigure provides a Serialize member function for reading and writing the CFigure data members from and to the disk. The classes that do not have an mThicnkess member can simply rely on the CFigure::Serialize function. However, each of the classes that has an mThickness data member must provide its own Serialize function to read and write the value of mThickness. (As you will see, each of these Serialize functions also explicitly calls the CFigure::Serialize function to read or write the data members defined in CFigure.)

Finally, CFigure provides a virtual member function, Draw, which does nothing itself:

```
virtual void Draw (CDC *PDC) {}
```

Defining this function, however, allows the program to use a single CFigure pointer to call the Draw function for each type of figure. The class for each type of figure provides an overriding version of the Draw function that performs the actual drawing, using a routine that is appropriate for the specific type of figure. As you will see, this use of polymorphism greatly simplifies the code in the view class that manages the drawing of the figures. For an explanation of class derivation, inheritance, virtual functions, and polymorphism, see Chapter 5.

Also in the CMinidrawDoc class definition, change the name of the GetNumLines member function to GetNumFigs, because this function now reports the total number of figures of all types.

Next, open the MINIDOC.CPP file and, at the end of this file, add the following code for implementing the member functions of the figure classes (this code should *replace* the existing code for the CLine class):

```
// implementation of figure classes:

IMPLEMENT_SERIAL (CFigure, CObject, 2)

CRect CFigure::GetDimRect ()
    {
    return CRect
      (min (mX1, mX2),
       min (mY1, mY2),
       max (mX1, mX2) + 1,
       max (mY1, mY2) + 1);
    }

void CFigure::Serialize (CArchive& ar)
    {
    if (ar.IsStoring ())
      ar << (WORD)mX1 << (WORD)mY1 << (WORD)mX2 << (WORD)mY2 << mColor;
```

```
   else
      ar >> (WORD &)mX1 >> (WORD &)mY1 >> (WORD &)mX2 >> (WORD &)mY2 >> mColor;
   }

IMPLEMENT_SERIAL (CLine, CFigure, 2)

CLine::CLine (int X1, int Y1, int X2, int Y2, COLORREF Color, int Thickness)
   {
   mX1 = X1;
   mY1 = Y1;
   mX2 = X2;
   mY2 = Y2;
   mColor = Color;
   mThickness = Thickness;
   }

void CLine::Serialize (CArchive& ar)
   {
   CFigure::Serialize (ar);
   if (ar.IsStoring ())
      ar << (WORD)mThickness;
   else
      ar >> (WORD &)mThickness;
   }

void CLine::Draw (CDC *PDC)
   {
   CPen Pen, *POldPen;

   // select pen/brush:
   Pen.CreatePen (PS_SOLID, mThickness, mColor);
   POldPen = PDC->SelectObject (&Pen);

   // draw figure:
   PDC->MoveTo (mX1, mY1);
   PDC->LineTo (mX2, mY2);

   // remove pen/brush:
   PDC->SelectObject (POldPen);
   }

IMPLEMENT_SERIAL (CRectangle, CFigure, 2)
```

```
CRectangle::CRectangle (int X1, int Y1, int X2, int Y2,
                        COLORREF Color, int Thickness)
    {
    mX1 = X1;
    mY1 = Y1;
    mX2 = X2;
    mY2 = Y2;
    mColor = Color;
    mThickness = Thickness;
    }

void CRectangle::Serialize (CArchive& ar)
    {
    CFigure::Serialize (ar);
    if (ar.IsStoring ())
        ar << (WORD)mThickness;
    else
        ar >> (WORD &)mThickness;
    }

void CRectangle::Draw (CDC *PDC)
    {
    CPen Pen, *POldPen;

    // select pen/brush:
    Pen.CreatePen (PS_INSIDEFRAME, mThickness, mColor);
    POldPen = PDC->SelectObject (&Pen);
    PDC->SelectStockObject (NULL_BRUSH);

    // draw figure:
    PDC->Rectangle (mX1, mY1, mX2, mY2);

    // remove pen/brush:
    PDC->SelectObject (POldPen);
    }

IMPLEMENT_SERIAL (CRectFill, CFigure, 2)

CRectFill::CRectFill (int X1, int Y1, int X2, int Y2, COLORREF Color)
    {
    mX1 = min (X1, X2);
    mY1 = min (Y1, Y2);
    mX2 = max (X1, X2);
    mY2 = max (Y1, Y2);
```

```
   mColor = Color;
   }

void CRectFill::Draw (CDC *PDC)
   {
   CBrush Brush, *POldBrush;
   CPen Pen, *POldPen;

   // select pen/brush:
   Pen.CreatePen (PS_INSIDEFRAME, 1, mColor);
   POldPen = PDC->SelectObject (&Pen);
   Brush.CreateSolidBrush (mColor);
   POldBrush = PDC->SelectObject (&Brush);

   // draw figure:
   PDC->Rectangle (mX1, mY1, mX2, mY2);

   // remove pen/brush:
   PDC->SelectObject (POldPen);
   PDC->SelectObject (POldBrush);
   }

IMPLEMENT_SERIAL (CRectRound, CFigure, 2)

CRectRound::CRectRound (int X1, int Y1, int X2, int Y2,
                        COLORREF Color, int Thickness)
   {
   mX1 = min (X1, X2);
   mY1 = min (Y1, Y2);
   mX2 = max (X1, X2);
   mY2 = max (Y1, Y2);
   mColor = Color;
   mThickness = Thickness;
   }

void CRectRound::Serialize (CArchive& ar)
   {
   CFigure::Serialize (ar);
   if (ar.IsStoring ())
      ar << (WORD)mThickness;
   else
      ar >> (WORD &)mThickness;
   }
```

```
void CRectRound::Draw (CDC *PDC)
   {
   CPen Pen, *POldPen;

   // select pen/brush:
   Pen.CreatePen (PS_INSIDEFRAME, mThickness, mColor);
   POldPen = PDC->SelectObject (&Pen);
   PDC->SelectStockObject (NULL_BRUSH);

   // draw figure:
   int SizeRound = (mX2 - mX1 + mY2 - mY1) / 6;
   PDC->RoundRect (mX1, mY1, mX2, mY2, SizeRound, SizeRound);

   // remove pen/brush:
   PDC->SelectObject (POldPen);
   }

IMPLEMENT_SERIAL (CRectRoundFill, CFigure, 2)

CRectRoundFill::CRectRoundFill (int X1, int Y1, int X2, int Y2, COLORREF Color)
   {
   mX1 = min (X1, X2);
   mY1 = min (Y1, Y2);
   mX2 = max (X1, X2);
   mY2 = max (Y1, Y2);
   mColor = Color;
   }

void CRectRoundFill::Draw (CDC *PDC)
   {
   CBrush Brush, *POldBrush;
   CPen Pen, *POldPen;

   // select pen/brush:
   Pen.CreatePen (PS_INSIDEFRAME, 1, mColor);
   POldPen = PDC->SelectObject (&Pen);
   Brush.CreateSolidBrush (mColor);
   POldBrush = PDC->SelectObject (&Brush);

   // draw figure:
   int SizeRound = (mX2 - mX1 + mY2 - mY1) / 6;
   PDC->RoundRect (mX1, mY1, mX2, mY2, SizeRound, SizeRound);
```

```
// remove pen/brush:
PDC->SelectObject (POldPen);
PDC->SelectObject (POldBrush);
}

IMPLEMENT_SERIAL (CCircle, CFigure, 2)

CCircle::CCircle (int X1, int Y1, int X2, int Y2,
                 COLORREF Color, int Thickness)
   {
   mX1 = min (X1, X2);
   mY1 = min (Y1, Y2);
   mX2 = max (X1, X2);
   mY2 = max (Y1, Y2);
   mColor = Color;
   mThickness = Thickness;
   }

void CCircle::Serialize (CArchive& ar)
   {
   CFigure::Serialize (ar);
   if (ar.IsStoring ())
      ar << (WORD)mThickness;
   else
      ar >> (WORD &)mThickness;
   }

void CCircle::Draw (CDC *PDC)
   {
   CPen Pen, *POldPen;

   // select pen/brush:
   Pen.CreatePen (PS_INSIDEFRAME, mThickness, mColor);
   POldPen = PDC->SelectObject (&Pen);
   PDC->SelectStockObject (NULL_BRUSH);

   // draw figure:
   PDC->Ellipse (mX1, mY1, mX2, mY2);

   // remove pen/brush:
   PDC->SelectObject (POldPen);
   }

IMPLEMENT_SERIAL (CCircleFill, CFigure, 2)
```

```
CCircleFill::CCircleFill (int X1, int Y1, int X2, int Y2, COLORREF Color)
   {
   mX1 = min (X1, X2);
   mY1 = min (Y1, Y2);
   mX2 = max (X1, X2);
   mY2 = max (Y1, Y2);
   mColor = Color;
   }

void CCircleFill::Draw (CDC *PDC)
   {
   CBrush Brush, *POldBrush;
   CPen Pen, *POldPen;

   // select pen/brush:
   Pen.CreatePen (PS_INSIDEFRAME, 1, mColor);
   POldPen = PDC->SelectObject (&Pen);
   Brush.CreateSolidBrush (mColor);
   POldBrush = PDC->SelectObject (&Brush);

   // draw figure:
   PDC->Ellipse (mX1, mY1, mX2, mY2);

   // remove pen/brush:
   PDC->SelectObject (POldPen);
   PDC->SelectObject (POldBrush);
   }
```

Each of the Draw functions uses the techniques that were described in this chapter to draw the appropriate figure. Notice that the Draw function for each class that draws an open figure selects the NULL_BRUSH stock object so that the interior of the figure is not painted. Notice, also, that the Draw functions for closed figures initialize the pen using the PS_INSIDEFRAME style so that the figure will lie completely within the bounding rectangle that the user drags within the view window. Notice, finally, that the two classes that draw rounded rectangles (CRectRound and CRectRoundFill) calculate the size of the ellipse for drawing the rounded corners as follows:

```
int SizeRound = (mX2 - mX1 + mY2 - mY1) / 6;
PDC->RoundRect (mX1, mY1, mX2, mY2, SizeRound, SizeRound);
```

This calculation makes the rounded corners circular, and makes the width of the circle used for the corners equal to one-third of the average length of the sides of the rectangle.

Other Code Modifications

In this section you will make a variety of changes to the code to support the draw-ing of different types of figures. First, in MINIDDOC.H, erase the declarations for the AddLine and GetLine member functions from the CMinidrawDoc class, add the following declarations for the AddFigure and GetFigure member functions, and change the name of the CMinidrawDoc::GetNumLines function to CMinidraw-Doc::GetNumFigs:

```
class CMinidrawDoc : public CDocument
{
protected: // create from serialization only
    CMinidrawDoc();
    DECLARE_DYNCREATE(CMinidrawDoc)

protected:
    CObArray mObArray;

public:
    void AddFigure (CFigure *PFigure);
    virtual void DeleteContents ();
    CFigure *GetFigure (int Index);
    int GetNumFigs ();
```

Likewise, in the MINIDDOC.CPP file, erase the implementations for AddLine and GetLine, and add the following implementations for the new AddFigure and Get-Figure member functions:

```
void CMinidrawDoc::AddFigure (CFigure *PFigure)
    {
    mObArray.Add (PFigure);
    SetModifiedFlag ();
    }

CFigure *CMinidrawDoc::GetFigure (int Index)
    {
    if (Index < 0 || Index > mObArray.GetUpperBound ())
        return 0;
    return (CFigure *)mObArray.GetAt (Index);
    }
```

The new functions work with any type of figure; they add or obtain CFigure object pointers rather than CLine pointers. Also, unlike the former AddLine function,

AddFigure does not invoke new to create the object; this task is now performed by the view class.

Next, in the MINIDVW.H file, define mPenDotted within the CMinidrawView class definition, as follows:

```
protected:
    CString mClassName;
    int mDragging;
    HCURSOR mHArrow;
    HCURSOR mHCross;
    CPen mPenDotted;
    CPoint mPointOld;
    CPoint mPointOrigin;
```

Then, in the MINIDVW.CPP file, add the following mPenDotted initialization to the CMinidrawView constructor:

```
CMinidrawView::CMinidrawView()
{
    // TODO: add construction code here

    mDragging = 0;
    mHArrow = AfxGetApp ()->LoadStandardCursor (IDC_ARROW);
    mHCross = AfxGetApp ()->LoadStandardCursor (IDC_CROSS);
    mPenDotted.CreatePen (PS_DOT, 1, RGB (0,0,0));
}
```

The mPenDotted data member will be used to draw dotted temporary lines (rather than solid lines) when the user drags the mouse pointer to draw a figure. All of the remaining changes are also made within the MINIDVW.CPP file.

Modify the OnMouseMove function as follows:

```
void CMinidrawView::OnMouseMove(UINT nFlags, CPoint point)
{
    // TODO: Add your message handler code here and/or call default

    CClientDC ClientDC (this);
    OnPrepareDC (&ClientDC);
    ClientDC.DPtoLP (&point);

    if (!mDragging)
        {
        CSize ScrollSize = GetTotalSize ();
        CRect ScrollRect (0, 0, ScrollSize.cx, ScrollSize.cy);
```

```
    if (ScrollRect.PtInRect (point))
        ::SetCursor (mHCross);
    else
        ::SetCursor (mHArrow);
    return;
    }

ClientDC.SetROP2 (R2_NOT);
ClientDC.SelectObject (&mPenDotted);
ClientDC.SetBkMode (TRANSPARENT);
ClientDC.SelectStockObject (NULL_BRUSH);

switch (((CMinidrawApp *)AfxGetApp ())->mCurrentTool)
    {
    case ID_TOOLS_LINE:
        ClientDC.MoveTo (mPointOrigin);
        ClientDC.LineTo (mPointOld);
        ClientDC.MoveTo (mPointOrigin);
        ClientDC.LineTo (point);
        break;

    case ID_TOOLS_RECTANGLE:
    case ID_TOOLS_RECTFILL:
        ClientDC.Rectangle (mPointOrigin.x, mPointOrigin.y,
                            mPointOld.x, mPointOld.y);
        ClientDC.Rectangle (mPointOrigin.x, mPointOrigin.y,
                            point.x, point.y);
        break;

    case ID_TOOLS_RECTROUND:
    case ID_TOOLS_RECTROUNDFILL:
        {
        int SizeRound = (abs (mPointOld.x - mPointOrigin.x) +
                         abs (mPointOld.y - mPointOrigin.y)) / 6;
        ClientDC.RoundRect (mPointOrigin.x, mPointOrigin.y,
                            mPointOld.x, mPointOld.y,
                            SizeRound, SizeRound);
        SizeRound = (abs (point.x - mPointOrigin.x) +
                     abs (point.y - mPointOrigin.y)) / 6;
        ClientDC.RoundRect (mPointOrigin.x, mPointOrigin.y,
                            point.x, point.y,
                            SizeRound, SizeRound);
        break;
        }
```

```
        case ID_TOOLS_CIRCLE:
        case ID_TOOLS_CIRCLEFILL:
            ClientDC.Ellipse (mPointOrigin.x, mPointOrigin.y,
                              mPointOld.x, mPointOld.y);
            ClientDC.Ellipse (mPointOrigin.x, mPointOrigin.y,
                              point.x, point.y);
            break;
        }

    mPointOld = point;

    CScrollView::OnMouseMove(nFlags, point);
}
```

The new code selects the drawing tools and sets the drawing attributes that are required to erase and draw the temporary figure in the view window (which marks the position where the figure would be drawn if the user released the mouse button). It then branches to an appropriate routine for erasing the previous temporary figure and drawing the new temporary figure, based upon the currently selected drawing tool.

You now need to modify the OnLButtonUp function, as follows:

```
void CMinidrawView::OnLButtonUp(UINT nFlags, CPoint point)
{
    // TODO: Add your message handler code here and/or call default
    if (!mDragging)
        return;

    mDragging = 0;
    ::ReleaseCapture ();
    ::ClipCursor (NULL);

    CClientDC ClientDC (this);
    OnPrepareDC (&ClientDC);
    ClientDC.DPtoLP (&point);
    ClientDC.SetROP2 (R2_NOT);
    ClientDC.SelectObject (&mPenDotted);
    ClientDC.SetBkMode (TRANSPARENT);
    ClientDC.SelectStockObject (NULL_BRUSH);

    CMinidrawApp *PApp = (CMinidrawApp *)AfxGetApp ();
    CFigure *PFigure;
```

```
switch (PApp->mCurrentTool)
   {
   case ID_TOOLS_LINE:
      ClientDC.MoveTo (mPointOrigin);
      ClientDC.LineTo (mPointOld);
      PFigure = new CLine
         (mPointOrigin.x, mPointOrigin.y,
         point.x, point.y,
         PApp->mCurrentColor,
         PApp->mCurrentThickness);
      break;

   case ID_TOOLS_RECTANGLE:
      ClientDC.Rectangle (mPointOrigin.x, mPointOrigin.y,
                          mPointOld.x, mPointOld.y);
      PFigure = new CRectangle
         (mPointOrigin.x, mPointOrigin.y,
         point.x, point.y,
         PApp->mCurrentColor,
         PApp->mCurrentThickness);
      break;

   case ID_TOOLS_RECTFILL:
      ClientDC.Rectangle (mPointOrigin.x, mPointOrigin.y,
                          mPointOld.x, mPointOld.y);
      PFigure = new CRectFill
         (mPointOrigin.x, mPointOrigin.y,
         point.x, point.y,
         PApp->mCurrentColor);
      break;

   case ID_TOOLS_RECTROUND:
      {
      int SizeRound = (abs (mPointOld.x - mPointOrigin.x) +
                       abs (mPointOld.y - mPointOrigin.y)) / 6;
      ClientDC.RoundRect (mPointOrigin.x, mPointOrigin.y,
                          mPointOld.x, mPointOld.y,
                          SizeRound, SizeRound);
      PFigure = new CRectRound
         (mPointOrigin.x, mPointOrigin.y,
         point.x, point.y,
         PApp->mCurrentColor,
```

```
            PApp->mCurrentThickness);
        break;
        }

    case ID_TOOLS_RECTROUNDFILL:
        {
        int SizeRound = (abs (mPointOld.x - mPointOrigin.x) +
                         abs (mPointOld.y - mPointOrigin.y)) / 6;
        ClientDC.RoundRect (mPointOrigin.x, mPointOrigin.y,
                            mPointOld.x, mPointOld.y,
                            SizeRound, SizeRound);
        PFigure = new CRectRoundFill
            (mPointOrigin.x, mPointOrigin.y,
            point.x, point.y,
            PApp->mCurrentColor);
        break;
        }

    case ID_TOOLS_CIRCLE:
        ClientDC.Ellipse (mPointOrigin.x, mPointOrigin.y,
                          mPointOld.x, mPointOld.y);
        PFigure = new CCircle
            (mPointOrigin.x, mPointOrigin.y,
            point.x, point.y,
            PApp->mCurrentColor,
            PApp->mCurrentThickness);
        break;

    case ID_TOOLS_CIRCLEFILL:
        ClientDC.Ellipse (mPointOrigin.x, mPointOrigin.y,
                          mPointOld.x, mPointOld.y);
        PFigure = new CCircleFill
            (mPointOrigin.x, mPointOrigin.y,
            point.x, point.y,
            PApp->mCurrentColor);
        break;
    }

ClientDC.SetROP2 (R2_COPYPEN);
PFigure->Draw (&ClientDC);
```

```
CMinidrawDoc* PDoc = GetDocument ();
PDoc->AddFigure (PFigure);

PDoc->UpdateAllViews (this, 0, PFigure);

CScrollView::OnLButtonUp(nFlags, point);
}
```

The new code selects the drawing tools and sets the drawing attributes for erasing the previously drawn temporary figure. It then branches to a routine for the current drawing tool. Each routine erases the temporary figure and then creates an object of the appropriate class to store and draw the new permanent figure, assigning the object's address to PFigure. After the switch statement, OnLButtonUp then calls SetROP2 to restore the default drawing mode and uses the PFigure pointer to call the Draw function; because Draw is a virtual function, this call automatically invokes the appropriate version of the Draw function for the current type of figure. Finally, the new code calls CMinidrawDoc::AddFigure to store the figure within the document class, and it calls UpdateAllViews to force redrawing of the other view window (in case two views are open).

Finally, you need to change several lines within the OnDraw function:

```
void CMinidrawView::OnDraw(CDC* pDC)
{
    CMinidrawDoc* pDoc = GetDocument ();

    // TODO: add draw code here

    CSize ScrollSize = GetTotalSize ();
    pDC->MoveTo (ScrollSize.cx, 0);
    pDC->LineTo (ScrollSize.cx, ScrollSize.cy);
    pDC->LineTo (0, ScrollSize.cy);

    CRect ClipRect;
    CRect DimRect;
    CRect IntRect;
    CFigure *PFigure;

    pDC->GetClipBox (&ClipRect);

    int NumFigs = pDoc->GetNumFigs ();
    for (int Index = 0; Index < NumFigs; ++Index)
        {
        PFigure = pDoc->GetFigure (Index);
```

```
DimRect = PFigure->GetDimRect ();
if (IntRect.IntersectRect (DimRect, ClipRect))
   PFigure->Draw (pDC);
}
}
```

The modified code uses the new `CFigure` class rather than `CLine`. It also draws the figures in the same order in which they were added (the previous version drew them in the opposite order), so that the figures will overlap in the order in which they were drawn.

The modifications to MINIDRAW are now complete, and you can build and run the program.

The MINIDRAW Source Code

Listings 16.9 through 16.16 contain the C++ source code for the version of the MINIDRAW program that you created in this chapter. A copy of these files can be obtained from the \MINIDRW6 companion disk subdirectory.

Listing 16.9

```
// minidraw.h : main header file for the MINIDRAW application
//

#ifndef __AFXWIN_H__
    #error include 'stdafx.h' before including this file for PCH
#endif

#include "resource.h"        // main symbols

/////////////////////////////////////////////////////////////////////////////
// CMinidrawApp:
// See minidraw.cpp for the implementation of this class
//

class CMinidrawApp : public CWinApp
{
public:
    CMinidrawApp();
```

```
// Overrides
    virtual BOOL InitInstance();

// Implementation

    //{{AFX_MSG(CMinidrawApp)
    afx_msg void OnAppAbout();
    afx_msg void OnLineDouble();
    afx_msg void OnUpdateLineDouble(CCmdUI* pCmdUI);
    afx_msg void OnLineSingle();
    afx_msg void OnUpdateLineSingle(CCmdUI* pCmdUI);
    afx_msg void OnLineTriple();
    afx_msg void OnUpdateLineTriple(CCmdUI* pCmdUI);
    afx_msg void OnUpdateToolsCircle(CCmdUI* pCmdUI);
    afx_msg void OnToolsCircle();
    afx_msg void OnToolsCirclefill();
    afx_msg void OnUpdateToolsCirclefill(CCmdUI* pCmdUI);
    afx_msg void OnUpdateToolsLine(CCmdUI* pCmdUI);
    afx_msg void OnToolsLine();
    afx_msg void OnToolsRectangle();
    afx_msg void OnUpdateToolsRectangle(CCmdUI* pCmdUI);
    afx_msg void OnUpdateToolsRectfill(CCmdUI* pCmdUI);
    afx_msg void OnToolsRectfill();
    afx_msg void OnToolsRectround();
    afx_msg void OnUpdateToolsRectround(CCmdUI* pCmdUI);
    afx_msg void OnUpdateToolsRectroundfill(CCmdUI* pCmdUI);
    afx_msg void OnToolsRectroundfill();
    afx_msg void OnColorBlack();
    afx_msg void OnUpdateColorBlack(CCmdUI* pCmdUI);
    afx_msg void OnColorBlue();
    afx_msg void OnUpdateColorBlue(CCmdUI* pCmdUI);
    afx_msg void OnColorCustom();
    afx_msg void OnUpdateColorCustom(CCmdUI* pCmdUI);
    afx_msg void OnColorCyan();
    afx_msg void OnUpdateColorCyan(CCmdUI* pCmdUI);
    afx_msg void OnColorGreen();
    afx_msg void OnUpdateColorGreen(CCmdUI* pCmdUI);
    afx_msg void OnColorMagenta();
    afx_msg void OnUpdateColorMagenta(CCmdUI* pCmdUI);
    afx_msg void OnColorRed();
    afx_msg void OnUpdateColorRed(CCmdUI* pCmdUI);
    afx_msg void OnColorWhite();
    afx_msg void OnUpdateColorWhite(CCmdUI* pCmdUI);
    afx_msg void OnColorYellow();
    afx_msg void OnUpdateColorYellow(CCmdUI* pCmdUI);
```

```
   //}}AFX_MSG
   DECLARE_MESSAGE_MAP()

// added data members:
public:
   COLORREF mCurrentColor;
   int mCurrentThickness;
   UINT mCurrentTool;
   UINT mIdxColorCmd;
};
```

//

Listing 16.10

```
// minidraw.cpp : Defines the class behaviors for the application.
//

#include "stdafx.h"
#include "minidraw.h"

#include "mainfrm.h"
#include "miniddoc.h"
#include "minidvw.h"

#ifdef _DEBUG
#undef THIS_FILE
static char BASED_CODE THIS_FILE[] = __FILE__;
#endif

////////////////////////////////////////////////////////////////////////////
// CMinidrawApp

BEGIN_MESSAGE_MAP(CMinidrawApp, CWinApp)
   //{{AFX_MSG_MAP(CMinidrawApp)
   ON_COMMAND(ID_APP_ABOUT, OnAppAbout)
   ON_COMMAND(ID_LINE_DOUBLE, OnLineDouble)
   ON_UPDATE_COMMAND_UI(ID_LINE_DOUBLE, OnUpdateLineDouble)
   ON_COMMAND(ID_LINE_SINGLE, OnLineSingle)
   ON_UPDATE_COMMAND_UI(ID_LINE_SINGLE, OnUpdateLineSingle)
   ON_COMMAND(ID_LINE_TRIPLE, OnLineTriple)
   ON_UPDATE_COMMAND_UI(ID_LINE_TRIPLE, OnUpdateLineTriple)
   ON_UPDATE_COMMAND_UI(ID_TOOLS_CIRCLE, OnUpdateToolsCircle)
   ON_COMMAND(ID_TOOLS_CIRCLE, OnToolsCircle)
   ON_COMMAND(ID_TOOLS_CIRCLEFILL, OnToolsCirclefill)
```

```
    ON_UPDATE_COMMAND_UI(ID_TOOLS_CIRCLEFILL, OnUpdateToolsCirclefill)
    ON_UPDATE_COMMAND_UI(ID_TOOLS_LINE, OnUpdateToolsLine)
    ON_COMMAND(ID_TOOLS_LINE, OnToolsLine)
    ON_COMMAND(ID_TOOLS_RECTANGLE, OnToolsRectangle)
    ON_UPDATE_COMMAND_UI(ID_TOOLS_RECTANGLE, OnUpdateToolsRectangle)
    ON_UPDATE_COMMAND_UI(ID_TOOLS_RECTFILL, OnUpdateToolsRectfill)
    ON_COMMAND(ID_TOOLS_RECTFILL, OnToolsRectfill)
    ON_COMMAND(ID_TOOLS_RECTROUND, OnToolsRectround)
    ON_UPDATE_COMMAND_UI(ID_TOOLS_RECTROUND, OnUpdateToolsRectround)
    ON_UPDATE_COMMAND_UI(ID_TOOLS_RECTROUNDFILL, OnUpdateToolsRectroundfill)
    ON_COMMAND(ID_TOOLS_RECTROUNDFILL, OnToolsRectroundfill)
    ON_COMMAND(ID_COLOR_BLACK, OnColorBlack)
    ON_UPDATE_COMMAND_UI(ID_COLOR_BLACK, OnUpdateColorBlack)
    ON_COMMAND(ID_COLOR_BLUE, OnColorBlue)
    ON_UPDATE_COMMAND_UI(ID_COLOR_BLUE, OnUpdateColorBlue)
    ON_COMMAND(ID_COLOR_CUSTOM, OnColorCustom)
    ON_UPDATE_COMMAND_UI(ID_COLOR_CUSTOM, OnUpdateColorCustom)
    ON_COMMAND(ID_COLOR_CYAN, OnColorCyan)
    ON_UPDATE_COMMAND_UI(ID_COLOR_CYAN, OnUpdateColorCyan)
    ON_COMMAND(ID_COLOR_GREEN, OnColorGreen)
    ON_UPDATE_COMMAND_UI(ID_COLOR_GREEN, OnUpdateColorGreen)
    ON_COMMAND(ID_COLOR_MAGENTA, OnColorMagenta)
    ON_UPDATE_COMMAND_UI(ID_COLOR_MAGENTA, OnUpdateColorMagenta)
    ON_COMMAND(ID_COLOR_RED, OnColorRed)
    ON_UPDATE_COMMAND_UI(ID_COLOR_RED, OnUpdateColorRed)
    ON_COMMAND(ID_COLOR_WHITE, OnColorWhite)
    ON_UPDATE_COMMAND_UI(ID_COLOR_WHITE, OnUpdateColorWhite)
    ON_COMMAND(ID_COLOR_YELLOW, OnColorYellow)
    ON_UPDATE_COMMAND_UI(ID_COLOR_YELLOW, OnUpdateColorYellow)
    //}}AFX_MSG_MAP
    // Standard file based document commands
    ON_COMMAND(ID_FILE_NEW, CWinApp::OnFileNew)
    ON_COMMAND(ID_FILE_OPEN, CWinApp::OnFileOpen)
END_MESSAGE_MAP()

/////////////////////////////////////////////////////////////////////////
// CMinidrawApp construction

CMinidrawApp::CMinidrawApp()
{
    // TODO: add construction code here,
    // Place all significant initialization in InitInstance

    mCurrentColor = RGB (0,0,0);
    mCurrentThickness = 1;
```

```
    mCurrentTool = ID_TOOLS_LINE;
    mIdxColorCmd = ID_COLOR_BLACK;
}


/////////////////////////////////////////////////////////////////////////
// The one and only CMinidrawApp object

CMinidrawApp NEAR theApp;

/////////////////////////////////////////////////////////////////////////
// CMinidrawApp initialization

BOOL CMinidrawApp::InitInstance()
{
    // Standard initialization
    // If you are not using these features and wish to reduce the size
    //  of your final executable, you should remove from the following
    //  the specific initialization routines you do not need.

    SetDialogBkColor();         // set dialog background color to gray
    LoadStdProfileSettings();   // Load standard INI file options (including MRU)

    // Register the application's document templates.  Document templates
    //  serve as the connection between documents, frame windows and views.

    AddDocTemplate(new CSingleDocTemplate(IDR_MAINFRAME,
            RUNTIME_CLASS(CMinidrawDoc),
            RUNTIME_CLASS(CMainFrame),      // main SDI frame window
            RUNTIME_CLASS(CMinidrawView)));

    // create a new (empty) document
    OnFileNew();

    m_pMainWnd->DragAcceptFiles ();

    if (m_lpCmdLine[0] != '\0')
    {
        // TODO: add command line processing here
    }

    return TRUE;
}


/////////////////////////////////////////////////////////////////////////
// CAboutDlg dialog used for App About
```

```
class CAboutDlg : public CDialog
{
public:
    CAboutDlg();

// Dialog Data
    //{{AFX_DATA(CAboutDlg)
    enum { IDD = IDD_ABOUTBOX };
    //}}AFX_DATA

// Implementation
protected:
    virtual void DoDataExchange(CDataExchange* pDX);    // DDX/DDV support
    //{{AFX_MSG(CAboutDlg)
        // No message handlers
    //}}AFX_MSG
    DECLARE_MESSAGE_MAP()
};

CAboutDlg::CAboutDlg() : CDialog(CAboutDlg::IDD)
{
    //{{AFX_DATA_INIT(CAboutDlg)
    //}}AFX_DATA_INIT
}

void CAboutDlg::DoDataExchange(CDataExchange* pDX)
{
    CDialog::DoDataExchange(pDX);
    //{{AFX_DATA_MAP(CAboutDlg)
    //}}AFX_DATA_MAP
}

BEGIN_MESSAGE_MAP(CAboutDlg, CDialog)
    //{{AFX_MSG_MAP(CAboutDlg)
        // No message handlers
    //}}AFX_MSG_MAP
END_MESSAGE_MAP()

// App command to run the dialog
void CMinidrawApp::OnAppAbout()
{
    CAboutDlg aboutDlg;
    aboutDlg.DoModal();
}
```

```
//////////////////////////////////////////////////////////////////////
// CMinidrawApp commands

void CMinidrawApp::OnLineDouble()
{
    // TODO: Add your command handler code here
    mCurrentThickness = 2;
}

void CMinidrawApp::OnUpdateLineDouble(CCmdUI* pCmdUI)
{
    // TODO: Add your command update UI handler code here
    pCmdUI->SetCheck (mCurrentThickness == 2 ? 1 : 0);
}

void CMinidrawApp::OnLineSingle()
{
    // TODO: Add your command handler code here
    mCurrentThickness = 1;
}

void CMinidrawApp::OnUpdateLineSingle(CCmdUI* pCmdUI)
{
    // TODO: Add your command update UI handler code here
    pCmdUI->SetCheck (mCurrentThickness == 1 ? 1 : 0);
}

void CMinidrawApp::OnLineTriple()
{
    // TODO: Add your command handler code here
    mCurrentThickness = 3;
}

void CMinidrawApp::OnUpdateLineTriple(CCmdUI* pCmdUI)
{
    // TODO: Add your command update UI handler code here
    pCmdUI->SetCheck (mCurrentThickness == 3 ? 1 : 0);
}

void CMinidrawApp::OnUpdateToolsCircle(CCmdUI* pCmdUI)
{
    // TODO: Add your command update UI handler code here
    pCmdUI->SetCheck (mCurrentTool == ID_TOOLS_CIRCLE ? 1 : 0);
}
```

```
void CMinidrawApp::OnToolsCircle()
{
    // TODO: Add your command handler code here
    mCurrentTool = ID_TOOLS_CIRCLE;
}

void CMinidrawApp::OnToolsCirclefill()
{
    // TODO: Add your command handler code here
    mCurrentTool = ID_TOOLS_CIRCLEFILL;
}

void CMinidrawApp::OnUpdateToolsCirclefill(CCmdUI* pCmdUI)
{
    // TODO: Add your command update UI handler code here
    pCmdUI->SetCheck (mCurrentTool == ID_TOOLS_CIRCLEFILL ? 1 : 0);
}

void CMinidrawApp::OnUpdateToolsLine(CCmdUI* pCmdUI)
{
    // TODO: Add your command update UI handler code here
    pCmdUI->SetCheck (mCurrentTool == ID_TOOLS_LINE ? 1 : 0);
}

void CMinidrawApp::OnToolsLine()
{
    // TODO: Add your command handler code here
    mCurrentTool = ID_TOOLS_LINE;
}

void CMinidrawApp::OnToolsRectangle()
{
    // TODO: Add your command handler code here
    mCurrentTool = ID_TOOLS_RECTANGLE;
}

void CMinidrawApp::OnUpdateToolsRectangle(CCmdUI* pCmdUI)
{
    // TODO: Add your command update UI handler code here
    pCmdUI->SetCheck (mCurrentTool == ID_TOOLS_RECTANGLE ? 1 : 0);
}
```

```
void CMinidrawApp::OnUpdateToolsRectfill(CCmdUI* pCmdUI)
{
    // TODO: Add your command update UI handler code here
    pCmdUI->SetCheck (mCurrentTool == ID_TOOLS_RECTFILL ? 1 : 0);
}

void CMinidrawApp::OnToolsRectfill()
{
    // TODO: Add your command handler code here
    mCurrentTool = ID_TOOLS_RECTFILL;
}

void CMinidrawApp::OnToolsRectround()
{
    // TODO: Add your command handler code here
    mCurrentTool = ID_TOOLS_RECTROUND;
}

void CMinidrawApp::OnUpdateToolsRectround(CCmdUI* pCmdUI)
{
    // TODO: Add your command update UI handler code here
    pCmdUI->SetCheck (mCurrentTool == ID_TOOLS_RECTROUND ? 1 : 0);
}

void CMinidrawApp::OnUpdateToolsRectroundfill(CCmdUI* pCmdUI)
{
    // TODO: Add your command update UI handler code here
    pCmdUI->SetCheck (mCurrentTool == ID_TOOLS_RECTROUNDFILL ? 1 : 0);
}

void CMinidrawApp::OnToolsRectroundfill()
{
    // TODO: Add your command handler code here
    mCurrentTool = ID_TOOLS_RECTROUNDFILL;
}

void CMinidrawApp::OnColorBlack()
{
    // TODO: Add your command handler code here
    mCurrentColor = RGB (0,0,0);
    mIdxColorCmd = ID_COLOR_BLACK;
}
```

```
void CMinidrawApp::OnUpdateColorBlack(CCmdUI* pCmdUI)
{
    // TODO: Add your command update UI handler code here
    pCmdUI->SetCheck (mIdxColorCmd == ID_COLOR_BLACK ? 1 : 0);
}

void CMinidrawApp::OnColorBlue()
{
    // TODO: Add your command handler code here
    mCurrentColor = RGB (0,0,255);
    mIdxColorCmd = ID_COLOR_BLUE;
}

void CMinidrawApp::OnUpdateColorBlue(CCmdUI* pCmdUI)
{
    // TODO: Add your command update UI handler code here
    pCmdUI->SetCheck (mIdxColorCmd == ID_COLOR_BLUE ? 1 : 0);
}

void CMinidrawApp::OnColorCustom()
{
    // TODO: Add your command handler code here
    CColorDialog ColorDialog;

    if (ColorDialog.DoModal () == IDOK)
        {
        mCurrentColor = ColorDialog.GetColor ();
        mIdxColorCmd = ID_COLOR_CUSTOM;
        }
}

void CMinidrawApp::OnUpdateColorCustom(CCmdUI* pCmdUI)
{
    // TODO: Add your command update UI handler code here
    pCmdUI->SetCheck (mIdxColorCmd == ID_COLOR_CUSTOM ? 1 : 0);
}

void CMinidrawApp::OnColorCyan()
{
    // TODO: Add your command handler code here
    mCurrentColor = RGB (0,255,255);
    mIdxColorCmd = ID_COLOR_CYAN;
}
```

```
void CMinidrawApp::OnUpdateColorCyan(CCmdUI* pCmdUI)
{
    // TODO: Add your command update UI handler code here
    pCmdUI->SetCheck (mIdxColorCmd == ID_COLOR_CYAN ? 1 : 0);
}

void CMinidrawApp::OnColorGreen()
{
    // TODO: Add your command handler code here
    mCurrentColor = RGB (0,255,0);
    mIdxColorCmd = ID_COLOR_GREEN;
}

void CMinidrawApp::OnUpdateColorGreen(CCmdUI* pCmdUI)
{
    // TODO: Add your command update UI handler code here
    pCmdUI->SetCheck (mIdxColorCmd == ID_COLOR_GREEN ? 1 : 0);
}

void CMinidrawApp::OnColorMagenta()
{
    // TODO: Add your command handler code here
    mCurrentColor = RGB (255,0,255);
    mIdxColorCmd = ID_COLOR_MAGENTA;
}

void CMinidrawApp::OnUpdateColorMagenta(CCmdUI* pCmdUI)
{
    // TODO: Add your command update UI handler code here
    pCmdUI->SetCheck (mIdxColorCmd == ID_COLOR_MAGENTA ? 1 : 0);
}

void CMinidrawApp::OnColorRed()
{
    // TODO: Add your command handler code here
    mCurrentColor = RGB (255,0,0);
    mIdxColorCmd = ID_COLOR_RED;
}

void CMinidrawApp::OnUpdateColorRed(CCmdUI* pCmdUI)
{
    // TODO: Add your command update UI handler code here
    pCmdUI->SetCheck (mIdxColorCmd == ID_COLOR_RED ? 1 : 0);
}
```

```
void CMinidrawApp::OnColorWhite()
{
    // TODO: Add your command handler code here
    mCurrentColor = RGB (255,255,255);
    mIdxColorCmd = ID_COLOR_WHITE;
}

void CMinidrawApp::OnUpdateColorWhite(CCmdUI* pCmdUI)
{
    // TODO: Add your command update UI handler code here
    pCmdUI->SetCheck (mIdxColorCmd == ID_COLOR_WHITE ? 1 : 0);
}

void CMinidrawApp::OnColorYellow()
{
    // TODO: Add your command handler code here
    mCurrentColor = RGB (255,255,0);
    mIdxColorCmd = ID_COLOR_YELLOW;
}

void CMinidrawApp::OnUpdateColorYellow(CCmdUI* pCmdUI)
{
    // TODO: Add your command update UI handler code here
    pCmdUI->SetCheck (mIdxColorCmd == ID_COLOR_YELLOW ? 1 : 0);
}
```

Listing 16.11

```
// miniddoc.h : interface of the CMinidrawDoc class
//
//////////////////////////////////////////////////////////////////////////

// class hierarchy for figures:

class CFigure : public CObject
{
protected:
    COLORREF mColor;
    int mX1, mY1, mX2, mY2;

    virtual void Serialize (CArchive& ar);
    DECLARE_SERIAL (CFigure)
```

```
public:
   virtual void Draw (CDC *PDC) {}
   CRect GetDimRect ();
};

class CLine : public CFigure
{
protected:
   int mThickness;

   CLine () {}
   virtual void Serialize (CArchive& ar);
   DECLARE_SERIAL (CLine)

public:
   CLine (int X1, int Y1, int X2, int Y2, COLORREF Color, int Thickness);
   virtual void Draw (CDC *PDC);
};

class CRectangle : public CFigure
{
protected:
   int mThickness;

   CRectangle () {}
   virtual void Serialize (CArchive& ar);
   DECLARE_SERIAL (CRectangle)

public:
   CRectangle (int X1, int Y1, int X2, int Y2, COLORREF Color, int Thickness);
   virtual void Draw (CDC *PDC);
};

class CRectFill : public CFigure
{
protected:
   CRectFill () {}
   DECLARE_SERIAL (CRectFill)

public:
   CRectFill (int X1, int Y1, int X2, int Y2, COLORREF Color);
   virtual void Draw (CDC *PDC);
};
```

```
class CRectRound : public CFigure
{
protected:
    int mThickness;

    CRectRound () {}
    virtual void Serialize (CArchive& ar);
    DECLARE_SERIAL (CRectRound)

public:
    CRectRound (int X1, int Y1, int X2, int Y2, COLORREF Color, int Thickness);
    virtual void Draw (CDC *PDC);
};

class CRectRoundFill : public CFigure
{
protected:
    CRectRoundFill () {}
    DECLARE_SERIAL (CRectRoundFill)

public:
    CRectRoundFill (int X1, int Y1, int X2, int Y2, COLORREF Color);
    virtual void Draw (CDC *PDC);
};

class CCircle : public CFigure
{
protected:
    int mThickness;

    CCircle () {}
    virtual void Serialize (CArchive& ar);
    DECLARE_SERIAL (CCircle)

public:
    CCircle (int X1, int Y1, int X2, int Y2, COLORREF Color, int Thickness);
    virtual void Draw (CDC *PDC);
};

class CCircleFill : public CFigure
{
protected:
    CCircleFill () {}
    DECLARE_SERIAL (CCircleFill)
```

```
public:
   CCircleFill (int X1, int Y1, int X2, int Y2, COLORREF Color);
   virtual void Draw (CDC *PDC);
};

// document class:

class CMinidrawDoc : public CDocument
{
protected: // create from serialization only
   CMinidrawDoc();
   DECLARE_DYNCREATE(CMinidrawDoc)

protected:
   CObArray mObArray;

public:
   void AddFigure (CFigure *PFigure);
   virtual void DeleteContents ();
   CFigure *GetFigure (int Index);
   int GetNumFigs ();

// Attributes
public:

// Operations
public:

// Implementation
public:
   virtual ~CMinidrawDoc();
   virtual void Serialize(CArchive& ar);   // overridden for document i/o
#ifdef _DEBUG
   virtual  void AssertValid() const;
   virtual  void Dump(CDumpContext& dc) const;
#endif
protected:
   virtual  BOOL  OnNewDocument();

// Generated message map functions
protected:
   //{{AFX_MSG(CMinidrawDoc)
   afx_msg void OnEditClearAll();
   afx_msg void OnUpdateEditClearAll(CCmdUI* pCmdUI);
```

```
    afx_msg void OnEditUndo();
    afx_msg void OnUpdateEditUndo(CCmdUI* pCmdUI);
    //}}AFX_MSG
    DECLARE_MESSAGE_MAP()
};
```

///

Listing 16.12

```
// miniddoc.cpp : implementation of the CMinidrawDoc class
//

#include "stdafx.h"
#include "minidraw.h"

#include "miniddoc.h"

#ifdef _DEBUG
#undef THIS_FILE
static char BASED_CODE THIS_FILE[] = __FILE__;
#endif

/////////////////////////////////////////////////////////////////////////
// CMinidrawDoc

IMPLEMENT_DYNCREATE(CMinidrawDoc, CDocument)

BEGIN_MESSAGE_MAP(CMinidrawDoc, CDocument)
    //{{AFX_MSG_MAP(CMinidrawDoc)
    ON_COMMAND(ID_EDIT_CLEAR_ALL, OnEditClearAll)
    ON_UPDATE_COMMAND_UI(ID_EDIT_CLEAR_ALL, OnUpdateEditClearAll)
    ON_COMMAND(ID_EDIT_UNDO, OnEditUndo)
    ON_UPDATE_COMMAND_UI(ID_EDIT_UNDO, OnUpdateEditUndo)
    //}}AFX_MSG_MAP
END_MESSAGE_MAP()

/////////////////////////////////////////////////////////////////////////
// CMinidrawDoc construction/destruction

CMinidrawDoc::CMinidrawDoc()
{
    // TODO: add one-time construction code here
}
```

```
CMinidrawDoc::~CMinidrawDoc()
{
}

BOOL CMinidrawDoc::OnNewDocument()
{
    if (!CDocument::OnNewDocument())
        return FALSE;
    // TODO: add reinitialization code here
    // (SDI documents will reuse this document)
    return TRUE;
}

/////////////////////////////////////////////////////////////////////////////
// CMinidrawDoc serialization

void CMinidrawDoc::Serialize(CArchive& ar)
{
    if (ar.IsStoring())
    {
        // TODO: add storing code here

    mObArray.Serialize (ar);
    }
    else
    {
        // TODO: add loading code here

    mObArray.Serialize (ar);
    }
}

/////////////////////////////////////////////////////////////////////////////
// CMinidrawDoc diagnostics

#ifdef _DEBUG
void CMinidrawDoc::AssertValid() const
{
    CDocument::AssertValid();
}

void CMinidrawDoc::Dump(CDumpContext& dc) const
{
    CDocument::Dump(dc);
}
```

```
#endif //_DEBUG

///////////////////////////////////////////////////////////////////////////////
// CMinidrawDoc commands

void CMinidrawDoc::AddFigure (CFigure *PFigure)
    {
    mObArray.Add (PFigure);
    SetModifiedFlag ();
    }

CFigure *CMinidrawDoc::GetFigure (int Index)
    {
    if (Index < 0 || Index > mObArray.GetUpperBound ())
        return 0;
    return (CFigure *)mObArray.GetAt (Index);
    }

int CMinidrawDoc::GetNumFigs ()
    {
    return mObArray.GetSize ();
    }

void CMinidrawDoc::DeleteContents ()
    {
    int Index = mObArray.GetSize ();
    while (Index--)
        delete mObArray.GetAt (Index);
    mObArray.RemoveAll ();
    }

void CMinidrawDoc::OnEditClearAll()
{
    // TODO: Add your command handler code here

    DeleteContents ();
    UpdateAllViews (0);
    SetModifiedFlag ();
}

void CMinidrawDoc::OnUpdateEditClearAll(CCmdUI* pCmdUI)
{
    // TODO: Add your command update UI handler code here
```

```
      pCmdUI->Enable (mObArray.GetSize ());
}

void CMinidrawDoc::OnEditUndo()
{
    // TODO: Add your command handler code here

    int Index = mObArray.GetUpperBound ();
    if (Index > -1)
        {
        delete mObArray.GetAt (Index);
        mObArray.RemoveAt (Index);
        }
    UpdateAllViews (0);
    SetModifiedFlag ();
}

void CMinidrawDoc::OnUpdateEditUndo(CCmdUI* pCmdUI)
{
    // TODO: Add your command update UI handler code here

    pCmdUI->Enable (mObArray.GetSize ());
}

// implementation of figure classes:

IMPLEMENT_SERIAL (CFigure, CObject, 2)

CRect CFigure::GetDimRect ()
    {
    return CRect
      (min (mX1, mX2),
       min (mY1, mY2),
       max (mX1, mX2) + 1,
       max (mY1, mY2) + 1);
    }

void CFigure::Serialize (CArchive& ar)
    {
    if (ar.IsStoring ())
        ar << (WORD)mX1 << (WORD)mY1 << (WORD)mX2 << (WORD)mY2 << mColor;
    else
        ar >> (WORD &)mX1 >> (WORD &)mY1 >> (WORD &)mX2 >> (WORD &)mY2 >> mColor;
    }
```

```
IMPLEMENT_SERIAL (CLine, CFigure, 2)

CLine::CLine (int X1, int Y1, int X2, int Y2, COLORREF Color, int Thickness)
    {
    mX1 = X1;
    mY1 = Y1;
    mX2 = X2;
    mY2 = Y2;
    mColor = Color;
    mThickness = Thickness;
    }

void CLine::Serialize (CArchive& ar)
    {
    CFigure::Serialize (ar);
    if (ar.IsStoring ())
       ar << (WORD)mThickness;
    else
       ar >> (WORD &)mThickness;
    }

void CLine::Draw (CDC *PDC)
    {
    CPen Pen, *POldPen;

    // select pen/brush:
    Pen.CreatePen (PS_SOLID, mThickness, mColor);
    POldPen = PDC->SelectObject (&Pen);

    // draw figure:
    PDC->MoveTo (mX1, mY1);
    PDC->LineTo (mX2, mY2);

    // remove pen/brush:
    PDC->SelectObject (POldPen);
    }

IMPLEMENT_SERIAL (CRectangle, CFigure, 2)

CRectangle::CRectangle (int X1, int Y1, int X2, int Y2,
                        COLORREF Color, int Thickness)
    {
    mX1 = X1;
    mY1 = Y1;
    mX2 = X2;
```

```
    mY2 = Y2;
    mColor = Color;
    mThickness = Thickness;
    }

void CRectangle::Serialize (CArchive& ar)
    {
    CFigure::Serialize (ar);
    if (ar.IsStoring ())
        ar << (WORD)mThickness;
    else
        ar >> (WORD &)mThickness;
    }

void CRectangle::Draw (CDC *PDC)
    {
    CPen Pen, *POldPen;

    // select pen/brush:
    Pen.CreatePen (PS_INSIDEFRAME, mThickness, mColor);
    POldPen = PDC->SelectObject (&Pen);
    PDC->SelectStockObject (NULL_BRUSH);

    // draw figure:
    PDC->Rectangle (mX1, mY1, mX2, mY2);

    // remove pen/brush:
    PDC->SelectObject (POldPen);
    }

IMPLEMENT_SERIAL (CRectFill, CFigure, 2)

CRectFill::CRectFill (int X1, int Y1, int X2, int Y2, COLORREF Color)
    {
    mX1 = min (X1, X2);
    mY1 = min (Y1, Y2);
    mX2 = max (X1, X2);
    mY2 = max (Y1, Y2);
    mColor = Color;
    }

void CRectFill::Draw (CDC *PDC)
    {
    CBrush Brush, *POldBrush;
    CPen Pen, *POldPen;
```

```
    // select pen/brush:
    Pen.CreatePen (PS_INSIDEFRAME, 1, mColor);
    POldPen = PDC->SelectObject (&Pen);
    Brush.CreateSolidBrush (mColor);
    POldBrush = PDC->SelectObject (&Brush);

    // draw figure:
    PDC->Rectangle (mX1, mY1, mX2, mY2);

    // remove pen/brush:
    PDC->SelectObject (POldPen);
    PDC->SelectObject (POldBrush);
    }

IMPLEMENT_SERIAL (CRectRound, CFigure, 2)

CRectRound::CRectRound (int X1, int Y1, int X2, int Y2,
                        COLORREF Color, int Thickness)
    {
    mX1 = min (X1, X2);
    mY1 = min (Y1, Y2);
    mX2 = max (X1, X2);
    mY2 = max (Y1, Y2);
    mColor = Color;
    mThickness = Thickness;
    }

void CRectRound::Serialize (CArchive& ar)
    {
    CFigure::Serialize (ar);
    if (ar.IsStoring ())
        ar << (WORD)mThickness;
    else
        ar >> (WORD &)mThickness;
    }

void CRectRound::Draw (CDC *PDC)
    {
    CPen Pen, *POldPen;

    // select pen/brush:
    Pen.CreatePen (PS_INSIDEFRAME, mThickness, mColor);
    POldPen = PDC->SelectObject (&Pen);
    PDC->SelectStockObject (NULL_BRUSH);
```

```
   // draw figure:
   int SizeRound = (mX2 - mX1 + mY2 - mY1) / 6;
   PDC->RoundRect (mX1, mY1, mX2, mY2, SizeRound, SizeRound);

   // remove pen/brush:
   PDC->SelectObject (POldPen);
   }

IMPLEMENT_SERIAL (CRectRoundFill, CFigure, 2)

CRectRoundFill::CRectRoundFill (int X1, int Y1, int X2, int Y2, COLORREF Color)
   {
   mX1 = min (X1, X2);
   mY1 = min (Y1, Y2);
   mX2 = max (X1, X2);
   mY2 = max (Y1, Y2);
   mColor = Color;
   }

void CRectRoundFill::Draw (CDC *PDC)
   {
   CBrush Brush, *POldBrush;
   CPen Pen, *POldPen;

   // select pen/brush:
   Pen.CreatePen (PS_INSIDEFRAME, 1, mColor);
   POldPen = PDC->SelectObject (&Pen);
   Brush.CreateSolidBrush (mColor);
   POldBrush = PDC->SelectObject (&Brush);

   // draw figure:
   int SizeRound = (mX2 - mX1 + mY2 - mY1) / 6;
   PDC->RoundRect (mX1, mY1, mX2, mY2, SizeRound, SizeRound);

   // remove pen/brush:
   PDC->SelectObject (POldPen);
   PDC->SelectObject (POldBrush);
   }

IMPLEMENT_SERIAL (CCircle, CFigure, 2)
```

```
CCircle::CCircle (int X1, int Y1, int X2, int Y2,
                  COLORREF Color, int Thickness)
   {
   mX1 = min (X1, X2);
   mY1 = min (Y1, Y2);
   mX2 = max (X1, X2);
   mY2 = max (Y1, Y2);
   mColor = Color;
   mThickness = Thickness;
   }

void CCircle::Serialize (CArchive& ar)
   {
   CFigure::Serialize (ar);
   if (ar.IsStoring ())
      ar << (WORD)mThickness;
   else
      ar >> (WORD &)mThickness;
   }

void CCircle::Draw (CDC *PDC)
   {
   CPen Pen, *POldPen;

   // select pen/brush:
   Pen.CreatePen (PS_INSIDEFRAME, mThickness, mColor);
   POldPen = PDC->SelectObject (&Pen);
   PDC->SelectStockObject (NULL_BRUSH);

   // draw figure:
   PDC->Ellipse (mX1, mY1, mX2, mY2);

   // remove pen/brush:
   PDC->SelectObject (POldPen);
   }

IMPLEMENT_SERIAL (CCircleFill, CFigure, 2)

CCircleFill::CCircleFill (int X1, int Y1, int X2, int Y2, COLORREF Color)
   {
   mX1 = min (X1, X2);
   mY1 = min (Y1, Y2);
   mX2 = max (X1, X2);
```

```
    mY2 = max (Y1, Y2);
    mColor = Color;
    }

void CCircleFill::Draw (CDC *PDC)
    {
    CBrush Brush, *POldBrush;
    CPen Pen, *POldPen;

    // select pen/brush:
    Pen.CreatePen (PS_INSIDEFRAME, 1, mColor);
    POldPen = PDC->SelectObject (&Pen);
    Brush.CreateSolidBrush (mColor);
    POldBrush = PDC->SelectObject (&Brush);

    // draw figure:
    PDC->Ellipse (mX1, mY1, mX2, mY2);

    // remove pen/brush:
    PDC->SelectObject (POldPen);
    PDC->SelectObject (POldBrush);
    }
```

Listing 16.13

```
// mainfrm.h : interface of the CMainFrame class
//
/////////////////////////////////////////////////////////////////////////////

class CMainFrame : public CFrameWnd
{
protected: // create from serialization only
    CMainFrame();
    DECLARE_DYNCREATE(CMainFrame)

protected:
    CSplitterWnd mSplitterWnd;
    CStatusBar mStatusBar;
    CToolBar mToolBar;

    virtual BOOL OnCreateClient (LPCREATESTRUCT lpcs, CCreateContext* pContext);
```

```
// Attributes
public:

// Operations
public:

// Implementation
public:
    virtual ~CMainFrame();
#ifdef _DEBUG
    virtual  void AssertValid() const;
    virtual  void Dump(CDumpContext& dc) const;
#endif


// Generated message map functions
protected:
    //{{AFX_MSG(CMainFrame)
    afx_msg int OnCreate(LPCREATESTRUCT lpCreateStruct);
    //}}AFX_MSG
    DECLARE_MESSAGE_MAP()
};
```

///

Listing 16.14

```
// mainfrm.cpp : implementation of the CMainFrame class
//

#include "stdafx.h"
#include "minidraw.h"

#include "mainfrm.h"

#ifdef _DEBUG
#undef THIS_FILE
static char BASED_CODE THIS_FILE[] = __FILE__;
#endif

/////////////////////////////////////////////////////////////////////////////
// CMainFrame

IMPLEMENT_DYNCREATE(CMainFrame, CFrameWnd)
```

```
BEGIN_MESSAGE_MAP(CMainFrame, CFrameWnd)
    //{{AFX_MSG_MAP(CMainFrame)
    ON_WM_CREATE()
    //}}AFX_MSG_MAP
END_MESSAGE_MAP()

// IDs for tool bar buttons:
static UINT ButtonIDs [] =
    {
    ID_TOOLS_LINE,
    ID_SEPARATOR,
    ID_TOOLS_RECTANGLE,
    ID_TOOLS_RECTFILL,
    ID_SEPARATOR,
    ID_TOOLS_RECTROUND,
    ID_TOOLS_RECTROUNDFILL,
    ID_SEPARATOR,
    ID_TOOLS_CIRCLE,
    ID_TOOLS_CIRCLEFILL,
    ID_SEPARATOR,
    ID_SEPARATOR,
    ID_LINE_SINGLE,
    ID_LINE_DOUBLE,
    ID_LINE_TRIPLE
    };

// IDs for status bar indicators:
static UINT IndicatorIDs [] =
    {
    ID_SEPARATOR,
    ID_INDICATOR_CAPS,
    ID_INDICATOR_NUM,
    ID_INDICATOR_SCRL
    };

/////////////////////////////////////////////////////////////////////////////
// CMainFrame construction/destruction

CMainFrame::CMainFrame()
{
    // TODO: add member initialization code here
}
```

```
CMainFrame::~CMainFrame()
{
}

///////////////////////////////////////////////////////////////////////
// CMainFrame diagnostics

#ifdef _DEBUG
void CMainFrame::AssertValid() const
{
    CFrameWnd::AssertValid();
}

void CMainFrame::Dump(CDumpContext& dc) const
{
    CFrameWnd::Dump(dc);
}

#endif //_DEBUG

///////////////////////////////////////////////////////////////////////
// CMainFrame message handlers

BOOL CMainFrame::OnCreateClient (LPCREATESTRUCT lpcs, CCreateContext* pContext)
    {
    return mSplitterWnd.Create
        (this,              // parent of splitter window
        1,                  // maximum rows
        2,                  // maximum columns
        CSize (15, 15),     // minimum pane size
        pContext);          // pass on context information
    }

int CMainFrame::OnCreate(LPCREATESTRUCT lpCreateStruct)
{
    if (CFrameWnd::OnCreate(lpCreateStruct) == -1)
        return -1;

    // TODO: Add your specialized creation code here

    if (!mToolBar.Create (this) ||
        !mToolBar.LoadBitmap (IDR_MAINFRAME) ||
```

```
    !mToolBar.SetButtons (ButtonIDs, sizeof (ButtonIDs) / sizeof (UINT)))
        return -1;

    if (!mStatusBar.Create (this) ||
        !mStatusBar.SetIndicators (IndicatorIDs,
        sizeof (IndicatorIDs) / sizeof (UINT)))
        return -1;

    return 0;
}
```

Listing 16.15

```
// minidvw.h : interface of the CMinidrawView class
//
///////////////////////////////////////////////////////////////////////////

class CMinidrawView : public CScrollView
{
protected: // create from serialization only
    CMinidrawView();
    DECLARE_DYNCREATE(CMinidrawView)

protected:
    CString mClassName;
    int mDragging;
    HCURSOR mHArrow;
    HCURSOR mHCross;
    CPen mPenDotted;
    CPoint mPointOld;
    CPoint mPointOrigin;

    virtual void OnInitialUpdate ();
    virtual void OnUpdate (CView* pSender, LPARAM lHint, CObject* pHint);
    virtual BOOL PreCreateWindow (CREATESTRUCT& cs);

// Attributes
public:
    CMinidrawDoc* GetDocument();

// Operations
public:
```

```
// Implementation
public:
    virtual ~CMinidrawView();
    virtual void OnDraw(CDC* pDC);   // overridden to draw this view
#ifdef _DEBUG
    virtual void AssertValid() const;
    virtual void Dump(CDumpContext& dc) const;
#endif

// Generated message map functions
protected:
    //{{AFX_MSG(CMinidrawView)
    afx_msg void OnLButtonDown(UINT nFlags, CPoint point);
    afx_msg void OnMouseMove(UINT nFlags, CPoint point);
    afx_msg void OnLButtonUp(UINT nFlags, CPoint point);
    //}}AFX_MSG
    DECLARE_MESSAGE_MAP()
};

#ifndef _DEBUG // debug version in minidvw.cpp
inline CMinidrawDoc* CMinidrawView::GetDocument()
    { return (CMinidrawDoc*) m_pDocument; }
#endif
```

//

Listing 16.16

```
// minidvw.cpp : implementation of the CMinidrawView class
//

#include "stdafx.h"
#include "minidraw.h"

#include "miniddoc.h"
#include "minidvw.h"

#ifdef _DEBUG
#undef THIS_FILE
static char BASED_CODE THIS_FILE[] = __FILE__;
#endif
```

//
```
// CMinidrawView
```

```
IMPLEMENT_DYNCREATE(CMinidrawView, CScrollView)

BEGIN_MESSAGE_MAP(CMinidrawView, CScrollView)
    //{{AFX_MSG_MAP(CMinidrawView)
    ON_WM_LBUTTONDOWN()
    ON_WM_MOUSEMOVE()
    ON_WM_LBUTTONUP()
    ON_WM_KEYDOWN()
    //}}AFX_MSG_MAP
END_MESSAGE_MAP()

///////////////////////////////////////////////////////////////////////////
// CMinidrawView construction/destruction

CMinidrawView::CMinidrawView()
{
    // TODO: add construction code here

    mDragging = 0;
    mHArrow = AfxGetApp ()->LoadStandardCursor (IDC_ARROW);
    mHCross = AfxGetApp ()->LoadStandardCursor (IDC_CROSS);
    mPenDotted.CreatePen (PS_DOT, 1, RGB (0,0,0));
}

CMinidrawView::~CMinidrawView()
{
}

///////////////////////////////////////////////////////////////////////////
// CMinidrawView drawing

void CMinidrawView::OnDraw(CDC* pDC)
{
    CMinidrawDoc* pDoc = GetDocument();

    // TODO: add draw code here

    CSize ScrollSize = GetTotalSize ();
    pDC->MoveTo (ScrollSize.cx, 0);
    pDC->LineTo (ScrollSize.cx, ScrollSize.cy);
    pDC->LineTo (0, ScrollSize.cy);

    CRect ClipRect;
    CRect DimRect;
```

```
    CRect IntRect;
    CFigure *PFigure;

    pDC->GetClipBox (&ClipRect);

    int NumFigs = pDoc->GetNumFigs ();
    for (int Index = 0; Index < NumFigs; ++Index)
        {
        PFigure = pDoc->GetFigure (Index);
        DimRect = PFigure->GetDimRect ();
        if (IntRect.IntersectRect (DimRect, ClipRect))
            PFigure->Draw (pDC);
        }
}

/////////////////////////////////////////////////////////////////////////////
// CMinidrawView diagnostics

#ifdef _DEBUG
void CMinidrawView::AssertValid() const
{
    CScrollView::AssertValid();
}

void CMinidrawView::Dump(CDumpContext& dc) const
{
    CScrollView::Dump(dc);
}

CMinidrawDoc* CMinidrawView::GetDocument() // non-debug version is inline
{
    ASSERT(m_pDocument->IsKindOf(RUNTIME_CLASS(CMinidrawDoc)));
    return (CMinidrawDoc*) m_pDocument;
}

#endif //_DEBUG

/////////////////////////////////////////////////////////////////////////////
// CMinidrawView message handlers

void CMinidrawView::OnLButtonDown(UINT nFlags, CPoint point)
{
    // TODO: Add your message handler code here and/or call default
```

```
    CClientDC ClientDC (this);
    OnPrepareDC (&ClientDC);
    ClientDC.DPtoLP (&point);

    // test whether cursor is within drawing area of view window:
    CSize ScrollSize = GetTotalSize ();
    CRect ScrollRect (0, 0, ScrollSize.cx, ScrollSize.cy);
    if (!ScrollRect.PtInRect (point))
        return;

    // save cursor position, capture mouse, & set dragging flag:
    mPointOrigin = point;
    mPointOld = point;
    SetCapture ();
    mDragging = 1;

    // clip mouse cursor:
    ClientDC.LPtoDP (&ScrollRect);
    CRect ViewRect;
    GetClientRect (&ViewRect);
    CRect IntRect;
    IntRect.IntersectRect (&ScrollRect, &ViewRect);
    ClientToScreen (&IntRect);
    ::ClipCursor (&IntRect);

    CScrollView::OnLButtonDown(nFlags, point);
}

void CMinidrawView::OnMouseMove(UINT nFlags, CPoint point)
{
    // TODO: Add your message handler code here and/or call default

    CClientDC ClientDC (this);
    OnPrepareDC (&ClientDC);
    ClientDC.DPtoLP (&point);

    if (!mDragging)
        {
        CSize ScrollSize = GetTotalSize ();
        CRect ScrollRect (0, 0, ScrollSize.cx, ScrollSize.cy);
        if (ScrollRect.PtInRect (point))
            ::SetCursor (mHCross);
        else
```

```
        ::SetCursor (mHArrow);
    return;
    }

ClientDC.SetROP2 (R2_NOT);
ClientDC.SelectObject (&mPenDotted);
ClientDC.SetBkMode (TRANSPARENT);
ClientDC.SelectStockObject (NULL_BRUSH);

switch (((CMinidrawApp *)AfxGetApp ())->mCurrentTool)
    {
    case ID_TOOLS_LINE:
        ClientDC.MoveTo (mPointOrigin);
        ClientDC.LineTo (mPointOld);
        ClientDC.MoveTo (mPointOrigin);
        ClientDC.LineTo (point);
        break;

    case ID_TOOLS_RECTANGLE:
    case ID_TOOLS_RECTFILL:
        ClientDC.Rectangle (mPointOrigin.x, mPointOrigin.y,
                            mPointOld.x, mPointOld.y);
        ClientDC.Rectangle (mPointOrigin.x, mPointOrigin.y,
                            point.x, point.y);
        break;

    case ID_TOOLS_RECTROUND:
    case ID_TOOLS_RECTROUNDFILL:
        {
        int SizeRound = (abs (mPointOld.x - mPointOrigin.x) +
                         abs (mPointOld.y - mPointOrigin.y)) / 6;
        ClientDC.RoundRect (mPointOrigin.x, mPointOrigin.y,
                            mPointOld.x, mPointOld.y,
                            SizeRound, SizeRound);
        SizeRound = (abs (point.x - mPointOrigin.x) +
                     abs (point.y - mPointOrigin.y)) / 6;
        ClientDC.RoundRect (mPointOrigin.x, mPointOrigin.y,
                            point.x, point.y,
                            SizeRound, SizeRound);
        break;
        }
    case ID_TOOLS_CIRCLE:
    case ID_TOOLS_CIRCLEFILL:
        ClientDC.Ellipse (mPointOrigin.x, mPointOrigin.y,
                          mPointOld.x, mPointOld.y);
```

```
        ClientDC.Ellipse (mPointOrigin.x, mPointOrigin.y,
                          point.x, point.y);
        break;
    }

    mPointOld = point;

    CScrollView::OnMouseMove(nFlags, point);
}

void CMinidrawView::OnLButtonUp(UINT nFlags, CPoint point)
{
    // TODO: Add your message handler code here and/or call default
    if (!mDragging)
        return;

    mDragging = 0;
    ::ReleaseCapture ();
    ::ClipCursor (NULL);

    CClientDC ClientDC (this);
    OnPrepareDC (&ClientDC);
    ClientDC.DPtoLP (&point);
    ClientDC.SetROP2 (R2_NOT);
    ClientDC.SelectObject (&mPenDotted);
    ClientDC.SetBkMode (TRANSPARENT);
    ClientDC.SelectStockObject (NULL_BRUSH);

    CMinidrawApp *PApp = (CMinidrawApp *)AfxGetApp ();
    CFigure *PFigure;

    switch (PApp->mCurrentTool)
        {
        case ID_TOOLS_LINE:
            ClientDC.MoveTo (mPointOrigin);
            ClientDC.LineTo (mPointOld);
            PFigure = new CLine
                (mPointOrigin.x, mPointOrigin.y,
                point.x, point.y,
                PApp->mCurrentColor,
                PApp->mCurrentThickness);
            break;
```

```
case ID_TOOLS_RECTANGLE:
    ClientDC.Rectangle (mPointOrigin.x, mPointOrigin.y,
                        mPointOld.x, mPointOld.y);
    PFigure = new CRectangle
        (mPointOrigin.x, mPointOrigin.y,
        point.x, point.y,
        PApp->mCurrentColor,
        PApp->mCurrentThickness);
    break;

case ID_TOOLS_RECTFILL:
    ClientDC.Rectangle (mPointOrigin.x, mPointOrigin.y,
                        mPointOld.x, mPointOld.y);
    PFigure = new CRectFill
        (mPointOrigin.x, mPointOrigin.y,
        point.x, point.y,
        PApp->mCurrentColor);
    break;

case ID_TOOLS_RECTROUND:
    {
    int SizeRound = (abs (mPointOld.x - mPointOrigin.x) +
                    abs (mPointOld.y - mPointOrigin.y)) / 6;
    ClientDC.RoundRect (mPointOrigin.x, mPointOrigin.y,
                        mPointOld.x, mPointOld.y,
                        SizeRound, SizeRound);
    PFigure = new CRectRound
        (mPointOrigin.x, mPointOrigin.y,
        point.x, point.y,
        PApp->mCurrentColor,
        PApp->mCurrentThickness);
    break;
    }

case ID_TOOLS_RECTROUNDFILL:
    {
    int SizeRound = (abs (mPointOld.x - mPointOrigin.x) +
                    abs (mPointOld.y - mPointOrigin.y)) / 6;
    ClientDC.RoundRect (mPointOrigin.x, mPointOrigin.y,
                        mPointOld.x, mPointOld.y,
                        SizeRound, SizeRound);
    PFigure = new CRectRoundFill
        (mPointOrigin.x, mPointOrigin.y,
        point.x, point.y,
        PApp->mCurrentColor);
```

```
                break;
                }

        case ID_TOOLS_CIRCLE:
            ClientDC.Ellipse (mPointOrigin.x, mPointOrigin.y,
                             mPointOld.x, mPointOld.y);
            PFigure = new CCircle
                (mPointOrigin.x, mPointOrigin.y,
                point.x, point.y,
                PApp->mCurrentColor,
                PApp->mCurrentThickness);
            break;

        case ID_TOOLS_CIRCLEFILL:
            ClientDC.Ellipse (mPointOrigin.x, mPointOrigin.y,
                             mPointOld.x, mPointOld.y);
            PFigure = new CCircleFill
                (mPointOrigin.x, mPointOrigin.y,
                point.x, point.y,
                PApp->mCurrentColor);
            break;
        }

    ClientDC.SetROP2 (R2_COPYPEN);
    PFigure->Draw (&ClientDC);

    CMinidrawDoc* PDoc = GetDocument();
    PDoc->AddFigure (PFigure);

    PDoc->UpdateAllViews (this, 0, PFigure);

    CScrollView::OnLButtonUp(nFlags, point);
    }

BOOL CMinidrawView::PreCreateWindow (CREATESTRUCT& cs)
    {
    mClassName = AfxRegisterWndClass
        (CS_HREDRAW | CS_VREDRAW,                    // class styles
        0,                                           // no cursor
        (HBRUSH)::GetStockObject (WHITE_BRUSH),      // set white background brush
        0);                                          // no icon
    cs.lpszClass = mClassName;
```

```
    return CScrollView::PreCreateWindow (cs);
    }

void CMinidrawView::OnInitialUpdate ()
    {
    SIZE Size = {640, 480};
    SetScrollSizes (MM_TEXT, Size);
    CScrollView::OnInitialUpdate ();
    }

void CMinidrawView::OnUpdate (CView* pSender, LPARAM lHint, CObject* pHint)
    {
    if (pHint != 0)
        {
        CRect InvalidRect = ((CFigure *)pHint)->GetDimRect ();
        CClientDC ClientDC (this);
        OnPrepareDC (&ClientDC);
        ClientDC.LPtoDP (&InvalidRect);
        InvalidateRect (&InvalidRect);
        }
    else
        CScrollView::OnUpdate (pSender, lHint, pHint);
    }
```

Summary

In this chapter you learned how to draw figures by using member functions of the CDC class.

The following is a brief summary of the main steps for drawing graphics:

- First, create a device context object. If you are drawing from an OnDraw member function of the view class, you can simply use the device context object that is passed to the function. Otherwise, you will have to create an instance of the CClientDC class, and—if you are drawing in a view window that supports scrolling—pass the object to the OnPrepareDC class before using it.

- Next, select a pen for drawing lines and the borders of closed figures, then select a brush for filling the interiors of closed figures.

- You can select a stock pen or brush by calling SelectStockObject.

- You can select a custom pen or brush by creating a CPen or CBrush object, calling the appropriate member function to initialize the pen or brush, and then calling CDC::SelectObject to select the pen or brush into the device context object. Save the handle of the previously selected object, which is returned by SelectObject.

- Then, use the CDC member functions listed in Table 16.3 to set any desired drawing attributes, such as the mapping mode that determines the coordinate system used to draw graphics.

- Finally, draw the graphics by calling member functions of the CDC class. This class provides functions for coloring individual pixels, for drawing straight or curved lines, and for drawing closed figures such as rectangles and ellipses.

- If you created and selected a custom pen or brush, remove it from the device context object by calling SelectObject to select the previous pen or brush object.

In the next chapter, you will learn how to create graphics by using bitmaps, as well as how to use bit operations to quickly transfer or modify blocks of graphic data.

SEVENTEEN

Using Bitmaps and Bit Operations

17

- Creating a bitmap

- Performing bit operations

- Displaying icons

- The BITDEMO program

A Windows *bitmap* is a data structure that stores an exact representation of a graphic image in memory or in a file. A bitmap stores the color of every pixel that is required to generate the image on a specific device, such as a monitor or printer. In this chapter, you will learn how to create bitmaps and how to display bitmaps on devices. You will also learn how to take advantage of the versatile and efficient bit-operation functions that Windows provides for transferring and modifying blocks of graphic data. At the end of the chapter you will create an example program named BITDEMO, which demonstrates the techniques for displaying a bitmap in a view window.

Creating a Bitmap

The MFC provides a class, CBitmap, for managing bitmaps. The first step in creating a bitmap, therefore, is to declare an instance of this class, as in the following example:

```
CBitmap mBitmap;
```

A bitmap object is typically declared as a data member of one of the main program classes, such as the view class.

Once you have declared a CBitmap object, you must call an appropriate CBitmap member function to initialize the object. In this chapter, you will learn how to initialize a CBitmap object either by calling the LoadBitmap member function to load the bitmap data from a program resource, or by calling CreateCompatibleBitmap to produce a blank bitmap in which you can draw the desired image at program run-time.

> **NOTE**
>
> In addition to the two methods described in this chapter, Windows provides several other ways to initialize a bitmap object. For example, you can call the `CBitmap::LoadOEMBitmap` function to load a predefined bitmap supplied by Windows, you can call `CBitmap::CreateBitmap` to create a bitmap conforming to a specific structure, or you can call `CBitmap::Attach` to initialize a bitmap object using a Windows bitmap handle. For general information, see the documentation on the `CBitmap` class in the *Reference Volume I, Class Library Reference* manual or in the *Foundation Classes* online help file.

Loading a Bitmap from a Resource

Including a bitmap as a program resource gives you the advantage that you can design the bitmap using App Studio or another bitmap editor (such as Windows Paintbrush). This method, therefore, is especially useful for creating relatively complex or nongeometric images, which are not easily generated using drawing commands.

To design the bitmap, open the program resource file in App Studio. (Usually you will first open the project in the Visual Workbench and then run App Studio from the Visual Workbench Tools menu.) In the App Studio resource dialog box, click the New... button and choose the Bitmap resource type. App Studio will then open the bitmap-designing window, which you used in Chapter 14 for creating tool bar buttons. You can now design the desired bitmap image.

When you open the bitmap-designing window, App Studio will display the default identifier for the bitmap in the window title bar (the first bitmap you create is assigned the identifier `IDB_BITMAP1`, the second bitmap is assigned the identifier `IDB_BITMAP2`, and so on). If you wish, you can assign a different identifier by choosing the Show Properties command on the Window menu and entering a different constant into the ID: text box. Whether you accept the default identifier or assign your own, remember the identifier, because you will need to use it when you load the bitmap from the program.

TIP

Rather than designing the bitmap using the App Studio bitmap-designing window, you can import a bitmap that you have created in another bitmap editor, such as Windows Paintbrush, by choosing the Import command on the Resource menu in App Studio and specifying the name of the .BMP file containing the image.

Once you have designed a bitmap in App Studio, you can use it to initialize a bit-map object in your program. To do this, call the CBitmap member function Load-Bitmap, as in the following example:

```
class CProgView : public CView
{
//...
   CBitmap mBitmap;
   void LoadBitmapImage ();
// ...
};


// ...

void CProgView::LoadBitmapImage ()
   {
   // ...

   mBitmap.LoadBitmap (IDB_BITMAP1);

   // ...
   }
```

The parameter passed to LoadBitmap is the identifier that was assigned to the bit-map in App Studio.

NOTE

The steps for designing a bitmap in App Studio and using this bitmap to initialize a bitmap object are described in the tutorial exercise for creating the BITDEMO program given near the end of the chapter.

Creating a Bitmap Using Drawing Functions

Rather than designing the bitmap in an editor, you can initialize a blank bitmap and then use the MFC drawing functions to draw the desired pattern at program runtime. The following is a summary of the required steps:

1. Initialize a blank bitmap.

2. Create a memory device context object.

3. Select the bitmap into the memory device context object.

4. Draw the desired image within the bitmap, using the member functions of the memory device context object.

To initialize a blank bitmap, you can call the function `CreateCompatibleBitmap`, as in the following example:

```
class CProgView : public CView
{
//...
   CBitmap mBitmap;
   void DrawBitmapImage ();
// ...
};

// ...

void CProgView::DrawBitmapImage ()
   {
   CClientDC ClientDC (this);

   mBitmap.CreateCompatibleBitmap (&ClientDC, 32, 32);

   // ...
   }
```

The first parameter passed to `CreateCompatibleBitmap` is the address of a device context object; the bitmap will be made compatible with the device that is associated with this object. The term *compatible* means that the graphic data in the bitmap will be structured in the same way that it is structured by the device; as a result of the compatibility, you will be able to transfer graphic data readily between the bitmap and the device. To create a bitmap that will be displayed on the screen, you should pass the address of a device context object for the screen (usually, a `CCli-entDC` device context object that you have explicitly defined, or the device context object that is passed to the `OnDraw` member function of the view class).

The second parameter passed to `CreateCompatibleBitmap` is the width of the bitmap, and the third parameter is the height; both of these dimensions are in pixels.

When you call `CreateCompatibleBitmap`, Windows reserves a block of memory for the bitmap. The pixel values stored within this bitmap are initially random; you must use drawing functions to create the desired image. Before you can draw within the bitmap, however, you need to create a device context object that is associated with the bitmap (just as you must have a device context object to send output to a device). Windows provides a special type of device context object for accessing a bitmap, which is known as a *memory device context object*. To create a memory device context object, you declare an instance of the `CDC` class and then call the `CDC` member function `CreateCompatibleDC`, as in the following example:

```
void CProgView::DrawBitmapImage ()
    {
    CClientDC ClientDC (this);
    CDC MemDC;

    mBitmap.CreateCompatibleBitmap (&ClientDC, 32, 32);

    MemDC.CreateCompatibleDC (&ClientDC);

    // ...
    }
```

The parameter passed to `CreateCompatibleDC` is the address of a device context object; this object should be associated with the *same* device as the object passed to `CreateCompatibleBitmap`. (In these examples, both the bitmap and the memory device context object are associated with the screen.)

TIP   If you pass NULL to `CreateCompatibleDC`, the function will automatically initialize a memory device context object that is compatible with the screen.

Next, you must use the CDC member function SelectObject to select the bitmap object into the memory device context object; the following is an example:

```
MemDC.SelectObject (&mBitmap);
```

The parameter passed to SelectObject is the address of the bitmap object.

You can now draw the desired image within the bitmap using the CDC member functions. You can display text or graphics within the bitmap using the functions discussed in chapters 15 and 16, just as if you were drawing within a window. You can also use any of the bit operations that will be discussed later in the chapter (for instance, the PatBlt function is useful for painting the background color within a bitmap). For example, the following code paints a white background and then draws a circle within the bitmap selected into the MemDC memory device context object:

```
// paint white background:
MemDC.PatBlt (0, 0, 32, 32, WHITENESS);

// draw a circle:
MemDC.Ellipse (2, 2, 30, 30);
```

This example assumes that the bitmap was given a size of 32 pixels by 32 pixels (in the call to CreateCompatibleBitmap).

The following code illustrates all of the steps discussed in this section; it initializes a bitmap and then draws an image within it:

```
class CProgView : public CView
{
//...
   CBitmap mBitmap;
   void DrawBitmapImage ();
// ...
};

// ...

void CProgView::DrawBitmapImage ()
{
   CClientDC ClientDC (this);   // window device context object
   CDC MemDC;                   // memory device context object

   // initialize a blank bitmap:
   mBitmap.CreateCompatibleBitmap (&ClientDC, 32, 32);
```

```
// initialize the memory device context object:
MemDC.CreateCompatibleDC (&ClientDC);

// select the bitmap object into the memory dc object:
MemDC.SelectObject (&mBitmap);

// use CDC member functions to draw within bitmap:

// draw white background:
MemDC.PatBlt (0, 0, 32, 32, WHITENESS);

// draw circle:
MemDC.Ellipse (2, 2, 30, 30);

// call other drawing functions ...
}
```

NOTE Usually, a bitmap object is declared as a data member of one of the main program classes (such as the view class), and therefore it typically persists throughout the entire course of the program. However, if the bitmap object is destroyed *before* the memory device context object, you should first remove it from the memory device context object. This is done as explained in Chapter 16 (for a drawing tool). Namely, when calling `SelectObject`, save the pointer to the default bitmap (a newly created memory device context object has a default bitmap consisting of a single pixel); when you have finished accessing the bitmap, call `SelectObject` again to select the default bitmap back into the device context object.

Displaying a Bitmap

After you have created and initialized a bitmap object, you can display the bitmap directly within a window or on another device. Neither the Windows API nor the MFC provides a single function that you can call to display a bitmap on a device. However, you can write your own function to perform this task, such as the following:

```
void DisplayBitmap (CDC *PDC, CBitmap *PBitmap, int X, int Y)
    {
    BITMAP BM;
    CDC MemDC;

    MemDC.CreateCompatibleDC (PDC);
    MemDC.SelectObject (PBitmap);
    PBitmap->GetObject (sizeof (BM), &BM);
    PDC->BitBlt
        (X,              // horizontal coordinate of destination
        Y,              // vertical coordinate of destination
        BM.bmWidth,     // width of block to transfer
        BM.bmHeight,    // height of block to transfer
        &MemDC,         // source dc for graphic data
        0,              // horizontal coordinate of block within source
        0,              // vertical coordinate of block within source
        SRCCOPY);       // code for type of transfer
    }
```

This function displays a bitmap on the device associated with the device context object specified by the first parameter. The second parameter supplies the address of the bitmap object, which must have been initialized using one of the techniques discussed in the chapter. The last two parameters specify the horizontal and vertical coordinates of the position within the target device where the upper-left corner of the bitmap is to be displayed.

DisplayBitmap first creates a memory device context object and selects the bitmap into this object, so that it can access the contents of the bitmap. It then calls the CGdiObject member function GetObject, which fills the fields of a BITMAP structure with information on the bitmap; the function obtains the size of the bitmap from the bmWidth and bmHeight fields of this structure. It next calls the CDC member function BitBlt, which transfers the graphic data contained in the bitmap directly to the target device.

The first two parameters passed to BitBlt specify the upper-left corner of the destination location, and the third and fourth parameters specify the width and height of the block of data to be transferred; DisplayBitmap transfers the entire bitmap by passing the bitmap width and height obtained from the bmWidth and bmHeight fields of the BITMAP structure. The fifth parameter (&MemDC) is the address of the device context object that is the source of the graphic data; DisplayBitmap specifies the memory device context object associated with the bitmap. The sixth and seventh parameters specify the upper-left corner of the block of graphic data to be transferred from the source device context object; because DisplayBitmap transfers the entire bitmap, it specifies the coordinates (0, 0). The last parameter is a code that indicates how the graphic data is to be transferred; the value SRCCOPY indicates that it should be copied without modification. The BitBlt function is one of the bit-operation functions that is described in the next section.

> **NOTE**
> The DisplayBitmap function assumes that the device context object for the target device uses the default mapping mode (MM_TEXT). It also assumes that the bitmap object passed as the second parameter is compatible with the device context object passed as the first parameter. (See the discussion above on the CBitmap::CreateCompatibleBitmap function.)

The following code illustrates how the DisplayBitmap function could be used to display a bitmap in the upper-left corner of the view window:

```
void CProgView::OnDraw(CDC* pDC)
{
    DisplayBitmap (pDC, &mBitmap, 0, 0);

}
```

This example assumes that mBitmap is a CBitmap object that has been defined as a member of the view class (CProgView), and that it has been initialized using one of the methods discussed previously. The BITDEMO program given at the end of the chapter demonstrates an alternative way to display a bitmap in the view window.

Other Ways to Use a Bitmap

An initialized bitmap object can be used for a variety of purposes in an MFC program, in addition to its use for displaying a bitmapped image on a device. For example, you can use an initialized bitmap object to:

- Create a custom push button control, using the MFC CBitmapButton class; a custom push button is labeled with a bitmapped image rather than text

- Display a custom check mark next to a menu command, by calling the `CMenu::SetMenuItemBitmaps` function

- Design a custom menu label, by calling the `CMenu::AppendMenu` function or one of several similar `CMenu` member functions, and specifying a bitmap rather than a text label

- Fill areas with a custom pattern by calling `CBrush::CreatePatternBrush` to create a brush, as described in Chapter 16

When performing any of these tasks, you must supply a `CBitmap` object that has been initialized using one of the methods discussed in the chapter. For information on any of these techniques, see the documentation on the class or member function mentioned in the list above in the *Reference Volume I, Class Library Reference* manual or in the *Foundation Classes* online help file.

Performing Bit Operations

The `CDC` class provides three versatile and efficient functions for transferring blocks of graphic data: `PatBlt`, `BitBlt`, and `StretchBlt`. You can use these functions when creating drawings; you can also use them for moving or copying drawings or portions of drawings, and for modifying drawings in simple or complex ways (for example, inverting colors or flipping images). Previously in the chapter, you saw how to use the `PatBlt` function to paint the background color in a bitmap, and you saw how to use the `BitBlt` to transfer a bitmap to a window or other device. In general, you can use these functions to transfer data within a single device context object or from one device context object to another.

> **NOTE** You can freely use the bit-operation functions with a device context object associated with the screen, or with a memory device context object that is compatible with the screen. These functions, however, might not be supported by other types of devices, such as certain printers or plotters. To determine whether a particular device supports the bit-operation functions, you can call the `GetDeviceCaps` member function of a device context object that is associated with the device. See the documentation on this function for an explanation of the information that it supplies.

PatBlt

You can use the `CDC` member function `PatBlt` to paint a rectangular area using the current brush. (See Chapter 16 for a description of the current brush.) In the context of bit operations, the current brush is usually referred to as the current *pattern*. Although you can also fill an area using the current pattern by calling the `CDC::Fill-Rect` function, the `PatBlt` function is more versatile. `PatBlt` has the following syntax:

```
BOOL PatBlt
    (int x, int y,            // upper-left corner of area to fill
    int nWidth, int nHeight,  // dimensions of area to fill
    DWORD dwRop);             // raster-operation code
```

The first two parameters specify the upper-left corner of the rectangular area that is to be painted, and the second two parameters specify the width and height of this area. All four of these parameters are in logical units.

> **NOTE** Specifying a raster-operation code when calling a bit-operation function is similar to setting the drawing mode, as explained in Chapter 16. The drawing mode, however, affects lines and the interiors of closed figures created using drawing commands; it does not affect the outcome of the bit-operations discussed here.

The last parameter, dwRop, is the *raster-operation code*. The raster-operation code is what gives PatBlt (as well as the other bit-operation functions) its versatility; it specifies the way that each pixel within the pattern is combined with the current pixel at the destination location, to derive the final destination pixel color. The raster-operation codes that you can pass to PatBlt are listed in Table 17.1. For each code, this table provides a Boolean expression (using C++ syntax) that describes the resulting color of each pixel within the area that is filled; in these expressions, D refers to the destination pixel and P refers to the pattern pixel.

TABLE 17.1: The Raster-Operation Codes You Can Pass to PatBlt

Raster-Operation Code	Boolean Expression	Description of Result on Destination Area
BLACKNESS	D = 0	Each pixel is set to black
DSTINVERT	D = ~D	The color of each pixel is inverted
PATCOPY	D = P	Each pixel is set to the color of the pattern pixel
PATINVERT	D = D ^ P	The color of each pixel is the result of combining the destination pixel and the pattern pixel using the Boolean XOR operator
WHITENESS	D = 1	Each pixel is set to white

NOTE Windows actually performs the specified raster operation on *each bit* that is used to encode the pixel's color. For a monochrome bitmap, only one bit is used for each pixel; for a color bitmap, however, several bits are used for each pixel. For example, when the color of a pixel is inverted (D = ~D), Windows inverts *each bit* used to encode the color; the exact resulting color depends upon the way that colors are represented by the current device.

For example, the following OnDraw function would paint the entire view window using the current pattern, completely replacing the current window contents:

```
void CProgView::OnDraw(CDC* pDC)
{
    RECT Rect;
    pDC->GetClientRect (&Rect);
```

```
pDC->PatBlt
    (Rect.left,
     Rect.top,
     Rect.right - Rect.left,
     Rect.bottom - Rect.top,
     PATCOPY);
}
```

BitBlt

The CDC member function BitBlt allows you to transfer a block of graphic data from one location to another. The source and destination locations can be within the same device context object, or within different device context objects. BitBlt has the following syntax:

```
BOOL BitBlt
    (int x, int y,              // u-l corner of destination block
     int nWidth, int nHeight,   // dimensions of block
     CDC* pSrcDC,               // source device context object
     int xSrc, int ySrc,        // u-l corner of block within source
     DWORD dwRop);              // raster-operation code
```

The first two parameters specify the upper-left corner of the destination location for the transfer, and the second two parameters specify the dimensions of the block of graphic data that is to be transferred. The fifth parameter (pSrcDC) is a pointer to the source device context object, and the sixth and seventh parameters (xSrc and ySrc) specify the location of the upper-left corner of the block within the source device context object. The last parameter (dwRop) is the raster-operation code. All measurements are in logical units.

BitBlt copies the block of graphic data *from* the device context object indicated by the fifth parameter *to* the device context object used to call the function. For example, the following call transfers a block of graphic data *from* a memory device context object (MemDC) *to* a view window device context object (*pDC):

```
pDC->BitBlt (X, Y, Width, Height, &MemDC, 0, 0, SRCCOPY);
```

When BitBlt paints the destination area, the final color of each pixel depends upon the current pixel color, the color of the corresponding pixel within the source device context object, *and* the color of the corresponding pixel within the current pattern (that is, the brush currently selected into the *destination* device context object). The way that BitBlt combines these color values depends upon the raster-operation code that you assign to the dwRop parameter. Because the raster-operation code passed to BitBlt affects the way the colors from *three* different pixels are combined, there are many more possible codes that you can specify than there are for PatBlt. (The raster-operation code passed to PatBlt affects the way only two pixels are combined.)

In fact, there are 256 different raster-operation codes that you can pass to BitBlt! Some of the most common ones are described in Table 17.2; for a complete list of these codes, see Appendix A in the *Programmer's Reference Volume 3* SDK manual (which is supplied with the Professional Edition of Microsoft Visual C++, and is also available separately from Microsoft). In the Boolean expressions given in Table 17.2, the symbol D refers to the destination pixel, S refers to the source pixel, and P refers to the pattern pixel. As with the PatBlt function, BitBlt performs the specified operation on *each bit* used to encode the pixel's color.

TABLE 17.2: Common Raster-Operation Codes You Can Pass to BitBlt or StretchBlt

Raster-Operation Code	Boolean Expression	Description of Result on Destination Area
MERGECOPY	D = P & S	The color of each pixel is the result of combining the pattern pixel and the source pixel using the Boolean AND operator
MERGEPAINT	D = ~S | D	The color of each pixel is the result of combining the inverted source pixel and the destination pixel using the Boolean OR operator
NOTSRCCOPY	D = ~S	Each pixel is set to the inverse of the source pixel color
NOTSRCERASE	D = ~(D | S)	The color of each pixel is the result of combining the destination pixel and the source pixel using the Boolean OR operator and then inverting the result
PATPAINT	D = ~S | P | D	The color of each pixel is the result of combining the inverse of the source pixel, the pattern pixel, and the destination pixel, using the Boolean OR operator

TABLE 17.2: Common Raster-Operation Codes You Can Pass to `BitBlt` or `StretchBlt` (continued)

Raster-Operation Code	Boolean Expression	Description of Result on Destination Area
SRCAND	D = D & S	The color of each pixel is the result of combining the destination pixel and the source pixel using the Boolean AND operator
SRCCOPY	D = S	Each pixel is set to the color of the source pixel
SRCERASE	D = ~D & S	The color of each pixel is the result of combining the inverse of the destination pixel and the source pixel using the Boolean AND operator
SRCINVERT	D = D ^ S	The color of each pixel is the result of combining the destination pixel and the source pixel using the Boolean XOR operator
SRCPAINT	D = D | S	The color of each pixel is the result of combining the destination pixel and the source pixel using the Boolean OR operator

Using BitBlt for Animation

You already saw how to use `BitBlt`, in conjunction with the `SRCCOPY` raster-operation code, to simply copy a block of graphic data from one device context object to another (see the `DisplayBitmap` function, given in the section "Displaying a Bitmap"). In this section, you will learn how to use several of the other raster-operation codes to perform animation.

When writing games or other types of applications, you sometimes need to move a small drawing across the window (you might move it in response to movements of the mouse, or move it automatically using a Windows timer). If the drawing is rectangular, you can simply call `BitBlt` with the `SRCCOPY` raster-operation code to display a bitmap containing the drawing at each new drawing location in the window. You can also use this method to display the drawing if the window has a uniform background color, regardless of the shape of the drawing. (In the source bitmap, simply paint the area surrounding the drawing using the window background color, so that this portion of the bitmap will be invisible when copied to the window.)

You might, however, need to animate a nonrectangular drawing within a window that contains various colors; an example would be moving a drawing of a chess piece within a window containing a chess board pattern. The problem is that the BitBlt function always transfers a *rectangular* block of graphics, and the pixels surrounding the drawing in the source bitmap would overwrite the existing pixels on the screen (thus, the chess piece would have an undesirable rectangular "aura" around it).

The solution to this problem is to create two source bitmaps: a *mask* bitmap and an *image* bitmap. In the mask bitmap, the drawing is colored black and the background is painted white. In the image bitmap, the drawing is given its normal colors and the background is painted black. Figure 17.1 illustrates mask and image bitmaps for a drawing of a cube.

To display the drawing at a particular location within the window, you use *two* calls to BitBlt. In the first call, you transfer the mask bitmap using the SRCAND raster-operation code, and in the second call, you transfer the image bitmap using the SRCINVERT raster-operation code, as in the following example function:

```
void CProgView::DisplayDrawing (int X, int Y)
{
    CClientDC ClientDC (this);
    CDC MemDC;
    MemDC.CreateCompatibleDC (&ClientDC);
```

FIGURE 17.1:

Mask and image bitmaps for a drawing of a cube

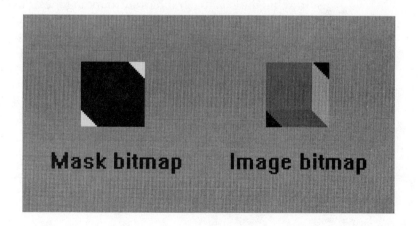

```
// transfer mask bitmap:
MemDC.SelectObject (&mMaskBitmap);
ClientDC.BitBlt
    (X, Y,
    BMWIDTH, BMHEIGHT,
    &MemDC,
    0, 0,
    SRCAND);

// transfer image bitmap:
MemDC.SelectObject (&mImageBitmap);
ClientDC.BitBlt
    (X, Y,
    BMWIDTH, BMHEIGHT,
    &MemDC,
    0, 0,
    SRCINVERT);
}
```

This example assumes that the program has already created and initialized two bitmap objects—mMaskBitmap for the mask bitmap and mImageBitmap for the image bitmap—and that the program has defined the constants BMWIDTH and BMHEIGHT equal to the width and height of these bitmaps.

The first call to BitBlt displays the drawing in black, without disturbing the existing graphics in the window surrounding the drawing. The second call to BitBlt then transfers a colored version of the drawing to the window, again without disturbing the existing graphics surrounding the drawing. The overall result is that a nonrectangular drawing is displayed within the window, and the drawing is surrounded by the existing window graphics. This two-step process is illustrated in Figure 17.2.

FIGURE 17.2:

The two-step process for displaying a nonrectangular drawing over existing background graphics

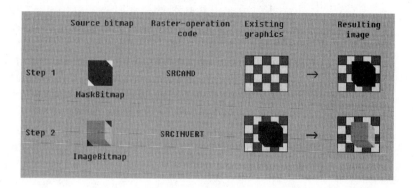

> **NOTE**   In a typical application, you would also need to save and restore the window graphics at each location where you temporarily display the moving drawing. You can do this by using another bitmap, which has the same size as the mask and image bitmaps. You could use BitBlt with the SRCCOPY raster-operation code first to copy the graphics from the screen to this bitmap (before the drawing is displayed), and then to copy the graphics from the bitmap back to the screen (after the drawing is displayed).

StretchBlt

The most versatile of the three bit-operation functions is StretchBlt. StretchBlt allows you to perform all of the operations that are possible using BitBlt; in addition, it permits you to *change the size* of the block of graphic data, or to flip the block (horizontally, vertically, or in both directions) as it is transferred. StretchBlt has the following syntax:

```
BOOL StretchBlt
    (int x, int y,                  // u-l corner of destination block
    int nWidth, int nHeight,        // dimensions of destination block
    CDC* pSrcDC,                    // source device context object
    int xSrc, int ySrc,            // u-l corner of block within source
    int nSrcWidth, int nSrcHeight,  // dimensions of source block
    DWORD dwRop);                   // raster-operation code
```

StretchBlt allows you to specify the size of both the source block *and* the destination block (recall that BitBlt allows you to specify only a single block size). If the destination size (nWidth, nHeight) is smaller than the source size (nSrcWidth, nSrcHeight), the image is compressed; if the destination size is larger than the source size, the image is expanded. If nWidth and nSrcWidth are given different signs (one positive, the other negative), the destination image will be a mirror image—in the horizontal direction—of the source image. Likewise, if nHeight and nSrcHeight are given different signs, the destination image will be a mirror image—in the vertical direction—of the source image. The BITDEMO program, presented later in the chapter, shows how to use StretchBlt to display a bitmap so that it fills the entire view window.

> **TIP**
>
> You can call the CDC member function SetStretchBltMode to fine-tune the way that StretchBlt processes eliminate pixels when a block of graphic data is compressed.

Displaying Icons

An icon is a special form of bitmap. Unlike a standard bitmap, it has a fixed size; on an EGA or VGA system, an icon is 32 pixels by 32 pixels. Also, when you design an icon using App Studio or another icon designer, as an alternative to assigning a specific color to a given pixel, you can assign it the *screen color* or the *inverse screen color*. When Windows displays the icon, the color of the existing pixel at the position of each screen-colored pixel is left unaltered; screen-colored portions of the icon are thus invisible. Likewise, the color of the existing pixel at the position of each inverse screen-colored pixel is inverted; inverse screen-colored portions of the icon are thus visible over almost any colored background.

You have already seen the following two ways for using icons:

- You can create a custom icon for a main program window (Chapter 8), or for a child window in an MDI program (Chapter 12), so that the icon is displayed when the window is minimized.

- You can display an icon within a dialog box (Chapter 13).

This section completes the discussion on icons by describing how to display an icon at any position within a program window.

The first step is to design the icon using App Studio, as explained in Chapter 8. Note that if the icon is assigned the IDR_MAINFRAME identifier, it is automatically assigned to the main frame window and is displayed when this window is minimized. If you do not want the icon you are designing to be assigned to the main frame window, you must give it a different identifier.

> **TIP**
>
> Like a bitmap, rather than designing an icon within App Studio, you can choose the Import... command on the App Studio Resource menu to import an icon from an .ICO file that you have created using another icon-editing program or one that you have obtained from another source.

Before displaying the icon in a program window, you must call the CWinApp member function LoadIcon to load the icon and obtain a handle to it, as in the following code:

```
HICON HIcon;

HIcon = AfxGetApp ()->LoadIcon (IDI_ICON1);
```

In this example, IDC_ICON1 is the identifier you assigned to the icon in App Studio. Notice that the AfxGetApp function is called to obtain a pointer to the program's application object, which is used to call LoadIcon.

> **TIP**
>
> Rather than calling LoadIcon to load a custom icon created in App Studio, you can call the CWinApp member function LoadStandardIcon to obtain a handle to a predefined icon provided by Windows. See the documentation on this function in the *Reference Volume I, Class Library Reference* manual or the *Foundation Classes* online help file for a description of the predefined icons that are available.

Finally, to display the icon within a window, call the CWnd member function DrawIcon:

```
BOOL DrawIcon (int x, int y, HICON hIcon);
```

The parameters x and y specify the coordinates of the upper-left corner of the position where the icon is to be displayed, and the hIcon parameter is the handle to the icon obtained from LoadIcon (or LoadStandardIcon).

As an example, the following function loads and displays an icon, which was created in App Studio, at the center of the view window:

```
void CProgView::DisplayIcon ()
    {
    CClientDC ClientDC (this);
    HICON HIcon;
    int IconHeight;
    int IconWidth;
    RECT Rect;

    HIcon = AfxGetApp ()->LoadIcon (IDI_ICON1);

    GetClientRect (&Rect);
    IconWidth = ::GetSystemMetrics (SM_CXICON);
    IconHeight = ::GetSystemMetrics (SM_CYICON);
    ClientDC.DrawIcon
        (Rect.right / 2 - IconWidth / 2,
        Rect.bottom / 2 - IconHeight / 2,
        HIcon);
    }
```

Notice that this function calls the Windows API function GetSystemMetrics to obtain the dimensions of the icon for the current video mode; this information is used to calculate the position of the icon's upper-left corner.

NOTE When you call the LoadIcon function, the mapping mode of the device context object must be set to the default MM_TEXT mode.

The BITDEMO Program

In this section, you will create a program named BITDEMO, which illustrates the techniques for designing a bitmap in App Studio and for displaying a bitmap in the view window. The BITDEMO program displays a checkerboard, which fills the view window. As you change the size of the window, the checkerboard pattern is stretched or compressed as necessary so that it always completely fills the window (see Figure 17.3).

Use AppWizard to generate the BITDEMO program source files, assigning the project name BITDEMO and choosing only the Generate Source Comments option in the AppWizard Options dialog box.

FIGURE 17.3:

The BITDEMO program window, showing that the checkerboard pattern always fills the window regardless of the window's size or proportions

Designing the Bitmap

Once the source files have been generated, begin by running App Studio so that you can design the bitmap that the program displays. In the App Studio resource dialog box, click the New... button, select the Bitmap item in the New Resource dialog box, and click OK. App Studio will open the bitmap-designing window (labeled "IDB_BIT-MAP1 (Bitmap)"). Now use the App Studio tools and commands to create the bitmap pattern, as described in Chapter 14 (in the section "Designing the Tool Bar Buttons"). The bitmap that was designed for the version of BITDEMO on the companion disk is shown in Figure 17.4. Be sure to accept the default bitmap identifier, `IDB_BITMAP1`.

> **TIP**
>
> When you design the bitmap, you will probably want to remove the tile grid (which you used for marking the positions of individual buttons when you designed the tool bar buttons in Chapter 14). Removing the tile grid will allow you to change the size of the bitmap in increments of a single pixel. To remove it, choose the Grid Settings... command on the Image menu and uncheck the Tile Grid option in the Grid Settings dialog box.

As an alternative method, you can design the bitmap in Windows Paintbrush or in any other drawing program that saves drawings in bitmap format. When you have completed the drawing, save it in a .BMP file and return to App Studio. You can then import the bitmap into App Studio by choosing the Import... command on the Resource menu and selecting the name of the .BMP file in which you saved the bitmap. Whether you create the bitmap in App Studio or import it from a file, make sure that it has the identifier `IDB_BITMAP1`.

Modifying the Code

To display the bitmap, you need to modify the program's view class. In BIT-DEVW.H, define the following data members at the end of the `CBitdemoView` class definition:

```
// new data members:
protected:
```

The **IDB_BITMAP**1 bitmap as it appears in App Studio

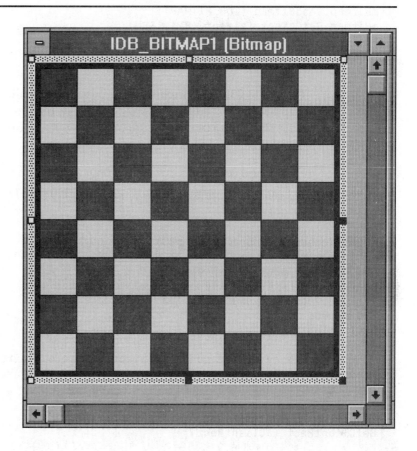

```
CBitmap mBitmap;
int mBitmapHeight;
int mBitmapWidth;
```

mBitmap is the bitmap object, while mBitmapHeight and mBitmapWidth store the dimensions of the bitmap. Next, in BITDEVW.CPP, initialize these data members within the class constructor, as follows:

```
CBitdemoView::CBitdemoView()
{
    // TODO: add construction code here
    BITMAP BM;
```

```
mBitmap.LoadBitmap (IDB_BITMAP1);
mBitmap.GetObject (sizeof (BM), &BM);
mBitmapWidth = BM.bmWidth;
mBitmapHeight = BM.bmHeight;
}
```

The call to CBitmap::LoadBitmap initializes the bitmap object by loading the bitmap pattern you created in App Studio. The dimensions of the bitmap are then obtained by calling CBitmap::GetObject, which returns information on the selected bitmap.

Finally, add code as follows to the OnDraw function to display the bitmap:

```
////////////////////////////////////////////////////////////////////////////
// CBitdemoView drawing

void CBitdemoView::OnDraw(CDC* pDC)
{
    CBitdemoDoc* pDoc = GetDocument();

    // TODO: add draw code here
    CDC MemDC;
    RECT ClientRect;

    // create memory device context object and select bitmap object into it:
    MemDC.CreateCompatibleDC (NULL);
    MemDC.SelectObject (&mBitmap);

    // get current dimensions of view window:
    GetClientRect (&ClientRect);

    // display bitmap, stretching it to fit view window:
    pDC->StretchBlt
        (0,                     // coordinates of u-l corner of destination rectangle
         0,
         ClientRect.right,      // width of destination rectangle
         ClientRect.bottom,     // height of destination rectangle
         &MemDC,                // source device context object
         0,                     // coordinates of u-l corner of source rectangle
         0,
         mBitmapWidth,          // width of source rectangle
         mBitmapHeight,         // height of source rectangle
         SRCCOPY);              // raster-operation code
}
```

OnDraw displays the bitmap in the same way as the example function `DisplayBit-map`, given previously in the chapter (in the section "Displaying a Bitmap"). However, rather than using `BitBlt` to transfer the bitmap in its original size, it uses `StretchBlt` to copy the bitmap to the view window and to compress or expand the bitmap as necessary so that it fits exactly within the window.

The BITDEMO Source Code

Listings 17.1 through 17.8 contain the C++ source code for the BITDEMO program. A copy of these files can be found in the \BITDEMO companion disk directory.

Listing 17.1

```
// bitdemo.h : main header file for the BITDEMO application
//

#ifndef __AFXWIN_H__
    #error include 'stdafx.h' before including this file for PCH
#endif

#include "resource.h"        // main symbols

/////////////////////////////////////////////////////////////////////////////
// CBitdemoApp:
// See bitdemo.cpp for the implementation of this class
//

class CBitdemoApp : public CWinApp
{
public:
    CBitdemoApp();

// Overrides
    virtual BOOL InitInstance();

// Implementation

    //{{AFX_MSG(CBitdemoApp)
    afx_msg void OnAppAbout();
        // NOTE - the ClassWizard will add and remove member functions here.
        //    DO NOT EDIT what you see in these blocks of generated code !
```

```
    //}}AFX_MSG
    DECLARE_MESSAGE_MAP()
};
```

//

Listing 17.2

```
// bitdemo.cpp : Defines the class behaviors for the application.
//

#include "stdafx.h"
#include "bitdemo.h"

#include "mainfrm.h"
#include "bitdedoc.h"
#include "bitdevw.h"

#ifdef _DEBUG
#undef THIS_FILE
static char BASED_CODE THIS_FILE[] = __FILE__;
#endif

//////////////////////////////////////////////////////////////////////
// CBitdemoApp

BEGIN_MESSAGE_MAP(CBitdemoApp, CWinApp)
    //{{AFX_MSG_MAP(CBitdemoApp)
    ON_COMMAND(ID_APP_ABOUT, OnAppAbout)
        // NOTE - the ClassWizard will add and remove mapping macros here.
        //    DO NOT EDIT what you see in these blocks of generated code !
    //}}AFX_MSG_MAP
    // Standard file based document commands
    ON_COMMAND(ID_FILE_NEW, CWinApp::OnFileNew)
    ON_COMMAND(ID_FILE_OPEN, CWinApp::OnFileOpen)
END_MESSAGE_MAP()

//////////////////////////////////////////////////////////////////////
// CBitdemoApp construction

CBitdemoApp::CBitdemoApp()
{
    // TODO: add construction code here,
    // Place all significant initialization in InitInstance
}
```

```
///////////////////////////////////////////////////////////////////////
// The one and only CBitdemoApp object

CBitdemoApp NEAR theApp;

///////////////////////////////////////////////////////////////////////
// CBitdemoApp initialization

BOOL CBitdemoApp::InitInstance()
{
   // Standard initialization
   // If you are not using these features and wish to reduce the size
   //  of your final executable, you should remove from the following
   //  the specific initialization routines you do not need.

   SetDialogBkColor();        // set dialog background color to gray
   LoadStdProfileSettings();  // Load standard INI file options (including MRU)

   // Register the application's document templates.  Document templates
   //  serve as the connection between documents, frame windows and views.

   AddDocTemplate(new CSingleDocTemplate(IDR_MAINFRAME,
         RUNTIME_CLASS(CBitdemoDoc),
         RUNTIME_CLASS(CMainFrame),      // main SDI frame window
         RUNTIME_CLASS(CBitdemoView)));

   // create a new (empty) document
   OnFileNew();

   if (m_lpCmdLine[0] != '\0')
   {
      // TODO: add command line processing here
   }

   return TRUE;
}

///////////////////////////////////////////////////////////////////////
// CAboutDlg dialog used for App About

class CAboutDlg : public CDialog
{
public:
   CAboutDlg();
```

```
// Dialog Data
   //{{AFX_DATA(CAboutDlg)
   enum { IDD = IDD_ABOUTBOX };
   //}}AFX_DATA

// Implementation
protected:
   virtual void DoDataExchange(CDataExchange* pDX);    // DDX/DDV support
   //{{AFX_MSG(CAboutDlg)
      // No message handlers
   //}}AFX_MSG
   DECLARE_MESSAGE_MAP()
};

CAboutDlg::CAboutDlg() : CDialog(CAboutDlg::IDD)
{
   //{{AFX_DATA_INIT(CAboutDlg)
   //}}AFX_DATA_INIT
}

void CAboutDlg::DoDataExchange(CDataExchange* pDX)
{
   CDialog::DoDataExchange(pDX);
   //{{AFX_DATA_MAP(CAboutDlg)
   //}}AFX_DATA_MAP
}

BEGIN_MESSAGE_MAP(CAboutDlg, CDialog)
   //{{AFX_MSG_MAP(CAboutDlg)
      // No message handlers
   //}}AFX_MSG_MAP
END_MESSAGE_MAP()

// App command to run the dialog
void CBitdemoApp::OnAppAbout()
{
   CAboutDlg aboutDlg;
   aboutDlg.DoModal();
}

/////////////////////////////////////////////////////////////////////////
// CBitdemoApp commands
```

Listing 17.3

```
// bitdedoc.h : interface of the CBitdemoDoc class
//
/////////////////////////////////////////////////////////////////////////////

class CBitdemoDoc : public CDocument
{
protected: // create from serialization only
    CBitdemoDoc();
    DECLARE_DYNCREATE(CBitdemoDoc)

// Attributes
public:

// Operations
public:

// Implementation
public:
    virtual ~CBitdemoDoc();
    virtual void Serialize(CArchive& ar);   // overridden for document i/o
#ifdef _DEBUG
    virtual  void AssertValid() const;
    virtual  void Dump(CDumpContext& dc) const;
#endif
protected:
    virtual  BOOL  OnNewDocument();

// Generated message map functions
protected:
    //{{AFX_MSG(CBitdemoDoc)
        // NOTE - the ClassWizard will add and remove member functions here.
        //     DO NOT EDIT what you see in these blocks of generated code !
    //}}AFX_MSG
    DECLARE_MESSAGE_MAP()
};


/////////////////////////////////////////////////////////////////////////////
```

Listing 17.4

```
// bitdedoc.cpp : implementation of the CBitdemoDoc class
//
```

```
#include "stdafx.h"
#include "bitdemo.h"

#include "bitdedoc.h"

#ifdef _DEBUG
#undef THIS_FILE
static char BASED_CODE THIS_FILE[] = __FILE__;
#endif

/////////////////////////////////////////////////////////////////////////
// CBitdemoDoc

IMPLEMENT_DYNCREATE(CBitdemoDoc, CDocument)

BEGIN_MESSAGE_MAP(CBitdemoDoc, CDocument)
    //{{AFX_MSG_MAP(CBitdemoDoc)
        // NOTE - the ClassWizard will add and remove mapping macros here.
        //     DO NOT EDIT what you see in these blocks of generated code !
    //}}AFX_MSG_MAP
END_MESSAGE_MAP()

/////////////////////////////////////////////////////////////////////////
// CBitdemoDoc construction/destruction

CBitdemoDoc::CBitdemoDoc()
{
    // TODO: add one-time construction code here
}

CBitdemoDoc::~CBitdemoDoc()
{
}

BOOL CBitdemoDoc::OnNewDocument()
{
    if (!CDocument::OnNewDocument())
        return FALSE;
    // TODO: add reinitialization code here
    // (SDI documents will reuse this document)
    return TRUE;
}
```

```
///////////////////////////////////////////////////////////////////////
// CBitdemoDoc serialization

void CBitdemoDoc::Serialize(CArchive& ar)
{
    if (ar.IsStoring())
    {
        // TODO: add storing code here
    }
    else
    {
        // TODO: add loading code here
    }
}


///////////////////////////////////////////////////////////////////////
// CBitdemoDoc diagnostics

#ifdef _DEBUG
void CBitdemoDoc::AssertValid() const
{
    CDocument::AssertValid();
}

void CBitdemoDoc::Dump(CDumpContext& dc) const
{
    CDocument::Dump(dc);
}

#endif //_DEBUG

///////////////////////////////////////////////////////////////////////
// CBitdemoDoc commands
```

Listing 17.5

```
// mainfrm.h : interface of the CMainFrame class
//
///////////////////////////////////////////////////////////////////////

class CMainFrame : public CFrameWnd
{
protected: // create from serialization only
    CMainFrame();
    DECLARE_DYNCREATE(CMainFrame)
```

```
// Attributes
public:

// Operations
public:

// Implementation
public:
    virtual ~CMainFrame();
#ifdef _DEBUG
    virtual  void AssertValid() const;
    virtual  void Dump(CDumpContext& dc) const;
#endif


// Generated message map functions
protected:
    //{{AFX_MSG(CMainFrame)
        // NOTE - the ClassWizard will add and remove member functions here.
        //    DO NOT EDIT what you see in these blocks of generated code !
    //}}AFX_MSG
    DECLARE_MESSAGE_MAP()
};
```

//

Listing 17.6

```
// mainfrm.cpp : implementation of the CMainFrame class
//

#include "stdafx.h"
#include "bitdemo.h"

#include "mainfrm.h"

#ifdef _DEBUG
#undef THIS_FILE
static char BASED_CODE THIS_FILE[] = __FILE__;
#endif

////////////////////////////////////////////////////////////////////////
// CMainFrame
```

```
IMPLEMENT_DYNCREATE(CMainFrame, CFrameWnd)

BEGIN_MESSAGE_MAP(CMainFrame, CFrameWnd)
    //{{AFX_MSG_MAP(CMainFrame)
        // NOTE - the ClassWizard will add and remove mapping macros here.
        //     DO NOT EDIT what you see in these blocks of generated code !
    //}}AFX_MSG_MAP
END_MESSAGE_MAP()

/////////////////////////////////////////////////////////////////////////////
// CMainFrame construction/destruction

CMainFrame::CMainFrame()
{
    // TODO: add member initialization code here
}

CMainFrame::~CMainFrame()
{
}

/////////////////////////////////////////////////////////////////////////////
// CMainFrame diagnostics

#ifdef _DEBUG
void CMainFrame::AssertValid() const
{
    CFrameWnd::AssertValid();
}

void CMainFrame::Dump(CDumpContext& dc) const
{
    CFrameWnd::Dump(dc);
}

#endif //_DEBUG

/////////////////////////////////////////////////////////////////////////////
// CMainFrame message handlers
```

Listing 17.7

```
// bitdevw.h : interface of the CBitdemoView class
//
/////////////////////////////////////////////////////////////////////////////
```

```
class CBitdemoView : public CView
{
protected: // create from serialization only
    CBitdemoView();
    DECLARE_DYNCREATE(CBitdemoView)

// Attributes
public:
    CBitdemoDoc* GetDocument();

// Operations
public:

// Implementation
public:
    virtual ~CBitdemoView();
    virtual void OnDraw(CDC* pDC);  // overridden to draw this view
#ifdef _DEBUG
    virtual void AssertValid() const;
    virtual void Dump(CDumpContext& dc) const;
#endif

// Generated message map functions
protected:
    //{{AFX_MSG(CBitdemoView)
        // NOTE - the ClassWizard will add and remove member functions here.
        //    DO NOT EDIT what you see in these blocks of generated code !
    //}}AFX_MSG
    DECLARE_MESSAGE_MAP()

// new data members:
protected:
    CBitmap mBitmap;
    int mBitmapHeight;
    int mBitmapWidth;
};

#ifndef _DEBUG // debug version in bitdevw.cpp
inline CBitdemoDoc* CBitdemoView::GetDocument()
    { return (CBitdemoDoc*) m_pDocument; }
#endif

/////////////////////////////////////////////////////////////////////////////
```

Listing 17.8

```cpp
// bitdevw.cpp : implementation of the CBitdemoView class
//

#include "stdafx.h"
#include "bitdemo.h"

#include "bitdedoc.h"
#include "bitdevw.h"

#ifdef _DEBUG
#undef THIS_FILE
static char BASED_CODE THIS_FILE[] = __FILE__;
#endif

/////////////////////////////////////////////////////////////////////////////
// CBitdemoView

IMPLEMENT_DYNCREATE(CBitdemoView, CView)

BEGIN_MESSAGE_MAP(CBitdemoView, CView)
    //{{AFX_MSG_MAP(CBitdemoView)
        // NOTE - the ClassWizard will add and remove mapping macros here.
        //    DO NOT EDIT what you see in these blocks of generated code !
    //}}AFX_MSG_MAP
END_MESSAGE_MAP()

/////////////////////////////////////////////////////////////////////////////
// CBitdemoView construction/destruction

CBitdemoView::CBitdemoView()
{
    // TODO: add construction code here
    BITMAP BM;

    mBitmap.LoadBitmap (IDB_BITMAP1);
    mBitmap.GetObject (sizeof (BM), &BM);
    mBitmapWidth = BM.bmWidth;
    mBitmapHeight = BM.bmHeight;
}

CBitdemoView::~CBitdemoView()
{
}
```

```
/////////////////////////////////////////////////////////////////////////////
// CBitdemoView drawing

void CBitdemoView::OnDraw(CDC* pDC)
{
    CBitdemoDoc* pDoc = GetDocument();

    // TODO: add draw code here
    CDC MemDC;
    RECT ClientRect;

    // create memory device context object and select bitmap object into it:
    MemDC.CreateCompatibleDC (NULL);
    MemDC.SelectObject (&mBitmap);

    // get current dimensions of view window:
    GetClientRect (&ClientRect);

    // display bitmap, stretching it to fit view window:
    pDC->StretchBlt
        (0,                 // coordinates of u-l corner of destination rectangle
         0,
         ClientRect.right,  // width of destination rectangle
         ClientRect.bottom, // height of destination rectangle
         &MemDC,            // source device context object
         0,                 // coordinates of u-l corner of source rectangle
         0,
         mBitmapWidth,      // width of source rectangle
         mBitmapHeight,     // height of source rectangle
         SRCCOPY);          // raster-operation code
}


/////////////////////////////////////////////////////////////////////////////
// CBitdemoView diagnostics

#ifdef _DEBUG
void CBitdemoView::AssertValid() const
{
    CView::AssertValid();
}

void CBitdemoView::Dump(CDumpContext& dc) const
{
```

```
    CView::Dump(dc);
}

CBitdemoDoc* CBitdemoView::GetDocument() // non-debug version is inline
{
    ASSERT(m_pDocument->IsKindOf(RUNTIME_CLASS(CBitdemoDoc)));
    return (CBitdemoDoc*) m_pDocument;
}

#endif //_DEBUG

///////////////////////////////////////////////////////////////////////////////
// CBitdemoView message handlers
```

Summary

In this chapter, you learned how to create and display bitmaps, as well as how to use bit-operation functions to transfer and manipulate blocks of graphic data. This chapter completes the discussion on the basic methods for displaying textual and graphic data within program windows. The following is a summary of some of the important concepts and methods discussed in the chapter:

- A bitmap stores an exact representation of an image by recording the state of every pixel used to create the image on a particular device.

- To create a bitmap, you first declare an instance of the MFC CBitmap class, and then call a CBitmap member function to initialize the object.

- You can initialize a bitmap object by calling CBitmap::LoadBitmap to load the bitmap data from a program resource. To use this method, you must have designed the bitmap in App Studio (or used App Studio to import the bitmap from a .BMP file you created with another drawing program).

- Alternatively, you can initialize a blank bitmap by calling the CBitmap::CreateCompatibleBitmap function, specifying the desired bitmap size. You can then draw the desired image within this bitmap by selecting the bitmap object into a memory device context object, and then using any of the drawing functions provided by the CDC class.

- You can display a bitmap within a window or on another device by selecting the bitmap into a memory device context object, and then using the CDC::BitBlt function to transfer the data from the memory device context object to a device context object for the window or other device.

- You can call the CDC::PatBlt function to paint a rectangular area using the current pattern (that is, the brush currently selected into the device context object). You pass PatBlt a raster-operation code that specifies the way the pixels in the pattern are to be combined with the pixels in the destination area.

- You can call the CDC::BitBlt function to transfer a block of graphics from one location to another location that is in the same or in a different device context object. The raster-operation code you pass to BitBlt specifies the way that the pixels within the source device context object, within the current pattern, and within the destination device context object are to be combined.

- The CDC::StretchBlt function provides all of the features of the BitBlt function, and additionally allows you to change the size of the block of graphics, or to flip the block, as it is transferred.

Printing and Print Previewing

18

- Basic printing and print previewing

- Advanced printing

- The MINIDRAW source code

In this chapter, you will learn how to print text and graphics, as well as how to provide a print preview feature that allows the user to view the printed appearance of a document before sending it to the printer. Specifically, you will learn how to implement the standard Print..., Print Preview, and Print Setup... commands on the program's File menu. Fortunately, because of Window's device-independent output model, you can use the techniques you have already learned for displaying text and graphics on the printer. The chapter focuses on the tasks that are unique to printing—selecting and setting up the printer, dividing the document into pages, and performing other steps necessary for managing a print job.

The chapter first explains how to provide basic printing support, which allows the program to print or preview a single page. It then presents the more advanced techniques required to print or preview all the pages of a document that does not fit on a single page. To illustrate the techniques, the chapter shows you how to add printing and print-previewing support to the MINIDRAW example program.

Basic Printing and Print Previewing

When you generate a new program using AppWizard, you can include basic printing and print-previewing support in the program by selecting the Printing and Print Preview item in the AppWizard Options dialog box. Selecting this option adds Print..., Print Preview, and Print Setup... commands to the program's File menu. As it is implemented by AppWizard, the Print... command prints as much of the document as will fit on a single page (any portion of the document that does not fit on a single page is ignored). Likewise, the Print Preview command displays the printed appearance of a single document page. As you will see, both the Print... command and the Print Preview command call your OnDraw function to generate the actual text and graphics output. The Print Setup... command displays the Print Setup common dialog box, which allows the user to select a printer and to specify printer settings.

In this section, you will add each of these printing features to the MINIDRAW program. When you finish these steps, the MINIDRAW program will have the same level of printer support that it would have if you had chosen the Printing and Print Preview option when you first generated the program using AppWizard. You will add each feature to the version of MINIDRAW you created in Chapter 16. (If you did not create this version, you can obtain a complete copy of the program source files from the \MINIDRW6 companion disk subdirectory.)

NOTE   As discussed in Chapter 8, if you derive the program's view class from the MFC CEditView class (which provides text editing), you do not need to write any code to support printing. You need only include a Print... command on the menu, assigning this command the identifier ID_FILE_PRINT. The CEditView class provides all code needed to print the document text when this command is chosen.

Modifying the Resources

After opening the MINIDRAW project in the Visual Workbench, choose the App Studio command on the Tools menu to edit the program resources. In App Studio, first open the menu-designing window for the IDR_MAINFRAME menu. Immediately below the existing Save As command on the File menu, add a separator, a Print... command, a Print Preview command, and a Print Setup... command. The properties of each of these menu items are shown in Table 18.1, and the completed File menu is shown in Figure 18.1.

TABLE 18.1: The Properties of the New File Menu Items

ID:	Caption:	Prompt:	Other Features
none	none	none	Separator
ID_FILE_PRINT	&Print...\tCtrl+P	Print the document	none
ID_FILE_PRINT_PREVIEW	Print Pre&view	Display full pages	none
ID_FILE_PRINT_SETUP	P&rint Setup...	Change the printer and printing options	none

FIGURE 18.1:

The completed File menu

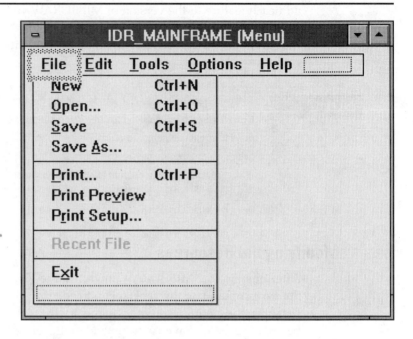

Next, open the accelerator dialog box for the IDR_MAINFRAME accelerator table to define the accelerator keystroke for the Print... command (Ctrl+P). Click the New button to open the properties dialog box, and then enter the identifier ID_FILE_PRINT and specify the keystroke Ctrl+P.

You now need to include some additional predefined resources in the MINIDRAW resource definition file. To do this, choose the Set Includes... command on the App Studio File menu. In the Set Includes dialog box, add the following line to the text within the Compile-Time Directives: text box:

```
#include "afxprint.rc"
```

The completed Set Includes dialog box is shown in Figure 18.2. Adding this new line causes the resource compiler to include the resource definitions that are contained in the resource script AFXPRINT.RC, which is provided by Visual C++. This script defines several resources that are used to support the program's Print and Print Preview commands (such as the Printing dialog box that is displayed while printing is in progress).

You can now save your work in App Studio and return to the Visual Workbench.

FIGURE 18.2:

The completed Set Includes dialog box

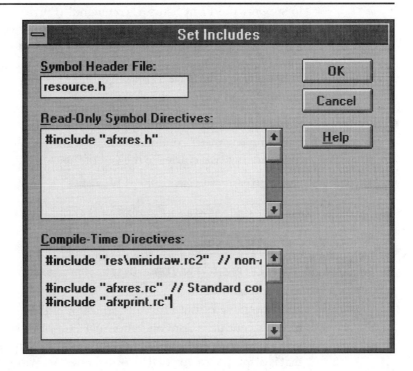

Modifying the Code

First, open the MINIDRAW.CPP file and add the following entry to the end of the message map belonging to the program's application class:

```
BEGIN_MESSAGE_MAP(CMinidrawApp, CWinApp)

    // other message map entries ...

    // Standard print setup command
    ON_COMMAND(ID_FILE_PRINT_SETUP, CWinApp::OnFilePrintSetup)
END_MESSAGE_MAP()
```

The new message-map entry causes the CWinApp::OnFilePrintSetup function to be called whenever the user chooses the Print Setup... command. OnFilePrint-Setup displays the Print Setup common dialog box, which allows the user to choose a printer and to set a variety of printing options. This is all you need to do to support the Print Setup... command! (Previously, ClassWizard automatically added the required message-map entry whenever you used ClassWizard to define a new message-handling function. In the present case, however, you do not use ClassWizard because you are merely activating a predefined message-handling function in a base class, rather than defining a new function. You must therefore manually add the required message-map entry.)

Similarly, you need to add message-map entries for processing the Print... and Print Preview menu commands. To do this, open the MINIDVW.CPP file and enter the following two entries to the end of the message map for the view class:

```
BEGIN_MESSAGE_MAP(CMinidrawView, CScrollView)

    // other message map entries ...

    // Standard printing commands
    ON_COMMAND(ID_FILE_PRINT, CView::OnFilePrint)
    ON_COMMAND(ID_FILE_PRINT_PREVIEW, CView::OnFilePrintPreview)
END_MESSAGE_MAP()
```

Both the CView::OnFilePrint function and the CView::OnFilePrintPreview function conduct a print operation; OnFilePrint, however, sends the output to the printer, while OnFilePrintPreview sends the output to a print preview window that is displayed on top of the normal program window. In the course of conducting the print job, these functions call a series of virtual functions that are defined within the CView class. These virtual functions provide limited default print processing. As you will see later in the chapter, you can define overriding versions of one or more of these functions to enhance the printing capabilities of the program. To provide basic printing and print-previewing support, however, you need to override only the OnPreparePrinting virtual function. To do this, include the following On-PreparePrinting declaration in the protected section of the CMinidrawView class definition in MINIDVW.H:

```
virtual BOOL OnPreparePrinting (CPrintInfo* pInfo);
```

Then, add the following function definition to the end of the MINIDVW.CPP file:

```
BOOL CMinidrawView::OnPreparePrinting(CPrintInfo* pInfo)
{
    return DoPreparePrinting(pInfo);
}
```

If the document is being *previewed*, DoPreparePrinting creates a device context object that is associated with the current default Windows printer and that is assigned the default printer settings. If, however, the document is being *printed*, DoPreparePrinting first displays the Print common dialog box, which allows the user to set several printing options and to choose a specific printer; it then creates a device context object that is associated with the chosen printer and is assigned the selected printer settings. This device context object is then used for printing or previewing the document. Note that you *must* provide an OnPreparePrinting function, because the default version of this function does *nothing* and would therefore cause the MFC to attempt to print or preview the document without a valid device context object.

> **NOTE**
> A CPrintInfo object is passed to all of the virtual printing functions. It contains information on the print job and is used by the virtual functions for both obtaining and changing print settings. For instance, if you know the number of printed pages in the document, you should call the CPrintInfo::SetMaxPage function from your OnPreparePrinting function (*before* the call to DoPreparePrinting); this number will then be displayed in the Print dialog box (in the To: text box).

After the MFC prepares the device context object for the printer, it calls the OnDraw member function of the view class, passing it the *printer* device context object rather than a device context object for the view window. Consequently, the graphics output appears on the printed page—or in the print preview window—rather than within the view window. This technique works because the OnDraw function and the CDC member functions that it calls are device-independent.

You can now build and run the new version of the MINIDRAW program. If you choose the Print Setup... command on the program's File menu, the Print Setup dialog box is displayed (see Figure 18.3), which allows you to choose a printer and specify print settings. If you choose the Print... command, the program opens the Print dialog box (see Figure 18.4). In the Print dialog box, you can choose several print options, and if you click the OK button, the program will proceed to print the drawing. If you click the Setup... button in the Print dialog box, the program will

FIGURE 18.3:

The Print Setup dialog box

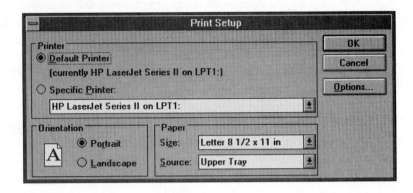

FIGURE 18.4:

The Print dialog box

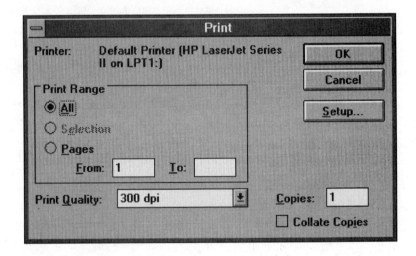

display the Print Setup dialog box (the same dialog box activated by the Print Setup... menu command), which allows you to choose an alternate printer or specify additional print settings immediately before printing the drawing. If the drawing is not printed too quickly, you will see a Printing dialog box while the drawing is being printed; you can click the Cancel button in this dialog box to stop the print job. (If you do this before the Windows Print Manager begins to send output to the printer, nothing will be printed.)

Finally, if you choose the Print Preview menu command, the program displays the print preview window (see Figure 18.5), which contains an image of the entire printed page, scaled to fit within the program window. The print preview window allows you to judge the appearance of the page layout, although it does not permit editing the drawing. (To edit, you must click the Close button to return to the normal view window.)

FIGURE 18.5:

The print preview window

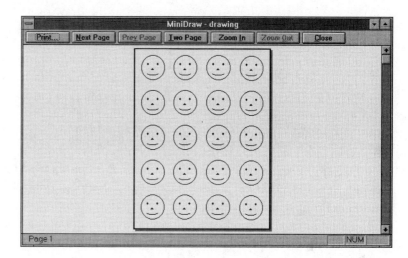

Advanced Printing

With the printing support that you have added so far, MINIDRAW prints or previews only the portion of the drawing that fits on a single printed page; the portion of the drawing (if any) that does not fit on this page is ignored. In this section, you will enhance the program so that it will always print the entire drawing; any parts of the drawing that do not fit on a single page will be printed on additional pages. As you will see, this enhancement is accomplished by overriding several other virtual print functions that are called during the print job.

Also, the current version of the OnDraw function always prints a border at the right and bottom of the drawing. This border, however, serves only to mark the boundaries of the drawing within the view window; it should *not* appear on the printed copy of the drawing. In this section, you will modify the OnDraw command so that it prints the borders only if the output is being sent to the view window.

Changing the Drawing Size

Recall from Chapter 11 that the MINIDRAW program sets the drawing size to 640 by 480 pixels. For most printers, a drawing of this size easily fits on a single page. To demonstrate the techniques for printing multiple pages, you should first modify the MINIDRAW program so that the drawing is *larger* than the typical size of a printed page. To do this, first define constant integers for the drawing width and height, at the beginning of the MINIDVW.H file, as follows:

```
// minidvw.h : interface of the CMinidrawView class
//
/////////////////////////////////////////////////////////////////////////////

const int DRAWWIDTH  = 4000;  // drawing width
const int DRAWHEIGHT = 6000;  // drawing height
```

Then, in the OnInitialUpdate function in the MINIDVW.H file, use these constants rather than the numeric values (640 and 480):

```
void CMinidrawView::OnInitialUpdate ()
    {
    SIZE Size = {DRAWWIDTH, DRAWHEIGHT};
    SetScrollSizes (MM_TEXT, Size);
    CScrollView::OnInitialUpdate ();
    }
```

Using the constants DRAWHEIGHT and DRAWWIDTH rather than fixed numeric values will make it easy to change the size of the drawing if desired (you will use the drawing size in several additional places in the code). The OnInitialUpdate function was explained in Chapter 11 (in the section "Limiting the Drawing Size").

Because you changed the drawing size, you should also change the version number used for serializing the document, so that the user cannot inadvertently read a file created by a previous version (or—when using a previous version of the program—try to read a file created by the current version). To do this, open the file MINID-DOC.CPP and change the version number from 2 to 3 in each occurrence of the

IMPLEMENT_SERIAL macro (you should find eight occurrences). For example, you should change the macro

```
IMPLEMENT_SERIAL (CFigure, CObject, 2)
```

to

```
IMPLEMENT_SERIAL (CFigure, CObject, 3)
```

Version numbers were explained in Chapter 10 (in the section "Serializing the Document Data").

> **NOTE** A full-featured drawing program would probably allow the user to set the size of each drawing, perhaps through a command on the program's Options menu. The drawing size would have to be saved on disk along with the data for the individual figures.

Overriding Virtual Printing Functions

As mentioned, when the MFC prints or previews a document, it calls a series of virtual functions defined within the CView class to perform various printing tasks. To enhance the printing process, you can define overriding versions of one or more of these functions within your view class, and can add code to these functions to - perform the desired tasks. Figure 18.6 illustrates the overall printing and print-previewing processes and shows where each of the virtual functions is called within the procedure. Note that the process passes through the loop shown in this figure once for each page that is to be printed.

Table 18.2 lists the virtual functions and describes the tasks that you might perform from each one. For details, see the documentation on each of these functions. Note that because the MFC calls the virtual functions when either printing or previewing a document, the overriding functions you define will affect *both* printing *and* print-previewing.

FIGURE 18.6:

The printing and print-previewing processes, and the CView virtual functions that are called

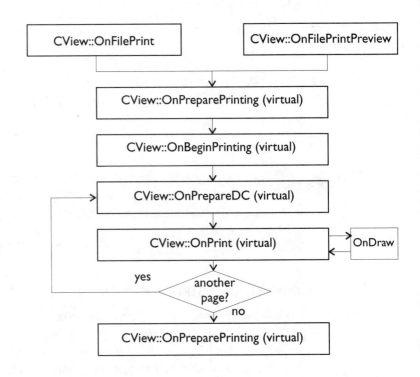

> **NOTE**   If you have written Windows printing code without using the MFC, you will be happy to know that the MFC provides all the code necessary for displaying the Printing dialog box while the document is being printed, which allows the user to cancel the print job. It also provides a function that processes messages during printing, so that the user can issue commands (such as clicking the Cancel button in the Printing dialog box) and can work in other programs; this function is known as an *abort procedure.*

TABLE 18.2: The `CView` Virtual Printing Functions

Function Name	Possible Tasks Performed by Overriding Version of Function
OnPreparePrinting	You *must* override this function and call `DoPreparePrinting` to create device context object; can also call `CPrintInfo::SetMaxPage` to set length of document
OnBeginPrinting	Set length or other features of document based upon device context object that has been created; store any required information on device context object; allocate any fonts, pens, brushes, and other objects used exclusively for printing
OnPrepareDC	Set text or drawing attributes for printing; modify viewport origin to print current page; if document length has *not* been set, terminate print loop at end of document (by assigning `FALSE` to `CPrintInfo::m_bContinuePrinting`)
OnPrint	Call `OnDraw` to perform output; before calling `OnDraw`, select any fonts or other objects allocated by `OnBeginPrinting`; after calling `OnDraw`, deselect objects; print headers or footers (which appear only in *printed* version of document); if printed output looks different from screen output, print it here *rather* than calling `OnDraw`
OnEndPrinting	Delect any objects allocated by `OnBeginPrinting` (by calling `CGdiObject::DeleteObject`)

You have already provided an overriding version of the `OnPreparePrinting` function (which is the only virtual printing function that *must* be overridden). To implement multiple-page printing, you will now define versions of the `OnBeginPrinting` and `OnPrepareDC` virtual functions. Before defining these functions, however, you need to add several data members to the view class. Open the MINIDVW.H file, and add the data member definitions marked in bold to the `CMinidrawView` class definition:

```
protected:
    CString mClassName;
    int mDragging;
    HCURSOR mHArrow;
    HCURSOR mHCross;
    int mNumCols, mNumRows;
    int mPageHeight, mPageWidth;
```

The data members `mNumCols` and `mNumRows` will be used to store the numbers of pages in the horizontal and vertical directions that are required to print the entire drawing, while `mPageHeight` and `mPageWidth` will be used to store the dimensions of the printed page.

Now add declarations for OnBeginPrinting and OnPrepareDC functions to the CMinidrawView definition:

```
protected:

    // other protected members ...

    virtual void OnBeginPrinting (CDC* pDC, CPrintInfo* pInfo);
    virtual void OnInitialUpdate ();
    virtual void OnPrepareDC (CDC* pDC, CPrintInfo* pInfo = NULL);

    // other protected members ...
```

Next, open the MINIDVW.CPP file and add the following definition for OnBeginPrinting to the end of the file:

```
void CMinidrawView::OnBeginPrinting (CDC* pDC, CPrintInfo* pInfo)
    {
    mPageHeight = pDC->GetDeviceCaps (VERTRES);
    mPageWidth = pDC->GetDeviceCaps (HORZRES);

    mNumRows = DRAWHEIGHT / mPageHeight  + (DRAWHEIGHT % mPageHeight > 0);
    mNumCols = DRAWWIDTH / mPageWidth  + (DRAWWIDTH % mPageWidth > 0);
    pInfo->SetMinPage (1);
    pInfo->SetMaxPage (mNumRows * mNumCols);
    }
```

As shown in Figure 18.6, the OnBeginPrinting virtual function is called once at the beginning of the print job, *after* the device context object for the printer has been created but *before* the printing process enters the loop for printing each page. CMinidrawView is the first of the virtual printing functions that has access to the device context object.

The code you added to OnBeginPrinting first uses the device context object to call the CDC member function GetDeviceCaps in order to obtain the dimensions of the printable area of the page. When passed VERTRES, GetDeviceCaps returns the height of the printable area of the page in pixels (which is saved in mPageHeight), and when passed HORZRES, it returns the width of the printable area in pixels (which is saved in mPageWidth).

OnBeginPrinting then uses the dimensions of the printed page and the dimensions of the drawing to calculate the number of pages that will be required to print the entire drawing. First, it calculates the number of pages required in the vertical direction and saves the result in mNumRows; it then calculates the number of pages required in the horizontal direction and saves the result in mNumCols. (Notice that the expressions used to calculate the numbers of pages both use the % operator to round the number of pages *up* to the nearest whole number.) The *total* number of pages required to print the entire drawing is mNumRows * mNumCols.

Finally, OnBeginPrinting reports the total number of pages to the MFC. It calls CPrintInfo::SetMinPage to specify the number of the first page (1), and it calls CPrintInfo::SetMaxPage to specify the number of the last page (mNumRows * mNumCols). The MFC printing code will print the specified number of pages; that is, it will call the OnPrepareDC and OnPrint virtual functions (which are shown in the print loop in Figure 18.6) once for each specified page.

> **NOTE**
>
> In the Print dialog box, the user can specify a limited range of pages *within* the range of pages that you specify using the SetMinPage and SetMaxPage functions; in this case, the MFC prints the limited range. Note, also, that if you do *not* call SetMaxPage to set the maximum number of pages, you must define an OnPrepareDC function (described later), which manually terminates the printing loop by assigning FALSE to CPrintInfo::m_bContinuePrinting when the last page has been printed.

The GetDeviceCaps and Escape Functions

The CDC class provides two useful member functions that you can call to help manage the print job once you have obtained a device context object for the printer: GetDeviceCaps and Escape. Typically, you would call these functions from an OnBeginPrinting, OnPrepareDC, or OnPrint virtual printing function that you have defined, or from the standard OnDraw member function of the view class.

You have already seen how to use GetDeviceCaps to obtain the size of the printable area of the page in *pixels*. Alternatively, you can obtain the width of the printable area in *millimeters* by assigning the index HORZSIZE, and the height in millimeters by assigning VERTSIZE. Note that GetDeviceCaps returns the dimensions of the portion of the page on which you can actually print; because many printers (notably, laser printers) cannot print all the way to the edge of the page, the dimensions returned by GetDeviceCaps are typically smaller than the physical page size.

When you modify the OnDraw function later in the chapter, you will see how to determine the type of device associated with the device context object by passing the index TECHNOLOGY to GetDeviceCaps.

When displaying data in a window, you generally assume that the display device is capable of performing all of the basic drawing and bitmap operations discussed in chapters 16 and 17. A printer or plotter, however, may not support all of these operations. You can call GetDeviceCaps to determine whether the associated printer is capable of supporting the specific operations you want to perform. To determine whether the printer is capable of performing the bitmap operations described in Chapter 17, you can pass Get-DeviceCaps the index RASTERCAPS. If the return code includes the value RC_BITBLT, then the device supports the PatBlt and BitBlt functions; if the return code includes the value RC_STRETCHBLT, then the device supports the StretchBlt function. The following code shows how you would test for bitmap operation capabilities:

```
int Caps;

Caps = pDC->GetDeviceCaps (RASTERCAPS);

if (Caps & RC_BITBLT)
    // then you can call 'PatBlt' or 'BitBlt'

if (Caps & RC_STRETCHBLT)
    // then you can call 'StretchBlt'
```

You can also determine the graphics drawing capabilities of the printer by passing GetDeviceCaps the index CURVECAPS (to determine its curve-drawing capabilities), LINECAPS (to determine its line-drawing capabilities), or POLYGONALCAPS (to determine its capabilities for drawing rectangles and other polygons). For a complete description of the information that is returned when you pass any of these indexes, as well as the information you can obtain by passing other indexes to GetDeviceCaps, see the documentation on GetDeviceCaps in the *Reference Volume I, Class Libraries Reference* manual, or in the *Foundation Classes* online help file.

You can call the general-purpose CDC member function Escape to gain a wide variety of services directly from the device driver for the printer that is associated with the device context object. Escape has the following syntax:

```
int Escape (int nEscape, int nCount, LPSTR lpInData, LPSTR lpOutData);
```

The first parameter, nEscape, is a code indicating the desired service or information. The second parameter, nCount, specifies the size of the data item pointed to by the third parameter. The third parameter, lpInData, is a pointer to a data item that is read by Escape, and the fourth parameter, lpOutData, is a pointer to a data item that is written by Escape.

The exact content of the Escape parameters depends upon the particular service that you request. For example, the following call to Escape causes the printer driver to print the number of copies specified by the third parameter (6); the printer driver writes the actual number of copies that it will print to the fourth parameter. (This value will be less that the requested number of copies if the requested number exceeds the printer's limit.)

```
int ActualCopies;
int NumCopies = 6;

pDC->Escape (SETCOPYCOUNT, sizeof (int), (LPSTR)&NumCopies, (LPSTR)&Actual-
Copies);
```

If the Escape function is successful, it returns a value greater than 0. If the service requested is not supported by the printer associated with the CDC object, Escape returns 0. If an error occurs, Escape returns a value less than 0. For a description of the different Escape calls you can make, see Chapter 5 of the *Programmer's Reference Volume 3* SDK manual (included with the Professional Edition of Visual C++, and available separately from Microsoft), or the *Windows 3.1 SDK* help file (the topic "Printer escapes").

You should now add the following definition for the OnPrepareDC function to the end of the MINIDVW.CPP file:

```
void CMinidrawView::OnPrepareDC (CDC* pDC, CPrintInfo* pInfo)
    {
    CScrollView::OnPrepareDC (pDC, pInfo);

    if (pInfo == NULL)
        return;

    int CurRow = pInfo->m_nCurPage / mNumCols +
                 (pInfo->m_nCurPage % mNumCols > 0);
    int CurCol = (pInfo->m_nCurPage - 1) % mNumCols + 1;

    pDC->SetViewportOrg
        (-mPageWidth * (CurCol - 1),
         -mPageHeight * (CurRow - 1));
    }
```

The added code first calls the base class version of the function, CScrollView::OnPrepareDC, to perform default processing. As you can see in Figure 18.6, the MFC calls OnPrepareDC before printing each page in the document, and its primary duty is to prepare the device context object for printing the current page. As explained in Chapter 11, the MFC *also* calls OnPrepareDC immediately before calling OnDraw to redraw the view window; in this case, its duty is to adjust the viewport origin for the current scrolled position of the document (provided that the view class is derived from CScrollView and therefore supports scrolling).

If OnPrepareDC has been called prior to redrawing the view window, pInfo will equal NULL; in this case, OnPrepareDC simply calls CScrollView::OnPrepareDC, which adjusts the device context object for the current scrolled position, and then exits. If OnPrepareDC has been called prior to printing a page, pInfo contains the address of the CPrintInfo object containing print information; in this case, On-PrepareDC proceeds to adjust the device context object so that the OnDraw function will print the next portion of the drawing on the current page.

OnPrepareDC adjusts the device context object using the *same* method employed by the CScrollView class when the document is scrolled; namely, it adjusts the viewport origin (see the explanation of the viewport origin in the section "Converting Coordinates" near the beginning of Chapter 11). Before each new page is printed, OnPrepareDC adjusts the viewport origin to shift the positions of the figures relative to the page so that the *next portion* of the document will be printed when OnDraw is called.

When the first page is printed, the viewport origin is set to 0, 0 (the default value) so that the upper-left portion of the document is printed. When the next page is printed, OnPrepareDC subtracts the width of a page from the horizontal setting of the viewport origin so that the next portion of the drawing to the right is printed. It continues in this way to print the entire document, row-by-row, as shown in Figure 18.7.

Note that OnPrepareDC is passed the number of the current page that is being printed in the m_nCurPage data member of the CPrintInfo object. It uses this value—together with the mNumCols data member set by OnBeginPrinting—to calculate the row (CurRow) and column (CurCol) position of the portion of the drawing that is to be printed on the current page. It then uses CurRow and CurCol—as well as the page dimensions stored in mPageWidth and mPageHeight—to calculate the new coordinates of the viewport origin, which it passes to the CDC member function SetViewportOrg.

Modifying the OnDraw Function

As you can see in Figure 18.6, after calling OnPrepareDC, the MFC calls the OnPrint virtual function. The default implementation of this function simply calls the OnDraw member function of your view class, passing it the device context object that was created by OnPreparePrinting and prepared by OnPrepareDC.

Because this device context object is associated with the printer, the output generated by OnDraw is automatically sent to the printer (or print preview window)

FIGURE 18.7:

The order in which portions of the drawing are printed on subsequent pages

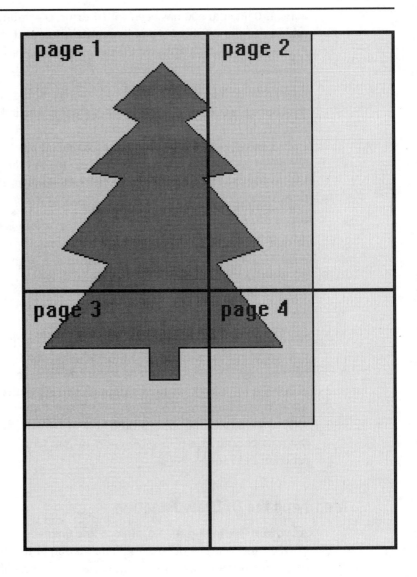

rather than the view window. Also, because the viewport origin of the device context object has been adjusted (by OnPrepareDC), OnDraw automatically prints the correct portion of the drawing (that is, the portion that is to appear on the current page).

NOTE The portion of the drawing that coincides with the physical printer page, and is therefore printed, depends upon the current coordinates of the viewport origin that were set by OnPrepareDC. The other portions of the drawing are *clipped* (that is, they are discarded because they fall outside the boundaries of the physical page). The OnDraw function, however, does not waste time calling drawing functions for any figure that is completely outside of the page. The call to GetClipBox returns the logical coordinates of the portion of the drawing that will appear on the physical page; OnDraw does *not* call CFigure::Draw for any figure that falls completely outside of these coordinates.

In general, the code in OnDraw should be device-independent, because this function is used to send output to a variety of target devices. However, the OnDraw function in MINIDRAW needs to print borders *only* if it is sending output to the view window. To prevent drawing borders when the output is being sent to a printer, place the code for drawing the lines within an if block, as follows:

```
void CMinidrawView::OnDraw(CDC* pDC)
{
    CMinidrawDoc* pDoc = GetDocument();

    // TODO: add draw code here

    if (pDC->GetDeviceCaps (TECHNOLOGY) == DT_RASDISPLAY)
        {
        CSize ScrollSize = GetTotalSize ();
        pDC->MoveTo (ScrollSize.cx, 0);
        pDC->LineTo (ScrollSize.cx, ScrollSize.cy);
        pDC->LineTo (0, ScrollSize.cy);
        }
```

Using Alternative Mapping Modes

Chapter 16 (in the section "The Mapping Mode") described the *mapping mode*, which is maintained by the device context object and affects the output of both text and graphics. Although using the default MM_TEXT mapping mode simplifies writing the program, the sizes of text and graphic images that the program displays *vary* depending upon the resolution of the output device (recall that in the MM_TEXT mapping mode all coordinates are specified in pixels; the number of pixels per physical inch *varies* according to the resolution). In this mapping mode, not only are the sizes of the images on the printer different from their sizes on the screen; the sizes also vary from one printer to another. Furthermore, on a laser printer or other high-resolution printer, the printed image sizes are quite small.

To produce images that are the *same* size regardless of the output device, you can use one of the alternative mapping modes: MM_HIENGLISH, MM_HIMETRIC, MM_LOENGLISH, MM_LOMETRIC, and MM_TWIPS. In each of these mapping modes, coordinates are specified in standard units of measurement (inches, millimeters, and so on), rather than in device-dependent pixels. (You could also employ one of the user-defined mapping modes, MM_ANISOMETRIC and MM_ISOMETRIC, provided that you set the units properly.) Using an alternative mapping mode changes the logic of the display code; a detailed discussion on the use of these mapping modes is beyond the scope of the book. For information, see the documentation on the CDC member function SetMap-Mode, as well as the other CDC mapping functions. For a list of all of the CDC mapping functions, see the general description of the CDC class in the *Reference Volume I, Class Library Reference*, or see the *Foundation Classes* online help file (the topic "CDC mapping functions").

When GetDeviceCaps is passed the index TECHNOLOGY, it returns a code indicating the type of device that is associated with the device context object. The code DT_RASDISPLAY indicates that the device is the screen; if OnDraw receives this code, it knows that the output is being sent to the view window (rather than the printer or the print preview window), and it proceeds to draw the borders. In general, you can use this technique whenever you need to customize the output generated by OnDraw for a particular target device. (See the GetDeviceCaps documentation for a description of the other codes it can return when it is passed the TECHNOLOGY index.)

You can now build and run the MINIDRAW program. The drawing will be much larger than in the previous version of the program, and you will have to use the scroll bars to access various portions of it. When you choose the Print Preview command on the File menu, you will now be able to view all of the pages required to print the drawing, and when you choose the Print... command, all pages of the drawing will now be printed (on a LaserJet Series II printer, the drawing will require four pages).

The MINIDRAW Source Code

Listings 18.1 through 18.8 contain the C++ source code for the latest (and final) version of the MINIDRAW program. You will find a copy of these files in the \MINIDRW7 companion disk subdirectory.

Listing 18.1

```
// minidraw.h : main header file for the MINIDRAW application
//

#ifndef __AFXWIN_H__
    #error include 'stdafx.h' before including this file for PCH
#endif

#include "resource.h"       // main symbols

/////////////////////////////////////////////////////////////////////////////
// CMinidrawApp:
// See minidraw.cpp for the implementation of this class
//
```

```
class CMinidrawApp : public CWinApp
{
public:
    CMinidrawApp();

// Overrides
    virtual BOOL InitInstance();

// Implementation

    //{{AFX_MSG(CMinidrawApp)
    afx_msg void OnAppAbout();
    afx_msg void OnLineDouble();
    afx_msg void OnUpdateLineDouble(CCmdUI* pCmdUI);
    afx_msg void OnLineSingle();
    afx_msg void OnUpdateLineSingle(CCmdUI* pCmdUI);
    afx_msg void OnLineTriple();
    afx_msg void OnUpdateLineTriple(CCmdUI* pCmdUI);
    afx_msg void OnUpdateToolsCircle(CCmdUI* pCmdUI);
    afx_msg void OnToolsCircle();
    afx_msg void OnToolsCirclefill();
    afx_msg void OnUpdateToolsCirclefill(CCmdUI* pCmdUI);
    afx_msg void OnUpdateToolsLine(CCmdUI* pCmdUI);
    afx_msg void OnToolsLine();
    afx_msg void OnToolsRectangle();
    afx_msg void OnUpdateToolsRectangle(CCmdUI* pCmdUI);
    afx_msg void OnUpdateToolsRectfill(CCmdUI* pCmdUI);
    afx_msg void OnToolsRectfill();
    afx_msg void OnToolsRectround();
    afx_msg void OnUpdateToolsRectround(CCmdUI* pCmdUI);
    afx_msg void OnUpdateToolsRectroundfill(CCmdUI* pCmdUI);
    afx_msg void OnToolsRectroundfill();
    afx_msg void OnColorBlack();
    afx_msg void OnUpdateColorBlack(CCmdUI* pCmdUI);
    afx_msg void OnColorBlue();
    afx_msg void OnUpdateColorBlue(CCmdUI* pCmdUI);
    afx_msg void OnColorCustom();
    afx_msg void OnUpdateColorCustom(CCmdUI* pCmdUI);
    afx_msg void OnColorCyan();
    afx_msg void OnUpdateColorCyan(CCmdUI* pCmdUI);
    afx_msg void OnColorGreen();
    afx_msg void OnUpdateColorGreen(CCmdUI* pCmdUI);
    afx_msg void OnColorMagenta();
    afx_msg void OnUpdateColorMagenta(CCmdUI* pCmdUI);
```

```
   afx_msg void OnColorRed();
   afx_msg void OnUpdateColorRed(CCmdUI* pCmdUI);
   afx_msg void OnColorWhite();
   afx_msg void OnUpdateColorWhite(CCmdUI* pCmdUI);
   afx_msg void OnColorYellow();
   afx_msg void OnUpdateColorYellow(CCmdUI* pCmdUI);
   //}}AFX_MSG
   DECLARE_MESSAGE_MAP()

// added data members:
public:
   COLORREF mCurrentColor;
   int mCurrentThickness;
   UINT mCurrentTool;
   UINT mIdxColorCmd;
};
```

///

Listing 18.2

```
// minidraw.cpp : Defines the class behaviors for the application.
//

#include "stdafx.h"
#include "minidraw.h"

#include "mainfrm.h"
#include "miniddoc.h"
#include "minidvw.h"

#ifdef _DEBUG
#undef THIS_FILE
static char BASED_CODE THIS_FILE[] = __FILE__;
#endif

/////////////////////////////////////////////////////////////////////////////
// CMinidrawApp

BEGIN_MESSAGE_MAP(CMinidrawApp, CWinApp)
   //{{AFX_MSG_MAP(CMinidrawApp)
   ON_COMMAND(ID_APP_ABOUT, OnAppAbout)
   ON_COMMAND(ID_LINE_DOUBLE, OnLineDouble)
   ON_UPDATE_COMMAND_UI(ID_LINE_DOUBLE, OnUpdateLineDouble)
   ON_COMMAND(ID_LINE_SINGLE, OnLineSingle)
```

```
    ON_UPDATE_COMMAND_UI(ID_LINE_SINGLE, OnUpdateLineSingle)
    ON_COMMAND(ID_LINE_TRIPLE, OnLineTriple)
    ON_UPDATE_COMMAND_UI(ID_LINE_TRIPLE, OnUpdateLineTriple)
    ON_UPDATE_COMMAND_UI(ID_TOOLS_CIRCLE, OnUpdateToolsCircle)
    ON_COMMAND(ID_TOOLS_CIRCLE, OnToolsCircle)
    ON_COMMAND(ID_TOOLS_CIRCLEFILL, OnToolsCirclefill)
    ON_UPDATE_COMMAND_UI(ID_TOOLS_CIRCLEFILL, OnUpdateToolsCirclefill)
    ON_UPDATE_COMMAND_UI(ID_TOOLS_LINE, OnUpdateToolsLine)
    ON_COMMAND(ID_TOOLS_LINE, OnToolsLine)
    ON_COMMAND(ID_TOOLS_RECTANGLE, OnToolsRectangle)
    ON_UPDATE_COMMAND_UI(ID_TOOLS_RECTANGLE, OnUpdateToolsRectangle)
    ON_UPDATE_COMMAND_UI(ID_TOOLS_RECTFILL, OnUpdateToolsRectfill)
    ON_COMMAND(ID_TOOLS_RECTFILL, OnToolsRectfill)
    ON_COMMAND(ID_TOOLS_RECTROUND, OnToolsRectround)
    ON_UPDATE_COMMAND_UI(ID_TOOLS_RECTROUND, OnUpdateToolsRectround)
    ON_UPDATE_COMMAND_UI(ID_TOOLS_RECTROUNDFILL, OnUpdateToolsRectroundfill)
    ON_COMMAND(ID_TOOLS_RECTROUNDFILL, OnToolsRectroundfill)
    ON_COMMAND(ID_COLOR_BLACK, OnColorBlack)
    ON_UPDATE_COMMAND_UI(ID_COLOR_BLACK, OnUpdateColorBlack)
    ON_COMMAND(ID_COLOR_BLUE, OnColorBlue)
    ON_UPDATE_COMMAND_UI(ID_COLOR_BLUE, OnUpdateColorBlue)
    ON_COMMAND(ID_COLOR_CUSTOM, OnColorCustom)
    ON_UPDATE_COMMAND_UI(ID_COLOR_CUSTOM, OnUpdateColorCustom)
    ON_COMMAND(ID_COLOR_CYAN, OnColorCyan)
    ON_UPDATE_COMMAND_UI(ID_COLOR_CYAN, OnUpdateColorCyan)
    ON_COMMAND(ID_COLOR_GREEN, OnColorGreen)
    ON_UPDATE_COMMAND_UI(ID_COLOR_GREEN, OnUpdateColorGreen)
    ON_COMMAND(ID_COLOR_MAGENTA, OnColorMagenta)
    ON_UPDATE_COMMAND_UI(ID_COLOR_MAGENTA, OnUpdateColorMagenta)
    ON_COMMAND(ID_COLOR_RED, OnColorRed)
    ON_UPDATE_COMMAND_UI(ID_COLOR_RED, OnUpdateColorRed)
    ON_COMMAND(ID_COLOR_WHITE, OnColorWhite)
    ON_UPDATE_COMMAND_UI(ID_COLOR_WHITE, OnUpdateColorWhite)
    ON_COMMAND(ID_COLOR_YELLOW, OnColorYellow)
    ON_UPDATE_COMMAND_UI(ID_COLOR_YELLOW, OnUpdateColorYellow)
    //}}AFX_MSG_MAP
    // Standard file based document commands
    ON_COMMAND(ID_FILE_NEW, CWinApp::OnFileNew)
    ON_COMMAND(ID_FILE_OPEN, CWinApp::OnFileOpen)
    // Standard print setup command
    ON_COMMAND(ID_FILE_PRINT_SETUP, CWinApp::OnFilePrintSetup)
END_MESSAGE_MAP()
```

```
/////////////////////////////////////////////////////////////////////////
// CMinidrawApp construction

CMinidrawApp::CMinidrawApp()
{
    // TODO: add construction code here,
    // Place all significant initialization in InitInstance

    mCurrentColor = RGB (0,0,0);
    mCurrentThickness = 1;
    mCurrentTool = ID_TOOLS_LINE;
    mIdxColorCmd = ID_COLOR_BLACK;
}

/////////////////////////////////////////////////////////////////////////
// The one and only CMinidrawApp object

CMinidrawApp NEAR theApp;

/////////////////////////////////////////////////////////////////////////
// CMinidrawApp initialization

BOOL CMinidrawApp::InitInstance()
{
    // Standard initialization
    // If you are not using these features and wish to reduce the size
    //  of your final executable, you should remove from the following
    //  the specific initialization routines you do not need.

    SetDialogBkColor();         // set dialog background color to gray
    LoadStdProfileSettings();  // Load standard INI file options (including MRU)

    // Register the application's document templates.  Document templates
    //  serve as the connection between documents, frame windows and views.

    AddDocTemplate(new CSingleDocTemplate(IDR_MAINFRAME,
            RUNTIME_CLASS(CMinidrawDoc),
            RUNTIME_CLASS(CMainFrame),      // main SDI frame window
            RUNTIME_CLASS(CMinidrawView)));

    // create a new (empty) document
    OnFileNew();
```

```
    m_pMainWnd->DragAcceptFiles ();

    if (m_lpCmdLine[0] != '\0')
    {
        // TODO: add command line processing here
    }

    return TRUE;
}

/////////////////////////////////////////////////////////////////////////////
// CAboutDlg dialog used for App About

class CAboutDlg : public CDialog
{
public:
    CAboutDlg();

// Dialog Data
    //{{AFX_DATA(CAboutDlg)
    enum { IDD = IDD_ABOUTBOX };
    //}}AFX_DATA

// Implementation
protected:
    virtual void DoDataExchange(CDataExchange* pDX);    // DDX/DDV support
    //{{AFX_MSG(CAboutDlg)
        // No message handlers
    //}}AFX_MSG
    DECLARE_MESSAGE_MAP()
};

CAboutDlg::CAboutDlg() : CDialog(CAboutDlg::IDD)
{
    //{{AFX_DATA_INIT(CAboutDlg)
    //}}AFX_DATA_INIT
}

void CAboutDlg::DoDataExchange(CDataExchange* pDX)
{
    CDialog::DoDataExchange(pDX);
    //{{AFX_DATA_MAP(CAboutDlg)
    //}}AFX_DATA_MAP
}
```

```
BEGIN_MESSAGE_MAP(CAboutDlg, CDialog)
    //{{AFX_MSG_MAP(CAboutDlg)
        // No message handlers
    //}}AFX_MSG_MAP
END_MESSAGE_MAP()

// App command to run the dialog
void CMinidrawApp::OnAppAbout()
{
    CAboutDlg aboutDlg;
    aboutDlg.DoModal();
}

/////////////////////////////////////////////////////////////////////////////
// CMinidrawApp commands

void CMinidrawApp::OnLineDouble()
{
    // TODO: Add your command handler code here
    mCurrentThickness = 2;
}

void CMinidrawApp::OnUpdateLineDouble(CCmdUI* pCmdUI)
{
    // TODO: Add your command update UI handler code here
    pCmdUI->SetCheck (mCurrentThickness == 2 ? 1 : 0);
}

void CMinidrawApp::OnLineSingle()
{
    // TODO: Add your command handler code here
    mCurrentThickness = 1;
}

void CMinidrawApp::OnUpdateLineSingle(CCmdUI* pCmdUI)
{
    // TODO: Add your command update UI handler code here
    pCmdUI->SetCheck (mCurrentThickness == 1 ? 1 : 0);
}

void CMinidrawApp::OnLineTriple()
{
```

```
    // TODO: Add your command handler code here
    mCurrentThickness = 3;
}

void CMinidrawApp::OnUpdateLineTriple(CCmdUI* pCmdUI)
{
    // TODO: Add your command update UI handler code here
    pCmdUI->SetCheck (mCurrentThickness == 3 ? 1 : 0);
}

void CMinidrawApp::OnUpdateToolsCircle(CCmdUI* pCmdUI)
{
    // TODO: Add your command update UI handler code here
    pCmdUI->SetCheck (mCurrentTool == ID_TOOLS_CIRCLE ? 1 : 0);
}

void CMinidrawApp::OnToolsCircle()
{
    // TODO: Add your command handler code here
    mCurrentTool = ID_TOOLS_CIRCLE;
}

void CMinidrawApp::OnToolsCirclefill()
{
    // TODO: Add your command handler code here
    mCurrentTool = ID_TOOLS_CIRCLEFILL;
}

void CMinidrawApp::OnUpdateToolsCirclefill(CCmdUI* pCmdUI)
{
    // TODO: Add your command update UI handler code here
    pCmdUI->SetCheck (mCurrentTool == ID_TOOLS_CIRCLEFILL ? 1 : 0);
}

void CMinidrawApp::OnUpdateToolsLine(CCmdUI* pCmdUI)
{
    // TODO: Add your command update UI handler code here
    pCmdUI->SetCheck (mCurrentTool == ID_TOOLS_LINE ? 1 : 0);
}

void CMinidrawApp::OnToolsLine()
{
    // TODO: Add your command handler code here
    mCurrentTool = ID_TOOLS_LINE;
}
```

```
void CMinidrawApp::OnToolsRectangle()
{
    // TODO: Add your command handler code here
    mCurrentTool = ID_TOOLS_RECTANGLE;
}

void CMinidrawApp::OnUpdateToolsRectangle(CCmdUI* pCmdUI)
{
    // TODO: Add your command update UI handler code here
    pCmdUI->SetCheck (mCurrentTool == ID_TOOLS_RECTANGLE ? 1 : 0);
}

void CMinidrawApp::OnUpdateToolsRectfill(CCmdUI* pCmdUI)
{
    // TODO: Add your command update UI handler code here
    pCmdUI->SetCheck (mCurrentTool == ID_TOOLS_RECTFILL ? 1 : 0);
}

void CMinidrawApp::OnToolsRectfill()
{
    // TODO: Add your command handler code here
    mCurrentTool = ID_TOOLS_RECTFILL;
}

void CMinidrawApp::OnToolsRectround()
{
    // TODO: Add your command handler code here
    mCurrentTool = ID_TOOLS_RECTROUND;
}

void CMinidrawApp::OnUpdateToolsRectround(CCmdUI* pCmdUI)
{
    // TODO: Add your command update UI handler code here
    pCmdUI->SetCheck (mCurrentTool == ID_TOOLS_RECTROUND ? 1 : 0);
}

void CMinidrawApp::OnUpdateToolsRectroundfill(CCmdUI* pCmdUI)
{
    // TODO: Add your command update UI handler code here
    pCmdUI->SetCheck (mCurrentTool == ID_TOOLS_RECTROUNDFILL ? 1 : 0);
}
```

```
void CMinidrawApp::OnToolsRectroundfill()
{
    // TODO: Add your command handler code here
    mCurrentTool = ID_TOOLS_RECTROUNDFILL;
}

void CMinidrawApp::OnColorBlack()
{
    // TODO: Add your command handler code here
    mCurrentColor = RGB (0,0,0);
    mIdxColorCmd = ID_COLOR_BLACK;
}

void CMinidrawApp::OnUpdateColorBlack(CCmdUI* pCmdUI)
{
    // TODO: Add your command update UI handler code here
    pCmdUI->SetCheck (mIdxColorCmd == ID_COLOR_BLACK ? 1 : 0);
}

void CMinidrawApp::OnColorBlue()
{
    // TODO: Add your command handler code here
    mCurrentColor = RGB (0,0,255);
    mIdxColorCmd = ID_COLOR_BLUE;
}

void CMinidrawApp::OnUpdateColorBlue(CCmdUI* pCmdUI)
{
    // TODO: Add your command update UI handler code here
    pCmdUI->SetCheck (mIdxColorCmd == ID_COLOR_BLUE ? 1 : 0);
}

void CMinidrawApp::OnColorCustom()
{
    // TODO: Add your command handler code here
    CColorDialog ColorDialog;

    if (ColorDialog.DoModal () == IDOK)
        {
        mCurrentColor = ColorDialog.GetColor ();
        mIdxColorCmd = ID_COLOR_CUSTOM;
        }
}
```

```
void CMinidrawApp::OnUpdateColorCustom(CCmdUI* pCmdUI)
{
    // TODO: Add your command update UI handler code here
    pCmdUI->SetCheck (mIdxColorCmd == ID_COLOR_CUSTOM ? 1 : 0);
}

void CMinidrawApp::OnColorCyan()
{
    // TODO: Add your command handler code here
    mCurrentColor = RGB (0,255,255);
    mIdxColorCmd = ID_COLOR_CYAN;
}

void CMinidrawApp::OnUpdateColorCyan(CCmdUI* pCmdUI)
{
    // TODO: Add your command update UI handler code here
    pCmdUI->SetCheck (mIdxColorCmd == ID_COLOR_CYAN ? 1 : 0);
}

void CMinidrawApp::OnColorGreen()
{
    // TODO: Add your command handler code here
    mCurrentColor = RGB (0,255,0);
    mIdxColorCmd = ID_COLOR_GREEN;
}

void CMinidrawApp::OnUpdateColorGreen(CCmdUI* pCmdUI)
{
    // TODO: Add your command update UI handler code here
    pCmdUI->SetCheck (mIdxColorCmd == ID_COLOR_GREEN ? 1 : 0);
}

void CMinidrawApp::OnColorMagenta()
{
    // TODO: Add your command handler code here
    mCurrentColor = RGB (255,0,255);
    mIdxColorCmd = ID_COLOR_MAGENTA;
}

void CMinidrawApp::OnUpdateColorMagenta(CCmdUI* pCmdUI)
{
    // TODO: Add your command update UI handler code here
    pCmdUI->SetCheck (mIdxColorCmd == ID_COLOR_MAGENTA ? 1 : 0);
}
```

```
void CMinidrawApp::OnColorRed()
{
    // TODO: Add your command handler code here
    mCurrentColor = RGB (255,0,0);
    mIdxColorCmd = ID_COLOR_RED;
}

void CMinidrawApp::OnUpdateColorRed(CCmdUI* pCmdUI)
{
    // TODO: Add your command update UI handler code here
    pCmdUI->SetCheck (mIdxColorCmd == ID_COLOR_RED ? 1 : 0);
}

void CMinidrawApp::OnColorWhite()
{
    // TODO: Add your command handler code here
    mCurrentColor = RGB (255,255,255);
    mIdxColorCmd = ID_COLOR_WHITE;
}

void CMinidrawApp::OnUpdateColorWhite(CCmdUI* pCmdUI)
{
    // TODO: Add your command update UI handler code here
    pCmdUI->SetCheck (mIdxColorCmd == ID_COLOR_WHITE ? 1 : 0);
}

void CMinidrawApp::OnColorYellow()
{
    // TODO: Add your command handler code here
    mCurrentColor = RGB (255,255,0);
    mIdxColorCmd = ID_COLOR_YELLOW;
}

void CMinidrawApp::OnUpdateColorYellow(CCmdUI* pCmdUI)
{
    // TODO: Add your command update UI handler code here
    pCmdUI->SetCheck (mIdxColorCmd == ID_COLOR_YELLOW ? 1 : 0);
}
```

Listing 18.3

```
// miniddoc.h : interface of the CMinidrawDoc class
//
//////////////////////////////////////////////////////////////////////////
```

```
// class hierarchy for figures:

class CFigure : public CObject
{
protected:
   COLORREF mColor;
   int mX1, mY1, mX2, mY2;

   virtual void Serialize (CArchive& ar);
   DECLARE_SERIAL (CFigure)

public:
   virtual void Draw (CDC *PDC) {}
   CRect GetDimRect ();
};

class CLine : public CFigure
{
protected:
   int mThickness;

   CLine () {}
   virtual void Serialize (CArchive& ar);
   DECLARE_SERIAL (CLine)

public:
   CLine (int X1, int Y1, int X2, int Y2, COLORREF Color, int Thickness);
   virtual void Draw (CDC *PDC);
};

class CRectangle : public CFigure
{
protected:
   int mThickness;

   CRectangle () {}
   virtual void Serialize (CArchive& ar);
   DECLARE_SERIAL (CRectangle)

public:
   CRectangle (int X1, int Y1, int X2, int Y2, COLORREF Color, int Thickness);
   virtual void Draw (CDC *PDC);
};
```

```
class CRectFill : public CFigure
{
protected:
    CRectFill () {}
    DECLARE_SERIAL (CRectFill)

public:
    CRectFill (int X1, int Y1, int X2, int Y2, COLORREF Color);
    virtual void Draw (CDC *PDC);
};

class CRectRound : public CFigure
{
protected:
    int mThickness;

    CRectRound () {}
    virtual void Serialize (CArchive& ar);
    DECLARE_SERIAL (CRectRound)

public:
    CRectRound (int X1, int Y1, int X2, int Y2, COLORREF Color, int Thickness);
    virtual void Draw (CDC *PDC);
};

class CRectRoundFill : public CFigure
{
protected:
    CRectRoundFill () {}
    DECLARE_SERIAL (CRectRoundFill)

public:
    CRectRoundFill (int X1, int Y1, int X2, int Y2, COLORREF Color);
    virtual void Draw (CDC *PDC);
};

class CCircle : public CFigure
{
protected:
    int mThickness;

    CCircle () {}
    virtual void Serialize (CArchive& ar);
    DECLARE_SERIAL (CCircle)
```

```
public:
   CCircle (int X1, int Y1, int X2, int Y2, COLORREF Color, int Thickness);
   virtual void Draw (CDC *PDC);
};

class CCircleFill : public CFigure
{
protected:
   CCircleFill () {}
   DECLARE_SERIAL (CCircleFill)

public:
   CCircleFill (int X1, int Y1, int X2, int Y2, COLORREF Color);
   virtual void Draw (CDC *PDC);
};

// document class:

class CMinidrawDoc : public CDocument
{
protected: // create from serialization only
   CMinidrawDoc();
   DECLARE_DYNCREATE(CMinidrawDoc)

protected:
   CObArray mObArray;

public:
   void AddFigure (CFigure *PFigure);
   virtual void DeleteContents ();
   CFigure *GetFigure (int Index);
   int GetNumFigs ();

// Attributes
public:

// Operations
public:

// Implementation
public:
   virtual ~CMinidrawDoc();
   virtual void Serialize(CArchive& ar);  // overridden for document i/o
```

```
#ifdef _DEBUG
   virtual  void AssertValid() const;
   virtual  void Dump(CDumpContext& dc) const;
#endif
protected:
   virtual  BOOL  OnNewDocument();

// Generated message map functions
protected:
   //{{AFX_MSG(CMinidrawDoc)
   afx_msg void OnEditClearAll();
   afx_msg void OnUpdateEditClearAll(CCmdUI* pCmdUI);
   afx_msg void OnEditUndo();
   afx_msg void OnUpdateEditUndo(CCmdUI* pCmdUI);
   //}}AFX_MSG
   DECLARE_MESSAGE_MAP()
};
```

//

Listing 18.4

```
// miniddoc.cpp : implementation of the CMinidrawDoc class
//

#include "stdafx.h"
#include "minidraw.h"

#include "miniddoc.h"

#ifdef _DEBUG
#undef THIS_FILE
static char BASED_CODE THIS_FILE[] = __FILE__;
#endif

////////////////////////////////////////////////////////////////////////
// CMinidrawDoc

IMPLEMENT_DYNCREATE(CMinidrawDoc, CDocument)

BEGIN_MESSAGE_MAP(CMinidrawDoc, CDocument)
   //{{AFX_MSG_MAP(CMinidrawDoc)
   ON_COMMAND(ID_EDIT_CLEAR_ALL, OnEditClearAll)
   ON_UPDATE_COMMAND_UI(ID_EDIT_CLEAR_ALL, OnUpdateEditClearAll)
   ON_COMMAND(ID_EDIT_UNDO, OnEditUndo)
```

```
    ON_UPDATE_COMMAND_UI(ID_EDIT_UNDO, OnUpdateEditUndo)
    //}}AFX_MSG_MAP
END_MESSAGE_MAP()

/////////////////////////////////////////////////////////////////////////////
// CMinidrawDoc construction/destruction

CMinidrawDoc::CMinidrawDoc()
{
    // TODO: add one-time construction code here
}

CMinidrawDoc::~CMinidrawDoc()
{
}

BOOL CMinidrawDoc::OnNewDocument()
{
    if (!CDocument::OnNewDocument())
        return FALSE;
    // TODO: add reinitialization code here
    // (SDI documents will reuse this document)
    return TRUE;
}

/////////////////////////////////////////////////////////////////////////////
// CMinidrawDoc serialization

void CMinidrawDoc::Serialize(CArchive& ar)
{
    if (ar.IsStoring())
    {
        // TODO: add storing code here

    mObArray.Serialize (ar);
    }
    else
    {
        // TODO: add loading code here

    mObArray.Serialize (ar);
    }
}
```

```
/////////////////////////////////////////////////////////////////////
// CMinidrawDoc diagnostics

#ifdef _DEBUG
void CMinidrawDoc::AssertValid() const
{
    CDocument::AssertValid();
}

void CMinidrawDoc::Dump(CDumpContext& dc) const
{
    CDocument::Dump(dc);
}

#endif //_DEBUG

/////////////////////////////////////////////////////////////////////
// CMinidrawDoc commands

void CMinidrawDoc::AddFigure (CFigure *PFigure)
    {
    mObArray.Add (PFigure);
    SetModifiedFlag ();
    }

CFigure *CMinidrawDoc::GetFigure (int Index)
    {
    if (Index < 0 ¦¦ Index > mObArray.GetUpperBound ())
       return 0;
    return (CFigure *)mObArray.GetAt (Index);
    }

int CMinidrawDoc::GetNumFigs ()
    {
    return mObArray.GetSize ();
    }

void CMinidrawDoc::DeleteContents ()
    {
    int Index = mObArray.GetSize ();
    while (Index--)
       delete mObArray.GetAt (Index);
    mObArray.RemoveAll ();
    }
```

```
void CMinidrawDoc::OnEditClearAll()
{
    // TODO: Add your command handler code here

    DeleteContents ();
    UpdateAllViews (0);
    SetModifiedFlag ();
}

void CMinidrawDoc::OnUpdateEditClearAll(CCmdUI* pCmdUI)
{
    // TODO: Add your command update UI handler code here

    pCmdUI->Enable (mObArray.GetSize ());
}

void CMinidrawDoc::OnEditUndo()
{
    // TODO: Add your command handler code here

    int Index = mObArray.GetUpperBound ();
    if (Index > -1)
        {
        delete mObArray.GetAt (Index);
        mObArray.RemoveAt (Index);
        }
    UpdateAllViews (0);
    SetModifiedFlag ();
}

void CMinidrawDoc::OnUpdateEditUndo(CCmdUI* pCmdUI)
{
    // TODO: Add your command update UI handler code here

    pCmdUI->Enable (mObArray.GetSize ());
}

// implementation of figure classes:

IMPLEMENT_SERIAL (CFigure, CObject, 3)

CRect CFigure::GetDimRect ()
    {
    return CRect
      (min (mX1, mX2),
```

```
      min (mY1, mY2),
      max (mX1, mX2) + 1,
      max (mY1, mY2) + 1);
   }

void CFigure::Serialize (CArchive& ar)
   {
   if (ar.IsStoring ())
      ar << (WORD)mX1 << (WORD)mY1 << (WORD)mX2 << (WORD)mY2 << mColor;
   else
      ar >> (WORD &)mX1 >> (WORD &)mY1 >> (WORD &)mX2 >> (WORD &)mY2 >> mColor;
   }

IMPLEMENT_SERIAL (CLine, CFigure, 3)

CLine::CLine (int X1, int Y1, int X2, int Y2, COLORREF Color, int Thickness)
   {
   mX1 = X1;
   mY1 = Y1;
   mX2 = X2;
   mY2 = Y2;
   mColor = Color;
   mThickness = Thickness;
   }

void CLine::Serialize (CArchive& ar)
   {
   CFigure::Serialize (ar);
   if (ar.IsStoring ())
      ar << (WORD)mThickness;
   else
      ar >> (WORD &)mThickness;
   }

void CLine::Draw (CDC *PDC)
   {
   CPen Pen, *POldPen;

   // select pen/brush:
   Pen.CreatePen (PS_SOLID, mThickness, mColor);
   POldPen = PDC->SelectObject (&Pen);

   // draw figure:
   PDC->MoveTo (mX1, mY1);
   PDC->LineTo (mX2, mY2);
```

```
   // remove pen/brush:
   PDC->SelectObject (POldPen);
   }

IMPLEMENT_SERIAL (CRectangle, CFigure, 3)

CRectangle::CRectangle (int X1, int Y1, int X2, int Y2,
                        COLORREF Color, int Thickness)
   {
   mX1 = X1;
   mY1 = Y1;
   mX2 = X2;
   mY2 = Y2;
   mColor = Color;
   mThickness = Thickness;
   }

void CRectangle::Serialize (CArchive& ar)
   {
   CFigure::Serialize (ar);
   if (ar.IsStoring ())
      ar << (WORD)mThickness;
   else
      ar >> (WORD &)mThickness;
   }

void CRectangle::Draw (CDC *PDC)
   {
   CPen Pen, *POldPen;

   // select pen/brush:
   Pen.CreatePen (PS_INSIDEFRAME, mThickness, mColor);
   POldPen = PDC->SelectObject (&Pen);
   PDC->SelectStockObject (NULL_BRUSH);

   // draw figure:
   PDC->Rectangle (mX1, mY1, mX2, mY2);

   // remove pen/brush:
   PDC->SelectObject (POldPen);
   }

IMPLEMENT_SERIAL (CRectFill, CFigure, 3)
```

```
CRectFill::CRectFill (int X1, int Y1, int X2, int Y2, COLORREF Color)
   {
   mX1 = min (X1, X2);
   mY1 = min (Y1, Y2);
   mX2 = max (X1, X2);
   mY2 = max (Y1, Y2);
   mColor = Color;
   }

void CRectFill::Draw (CDC *PDC)
   {
   CBrush Brush, *POldBrush;
   CPen Pen, *POldPen;

   // select pen/brush:
   Pen.CreatePen (PS_INSIDEFRAME, 1, mColor);
   POldPen = PDC->SelectObject (&Pen);
   Brush.CreateSolidBrush (mColor);
   POldBrush = PDC->SelectObject (&Brush);

   // draw figure:
   PDC->Rectangle (mX1, mY1, mX2, mY2);

   // remove pen/brush:
   PDC->SelectObject (POldPen);
   PDC->SelectObject (POldBrush);
   }

IMPLEMENT_SERIAL (CRectRound, CFigure, 3)

CRectRound::CRectRound (int X1, int Y1, int X2, int Y2,
                        COLORREF Color, int Thickness)
   {
   mX1 = min (X1, X2);
   mY1 = min (Y1, Y2);
   mX2 = max (X1, X2);
   mY2 = max (Y1, Y2);
   mColor = Color;
   mThickness = Thickness;
   }

void CRectRound::Serialize (CArchive& ar)
   {
   CFigure::Serialize (ar);
   if (ar.IsStoring ())
```

```
      ar << (WORD)mThickness;
   else
      ar >> (WORD &)mThickness;
   }

void CRectRound::Draw (CDC *PDC)
   {
   CPen Pen, *POldPen;

   // select pen/brush:
   Pen.CreatePen (PS_INSIDEFRAME, mThickness, mColor);
   POldPen = PDC->SelectObject (&Pen);
   PDC->SelectStockObject (NULL_BRUSH);

   // draw figure:
   int SizeRound = (mX2 - mX1 + mY2 - mY1) / 6;
   PDC->RoundRect (mX1, mY1, mX2, mY2, SizeRound, SizeRound);

   // remove pen/brush:
   PDC->SelectObject (POldPen);
   }

IMPLEMENT_SERIAL (CRectRoundFill, CFigure, 3)

CRectRoundFill::CRectRoundFill (int X1, int Y1, int X2, int Y2, COLORREF Color)
   {
   mX1 = min (X1, X2);
   mY1 = min (Y1, Y2);
   mX2 = max (X1, X2);
   mY2 = max (Y1, Y2);
   mColor = Color;
   }

void CRectRoundFill::Draw (CDC *PDC)
   {
   CBrush Brush, *POldBrush;
   CPen Pen, *POldPen;

   // select pen/brush:
   Pen.CreatePen (PS_INSIDEFRAME, 1, mColor);
   POldPen = PDC->SelectObject (&Pen);
   Brush.CreateSolidBrush (mColor);
   POldBrush = PDC->SelectObject (&Brush);
```

```
// draw figure:
int SizeRound = (mX2 - mX1 + mY2 - mY1) / 6;
PDC->RoundRect (mX1, mY1, mX2, mY2, SizeRound, SizeRound);

// remove pen/brush:
PDC->SelectObject (POldPen);
PDC->SelectObject (POldBrush);
}

IMPLEMENT_SERIAL (CCircle, CFigure, 3)

CCircle::CCircle (int X1, int Y1, int X2, int Y2,
                 COLORREF Color, int Thickness)
   {
   mX1 = min (X1, X2);
   mY1 = min (Y1, Y2);
   mX2 = max (X1, X2);
   mY2 = max (Y1, Y2);
   mColor = Color;
   mThickness = Thickness;
   }

void CCircle::Serialize (CArchive& ar)
   {
   CFigure::Serialize (ar);
   if (ar.IsStoring ())
      ar << (WORD)mThickness;
   else
      ar >> (WORD &)mThickness;
   }

void CCircle::Draw (CDC *PDC)
   {
   CPen Pen, *POldPen;

   // select pen/brush:
   Pen.CreatePen (PS_INSIDEFRAME, mThickness, mColor);
   POldPen = PDC->SelectObject (&Pen);
   PDC->SelectStockObject (NULL_BRUSH);

   // draw figure:
   PDC->Ellipse (mX1, mY1, mX2, mY2);
```

```
    // remove pen/brush:
    PDC->SelectObject (POldPen);
    }

IMPLEMENT_SERIAL (CCircleFill, CFigure, 3)

CCircleFill::CCircleFill (int X1, int Y1, int X2, int Y2, COLORREF Color)
    {
    mX1 = min (X1, X2);
    mY1 = min (Y1, Y2);
    mX2 = max (X1, X2);
    mY2 = max (Y1, Y2);
    mColor = Color;
    }

void CCircleFill::Draw (CDC *PDC)
    {
    CBrush Brush, *POldBrush;
    CPen Pen, *POldPen;

    // select pen/brush:
    Pen.CreatePen (PS_INSIDEFRAME, 1, mColor);
    POldPen = PDC->SelectObject (&Pen);
    Brush.CreateSolidBrush (mColor);
    POldBrush = PDC->SelectObject (&Brush);

    // draw figure:
    PDC->Ellipse (mX1, mY1, mX2, mY2);

    // remove pen/brush:
    PDC->SelectObject (POldPen);
    PDC->SelectObject (POldBrush);
    }
```

Listing 18.5

```
// mainfrm.h : interface of the CMainFrame class
//
/////////////////////////////////////////////////////////////////////////

class CMainFrame : public CFrameWnd
{
protected: // create from serialization only
```

```
    CMainFrame();
    DECLARE_DYNCREATE(CMainFrame)

protected:
    CSplitterWnd mSplitterWnd;
    CStatusBar mStatusBar;
    CToolBar mToolBar;

    virtual BOOL OnCreateClient (LPCREATESTRUCT lpcs, CCreateContext* pContext);

// Attributes
public:

// Operations
public:

// Implementation
public:
    virtual ~CMainFrame();
#ifdef _DEBUG
    virtual  void AssertValid() const;
    virtual  void Dump(CDumpContext& dc) const;
#endif


// Generated message map functions
protected:
    //{{AFX_MSG(CMainFrame)
    afx_msg int OnCreate(LPCREATESTRUCT lpCreateStruct);
    //}}AFX_MSG
    DECLARE_MESSAGE_MAP()
};
```

//

Listing 18.6

```
// mainfrm.cpp : implementation of the CMainFrame class
//

#include "stdafx.h"
#include "minidraw.h"

#include "mainfrm.h"
```

```
#ifdef _DEBUG
#undef THIS_FILE
static char BASED_CODE THIS_FILE[] = __FILE__;
#endif

/////////////////////////////////////////////////////////////////////////////
// CMainFrame

IMPLEMENT_DYNCREATE(CMainFrame, CFrameWnd)

BEGIN_MESSAGE_MAP(CMainFrame, CFrameWnd)
    //{{AFX_MSG_MAP(CMainFrame)
    ON_WM_CREATE()
    //}}AFX_MSG_MAP
END_MESSAGE_MAP()

// IDs for tool bar buttons:
static UINT ButtonIDs [] =
    {
    ID_TOOLS_LINE,
    ID_SEPARATOR,
    ID_TOOLS_RECTANGLE,
    ID_TOOLS_RECTFILL,
    ID_SEPARATOR,
    ID_TOOLS_RECTROUND,
    ID_TOOLS_RECTROUNDFILL,
    ID_SEPARATOR,
    ID_TOOLS_CIRCLE,
    ID_TOOLS_CIRCLEFILL,
    ID_SEPARATOR,
    ID_SEPARATOR,
    ID_LINE_SINGLE,
    ID_LINE_DOUBLE,
    ID_LINE_TRIPLE
    };

// IDs for status bar indicators:
static UINT IndicatorIDs [] =
    {
    ID_SEPARATOR,
    ID_INDICATOR_CAPS,
    ID_INDICATOR_NUM,
    ID_INDICATOR_SCRL
    };
```

```
///////////////////////////////////////////////////////////////////////////
// CMainFrame construction/destruction

CMainFrame::CMainFrame()
{
    // TODO: add member initialization code here
}

CMainFrame::~CMainFrame()
{
}

///////////////////////////////////////////////////////////////////////////
// CMainFrame diagnostics

#ifdef _DEBUG
void CMainFrame::AssertValid() const
{
    CFrameWnd::AssertValid();
}

void CMainFrame::Dump(CDumpContext& dc) const
{
    CFrameWnd::Dump(dc);
}

#endif //_DEBUG

///////////////////////////////////////////////////////////////////////////
// CMainFrame message handlers

BOOL CMainFrame::OnCreateClient (LPCREATESTRUCT lpcs, CCreateContext* pContext)
    {
    return mSplitterWnd.Create
        (this,              // parent of splitter window
        1,                  // maximum rows
        2,                  // maximum columns
        CSize (15, 15),     // minimum pane size
        pContext);          // pass on context information
    }

int CMainFrame::OnCreate(LPCREATESTRUCT lpCreateStruct)
{
    if (CFrameWnd::OnCreate(lpCreateStruct) == -1)
        return -1;
```

```
    // TODO: Add your specialized creation code here

    if (!mToolBar.Create (this) ||
        !mToolBar.LoadBitmap (IDR_MAINFRAME) ||
        !mToolBar.SetButtons (ButtonIDs, sizeof (ButtonIDs) / sizeof (UINT)))
        return -1;

    if (!mStatusBar.Create (this) ||
        !mStatusBar.SetIndicators (IndicatorIDs,
        sizeof (IndicatorIDs) / sizeof (UINT)))
        return -1;

    return 0;
}
```

Listing 18.7

```
// minidvw.h : interface of the CMinidrawView class
//
//////////////////////////////////////////////////////////////////////////////

const int DRAWWIDTH  = 4000;   // drawing width
const int DRAWHEIGHT = 6000;   // drawing height

class CMinidrawView : public CScrollView
{
protected: // create from serialization only
    CMinidrawView();
    DECLARE_DYNCREATE(CMinidrawView)

protected:
    CString mClassName;
    int mDragging;
    HCURSOR mHArrow;
    HCURSOR mHCross;
    int mNumCols, mNumRows;
    int mPageHeight, mPageWidth;
    CPen mPenDotted;
    CPoint mPointOld;
    CPoint mPointOrigin;

    virtual void OnBeginPrinting (CDC* pDC, CPrintInfo* pInfo);
    virtual void OnInitialUpdate ();
    virtual void OnPrepareDC (CDC* pDC, CPrintInfo* pInfo = NULL);
```

```
    virtual BOOL OnPreparePrinting (CPrintInfo* pInfo);
    virtual void OnUpdate (CView* pSender, LPARAM lHint, CObject* pHint);
    virtual BOOL PreCreateWindow (CREATESTRUCT& cs);

// Attributes
public:
    CMinidrawDoc* GetDocument();

// Operations
public:

// Implementation
public:
    virtual ~CMinidrawView();
    virtual void OnDraw(CDC* pDC);   // overridden to draw this view
#ifdef _DEBUG
    virtual void AssertValid() const;
    virtual void Dump(CDumpContext& dc) const;
#endif

// Generated message map functions
protected:
    //{{AFX_MSG(CMinidrawView)
    afx_msg void OnLButtonDown(UINT nFlags, CPoint point);
    afx_msg void OnMouseMove(UINT nFlags, CPoint point);
    afx_msg void OnLButtonUp(UINT nFlags, CPoint point);
    //}}AFX_MSG
    DECLARE_MESSAGE_MAP()
};

#ifndef _DEBUG // debug version in minidvw.cpp
inline CMinidrawDoc* CMinidrawView::GetDocument()
    { return (CMinidrawDoc*) m_pDocument; }
#endif
```

//

Listing 18.8

```
// minidvw.cpp : implementation of the CMinidrawView class
//

#include "stdafx.h"
#include "minidraw.h"
```

```
#include "miniddoc.h"
#include "minidvw.h"

#ifdef _DEBUG
#undef THIS_FILE
static char BASED_CODE THIS_FILE[] = __FILE__;
#endif

/////////////////////////////////////////////////////////////////////////////
// CMinidrawView

IMPLEMENT_DYNCREATE(CMinidrawView, CScrollView)

BEGIN_MESSAGE_MAP(CMinidrawView, CScrollView)
    //{{AFX_MSG_MAP(CMinidrawView)
    ON_WM_LBUTTONDOWN()
    ON_WM_MOUSEMOVE()
    ON_WM_LBUTTONUP()
    ON_WM_KEYDOWN()
    //}}AFX_MSG_MAP
    // Standard printing commands
    ON_COMMAND(ID_FILE_PRINT, CView::OnFilePrint)
    ON_COMMAND(ID_FILE_PRINT_PREVIEW, CView::OnFilePrintPreview)
END_MESSAGE_MAP()

/////////////////////////////////////////////////////////////////////////////
// CMinidrawView construction/destruction

CMinidrawView::CMinidrawView()
{
    // TODO: add construction code here

    mDragging = 0;
    mHArrow = AfxGetApp ()->LoadStandardCursor (IDC_ARROW);
    mHCross = AfxGetApp ()->LoadStandardCursor (IDC_CROSS);
    mPenDotted.CreatePen (PS_DOT, 1, RGB (0,0,0));
}

CMinidrawView::~CMinidrawView()
{
}

/////////////////////////////////////////////////////////////////////////////
// CMinidrawView drawing
```

```
void CMinidrawView::OnDraw(CDC* pDC)
{
    CMinidrawDoc* pDoc = GetDocument();

    // TODO: add draw code here

    if (pDC->GetDeviceCaps (TECHNOLOGY) == DT_RASDISPLAY)
        {
        CSize ScrollSize = GetTotalSize ();
        pDC->MoveTo (ScrollSize.cx, 0);
        pDC->LineTo (ScrollSize.cx, ScrollSize.cy);
        pDC->LineTo (0, ScrollSize.cy);
        }

    CRect ClipRect;
    CRect DimRect;
    CRect IntRect;
    CFigure *PFigure;

    pDC->GetClipBox (&ClipRect);

    int NumFigs = pDoc->GetNumFigs ();
    for (int Index = 0; Index < NumFigs; ++Index)
        {
        PFigure = pDoc->GetFigure (Index);
        DimRect = PFigure->GetDimRect ();
        if (IntRect.IntersectRect (DimRect, ClipRect))
            PFigure->Draw (pDC);
        }
}

/////////////////////////////////////////////////////////////////////////////
// CMinidrawView diagnostics

#ifdef _DEBUG
void CMinidrawView::AssertValid() const
{
    CScrollView::AssertValid();
}

void CMinidrawView::Dump(CDumpContext& dc) const
{
    CScrollView::Dump(dc);
}
```

```
CMinidrawDoc* CMinidrawView::GetDocument() // non-debug version is inline
{
    ASSERT(m_pDocument->IsKindOf(RUNTIME_CLASS(CMinidrawDoc)));
    return (CMinidrawDoc*) m_pDocument;
}

#endif //_DEBUG

/////////////////////////////////////////////////////////////////////////////
// CMinidrawView message handlers

void CMinidrawView::OnLButtonDown(UINT nFlags, CPoint point)
{
    // TODO: Add your message handler code here and/or call default

    CClientDC ClientDC (this);
    OnPrepareDC (&ClientDC);
    ClientDC.DPtoLP (&point);

    // test whether cursor is within drawing area of view window:
    CSize ScrollSize = GetTotalSize ();
    CRect ScrollRect (0, 0, ScrollSize.cx, ScrollSize.cy);
    if (!ScrollRect.PtInRect (point))
        return;

    // save cursor position, capture mouse, & set dragging flag:
    mPointOrigin = point;
    mPointOld = point;
    SetCapture ();
    mDragging = 1;

    // clip mouse cursor:
    ClientDC.LPtoDP (&ScrollRect);
    CRect ViewRect;
    GetClientRect (&ViewRect);
    CRect IntRect;
    IntRect.IntersectRect (&ScrollRect, &ViewRect);
    ClientToScreen (&IntRect);
    ::ClipCursor (&IntRect);

    CScrollView::OnLButtonDown(nFlags, point);
}
```

```
void CMinidrawView::OnMouseMove(UINT nFlags, CPoint point)
{
    // TODO: Add your message handler code here and/or call default

    CClientDC ClientDC (this);
    OnPrepareDC (&ClientDC);
    ClientDC.DPtoLP (&point);

    if (!mDragging)
        {
        CSize ScrollSize = GetTotalSize ();
        CRect ScrollRect (0, 0, ScrollSize.cx, ScrollSize.cy);
        if (ScrollRect.PtInRect (point))
            ::SetCursor (mHCross);
        else
            ::SetCursor (mHArrow);
        return;
        }

    ClientDC.SetROP2 (R2_NOT);
    ClientDC.SelectObject (&mPenDotted);
    ClientDC.SetBkMode (TRANSPARENT);
    ClientDC.SelectStockObject (NULL_BRUSH);

    switch (((CMinidrawApp *)AfxGetApp ())->mCurrentTool)
        {
        case ID_TOOLS_LINE:
            ClientDC.MoveTo (mPointOrigin);
            ClientDC.LineTo (mPointOld);
            ClientDC.MoveTo (mPointOrigin);
            ClientDC.LineTo (point);
            break;

        case ID_TOOLS_RECTANGLE:
        case ID_TOOLS_RECTFILL:
            ClientDC.Rectangle (mPointOrigin.x, mPointOrigin.y,
                                mPointOld.x, mPointOld.y);
            ClientDC.Rectangle (mPointOrigin.x, mPointOrigin.y,
                                point.x, point.y);
            break;

        case ID_TOOLS_RECTROUND:
        case ID_TOOLS_RECTROUNDFILL:
            {
            int SizeRound = (abs (mPointOld.x - mPointOrigin.x) +
```

```
                            abs (mPointOld.y - mPointOrigin.y)) / 6;
          ClientDC.RoundRect (mPointOrigin.x, mPointOrigin.y,
                              mPointOld.x, mPointOld.y,
                              SizeRound, SizeRound);
          SizeRound = (abs (point.x - mPointOrigin.x) +
                       abs (point.y - mPointOrigin.y)) / 6;
          ClientDC.RoundRect (mPointOrigin.x, mPointOrigin.y,
                              point.x, point.y,
                              SizeRound, SizeRound);
          break;
          }
      case ID_TOOLS_CIRCLE:
      case ID_TOOLS_CIRCLEFILL:
          ClientDC.Ellipse (mPointOrigin.x, mPointOrigin.y,
                            mPointOld.x, mPointOld.y);
          ClientDC.Ellipse (mPointOrigin.x, mPointOrigin.y,
                            point.x, point.y);
          break;
      }

   mPointOld = point;

   CScrollView::OnMouseMove(nFlags, point);
}

void CMinidrawView::OnLButtonUp(UINT nFlags, CPoint point)
{
   // TODO: Add your message handler code here and/or call default
   if (!mDragging)
      return;

   mDragging = 0;
   ::ReleaseCapture ();
   ::ClipCursor (NULL);

   CClientDC ClientDC (this);
   OnPrepareDC (&ClientDC);
   ClientDC.DPtoLP (&point);
   ClientDC.SetROP2 (R2_NOT);
   ClientDC.SelectObject (&mPenDotted);
   ClientDC.SetBkMode (TRANSPARENT);
   ClientDC.SelectStockObject (NULL_BRUSH);

   CMinidrawApp *PApp = (CMinidrawApp *)AfxGetApp ();
   CFigure *PFigure;
```

```
switch (PApp->mCurrentTool)
    {
    case ID_TOOLS_LINE:
        ClientDC.MoveTo (mPointOrigin);
        ClientDC.LineTo (mPointOld);
        PFigure = new CLine
            (mPointOrigin.x, mPointOrigin.y,
            point.x, point.y,
            PApp->mCurrentColor,
            PApp->mCurrentThickness);
        break;

    case ID_TOOLS_RECTANGLE:
        ClientDC.Rectangle (mPointOrigin.x, mPointOrigin.y,
                            mPointOld.x, mPointOld.y);
        PFigure = new CRectangle
            (mPointOrigin.x, mPointOrigin.y,
            point.x, point.y,
            PApp->mCurrentColor,
            PApp->mCurrentThickness);
        break;

    case ID_TOOLS_RECTFILL:
        ClientDC.Rectangle (mPointOrigin.x, mPointOrigin.y,
                            mPointOld.x, mPointOld.y);
        PFigure = new CRectFill
            (mPointOrigin.x, mPointOrigin.y,
            point.x, point.y,
            PApp->mCurrentColor);
        break;

    case ID_TOOLS_RECTROUND:
        {
        int SizeRound = (abs (mPointOld.x - mPointOrigin.x) +
                        abs (mPointOld.y - mPointOrigin.y)) / 6;
        ClientDC.RoundRect (mPointOrigin.x, mPointOrigin.y,
                            mPointOld.x, mPointOld.y,
                            SizeRound, SizeRound);
        PFigure = new CRectRound
            (mPointOrigin.x, mPointOrigin.y,
            point.x, point.y,
            PApp->mCurrentColor,
```

```
          PApp->mCurrentThickness);
      break;
      }

   case ID_TOOLS_RECTROUNDFILL:
      {
      int SizeRound = (abs (mPointOld.x - mPointOrigin.x) +
                       abs (mPointOld.y - mPointOrigin.y)) / 6;
      ClientDC.RoundRect (mPointOrigin.x, mPointOrigin.y,
                          mPointOld.x, mPointOld.y,
                          SizeRound, SizeRound);
      PFigure = new CRectRoundFill
         (mPointOrigin.x, mPointOrigin.y,
         point.x, point.y,
         PApp->mCurrentColor);
      break;
      }

   case ID_TOOLS_CIRCLE:
      ClientDC.Ellipse (mPointOrigin.x, mPointOrigin.y,
                        mPointOld.x, mPointOld.y);
      PFigure = new CCircle
         (mPointOrigin.x, mPointOrigin.y,
         point.x, point.y,
         PApp->mCurrentColor,
         PApp->mCurrentThickness);
      break;

   case ID_TOOLS_CIRCLEFILL:
      ClientDC.Ellipse (mPointOrigin.x, mPointOrigin.y,
                        mPointOld.x, mPointOld.y);
      PFigure = new CCircleFill
         (mPointOrigin.x, mPointOrigin.y,
         point.x, point.y,
         PApp->mCurrentColor);
      break;
   }

ClientDC.SetROP2 (R2_COPYPEN);
PFigure->Draw (&ClientDC);

CMinidrawDoc* PDoc = GetDocument();
PDoc->AddFigure (PFigure);
```

```
    PDoc->UpdateAllViews (this, 0, PFigure);

    CScrollView::OnLButtonUp(nFlags, point);
    }

BOOL CMinidrawView::PreCreateWindow (CREATESTRUCT& cs)
    {
    mClassName = AfxRegisterWndClass
        (CS_HREDRAW | CS_VREDRAW,                  // class styles
        0,                                         // no cursor
        (HBRUSH)::GetStockObject (WHITE_BRUSH),    // set white background brush
        0);                                        // no icon
    cs.lpszClass = mClassName;

    return CScrollView::PreCreateWindow (cs);
    }

void CMinidrawView::OnInitialUpdate ()
    {
    SIZE Size = {DRAWWIDTH, DRAWHEIGHT};
    SetScrollSizes (MM_TEXT, Size);
    CScrollView::OnInitialUpdate ();
    }

void CMinidrawView::OnUpdate (CView* pSender, LPARAM lHint, CObject* pHint)
    {
    if (pHint != 0)
        {
        CRect InvalidRect = ((CFigure *)pHint)->GetDimRect ();
        CClientDC ClientDC (this);
        OnPrepareDC (&ClientDC);
        ClientDC.LPtoDP (&InvalidRect);
        InvalidateRect (&InvalidRect);
        }
    else
        CScrollView::OnUpdate (pSender, lHint, pHint);
    }

BOOL CMinidrawView::OnPreparePrinting(CPrintInfo* pInfo)
{
    return DoPreparePrinting(pInfo);
}

void CMinidrawView::OnBeginPrinting (CDC* pDC, CPrintInfo* pInfo)
    {
```

```
   mPageHeight = pDC->GetDeviceCaps (VERTRES);
   mPageWidth = pDC->GetDeviceCaps (HORZRES);

   mNumRows = DRAWHEIGHT / mPageHeight  + (DRAWHEIGHT % mPageHeight > 0);
   mNumCols = DRAWWIDTH / mPageWidth  + (DRAWWIDTH % mPageWidth > 0);
   pInfo->SetMinPage (1);
   pInfo->SetMaxPage (mNumRows * mNumCols);
   }

void CMinidrawView::OnPrepareDC (CDC* pDC, CPrintInfo* pInfo)
   {
   CScrollView::OnPrepareDC (pDC, pInfo);

   if (pInfo == NULL)
      return;

   int CurRow = pInfo->m_nCurPage / mNumCols +
               (pInfo->m_nCurPage % mNumCols > 0);
   int CurCol = (pInfo->m_nCurPage - 1) % mNumCols + 1;

   pDC->SetViewportOrg
      (-mPageWidth * (CurCol - 1),
       -mPageHeight * (CurRow - 1));
   }
```

Summary

In this chapter, you learned how to provide the code to support the standard Print...,
Print Preview, and Print Setup... commands on the File menu. The following is a
summary of the main concepts and techniques that were presented:

- If you are creating a new program using AppWizard, you can include
  Print..., Print Preview, and Print Setup... commands on the program's File
  menu by selecting the Printing and Print Preview option in the AppWizard
  Options dialog box. The Print... and Print Preview commands, however, will
  print or preview only the portion of a document that fits on a single page.

- You can also add Print..., Print Preview, and Print Setup... commands to an
  existing program, and can modify the program code to support these commands. In App Studio, in addition to including the print commands in the
  program menu, you must choose the Set Includes... command on the File

menu, and must specify the prewritten file AFXPRINT.RC, so that the resources defined in this file (which are used for printing) are included in the program.

- To process the Print Setup... command, you must add a message-map entry to the application class, which invokes the `CWinApp::OnFilePrintSetup` function.

- To process the Print... and Print Preview commands, you must add message-map entries to the view class, which invoke the `CView::OnFilePrint` and `CView::OnFilePrintPreview` functions.

- When the `OnFilePrint` and `OnFilePrintPreview` functions conduct the print or print preview job, they call a series of virtual functions defined within the `CView` class. You *must* provide an overriding version of the OnPreparePrinting virtual function; your function must call CView:: DoPreparePrinting to create a device context object for the printer.

- If your program is to print more than one page, you should call the `CPrintInfo` member functions `SetMinPage` and `SetMaxPage` to specify the numbers of the first and last pages. You normally call these functions in an overriding version of the `OnBeginPrinting` virtual function.

- To support multiple-page printing, you should also provide an overriding version of the `OnPrepareDC` virtual function, which is called before each page is printed. Your function should adjust the viewport origin so that the standard output function, `OnDraw`, will print the portion of the document that is to appear on the current page.

- After calling `OnPrepareDC`, the MFC calls the `OnPrint` virtual function; the default version of this function simply calls `OnDraw` to display output on the current page.

- The device-independent code in `OnDraw` serves to display output on a variety of devices. To customize the output for a specific device, you can pass the index `TECHNOLOGY` to the `GetDeviceCaps` function to determine the type of the target device.

Exchanging Data Using the Clipboard and OLE

19

- Using the Clipboard

- Using OLE

In this chapter you will learn how to use two different mechanisms for exchanging data: the Windows Clipboard and the Object Linking and Embedding protocol (OLE). You will first learn how to use the Clipboard to perform simple transfers of standard text, bitmaps, or privately formatted data, either within a single program or from one program to another. You will then learn how to use the more versatile OLE mechanism, which allows you to transfer data in an unlimited variety of formats; specifically, you will learn how to create an OLE *client*, which is a program that receives OLE data objects from other OLE-aware applications. To implement OLE capability, you will learn how to use AppWizard and the MFC OLE classes, which greatly simplify an otherwise daunting programming task.

Using the Clipboard

In the following sections, you will learn how to use the Windows Clipboard to transfer data within your program and to exchange data with other programs. The first section describes the commands that your program should provide if it makes use of the Clipboard. The following sections then explain how to use the Clipboard to transfer plain text, graphic images in bitmap format, and data that conforms to a private format.

The Clipboard Commands

If your program makes use of the Windows Clipboard facilities, it should generally provide Cut, Copy, and Paste commands on the program's Edit menu. If you use AppWizard to generate your program, AppWizard will add Cut, Copy, and Paste commands to the initial Edit menu. (In many of the example programs given in this book, you have been instructed to remove these menu commands because the program has not used them.) Table 19.1 lists these menu commands as they are defined by AppWizard, and Figure 19.1 illustrates the initial Edit menu generated by AppWizard, showing the Cut, Copy, and Paste commands. (As you will learn later in the chapter, the Edit menu will have several additional commands if you choose the OLE Client option in AppWizard.)

AppWizard also defines two accelerator keystrokes for each of the Cut, Copy, and Paste menu commands. One accelerator keystroke conforms to the older keystroke convention, and the other keystroke conforms to the newer convention. The user

TABLE 19.1: The Properties of the Cut, Copy, and Paste Menu Commands Generated by AppWizard

ID:	Caption:	Prompt:	Other Features
ID_EDIT_CUT	Cu&t\tCtrl+X	Cut the selection and put it on the Clipboard	none
ID_EDIT_COPY	&Copy\tCtrl+C	Copy the selection and put it on the Clipboard	none
ID_EDIT_PASTE	&Paste\tCtrl+V	Insert Clipboard contents	none

FIGURE 19.1:

The initial Edit menu generated by AppWizard, showing the Cut, Copy, and Paste commands

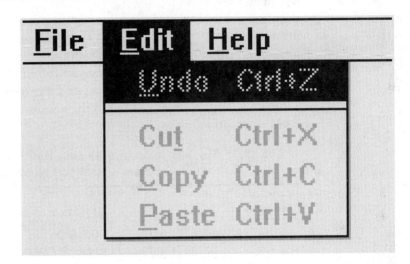

can thus use *either* the older *or* the newer keystroke to activate a given command. Note that the menu captions display the keystrokes conforming to the newer convention. These accelerator keystrokes are described in Table 19.2.

AppWizard does not, however, provide handlers for the Cut, Copy, and Paste commands. Therefore, these menu commands are initially disabled. As usual, you can define message-handling functions for these commands using ClassWizard. You should normally add these message handlers to the program's view class,

TABLE 19.2: Accelerator Keystrokes for the Cut, Copy, and Paste Commands
Generated by AppWizard

Menu Command	ID of Menu Command and Accelerator	Keystroke for Older Convention	Keystroke for Newer Convention
Cut	ID_EDIT_CUT	Shift+Del	Ctrl+X
Copy	ID_EDIT_COPY	Ctrl+Ins	Ctrl+C
Paste	ID_EDIT_PASTE	Shift+Ins	Ctrl+V

because—like other editing commands—these commands directly affect the content of the view window. Also, for each of the Cut, Copy, and Paste commands, you should provide both a COMMAND handler and an UPDATE_COMMAND_UI handler. The UPDATE_COMMAND_UI handler receives control when the user first opens the Edit menu, and either enables or disables the command based upon the current state of the Clipboard or the view window. The COMMAND handler receives control when the user chooses the command and it carries out the Clipboard operation. Table 19.3 lists the default names of the handlers that ClassWizard generates for these commands.

TABLE 19.3: The Default Message-Handling Functions that ClassWizard Defines for the Cut, Copy, and Paste Menu Commands

Command	ID:	Message	Message-Handling Function
Cut	ID_EDIT_CUT	COMMAND	OnEditCut
Cut	ID_EDIT_CUT	UPDATE_COMMAND_UI	OnUpdateEditCut
Copy	ID_EDIT_COPY	COMMAND	OnEditCopy
Copy	ID_EDIT_COPY	UPDATE_COMMAND_UI	OnUpdateEditCopy
Paste	ID_EDIT_PASTE	COMMAND	OnEditPaste
Paste	ID_EDIT_PASTE	UPDATE_COMMAND_UI	OnUpdateEditPaste

NOTE If you choose the Initial Toolbar AppWizard option, AppWizard will add tool bar buttons for the Cut, Copy, and Paste commands. Because these buttons are assigned the *same* identifiers as the corresponding menu commands, they will be processed by the menu message handlers that you define; you do not need to provide any additional code to respond to the buttons.

The COMMAND handlers for the Cut and Copy commands should transfer the selected data (text or graphics) into the Clipboard. In addition, the Cut COMMAND handler should delete the data from the document. The UPDATE_COMMAND_UI handlers for the Cut and Copy commands should enable the command only if the user has selected document data within the view window.

NOTE A program might also provide a Delete command for deleting the selected data *without* copying it to the Clipboard.

After the data has been transferred to the Clipboard, the user can insert it into another position within the same document, into another document in the same program, or into another Windows or DOS program (DOS programs can receive only textual data).

The COMMAND handler for the Paste command should insert the contents of the Clipboard into the current document. The data might have been obtained from the current document, from another document within the same program, or from another Windows or DOS program. The textual or graphic data is generally inserted at the position of the caret that marks the text insertion point in the view window (for example, in a word processing application). Alternatively, graphic data might be inserted at an arbitrary location within the view window, and be selected so that the user can move it to the desired position (for example, in a drawing program).

The UPDATE_COMMAND_UI handler for the Paste command should enable the command only if the Clipboard contains data in the appropriate format. The technique for testing for specific formats is discussed later in the chapter.

The way that the COMMAND and UPDATE_COMMAND_UI handlers work depends upon the format of the data that is being transferred. Details are given in the following sections.

Using the Clipboard to Transfer Text

In this section, you will learn how to use the Clipboard to transfer plain text (that is, text consisting of a simple stream of characters without formatting codes, such as the text displayed by the Windows NotePad editor). To transfer text containing proprietary formatting codes (for example, the formatted text displayed in a word processor), you can use the techniques given later in the chapter, in the section "Using the Clipboard to Transfer Private Data Formats." You will first learn how to transfer text to the Clipboard, and then learn how to obtain text from the Clipboard.

> **NOTE**
>
> If you derive the program's view class from the MFC CEditView class (which provides text editing as discussed in Chapter 8), you do not need to write any code to support the Cut, Copy, and Paste commands for transferring view window text. You need only make sure that the program's Edit menu includes Cut, Copy, and Paste commands, and that these commands have the identifiers given in Table 19.1. The CEditView class provides a full set of message handlers for these commands.

Adding Text to the Clipboard

Text is transferred to the Clipboard in response to the Cut or Copy command. The UPDATE_COMMAND_UI message handlers for these commands should enable the command only if the user has selected a block of text, as in the following examples:

```
void CProgView::OnUpdateEditCut(CCmdUI* pCmdUI)
{
    // TODO: Add your command update UI handler code here
    pCmdUI->Enable (mIsSelection);
}

void CProgView::OnUpdateEditCopy(CCmdUI* pCmdUI)
{
```

```
// TODO: Add your command update UI handler code here
pCmdUI->Enable (mIsSelection);
}
```

These examples assume that `mIsSelection` is a `BOOL` data member of the view class that is set to `TRUE` only when a block of text is selected.

The `COMMAND` message handlers for the Cut and Copy commands must add the selected block of text to the Clipboard. The following are the general steps for doing this:

1. Call `GlobalAlloc` to allocate a block of global memory that is large enough to hold the text that is to be inserted into the Clipboard.

2. Call `GlobalLock` to lock the global memory and obtain a pointer to it.

3. Copy the text into the global memory block.

4. Call `GlobalUnlock` to unlock the global memory.

5. Call `OpenClipboard` to open the Clipboard.

6. Call `EmptyClipboardData` to remove the current Clipboard contents.

7. Call `SetClipboardData` to supply the global memory handle to the Clipboard.

8. Call `CloseClipboard` to close the Clipboard.

9. The `COMMAND` handler for the Cut command should remove the selected data from the document.

The text you add to the Clipboard using the procedure discussed in this section must conform to the standard text format, which has the following three characteristics:

- The text consists of a simple stream of ANSI characters, without embedded formatting or control codes.

- Each line is terminated with a carriage-return and a linefeed character.

- The entire block of text is terminated with a single `NULL` character.

If the text stored in your program does not conform to this format, you can translate it into the proper format as you copy it to the Clipboard.

When you add text to the Clipboard, the Windows Clipboard facility does not store the data for you. Rather, you must explicitly allocate a global memory block, copy the text to this block, and then supply the global memory handle to the Clipboard. The Clipboard stores only the handle (and supplies the handle to any program that wants to access the data in the Clipboard).

Accordingly, the first step in adding text to the Clipboard is to allocate a global memory block (that is, a block outside of the program's data segment) by calling the Windows API function GlobalAlloc:

```
HGLOBAL GlobalAlloc (UINT fuAlloc, DWORD cbAlloc);
```

You assign the first parameter, fuAlloc, one or more flags describing the block of memory. For example, the flag GMEM_MOVEABLE indicates that the memory block is to be moveable (that is, Windows will be able to move the block if necessary to defragment the remaining free memory). Also, if you include the flag GMEM_ZEROINIT, the block of memory will be initialized with all zeros. See the documentation on the GlobalAlloc function for a description of the other flags you can assign (in the *Programmer's Reference, Volume 2* SDK manual, or in the *Windows 3.1 SDK* online help file).

The second parameter, cbAlloc, specifies the desired size of the memory block. When you specify the memory block size, be sure to allow room for the NULL character that must terminate the text. If successful, GlobalAlloc returns the handle of the global memory block; if, however, it cannot allocate the requested memory, it returns NULL.

Assume, for example, that the text you want to add to the Clipboard is contained within the character array Buffer, and that this text is properly formatted and is NULL terminated. You could then allocate memory as follows:

```
HGLOBAL HGlobalMem;

HGlobalMem = ::GlobalAlloc (GMEM_MOVEABLE, strlen (Buffer) + 1);
if (HGlobalMem == NULL)
    {
    MessageBox ("Error copying data to the Clipboard.");
    return;
    }
```

Before you can access the block of global memory, you must call the Windows API function GlobalLock,

```
void FAR* GlobalLock (HGLOBAL hglb);
```

where hglb is the handle obtained from GlobalAlloc. If successful, GlobalLock returns a far pointer to the beginning of the memory block; if an error occurs, it returns NULL. The following code obtains a pointer to the memory allocated in the previous example:

```
char FAR* PGlobalMem;

PGlobalMem = ::GlobalLock (HGlobalMem);
if (PGlobalMem == NULL)
    {
    ::GlobalFree (HGlobalMem);
    MessageBox ("Error copying data to the Clipboard.");
    return;
    }
```

In this example, notice that if the call to GlobalLock fails, the memory block is released before the function exits by passing the memory handle to the Windows API function GlobalFree.

Next, you need to copy the text that you want to add to the Clipboard into the global memory block. To do this, you might use the Windows API function lstrcpy, as in the following example:

```
::lstrcpy (PGlobalMem, Buffer);
```

Like the standard C++ library function strcpy, lstrcpy copies a NULL-terminated string from the location given by the second parameter to the location given by the first parameter. The advantage of lstrcpy is that either of the parameters can be a near pointer *or* a far pointer. If the text you want to add to the Clipboard does not conform to the standard text format, or does not contain a NULL termination, you can write your own copy routine to perform the necessary translations as the data is copied.

Next, you must prepare the global memory handle, so that it can be passed to the Clipboard, by calling the Windows API function GlobalUnlock, as in the following example:

```
::GlobalUnlock (HGlobalMem);
```

Before you can access the Clipboard, you must open it by calling the CWnd member function OpenClipboard:

```
BOOL OpenClipboard ();
```

OpenClipboard returns TRUE if successful. If, however, another program has already opened the Clipboard and has not yet closed it, OpenClipboard returns FALSE; in this case, you cannot complete the Clipboard operation. The following is an example:

```
if (!OpenClipboard ())
    {
    ::GlobalFree (HGlobalMem);
    MessageBox ("Clipboard not available.");
    }
```

After opening the Clipboard, you must remove the current Clipboard contents by calling the Windows API function EmptyClipboard:

```
BOOL EmptyClipboard (void);
```

You can now add your text to the Clipboard by calling the Windows API function SetClipboardData:

```
HANDLE SetClipboardData (UINT uFormat, HANDLE hData);
```

The first parameter, uFormat, specifies the format of the data you are adding to the Clipboard; to add text, you pass the value CF_TEXT. (See the documentation on this function for a description of the other standard formats you can specify.) The second parameter, hData, is the handle to the global memory allocation that contains the data. The following is an example:

```
::SetClipboardData (CF_TEXT, HGlobalMem);
```

After calling SetClipboardData, you must *not* use the global memory handle (specifically, you must *not* attempt to read or write to the memory, nor call GlobalFree to free the memory block; the handle now belongs to Windows, which will automatically free the memory block when appropriate). To avoid the temptation to use the handle, you might set the variable containing the handle to NULL immediately after calling SetClipboardData. If you need to access the memory block after calling SetClipboardData, you must use the standard procedure for obtaining Clipboard data in response to the Paste command, which is described in the next section.

> **NOTE** If you use the `GlobalAlloc` function to obtain a block of memory that you do *not* pass to the Clipboard, you must call `GlobalUnlock` and then `GlobalFree` when you have finished using the memory. Note, also, that as long as your program is never run under the Real mode of Windows 3.0 (the programs in this book *cannot* run in Real mode), you do not need to call `GlobalUnlock` until you are ready to free the memory (unlocking memory is useful only in Real mode).

Finally, you must close the Clipboard by calling the Windows API function `Close-Clipboard`:

```
BOOL CloseClipboard (void);
```

Because only one program can have the Clipboard open at a given time, you must close the Clipboard before you return control from the current message-handling function or perform any other action that allows other programs to run (such as displaying a message box or modal dialog box).

The following is an example of a COMMAND message-handling function for the Copy command (defined as a member function of the view class), which illustrates all of the steps discussed in this section:

```
void CProgView::OnEditCopy()
{
    // TODO: Add your command handler code here

    HGLOBAL HGlobalMem;
    char FAR* PGlobalMem;

    // 1. allocate global memory:
    HGlobalMem = ::GlobalAlloc(GMEM_MOVEABLE, strlen(Buffer) + 1);
    if (HGlobalMem == NULL)
        {
        MessageBox ("Error copying data to the Clipboard.");
        return;
        }

    // 2. lock global memory and obtain a pointer:
    PGlobalMem = ::GlobalLock (HGlobalMem);
    if (PGlobalMem == NULL)
```

```
   {
   ::GlobalFree (HGlobalMem);
   MessageBox ("Error copying data to the Clipboard.");
   return;
   }

// 3. copy selected text into global memory block:
::lstrcpy (PGlobalMem, Buffer);

// 4. unlock global memory:
::GlobalUnlock (HGlobalMem);

// 5. open Clipboard:
if (!OpenClipboard ())
   {
   ::GlobalFree (HGlobalMem);
   MessageBox ("Error copying data to the Clipboard.");
   }

// 6. remove current Clipboard contents:
::EmptyClipboard ();

// 7. supply the global memory handle to the Clipboard:
::SetClipboardData (CF_TEXT, HGlobalMem);

// 8. close Clipboard:
::CloseClipboard ();
}
```

This example assumes that `Buffer` is a global character array containing the currently selected text, and that this text is `NULL` terminated. The `COMMAND` message handler that processes the Cut command (`OnEditCut`) could call this function and then proceed to remove the selected text from the document.

Obtaining Text from the Clipboard

If your program allows the user to paste only standard text from the Clipboard, the `UPDATE_COMMAND_UI` message-handling function for the Paste command should enable the command only if the Clipboard currently contains text. To determine whether the Clipboard contains data that conforms to a specific format, you can call the Windows API function `IsClipboardFormatAvailable`:

```
BOOL IsClipboardFormatAvailable (UINT uFormat);
```

The parameter uFormat specifies the desired format. The following is an example of an UPDATE_COMMAND_UI message-handling function that enables or disables the Paste command, depending upon whether or not the Clipboard contains text:

```
void CProgView::OnUpdateEditPaste(CCmdUI* pCmdUI)
{
    // TODO: Add your command update UI handler code here

    BOOL EnableIt = FALSE;

    if (OpenClipboard ())
        {
        if (::IsClipboardFormatAvailable (CF_TEXT) ||
            ::IsClipboardFormatAvailable (CF_OEMTEXT))
          EnableIt = TRUE;
        ::CloseClipboard ();
        }
    pCmdUI->Enable (EnableIt);
}
```

Notice that you must open the Clipboard before calling IsClipboardFormat-Available. The example OnUpdateEditPaste function checks both for standard Windows text (the CF_TEXT format), as well as text conforming to the CF_OEMTEXT format. The CF_OEMTEXT format is the same as the CF_TEXT format, except that the text uses the OEM character set (that is, the character set displayed by DOS text-mode programs). If neither format is available, or if Clipboard cannot be opened, the Paste command is disabled; otherwise, it is enabled.

The COMMAND message handler for the Paste command must obtain a copy of the text contained in the Clipboard. The following are the general steps for doing this:

1. Call OpenClipboard to open the Clipboard.

2. Call GetClipboardData to obtain a handle to the block of global memory holding the Clipboard text.

3. Allocate a block of program memory to store a copy of the Clipboard text.

4. Call GlobalLock to lock the handles for the Clipboard and program memory blocks and to obtain pointers to these blocks.

5. Copy the text from the Clipboard memory to the program memory.

6. Call GlobalUnlock to unlock the Clipboard memory.

7. Call `CloseClipboard` to close the Clipboard.

8. After you have finished using the copy of the text contained in the program memory, unlock and free this memory block.

After you have opened the Clipboard, you can obtain a handle to the block of global memory holding the text by calling the `GetClipboardData` Windows API function, as in the following example:

```
HGLOBAL HClipText;

HClipText = ::GetClipboardData (CF_TEXT);
if (HClipText == NULL)
    {
    ::CloseClipboard ();
    MessageBox ("Error obtaining text from Clipboard.");
    return;
    }
```

The parameter you pass to `GetClipboardData` specifies the desired data format. If the Clipboard does not contain data in the specified format, it returns NULL. (Theoretically, this error should not occur—if your UPDATE_COMMAND_UI message handler enables the Paste command only when `IsClipboardFormatAvailable` indicates that the desired format is available.) Note that you need request only the CF_TEXT format; if the Clipboard contains only text that conforms to the CF_OEMTEXT format, it will automatically convert the text to the CF_TEXT format.

The handle you obtain by calling `GetClipboardData` does *not* belong to your program, and the handle remains valid only until you call `CloseClipboard`. You can read or copy the data from the associated memory block, but you must *not* alter it. (This block must remain unaltered so that the Clipboard can supply the data in response to subsequent requests by your program or other programs.)

After you have successfully obtained a handle to the global memory containing the Clipboard text, you can allocate a block of memory to hold a copy of the text. Call the Windows API function `GlobalSize` to determine the size of the Clipboard's global memory block. As an example, the following code allocates a block of global memory that is large enough to hold the text from the Clipboard:

```
HGLOBAL HProgText;

HProgText = GlobalAlloc (GMEM_MOVEABLE, ::GlobalSize (HClipText));
if (HProgText == NULL)
```

```
    {
    ::CloseClipboard ();
    MessageBox ("Out of memory!");
    return;
    }
```

In this example, HClipText is the global memory handle that was returned by GetClipboardData.

Before you can access either the Clipboard memory or the private program memory, you must call GlobalLock to obtain pointers to these memory blocks:

```
char FAR *PClipText;
char FAR *PProgText;

PClipText = ::GlobalLock (HClipText);
PProgText = ::GlobalLock (HProgText);
```

Before closing the Clipboard, be sure to call GlobalUnlock to unlock the Clipboard memory:

```
::GlobalUnlock (HClipText);
::CloseClipboard ();
```

After calling CloseClipboard, you *cannot* use the handle to the memory that was obtained from the Clipboard.

The following is an example of a COMMAND message-handling function (defined as a member of the view class) that obtains text from the Clipboard in response to the Paste command:

```
void CProgView::OnEditPaste()
{
    // TODO: Add your command handler code here

    HGLOBAL HClipText;
    HGLOBAL HProgText;
    char FAR *PClipText;
    char FAR *PProgText;

    // 1. open Clipboard:
    if (!OpenClipboard ())
        {
        MessageBox ("Could not open Clipboard.");
        return;
        }
```

```
// 2. obtain handle to Clipboard data:
HClipText = GetClipboardData (CF_TEXT);
if (HClipText == NULL)
    {
    ::CloseClipboard ();
    MessageBox ("Error obtaining text from Clipboard.");
    return;
    }

// 3. allocate a block of memory to store text from Clipboard:
HProgText = GlobalAlloc (GMEM_MOVEABLE, ::GlobalSize (HClipText));
if (HProgText == NULL)
    {
    ::CloseClipboard ();
    MessageBox ("Out of memory!");
    return;
    }

// 4. lock memory handles and obtain pointers:
PClipText = ::GlobalLock (HClipText);
PProgText = ::GlobalLock (HProgText);

// 5. copy text from Clipboard:
::lstrcpy (PProgText, PClipText);

// 6. unlock Clipboard memory block:
::GlobalUnlock (HClipText);

// 7. close Clipboard
::CloseClipboard ();

InsertText (PProgText);

// 8. unlock and free program memory block:
::GlobalUnlock (HProgText);
::GlobalFree (HProgText);
}
```

This example assumes that the function InsertText inserts the text from the NULL-terminated buffer that is passed to it, into the current document.

> **NOTE** For simplicity, the example function did not check for errors when calling `GlobalLock` to lock the memory blocks. Rather, it made the relatively safe assumption that if a valid handle is passed to `GlobalLock`, the function will be successful.

Using the Clipboard to Transfer Graphics

You can transfer graphic information within a program or among separate programs by using the Clipboard to exchange bitmaps. In this section you will learn how to add a bitmap to the Clipboard and how to obtain a bitmap from the Clipboard. The procedures you learn here will be useful for developing drawing programs, word processors, or other programs that display graphics in bitmap format.

Adding a Bitmap to the Clipboard

As with a block of text, a bitmap is transferred to the Clipboard in response to the Cut or Copy command. The UPDATE_COMMAND_UI message-handlers for these commands should enable the command only if the user has selected a bitmap, as in the following examples:

```
void CProgView::OnUpdateEditCut(CCmdUI* pCmdUI)
{
    // TODO: Add your command update UI handler code here
    pCmdUI->Enable (mIsSelection);
}

void CProgView::OnUpdateEditCopy(CCmdUI* pCmdUI)
{
    // TODO: Add your command update UI handler code here
    pCmdUI->Enable (mIsSelection);
}
```

These examples assume that mIsSelection is a BOOL data member of the view class that is set to TRUE only when a bitmap is selected (or, if the program also permits the user to transfer text to the Clipboard, that mIsSelection would be set to TRUE if either text or a bitmap is selected).

The bitmap is added to the Clipboard by the COMMAND message handlers for the Cut and Copy commands. The following is the general procedure for doing this:

1. Call OpenClipboard to open the Clipboard.

2. Call EmptyClipboard to remove the current Clipboard contents.

3. Call SetClipboardData, passing this function the code CF_BITMAP as the first parameter, and the handle of the bitmap you want to place in the Clipboard as the second parameter. (As you saw in Chapter 17, there are several different ways to create a bitmap and obtain a bitmap handle. The example code that follows creates an empty bitmap and copies data into it.)

4. Call CloseClipboard to close the Clipboard.

5. The COMMAND message handler for the Cut command should remove the graphic data from the document.

As an example, the following COMMAND message handler for the Copy command creates a bitmap that contains the current contents of the view window. It then adds this bitmap to the Clipboard.

```
void CProgView::OnEditCopy()
{
    // TODO: Add your command handler code here

    CBitmap BitmapClip;
    CClientDC ClientDC (this);
    CDC MemDC;
    RECT Rect;

    // create an empty bitmap:
    GetClientRect (&Rect);
    BitmapClip.CreateCompatibleBitmap
        (&ClientDC,
        Rect.right - Rect.left,
        Rect.bottom - Rect.top);

    // create a memory DC object and select bitmap into it:
    MemDC.CreateCompatibleDC (&ClientDC);
    MemDC.SelectObject (&BitmapClip);
```

```
// copy contents of view window into bitmap:
MemDC.BitBlt
   (0,
   0,
   Rect.right - Rect.left,
   Rect.bottom - Rect.top,
   &ClientDC,
   0,
   0,
   SRCCOPY);

// 1. open Clipboard:
if (!OpenClipboard ())
   return;

// 2. remove current Clipboard contents:
::EmptyClipboard ();

// 3. give bitmap handle to Clipboard:
::SetClipboardData (CF_BITMAP, BitmapClip.m_hObject);

// avoid destroying the bitmap:
BitmapClip.Detach ();

// 4. close Clipboard:
::CloseClipboard ();
}
```

The example `OnEditCopy` function begins by calling `CreateCompatibleBitmap` to create an empty bitmap the size of the entire view window. It then creates a memory device context and selects the new bitmap into it. Next, it calls `BitBlt` to copy the contents of the view window to the bitmap (that is, it copies whatever text or graphics happen to be displayed in the view window).

NOTE See Chapter 17 for information on creating bitmaps and on calling functions for performing bit operations (such as `BitBlt`).

`OnEditCopy` calls `SetClipboardData` to add the bitmap to the opened Clipboard. It assigns the first parameter the value `CF_BITMAP` to specify the bitmap format, and it assigns the second parameter `BitmapClip.m_hObject`, which contains the handle of the bitmap (m_hObject is a data member that the CBitmap class inherits from CGdiObject).

After calling SetClipboardData to supply the bitmap to the Clipboard, you must *not* use or destroy the bitmap. Accordingly, the example OnEditCopy function calls the CGdiObject member function Detach to remove the bitmap handle from the BitmapClip object. If this step were not performed, the CBitmap destructor would automatically destroy the bitmap when the BitmapClip object goes out of scope (that is, when the OnEditCopy function returns).

> **NOTE** If the program also supports copying text to the Clipboard, the OnEditCopy function would have to determine the format of the selected data and switch to an appropriate routine.

Obtaining a Bitmap from the Clipboard

Your UPDATE_COMMAND_UI message-handling function for the Paste command can pass the flag CF_BITMAP to the IsClipboardFormatAvailable function to determine whether the Clipboard currently contains data in the bitmap format. It can then use this information to enable or disable the Paste command, as in the following example:

```
void CProgView::OnUpdateEditPaste(CCmdUI* pCmdUI)
{
    // TODO: Add your command update UI handler code here

    BOOL EnableIt = FALSE;

    if (OpenClipboard ())
        {
        if (::IsClipboardFormatAvailable (CF_BITMAP)
            EnableIt = TRUE;
        ::CloseClipboard ();
        }
    pCmdUI->Enable (EnableIt);
}
```

(If the program supports the pasting of text as well as bitmaps, the OnUpdateEdit-Paste function should also test for the CF_TEXT and CF_OEMTEXT formats, which were described previously.)

The COMMAND message handler for the Paste command must obtain the bitmap from the Clipboard. The following is the general procedure for doing this:

1. Call OpenClipboard to open the Clipboard.

2. Pass the value CF_BITMAP to the function GetClipboardData to obtain a handle to the bitmap.

3. Use the bitmap handle to copy or display the bitmap, but do *not* alter the bitmap contents.

4. Call CloseClipboard to close the Clipboard.

As an example, the following COMMAND message handler for the Paste command obtains a bitmap from the Clipboard and displays it within the view window (the upper-left corner of the bitmap is placed at the upper-left corner of the window):

```
void CProgView::OnEditPaste()
{
    // TODO: Add your command handler code here

    CClientDC ClientDC (this);
    CBitmap BitmapClip;
    BITMAP BitmapClipInfo;
    HANDLE HBitmapClip;
    CDC MemDC;

    // 1. open Clipboard:
    if (!OpenClipboard ())
        return;

    // 2. obtain bitmap handle from Clipboard:
    HBitmapClip = ::GetClipboardData (CF_BITMAP);
    if (HBitmapClip == NULL)
        {
        ::CloseClipboard ();
        return;
        }

    // 3. use bitmap handle to display bitmap:

    // initialize bitmap object using handle from Clipboard:
    BitmapClip.Attach (HBitmapClip);
```

```
// get information on bitmap:
BitmapClip.GetObject (sizeof (BITMAP), &BitmapClipInfo);

// create a memory device context and select bitmap into it:
MemDC.CreateCompatibleDC (&ClientDC);
MemDC.SelectObject (&BitmapClip);

// copy bitmap contents to client area:
ClientDC.BitBlt
   (0,
    0,
    BitmapClipInfo.bmWidth,
    BitmapClipInfo.bmHeight,
    &MemDC,
    0,
    0,
    SRCCOPY);

// remove the bitmap handle from the bitmap object:
BitmapClip.Detach ();

// 4. close Clipboard:
::CloseClipboard ();
}
```

The OnEditPaste function declares a CBitmap object, BitmapClip, to manage the bitmap that is obtained from the Clipboard. After it calls GetClipboardData to get the bitmap handle, it passes the handle to the CGdiObject member function Attach to initialize the bitmap object with the bitmap from the Clipboard. It then calls the CGdiObject member function GetObject to obtain information on this bitmap. (The information is written to the fields of the BITMAP structure BitmapClipInfo.)

Next, OnEditPaste creates a memory device context, selects the bitmap into it, and calls BitBlt to copy the bitmap to the client area of the window. The width and height of the bitmap are obtained from the bmWidth and bmHeight fields of the BITMAP structure.

If the bitmap is larger than the view window, Windows automatically clips the portion that falls outside of this window.

Before closing the Clipboard, OnPaste calls Detach to remove the bitmap handle from the BitmapClip object. (As with the example OnEditCopy function given in the previous section, this is done to prevent the CBitmap destructor from destroying the bitmap that belongs to the Clipboard.) After calling CloseClipboard, the program must *not* use the bitmap handle.

If the program also supports the pasting of text, OnEditPaste must test for *both* the CF_BITMAP *and* the CF_TEXT formats, and branch to an appropriate routine according to the format that is found. (GetClipboardData will return NULL if the specified format is not contained in the Clipboard.) If the Clipboard contains data in *both* formats, the program would have to choose one.

Using the Clipboard to Transfer Private Data Formats

All of the standard Clipboard formats are described in the documentation on the SetClipboardData function in the *Programmer's Reference, Volume 2* SDK manual, and in the *Windows 3.1 SDK* online help file. The data you want to transfer, however, may not conform to one of these formats. For example, if you are writing a word processor, you might store formatted text using your own format (the text characters might be stored along with embedded codes indicating fonts and other text features). You can, however, still use the Clipboard to transfer your data by calling RegisterClipboardFormat to register your private data format:

```
UINT RegisterClipboardFormat (LPCSTR lpszFormatName):
```

You can pass any name you want to RegisterClipboardFormat, and the function will return a format identifier. You can then use the other Clipboard functions to transfer the formatted text, using the same techniques that are employed for transferring plain text; however, rather than specifying the CF_TEXT format identifier, you specify the format identifier returned from `RegisterClipboardFormat`. For example, if you register a private text format as follows,

```
UINT TextFormat;

TextFormat = ::RegisterClipboardFormat ("MyAppText");
```

you could add text that conforms to this format to the Clipboard, using the following call:

```
::SetClipboardData (TextFormat, HMyText);
```

In this call, `HMyText` is a handle to a global memory block containing the formatted text. Similarly, you could pass `TextFormat`—rather than the identifier for a standard format—to the `IsClipboardFormatAvailable` and `GetClipboardData` functions.

How can the user paste the text into another program or view the text in the Windows Clipboard Viewer utility (CLIPBRD.EXE), given that other programs do not know how to interpret your private format? Fortunately, Windows allows you to add several blocks of data to the Clipboard, provided that each block has a different format. Therefore, whenever you add a block of data in your private format, you could also add a block of equivalent data conforming to a standard format; other applications or the Clipboard Viewer could then use the standard format to access or display the data (in this case, some of the formatting information would inevitably be lost). For example, to copy text to the Clipboard, you could issue the commands

```
::SetClipboardData (TextFormat, HFormattedText);
::SetClipboardData (CF_TEXT, HPlainText);
```

where `HFormattedText` is a handle to a block of text in your private format, `HPlainText` is a handle to a block of text that conforms to the standard Clipboard text format, and `TextFormat` is the index of the private format returned by `RegisterClipboardFormat`.

Using OLE

When you use the Clipboard to transfer data as described in the previous sections, the data must be in a format that the receiving application can understand (for example, plain text or a standard bitmap). Once the data has been pasted, the receiving application is fully responsible for displaying, editing, and performing other processing on the data. The variety of types of data that a program can receive via the Clipboard is thus strictly limited.

In contrast, when you transfer data using the Object Linking and Embedding protocol (OLE), the target application does *not* need to understand the data format. With OLE, the *source* application is responsible for displaying, editing, and processing the data. The target application can thus receive data from *any* application that supports the OLE protocol; in doing so, the target application can create documents consisting of a wide variety of different data types, such as text, drawings, charts, and spreadsheet cells. Such a document is known as a *compound document*.

With OLE, the source application is called the *server*, and the target application is called the *client*. A data object in the client can be either *linked* or *embedded*. If the object displayed in a client document is *linked*, the complete data for this object is stored in a separate document maintained by the server. To edit the object, the user runs the server application, usually by double-clicking the data object in the client or by choosing the Object command on the client's Edit menu. The server then opens the source document (if it is not already open), and the user can make the desired changes to the linked data within this document. When the desired changes are made, the user chooses the Save command to save the source document. The data displayed in the client is automatically or manually updated to reflect these changes, via the link that exists between the server and client.

In contrast, if the object displayed in the client document is *embedded*, the complete data for this object is stored as an integral part of the client document (there is *no* separate source document). To edit the data, the user runs the server application, usually by double-clicking the data object in the client or by choosing the Object command on the Edit menu. The server application then opens an editing window that displays the object contained in the client, and the user can use the facilities of the server to edit the object data. When the desired changes are made, rather than choosing the client's Save command to save the data in a separate disk file, the user chooses the Update command to update the single copy of the data stored within the client document.

In the following sections, you will create a simple OLE *client* application named OLEDEMO. This program allows you to insert a linked or embedded object from any OLE server program that is installed on your system. OLEDEMO displays the object and permits you to activate the server program to edit the object. For simplicity, OLEDEMO allows you to paste only one object at a time (when you paste a new object, it replaces the previous one), and the object data cannot be saved in a disk file. As you will see, the basic program template is created using AppWizard, and the OLE support is derived primarily from two MFC classes: `COleClientDoc` and `COleClientItem`.

For information on creating an OLE server application, see the *Class Library User's Guide* manual (Chapter 18, "OLE Support").

> **NOTE**
> In the context of the MFC, a linked or embedded data object is known as an *item* (presumably to avoid confusing an OLE data object from the C++ class object that manages it). Accordingly, the remainder of the chapter will use the term *OLE item* or simply *item* to refer to a linked or embedded data object.

Generating the Program

Generate the program source files using AppWizard, specifying OLEDEMO as the project name, and choosing only the OLE Client and Generate Source Comments options in the Options dialog box.

Choosing the OLE Client option causes AppWizard to derive the program's document class from the MFC class `COleClientDoc`, which provides support for an OLE client application, and it causes it to define several member functions for implementing OLE. The OLE Client option also causes AppWizard to add four new commands to the Edit menu: Paste Link, Insert New Object..., Links..., and Object (see Figure 19.2). AppWizard, however, provides little of the code for implementing these commands (it provides only a handler for the Links... command, and partially implemented handlers for the Insert New Object... and Object commands). Your primary programming task will be to add the code required to process the new OLE commands on the Edit menu, as well as the standard Cut, Copy, and Paste commands.

FIGURE 19.2:

The OLEDEMO Edit menu; AppWizard adds the last four commands to support OLE when you select the OLE Client AppWizard option

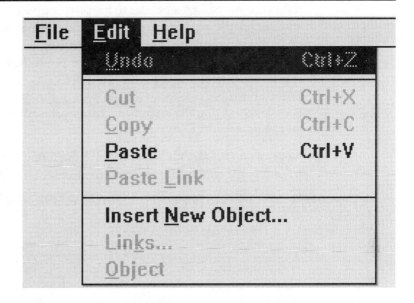

Defining the Item Class

Before defining the required message-handling functions, you need to define a class to manage the OLE linked and embedded items that are inserted into the OLEDEMO program. This class must be derived from the MFC `COleClientItem` class. To define the new class, open the OLEDEDOC.H file and add the following definition at the end of the file:

```
class CDemoOleClientItem : public COleClientItem
{
public:
    CDemoOleClientItem (COleClientDoc* pContainerDoc) :
        COleClientItem (pContainerDoc)
        { }

    virtual void OnChange (OLE_NOTIFICATION wNotification);

};
```

As you will see, whenever an OLE item is inserted into the program (through the Paste, Paste Link, or Insert New Object... commands), the program creates an instance of the `CDemoOleClientItem` class to manage the item. Notice that the class constructor is passed a pointer to the program's document object, and that the constructor simply passes this pointer to the constructor belonging to the base class, COleClientItem. The base class constructor then stores the address of the new CDemoOleClientItem object within the program's document object. One of the special tasks performed by the document class used in an OLE client program, COleClientDoc, is to store the address of the object for each OLE item that has been inserted into the document. Later, you will see how these addresses can be accessed.

Next, open OLEDEDOC.CPP and add the following definition for the CDemoOle-ClientItem::OnChange function to the end of the file:

```
void CDemoOleClientItem::OnChange (OLE_NOTIFICATION wNotification)
    {
    GetDocument ()->UpdateAllViews (NULL);
    }
```

Whenever the OLE item is updated by the server application, the COle-ClientItem::OnChange virtual member function of the object managing the item is called. The default version of this function does nothing. The overriding version that you defined calls CDocument::UpdateAllViews to cause the view window to be erased and the OnDraw function to redraw the updated OLE item within the view window. (Later, you will see how OnDraw draws the item.)

> **TIP**
>
> A full-featured program would typically allow the user to insert *several* OLE items into a document (OLEDEMO allows only one item to be inserted at a time). In such a program, you could make redrawing of the view window more efficient by passing hint information to UpdateAllViews, and defining an overriding version of the CView::OnUpdate function, which uses the hint information to invalidate *only* the area of the view window that contains the updated OLE item. See Chapter 11 (the section "Redrawing Efficiently") for a complete discussion on the use of hint information to optimize redrawing of the view window.

Supporting the Insert New Object Command

The Insert New Object... command on the File menu allows the user to embed an OLE item by running an OLE server application (the user chooses the specific type of item from a list). AppWizard provides a partially implemented message handler for this function, which is named `OnInsertObject`. To complete the definition of this function, open the OLEDEVW.CPP file, and *erase* the following lines from the `OnInsertObject` definition:

```
char szT[300];
wsprintf(szT, "TODO: this function is not completely implemented.\n"
    "You must add code to create a COleClientItem\n"
    " with a type name of '%s'.\n"
    "See COledemoView::OnInsertObject in"
        " OLEDEVW.CPP for more info.", (LPCSTR)strTypeName);
AfxMessageBox(szT);
```

Then, add the following bold lines to the definition:

```
void COledemoView::OnInsertObject()
{
    CString strTypeName;

    if (!AfxOleInsertDialog(strTypeName))
        return;      // no OLE class selected

    TRACE("Trying to Insert OLE item with type '%s'\n",
            (const char*)strTypeName);

    // TODO: create an embedded OLE object with that class name

    COledemoDoc* PDoc = GetDocument();

    POSITION Pos = PDoc->GetStartPosition ();
    if (Pos != NULL)
        delete PDoc->GetNextItem (Pos);

    CDemoOleClientItem *POleClientItem = new CDemoOleClientItem (PDoc);

    POleClientItem->CreateNewObject (strTypeName, "Demo Object");
}
```

The call to `AfxOleInsertDialog` displays the Insert New Object dialog box, which contains a list of the different types of embedded items that can be provided by the

OLE client applications that are installed in Windows (see Figure 19.3). AfxOle-InsertDialog copies to strTypeName the name of the item type that the user selected.

The code you added then deletes the previous OLE item—if any—that was embedded in the program (recall that OLEDEMO allows only one item to be embedded at a time). It does this by calling the GetStartPosition member function of the document object to obtain the position of the first (and only) OLE item in the document. If the position value is non-NULL (indicating that an OLE item has been inserted), it then calls GetNextItem to obtain the address of the CDemoOleClientItem object that manages the OLE item. By invoking delete on this object, it deletes the object (the object's destructor then automatically deletes the OLE item itself *and* removes the object's address from the document object):

```
POSITION Pos = PDoc->GetStartPosition ();
if (Pos != NULL)
    delete PDoc->GetNextItem (Pos);
```

Next, the added code creates an instance of the CDemoOleClientItem class to manage the OLE item:

```
CDemoOleClientItem *POleClientItem = new CDemoOleClientItem (PDoc);
```

Finally, the added code calls the COleClientItem::CreateNewObject function to embed the new item:

```
POleClientItem->CreateNewObject (strTypeName, "Demo Object");
```

FIGURE 19.3:

The Insert New Object dialog box; in this dialog box, the user chooses the type of OLE item that is to be embedded

The first parameter passed to CreateNewObject is the type name for the OLE item that the user selected in the Insert New Object dialog box, and the second parameter is a name that will be assigned to the particular item that is embedded. (If the document contains more than one embedded or linked item, each one must be given a *unique* name.)

The CreateNewObject function runs the server application, allowing the user to create the new OLE item. When the user has completed designing the item and chooses the Update command in the server, the data is transferred to the new CDemoOleClientItem object in the client, and the object's OnChange function is called. As explained previously, OnChange then causes the new item to be drawn in the view window.

Displaying the OLE Item

Once the user has embedded (or linked, as described later) a new OLE item, the OnDraw member function of the view class is responsible for drawing the item. To perform this task, add code as follows to the OnDraw function definition in the OLEDEVW.CPP file:

```
void COledemoView::OnDraw(CDC* pDC)
{
    COledemoDoc* pDoc = GetDocument();

    // TODO: add draw code here

    POSITION Pos = pDoc->GetStartPosition ();
    if (Pos == NULL)
        return;
    COleClientItem *PItem = (COleClientItem *)pDoc->GetNextItem (Pos);

    RECT Rect;
    PItem->GetBounds (&Rect);

    pDC->SetMapMode (MM_HIMETRIC);

    PItem->Draw (pDC, &Rect);
}
```

The added code first calls the GetStartPosition and GetNextItem member functions of the document object (which were explained previously) to obtain a pointer to the `CDemoOleClientItem` object that manages the OLE item that is currently embedded in or linked to the program.

Next, the code calls the OLE object's `GetBounds` member function, which copies the coordinates of the OLE item to the `RECT` structure that is passed to this function. The `left` and `top` fields of this structure are always set to 0, and the `right` and `bottom` fields are set to the width and height of the OLE item. The code then sets the mapping mode to the `MM_HIMETRIC` setting; this is done because the coordinates supplied by `GetBounds` assume that the `MM_HIMETRIC` mapping mode is in effect. (For an explanation of mapping modes, see the section "The Mapping Mode" in Chapter 16.)

Finally, the code calls the OLE object's `Draw` member function, which causes the OLE item to be drawn. The `RECT` structure passed to `Draw` specifies the area in which the OLE item is to be drawn. Because `Rect` contains the coordinates of the item supplied by `GetBounds`, the item is positioned in the upper-left corner of the window and is drawn in its original size (that is, its size in the server application; if you specify a smaller or larger rectangle, the item will be compressed or expanded to fill the specified rectangle).

At this time, you might want to build and run the OLEDEMO program. If, after you run the program, you choose the Insert New Object... command on the Edit menu and select a particular type of OLE item, the server application will be launched and you can use it to create an OLE item. For example, if you choose the Paintbrush Picture item type and click OK in the Insert New Object dialog box, the Windows Paintbrush program will begin running. You can then create a drawing in Paintbrush and choose the Update command on the Paintbrush File menu when you are done. The drawing will then appear in the view window of the OLEDEMO program.

Implementing the Paste and Paste Link Commands

You will now add code to support the Paste and Paste Link commands. The Paste command allows you to embed an OLE item in the program using the following alternative method: Run an OLE server application (such as Paintbrush), select the data that you want to embed in the client application, and choose the Cut or Copy command on the server's Edit menu. Then, switch to the OLEDEMO program and choose the Paste command; the OLE item will then be embedded in the program and appear in the view window. The advantage of using the Paste command is that you can embed a selected *portion* of the server document rather than embedding the entire document.

The Paste Link command works like the Paste command except that it inserts a *linked* OLE item into the document. In the server application, you must create or open the source document, select the text or graphics you want to insert into the client program, and choose the Cut or Copy command on the server's Edit menu. Then, switch to the OLEDEMO client program and choose the Paste Link command. The selected data will appear in the OLEDEMO view window, and will be linked to the selected data in the server document; as a result, whenever you modify the data in the server document, the same modification will automatically be made to the data displayed in OLEDEMO.

To provide handlers for the Paste and Paste Link commands, run the ClassWizard tool, and select the COledemoView class in the Class Name: list. To define the Paste command handler, select the ID_EDIT_PASTE identifier in the Object IDs: list, select the COMMAND item in the Messages: list, and click the Add Function... button; accept the default function name, OnEditPaste. In the same way, define a handler for the Paste Link command; you should select the ID_EDIT_PASTE_LINK identifier in the Object IDs: list and accept the default name, OnEditPasteLink.

Next, add code as follows to the OnEditPaste function in the OLEDEVW.CPP file:

```
void COledemoView::OnEditPaste()
{
    // TODO: Add your command handler code here
    if (OpenClipboard () == 0)
        return;

    COledemoDoc* PDoc = GetDocument();

    POSITION Pos = PDoc->GetStartPosition ();
    if (Pos != NULL)
        delete PDoc->GetNextItem (Pos);

    CDemoOleClientItem *POleClientItem = new CDemoOleClientItem (PDoc);

    if (POleClientItem->CreateFromClipboard ("Demo Object") == 0)
        POleClientItem->CreateStaticFromClipboard ("Demo Object");

    CloseClipboard ();
```

```
    PDoc->UpdateAllViews (NULL);
}
```

Because the information on the OLE item is transferred using the Windows Clipboard, OnEditPaste must call OpenClipboard to open the Clipboard at the beginning of the function, and it must call CloseClipboard to close the Clipboard after it has completed accessing the information (opening and closing the Clipboard was explained previously in the chapter).

OnEditPaste then deletes the object for the previous OLE item stored by the program, if any, and creates a new CDemoOleClientItem object to manage the new OLE item that is to be embedded. It performs these steps using the same technique as the OnInsertObject function, described previously:

```
POSITION Pos = PDoc->GetStartPosition ();
if (Pos != NULL)
    delete PDoc->GetNextItem (Pos);

CDemoOleClientItem *POleClientItem = new CDemoOleClientItem (PDoc);
```

Next, OnEditPaste calls the COleClientItem::CreateFromClipboard function, which initializes the CDemoOleClientItem object using the information in the Clipboard, creating an embedded item. The Clipboard, however, may contain information only for a special type of embedded OLE item known as a *static embedded item*; a static item can be displayed in the client program, but cannot subsequently be edited by the server program. In this case, CreateFromClipboard will return FALSE and OnEditPaste calls the CreateStaticFromClipboard function to create the static item:

```
if (POleClientItem->CreateFromClipboard ("Demo Object") == 0)
    POleClientItem->CreateStaticFromClipboard ("Demo Object");
```

Before exiting, OnEditPaste calls UpdateAllViews to cause the newly embedded item to be drawn in the view window.

> **NOTE** Typically, in a full-featured program, the Paste command would also be used to paste non-OLE data, as described in the first portion of this chapter. In this case, the OnEditPaste function could initially attempt to embed an OLE item by calling CreateFromClipboard and then CreateStaticFromClipboard. If both of these functions fail, it could then call GetClipboardData to attempt to obtain a handle to non-OLE data in the required format, as described previously in the chapter. In such a program, the Paste command should be enabled if either OLE data or non-OLE data is contained in it; enabling the Paste and Paste Link commands is discussed later.

Next, you should implement the OnEditPasteLink function, as follows:

```
void COledemoView::OnEditPasteLink()
{
    // TODO: Add your command handler code here
    if (OpenClipboard () == 0)
        return;

    COledemoDoc* PDoc = GetDocument();

    POSITION Pos = PDoc->GetStartPosition ();
    if (Pos != NULL)
        delete PDoc->GetNextItem (Pos);

    CDemoOleClientItem *POleClientItem = new CDemoOleClientItem (PDoc);

    POleClientItem->CreateLinkFromClipboard ("Demo Object");

    CloseClipboard ();

    PDoc->UpdateAllViews (NULL);
}
```

The OnEditPasteLink function works just like OnEditPaste, except that it calls CreateLinkFromClipboard to create a *linked* OLE item from the information in the Clipboard.

In the OLEDEMO program, you do *not* need to provide UPDATE_COMMAND_UI message handlers for the Paste or Paste Link commands, because the MFC provides them for you (they are defined as members of the COleClientDoc class). The MFC update handler for the Paste command enables the command only if the Clipboard currently contains information for an embedded OLE item (normal or static). The MFC update handler for the Paste Link command enables the command only if the Clipboard contains information for a linked OLE item.

> **NOTE**   If the Paste command is used in your program to insert non-OLE data as well as OLE embedded items, you should define your own UPDATE_COMMAND_UI message handler for the Paste command. Your handler can test for the presence of an OLE embedded item in the Clipboard by calling the COleClientItem::CanPaste function (because this is a static member function, you do not need a class object to call it, as explained in Chapter 4). Your handler can test for the presence of non-OLE data by calling IsClipboardFormatAvailable, as described previously in the chapter.

The Edit Links... Command

If a linked item has been inserted into the program, the user can choose the Edit Links... command on the Edit menu. This command displays the Links dialog box (see Figure 19.4), which allows the user to update, cancel, or modify the linked item.

The MFC provides both the COMMAND handler and the UPDATE_COMMAND_UI handler for the Edit Links... command. (The update handler enables the command only if the document currently contains a linked OLE item.) You do not need to write any code to support this command.

FIGURE 19.4:

The Links dialog box

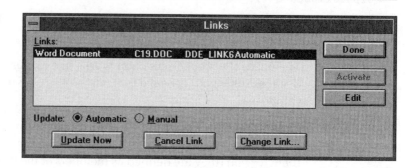

Supporting the Object Command

The next step is to complete the implementation of the Object command on the Edit menu. The MFC provides both an UPDATE_COMMAND_UI and a COMMAND handler for this command. The update handler enables the command only if an OLE item (linked or embedded) is currently selected, and it sets the command caption according to the type of the item. For example, if the selected OLE item is a drawing from Paintbrush, it sets the caption to "Edit Paintbrush Picture Object." To determine whether an item is selected, and to ascertain the type of the item, the MFC update handler accesses each OLE item stored in the document (in OLEDEMO there can be only one), and for each item it calls the IsSelected member function of the view class, passing this function the address of the object that manages the item.

AppWizard generates the following default version of the IsSelected function:

```
BOOL COledemoView::IsSelected(const CObject* pDocItem) const
{
    // TODO: implement this function that tests for a selected OLE client item
    return FALSE;
}
```

A FALSE return value indicates that the item is *not* selected; because the default function always returns FALSE, the Object command is never enabled. To cause the Object command to be enabled whenever an item has been inserted into the program, simply change the return value to TRUE:

```
BOOL COledemoView::IsSelected(const CObject* pDocItem) const
{
    // TODO: implement this function that tests for a selected OLE client item
    return TRUE;
}
```

> **NOTE** An application that allows the user to insert more than one OLE item should let the user select a specific item (normally by clicking on it), and it should mark the selected item (for example, by reversing its colors or by drawing a selection rectangle around it). Also, the IsSelected function should return TRUE only if the item passed to it (pDocItem) is selected.

The MFC COMMAND handler for the Object command causes the server for the OLE item to execute an action known as the *primary verb*. Usually, when the server executes the primary verb it displays the OLE item in a window and allows the user to edit it. Some servers, however, perform a different action in response to the primary verb; for example, the Windows Sound Recorder plays the sound.

> **NOTE**
>
> An OLE client application normally allows the user to execute the primary verb by double-clicking the OLE item, as well as by choosing the Object menu command. To provide this feature, you would have to define a message-handling function for the WM_LBUTTONDBLCLK message. If your function determines that the mouse cursor is on an OLE item, it can execute the primary verb by calling the DoVerb member function of the object that manages the item. For information, see the documentation on the COleClientItem::DoVerb function.

Implementing the Cut and Copy Commands

The final task is to define handlers for the Copy and Cut commands on the Edit menu. These commands allow the user to transfer the current OLE item to the Windows Clipboard, so that the item can be inserted into another program. The Cut command also removes the item from the document.

To define these commands, run ClassWizard and select the COledemoView class in the Class Name: list. Then define COMMAND and UPDATE_COMMAND_UI handlers for both the Copy and the Cut command; in all cases, accept the default function name. For each function you are to define, Table 19.4 lists the command, the command identifier, the message identifier, and the default function name.

In the OLEDVW.CPP file, add code as follows to the OnUpdateEditCopy function:

```
void COledemoView::OnUpdateEditCopy(CCmdUI* pCmdUI)
{
    // TODO: Add your command update UI handler code here
    COledemoDoc* PDoc = GetDocument();
    pCmdUI->Enable ((BOOL)PDoc->GetStartPosition ());
}
```

The code you added to the update function enables the Copy command only if the GetStartPosition function returns a nonzero value, indicating that the document

TABLE 19.4: Message-Handling Functions for the Cut and Copy Commands

Command	Object ID:	Message	Default Function Name
Copy	ID_EDIT_COPY	COMMAND	OnEditCopy
Copy	ID_EDIT_COPY	UPDATE_COMMAND_UI	OnUpdateEditCopy
Cut	ID_EDIT_CUT	COMMAND	OnEditCut
Cut	ID_EDIT_CUT	UPDATE_COMMAND_UI	OnUpdateEditCut

currently contains an OLE item.

Then add the following statements to the OnEditCopy function:

```
void COledemoView::OnEditCopy()
{
    // TODO: Add your command handler code here
    if (OpenClipboard () == 0)
        return;

    COledemoDoc* PDoc = GetDocument();
    POSITION Pos = PDoc->GetStartPosition ();
    COleClientItem *PItem = (COleClientItem *)PDoc->GetNextItem (Pos);

    PItem->CopyToClipboard ();

    CloseClipboard ();
}
```

The added code opens the Clipboard, calls GetStartPosition and GetNextItem to obtain the address of the object managing the OLE item, and then calls the object's CopyToClipboard member function, which copies the information for the item to the Clipboard.

Finally, implement the OnUpdateEditCut and OnEditCut functions as follows:

```
void COledemoView::OnUpdateEditCut(CCmdUI* pCmdUI)
{
    // TODO: Add your command update UI handler code here
    COledemoDoc* PDoc = GetDocument();
    pCmdUI->Enable ((BOOL)PDoc->GetStartPosition ());
}
```

```
void COledemoView::OnEditCut()
{
    // TODO: Add your command handler code here
    if (OpenClipboard () == 0)
        return;

    COledemoDoc* PDoc = GetDocument();
    POSITION Pos = PDoc->GetStartPosition ();
    COleClientItem *PItem = (COleClientItem *)PDoc->GetNextItem (Pos);

    PItem->CopyToClipboard ();

    CloseClipboard ();

    delete PItem;

    PDoc->UpdateAllViews (NULL);
}
```

These two handlers work just like the handlers for the Copy command, except that the OnEditCut function invokes delete to remove the OLE item after it has been copied to the Clipboard.

NOTE   The update handlers you defined in this section enable the Cut and Copy commands only if an *OLE* item is selected, and the command handlers transfer only an OLE item to the Clipboard. A full-featured application, however, would also typically allow the user to cut or copy non-OLE data using the Cut or Copy commands. In such an application, the update handlers must enable the Cut and Copy commands if *either* OLE *or* non-OLE data is selected. The command handlers must branch to an appropriate routine to transfer the selected data; to transfer non-OLE data, the function could use the methods described in the first portion of this chapter.

The OLEDEMO Source Code

The following listings, Listing 19.1 through Listing 19.8, contain the C++ source code for the OLEDEMO program that you created in this chapter. You will find a copy of these files in the \OLEDEMO subdirectory of the directory in which you installed the companion disk.

Listing 19.1

```
// oledemo.h : main header file for the OLEDEMO application
//

#ifndef __AFXWIN_H__
    #error include 'stdafx.h' before including this file for PCH
#endif

#include "resource.h"        // main symbols

/////////////////////////////////////////////////////////////////////////////
// COledemoApp:
// See oledemo.cpp for the implementation of this class
//

class COledemoApp : public CWinApp
{
public:
    COledemoApp();

// Overrides
    virtual BOOL InitInstance();

// Implementation

    //{{AFX_MSG(COledemoApp)
    afx_msg void OnAppAbout();
        // NOTE - the ClassWizard will add and remove member functions here.
        //    DO NOT EDIT what you see in these blocks of generated code !
    //}}AFX_MSG
    DECLARE_MESSAGE_MAP()
};

/////////////////////////////////////////////////////////////////////////////
```

Listing 19.2

```
// oledemo.cpp : Defines the class behaviors for the application.
//

#include "stdafx.h"
#include "oledemo.h"
```

```
#include "mainfrm.h"
#include "olededoc.h"
#include "oledevw.h"

#ifdef _DEBUG
#undef THIS_FILE
static char BASED_CODE THIS_FILE[] = __FILE__;
#endif

//////////////////////////////////////////////////////////////////////
// COledemoApp

BEGIN_MESSAGE_MAP(COledemoApp, CWinApp)
    //{{AFX_MSG_MAP(COledemoApp)
    ON_COMMAND(ID_APP_ABOUT, OnAppAbout)
        // NOTE - the ClassWizard will add and remove mapping macros here.
        //    DO NOT EDIT what you see in these blocks of generated code !
    //}}AFX_MSG_MAP
    // Standard file based document commands
    ON_COMMAND(ID_FILE_NEW, CWinApp::OnFileNew)
    ON_COMMAND(ID_FILE_OPEN, CWinApp::OnFileOpen)
END_MESSAGE_MAP()

//////////////////////////////////////////////////////////////////////
// COledemoApp construction

COledemoApp::COledemoApp()
{
    // TODO: add construction code here,
    // Place all significant initialization in InitInstance
}

//////////////////////////////////////////////////////////////////////
// The one and only COledemoApp object

COledemoApp NEAR theApp;

//////////////////////////////////////////////////////////////////////
// COledemoApp initialization

BOOL COledemoApp::InitInstance()
{
    // Standard initialization
    // If you are not using these features and wish to reduce the size
```

```
//   of your final executable, you should remove from the following
//   the specific initialization routines you do not need.

SetDialogBkColor();            // set dialog background color to gray
LoadStdProfileSettings();   // Load standard INI file options (including MRU)

// Register the application's document templates.  Document templates
//   serve as the connection between documents, frame windows and views.

AddDocTemplate(new CSingleDocTemplate(IDR_MAINFRAME,
      RUNTIME_CLASS(COledemoDoc),
      RUNTIME_CLASS(CMainFrame),       // main SDI frame window
      RUNTIME_CLASS(COledemoView)));

// create a new (empty) document
OnFileNew();

if (m_lpCmdLine[0] != '\0')
{
    // TODO: add command line processing here
}

return TRUE;
}

/////////////////////////////////////////////////////////////////////////////
// CAboutDlg dialog used for App About

class CAboutDlg : public CDialog
{
public:
   CAboutDlg();

// Dialog Data
   //{{AFX_DATA(CAboutDlg)
   enum { IDD = IDD_ABOUTBOX };
   //}}AFX_DATA

// Implementation
protected:
   virtual void DoDataExchange(CDataExchange* pDX);    // DDX/DDV support
   //{{AFX_MSG(CAboutDlg)
      // No message handlers
   //}}AFX_MSG
```

```
   DECLARE_MESSAGE_MAP()
};

CAboutDlg::CAboutDlg() : CDialog(CAboutDlg::IDD)
{
   //{{AFX_DATA_INIT(CAboutDlg)
   //}}AFX_DATA_INIT
}

void CAboutDlg::DoDataExchange(CDataExchange* pDX)
{
   CDialog::DoDataExchange(pDX);
   //{{AFX_DATA_MAP(CAboutDlg)
   //}}AFX_DATA_MAP
}

BEGIN_MESSAGE_MAP(CAboutDlg, CDialog)
   //{{AFX_MSG_MAP(CAboutDlg)
      // No message handlers
   //}}AFX_MSG_MAP
END_MESSAGE_MAP()

// App command to run the dialog
void COledemoApp::OnAppAbout()
{
   CAboutDlg aboutDlg;
   aboutDlg.DoModal();
}

/////////////////////////////////////////////////////////////////////////
// COledemoApp commands
```

Listing 19.3

```
// olededoc.h : interface of the COledemoDoc class
//
/////////////////////////////////////////////////////////////////////////

class COledemoDoc : public COleClientDoc
{
protected: // create from serialization only
   COledemoDoc();
   DECLARE_DYNCREATE(COledemoDoc)
```

```
// Attributes
public:

// Operations
public:

// Implementation
public:
    virtual ~COledemoDoc();
    virtual void Serialize(CArchive& ar);   // overridden for document i/o
    virtual  void DeleteContents();
#ifdef _DEBUG
    virtual  void AssertValid() const;
    virtual  void Dump(CDumpContext& dc) const;
#endif
protected:
    virtual  BOOL  OnNewDocument();

// Generated message map functions
protected:
    //{{AFX_MSG(COledemoDoc)
        // NOTE - the ClassWizard will add and remove member functions here.
        //    DO NOT EDIT what you see in these blocks of generated code !
    //}}AFX_MSG
    DECLARE_MESSAGE_MAP()
};

////////////////////////////////////////////////////////////////////////////

class CDemoOleClientItem : public COleClientItem
{
public:
    CDemoOleClientItem (COleClientDoc* pContainerDoc) :
        COleClientItem (pContainerDoc)
        { }

    virtual void OnChange (OLE_NOTIFICATION wNotification);

};
```

Listing 19.4

```
// olededoc.cpp : implementation of the COledemoDoc class
//
```

```
#include "stdafx.h"
#include "oledemo.h"

#include "olededoc.h"

#ifdef _DEBUG
#undef THIS_FILE
static char BASED_CODE THIS_FILE[] = __FILE__;
#endif

/////////////////////////////////////////////////////////////////////////////
// COledemoDoc

IMPLEMENT_DYNCREATE(COledemoDoc, COleClientDoc)

BEGIN_MESSAGE_MAP(COledemoDoc, COleClientDoc)
    //{{AFX_MSG_MAP(COledemoDoc)
        // NOTE - the ClassWizard will add and remove mapping macros here.
        //    DO NOT EDIT what you see in these blocks of generated code !
    //}}AFX_MSG_MAP
END_MESSAGE_MAP()

/////////////////////////////////////////////////////////////////////////////
// COledemoDoc construction/destruction

COledemoDoc::COledemoDoc()
{
    // TODO: add one-time construction code here
}

COledemoDoc::~COledemoDoc()
{
}

BOOL COledemoDoc::OnNewDocument()
{
    if (!COleClientDoc::OnNewDocument())
        return FALSE;
    // TODO: add reinitialization code here
    // (SDI documents will reuse this document)
    return TRUE;
}
```

```
/////////////////////////////////////////////////////////////////////////
// COledemoDoc serialization

void COledemoDoc::Serialize(CArchive& ar)
{
    if (ar.IsStoring())
    {
        // TODO: add storing code here
        // you must save client items as well
    }
    else
    {
        // TODO: add loading code here
        // you must load client items as well
    }
}

void COledemoDoc::DeleteContents()
{
    // TODO: add additional cleanup before doc-items are deleted
    COleClientDoc::DeleteContents(); // delete doc-items
}

/////////////////////////////////////////////////////////////////////////
// COledemoDoc diagnostics

#ifdef _DEBUG
void COledemoDoc::AssertValid() const
{
    COleClientDoc::AssertValid();
}

void COledemoDoc::Dump(CDumpContext& dc) const
{
    COleClientDoc::Dump(dc);
}

#endif //_DEBUG

/////////////////////////////////////////////////////////////////////////
// COledemoDoc commands
```

```
void CDemoOleClientItem::OnChange (OLE_NOTIFICATION wNotification)
   {
   GetDocument ()->UpdateAllViews (NULL);
   }
```

Listing 19.5

```
// mainfrm.h : interface of the CMainFrame class
//
/////////////////////////////////////////////////////////////////////////////

class CMainFrame : public CFrameWnd
{
protected: // create from serialization only
   CMainFrame();
   DECLARE_DYNCREATE(CMainFrame)

// Attributes
public:

// Operations
public:

// Implementation
public:
   virtual ~CMainFrame();
#ifdef _DEBUG
   virtual  void AssertValid() const;
   virtual  void Dump(CDumpContext& dc) const;
#endif

protected:
   BOOL OnCommand(UINT wParam, LONG lParam);

// Generated message map functions
protected:
   //{{AFX_MSG(CMainFrame)
      // NOTE - the ClassWizard will add and remove member functions here.
      //    DO NOT EDIT what you see in these blocks of generated code !
   //}}AFX_MSG
   DECLARE_MESSAGE_MAP()
};

/////////////////////////////////////////////////////////////////////////////
```

Listing 19.6

```cpp
// mainfrm.cpp : implementation of the CMainFrame class
//

#include "stdafx.h"
#include "oledemo.h"

#include "mainfrm.h"

#ifdef _DEBUG
#undef THIS_FILE
static char BASED_CODE THIS_FILE[] = __FILE__;
#endif

/////////////////////////////////////////////////////////////////////////////
// CMainFrame

IMPLEMENT_DYNCREATE(CMainFrame, CFrameWnd)

BEGIN_MESSAGE_MAP(CMainFrame, CFrameWnd)
    //{{AFX_MSG_MAP(CMainFrame)
        // NOTE - the ClassWizard will add and remove mapping macros here.
        //    DO NOT EDIT what you see in these blocks of generated code !
    //}}AFX_MSG_MAP
END_MESSAGE_MAP()

/////////////////////////////////////////////////////////////////////////////
// CMainFrame construction/destruction

CMainFrame::CMainFrame()
{
    // TODO: add member initialization code here
}

CMainFrame::~CMainFrame()
{
}

// Disable menu commands while waiting for OLE server
BOOL CMainFrame::OnCommand(UINT wParam, LONG lParam)
{
    if (COleClientItem::InWaitForRelease())
    {
        AfxMessageBox(IDP_BUSY);
```

```
      return TRUE;           // handled
   }
   return CFrameWnd::OnCommand(wParam, lParam);
}

//////////////////////////////////////////////////////////////////////////
// CMainFrame diagnostics

#ifdef _DEBUG
void CMainFrame::AssertValid() const
{
   CFrameWnd::AssertValid();
}

void CMainFrame::Dump(CDumpContext& dc) const
{
   CFrameWnd::Dump(dc);
}

#endif //_DEBUG

//////////////////////////////////////////////////////////////////////////
// CMainFrame message handlers
```

Listing 19.7

```
// oledevw.h : interface of the COledemoView class
//
//////////////////////////////////////////////////////////////////////////

class COledemoView : public CView
{
protected: // create from serialization only
   COledemoView();
   DECLARE_DYNCREATE(COledemoView)

// Attributes
public:
   COledemoDoc* GetDocument();

// Operations
public:
```

```
// Implementation
public:
    virtual ~COledemoView();
    virtual void OnDraw(CDC* pDC);   // overridden to draw this view
#ifdef _DEBUG
    virtual void AssertValid() const;
    virtual void Dump(CDumpContext& dc) const;
#endif

    // OLE Client support
    virtual BOOL IsSelected(const CObject* pDocItem) const;

// Generated message map functions
protected:
    //{{AFX_MSG(COledemoView)
    afx_msg void OnInsertObject();    // OLE support
    afx_msg void OnEditPaste();
    afx_msg void OnEditPasteLink();
    afx_msg void OnEditCopy();
    afx_msg void OnUpdateEditCopy(CCmdUI* pCmdUI);
    afx_msg void OnEditCut();
    afx_msg void OnUpdateEditCut(CCmdUI* pCmdUI);
    //}}AFX_MSG
    DECLARE_MESSAGE_MAP()
};

#ifndef _DEBUG // debug version in oledevw.cpp
inline COledemoDoc* COledemoView::GetDocument()
    { return (COledemoDoc*) m_pDocument; }
#endif
```

//

Listing 19.8

```
// oledevw.cpp : implementation of the COledemoView class
//

#include "stdafx.h"
#include "oledemo.h"

#include "olededoc.h"
#include "oledevw.h"
```

```
#ifdef _DEBUG
#undef THIS_FILE
static char BASED_CODE THIS_FILE[] = __FILE__;
#endif

/////////////////////////////////////////////////////////////////////////////
// COledemoView

IMPLEMENT_DYNCREATE(COledemoView, CView)

BEGIN_MESSAGE_MAP(COledemoView, CView)
    //{{AFX_MSG_MAP(COledemoView)
    ON_COMMAND(ID_OLE_INSERT_NEW, OnInsertObject)
    ON_COMMAND(ID_EDIT_PASTE, OnEditPaste)
    ON_COMMAND(ID_EDIT_PASTE_LINK, OnEditPasteLink)
    ON_COMMAND(ID_EDIT_COPY, OnEditCopy)
    ON_UPDATE_COMMAND_UI(ID_EDIT_COPY, OnUpdateEditCopy)
    ON_COMMAND(ID_EDIT_CUT, OnEditCut)
    ON_UPDATE_COMMAND_UI(ID_EDIT_CUT, OnUpdateEditCut)
    //}}AFX_MSG_MAP
END_MESSAGE_MAP()

/////////////////////////////////////////////////////////////////////////////
// COledemoView construction/destruction

COledemoView::COledemoView()
{
    // TODO: add construction code here
}

COledemoView::~COledemoView()
{
}

/////////////////////////////////////////////////////////////////////////////
// COledemoView drawing

void COledemoView::OnDraw(CDC* pDC)
{
    COledemoDoc* pDoc = GetDocument();

    // TODO: add draw code here

    POSITION Pos = pDoc->GetStartPosition ();
    if (Pos == NULL)
```

```
       return;
    COleClientItem *PItem = (COleClientItem *)pDoc->GetNextItem (Pos);

    RECT Rect;
    PItem->GetBounds (&Rect);

    pDC->SetMapMode (MM_HIMETRIC);

    PItem->Draw (pDC, &Rect);
}

////////////////////////////////////////////////////////////////////////////
// OLE Client support and commands

BOOL COledemoView::IsSelected(const CObject* pDocItem) const
{
    // TODO: implement this function that tests for a selected OLE client item
    return TRUE;
}

void COledemoView::OnInsertObject()
{
    CString strTypeName;

    if (!AfxOleInsertDialog(strTypeName))
        return;      // no OLE class selected

    TRACE("Trying to Insert OLE item with type '%s'\n",
          (const char*)strTypeName);

    // TODO: create an embedded OLE object with that class name

    COledemoDoc* PDoc = GetDocument();

    POSITION Pos = PDoc->GetStartPosition ();
    if (Pos != NULL)
        delete PDoc->GetNextItem (Pos);

    CDemoOleClientItem *POleClientItem = new CDemoOleClientItem (PDoc);

    POleClientItem->CreateNewObject (strTypeName, "Demo Object");
}

////////////////////////////////////////////////////////////////////////////
// COledemoView diagnostics
```

```
#ifdef _DEBUG
void COledemoView::AssertValid() const
{
   CView::AssertValid();
}

void COledemoView::Dump(CDumpContext& dc) const
{
   CView::Dump(dc);
}

COledemoDoc* COledemoView::GetDocument() // non-debug version is inline
{
   ASSERT(m_pDocument->IsKindOf(RUNTIME_CLASS(COledemoDoc)));
   return (COledemoDoc*) m_pDocument;
}

#endif //_DEBUG

/////////////////////////////////////////////////////////////////////////////
// COledemoView message handlers

void COledemoView::OnEditPaste()
{
   // TODO: Add your command handler code here
   if (OpenClipboard () == 0)
      return;

   COledemoDoc* PDoc = GetDocument();

   POSITION Pos = PDoc->GetStartPosition ();
   if (Pos != NULL)
      delete PDoc->GetNextItem (Pos);

   CDemoOleClientItem *POleClientItem = new CDemoOleClientItem (PDoc);

   if (POleClientItem->CreateFromClipboard ("Demo Object") == 0)
      POleClientItem->CreateStaticFromClipboard ("Demo Object");

   CloseClipboard ();

   PDoc->UpdateAllViews (NULL);
}
```

```
void COledemoView::OnEditPasteLink()
{
    // TODO: Add your command handler code here
    if (OpenClipboard () == 0)
        return;

    COledemoDoc* PDoc = GetDocument();

    POSITION Pos = PDoc->GetStartPosition ();
    if (Pos != NULL)
        delete PDoc->GetNextItem (Pos);

    CDemoOleClientItem *POleClientItem = new CDemoOleClientItem (PDoc);

    POleClientItem->CreateLinkFromClipboard ("Demo Object");

    CloseClipboard ();

    PDoc->UpdateAllViews (NULL);
}

void COledemoView::OnEditCopy()
{
    // TODO: Add your command handler code here
    if (OpenClipboard () == 0)
        return;

    COledemoDoc* PDoc = GetDocument();
    POSITION Pos = PDoc->GetStartPosition ();
    COleClientItem *PItem = (COleClientItem *)PDoc->GetNextItem (Pos);

    PItem->CopyToClipboard ();

    CloseClipboard ();
}

void COledemoView::OnUpdateEditCopy(CCmdUI* pCmdUI)
{
    // TODO: Add your command update UI handler code here
    COledemoDoc* PDoc = GetDocument();
    pCmdUI->Enable ((BOOL)PDoc->GetStartPosition ());
}

void COledemoView::OnEditCut()
{
```

```
    // TODO: Add your command handler code here
    if (OpenClipboard () == 0)
        return;

    COledemoDoc* PDoc = GetDocument();
    POSITION Pos = PDoc->GetStartPosition ();
    COleClientItem *PItem = (COleClientItem *)PDoc->GetNextItem (Pos);

    PItem->CopyToClipboard ();

    CloseClipboard ();

    delete PItem;

    PDoc->UpdateAllViews (NULL);
}

void COledemoView::OnUpdateEditCut(CCmdUI* pCmdUI)
{
    // TODO: Add your command update UI handler code here
    COledemoDoc* PDoc = GetDocument();
    pCmdUI->Enable ((BOOL)PDoc->GetStartPosition ());
}
```

Summary

In this chapter, you learned how to use the Clipboard to perform simple transfers of data in standard formats. You then learned how to use the more versatile OLE mechanism for exchanging data in an unlimited variety of formats.

The following is a summary of the discussion on performing simple data transfers using the Clipboard:

- When you use the Clipboard to perform a simple data transfer (that is, you do not use OLE), the target program must understand the data format, and the target program is fully responsible for displaying, editing, and storing the data. Therefore, the number of formats that can be exchanged using this method is limited by the capabilities of the target application.

- A program normally provides access to the Clipboard by including Cut, Copy, and Paste commands on the Edit menu.

- You can exchange textual information by adding a block of text to the Clipboard in response to the Cut or Copy command, and by obtaining text from the Clipboard in response to the Paste command.

- You add plain text to the Clipboard by allocating a block of global memory, copying the text to this block, and then supplying the global memory handle to the Clipboard.

- You obtain text from the Clipboard by requesting a handle to the block of global memory that contains the text. You can then use this handle to copy the text from the Clipboard memory into a private memory area that your program has allocated.

- You can exchange graphics information by adding a bitmap to the Clipboard or obtaining a bitmap from the Clipboard.

- To add a bitmap, you supply the bitmap handle to the Clipboard.

- To obtain a bitmap from the Clipboard, you request the bitmap handle and then display or make a private copy of the bitmap within your program.

- You can exchange data that does not conform to one of the standard Clipboard formats by calling `RegisterClipboardFormat` to register your own format. You then follow the procedures for exchanging text with the Clipboard; however, rather than passing an index for a standard format, you pass the index returned by `RegisterClipboardFormat`.

- You can call the `IsClipboardFormatAvailable` function to determine whether the Clipboard currently contains data conforming to a specific format.

The following is a summary of the discussion on exchanging data using OLE:

- When you transfer data using OLE, the target application does *not* need to understand the data format, because the source application is responsible for displaying and editing the data. OLE can thus be used to create *compound documents*, which are documents that contain data originating from a wide variety of source programs.

- The document that is the source of the data is known as the *server*, and the document that receives the data is known as the *client*.

- A block of data transferred using OLE is commonly known as an *object*. However, in the context of MFC programming, it is known as an *item* to distinguish it from the class instance (or *object*) that manages it.

- An OLE item can be *linked* or *embedded*. If it is linked, the complete data for the item is stored in a separate source document that is maintained by the server. If it is embedded, the complete data for the item is stored within the compound document maintained by the client, and there is *no* separate source document.

- You can use AppWizard to generate the basic source code for a client OLE program by choosing the OLE Client option. The remaining techniques discussed in this summary are for writing an OLE *client* program.

- You must define a class for managing the OLE items that are linked or embedded in the client program. You must derive this class from the MFC COleClientItem class, and you must define an overriding version of the COleClientItem::OnChange virtual function, which redraws the view window whenever an OLE item is updated.

- The Insert New Object... menu command runs a server application and embeds an OLE item in the program. You must add code to the handler for this command, which creates an object for managing the item and calls the object's CreateNewObject function to launch the server application.

- The program's document object maintains a list of the OLE items that have been linked or embedded in the document.

- To display an OLE item from your OnDraw function, call the Draw member function of the object that manages the item. You can obtain the address of each object by calling the GetStartPosition and GetNextItem member functions of the document class.

- The user can also transfer an OLE item by selecting the data in the server and then choosing the Paste or Paste Link menu command on the Edit menu of the client. The information is transferred using the Clipboard.

- The Paste menu command inserts an embedded item; you must define a handler for this command that opens the Clipboard, creates an object to manage the new item, and then calls the CreateFromClipboard member function of the object. If this function fails, it can call CreateStaticFromClipboard to try to create a *static embedded item*, which is a special type of OLE item that can be displayed but not edited.

- The Paste Link menu command inserts a linked item; you must also define a handler for this command. The handler is defined just like the one for the Paste command, except that rather than calling `CreateFromClipboard` and `CreateStaticFromClipboard`, it calls `CreateLinkFromClipboard`.

- The MFC provides an Edit Links… command on the Edit menu, which allows the user to update, cancel, or modify a linked item. You do not need to write any code for this command.

- The Object command on the Edit menu executes the *primary verb* for the selected OLE item. Usually, executing the primary verb allows the user to edit the item using the facilities of the server application. The MFC provides the handlers for this command; however, you must modify the `IsSelected` member function of your view class to return `TRUE` if the item that is passed to this function is currently selected. (The MFC calls `IsSelected` for each item to determine whether it should enable the Object command.)

- You should also provide handlers for the Cut and Copy commands, which insert the selected OLE item into the Clipboard (so that it can be transferred to another program). To do this, your handlers should call the `CopyToClipboard` member function of the object that manages the selected item. Your Cut handler should also invoke `delete` on the object to remove the item from the document.

PART IV

MS-DOS and QuickWin Programming with the iostream Library

In this part of the book you will learn how to write MS-DOS and QuickWin programs using Visual C++, as well as how to perform input and output from these programs with the C++ iostream class library. Chapter 20 discusses some general guidelines for writing MS-DOS and QuickWin programs, and it explains how to build and run these programs using Visual Workbench projects. Chapter 21 then introduces the iostream library, which is the standard, general-purpose C++ class library for performing input and output; this library can be used by both MS-DOS and QuickWin programs.

CHAPTER

TWENTY

Writing MS-DOS and QuickWin Programs

- Creating MS-DOS programs

- Creating QuickWin programs

20

In this chapter, you will learn how to use Visual C++ to create MS-DOS and Quick-Win programs. An MS-DOS program is one that is run from the MS-DOS command prompt, either independently of Windows or within a Windows MS-DOS session. A QuickWin program is one that is written using MS-DOS programming techniques but is linked with the Microsoft QuickWin library, which allows it to run as a standard (although not full-featured) Windows application.

For each of these types of programs, the chapter explains how to create a project and build the program using the Visual Workbench. It also provides some general guidelines for writing the program code. Chapter 21 will describe the `iostream` class library, which provides a set of classes that can be used for performing basic I/O from both MS-DOS and QuickWin programs written in C++.

> **NOTE** Although MS-DOS and QuickWin programs can be written in either C or C++, this chapter emphasizes C++.

Creating MS-DOS Programs

To develop MS-DOS programs, you need to have the Professional Edition of Visual C++, and you must have installed an MS-DOS version of the run-time library. See Chapter 1 for a description of the different versions of Visual C++, and for instructions on installing the required run-time libraries using the Setup program. (To build the example program given in this section, you need the medium-memory model version of the MS-DOS run-time library.)

> **TIP** If you do not have the Professional Edition of Visual C++, you can develop and test programs using the QuickWin library as described in the second portion of the chapter. You can later port these programs to MS-DOS, provided that you do not use any of the enhanced QuickWin features described in the section "Enhancing QuickWin Programs."

Building an Example Program

Chapter 2 described the basic techniques for creating a project and for building, running, and debugging a program using the Visual Workbench. In this section, you will learn the specific Visual Workbench techniques required to prepare an MS-DOS program. You will learn these techniques by creating an example C++ program, DOSGREET, which is an MS-DOS version of the GREET program presented in Chapter 2.

Creating the Project File

The first step in developing the DOSGREET program is to run the Visual Workbench and define a project. (Because you cannot use AppWizard to generate an MS-DOS program, you have to manually create the project and each program source file.) The following are the steps for defining the project:

1. Create a new directory to contain the project files, if necessary. It is a good idea to put the files for each project in a separate directory that is reserved exclusively for those files. You might, for example, create a directory for the DOSGREET program named C:\SAMPLES\DOSGREET.

2. Choose the New... command on the Visual Workbench Project menu, which will open the New Project dialog box.

3. Into the Project Name: text box, enter the name of the project, DOSGREET, including the full path name of the directory you created in step 1. For example, if the project directory is C:\SAMPLES\DOSGREET, enter C:\SAMPLES\DOSGREET\DOSGREET. (You do not need to include the .MAK extension because the Visual Workbench automatically appends it to the project file name.)

   Alternatively, you can click the Browse... button, select the desired project directory in the Browse dialog box, enter the simple project name, DOSGREET, into the File Name: text box, and click the OK button

4. In the New Project dialog box, select the "MS-DOS application (.EXE)" project type in the Project Type: list to create a standard executable MS-DOS program.

The Project Type: list contains the names of four different types of MS-DOS applications that you can create using the Visual C++ Professional Edition. Table 20.1 briefly explains each of these. Choosing a specific project type causes the Visual Workbench to set the build options (that is, the compiler and linker options) to an initial set of values that are appropriate for the type of program that is being developed. You can later change any of these options by choosing the Project... command on the Options menu.

TABLE 20.1: MS-DOS Project Types

Project Type:	Type of Program Created
MS-DOS application (.EXE)	A standard MS-DOS program that runs from the MS-DOS command prompt.
MS-DOS P-code application (.EXE)	An MS-DOS program whose executable file contains p-code, which is more compact than machine code but must be interpreted (that is, translated into machine code) at run-time. A p-code application thus tends to be smaller but slower than a standard MS-DOS program (which consists of machine code).
MS-DOS Overlaid application (.EXE)	An MS-DOS program that is loaded in segments (using the Microsoft Overlaid Virtual Environment, or *MOVE*). Each segment is loaded only as needed, allowing the program to be much larger than if the entire program had to be loaded into conventional memory at once.
MS-DOS COM application (.COM)	A fast-loading MS-DOS program having the .COM extension. The program must be compiled using the *tiny*-memory model (produced with the /AT compiler flag), and the total size of its code plus data must be less than 64KB.

5. In the New Project dialog box, disable the Use Microsoft Foundation Classes option, because the DOSGREET program does not use any of the MFC classes. Figure 20.1 shows the completed New Project dialog box.

Selecting the Use Microsoft Foundation Classes option adds the appropriate MFC library file to the list of library files linked to the program. Using the MFC in an MS-DOS program is discussed later in the chapter (in the section "Guidelines for Writing MS-DOS Code").

FIGURE 20.1:

The completed New Project dialog box for creating the DOSGREET project; the text in the Project Name: text box is not completely visible

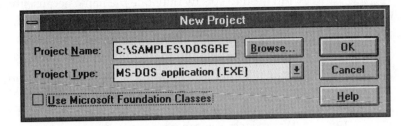

6. Click the OK button in the New Project dialog box. The Edit dialog box (titled "Edit - DOSGREET.MAK") will now appear. In this dialog box, the project directory specified in step 3 will be selected.

7. Enter the name of the program source file, DOSGREET.CPP, into the File Name: text box and click the Add button (the full path name of this file will then be displayed in the Files in Project: list at the bottom of the dialog box). Figure 20.2 shows the completed Edit dialog box.

FIGURE 20.2:

The completed Edit dialog box for specifying the source file for the DOSGREET program

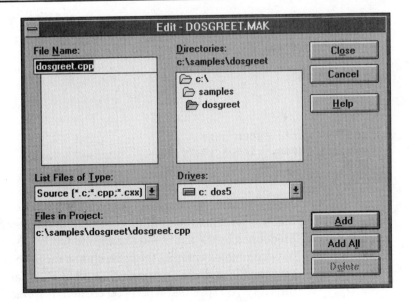

You need to specify only one file name because the DOSGREET program consists of a single source file. Like Windows programs, MS-DOS programs often consist of several source files. You can add or remove source files from the project at any time by choosing the Edit... command on the Project menu.

8. Click the Close button to remove the Edit dialog box.

After you close the Edit dialog box, the DOSGREET project is opened in the Visual Workbench. You can now proceed to create the program source file as explained in the next section. If you close the project, you can later open it again by choosing the Open... command on the Project menu and selecting the project file, DOS-GREET.MAK.

Editing the Source Code

To create the C++ source code file for the DOSGREET program, choose the New command on the File menu to open a new file, and enter the code shown in Listing 20.1 into this file.

Listing 20.1

```
// DOSGREET.CPP: The C++ source code for the DOSGREET program.

#include <iostream.h>

char Name [16];

void main ()
    {
    cout << "enter your name: ";
    cin.get (Name, sizeof (Name));
    cout << "\ngreetings, " << Name;
    }
```

This code is the same as the code you entered into the GREET QuickWin program that was presented and briefly explained in Chapter 2. The cout and cin objects are predefined by the iostream library, and will be discussed in Chapter 21. When you have completed entering the code, choose the Save command on the File menu, and save the file under the name DOSGREET.CPP. (Make sure you save it in the project directory you specified when you created the project.)

TIP For a summary of the Visual Workbench editing commands, see Table 2.1.

You can now build the program by choosing the "Build DOSGREET.EXE" command on the Project menu. To run the program, choose the "Execute DOS-GREET.EXE" command on the Project menu; the Visual Workbench will start an MS-DOS session and run DOSGREET within it. You can also run the program by typing DOSGREET at the MS-DOS command prompt (in a Windows MS-DOS session, or outside of Windows), provided that the directory containing the program is the current directory, or is in your directory path.

TIP When the Visual Workbench executes an MS-DOS program, Windows uses the settings in the _DEFAULT.PIF program information file to run the MS-DOS session. You can specify two settings in this file that make it easier to run MS-DOS programs from the Visual Workbench. To do this, run the Windows PIF Editor program, and open _DEFAULT.PIF (which is located in the Windows directory). First, you can choose the Windowed display usage option, so that MS-DOS programs will be run in a window on the Windows desktop rather than within a full screen. Second, you can disable the Close Window on Exit option, so that the program window will remain open after the program stops running, allowing you to contemplate the program output (otherwise the window is closed immediately after the program quits).

To debug the program, you can run the MS-DOS version of the CodeView debugger by choosing the "CodeView for MS-DOS" command on the Tools menu (you must, of course, have installed MS-DOS CodeView using the Setup program). You *cannot* use the integrated Visual Workbench debugger for MS-DOS programs. For information on using CodeView for MS-DOS, see the *CodeView Debugger User's Guide* manual, or the online help available through the CodeView Help menu.

Guidelines for Writing MS-DOS Code

When you write a program for MS-DOS, you have much more freedom than you do when you develop a Windows application. When an MS-DOS program runs, it essentially owns the entire machine (or the entire *virtual* machine if it is being run in an MS-DOS session of 386 Enhanced mode Windows). Unlike a Windows program, it does *not* need to conform to a strict architecture enabling it to receive messages from other processes, share resources, and yield control to other programs. Windows programs perform most actions in response to messages, and are thus described as *message-oriented*; in contrast, MS-DOS programs typically initiate a sequence of procedures, and are thus described as *procedural*.

Also, an MS-DOS program can be written at many different levels. At the lowest level, it can directly access I/O ports and system memory addresses, and it can accelerate text and graphics output by writing directly to video memory. At a higher level, it can issue software interrupt instructions to invoke the services provided by the system BIOS and the MS-DOS operating system. At an even higher level, it can call the functions in the standard C/C++ run-time library—or, if it is written in C++, it can use the `iostream` class library to perform object-oriented input and output (as discussed in Chapter 21).

Creating QuickWin Programs

As you learned in Part III of this book, when writing a Windows application you must normally conform to a rather strict program architecture and make extensive use of the special functions provided by the Windows API or the MFC library. The Microsoft QuickWin library, however, allows you to create simple Windows programs using the same programming techniques that you normally employ for writing MS-DOS applications. Linking a program with the QuickWin library provides all the code necessary for running the program as a Windows application; that is, for running it within a standard window on the Windows desktop. The QuickWin library manages the window interface, and it processes calls to standard C++ I/O functions—such as `printf`, `scanf`, and member functions of the `iostream` class— by sending all output to the program window.

The advantage of employing the QuickWin library is that you can use your existing MS-DOS programs and MS-DOS programming skills to immediately create programs for Windows that enjoy many of the benefits of the Windows environment. For example, QuickWin programs run in standard windows that can be resized, minimized, or maximized. QuickWin programs store window output and allow the user to scroll through output that is not visible in the window. QuickWin programs

Using the MFC in an MS-DOS Program

Although the Microsoft Foundation Classes library is designed primarily for developing Windows applications, you can use some of the general-purpose MFC classes in an MS-DOS program. These classes include CObject; CRuntimeClass; the file classes, such as CFile and CArchive; the collection classes, such as CByteArray and CObList; and the simple value classes, such as CString and CRect. For an overview of the general-purpose classes, see the *Reference Volume I, Class Library Reference* manual (Chapter 6, "The General-Purpose Classes").

To use the MFC classes in an MS-DOS program, you must select the Use Microsoft Foundation Classes option in the New Project dialog box when you first create the project, or later choose the Project... command on the Options menu and select this option in the Project Options dialog box. The Use Microsoft Foundation Classes option adds an MS-DOS version of the MFC library to the list of library files that are linked with the program (specifically, the MS-DOS library version that is appropriate for the current memory model). Note that you must manually build the required MS-DOS version of the MFC library, because the Setup program prebuilds only Windows library versions. For information on building MFC libraries, see Appendix B in the *Class Library User's Guide* manual.

run within Windows' protected mode memory space, so that their use of memory is not limited to conventional memory. Also, the user of a QuickWin program can easily exchange data with other Windows programs through the standard commands provided on the Edit menu.

QuickWin programs, however, are considerably more limited than standard Windows programs. For example, QuickWin programs cannot call either Windows API functions or the equivalent functions provided by the MFC (using the MFC in QuickWin programs is discussed later). QuickWin programs cannot read mouse input. QuickWin programs cannot display Windows controls (such as push buttons) or dialog boxes, nor can they customize the standard menu (all QuickWin programs have a standard menu). Finally, QuickWin programs cannot provide their own online help (all QuickWin programs have a standard help file).

As you will see later in the chapter, you can take greater advantage of the Windows environment by enhancing a QuickWin program, but if you do so, the program can no longer be ported to MS-DOS.

In Chapter 2, you created a simple C++ QuickWin program named GREET. The following sections provide a more detailed description of the QuickWin program interface, and discuss additional guidelines for creating and enhancing QuickWin programs.

The QuickWin Program Interface

A QuickWin program runs as a multiple document interface (MDI) application, consisting of a main frame window and one or more child frame windows (MDI applications were discussed in Chapter 12). A QuickWin program is shown in Figure 20.3.

FIGURE 20.3:

A QuickWin program

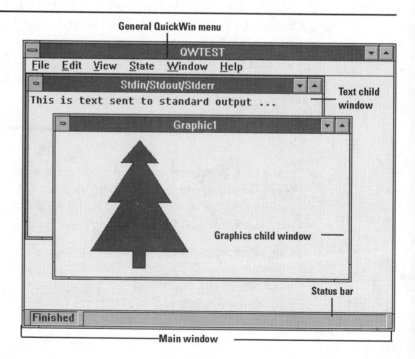

The Main Window

The QuickWin main window contains the standard components found on an MDI main frame window. The title bar displays the name of the program, and the window includes a status bar that is used to report the current status of the program (it displays messages such as "Running," "Input pending in Stdin/Stdout/Stderr," "Finished," and so on). The program menu provides a set of standard commands that can be used for any QuickWin program; these commands are summarized in Table 20.2.

These user interface elements are designed for all types of QuickWin programs. The QuickWin code creates and manages these elements for you, and you cannot modify or control them from your code (however, as you will see in the section "Enhancing QuickWin Programs," you can customize the program icons and the text displayed in the About dialog box).

TABLE 20.2: The Menu Commands on a Quickwin Program

Pop-Up Menu	Command	Description
File	Exit	Terminates the program and closes all program windows
Edit	Mark	Puts the active child window in "mark mode," allowing the user to select text with the keyboard or mouse
Edit	Paste	Inserts text from the Clipboard into the program's input buffer; while text is in this buffer, program reads (for example, calls to scanf) will take text from this buffer rather than from the standard input stream
Edit	Copy Tabs	Copies the selected text into the Clipboard; each sequence of one or more blanks (except leading blanks) is converted into a single tab character
Edit	Copy	Copies the selected text into the Clipboard, without translating blanks to tabs; if a graphics child window is active, this command copies the entire window contents into the Clipboard (as a bitmap)
Edit	Select All	Selects all text in the active window
View	Size To Fit	Expands or compresses the graphics in the active graphics child window to fit exactly within this window
View	Full Screen	Expands or compresses the graphics in the active graphics child window to fit within the entire screen
State	Pause	Temporarily suspends the program
State	Resume	Restarts a suspended program

TABLE 20.2: The Menu Commands on a Quickwin Program (continued)

Pop-Up Menu	Command	Description
Window	Cascade	Arranges child windows in an overlapping pattern
Window	Tile	Arranges child windows in a nonoverlapping pattern so that they are all visible
Window	Arrange Icons	Places icons for any minimized child windows in a row along the bottom of the main window
Window	Input	Activates the graphics child window with pending input
Window	Clear Paste	Empties the program's input buffer (which is filled through the Paste command), so that subsequent program input will come from the standard input stream
Window	Status Bar	Displays or removes the status bar
Window	*n title*	Activates a specific child window (*n* is the number of the window, and *title* is its caption)
Help	Index	Displays the index to a general help file that explains how to use QuickWin programs
Help	Using Help	Displays help on using the help facility
Help	About	Displays the About dialog box

> **NOTE** After your code exits (for example, by returning from the `main` function), the QuickWin windows remain open, so that the program output will remain visible. The user can close these windows by choosing the Exit command on the QuickWin File menu, or by pressing Ctrl+C.

The Stdin/Stdout/Stderr Child Window

The child window labeled Stdin/Stdout/Stderr displays the text that your program sends to the standard output and standard error streams (using, for example, the `printf` function or the `cout` object). Also, when your program reads from the standard input stream (using, for example, the `scanf` function or the `cin` object), the blinking caret and the echoed input characters are displayed in this window. (Input and output streams are explained in Chapter 21.) The QuickWin code stores up to 2048 bytes of output text, and displays scroll bars in the text window that allow the user to scroll through portions of the text that are not currently visible in the window. (As you will see in the section "Enhancing QuickWin Programs," you can change the size of the buffer that stores output text.) The user can also scroll through the text using the arrow, PgUp, and PgDn keys.

The Graphics Child Window

If your QuickWin program displays graphics (as explained later), the graphics output will appear in a *separate* child window, which is labeled Graphic1. If the graphics do not fit within this window, scroll bars will be displayed so that the user can view various portions of the output. (As with text, the user can also scroll through graphic output using the arrow, PgUp, and PgDn keys.)

As you will see in the section "Enhancing QuickWin Programs," an enhanced QuickWin program can display more than one text or graphics child window, and can provide a custom title for each window. Each child window—whether text or graphics—can be independently sized, minimized, or maximized. When the user clicks in a particular child window or chooses its title from the Window menu, it becomes the *active* child window, which means that it is displayed on top of any other child window and that it has the input focus.

Guidelines for Writing QuickWin Programs

The techniques for building, running, and debugging a QuickWin program using the Visual Workbench were discussed in Chapter 2 (in that chapter you created a simple QuickWin program named GREET; you might want to review this information before continuing). This section discusses some general guidelines for writing the actual code for a QuickWin program. Specifically, it describes some of the things that you can and cannot do within a QuickWin program.

What You Can Do

In general, you can write a QuickWin program using the same procedural programming techniques that you use for writing an MS-DOS program, and you can use almost all of the library functions that can be used for MS-DOS.

First, you can use most of the standard C/C++ run-time library functions, such as `printf`, `scanf`, `getchar`, `strcpy`, `fopen`, and `fprintf` (the functions that you cannot use are discussed in the next section).

Also, you can call any of the Microsoft run-time library graphics functions contained in the GRAPHICS.LIB library, such as _clearscreen, _setcolor, _lineto, and _ellipse. As mentioned previously, when you display graphics, the output appears in a separate graphics window, which has the default title Graphic1. Note that some of the graphics functions work differently than they do in an MS-DOS program; the differences are described in the *Programming Techniques* manual, Chapter 7 (the section "Differences Between MS-DOS Graphics and QuickWin Graphics").

The C/C++ run-time functions, including the graphics functions, are documented in the *Reference Volume III, Run-Time Library Reference* manual, and in the *C/C++ Language* online help file.

Additionally, you can use the iostream class library in a QuickWin program in the same way that you use it in an MS-DOS program. The techniques are described in Chapter 21.

Finally, you can use the same general-purpose MFC classes that you can use in an MS-DOS program. These functions, and the techniques for using them, were described previously, in the sidebar titled "Using the MFC in an MS-DOS Program." Note, however, that choosing the Use Microsoft Foundation Classes option links a *Windows* version of the MFC library to the program. Thus, if you are using the medium- or large-memory model, you will not have to build a new library version.

What You Cannot Do

Several categories of C/C++ run-time functions are compatible with MS-DOS programs, but are off-limits for QuickWin programs.

First, you cannot call any of the console or port I/O functions that are declared in the CONIO.H header file. The following is a list of these functions:

```
_cgets
_cprintf
_cputs
_cscanf
_getch
_getche
_inp
_inpw
_kbhit
```

```
_outp
_outpw
_putch
_ungetch
```

In QuickWin programs, however, you can perform console I/O either by calling functions that read from standard input (such as `getchar` and `scanf`) or that write to standard output (such as `putchar` and `printf`), or by using the `iostream` class library as explained in Chapter 21.

To perform port I/O from QuickWin programs, you must write routines in assembly language, which invoke the machine instructions `in` and `out`. (Performing direct port I/O from Windows applications, however, may not be permitted in future versions of Windows.) You can add assembly language routines to your C++ code using the __asm keyword; for an explanation, see the *Programming Techniques* manual (Chapter 4, "Using the 16-Bit Inline Assembler") or the *C/C++ Language* help file (the topic "__asm").

Also, in a QuickWin program you cannot call any of the run-time library functions that spawn other processes. These functions include the `_spawn` function family (`_spawnl`, `_spawnle`, and so on), as well as the `_exec` function family (`_execl`, `_execle`, and so on).

Although a QuickWin program can use any of the graphics functions contained in the GRAPHICS.LIB library, it *cannot* use the presentation graphics functions contained in PGCHART.LIB; these functions all begin with the characters `_pg_` (such as `_pg_chart` and `_pg_setpalette`).

This section mentioned some, but *not* all, of the run-time functions that you cannot call from a QuickWin program. To determine whether a particular function can be used from a QuickWin program, see the Compatibility section of the documentation on the function in the *Reference Volume III, Run-Time Library Reference* manual, or click the Compatibility button in the online documentation on the function in the *C/C++ Language* online help file.

Enhancing QuickWin Programs

You can enhance a QuickWin program by using a set of special run-time functions that are provided by the QuickWin library. The QuickWin functions allow you to take greater advantage of the Windows environment as well as to customize features of the program windows. However, because these functions are unique to the

QuickWin library, if you use them in your program, you can no longer rebuild the program to run under MS-DOS. (To port the program to MS-DOS, you would first have to remove all calls to QuickWin functions.)

The following is a summary of the tasks you can perform using the QuickWin functions, together with the specific functions that are used to perform each type of task:

- Open or close a new text child window (_fwopen, _wopen, _wclose)
- Activate a text child window, or obtain the text child window that is currently active (_wsetfocus, _wgetfocus)
- Get or set the size and position of a text child window (_wgetsize, _wsetsize)
- Change the size of the buffer used to store output sent to a text child window, or obtain the current buffer size (_wsetscreenbuf, _wgetscreenbuf)
- Open or close a graphics child window (_wgopen, _wgclose)
- Activate a graphics child window, or obtain the graphics child window (if any) that is currently active (_wgsetactive, _wggetactive)
- Read a character when a graphics child window is active (_inchar)
- Execute one of the commands on the Window menu, simulating the user's choosing the command (_wmenuclick)
- Customize the text displayed in the About dialog box (_wabout)
- Allow Windows to process messages, so that other applications can run (_wyield)
- Modify or obtain the program's exit behavior—that is, whether the program windows are left open after the program exits (_wsetexit, _wgetexit)

For details on performing any of these tasks, see the documentation on the individual QuickWin functions in the *Reference Volume III, Run-Time Library Reference* manual, or in the *C/C++ Language* help file.

> **NOTE**
>
> You can also create a custom icon that is displayed when the main window or a child window is minimized. For instructions, see the *Programming Techniques* manual, Chapter 7 (the heading "Using Custom Icons").

> **TIP**
>
> When you write an enhanced QuickWin program, you lose some of the most important benefits of QuickWin programming—namely, the ability to directly port the program to MS-DOS, plus the ability to program quickly without learning new techniques and function calls. Accordingly, if you are targeting your program for Windows only, you might consider writing a standard Windows application, using the techniques presented in Part III of this book, rather than writing an enhanced QuickWin program. You would then be able to employ the full range of the Windows API and the MFC library, and you could make use of the timesaving Windows development tools provided by Visual C++.

Summary

In this chapter, you learned how to use the Visual Workbench to create projects for MS-DOS and QuickWin programs, and to build and run these programs. The chapter also presented a number of guidelines for coding MS-DOS and QuickWin programs. The following are some of the main concepts and techniques that were discussed:

- An MS-DOS program is one that is run from the MS-DOS command prompt, either independently of Windows or within a Windows MS-DOS session.

- To build an MS-DOS program, you need the Professional Edition of Visual C++.

- When you create a Visual Workbench project for a standard MS-DOS program, you should select the "MS-DOS application (.EXE)" project type in the Project Type: list of the New Project dialog box. Visual Workbench provides several other project types for creating special types of MS-DOS programs.

- Although most of the classes in the MFC are designed for Windows programs, you can use some of the general-purpose classes in a MS-DOS program. To do so, you must choose the Use Microsoft Foundation Classes option when creating the project or when changing the project options through the Project command on the Options menu. You must also build a version of the MFC library that is suitable for MS-DOS programs.

- A QuickWin program is one that is written using MS-DOS programming techniques but is linked with the Microsoft QuickWin library, which allows it to run as a Windows application.

- A QuickWin program conforms to the MDI program model. The main window provides a menu of general-purpose commands, as well as a status bar. Text output is displayed in a text child window, and graphics output is displayed in a graphics child window. The QuickWin library provides all the code for creating the windows and managing the user interface.

- When you create a project for a QuickWin program, you select the "Quick-Win application (.EXE)" project type in the Project Type: list of the New Project dialog box.

- In a QuickWin program, you can call most of the standard C/C++ run-time library functions, and you can call all of the Microsoft graphics run-time functions contained in GRAPHICS.LIB. You can also use the classes of the `iostream` library, as well as the general-purpose classes of the MFC library.

- In a QuickWin program, however, you *cannot* call the following groups of run-time functions: the console and port I/O functions declared in CONIO.H, the _spawn and _exec function families for spawning processes, the presentation graphics functions contained in PGCHART.LIB, and other individual functions. To determine whether you can use a particular function, see the Compatibility section of the documentation on the function.

- You can use a set of functions provided by the QuickWin library to enhance a QuickWin program. If you do so, however, you cannot build the program to run under MS-DOS. The QuickWin functions allow you to create additional text and graphics child windows, to manage child windows, to customize the About dialog box, and to perform other tasks.

TWENTY-ONE

Using the iostream Class Library

- The iostream library

- Performing standard stream I/O

- Performing file I/O

21

This chapter introduces you to the iostream class library, which is the standard collection of classes for performing object-oriented input and output from C++ programs. The authors of C++ designed the iostream library primarily for typical text-mode programs that display characters on the monitor and on other devices in teletype fashion. Among the Visual C++ program types, it is useful chiefly for MS-DOS and QuickWin programs, which were discussed in the previous chapter (although Windows programs *can* use the file and string I/O classes).

The chapter first describes the general features of the iostream library. It then explains how to use iostream for reading and writing to the standard I/O streams, which are normally associated with the console but may be redirected to other devices. Finally, it explains how to use iostream to read or write both to files and to other devices.

The iostream Library

The term *stream* refers to a source of or a destination for a sequence of byte values, usually characters. A stream can be associated with a variety of different devices, such as the console (the monitor and keyboard), a disk file, a printer, a serial port, or a memory buffer. Performing I/O with a particular type of stream results in reading or writing to the associated device. Because MS-DOS—and therefore Quick-Win—uses a common I/O model for all of these devices, the techniques for reading or writing to any of these types of streams are quite similar. (There are, of course, some differences in techniques due to physical differences in devices; for example, console I/O is sequential, while disk I/O can be sequential or random.)

The standard C/C++ run-time library provides a set of *stream functions* for reading and writing to streams; these functions are defined in STDIO.H and include such functions as printf, scanf, putchar, getchar, fputc, fgetc, fopen, and fclose. The iostream library consists of a set of *stream classes*, which provide the C++ programmer with an object-oriented alternative to the stream run-time functions. The iostream library offers much of the same functionality as the stream run-time functions; because it is based upon C++ classes, however, it is more versatile.

Like the stream run-time functions, the iostream stream classes usually perform buffered I/O (although, in some cases, buffering can be disabled). Buffering minimizes the number of device read or write operations and therefore increases I/O efficiency. If input is buffered, a block of data (typically larger than the requested block) is read into a memory buffer; subsequent read requests are then filled from the buffer until it is empty. If output is buffered, data is written to a memory buffer until the buffer becomes full—or until it is *flushed* for some other reason; the entire buffer contents are then written to the device.

Figure 21.1 shows the hierarchy of iostream classes that are discussed in this chapter, including their base classes. For a complete hierarchy chart of *all* the iostream classes, see the *Reference Volume II, iostream Class Library Reference*, Chapter 2.

The following are some general rules that apply to using the iostream library for all types of input and output discussed in the chapter:

- You must include the IOSTREAM.H header file at the beginning of any source file that uses the iostream classes. This header file contains most of the required declarations. When using certain iostream features, however, you must include other header files; these headers are discussed in the relevant sections.

- You can use any of the classes and techniques discussed in this chapter in MS-DOS or QuickWin programs.

FIGURE 21.1:

The hierarchy of iostream classes discussed in this chapter, including their base classes

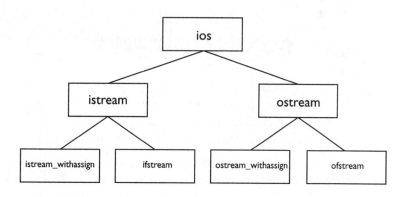

- In Windows programs, you can use *only* the file and string I/O classes (the file classes are discussed in the section "Performing File I/O"). You *cannot* use the classes for standard stream I/O because Windows programs do not use streams for reading characters from the keyboard or writing text to a window (rather, they read keyboard input in response to messages, and write text to a graphics display surface).

- You cannot use `iostream` in programs that have been compiled using the tiny-memory model (such programs cannot support the predefined class objects, such as `cin` and `cout`).

NOTE   In addition to the classes for performing I/O to disk files and devices, the `iostream` library provides classes for reading and writing to character arrays (that is, strings) in program memory. Although these classes are not discussed in this chapter, the techniques are quite similar to those that are described. For information, see the documentation on the `ostrstream`, `istrstream`, and `strstream` classes, in the *Reference Volume III, iostream Class Library Reference* manual, or in the *C/C++ Language* online help file.

Performing Standard Stream I/O

You will first learn how to perform I/O with the three *standard streams*: the standard input stream, the standard output stream, and the standard error stream. The standard streams have the following special properties:

- The standard streams are preopened, and the `iostream` library provides predefined objects for them, which will be described later. (For file streams, discussed later in the chapter, you must define your own object and explicitly open the stream.)

- Normally, the standard streams are associated with the console. That is, reading from the standard input stream obtains characters from the keyboard, while writing to the standard output or standard error stream displays characters on the monitor (or in a text child window of a QuickWin program).

- When running the program, however, the user can *redirect* the standard input stream (using the < operator) so that the input comes from a disk file or from another device (a printer or serial port). Similarly, the user can redirect the standard output stream (using the > or >> operator) so that the output goes to a disk file or another device. Under MS-DOS, the user cannot redirect the standard error stream. For details on redirecting input and output, see an MS-DOS manual.

Because of the third property, when using the standard streams you cannot assume that you are reading or writing to a particular device. (Although the user cannot redirect the standard error stream, it can be redirected by another application that spawns your program as a child process.) Therefore, for example, you should not attempt to perform random I/O (reading or writing to particular character positions), which would work only for a disk file.

Performing Output

The `iostream` library provides predefined objects for writing to the standard output stream or to the standard error stream. Each of these objects is an instance of the `ostream_withassign` class. (Figure 21.1 shows where this class fits into the hierarchy of `iostream` classes.) The objects are as follows:

- `cout`—this object writes to the standard output stream.
- `cerr`—this object writes to the standard error stream, using minimal buffering.
- `clog`—this object writes to the standard error stream, using full buffering.

Usually, you use one of these predefined objects rather than defining your own object.

There are three basic ways that you make use of these predefined objects: performing output with the insertion operator; using manipulators in conjunction with the insertion operator to format the output; and calling member functions to display output, format output, and perform other operations.

Using the Insertion Operator

The ostream class (which is the base class of ostream_withassign) overloads the C++ << operator, so that it can be used with cout, cerr, clog or another output stream object to write a data item to the stream. When used for this purpose, the << operator is known as the *insertion operator*.

The insertion operator can display the value of any variable that has a standard C++ data type; all values are written as text strings (when numeric values are converted to text strings, the output is described as *formatted*). For example, the following program displays various data types on the standard output and standard error streams:

```
#include <iostream.h>

void main ()
    {
    // display data items on standard output:
    cout << 25;        // display integer
    cout << '\n';      // display newline character
    cout << "string";  // display string
    cout << '\n';      // display newline character
    long John = 100000;
    cout << John;      // display long
    cout << '\n';      // display newline character

    // display data items on standard error, with minimal buffering:
    cerr << 45.96;     // display double
    cerr << '\n';      // display newline character

    // display data items on standard error, with full buffering:
    float Boat = 25.43;
    clog << Boat;      // display double
    clog << '\n';      // display newline character
    }
```

This program produces the following output (assuming that the standard output stream has not been redirected):

```
25
string
100000
45.96
25.43
```

You can also chain a series of insertion operators in a single expression, as in the code

```
int Number = 25;

cout << "the value of Number is " << Number << '\n';
```

which would print the following line on the standard output device:

```
the value of Number is 25
```

> **NOTE** For an explanation of how chaining of overloaded operators works, see Chapter 6 (the section "Overloading the Assignment Operator").

Using Member Functions and Manipulators

The `ios` and `ostream` classes (the base classes of `ostream_withassign`) provide a set of member functions that you can use in conjunction with `cout`, `cerr`, `clog`, and other types of output stream objects. These functions can be used to write data, to format the output, and to perform other operations. The `iostream` library also provides a set of *manipulators*, which are special nonmember functions that you can use in conjunction with the insertion operator to format output or to perform other tasks. In the following sections, you will learn how to use these member functions and manipulators to display and format output and to flush the output buffer.

As you will see, some of the manipulators take arguments, and some do not. To use any of the manipulators that take arguments, you must include the IOMANIP.H header file in your program:

```
#include iomanip.h
```

If you include IOMANIP.H, you do not need to include IOSTREAM.H because IOMANIP.H includes it for you.

Setting Field Widths and Fill Characters   By default, each data item sent to a stream is displayed within a field that is the same width as the item itself. You can, however, specify field widths that are larger than the item widths, so that individual items can be separated and can be aligned. One way to set field widths is to use the `ios::width` function, as in the following program:

```
#include <iostream.h>
#include <stdlib.h>

void main ()
    {
    for (int i = 1; i <= 5; ++i)
        {
        cout.width (10);
        cout << rand ();
        cout.width (10);
        cout << rand ();
        cout.width (10);
        cout << rand () << '\n';
        }
    }
```

This program produces the following output:

```
        41     18467      6334
     26500     19169     15724
     11478     29358     26962
     24464      5705     28145
     23281     16827      9961
```

Each data item is right-aligned within a field that is ten characters wide, and the remaining character positions to the left are filled with blanks. Note that if a data item is wider than the specified field width, the field is expanded to accommodate the item; the data is *not* truncated to fit within the specified field.

Note, also, that setting the width (using the `width` function, or the `setw` manipulator to be discussed next) affects only the output generated by the *next* insertion operation; the width then reverts to its default value. In contrast, when you set any of the other formatting features, such as the text alignment, the new feature remains in effect until you explicitly change it.

Alternatively, you can set the field width for the next output operation using the `setw` manipulator. The `setw` manipulator allows you to set the width for each of a series of output operations contained in a single expression, as in the following program (this program produces the same output as the previous example):

```
#include <iomanip.h>
#include <stdlib.h>

void main ()
    {
    for (int i = 1; i <= 5; ++i)
        cout << setw (10) << rand () << setw (10) << rand ()
            << setw (10) << rand () << '\n';
    }
```

Note the inclusion of the IOMANIP.H header file, required because setw is one of the manipulators that is passed one or more parameters.

NOTE In the initial release of Visual C++, using a manipulator that takes one or more parameters generates a rather complex (and undocumented) warning message. These warnings do not go away until you set the compiler warning level to 1 (with the /W1 compiler flag). The manipulators, however, work properly.

By default, unused character positions in a field are filled with blanks. To specify an alternative fill character, you can call the ios::fill function, as in the following example:

```
#include <iostream.h>
#include <stdlib.h>

void main ()
    {
    cout.fill ('.');
    cout << "total amount due";
    cout.width (20);
    cout << "$1024.64";
    }
```

This program produces the following output:

```
total amount due...........$1024.64
```

Alternatively, you can use the `setfill` manipulator, as in the following example program (which produces the same output as the previous example):

```
#include <iomanip.h>
#include <stdlib.h>

void main ()
   {
   cout << setfill ('.') << "total amount due" << setw (20) << "$1024.64";
   }
```

Setting the Alignment   When you specify a field that is wider than the data item, the data item—by default—is right-justified within the field. To left-justify data items, you can pass the enumerator `ios::left` to the `ios::flags` function, as in the following example:

```
#include <iomanip.h>
#include <stdlib.h>

void main ()
   {
   cout.flags (ios::left);
   for (int i = 1; i <= 5; ++i)
      cout << setw (10) << rand () << setw (10) << rand ()
           << setw (10) << rand () << '\n';
   }
```

This program would generate the following output:

```
41        18467      6334
26500     19169      15724
11478     29358      26962
24464     5705       28145
23281     16827      9961
```

Alternatively, you can set the alignment using the `setiosflags` manipulator, as in the following equivalent code:

```
#include <iomanip.h>
#include <stdlib.h>

void main ()
   {
   cout << setiosflags (ios::left);
   for (int i = 1; i <= 5; ++i)
```

```
cout << setw (10) << rand () << setw (10) << rand ()
     << setw (10) << rand () << '\n';
}
```

To change the alignment back to the default right-alignment style, you can pass the enumerator `ios::right` to either the `ios::flags` function or the `setiosflags` manipulator.

Note that you can also call the `ios::setf` function to set the alignment style. For a complete list of the formatting features you can set using the `ios::flags` or `ios::setf` function or the `setiosflags` manipulator, see the documentation on `ios::flags` in the *Reference Volume III, iostream Class Library Reference* manual, or in the *C/C++ Language* online help file.

Setting the Precision   The following program prints a column of floating point numbers:

```
#include <iomanip.h>
#include <stdlib.h>

void main ()
    {
    for (int i = 1; i <= 10; ++i)
        cout << setw (10) << rand () / 165.37 << '\n';
    }
```

Here is the program output:

```
 0.247929
 111.671
  38.302
 160.247
 115.916
 95.0838
  69.408
 177.529
  163.04
 147.935
```

Notice that the number of digits displayed after the decimal point varies, and that the decimal points are therefore not vertically aligned. As an alternative, you can display numbers that are rounded to a fixed number of digits after the decimal point by calling the `ios::precision` function or using the `setprecision` manipulator. However, if you simply call this function or use this manipulator, you will set the total number of *significant digits* rather than the number of digits after the decimal point (remember the confusing discussion on significant digits in the first chapter of your high school physics book?). To set the number of decimal places, you must first pass the enumerator `ios::fixed` to the `ios::flags` function or the `setiosflags` manipulator, and then specify the precision. The following version of the previous program uses this method to display each number with two digits following the decimal point:

```
#include <iomanip.h>
#include <stdlib.h>

void main ()
    {
    cout.flags (ios::fixed);
    cout.precision (2);

    for (int i = 1; i <= 10; ++i)
        cout << setw (10) << rand () / 165.37 << '\n';
    }
```

The program output is as follows:

```
      0.25
    111.67
     38.30
    160.25
    115.92
     95.08
     69.41
    177.53
    163.04
    147.93
```

Specifying the Radix   You can display numbers in octal format by passing the `ios::oct` value to `ios::flags` or `setiosflags`, you can display numbers in hexadecimal format by passing `ios::hex`, and you can display numbers in decimal format (the default) by passing `ios::dec`. Alternatively, you can use an equivalent manipulator: `oct`, `hex`, or `dec`.

Also, if you pass the `ios::uppercase` flag to `ios::flags` or `setiosflags`, any letters (*a* through *f*) contained in hexadecimal numbers will be displayed in uppercase.

Turning Formatting Flags On and Off

As explained, you can specify formatting options by passing various prede-fined enumerator values to the `ios::flags` (or `ios::setf`) function or the `setiosflags` manipulator. If you want to select more than one option, you must combine the enumerators using the ¦ operator. For example, the follow-ing function call turns on the left-alignment option *and* an option for display-ing a + sign in front of positive numbers:

```
cout.flags (ios::left ¦ ios::showpos);
```

When you call `flags` or `setiosflags`, any option that you do *not* specify is turned *off*. For example, the two function calls

```
cout.flags (ios::left ¦ ios::showpos);
cout.flags (ios::fixed);
```

would select *only* the `ios::fixed` option, because the second call turns *off* the `ios::left` and `ios::showpos` options (as well as any other options that might have been selected since the program began running).

Once you have turned on a particular option, you can turn it off—without affecting other options—by passing the enumerator for the option to the `ios::unsetf` function or the `resetiosflags` manipulator. For example, the following code selects a set of formatting options and then later turns off only *one* of these options, leaving the others set:

```
// set three formatting options:
cout.flags (ios::left ¦ ios::showpos ¦ ios::fixed);

// send output to cout ...

// turn off just one option:
cout.unsetf (ios::showpos);

// send more output to cout ...
```

Displaying Characters　　Rather than using the insertion operator to display a single character,

```
cout << 'X';
```

you can use the `ostream::put` function,

```
cout.put ('X');
```

Unlike the insertion operator, the `put` function is *not* affected by the formatting options discussed in the previous sections.

You can also display characters using the `ostream::write` function; however, this function is not explained until the section "Writing the Data," because it is most useful for writing data to disk files.

Flushing the Buffer　　When you send output to `cout` or `clog`, the characters typically do not appear immediately because they are stored in an output buffer. This buffer is automatically flushed—causing the characters to appear—if the buffer becomes full, if the program terminates, or if the program reads from `cin`. You can also force the buffer to be flushed at any time by calling the `ostream::flush` function or using the `flush` manipulator.

For example, you might want to display a message before the program performs some lengthy process. You can flush the buffer to make sure that the message appears before the process starts. The following is an example using the `flush` function,

```
cout << "sorting records ..." << '\n';
cout.flush ();

// sort records ...
```

and the following is an example using the `flush` manipulator:

```
cout << "sorting records ..." << '\n' << flush;

// sort records ...
```

As a shortcut, you can use the manipulator `endl`, which inserts a newline character (`'\n'`) *and* flushes the buffer. The following code uses `endl`, and is equivalent to the previous example:

```
cout << "sorting records ..." << endl;

// sort records ...
```

TIP   Output sent to the `cerr` object is automatically flushed immediately after each insertion operation. You can make the `cin` or `clog` object behave in this way by passing the `ios::unitbuf` flag to `ios:flags` or `setiosflags`.

Performing Input

The `iostream` library provides a predefined object, `cin`, for reading input from the standard input stream. This object is an instance of the `istream_withassign` class. You use the `cin` object to perform input with the extraction operator and to read and format input with member functions and manipulators.

Using the Extraction Operator

The `istream` class (which is the base class of `istream_withassign`) overloads the C++ `>>` operator, so that it can be used with `cin` or other input stream objects to read data from the stream. When used for this purpose, the `>>` operator is known as the *extraction operator*.

The extraction operator reads a text string and assigns the value that is expressed by the text to a variable of any standard C++ type. (When strings are converted to numeric values, the input is described as *formatted*.) For example, the following extraction operation reads the characters typed by the user, converts the resulting text string to an integer value, and assigns this value to `Number`:

```
int Number;
cin >> Number;
```

NOTE   Recall that the input can come from a file rather than the keyboard if standard input has been redirected.

Similarly, the following extraction operation reads characters and converts the text to a floating point number:

```
float RealNumber;
cin >> RealNumber;
```

Finally, the following operation reads characters and copies them directly to a string (no conversion is necessary):

```
char String;
cin >> String;
```

Like the insertion operator, you can chain extraction operators within a single expression. For example, the following code is equivalent to the previous three examples combined:

```
int Number;
float RealNumber;
char String;

cin >> Number >> RealNumber >> String;
```

The extraction operator reads and converts characters from the input stream until it encounters a white space character (that is, either a space, a tab, or a newline character). The next extraction operation then begins reading the first character *beyond* the white space character or characters; in other words, the operator skips white space. (If the extraction operator is reading a numeric value, it also stops reading the input if it encounters a nonnumeric character.) Consequently, the individual data items that are read must be separated by white space characters; they cannot be separated by other characters such as commas. Also, a single extraction operation cannot read a string that contains an embedded space or other white space character. To overcome this limitation, you can use the `istream::get` or `istream::getline` function; these functions allow you to specify the terminating character (that is, the character that stops the function from reading input; these functions are discussed in the next section).

Another problem with using the extraction operator to read a string is that you cannot limit the number of characters that are read from the input stream; the input characters might therefore be written past the end of the string. This problem can also be solved by using the `get` function or the `getline` function, which allow you to limit the number of characters that are extracted.

If, when reading a numeric value, the first character that the extraction operator encounters is not a valid numeric character, the operator assigns 0 to the variable. It also sets an internal error flag, which causes all subsequent extraction operations on cin to fail (that is, it causes them to return immediately, without assigning a value to the variable). You can test for this error condition by calling the ios::fail function, and you can clear the error flag by calling ios::clear. These functions will be discussed in the section "Testing for Errors," later in the chapter.

Using Member Functions and Manipulators

In this section, you will learn about some of the useful manipulators and member functions you can use with the cin input object.

You can use the radix functions or manipulators described previously (in the section "Specifying the Radix") to control the way that the extraction operator interprets characters when reading a numeric value. For example, if you specify the ios::hex option, the extraction operator will interpret characters as hexadecimal digits (thus, the letters *a* through *f* will be considered valid numeric characters). With the hex option, the input characters 10 will be converted to the decimal value 16, and the characters 1a will be converted to the decimal value 26.

You can call the istream::get function to read *unformatted* input, that is, to simply read one or more characters without converting the character string to a numeric value. To read a single character, you can call get without passing it any parameters, as in the following example:

```
char Ch;

Ch = cin.get ();
```

This form of get always reads the *next* character from the input, even if it is a white space character.

You can read an entire string of characters by calling the following version of get:

```
istream& get (unsigned char* puch, int nCount, char delim = '\n');
```

The puch parameter is the address of the buffer to receive the string, nCount is the maximum number of characters to read into this buffer (including a NULL written at the end), and delim is the terminating character—that is, the character that *stops* the function from reading further characters. (This parameter defaults to a newline if you do not pass a different character.) For example, the following code reads a character string into String:

```
char String [128];
```

```
cin.get (String, sizeof (String));
```

In this call, `get` extracts characters from the input stream and stores them in `String`, until 127 characters have been read and stored *or* it encounters a newline. It then writes a `NULL` character to `String`.

The `get` function, however, does *not* extract the terminating character from the input stream; consequently, if you call it a second time, specifying the same terminating character, it returns without reading further input (because it immediately encounters the terminating character that remains in the input stream). The following form of the `istream::getline` function, however, works just like `get` except that it extracts the terminating character (it merely extracts this character from the input; it does *not* store it in the receiving buffer):

```
istream& getline (char* pch, int nCount, char delim = '\n');
```

The `istream::read` function is especially useful for reading data from files, and will be described later (in the section "Reading the Data"). The `istream` class provides the following additional input functions, which you might find useful in your program: `ignore`, `peek`, `gcount`, `eatwhite`. For information, see the description of these functions in the *Reference Volume III, iostream Class Library Reference* manual, or in the *C/C++ Language* online help file.

Performing File I/O

In this section, you will learn how to use the `iostream` library to read or write to files, as well as other devices such as printers or serial ports (which are treated like files under MS-DOS). When reading or writing to files, you can use most of the `iostream` I/O facilities discussed in previous sections, such as the insertion and extraction operators, manipulators, and member functions of the input or output object.

There are, however, some differences in the I/O techniques used for files. For example, when performing file I/O, you must create your own input or output stream object, specifying the file name and the file open mode. Also, with files, you can perform either sequential or random I/O (with the standard streams, I/O is sequential). The following sections focus on the techniques that are unique to file I/O, as well as techniques that are especially useful for working with files.

To use the output and input file stream classes, you must include the header file FSTREAM.H in your program:

```
#include <fstream.h>
```

(You do not need to include IOSTREAM.H because FSTREAM.H includes it for you.)

Performing Output

To perform output to a file, you must first create an output stream object. Creating this object opens the file and sets the file mode. You can then use the insertion operator or the object's member functions to perform either sequential or random output to the file. You can also call member functions of the object to test for errors.

Creating the Output Stream Object

To create a stream object for writing to a file, you should define an instance of the ofstream class. The easiest way to do this is to use the following ofstream constructor:

```
ofstream (const char* szName, int nMode = ios::out);
```

> **NOTE** You can pass a third parameter to the ofstream constructor to specify the file sharing mode. The ofstream class also provides several alternative constructors that allow you to create the output object and open the file in different ways. For information, see the ofstream documentation.

The szName parameter is the name of the file that is to be opened for receiving output. You can supply the name of a disk file, or the name of one of the standard MS-DOS devices listed in Table 21.1. When the object is destroyed, the destructor will automatically close the file.

For example, the following statement creates an object that writes data to the file OUTPUT.DAT,

```
ofstream OFStream ("OUTPUT.DAT");
```

and the following statement creates an object for displaying data on the printer:

```
ofstream OFStream ("PRN");
```

TABLE 21.1: The Standard MS-DOS Devices You Can Open with the `ofstream` Constructor

Name Passed to ofstream Constructor	Device Opened
AUX	Same as COM1
COM1, COM2, COM3, or COM4	Serial port number 1, 2, 3, or 4
CON	Console (that is, the monitor and the keyboard)
LPT1, LPT2, or LPT3	Printer on first, second, or third parallel port
PRN	Same as LPT1

You assign the nMode parameter one or more flags indicating the mode in which you want to open the file (if you do not pass a value, this parameter defaults to the flag `ios::out`). To specify a flag, use one of the enumerators described in Table 21.2; you can specify several flags by combining enumerators using the ¦ operator.

Opening Existing Files   Normally, if the file you want to open does not exist, of-stream creates it for you. (If, for some reason, you do not want to create a new file, you should specify the `ios::nocreate` nMode parameter flag.) If the file already exists, however, there are various ways to handle it. By default (that is, if you do *not* specify the `ios::app`, `ios::ate`, `ios::in`, or `ios::noreplace` flag), an existing file is truncated to zero length.

If you specify the `ios::app` nMode parameter flag,

```
ofstream OFStream ("OUTPUT.DAT", ios::app);
```

an existing file is *not* truncated, and all data you write to it is appended *after* the file contents (you *cannot* overwrite the existing file data).

If you specify the `ios::ate` or `ios::in` flag, an existing file is not truncated, and you can write data to *any* position within the file, using the techniques for positioning the output pointer that will be described later. The `ios::ate` flag initially positions the output pointer at the end of the file, while `ios::in` positions it at the beginning; with either flag, you can reposition the pointer to any position.

Finally, if you specify the `ios::noreplace` flag, the file open fails if the file already exists; that is, an existing file is *not* opened. To test for a file-open failure, you can call the `ios::fail` function, as shown in the following example:

```
ofstream OFStream ("OUTPUT.DAT", ios::noreplace);
if (OFStream.fail ())
    {
    cerr << "sorry, file already exists" << endl;
    return;
    }
```

The Binary and Text Modes   By default, a file is opened in *text mode*. In text mode, each newline character (which has an ASCII value of 10) is translated into a carriage-return and newline character pair (ASCII values 13 and 10). Text mode is suitable for processing standard text strings and buffers. (By convention, in C++ programs a line is terminated with a single newline character, while in a standard text file it is terminated with a carriage-return and newline character pair.)

If, however, you specify the `ios::binary nMode` flag, the file is opened in *binary mode*. In binary mode, characters are *not* translated. This mode is thus suitable for storing nontext data, such as numeric variables and data structures containing numeric values.

> **NOTE**   You can also switch between binary and text mode *after* the object has been constructed and the file opened. To do this, you can call the `ofstream::setmode` function, passing it either `filebuf::binary` or `filebuf::text`. You can also use the `binary` and `text` manipulators.

Writing the Data

You can write formatted data to a file stream using the insertion operator, and you can write individual characters using the `ostream::put` function, as described previously in the chapter. The best way to write blocks of unformatted binary data, however, is to open the file in binary mode and use the `ostream::write` function:

```
ostream& write (const char* pch, int nCount);
```

The parameter `pch` is a pointer to the block of data to write, and `nCount` is the number of bytes to write.

Suppose, for example, that you are creating an inventory data file to consist of a series of records that match the format of the following structure:

```
struct
    {
    int CatNumber;
    char Description [64];
    double Cost;
    int Quantity;
    }
Item;
```

Once you have assigned a value to each of the fields of the Item structure, you could write the record data to the file using the write function, as in the following code:

```
ofstream OFStream ("INVENTRY.DAT", ios::binary);

OFStream.write ((char *)&Item, sizeof (Item));
```

Setting the Output Pointer   An output stream object maintains an internal pointer marking the position where the next byte will be written to the stream. Usually, when you first open a file, the output pointer is at the first position in the file (that is, at position 0; as shown in Table 21.2, however, when you open an existing file in certain modes, the output pointer is positioned at the *end* of the file). Each time you perform a write operation, the pointer is moved to the end of the data that is written. Because of this mechanism, a series of output operations automatically writes data to a file *sequentially*.

To write data *randomly* (that is, to write individual data items to specific positions in the file), you can explicitly move the output pointer by calling the ostream::seekp function:

```
ostream& seekp (streampos pos);
```

The parameter pos is a long value that specifies the desired position of the output pointer, as the number of bytes from the beginning of the file (thus, the value 0 would position the pointer at the beginning of the file, the value 1 would place it one byte from the beginning of the file, and so on).

TABLE 21.2: File Mode Flags You Can Assign to the nMode Parameter of the ofstream Constructor

Value	Effect
ios::out	The file is opened for output (the default, implied mode); if the file exists, and if you have *not* specified the ios::app, ios::ate, or ios::in value, the file is truncated
ios::trunc	If the file exists, it will be truncated to zero length; this mode is implied if you specify ios::out but do *not* specify ios::app, ios::ate, or ios::in
ios::app	If the file exists, it is *not* truncated; the output pointer is initially positioned at the end of the file, and all new data is appended to the *end* of the file (you cannot overwrite the existing file data)
ios::ate	If the file exists, it is *not* truncated; the output pointer is initially positioned at the end of the file, and new data can be written to *any* position in the file
ios::in	If the file exists, it is *not* truncated; the output pointer is initially positioned at the beginning of the file, and new data can be written to *any* position in the file
ios::noreplace	If the file exists, the file open fails
ios::nocreate	If the file does not exist, the file open fails (it does *not* create a new file)
ios::binary	The file is opened in binary mode rather than in the default text mode

Consider the inventory file example that was given in the previous section. You could open an existing inventory file, and use the seekp function to update a specific record:

```
ofstream OFStream ("INVENTRY.DAT", ios::in);
OFStream.seekp (sizeof (Item) * 5);
OFStream.write ((char *)&Item, sizeof (Item));
```

This example assumes that the fields of the Item structure have been assigned the desired new values. The code first opens the existing file using the ios::in flag, so that the file is *not* truncated. It then calls seekp to move the output pointer to the beginning of the sixth record, and finally it calls write to write the record data.

To *obtain* the current position of the output pointer, you can call ostream::tellp:

```
streampos tellp ( );
```

> **NOTE** If you open an existing file in append mode (by specifying the `ios::app` flag when creating the stream object), all data will be written sequentially to the end of the file, beyond the existing file data. Calls to `seekp` will have no effect.

Testing for Errors

Whenever you perform an operation with a stream object, the `iostream` library sets the bits of an internal flag indicating the current error state. You can obtain a copy of this flag by calling the `ios::rdstate` function:

```
int rdstate ( ) const;
```

Table 21.3 lists masks that you can use to access each bit of this flag, as well as the meaning of each bit. For example, the following code tests for both a minor error and a serious error after performing a write operation (from the previous example):

```
OFStream.write ((char *)&Item, sizeof (Item));

if (OFStream.rdstate () & ios::badbit || OFStream.rdstate () & ios::failbit)
   cerr << "error writing to file" << endl;
```

(You cannot ascertain the success of a write operation by simply checking the `ios::goodbit` bit, because this bit will be turned off whenever the output pointer is positioned at the end of the file, even if the write operation was successful.)

TABLE 21.3: Bits of the `iostream` Error State Flag

Bit Mask	Meaning of Bit
`ios::badbit`	A serious (unrecoverable) error has occurred
`ios::eofbit`	End of file has been reached
`ios::failbit`	A minor (possibly recoverable) error has occurred
`ios::goodbit`	No error has occurred (that is, *none* of the other bits are set)

Rather than checking both the `ios::badbit` and the `ios::failbit` error state bits, you can simply call the `ios:fail` function, which returns a nonzero value if *either* of these bits is set, as shown in the following shorter code:

```
OFStream.write ((char *)&Item, sizeof (Item));

if (OFStream.fail ())
    cerr << "error writing to file" << endl;
```

Table 21.4 summarizes `rdstate`, `fail`, and the other `ios` error functions.

TABLE 21.4: The `ios` Error Functions

Function	Purpose
`ios::bad`	Returns TRUE if `ios::badbit` error state bit is set
`ios::clear`	Clears *all* error state bits (if no parameter is passed)
`ios::eof`	Returns TRUE if `ios::eofbit` is set
`ios::fail`	Returns TRUE if *either* `ios::failbit` *or* `ios::badbit` error state bit is set
`ios::good`	Returns TRUE if `ios::goodbit` error state bit is set
`ios::rdstate`	Returns the current error state flag (which contains the error state bits)

Also, the `ios` class overloads the `!` operator so that, when it is used in conjunction with a stream object, it returns TRUE if either the `ios::badbit` or the `ios::failbit` bit is set. Thus, the expression

```
if (!OFStream)
```

is equivalent to

```
if (OFStream.fail ())
```

You could therefore further simplify the test in the previous example to the following:

```
OFStream.write ((char *)&Item, sizeof (Item));

if (!OFStream)
    cerr << "error writing to file" << endl;
```

> **NOTE** You can use the error functions discussed in this section with any type of stream object. They are presented here because they are most useful when performing file I/O (that is, file operations are the most error-prone).

Performing Input

To read data from a file, you must first create an input stream object. Creating this object opens the file and sets the file mode. You can then use the extraction operator or the object's member functions to perform either sequential or random input from the file. Also, when creating the input object or performing an input operation, you can check for errors using the methods discussed in the previous section.

Creating the Input Stream Object

To create a stream object for reading a file, you should define an instance of the `ifstream` class. The easiest way to do this is to use the following `ifstream` constructor:

```
ifstream (const char* szName, int nMode = ios::in);
```

> **NOTE** You can pass a third parameter to the `ifstream` constructor to specify the file sharing mode. The `ifstream` class also provides several alternative constructors that allow you to create the input object and open the file in different ways. For information, see the `ifstream` documentation.

The `szName` parameter is the name of the file that is to be opened for input. You can supply the name of a disk file, or the name of one of the standard MS-DOS devices listed in Table 21.1 (except `PRN`, `LPT1`, `LPT2`, or `LPT3`, because the printer is an output-only device). When the object is destroyed, the destructor will automatically close the file.

For example, the following statement creates an object for reading data from the file INPUT.DAT:

```
ifstream IFStream ("INPUT.DAT");
```

You can assign the nMode parameter one or more flags indicating the mode in which you want to open the file (if you do not pass a value, this parameter defaults to the flag ios::in). The default ios::in flag simply opens the file for input.

Normally, if the file does not already exist, ifstream will *create* an empty file, even though the file will contain no data that can be read. (Note, however, that you could also create an output stream object and use it to write data to the file; you could then use the input stream object to read this data.) If, however, you specify the ios::nocreate flag and the file does not exist, the file open will fail (this is a safe way to determine whether a particular file exists). As explained previously, you can test for a file-open failure by calling the ios::fail function, as shown in the following example:

```
ifstream IFStream ("INPUT.DAT", ios::nocreate);
if (IFStream.fail ())
    // then INPUT.DAT does not exist ...
```

If you specify the ios::binary flag, the file will be opened in binary mode rather than text mode. When you read a file in text mode, each carriage-return and new-line character pair is converted to a newline character. Also, an input function stops reading if it encounters a Ctrl+Z character (ASCII character 26), even if the physical end of the file has not been reached. In binary mode, no characters are translated and input functions read to the physical end of the file.

> **TIP**
>
> If you need to read *and* write to the same file, you can create an input stream object (an ifstream instance) that you use for reading the file, *and* an output stream object (an ofstream instance) that you use for writing to the file. Alternatively, you can create a single object of the fstream class, which you can use for performing both input and output operations. For details, see the documentation on fstream.

Reading the Data

You can read formatted data from a file stream using the extraction operator, and you can read one or more characters using the istream::get or istream::getline function, as described previously in the chapter. The best way to read blocks of unformatted binary data, however, is to open the file in binary mode and use the `istream::read` function:

```
istream& read (char* pch, int nCount);
```

The parameter pch is a pointer to the block of data to read, and nCount is the number of bytes to read.

Sequential and Random Reading   Like an output stream object, an input stream object maintains an internal pointer marking the position of the next byte that will be read. When you open a file for input, the pointer is initially set at position 0. Each time you perform a read operation, the pointer is advanced to the end of the data that was read. You can thus read a file sequentially by simply performing a series of read operations.

To read an entire file sequentially, you should test for the end of the file before performing each read operation. To do this, you can call the `ios::eof` function (which was described in the section "Testing for Errors"). As an example, consider the inventory file example given previously; recall that this file consists of a series of records that match the format of the following structure:

```
struct
    {
    int CatNumber;
    char Description [64];
    double Cost;
    int Quantity;
    }
Item;
```

The following code would read the entire file sequentially:

```
ifstream IFStream ("INVENTRY.DAT", ios::binary | ios::nocreate);
if (!IFStream)
    {
    cerr << "file not found" << endl;
    return;
    }

while (!IFStream.eof ())
    {
    IFStream.read ((char *)&Item, sizeof (Item));
```

```
// now display or process record ...

}
```

 Rather than reading the file until `ios::eof` returns a nonzero value, you could read it until `ios::good` returns zero; in this way, reading would stop if *either* the end of file is reached *or* an error is encountered. For a description of the error-testing functions you can use when reading the file, see the section "Testing for Errors."

To read a file *randomly* (that is, to read individual records at specific positions), you can explicitly move the input pointer by calling the `istream::seekg` function:

```
istream& seekg (streampos pos);
```

The parameter `pos` is a `long` value that specifies the desired position of the input pointer, as the number of bytes from the beginning of the file. As an example, you could read the sixth record in the inventory file as follows:

```
IFStream.seekg (sizeof (Item) * 5);
IFStream.read ((char *)&Item, sizeof (Item));
```

(This example assumes that the file has been opened as shown above and that you have already ascertained that the file contains at least six records.)

To *obtain* the current position of the input pointer, you can call `istream::tellg`:

```
streampos tellg ();
```

Summary

In this chapter, you learned how to perform object-oriented input and output from your MS-DOS and QuickWin C++ programs, using the standard `iostream` class library. The following are some of the important concepts that were discussed:

- A *stream* is a source of or a destination for a sequence of byte values (usually characters). A stream is associated with a particular device, such as the console or a disk file, and is used for reading or writing to that device.

- The `iostream` library provides a set of classes and objects for reading or writing to streams. These stream classes offer an object-oriented alternative to using the stream functions in the C/C++ run-time library (that is, the functions defined in STDIO.H, such as `printf` and `scanf`).

- I/O with the `iostream` library is almost always buffered.

- The `iostream` library predefines objects for reading or writing to the standard streams: standard output (`cout`), standard error (`cerr` and `clog`), and standard input (`cin`).

- The standard streams are associated with the console (the monitor and keyboard) unless the user has redirected them to a disk file or another device.

- You can write formatted data to the standard output or standard error stream by using the insertion operator (`<<`) in conjunction with the `cout`, `cerr`, or `clog` stream object. This operator converts a variable of any C++ data type to a string in the output stream. You can write unformatted data by calling the `put` or `write` member functions of the stream object.

- You can read formatted data from the standard input stream by using the extraction operator (`>>`) in conjunction with the `cin` stream object. You can read unformatted data by calling the `get`, `getline`, or `read` member function of the stream object.

- You can format data written to the standard output or standard error stream by calling member functions of the stream object, or by using special nonmember functions known as *manipulators* in conjunction with the insertion operator.

- You can also use the `iostream` library to read or write to files or other devices (such as printers or serial ports). To do so, however, you must define your own stream object, which opens the file or device and specifies the open mode. To read or write raw data, you should open the file in *binary* mode, which suppresses the character translations that occur in the default *text* mode.

- To write to a file or device, you must define a stream object that belongs to the `ofstream` class. You can use the same output techniques that you use for writing to a standard stream. The `write` function is especially useful for writing blocks of unformatted data.

- You can also perform random output to a file by calling the `ostream::seekp` function to place the output pointer at the position where you want to write the data.

- To read from a file or device, you must define a stream object that belongs to the `ifstream` class. You can use the same input techniques that you use for reading from a standard stream. The `read` function is especially useful for reading blocks of unformatted data.

- You can perform random input from a file by calling the `istream::seekg` function to position the input pointer.

INDEX

Note to the Reader: **Boldfaced** page numbers indicate definitions of terms or principal discussions of topics. *Italic* page numbers indicate illustrations.

Symbols

& (ampersands)
  for dialog box controls, 423, 426
  for menu items, 239
  for reference types, 52–54
* (asterisks)
  for comments, 43–44
  as operator, overloading, 142
: (colons)
  for member initializer lists, 90
  for scope resolution operator, 47–48
, (commas)
  with extraction operators, 920
  for member initializer lists, 90
{} (curly brackets)
  for arrays, 159
  for blocks, 44
. (dot operator) for member access, 80
= (equal sign) operator
  overloading, **144–148**
  with reference types, 54
> (greater than signs)
  in extraction operator, **919–920**
  for redirection, 909
  for serializing objects, 298
< (less than signs)
  as insertion operator, 23–24, 298,
    910–911
  for redirection, 909
  for serializing objects, 298
- (minus sign) operator, overloading, 142
  for constructors, 88
  for member initializer lists, 90

+ (plus sign) operator, overloading,
  134–142, 155–156
/ (slashes)
for comments, 43–44
as operator, overloading, 142
[] (square brackets) for arrays, 70–71, 95
~ (tildes) for destructors, 92
~ ¦ (vertical bars) with formatting
  flags, 917

A

abort procedures, 774
About command
  for QuickWin programs, 898
  tool bar button for, 474, *475*
  for WINGREET, 175
accelerator dialog box, 241
accelerator keys, **240–241**
  for Clipboard commands, 826–828, *827*
  copying, 399
  identifiers for, 270–271
  for MINIEDIT, 397, 399
accelerator properties dialog box, 241
access specifiers, **79–81**
accessing class members, **79–85**
  with friend classes, 138–139
  with inheritance, **112–116**
  static members, 102–103
active windows, 552
  child, 386, 552
  in QuickWin programs, 902
Add Class dialog box, 427, *428*
Add function (CObArray), 261

Add Function button, 207, 266
Add Member Function dialog box, 266, 433
Add Member Variable dialog box, 429–431, *430*, 436
Add Variable button, 429, 432
AddDocTemplate functions
  in CMinieditApp, 393, 403
  in CWingreetApp, 182, **195–196**
AddFigure function (CMinidrawDoc), **676–677**, 682, 700
AddLine function (CMinidrawDoc)
  deleting, 676
  for file I/O, 309
  for storing documents, 259–262, 278, 299
  for updating views, 358–359, 371
addresses
  of derived classes, 121
  of virtual functions, 124
AfxGetApp function (MFC), 204, 743
AFX_IDS_IDLEMESSAGE identifier, 499
AfxOleInsertDialog function (MFC), 853
AFXPRINT.RC resource script, 766
AfxRegisterWndClass function (MFC), **222–223**
aliases. *See* reference types and parameters
aligning text
  alignment points for, *532*, 534
  enumerators for, 434
  functions for, 533–534
  identifier for, 421–422
  in stream output, 912, **914–915**
allocating memory blocks, **68–72**, **831–835**, **837–841**
Alt key
  for debugging, 29
  for dialog box controls, 423, 426
  for editing source files, 22
  message handler for, 553
ambiguous functions, 68, 153
ampersands (&)
  for dialog box controls, 423, 426
  for menu items, 239
  for reference types, 52–54
AND operator with bit operations, 738
animation, bitmaps for, **738–741**

ANSI character sets
  LOGFONT field for, 539, 579
  TEXTMETRIC field for, 544, 583
ANSI_FIXED_FONT value, 549, *549*
ANSI_VAR_FONT value, 549, *549*
API (application program interface), 166, 895
app flag (ios), 924, 927–928
App Studio tool, 9, 11, **216**
  for bitmaps, 725, 746
  for copying, **398**, **400**
  for dialog boxes, 418, *419*, 420, 467
  for icons, **220**, **400**, 743
  for MDI programs, **395–397**, **399–400**
  for menus, **218–219**, **239–241**, 263–265, **398**
  for tab order of controls, 425–426, *427*
  for tool bars, **477–484**
appending file output, 924
AppendMenu function (CMenu), 733
application classes, **176–178**
  for MDI programs, 390
  message-handling by, 205
  for tool bar messages, 488
application program interface (API), 166, 895
applications. *See also* MS-DOS programs; QuickWin programs; Windows programs
  building, **26–27**, **174–176**
  debugging, **28–33**
  initializing, **194–197**
  MDI. *See* multiple document interface (MDI)
  running, **28**, **174–176**
AppWizard editor, 8, 166–167
  for classes, **176–179**
  for document type, 219
  for MDI programs, 388, *389*, 390
  for message maps, 210
  for source code
    editing, **170–174**
    generating, **167–170**, **202–203**
Arc function (CDC), 612
  attributes for, 620
  pens for, 613
  using, **648**, *649*

Arrange Icons command, 898
arranging
  MDI windows, 388
  QuickWin windows, 898
arrays
  allocating, 70–71
  constructors for, **94–95**
  dimensioning, 60
  initializing, 95, **159–160**
  reading and writing, 908
  for status bars, 497–499, 515
  for storing text, 534, 538–547, 578–584
  for tool bars, 485–488, 515
arrow cursor
  hot spot in, 217
  identifier for, 204
arrow keys
  for editing source files, 21
  for radio buttons, 426
  for scrolling, 559
  virtual key codes for, 553–554
ascent of text, TEXTMETRIC field for,
    532, 542, 581
__asm keyword, 901
assignment operator, overloading,
    144–148
assignments to base class pointers, 121
associativity of overloaded operators, 142
asterisks (*)
  for comments, 43–44
  as operator, overloading, 142
ate flag (ios), 924, 927
Attach function (CBitmap), 725, 846
attributes
  for drawings, **620–624**
  for text, **532–533**
Auto property for buttons, 426
auto_inline pragma, 49
automatic variables with reference types,
    58
AUX device, 924

B

background color
  in dialog boxes, 452

  for drawings, 620
  for text, 532–533
  for tool bar buttons, 480
Backspace key
  for editing source files, 22
  handling, 564–565
bad function (ios), 929
badbit flag (ios), 928–929
bars (¦) with formatting flags, 917
base classes, 108, 112, 116–117
  pointers to, **121**
  virtual functions with, **127–129**
BEGIN_MESSAGE_MAP macro, 211
binary file mode, 925
binary flag (ios), 925, 931
binary manipulator, 925
binary operators, overloading, **142–143**
binding, 124
bit operations, **733–734**
  BitBlt, **736–741**
  with Clipboard commands, 843, 846
  device support for, 778
  PatBlt, **734–736**
  StretchBlt, **741–742**
BitBlt function (CDC), 731–732, **736–741**
  with Clipboard commands, 843, 846
  device support for, 778
BITDEDOC.CPP file, 753–755
BITDEDOC.H file, 753
BITDEMO program, **745**, *745*
  coding, 746–749
  designing bitmaps in, **746**
BITDEVW.CPP file, 759–761
BITDEVW.H file, 757–758
BITMAP.CPP file, 750–752
bitmap-designing window, 479, *480, 481,*
    725
BITMAP.H file, 749–750
bitmap properties dialog box, 478, *478*
BITMAP structure, 731, 846
BitmapClipInfo structure, 846
bitmaps, **724**
  for animation, **738–741**
  for brushes, 618, 733
  for check marks, 733
  class for, 437
  color for, **735–738**

for controls, 732
copying, **736–742, 841–844**
creating, **724–730**
designing, **746**
displaying, **730–732**
drawing functions for, **727–730**
for icons, **742–744**
importing, 726, 746
memory device context objects for,
   728–732
for menu labels, 733
moving, **736–742**
painting, **733–736**
pasting, **844–848**
printer capabilities for, 778
size of, 478–479, 481, 728, 731, 734,
   741–742, 747
for tool bars, **478–481**
black color
for bitmaps, 735
drawing mode for, 649–650
functions for, 660–661, 691–692
for pen, 613–614
BLACKNESS raster-operation code, 735
BLACK_PEN value, 613–614
blanks
with extraction operators, 920
in output fields, 913
blinking caret, 30
in ECHO, **567–571**
inserting Clipboard data at, 829
blocks, 44. *See also* memory
allocating and releasing, **68–72**
initializing, 832
reading and writing, 322
blue drawing color, functions for,
   660–661, 692
BN_CLICKED messages, 433, 445
bold lines in source listings, 172
bold style
data member for, 429, *430*
identifier for, 421–422
message handler for, 433, 437
for System font, 418
bookmarks, 23
BOOL type, 429

borders
class for, 177
for default buttons, 423
dotted lines for, 656
for drawing areas, 347
for figures, 612, 655
for group boxes, 424
for modeless dialog boxes, 467
printing, 771–772, 783, 785
for program windows, *175*
for tool bar buttons, 480
width of, 568
bounding rectangles, 357–358, 360, 668
brackets (({}, []))
for arrays, 70–71, 95, 159
for blocks, 44
Breakpoint button, 30, *30*
breakpoints, 30–31
Browse dialog box, 18
brushes, 223, 612
for bitmaps, 734
bitmaps for, 618, 733
color of, 617
creating, **614–619**
device context objects for, 614–615,
   618–619
for figures, 655
initializing, 617–618
origins for, 620
patterns with, 617–618, *617*, 655
selecting, **612–614**
buffers
for CEditView window, 320
flushing, 907, **918–919**
for I/O, 24, 906–907, 909
in QuickWin programs, 902
BUFFERS= statement, 5
Build All button, 27, *27*
Build button, 26, *27*, 174, *174*
Build command, 26, 174, 893
build options, **24–26**
building programs, **26–27**, **174–176**
bullets for menu items, 269
ButtonIDs array, 485–487, 515
buttons. *See also* controls; tool bars
classes for, 437
functions for, 440–441

buttons array, 488
BYTE data type, serializing, 298

C

C++
  comments in, **43–44**
  constant types in, **59–66**
  converting C programs to, **38–43**
  declaration statements in, **44–46**
  default function parameters in, **51–52**
  inline functions in, **48–50**
  new and delete operators in, **68–72**
  overloaded functions in, **66–68**
  reference types in, **52–59**
  scope resolution operator in, **47–48**
CAboutDlg class, 182–183
Cancel buttons
  default message handlers for, 445
  in initial dialog boxes, 418, *419*
CanPaste function (COleClientItem), 860
Caps Lock key
  indicator for, 476, 497, 499
  testing state of, 557
Caption: text box for resources, 219, 239,
    263, 292
capturing of mouse, 209, 215
CArchive class, 294–295, 322, 895
carets, 30. *See also* cursors
  in ECHO, **567–571**
  inserting Clipboard data at, 829
carriage returns, handling, 564–565
Cascade command, 898
cascading menus, 265
cascading windows
  for MDI, 388
  for QuickWin, 898
cast notation, alternate syntax of, 152
CBitdemoApp class, 749–752
CBitdemoDoc class, 753–755
CBitdemoView class, **746–749**, 757–761
CBitmap class, 724–725
CBitmapButton class, 437, 732
CBlock class, 114–115
CBLOCK.H file, 114–115
CBrush class, 614–615

CButton class, 437
CByteArray class, 895
C/C++ Compiler Options dialog box,
    25–26, *26*
CCircle class, 667, *668*, 674, 696, 705–706
CCircleFill class, 667, *668*, 674–675,
    696–697, 706–707
CClientDC class, 565, 611, 728
CCmdTarget class, 206
CCmdUI class
  for menus, 268–269
  for tool bars, 493, **495–496**
CColorDialog class, 469
CComboBox class, 437
CControlBar class, *486*
CCURR.H file, 156–157
CCurrency class, **134–145**, **152–157**
CDC class, 174
CDemoOleClientItem class, **851–852**
CDialog class, 440
CDialogBar class, *486*, 500
CDocument class, 171, 177–178, 293
CEchoApp class, 593–596
CEchoDoc class, 564, 596–599
CEchoView class, **563–571**, 601–606
CEdit class, 432, 437
CEditView class, 237, *339*, 830
centering text
  identifier for, 421–422
  message handler for, 433, 438
cerr object, 909–910, 919
CF_BITMAP format, 842–845, 847
CFigure class, **664–675**, *668*, 694–697
CFile class, 895
CFileDialog class, 469
CFindReplaceDialog class, 469
CF_OEMTEXT format, 837–838
CFont class, 538
CFontdemoApp class, 453–456
CFontdemoDoc class, **448–449**, 457–460
CFontdemoView class, **449–452**, 463–467
CFontDialog class, 469, 545
CFormat class
  coding for, **434–444**
  members of, **428–432**
  message handlers for, **432–433**, *434*
CFormView class, *339*, 468–469

CFrameWnd class, 177–178, 390–391, *392*
CF_TEXT format, 834, 837–838, 847
_cgets function, 900
character sets
  LOGFONT field for, 539–540, 579–580
  TEXTMETRIC field for, 544, 583–584
characters
  displaying, **918**
  fill, **913–914**
  reading, 24, **919–921**
    WM_CHAR messages for, **560–566**
    WM_KEYDOWN messages for,
      552–559
  in streams, 906
check boxes
  Alt key with, 423
  class for, 437
  control palette for, *420*
  data members for, 429
  message handlers for, 433, 437–438
  properties of, 422
  using, 424
check marks
  bitmaps for, 733
  for menu items, 269, 493, *494*
CheckDlgButton function (CWnd), 440
checkerboard program (BITDEMO), **745**,
  745
  coding, 746–749
  designing bitmaps in, **746**
CheckRadioButton function (CWnd), 440
child frame window classes, 390–391,
  392, 393
child windows, 177
  active, 386, 552
  in MDI, 386, *387*
  in QuickWin programs, **899**, 902
  QuickWin programs as, 896, *896*
  splitter windows as, 355
Chord function (CDC)
  drawing attributes for, 620
  pens and brushes for, 613
  using, 651, 653, *653*
cin object, 24, 919–920
  in MS-DOS programs, 892
  in QuickWin programs, 898
Circle command in MINIDRAW, 482, *483*

Circle Fill command in MINIDRAW, 482,
  483
Circle tool bar button, *477*
circles
  drawing, 651
  tools for, *477*, 482
Class Name: list with ClassWizard, 206
classes. *See also* Microsoft Foundation
  Classes (MFC)
  accessing members of, **79–85, 112–116,**
    138–139
  collection, 260
  constructors for, **85–92**
  defining, **76–77**
  derived, **108–117**
  destructors for, **92–95**
  for dialog boxes, **427–432**
  for drawings, **664–675**
  for encapsulation, **80–85**
  friend, 116, **138–139,** 143, 146
  functions in, 209
  hierarchies of, **116–120,** *118*
  inheritance in, **112–116**
  inline functions in, **95–97**
  instances of, **78–79**
  libraries for, 117
  for MDI, **390–393**
  pointers to, **121**
  static members in, **101–104**
  stream. *See* iostream class
  this pointer for, **99–101**
  virtual functions in, **120–129**
  for WINGREET, **176–179**
Classes button, 169, 292
Classes dialog box, 388, *389*
ClassName: list, 266
ClassWizard editor, 8, 166, 206–207, *208*,
  211–212, *212*
  for dialog boxes, **427–432**
  files for, 179
  for menu commands, 266–267, *267*
  for message-handling, **205–208,** 210–
    212, 432–433, *434*
Clear command in ECHO, 561, *562*
clear function (ios), 921, 929
Clear Paste command, 898
_clearscreen function, 900

clicking on MDI windows, 386
client area, 177
client coordinates, converting, 208–209, 359, 435
clients in OLE, 849
ClientToScreen function (CWnd), 208–209, 349
CLine class
  for drawings, 664–665, *668*, 670, 695, 702
  for file I/O, **296–298**, 305
  for split windows, **357–358**, **360–361**
  for storing documents, **259–260**
Clipboard, **826**
  closing, 831, 835, 837, 839, 842, 845, 847, 858
  commands for, **826–830**
  copying and cutting to, **830–836**, **841–844**
  deleting contents of, 831, 834, 842
  formats with, 834, 836–838, 842–845, **847–848**
  with graphics, **841–848**
  with icons, 400
  memory for, **831–835**, **837–841**
  for OLE items, **858–860**
  opening, 831, 834, 837, 842, 845, 858
  pasting from, **836–841**, **844–848**
  for QuickWin programs, 897
  with text, **830–841**
Clipboard Viewer (CLIPBRD.EXE) utility, 848
ClipCursor function (API), 208–210, 215, 349
clipped regions
  in drawings, 362
  in printing, 783
CListBox class, 437
clog object, 909–910, 918–919
Close Window on Exit option, 893
CloseClipboard function (API), 831, 835, 837, 839, 842, 845, 847, 858
closed figures, drawing, **650–655**
closing
  Clipboard, 831, 835, 837, 839, 842, 845, 847, 858
  dialog boxes, 441, **445**, 468
  MDI windows, 386

CMainFrame class, 177–178, 187–189
  for BITDEMO, 755–757
  for ECHO, 599–601
  for FONTDEMO, 460–462
  for MANDEL, 639–641
  for MINIDRAW, 230–232
    for drawings, 707–711
    for file I/O, 310–312
    for printing and print previewing, 809–813
    for scrolling, 372–375
    for splitting windows, 353, 372–375
    for status bars, **497–499**, 513–517
    for storing documents, 280–282
    for tool bars, **485–488**, 513–517
  for MINIEDIT, 249–252
    for file I/O, 329–331
    for MDI, 391, 408–410
  for OLEDEMO, 872–874
  for TEXTDEMO, 584–586
CMandelApp class, **627–628**, 632–636
CMandelDoc class, 636–638
CMandelView class, **628–632**, 641–645
CMDIChildWnd class, 391, *392*, 393
CMDIFrameWnd class, 390, *392*
CMESS.H file, 158–159
CMessage class, **145–148**, 150–151, 153–154, 158–159
CMinidrawApp class, 204, 224–227
  for drawings, **660–664**, 683–694
  for file I/O, **301–305**
  for printing and print previewing, **767–768**, 785–796
  for scrolling and splitting, 363–367
  for status bars, 499–507
  for storing documents, 271–275
  for tool bars, **488–494**, 499–507
CMinidrawDoc class, 227–230
  for drawings, **676–677**, 694–707
  for file I/O, **292–300**, 305–310
  for printing and print previewing, 796–809
  for scrolling and splitting, 368–372
  for storing documents, **265–268**, **270–271**, 275–280
  for tool bars and status bars, 507–513

CMinidrawView class, **203–204**, **206–216**, **222–223**, 232–237
  for drawings, **677–683**, 711–720
  for file I/O, 312–317
  for printing and print previewing, **768–769**, **772–773**, **776–777**, **780–781**, **783**, **785**, 813–823
  for scrolling, **342–352**, 375–381
  for split windows, **356–363**, 375–381
  for storing documents, **260–263**, 282–286
  for tool bars and status bars, 517–523
CMinieditApp class, 243–246
  for file I/O, **321–326**
  for MDI, 390, 401–405
CMinieditDoc class, 247–249
  for file I/O, **319–320**, 326–329
  for MDI, 390, **393–394**, 405–408
CMinieditView class, 251–254
  for file I/O, 331–334
  for MDI, 410–412
CMultiDocTemplate class, 393
CObArray class, 260, **295–296**
CObject class, 260, 298, *668*, 895
CObList class, 895
code reuse, 118–119
CodeView debuggers, 29, 893
COleClientDoc class, 850, 859
COleClientItem class, 850–852
COledemoApp class, 865–868
COledemoDoc class, 868–872
COledemoView class, **853–864**, 874–880
collection classes, 260
colons (:)
  for member initializer lists, 90
  for scope resolution operator, 47–48
color
  for bitmaps, **735–738**
  for brushes, 617
  dialog box class for, 469
  in dialog boxes, **452**
  for drawings, 620, 625, 631
  for filling, 656
  for hatch lines, 617
  for icons, 742
  for lines, 615–616, 648–650
  menu for, **657–658**, *659*, **660**
  for pen, 615–616, 648–650

  for text, 452, 531–533, 545–546, 565
  for tool bar buttons, 480–481
Color common dialog box, 664, *665*
Color menu for MINIDRAW, **657–658**, *659*, **660**
ColorTable array, 629
COLOR_WINDOWTEXT value, 565
columns in printing area, 775–777, 781
COM devices, 924
.COM extension, 890
combo boxes
  class for, 437
  control palette for, *420*
  functions for, 440
  using, 424
COMMAND handler, 266
  for Clipboard, 828–831, 836–837, 839, 842
  for drawings, 658, 660
  for OLE items, 860–862
  for tool bars, 489
Command Line: text box, 12
command messages, 205
commas (,)
  with extraction operators, 920
  for member initializer lists, 90
comments
  in C++, **43–44**
  option for, 169, 238
  in source code, 173
common dialog boxes, **469**, 545
Common User Access standard, 21
companion disk, installing, 11–13
compatibility of C and C++, **38–43**
compatible bitmaps, 727
compiler, 8, 11
  constructors generated by, 88, 90
  modes for, 24–25
  options for, 25
Compiler button, 25
Compiler Options dialog box, 25
Compile-Time Directives: text box, 766, *767*
compound documents, 849
compressed files, 7, 12
CON device, 924
condensed text, 533
CONFIG.SYS file, 5

CONIO.H file, 900–901
console I/O
  in QuickWin programs, 900–901
  and streams, 906, 908
constants and constant types, **59–60**
  definition files for, 179
  and functions, **63–67**
  initializing, 59, 63
  with overloading, 67
  and pointers, **60–62**
  with references, 53, 56–57, **62–63**
construction, order of, **112**
constructors, **85–87**
  calling, **94–95**
  conversion, **152–160**
  copy, **148–152, 159–160**
  default, **87–88**, 90, 92, 193
  for derived classes, **111–112**
  initialization in, 85–87, **90–92**
  new for, 70
  overloaded, **88–90**
control codes, entering, 564–565
Control IDs: list box, 429, 432
control palette for dialog boxes, 418, *419*,
      420, *420*
controls
  adding, **421–425**
  bitmaps for, 732
  classes for, **427–432, 436–437**
  coding for, **434–444**
  form views for, **468–469**
  identifiers for, **421–423**
  message handlers for, **432–433**, *434*
  position of, 421–422, 425, 441
  properties of, **421–422**
  in QuickWin programs, 895
  size of, 421–423, 425
  tab order of, **425–426**, *427*
  using, **424–425**
conversion constructors, **152–160**
conversion functions, 159
converting
  coordinates
    device and logical, 342–344, *342*, 349,
        361, 624
    screen and client, 208–209, 359, 435

with overloaded functions, 67
programs
  C to C++, **38–43**
  SDI to MDI, 394
coordinates
  for bitmaps, 731
  for controls, 441
  converting
    device and logical, 342–344, *342*, 349,
        361, 624
    screen and client, 208–209, 359, 435
  for cursor, 208–209
  for dialog boxes, 435
  for drawings, 349, *349*, *350*, 625
  for figures, 667–668
  for icons, 743–744
  for lines, 259
  in mapping modes, 346, **621–624**, *622*
  with mouse messages, 217
  for OLE items, 856
  for printing, 784
  for text, 534
copies in printing, 779
Copy command
  for Clipboard, 826–829, *827*
  for graphics, **841–844**
  for icons, 400
  for OLE items, 857, **862–864**
  for QuickWin programs, 897
  for text, **830–836**
  tool bar button for, 474, *475*, 829
copy constructors, **148–152, 159–160**
Copy Tabs command, 897
copying
  accelerator keystrokes, 399
  bitmaps, **736–742, 811–844**
  with Clipboard, **830–846**
  companion disk files, 12
  graphics, **841–844**
  icons, **400**
  menu items, **398**
  OLE items, **862–864**
  in QuickWin programs, 897
  in source files, 22
  text, **830–836**
cout object, 23–24, 909–911
  flushing buffers with, 918–919

in MS-DOS programs, 892
in QuickWin programs, 898
CPaintDC class, 444, 611
CPen class, 614–615
.CPP extension, 23, 38
CPrintDialog class, 469
_cprintf function, 900
CPrintInfo class, 769
_cputs function, 900
Create functions
in CDialog, 468
in CSplitterWnd, 355
in CStatusBar, 498
in CToolBar, 487
CreateBitmap function (CBitmap), 725
CreateCompatibleBitmap function (CBit-
map), 724, **727–729**, 843
CreateFontIndirect function (CFont), 544,
546
CreateFromClipboard function (COleCli-
entItem), 858–859
CreateHatchBrush function (CBrush),
617, 655
CreateLinkFromClipboard function
(COleClientItem), 859
CreateNewObject function
(COleClientItem), 854–855
CreatePatternBrush functions
in CBrush, 618, 655
in CDC, 733
CreatePen function (CPen), 615
CreateSolidBrush function (CBrush), 617
CreateSolidCaret function (CWnd),
568–569
CreateStaticFromClipboard function
(COleClientItem), 858–860
CREATESTRUCT structure, 222
CRect class, 348–349, 895
CRectangle class, 98–99, 113–114, 666,
668, 670–671, 695,
CRECT.CPP file, 99
CRectFill class, 666, *668*, 671–672, 695,
703–704
CRECT.H file, 98–99
CRECT1.H file, 113–114, 702–703

CRectRound class, 666, *668*, 672–673, 675,
696, 704–705
CRectRoundFill class, 666–667, *668*,
673–675, 696, 705
cross hatch patterns, *617*
crosshairs cursor, 204
cross-shaped cursor
changing to, **350–352**
hot spot in, 217
CRoundBlock class, 116–117
CRunTime class, 895
CS_ class styles, 222
_cscanf function, 900
CScrollBar class, 437
CScrollView class, 338, *339*, 780–781
CSingleDocTemplate class, 196, 393
CSplitterWnd class, 355
CStatic class, 437
CStatusBar class, *486*, 496
CString class, 895
CTextdemoApp class, 571–575
CTextdemoDoc class, **537–549**, 575–584
CTextdemoView class, **527–534**, **550–559**,
587–592
CToolBar class, 485, *486*, 488
Ctrl key
bit mask for, 218
for copying menu items, 398
for debugging, 29
for editing source files, 21–23
for scrolling, 559
virtual key code for, 556
curly brackets ({})
for arrays, 159
for blocks, 44
current line in debugging, 31
current objects, 100
current point, 646–648
current position, 620
cursors, 30. *See also* carets
changing, **350–352**
coordinates of, 208–209
for delays, **214**
displaying, **221–223**
identifiers for, 204
CURVECAPS index for device
capabilities, 779

curved lines, 612
  device support for, 779
  drawing, **648–650**
custom drawing color, 660, 662, 664, *665*,
    692
customizing
  building options, 25
  installation configuration, 6–7
  strings, 219
  windows, **221–223**
Cut command
  for Clipboard, 826–829, *827*
  for graphics, **841–844**
  for OLE items, 857, **862–864**
  for text, **830–836**
  tool bar button for, 474, *475*, 829
cutting
  graphics, **841–844**
  OLE items, **862–864**
  in source files, 22
  text, **830–836**
CVBControl class, 437
CView class, 173, 177–178, 200, 209
  hierarchy of, 338, *339*
  OnPaint handlers in, 444
  for printing and print previewing,
    773–774, *774*
CWinApp class, 177–178, **192–194**, 292
CWingreetApp class, 177–178, 180–182,
    192–193
CWingreetDoc class, 171, 177–178, 184–
    186
CWingreetView class, **173–174**, 177–178,
    189–191
CWnd class, 209, *392*, 440, *486*
.CXX extension, 38
cyan drawing color, functions for, 660,
    662, 692–693

D

data, exchanging. *See* Clipboard; mes-
    sages and message handlers; OLE
    (Object Linking and Embedding)
data members, 77
  accessing, **79–85**

  for derived classes, 109
  inheriting, 108
  initializing, 85–87, **90–92**
  static, **101–104**
data types
  in inline functions vs. macros, 50
  with memory allocation, **68–69**
  with overloaded functions, 66–67
  serializing, 298
Debug build mode, 24–25
debugging programs, **28–33**
  and const variables, 60
  MS-DOS, 893
dec enumerator (ios), 916
dec manipulator, 916
decimal output, 916
declarations, 39, **44–46**
DECLARE_SERIAL macro, 296, 305
decorative font family
  LOGFONT field for, 540, 580
  TEXTMETRIC field for, 543, 583
Default Button property, 423
default character set
  LOGFONT field for, 539, 579
  TEXTMETRIC field for, 544, 584
default constructors, **87–88**, 90, 92,
    111–112, 193
default function parameters, **51–52**, 68
_DEFAULT.PIF file, 893
default text pitch
  LOGFONT field for, 540, 580
  TEXTMETRIC field for, 543, 582
defaults
  for alignment points, *532*
  for bitmap identifiers, 725, 746
  for brushes, 612
  for drawing attributes, **620–621**
  for file extensions, 292, 388, *389*, 390
  for file names, 293
  for fonts, 549, *549*
  for installation configuration, 6
  for message-handling, 205, 211, 445
  for pens, 612
  for push buttons, 441
#define preprocessor directive, 50, 60
defining
  classes, **76–77**

functions, 39
static members, 102
Del key, 22
delays, cursor for, **214**
Delete All command in MINIDRAW,
    263–264, *264*, **266–268**
delete operator, **68–70**
  for arrays, **71**
  for dialog boxes, 468
  for instances, 79, 95
  for OLE items, 854
DeleteContents functions
  in CDocument, 267–268, 299, 319–320,
    394
  in CMinidrawDoc, 260, **265**, 279
DeleteObject functions
  in CDC, 546
  in CGdiObject, 775
deleting
  Clipboard contents, 831, 834, 842
  document data, **265**
  menu items, 218–219
  objects. *See* delete operator
  project source files, 19
  in source files, 22
  text, **830–836**
derived classes, **108–111**, 116–117
  accessing members in, **112–116**
  constructors for, **111–112**
  for serialized objects, 298
descent of text, TEXTMETRIC field for,
    532, 542, 581
descriptions in status bar, 476, 498
designing
  bitmaps, **746**
  dialog boxes, **418–426**, *421*, *427*
  tool bar buttons, **478–481**
DestroyCaret function (API), 569
DestroyWindow function, 468
destruction, order of, **112**
destructors, **92–94**
  calling, **94–95**
  overloaded, 88
Detach function (CGdiObject), 844, 847
device capabilities for printing, **776–779**
device context objects, 174, 213
  for bitmaps, 728–732, 734

for brushes, 614–615, 618–619
for character input, 565
for converting coordinates, 343
current point of, 647
for dialog boxes, 444
for drawings, **610–612**
for fonts, 530, 545, 547
mapping modes with, 346
for pens, 614–615, 618–619
for printing and print previewing, 769,
    775, 781
device coordinates, **340–344**, *342*, 349,
    621–624
DEVICE_DEFAULT_FONT value, 549,
    549
device size of drawings, 624
device units, 621
diagonal hatch patterns, *617*
dialog bars, 496, **500**
dialog box units for control size, 423
dialog boxes, 9, **416**, *417*, **418**
  classes for, **427–432**
  closing, 441, **445**, 468
  coding for, **434–444**
  colors in, **452**
  common, **469**, 545
  controls in. *See* controls
  designing, **418–426**, *421*, *427*
  displaying, **444**, **446–452**, 468
  and form views, **468–469**
  graphics in, 611
  message handlers for, **432–433**, *434*, 445
  MFC functions for, **440–441**
  modeless, **467–468**
  in QuickWin programs, 896
  resources for, **444**, **446–447**
dialog properties window, 421–422
dialog-designing window, 418, *420*
dimensioning arrays, 60
dimensions. *See* size
direct base classes, 117
directly derived classes, 117
directories
  for companion disk files, 12
  for installation, 6–7
  in list boxes, 440
  for programs, 23, 168

for project files, 18
Directory: list box in AppWizard, 168
disabled menu items, 268
disabling tool bar buttons, 495
Display function (CMessage), 158
displaying
  bitmaps, **730–732**
  caret, 569–570
  characters, **918**
  command descriptions, 476, 498
  cursor, **221–223**
  dialog boxes, **444**, **446–452**, 468
  icons, 223, **742–744**
  MDI windows, 391
  OLE items, **855–856**
  text, **527–535**
  title and document type, 219
  variables, 910
  view class for, 177–178
dithered colors, 615–616
dividing windows, **352–363**, *354*
DKGRAY_BRUSH value, 614
DlgDirList function (CWnd), 440
DlgDirListComboBox function (CWnd),
  440
DlgDirSelect function (CWnd), 440
DlgDirSelectComboBox function
  (CWnd), 440
document classes, 171, **176–178**
  for MDI programs, 390
  message-handling by, 205
document data
  deleting, **265**
  modified flag for, **299–300**
  serializing, **294–298**
  storing, **290–301**, **317–321**
document templates, 182, **195–196**
document type, displaying, 219
DoModal function (CDialog), 449
DoPreparePrinting function, 768–769
DOS version requirements, 5
DOSGREET program
  project files for, **889–892**
  source code for, **892–893**
DOSGREET.CPP file, 892
dot operator (.) for member access, 80

dotted lines
  for borders, 656
  for temporary lines, 677
double-clicking OLE items, 862
Double command in MINIDRAW, 483,
  484
double data type, serializing, 298
double-thick lines
  functions for, 488–491, 493–494, 505
  identifier for, 483, 488–489, 658
  tool bar button for, 477
DoVerb function (COleClientItem), 862
DPtoLP function (CDC), 342–344, 624
drag operations, 209
DragAcceptFiles function (CWnd), 300–
  301, 321, 395
drag-drop feature, **300–301**, 321, 395
Draw functions
  in CBlock, 114
  in CCircle, 674, 706
  in CCircleFill, 675, 707
  in CFigure, 669
  in CLine, **259–260**, 263, 278, 670, 702
  in CRectangle, 99, 671, 703
  in CRectFill, 672, 703–704
  in CRectRound, 673, 704–705
  in CRectRoundFill, 673–674, 705
  in CRoundBlock, 116
  for OLE items, 856
DrawCol function (CMandelView),
  628–631, 645
DrawFocusRect function (CDC), 656
DrawIcon function (CWnd), 744
drawing area
  for printing and print previewing,
    772–773, *775–778*, *781*
  for scrolling, **344–352**
drawings. *See also* MINIDRAW program
  attributes for, **620–624**
  and bitmaps, **727–730**
  classes for, **664–675**
  closed figures, **650–655**
  coding for, **676–683**
  device context objects for, **610–612**
  device support for, 779
  fractal program for, **626–632**, *626*
  lines, 612, **646–650**

mapping modes for, **620–624**
menus for, **657–660**, *659*
message handlers for, **660–664**
modes for, 620, **648–650**
points, **625–626**
tools for, **612–619**
view class for, 173
DrawText function (CDC), 174, 535
Drive: list box in AppWizard, 168
drives for programs, 168, 440
drop-down combo boxes, 424
drop-list combo boxes, 424
DSTINVERT raster-operation code, 735
DT_CENTER flag, 174
DT_RASDISPLAY flag, 785
DT_VCENTER flag, 174
DWORD data type, serializing, 298
dynamic binding, 124
dynamic memory objects, **70**
dynamic variables, 58

E

early binding, 124
eatwhite function (istream), 922
ECHO program, 560, *561*
  caret management in, **567–571**
  coding for, **563–566**
  icon for, 562, *563*
  menus for, **560–561**, *562*
  message handlers for, **562–563**
  resources for, **560–562**
ECHO.CPP file, 593–596
ECHODOC.CPP file, 597–599
ECHODOC.H file, 596–597
ECHO.H file, 593
ECHOVIEW.CPP file, 602–606
ECHOVIEW.H file, 601–602
EDIT class, 320
Edit Code button, 267
Edit command for project files, 19
edit controls, 320
  class for, 437
  control palette for, *420*
  data members for, 431–432
  limiting entries for, 435–436

properties of, 422
using, 424
Edit dialog box, 891–892, *891*
Edit Links command in OLEDEMO, 860
Edit Member Variables dialog box,
    429–432, *429*, *431*, 436
Edit menu
  for Clipboard, 826–828, *827*
  for ECHO, **560–561**, *562*
  for MINIDRAW, 219, 263–264, *264*
  for MINIEDIT, **239–240**, 386, 396–397,
    397
  for OLEDEMO, 850
  for QuickWin programs, 897
  tool bar buttons for, 474, *475*
  for WINGREET, 175
Edit Project dialog box, 18, *19*
Edit Variables button, 429
editing
  icons, **220**
  OLE objects, 849
  source files, **20–24**, **170–174**, **892–893**
editors. *See* App Studio tool; MINIEDIT
    program; Visual Workbench
_ellipse function, 900
Ellipse function (CDC)
  drawing attributes for, 620
  pens and brushes for, 613
  using, 651, *652*
ellipses
  drawing, 651, *652*
  tool for, 482
embedded objects, 849–850, 858. *See also*
    OLEDEMO program
Empty function (CString), 566
EmptyClipboard function (API), 831, 834,
    842
emulation math support, 9
EN_CHANGE messages, 433
Enable function (CCmdUI), 269, 495
enabling
  menu items, 269
  tool bar buttons, 495
encapsulation, **80–85**
End key
  for editing source files, 21
  for scrolling, 559

virtual key codes for, 554, 556
EndDialog function (CDialog), 441, 445, 468
endl manipulator, 918
Enter key for default buttons, 423
enum tags, C vs. C++, **40–43**
eof function (ios), 929, 932–933
eofbit flag (ios), 928
equal sign (=) operator
  overloading, **144–148**
  with reference types, 54
erasing. *See* deleting
error testing
  encapsulation for, 84–85
  in file output, **928–930**
errors
  with extraction operators, 920–921
  warning messages for, 25, 27, 913
Esc button, default message handlers for, 445
Esc key, handling, 564–565
Escape function (CDC), **779–780**
example programs, 9, 11
exchanging data. *See* Clipboard; messages and message handlers; OLEDEMO program
_exec functions, 901
Execute command, 28, 174, 893
Exit command
  for FONTDEMO, 444
  message-handling for, 206
  for QuickWin programs, 897
  for WINGREET, 175
ExitInstance function (CWinApp), 194
EXPAND utility, 12
expanded text, 533
expanding variables in debugging, 31
expressions
  for default function parameters, 51
  in inline functions vs. macros, 50
extensions, default, 292, 388, *389*, 390
extern specifier, C vs. C++, 40
external leading, 531, *532*, 542, 582
ExtFloodFill function (CDC), 613, 656
extraction operators, **919–920**
ExtTextOut function (CDC), 535

F

fail function (ios), 921, 925, 929, 931
failbit flag (ios), 928–929
fclose function, 906
fgetc function, 906
figures. *See also* drawings; MINIDRAW program
  coordinates and size of, 667–668
  drawing, **650–655**
File Extension: text box, 292
file I/O, **922–923**
  input, **930–933**
  for MINIDRAW, 290–301
  for MINIEDIT, **317–321**
  output, 923–930
File menu
  for MINIDRAW, 218
    for file I/O, 290–292, *291*
    for printing, **765–766**, *766*
  for MINIEDIT, **239**, *240*
    for file I/O, **317–318**, *319*
    for MDI, 386, 395, *396*, 397
  for QuickWin programs, 897
  tool bar buttons for, 474, *475*
  for WINGREET, 175
File Name: text box, 18–19, 23, 293
File Open dialog box, 292, *293*
  with default extensions, 390
  for WINGREET, 175
File Save As dialog box, 293, *294*, 390
file sharing modes, 923, 930
files
  default extensions for, 292, 388, *389*, 390
  header, 49, 60, 97, 179
  help, 10–11, 17
  for icons, 179
  in list boxes, 440
  opening, 171, **300–301**, 469, **924–925**
  printing, 469
  and streams, 906
FILES= statement, 5
fill characters in output, **913–914**
fill function (ios), 913
Filled Circle tool bar button, *477*

filled circles and rectangles
    functions for, 489, 491–493, 506–507
    identifiers for, 482, 487, 489
    tool for, *477*, 482
Filled Rect tool bar button, *477*
Filled Rnd Rect tool bar button, *477*
filling areas, 655–656
FillRect function (CDC), 656, 734
Find command in MINIEDIT, 239–240,
        241, 396, *397*
Find Next command in MINIEDIT,
        239–240, *241*, 396–397, *397*
finding text
    dialog box class for, 469
    in source files, 22
fixed enumerator (ios), 916–917
fixed text pitch
    fonts for, 549, *549*
    identifier for, 421–422
    LOGFONT field for, 540, 580
    message handler for, 433, 438
    TEXTMETRIC field for, 543, 582
flags function (ios), 914–917, 919
flicker, 221–223, 566
flipping bitmaps, 741
float data type, serializing, 298
FloodFill function (CDC), 613, 656
floppy disk requirements, 4
flow control in WINGREET, **192–195**
flush function (ostream), 918
flush manipulator, 918
flushing buffers, 907, **918–919**
focus, 552, **568–569**
    for controls, 441
    in QuickWin programs, 902
Font dialog box, 526, *527*, **535–549**
Font: list, 546
FONTDDOC.CPP file, 458–460
FONTDDOC.H file, 457–458
FONTDEMO program, 416, *417*
    classes for, **427–432**
    coding for, **434–444**
    designing dialog boxes for, **418–426**,
        421, *427*
    displaying dialog boxes in, **444**, **446–452**
    generating, 418
    message handlers for, **432–433**, *434*
FONTDEMO.CPP file, 454–456
FONTDEMO.H file, 453
FONTDVW.CPP file, 464–467
FONTDVW.H file, 463
fonts
    and control size, 423
    dialog box class for, 469
    selecting, **530–531**
    size of, 531, *532*, 546, 551
    stock, **548–549**, *549*
fopen function, 899, 906
for statements, declaring variables in, 45
foreground color for tool bar buttons, 480
form views, **468–469**
Format command in FONTDEMO, 444,
        446
Format dialog box, 416, *417*, 418
    adding controls to, **421–425**
    class for, **427–432**
    coding for, **434–444**
    designing, **418–426**, *421*, *427*
    displaying, **444**, **446–452**
    members for, **428–432**
    message handlers for, **432–433**, *434*
    resources for, **444**, **446–447**
FORMAT.CPP file, 427
FORMAT.H file, 427
formats
    for Clipboard, 834, 836–838, 842–845,
        847–848
    version numbers for, 297
formatted I/O, 910, 919
formatting flags, **917**
foundation classes. *See* Microsoft Founda-
        tion Classes (MFC)
fprintf function, 899
fputc function, 906
fractal patterns program, **626–632**, *626*
FrameRect function (CDC), 656
free store, allocating and releasing mem-
        ory in, **68–72**
friend classes, 116, **138–139**, 143, 146
fstream class, 931
FSTREAM.H file, 923
Full Screen command, 897
function keys
    for debugging, 29

virtual key codes for, 556
functions
  C vs. C++, 39
  and constant types, **63–66**
  conversion, 159
  declarations and definitions for, 39
  inline, **95–97**
  member. *See* member functions and
    data members
  overloaded. *See* overloaded functions
  parameters for. *See* parameters
  and reference variables, **54–59**
  virtual, **120–129**
_fwopen function, 902

G

games, animation for, **738–741**
gcount function (istream), 922
Generate Source Comments option, 169
get function (istream), 24, 920–922, 931
GetActiveView function (CFrameWnd),
  627
GetAmount function (CCurrency), 157
GetAsyncKeyState function (API), 557
GetAt function (CObArray), 261, 265, 270
GetBkColor function (CDC), 533
GetBkMode function (CDC), 533
GetBounds function, 856
_getch function, 900
getchar function, 899, 901, 906
_getche function, 900
GetCheckedRadioButton function
  (CWnd), 440
GetClientRect function (CWnd), 174, 207,
  209, 559, 624
GetClipboardData function (API),
  837–838, 845–846, 848, 859
GetClipBox function (CDC), 362, 533–534,
  783
GetColor function (CFontDialog), 545
GetCoord function (CRectangle), 98–99
GetDefID function (CDialog), 441
GetDeviceCaps function (CDC)
  for bitmap operations, 734
  for printing operations, **776–779**

GetDimRect functions
  in CFigure, 668–669, 701
  in CLine, 357–358, 360, 362
GetDlgItem function (CWnd), 436, 440
GetDlgItemInt function (CWnd), 440, 442
GetDlgItemText function (CWnd), 440
GetDocument function (CView), 173, 189,
  262
GetFaceName function (CFontDialog),
  546
GetFigure function (CMinidrawDoc),
  676, 700
GetFirstViewPosition function (CDocu-
  ment), 319–321
GetKeyState function (API), 556–557
GetLength function (CDC), 551
GetLine function (CMinidrawDoc), 260–
  261, 263, 278–279, 676
getline function (istream), 920, 922, 931
GetMapMode function (CDC), 532–533
GetMessage function (CWingreetDoc),
  171, 173, 185
GetNextDlgGroupItem function (CWnd),
  440
GetNextDlgTabItem function (CWnd),
  441
GetNextItem function, 854–855, 863–864
GetNextView function (CDocument),
  320–321
GetNumFigs function (CMinidrawDoc),
  669, 676, 700
GetNumLines function (CMinidrawDoc),
  260–261, 263, 279, 669, 676
GetObject functions
  in CBitmap, 748
  in CGdiObject, 731, 846
GetParentFrame function (CWnd), 631
GetSize functions
  in CFontDialog, 546
  in CObArray, 261, 265
GetStartPosition function, 854–855,
  863–864
GetSysColor function (API), 452, 565
GetSystemMetrics function (API), 568, 744
GetTextAlign function (CDC), 533
GetTextCharacterExtra function (CDC),
  533

GetTextColor function (CDC), 533
GetTextExtent function (CDC), 570
GetTextMetrics function (CDC), 531–532,
    532, 545, 547, 551, 568
GetTotalSize function (CScrollView),
    347–348, 559
GetUpperBound function (CObArray),
    261, 270
global data objects and variables
    C vs. C++, 40
    constructors for, 94
    for default function parameters, 51
    with reference types, 58
    scope resolution operator for, **47–48**
GlobalAlloc function (API), 831–833, 835,
    838–839
GlobalFree function (API), 833–835
GlobalLock function (API), 831, 833, 837,
    839–841
GlobalSize function (API), 838
GlobalUnlock function (API), 831,
    833–835, 837, 839
GMEM_MOVEABLE flag, 832
GMEM_ZEROINT flag, 832
Go button for debugger, 31–32, *31*
Go command for debugger, 31–32
Go To button for help, 17
good function (ios), 929, 933
goodbit flag (ios), 928
GotoDlgCtrl function (CDialog), 441
graphics. *See also* drawings; MINIDRAW
        program
    copying, **841–844**
    device support for, 779
    origins for, 340
    pasting, **844–848**
    in QuickWin programs, **897–899**, 902
    saving, **258–262**
Graphics Editor tool, 220
GRAPHICS.LIB library, 900–901
GRAY_BRUSH value, 614
grayed menu items, 268
greater than signs (>)
    in extraction operator, **919–920**
    for redirection, 909
    for serializing objects, 298

green drawing color, functions for, 660,
    662, 693
GREET program
    build options for, **24–26**
    building, **26–27**
    creating, 18
    debugging, **28–33**
    running, **28**, *28*
GREET.CPP file, 19–21, 23
GREET.MAK file, 20, 29
GREET.VCW file, 20
GREET.WSP file, 20
grid lines for bitmaps, 478, 746
Grid Settings dialog box, 479, *479*, 746
group boxes
    class for, 437
    control palette for, *420*
    properties of, 422
    using, 424
Group property for controls, 423
groups of controls
    data members for, 430
    tab order for, 426

H

hard disk requirements, 4, 11
hardware requirements, **4**
hatched patterns, 617–618, *617*, 655
header files, 97, 179
    for constants, 60
    for inline functions, 49
heap, allocating and releasing memory
        in, **68–72**
height
    of bitmaps, 478–479, 728, 731, 734, 747
    of carets, 567–568
    of printing area, 775–778, 781
    of text, 551
        LOGFONT field for, 539, 579
        TEXTMETRIC field for, 531, 541, 581
help and help files, 10–11, **17**
    for editing icons, 220
    for installation, 6
    in QuickWin programs, 896, 898
Help Files installation option, 10

Help menu
  for QuickWin programs, 898
  tool bar buttons for, 474
  for WINGREET, 175
Help window, 17
hex enumerator (ios), 916, 921
hex manipulator, 916
hexadecimal input, 921
hexadecimal output, 916
HideCaret function (CWnd), 570
hiding
  caret, 569–570
  MDI windows, 391
hierarchies of classes, **116–120**, *118*
hints with UpdateAllViews, **359–361**, 852
Home key
  for editing source files, 21
  for scrolling, 559
  virtual key codes for, 554, 556
horizontal hatch patterns, *617*
horizontal scroll bars, 338, *339*
  control palette for, *420*
  using, 425
horizontal splitting of windows, 355–356
HORZRES index for device capabilities,
    776
HORZSIZE index for device capabilities,
    778
hot spot, 217
hourglass cursor, 204, **214**
HS_ brush patterns, 617, *617*

I

I-beam cursor, 204
icon-designing window, 400, 562
icons, 9
  copying, **400**
  displaying, 223, **742–744**
  for ECHO, 562, *563*
  files for, 179
  for MANDEL, 645, *646*
  for MINIDRAW, **220**, *220*
  for MINIEDIT, 242, *242*, 400
  for QuickWin programs, 898, 903
  reducing MDI windows to, 388

  for TEXTDEMO, **536–537**, *537*
ID: text box, 725
ID_APP_EXIT identifier, 446, 535, 561
ID_COLOR_ identifiers, 658, 660
ID_EDIT_CLEAR identifier, 561, 563
ID_EDIT_CLEAR_ALL identifier, 264, 266
ID_EDIT_COPY identifier, 827–828, 863
ID_EDIT_CUT identifier, 827–828, 863
ID_EDIT_FIND identifier, 239, 396
ID_EDIT_PASTE identifier, 827–828, 857
ID_EDIT_PASTE_LINK identifier, 857
ID_EDIT_REPEAT identifier, 239, 396–397
ID_EDIT_REPLACE identifier, 239, 396
ID_EDIT_SELECT_ALL identifier, 239,
    396
ID_EDIT_UNDO identifier, 264, 268,
    270–271
ID_FILE_MRU_FILE1 identifier, 291, 318
ID_FILE_NEW identifier, 318
ID_FILE_OPEN identifier, 291, 318
ID_FILE_PRINT identifier, 239, 395, 397,
    765
ID_FILE_PRINT_PREVIEW identifier, 765
ID_FILE_PRINT_SETUP identifier, 765
ID_FILE_SAVE identifier, 291, 318
ID_FILE_SAVE_AS identifier, 291, 318
ID_INDICATOR_CAPS identifier, 497
ID_INDICATOR_NUM identifier, 497
ID_INDICATOR_SCRL identifier, 497
ID_LINE_DOUBLE identifier, 483,
    488–489, 658
ID_LINE_SINGLE identifier, 483, 489, 658
ID_LINE_TRIPLE identifier, 483, 489, 658
ID_OPTIONS_FONT identifier, 535
ID_SEPARATOR identifier, 487, 497
ID_TEXT_FORMAT identifier, 446–447
ID_TOOLS_CIRCLE identifier, 482, 489
ID_TOOLS_CIRCLEFILL identifier, 482,
    489
ID_TOOLS_LINE identifier, 482, 487, 489
ID_TOOLS_RECTANGLE identifier, 482,
    487, 489
ID_TOOLS_RECTFILL identifier, 482,
    487, 489
ID_TOOLS_RECTROUND identifier, 482,
    487, 489

ID_TOOLS_RECTROUNDFILL identifier, 482, 489
IDB_BITMAP1 identifier, 725, 746, *747*
IDCANCEL identifier, 421–422, 445
IDC_BOLD identifier, 421–422
  data member for, 429, *430*
  message handler for, 433
IDC_CENTER identifier, 421–422, 433
IDC_CROSS identifier, 204
IDC_ cursor identifiers, 204
IDC_FIXED identifier, 421–422, 433
IDC_ITALIC identifier, 421–422
  data member for, 429
  message handler for, 433
IDC_LEFT identifier, 421–422, 430, 433
IDC_RIGHT identifier, 421–422, 433
IDC_SAMPLE identifier, 421–422
IDC_SPACING identifier, 421–422
  data member for, 431–432
  limiting entries for, 435
  message handler for, 433
IDC_STATIC identifier, 421–423
IDC_UNDERLINE identifier, 421–422
  data member for, 429
  message handler for, 433
IDC_VARIABLE identifier, 421–422, 430–431, 433
IDD_DIALOG1 identifier, 421–422
identifiers
  C vs. C++, 38–39
  for controls, **421–423**
idle prompts, 499
IDOK identifier, 421–422, 445, 449
IDR_MAINFRAME identifier, 218–220, 239, 242, 263, 290–292
IDR_RESOURCE string, 318
IDR_TEXTTYPE identifier, 393, 395, 400
IDs: list for resources, 291
ifstream class, *907*, 930
ignore function (istream), 922
image bitmaps, 739–740, *739*
implementation files, 98
IMPLEMENT_SERIAL macro, 296–297, 773
Import command, 726, 746
importing
  bitmaps, 726, 746

icons, 743
in flag (ios), 924, 927, 931
in instruction, 901
_inchar function, 902
including header files, 97
indeterminate button states, 495
Index command for QuickWin programs, 898
IndicatorIDs array, 497–498, 515
indicators array, 499
indicators on status bars, 476, 497–499
indirect base classes, 117
indirectly derived classes, 117
inheritance, 108
  access with, **112–116**
  advantages of, **118–120**
  multiple, 118
Initial Tool bar option, 474, 499, 829
initialization (.INI) files, 176, 293
initializing
  applications, **194–197**
  arrays, 95, **159–160**
  bitmaps, 725–727, 748
  block allocations, **71–72**
  brushes, 614–615, 617–618
  constant pointers, 61
  constants, 59, 63
  constructors for, 85–87, **90–92**
  in definitions, 149–151
  font objects, 530, 546
  MDI programs, 390
  memory blocks, 832
  menu commands, 268–269
  pens, 614–615, 617–618
  reference types, 53
  static members, 102
  variables, 45–46
InitInstance functions
  in CBitdemoApp, 751
  in CEchoApp, 594–595
  in CFontdemoApp, 455
  in CMandelApp, 634
  in CMinidrawApp, 226, 273–274, 300, 303–304
  in CMinieditApp, 245, 321, 324–325, 403–404
  in COledemoApp, 866–867

in CTextdemoApp, 573–574
in CWingreetApp, 182, **194–197**
in MDI programs, 390–391, 393
inline expansion, 49
Inline Expansion of Functions: list, 49
Inline Function Size: list, 49
inline functions, **48–50**, **95–97**
_inp function, 900
input. *See* iostream class
Input command, 898
input focus, 552, **568–569**
  for controls, 441
  in QuickWin programs, 902
_inpw function, 900
Ins key, 22
Insert New Object command in
    OLEDEMO, 850, *851*, **853–856**
Insert New Object dialog box, 853–856,
    854
inserting data. *See* pasting
insertion operator, **910–911**
insertion point in source files, 21–22
Install program, 12
Installation Options dialog box, 6–7, *7*,
    9–10
installing
  companion disk, 11–13
  Visual C++, **4–8**
instances
  constructors for, 85
  creating, **78–80**, 87, 94–95
  of dialog boxes, 449
  initialization in, **90–92**
int data type
  for data members, 431
  serializing, 298
integrated debugger, 28
integrated development environment. *See*
    Visual Workbench
internal leading, 531, *532*, 542, 582
interrupts in MS-DOS programs, 894
IntersectRect function (CRect), 349, 362
IntRect object (CRect), 349
InvalidateRect function (CWnd), 360–361
invalidating areas, 361–362
inverting colors, 656
  for bitmaps, 735, 737–739

drawing mode for, 649–650
  for icons, 742
InvertRect function (CDC), 656
InWaitForRelease function
    (COleClientItem), 873–874
I/O. *See also* file I/O; iostream class
  in MS-DOS programs, 894
  in QuickWin programs, **900–901**
IOMANIP.H file, 911, 913
ios class, *907*
iostream class, **23–24**, 117, **906–908**
  input with
    extraction operator for, **919–920**
    file input, **930–933**
    functions and manipulators for,
      921–922
    standard stream, **919–922**
  for MS-DOS programs, 892
  output with
    alignment in, **914–915**
    displaying characters in, **918**
    error testing for, **928–930**
    field widths in, **911–913**
    file output, **922–930**
    fill characters in, **913–914**
    flushing buffers in, **918–919**
    formatting flags for, **917**
    functions and manipulators for,
      911–919
    insertion operator for, **910–911**
    precision in, **915–916**
    radix in, **916**
    standard stream, **909–919**
    writing data for, **925–928**
  overloaded operators in, 143
  for QuickWin programs, 900–901
IOSTREAM.H file, 23, 907
IsClipboardFormatAvailable function
    (API), 836–838, 844, 848, 860
IsDlgButtonChecked function (CWnd),
    438–439, 441
IsIconic function (CWnd), 631
IsSelected function (COledemoView),
    861, 877
IsStoring function (CArchive), 295
istream class, *907*
istream_withassign class, *907*, 919

istrstream class, 908
italic style
  data member for, 429
  identifier for, 421–422
  LOGFONT field for, 539, 579
  message handler for, 433, 437–438
  TEXTMETRIC field for, 542, 582

J

justifying text
  alignment points for, 532, 534
  enumerators for, 434
  functions for, 533–534
  identifier for, 421–422
  in stream output, 912, **914–915**

K

_kbhit function, 900
keyboard
  for debugging, 28–29
  for editing source files, **21–23**
  and mouse messages, 217
  reading
    standard streams for, 906, 908
    WM_CHAR messages for, **560–566**
    WM_KEYDOWN messages for,
      552–559
keyboard shortcuts, **240–241**
  for Clipboard commands, 826–828, 827
  copying, 399
  identifiers for, 270–271
  for MINIEDIT, 397, 399

L

late binding, 124
leading, 531, 532, 542, 582
left alignment
  identifier for, 421–422
  with iostream, 914, 917
  message handler for, 433, 438–439
left enumerator (ios), 914, 917

less than signs (<)
  as insertion operator, 23–24, 298, 910–911
  for redirection, 909
  for serializing objects, 298
lHint parameter with UpdateAllViews,
    359–360
libraries. See also Microsoft Foundation
      Classes (MFC)
  for classes, 117
  for MS-DOS programs, 888
  for QuickWin programs, 894, **899–902**
  run-time, 9, 11
Libraries installation option, 7, 9
lifetime of objects, 70
limiting
  drawing size, **344–352**
  edit control input, 435–436
LimitText function (CEdit), 435–436
Line command in MINIDRAW, 483
line feeds, handling, 564–565
Line menu for MINIDRAW, 483, 484
Line Thickness menu for MINIDRAW,
    658, 659
LINECAPS index for device capabilities,
    779
lines. See also MINIDRAW program
  device support for, 779
  drawing, 612, **646–650**
  thickness of. See thickness of lines
  tool for, 482
  tool bar buttons for, 476–477, 477
_lineto function, 900
LineTo function (MFC), 212–213, 260, 612,
    646–647
  coordinates with, 340
  drawing attributes for, 620
  pens for, 613
linking
  implementation files, 98
  modes for, 24
  objects. See OLEDEMO program
  QuickWin programs, 894
Links command in OLEDEMO, 850, 851
Links dialog box, 860, 860
list boxes
  class for, 437
  control palette for, 420

functions for, 440
using, 424
LoadBitmap function (CBitmap), 487,
  724, 726, 748
LoadFrame function (CFrameWnd), 391
LoadIcon function (CWinApp), 743
LoadOEMBitmap function (CBitmap), 725
LoadStandardCursor function
  (CWinApp), 204, 214
LoadStandardIcon function (CWinApp),
  743
local objects
  constructors for, 94
  declaring, **44–46**
locking memory, 831, 833, 835, 837, 839
LOGFONT structure, 539–541, 546–547,
  549, 578–581
logical coordinates
  converting, 342–344, *342*, 349, 361, 624
  in mapping modes, **621–624**
logical units for pen width, 615
LONG data type, serializing, 298
lpszClass field (CREATESTRUCT), 222
LPT devices, 924
LPtoDP function (CDC), 349, 361, 624
lstrcpy function (API), 833
LTGRAY_BRUSH value, 614

M

macros
  vs. inline functions, 50
  mapping, 181
magenta drawing color, functions for,
  660, 663, 693
main frame window classes, **176–178**,
  390–391, *392*
main window in QuickWin programs,
  897–898
MAINFRM.CPP file, 177–178
  for BITDEMO, 756–757
  for ECHO, 600–601
  for FONTDEMO, 461–462
  for MANDEL, 640–641
  for MINIDRAW, 231–232
    for drawings, 708–711

for file I/O, 311–312
for printing and print previewing,
  810–813
for scrolling and splitting, 373–375
for storing documents, 281–282
for tool bars and status bars, 514–517
for MINIEDIT, 250–251
  for file I/O, 330–331
  for MDI, 408–410
for OLEDEMO, 873–874
for TEXTDEMO, 585–586
for WINGREET, 187–189
MAINFRM.H file, 177–178
  for BITDEMO, 755–756
  for ECHO, 599–600
  for FONTDEMO, 460–461
  for MANDEL, 639–640
  for MINIDRAW, 230–231
    for drawings, 707–708
    for file I/O, 310–311
for printing and print previewing,
  809–810
  for scrolling and splitting, 372–373
  for storing documents, 280
  for tool bars and status bars, 513–514
for MINIEDIT, 249–250
  for file I/O, 329–330
  for MDI, 408
for OLEDEMO, 872
for TEXTDEMO, 584–585
for WINGREET, 187
malloc functions, 70
MANDEDOC.CPP file, 637–638
MANDEDOC.H file, 636–637
MANDEL program, **626–632**, *626*, 645, *646*
MANDEL.CPP file, 633–636
MANDEL.H file, 632–633
MANDEL.ICO file, 645, *646*
MANDEVW.CPP file, 642–645
MANDEVW.H file, 641–642
manipulators
  for input, **921–922**
  for output, **911–919**
MapDialogRect function (CDialog), 441
mapping macros, 181
mapping modes
  for bitmaps, 732

for drawings, **620–624**
for icons, 744
for OLE items, 856
for pen width, 612
for printing, **784**
for scrolling, 346, *346*
for text, 533
maps, message, 207, **210–211**, **767–768**,
   787–788, 815
Mark command and mark mode in
   QuickWin programs, 897
mask bitmaps, 739–740, *739*
math support option, 9
__max macro, 82–84
max macro, 358
maximize buttons, *175*
  class for, 177
  for MDI windows, 386, *387*
Maximum Value: box, 431
m_bContinuePrinting data member
   (CPrintInfo), 775, 777
mBold data member (CFormat), 429, *430*,
   437, 443, 447–448
mCaretPos data member (CEchoView),
   567
mColor data member (CTextdemoDoc),
   538, 545
mCurrentColor data member
   (CMinidrawApp), 661, 686
mCurrentThickness data member
   (CMinidrawApp), 490–491, 493
mCurrentTool data member
   (CMinidrawApp), 490–494
MDI. *See* multiple document interface
   (MDI)
mDragging data member (CWnd), 209
measurements for controls, 423
Medium memory model, 9
member functions and data members,
   24, 77
  accessing, **79–85**
  conversion functions, 159
  for derived classes, 109
  inheriting, 108
  initializing, 85–87, **90–92**
  inline, **95–97**
  static, **101–104**

member initializer lists, **90–92**, 111
Member Variable Name: text box, 432
memory
  allocating and releasing, **68–72**
  for bitmaps, 728
  for Clipboard, **831–835**, **837–841**
  for instances, 78–79
  for objects, 145–146
  for reference types, 54
  requirements for, 4
  and streams, 906
memory device context objects, 728–732
memory models, 9
menu bars, *175*, 177
menu item properties dialog box, 239,
   263, 290–291
menu labels, bitmaps for, 733
menu-designing window, 290, 395, 482
menus, 9
  class for, 177
  for Clipboard commands, 826–828, *827*
  copying items on, **398**
  for ECHO, **560–561**, *562*
  for FONTDEMO, **444**, **446–447**, *446*
  initializing commands on, 268–269
  implementing commands on, **266–271**
  messages for, 205
  for MINIDRAW, **218–219**
    for drawings, **657–660**, *659*
    for file I/O, **290–292**
    for printing, **765–766**
    for storing documents, **263–271**
    for tool bars, **482–484**
  for MINIEDIT, **239–241**, *240*, *241*
    for file I/O, **317–319**
    for MDI, **395–397**, 399
    for scrolling and splitting, 386
  for OLEDEMO, 850, *851*
  in QuickWin programs, 896
  for TEXTDEMO, **535–536**, *536*
  for WINGREET, 175
MERGECOPY raster-operation code, 737
MERGEPAINT raster-operation code, 737
message maps, 207, **210–211**, **767–768**,
   787–788, 815
MessageBeep function, 564

messages and message handlers,
177–178, **204–216**
for dialog boxes, **432–433**, *434*, 445
for drawings, **660–664**
parameters for, **217–218**
for reading keyboard, **552–566**
for scrolling, **557–559**
for storing documents, **266–271**
for tool bars, **484–494**
for windows, **205–206**
WinMain processing of, **194–195**
MFC. *See* Microsoft Foundation Classes
(MFC)
MFC AppWizard dialog box, 168, *168*,
202, *202*, 238, 388, 390
mFont data member (CFont), 538, 544
mHArrow data member
(CMinidrawView), 350–351
m_hObject data member (CGdiObject),
843–844
Microsoft Foundation Classes (MFC),
8–9, 11, 117, 166–167
for controls, **436–437**
for dialog boxes, **440–441**
for messages, 205–206
for QuickWin programs, 900
Microsoft Overlaid Virtual Environment
(MOVE), 890
Microsoft Visual C++ group, 16
mIdxColorCmd data member
(CMinidrawApp), 661, 687
__min macro, 82–84
min macro, 358
MINIDDOC.CPP file, 228–230
for drawings, 698–707
for file I/O, 306–310
for printing and print previewing,
800–809
for scrolling and splitting, 368–372
for storing documents, 276–280
for tool bars and status bars, 509–513
MINIDDOC.H file, 227–228
for drawings, 694–698
for file I/O, 305–306
for printing and print previewing,
796–800
for scrolling and splitting, 367–368

for storing documents, 275–276
for tool bars and status bars, 507–509
MINIDRAW program, **200–201**, *201*
classes in, **664–675**
deleting document data in, **265**
drag-drop feature in, **300–301**
drawing features in, **656–683**
figures in, **664–675**
file I/O in, **290–301**
icons for, **220**, *220*
members for, **203–204**
menus for, **218–219**, **263–271**
for drawings, **657–660**, *659*
for file I/O, **290–292**
for printing, **765–766**
for storing documents, **263–271**
for tool bars, **482–484**
message handlers for, **204–216**, **660–664**
message maps for, **767–768**
modified flag for, **299–300**
printing features in, **764–785**
program window for, *657*
redrawing windows in, **262–263**
resources for, **216**, **218–221**, **477–484**,
657–660
scrolling in, **338–352**
serializing data in, **292–298**
source files for, **202–203**
splitting windows in, **352–363**, *354*
status bars for, **496–499**, *496*
storing data in, **258–262**
tool bars for, **476–496**, *477*
windows for, **221–223**
MINIDRAW.CPP file, 225–227
for drawings, 685–694
for file I/O, 302–305
for printing and print previewing,
787–796
for scrolling and splitting, 364–367
for storing documents, 272–275
for tool bars and status bars, 501–507
MINIDRAW.H file, 224
for drawings, 683–685
for file I/O, 301–302
for printing and print previewing,
785–787
for scrolling and splitting, 363–364

for storing documents, 271–272
for tool bars and status bars, 499–501
MINIDRAW.ICO file, 221
MINIDRAW.INI file, 293
MINIDRAW.RC file, 221
MINIDVW.CPP file, 207, 234–237
  for drawings, 712–720
  for file I/O, 313–317
  for printing and print previewing,
    814–823
  for scrolling and splitting, 376–381
  for storing documents, 283–286
  for tool bars and status bars, 518–523
MINIDVW.H file, 203–204, 207, 210,
    232–233
  for drawings, 711–712
  for file I/O, 312–313
  for printing and print previewing,
    813–814
  for scrolling and splitting, 375–376
  for storing documents, 282–283
  for tool bars and status bars, 517–518
MINIEDIT program, **237–238**, *238*
  classes and files for, **390–393**
  creating, **238–242**
  drag-drop feature in, 321
  file I/O in, **317–321**
  icons for, 242, *242*, 400
  MDI with, 386, *387*, **388–400**
  menus for, **239–241**
    for file I/O, **317–319**
    for MDI, **395–397**, 399
    for scrolling and splitting, 386
  resources for, **395–397**, **399–400**
  serializing data in, **320–321**
MINIEDIT.CPP file, 244–246
  for file I/O, 323–326
  for MDI, 402–405
MINIEDIT.H file, 243–244
  for file I/O, 322–323
  for MDI, 401
MINIEDOC.CPP file, 247–249
  for file I/O, 327–329
  for MDI, 406–408
MINIEDOC.H file, 247
  for file I/O, 326–327
  for MDI, 405–406

MINIEVW.CPP file, 238, 252–254
  for file I/O, 332–334
  for MDI, 411–412
MINIEVW.H file, 238, 251–252
  for file I/O, 331–332
  for MDI, 410–411
minimize buttons, *175*
  class for, 177
  for MDI windows, *387*, 388
Minimum Value: box, 431
minus sign (-) operator, overloading, 142
mItalic data member (CFormat), 429, 438,
    443, 447–448
mJustify data member (CFormat), 430,
    438–439, 443, 447–448
MK_ bit masks, 218
m_lf data member (CFontDialog), 546
mLineTable array (CTextdemoDoc), 534,
    538–547, 578–584
MM_ANISOMETRIC mapping mode,
    623–624, 784
MM_HIENGLISH mapping mode,
    622–623, 784
MM_HIMETRIC mapping mode, 622–623
  for OLE items, 856
  for printing, 784
MM_ISOMETRIC mapping mode,
    623–624, 784
MM_LOENGLISH mapping mode,
    622–623, 784
MM_LOMETRIC mapping mode,
    622–623, 784
MM_TEXT mapping mode, 621–622, *622*
  for bitmaps, 732
  for icons, 744
  for printing, 784
  for scrolling, 346, *346*
MM_TWIPS mapping mode, 622–623, 784
m_nCurPage data member (CPrintInfo),
    781
modal dialog boxes, 418
modeless dialog boxes, **467–468**
modern font family
  LOGFONT field for, 541, 580
  TEXTMETRIC field for, 543, 583
modified flag, **299–300**
module-definition files, 179

monitor
  requirements for, 4
  stream output to, 908
mouse
  capturing, 209
  for controls, 421–422
  messages for, **205–218**, 433, 624, 862
  in QuickWin programs, 895
  releasing, 215
mouse cursor. *See* cursors
MOVE (Microsoft Overlaid Virtual Environment), 890
moveable memory blocks, 832
MoveTo function (MFC), 212–213, 260, 340, 620, 646–647
MoveWindow function, 624
moving
  bitmaps, **736–742**
  graphics, **841–844**
  menu items, 398
  text, **830–836**
m_ prefix, 172
mPenDotted data member (CMinidrawView), 678
mPitch data member (CFormat), 438–439, 443, 448
m_pMainWnd data member (CWinApp), 300, 391, 627
mRectSample data member (CFormat), 435
MS-DOS programs, **888**
  editing source code for, **892–893**
  guidelines for, **893–894**
  importing QuickWin programs to, 903
  MFC in, **895**
  project files for, **889–892**
MS-DOS project types, **889–890**
MS-DOS.EXE targets option, 9
mSpacing data member (CFormat), 431, 441, 448
mSpacingEdit data member (CFormat), 435
mSplitterWnd data member (CMainFrame), 355
mTextLine data member (CEchoDoc), 564
mThickness data member (CFigure), 669

mTool bar data member (CMainFrame), 485
multiline controls, 424
multiple document interface (MDI), **386**, *387*, **388**
  classes and files for, **390–393**
  coding for, **393–395**
  generating programs for, **388–393**
  QuickWin programs as, 896, *896*
  resources for, **395–397**, **399–400**
Multiple Document Interface option, 388, *389*
multiple inheritance, 118
mUnderline data member (CFormat), 429, 438, 443, 448
m_wndToolBar object (CToolBar), 488

N

named constants. *See* constants and constant types
names
  C vs. C++, **40–43**
  of classes, 176, 178
  of constructors, 85
  of fonts, 546
  of overloaded functions, 66
  of program files, 18–19, 23, 168, 176, 178, 293
New Application Classes: list, 292
New Application Information dialog box, 169–170, *170*
New button for accelerator keys, 241
New command
  in MINIDRAW, 265
  in MINIEDIT, 317–318, *319*, 386, 395
  for projects, 18
  for source files, 20
  tool bar button for, 474, *475*
new operator, **68–70**
  for arrays, **70–71**
  for dialog boxes, 468
  for document templates, 196
  and initializing allocations, **71–72**
  for instances, 78–80, 87, 94–95

New Project dialog box, 18, *19*, 890–891, *891*, 895

New Resource dialog box, 418, *419*

New Window command in MINIEDIT, 397, **399**

newline characters
with extraction operators, 920
in files, 925

Next Error command, 27

Next Key Typed button, 241

NextDlgCtrl function (CDialog), 441

nFlags parameter for mouse messages, **217–218**

nIndex parameter
for CreateHatchBrush, 617
for SelectStockObject, 548–549, 612

nocreate flag (ios), 924, 927, 931

noreplace flag (ios), 924–925, 927

NOTSRCCOPY raster-operation code, 737

NOTSRCERASE raster-operation code, 737

NULL_BRUSH value, 614, 655, 675

NULL_PEN value, 614

Num Lock key
indicator for, 476, 497, 499
testing state of, 557

O

Object command in OLEDEMO, 850, *851*, **861–862**

Object IDs: list with ClassWizard, 206, 268

Object Linking and Embedding (OLE).
See OLEDEMO program

objects, 78
memory for, 145–146
as parameters, 151
virtual functions for, **125–127**

oct enumerator (ios), 916

oct manipulator, 916

octal output, 916

OEM character set
Clipboard formats for, 837–838
LOGFONT field for, 540, 580
TEXTMETRIC field for, 544, 584

OEM_FIXED_FONT value, 549, *549*

ofstream class, *907*, 923

OK buttons, 423
default message handlers for, 445
in initial dialog boxes, 418, *419*

OLE (Object Linking and Embedding).
See OLEDEMO program

OLEDEDOC.CPP file, 869–872

OLEDEDOC.H file, 868–869

OLEDEMO program, **848–850**
class for, **851–852**
cutting and copying items in, **862–864**
displaying items in, **855–856**
executing items in, **861–862**
generating, 850
inserting items in, **853–855**
linking items in, **856–860**
menus for, 850, *851*

OLEDEMO.CPP file, 865–868

OLEDEMO.H file, 865

OLEDEVW.CPP file, 875–880

OLEDEVW.H file, 874–875

ON_WM_LBUTTONDOWN macro, 211

ON_WM_LBUTTONUP macro, 211

ON_WM_MOUSEMOVE macro, 211

OnBeginPrinting functions
in CMinidrawView, **776–777**
in CView, 774–775

OnCancel function (CDialog), 445

OnChange function
(CDemoOleClientItem), 852, 855

OnChangeSpacing function (CFormat), 433, 441

OnChar function (CEchoView), 530, **564–565**, **569–570**, 604–605

OnClickedBold function (CFormat), 433, 437

OnClickedCenter function (CFormat), 433, 438

OnClickedFixed function (CFormat), 433, 438

OnClickedItalic function (CFormat), 433, 437–438

OnClickedLeft function (CFormat), 433, 438–439

OnClickedRight function (CFormat), 433, 439

OnClickedUnderline function (CFormat), 433, 438

OnClickedVariable function (CFormat), 433, 439

OnColorBlack function (CMinidrawApp), 660–661, 691

OnColorBlue function (CMinidrawApp), 660–661, 692

OnColorCustom function (CMinidrawApp), 660, 662, 664, *665*, 692

OnColorCyan function (CMinidrawApp), 660, 662, 692

OnColorGreen function (CMinidrawApp), 660, 662, 693

OnColorMagenta function (CMinidrawApp), 660, 663, 693

OnColorRed function (CMinidrawApp), 660, 663, 693

OnColorWhite function (CMinidrawApp), 660, 663, 694

OnColorYellow function (CMinidrawApp), 660, 663, 694

OnCreate functions
  in CEchoView, **567–569**, 605
  in CMainFrame, 485, **487–488**, **498**, 516–517

OnCreateClient function (CMainFrame), 353, 355

OnDraw functions
  in CBitdemoView, **748–749**, 760
  in CEchoView, **566**, 570, 603–604
  in CFontdemoView, 449–452, 465–466
  in CMandelView, 631–632, 643–644
  in CMinidrawView, 270
    device context objects for, 343
    for drawings, **682–683**, 713–714
    for printing, 781, **783**, **785**, 816
    for scrolling, 340, **347**, 377–378
    for split windows, 356–357, 377–378
    for storing documents, 262–263
    for updating windows, 361–363
  in CMinieditView, 253, 284
  in COledemoView, **855–856**, 876–877
  in CTextdemoView, **529–534**, 545, 547, 588–589
  in CWingreetView, 173–174, 192

for graphics, 610–611, 619
for printing, 764, 769, 775

OnEditClear function (CEchoView), 563, 566, **570–571**, 605

OnEditClearAll function (CMinidraw-Doc)
  for file I/O, 299, 309–310
  for storing documents, **266–268**, 279

OnEditCopy function
  for Clipboard, 828, **835–836**, **842–844**
  in COledemoView, 863, 879

OnEditCut function
  for Clipboard, 828, 836
  in COledemoView, 864

OnEditPaste functions
  for Clipboard, 828, **839–840**, **845–847**
  in COledemoView, **857–859**, 878

OnEditPasteLink function (COledemoView), **859–860**, 879

OnEditUndo function (CMinidrawDoc)
  for file I/O, 310
  for storing documents, 270–271, 279, 299–300

OnEndPrinting function (CView), 775

OnFileNew function (CWinApp), 182, 196–197, 265, 300

OnFileOpen function (CWinApp), 292

OnFilePrint function (CView), 768, 774

OnFilePrintPreview function (CView), 768, 774

OnFilePrintSetup function (CWinApp), 767

OnFileSave function (CDocument), 293

OnFileSaveAs function (CDocument), 293

OnIdle function (CMandelApp), **627–628**, 636

OnInitDialog function (CFormat), 432, 435

OnInitialUpdate function (CMinidrawView)
  for printing and print previewing, **772–773**, 822
  for scrolling and splitting, 344–345, 360, 381

OnInsertObject function (COledemoView), **853–854**, 877

OnKeyDown function (CTextdemoView), **553–559**, 591–592

OnKillFocus function (CEchoView), 567,
569, 605–606
OnLButtonDown function
(CMinidrawView), **206–211**,
235–236, **342–343**, **347–349**, 378–379
OnLButtonUp function
(CMinidrawView), **214–216**,
236–237
for drawings, **679–682**, 717–719
for storing documents, **261–262**, 286
for updating views, **356–357**, **359**
online help, 10–11, **17**
for editing icons, 220
for installation, 6
in QuickWin programs, 896
Online Help Files installation option, 7
OnLineDouble function
(CMinidrawApp), 488–490, 493, 505
OnLineSingle function (CMinidrawApp),
489, 491, 505
OnLineTriple function (CMinidrawApp),
489, 491, 505
OnModal function (CFontDialog), 545
OnMouseMove function
(CMinidrawView), **211–214**, 236
for drawings, **677–679**, 715–717
for scrolling, **343–344**, **351**, 379–380
OnNewDocument functions
in CMinidrawDoc, 229, 277
in CWingreetDoc, 186
OnOK functions
in CDialog, 445
in CFormat, 445
OnOptionsFont function (CTextdemo-
Doc), **538–549**, 551, 578–584
OnPaint function, 611
in CFormat, 432, 437, **442–443**
in CView, 444
OnPrepareDC functions
in CMinidrawView, **780–781**, 823
in CScrollView, 342–344, 361, 611, 780
in CView, 565, 774–775
OnPreparePrinting functions
in CMinidrawApp, **768–769**
in CView, 774–775
OnPrint function (CView), 774–775

OnSetFocus function (CEchoView),
567–569, 606
OnSize function (CMandelView), 631, 644
OnTextFormat function (CFontDemo-
Doc), **448–449**, 460
OnToolsCircle function
(CMinidrawApp), 489, 491, 506
OnToolsCirclefill function
(CMinidrawApp), 489, 491, 506
OnToolsLine function (CMinidrawApp),
489, 492, 506
OnToolsRectangle function
(CMinidrawApp), 489, 492, 506
OnToolsRectfill function
(CMinidrawApp), 489, 492, 507
OnToolsRectround function
(CMinidrawApp), 489, 492–493, 507
OnToolsRectroundfill function
(CMinidrawApp), 489, 493, 507
OnUpdate functions
in CMinidrawView, 360, 362, 381
in CScrollView, 552
in CTextdemoView, **550–551**, 590–591
in CView, 852
OnUpdateColorBlack function
(CMinidrawApp), 660–661, 692
OnUpdateColorBlue function
(CMinidrawApp), 660–661, 692
OnUpdateColorCustom function
(CMinidrawApp), 660, 662, 692
OnUpdateColorCyan function
(CMinidrawApp), 660, 662, 693
OnUpdateColorGreen function
(CMinidrawApp), 660, 662, 693
OnUpdateColorMagenta function
(CMinidrawApp), 660, 663, 693
OnUpdateColorRed function
(CMinidrawApp), 660, 663, 693
OnUpdateColorWhite function
(CMinidrawApp), 660, 663, 694
OnUpdateColorYellow function
(CMinidrawApp), 660, 664, 694
OnUpdateEditClearAll function
(CMinidrawDoc), 268, 279
OnUpdateEditCopy function
for Clipboard, 828, 830–831, 841
in COledemoView, 862–863, 879–880

OnUpdateEditCut function
  for Clipboard, 828, 830–831, 841
  in COledemoView, 863, 880
OnUpdateEditPaste function, 828, 837,
    844
OnUpdateEditUndo function
    (CMinidrawDoc), 270–271, 280
OnUpdateLineDouble function
    (CMinidrawApp), 488–491,
    493–494, 505
OnUpdateLineSingle function
    (CMinidrawApp), 489, 491, 494, 505
OnUpdateLineTriple function
    (CMinidrawApp), 489, 491, 494, 505
OnUpdateToolsCircle function
    (CMinidrawApp), 489, 491, 505–506
OnUpdateToolsCirclefill function
    (CMinidrawApp), 489, 492, 506
OnUpdateToolsLine function
    (CMinidrawApp), 489, 492, 506
OnUpdateToolsRectangle function
    (CMinidrawApp), 489, 492, 506
OnUpdateToolsRectfill function
    (CMinidrawApp), 489, 492, 507
OnUpdateToolsRectround function
    (CMinidrawApp), 489, 493, 507
OnUpdateToolsRectroundfill function
    (CMinidrawApp), 489, 493, 507
OPAQUE background mode, 532, 650
Open command
  in MINIDRAW, 290, 291, 292
  in MINIEDIT, 317–318, 319, 386
  for projects, 30
  tool bar button for, 474, 475
  in WINGREET, 175
Open dialog boxes
  default extensions for, 292
  for resources, 398
Open Project File button, 30, 30, 171, 171
OpenClipboard function (API), 831, 834,
    837, 842, 845, 858
opening
  Clipboard, 831, 834, 837, 842, 845, 858
  dialog boxes, 444, 446–447
  files, 171, 300–301, 469, 924–925
  MDI windows, 386, 388

projects, 20, 29–30
QuickWin windows, 902
operators, overloading, 24, 134–137
  assignment, 144–148
  defining additional functions in, 137–142
  guidelines for, 142–143
  new and delete, 70
Optimizations option, 49
optimized code, 24–25
Options dialog box, 169, 169, 238
  for MDI programs, 388, 389
  for tool bars, 474, 475, 476
Options menu
  for MINIDRAW, 657–658, 659
  for TEXTDEMO, 535–536, 536
OR operator with bit operations, 737–738
order
  of construction and destruction, 112
  of controls, 425–426, 427
  in printing, 781, 782
  of tool bar buttons, 479–480
origins, 340, 343
  for brushes, 620
  in mapping modes, 621
  in printing, 781, 783
ostream class, 907
ostream_withassign class, 907, 909–910
ostrstream class, 908
out flag (ios), 924, 927
out instruction, 901
_outp function, 901
output. See iostream class
output pointers, 926–928, 933
_outpw function, 901
overlapped windows
  for MDI, 388
  for QuickWin, 898
overloaded constructors, 88–90
overloaded functions, 66–68, 154–156
overloaded operators, 24, 134–137
  assignment, 144–148
  defining additional functions in, 137–142
  guidelines for, 142–143
  for new and delete, 70
overriding, 130–131

P

p-code for MS-DOS applications, 890
painting, 222–223, **262–263**
  bitmaps, **733–736**
  dialog boxes, **442–443**
  message for, 432
  with scrolling, 340
  with split views, **356–363**
  view class for, 173
panes, 352
parameters
  C vs. C++, 39
  constants as, **63–64**
  with constructors, 85–88, 91, 148–149, 152
  default, **51–52**, 68
  in inline functions vs. macros, 50
  for mouse messages, **217–218**
  for overloaded functions, **66–68**
  for overloaded operators, 140
  reference types as, **54–56**
parentheses ()
  for constructors, 88
  for member initializer lists, 90
Paste command
  for Clipboard, 826–829, *827*
  for graphics, **844–848**
  for icons, 400
  for OLE items, 856–857, 860
  for QuickWin programs, 897
  for text, **836–841**
  tool bar button for, 474, *475*, 829
Paste Link command in OLEDEMO, 850, *851*, **857–860**
pasting
  graphics, **844–848**
  OLE items, **856–860**
  in source files, 22
  text, **836–841**
PatBlt function (CDC), **734–736**, 778
PATCOPY raster-operation code, 735
PATINVERT raster-operation code, 735
PATPAINT raster-operation code, 737
patterns
  for bitmaps, 734, 736–737
  for brushes, 617–618, *617*, 655
Pause command for QuickWin programs, 897
peek function (istream), 922
pens, 612
  color of, 615–616, 648–650
  creating, **614–619**
  device context objects for, 614–615, 618–619
  drawing modes for, **648–650**
  initializing, 614–615
  for lines, 648
  selecting, **612–614**
  style of, 615
periods (.) for member access, 80
_pg_ functions, 901
PGCHART.LIB library, 901
PgUp and PgDn keys
  for editing source files, 21
  for scrolling, 559
  virtual key codes for, 554–555
pHint parameter with UpdateAllViews, 359–361
picture controls
  control palette for, *420*
  using, 424
Pie function (CDC), 651
  drawing attributes for, 620
  pens and brushes for, 613
  using, 653–654, *654*
PIF (program information file) editor, 893
pitch of text, 551
  enumerators for, 434
  fonts for, 549, *549*
  identifiers for, 421–422
  LOGFONT field for, 540, 580
  message handlers for, 433, 438–439, 443
  TEXTMETRIC field for, 542–543, 582–583
Pixel Grid option, 478
pixels
  color of, 625, 649–650, 735, 737–739
  in mapping modes, 346, 621
plus sign (+) operator, overloading, **134–142**, **155–156**
PMVC directory, 12
point parameter for mouse messages, **217**

POINT structure, 626, 647–648, 654
pointers. *See also* cursors; output pointers
  to application class objects, 204
  to base classes, **121**
  to brushes, 618
  C vs. C++, 40
  to CObject objects, 260
  and constant types, **60–62**
  to control objects, 436
  and inlining, 49
  to instances, 80
  as parameters, 56, 63–64
  to pens, 618
  vs. reference variables, 54, *55*
  as return types, 65
  this, **99–101**
points, drawing, **625–626**
Polygon function (CDC), 651, 654–655
  drawing attributes for, 620
  pens and brushes for, 613
POLYGONCAPS index for device
    capabilities, 779
polygons
  device support for, 779
  drawing, 654–655
  filling, 620
PolyLine function (CDC), 647, 655
  drawing attributes for, 620
  pens for, 613
polymorphism, **125**
PolyPolygon function (CDC), 651, 655
  drawing attributes for, 620
  pens and brushes for, 613
port access
  in MS-DOS programs, 894
  in QuickWin programs, 900–901
  and streams, 906
position
  of bitmaps, 731
  of brushes, 620
  of caret, 569–571
  of controls, 421–422, 425, 441
  of cursor, 208–209
  of dialog boxes, 435
  of drawings, 349, *349*, *350*, 625
  of figures, 667–668
  of icons, 743–744

  of lines, 259
  of OLE items, 856
  of Quickwin windows, 902
  of text, 534
PostQuitMessage function (API), 195
precedence of overloaded operators, 136,
    142
precision
  with inline functions vs. macros, 50
  in output, **915–916**
precision function (ios), 915
PreCreateWindow function
    (CMinidrawView), **221–222**, 237
preliminary tool bars, 474, 499, 829
PrevDlgCtrl function (CDialog), 441
Previous Error command, 27
primary verbs in OLE, 862
Print command, 764
  in MINIDRAW, 765, *766*, **768–770**
  in MINIEDIT, 239, *240*, 386, 395, *396*, 397
  tool bar button for, 474, *475*
Print dialog box, 769, *770*, 777
Print Preview command, 764–765, *766*,
    768–771
print preview window, 768, 771, *771*
Print Setup command, 764–765, *766*,
    767–769
Print Setup common dialog box, 764, 767,
    769–770, *770*
PrintAmount function (CCurrency), 157
printers
  file output to, 923
  and streams, 906
printf function, 898–899, 901, 906
printing and print previewing, **764–765**
  advanced, **771–785**
  coding for, **768–771**
  device capabilities for, **776–779**
  dialog box class for, 469
  drawing size for, **772–773**, 775–778, 781
  escape services for, **779–780**
  mapping modes for, **784**
  message maps for, **767–768**, 787–788, 815
  order in, 781, *782*
  overriding virtual functions for,
    773–777, **780–781**
  resources for, **765–766**

Printing dialog box, 770, 774
private access specifier, 79–81, 115
private formats with Clipboard, **847–848**
PRN device, 924
procedural programs, 894
processor requirements, 4
program information files (PIF), 893
program titles, strings for, 219
program window for WINGREET,
 174–175, *175*
programs. *See also* MS-DOS programs;
 QuickWin programs; Windows
 programs
 building, **26–27**, **174–176**
 debugging, **28–33**
 initializing, **194–197**
 MDI. *See* multiple document interface
  (MDI)
 running, **28**, **174–176**
Project command, 24, 49
project files, 20, 179, **889–892**
project manager, 8
Project Name: text box, 168
Project Options dialog box, 24–26, *25*, 895
Project Type list, 18, 25
projects
 creating, **18–20**, 170
 opening, 20, 29–30
Prompt: text box, 482, 498
properties
 of accelerators, 241
 of bitmaps, 478, *478*
 of controls, **421–422**
 of menus, 239, 263, 290–291
 of strings, 219, 292, 399–400
Property: list, 429, 432, 436
protected access specifier, 82
 for constructors, 86
 for derived classes, **113–115**
PrtSc key, 553
PS_ pen styles, 615, *616*, 650, 655, 675
PtInRect function (CRect), 348
public access specifier, 79–81
 for constructors, 86
 for derived classes, 109, 115
 for overloading operators, 136
pure colors, 615

push buttons
 Alt key with, 423
 bitmaps for, 732
 class for, 437
 control palette for, *420*
 properties of, 422
 using, 424
put function (ostream), 918, 925
_putch function, 901
putchar function, 901, 906

Q

QuickWin .EXE targets option, 9
QuickWin library, 894, **901–902**
QuickWin programs, 18, 25, **894–896**
 enhancing, **901–903**
 graphics window in, **899**
 guidelines for, **899–901**
 I/O in, **900–901**
 main window in, **897–898**
 program interface for, **896–899**, *896*
 Stdin/Stdout/Stderr window in,
  898–899

R

R2_ drawing modes, 649–650
radio buttons
 Alt key with, 423
 check marks for, 426
 class for, 437
 control palette for, *420*
 data members for, 430
 enumerators for, 434
 functions for, 440
 message handlers for, 433, 438
 properties of, 422
 using, 424
radix
 in input, 921
 in output, **916**
RAM (random access memory) requirements, 4. *See also* memory
random file I/O, 926–928, 933

ranges for control values, 431
RASTERCAPS index for device capabilities, 778
raster-operation codes, **734–738**
RC_BITBLT index for device capabilities, 778
RC_COPYPEN drawing mode, 649–650
RC.EXE program, 221
RC_NOTCOPYPEN drawing mode, 649
RC_STRETCHBLT index for device capabilities, 778
rdstate function (ios), **928–929**
Read function (CArchive), 322
read function (istream), 922, 932
Read me icon, 8
reading
  from arrays, 908
  blocks, 322
  characters, 24, **919–921**
  document data, **294–298**
  file input, **931–933**
  keyboard
    standard streams for, 906, 908
    WM_CHAR messages for, **560–566**
    WM_KEYDOWN messages for, **552–559**
README.TXT files, 178
ReadObject function (CArchive), 296
read-only aliases, 62
Rebuild All command, 27
Recent File command
  in MINIDRAW, 290, *291*
  in MINIEDIT, 317–318, *319*
Rect Fill command in MINIDRAW, 482, *483*
Rect Round command in MINIDRAW, 482, *483*
Rect Round Fill command in MINIDRAW, 482, *483*
RECT structure for OLE items, 856
Rect tool bar button, *477*
Rectangle command in MINIDRAW, 482, *483*
Rectangle function (CDC)
  drawing attributes for, 620
  pens and brushes for, 613
  using, 650–651, *652*

rectangles
  bounding, 357–358, 360, 668
  device support for, 779
  drawing, 651, *652*
  filling, 482, 656
  tool for, 482
rectangular cursor, 204
recursive functions, inlining, 49
red drawing color, functions for, 660, 663, 693
redirecting streams, 909
redrawing, 222–223, **262–263**
  dialog boxes, **442–443**
  message for, 432
  for scrolling, 340
  for split views, **356–363**
  view class for, 173
reference types and parameters, **52–54**, 63–64
  and constant types, **62–63**
  with copy constructors, 149, 151
  and functions, **54–59**
  with overloaded functions, 67, 137
  as return types, 54, **56–58**, 65
RegisterClipboardFormat function (API), 847–848
Release build mode, 24, 33
ReleaseCapture function (API), 215
releasing
  blocks, **68–72**
  mouse, 215
RemoveAll function (CObArray), 265
removing. *See* deleting
repainting, 222–223, **262–263**
  dialog boxes, **442–443**
  message for, 432
  for scrolling, 340
  for split views, **356–363**
  view class for, 173
Replace command in MINIEDIT, 239–240, *241*, 396, *397*
replacing text, dialog box class for, 469
requirements, hardware and software, **4–5**
resetiosflags manipulator, 917
resolution for printing, 784
resource dialog box, 218, *218*
resource editor. *See* App Studio tool

Resource Editor program, 221
RESOURCE.H file, 179
resources, 179. *See also* icons; menus
  for dialog boxes, **444, 446–447**
  for ECHO, **560–562**
  for MDI programs, **395–397, 399–400**
  for MINIDRAW, **216, 218–221, 657–660**
  for MINIEDIT, **239–242, 318**
  options for, 25
  for printing and print previewing, **765–766**
  scripts for, 221
  for tool bars, **477–484**
Resources button, 25
Resources: list, 292
Resume command for QuickWin programs, 897
return types
  constants as, **65–66**
  with constructors, 85
  with destructors, 93
  objects as, 151
  reference types as, 54, **56–58**
RGB macro, 452, 615
right alignment
  identifier for, 421–422
  with iostream, 915
  message handler for, 433, 439
right enumerator (ios), 915
roman font family
  LOGFONT field for, 541, 580
  TEXTMETRIC field for, 543, 583
Round Rect tool bar button, 477
rounded rectangles
  drawing, 651, *652,* 675
  tool for, 482
rounding in output, 915
RoundRect function (CDC), 650
  drawing attributes for, 620
  pens and brushes for, 613
  using, 651, *652*
routing messages, 205–206
rows in printing area, 775–776, 781
Run dialog box, 6, 12
Run function, 195
running programs, **28, 174–176**

RUNTIME_CLASS macro (MPC), 196
run-time libraries, 6–7, 9, 11, 888
Run-Time Libraries installation option, 6–7

S

sample programs, 9, 11
Sample Source Code installation option, 6–7
Samples button, 9
Save command
  for dialog boxes, 426
  message-handling for, 206
  in MINIDRAW, 290, *291,* 293
  in MINIEDIT, 317–318, *319,* 386
  for resources, 221
  tool bar button for, 474, *475*
Save As command
  in MINIDRAW, 290, *291,* 293
  in MINIEDIT, 317–318, *319,* 386
Save As dialog box
  default extensions for, 292
  for source files, 23
  for WINGREET, 175
Save File button, 23, *23*
saving
  document data
    modified flag for, **299–300**
    serialization for, **294–298**
  graphic data, **258–262**
  project settings, 26
  resource changes, 221
  source files, 23
SB_ codes, **557–559,** *558*
scales for control size, 423
scanf function, 898–899, 901, 906
scope resolution operator (::), **47–48**
  for API functions, 210
  for derived classes, 110
  for functions, 96, 101
  for static members, 102–103
scope of variables, 44
screen color for icons, 742
screen coordinates, converting, 208–209, 359, 435

script font family
 LOGFONT field for, 541, 581
 TEXTMETRIC field for, 543, 583
scripts, resource, 221
scroll bars, 338, *339*, *420*
 class for, 437
 using, 425
Scroll Lock key
 indicator for, 476, 497, 499
 testing state of, 557
scrolling, **338**, *341*
 converting coordinates for, **340–344**, *342*
 cursor changes in, **350–352**
 for graphics, 611
 limiting drawing size for, **344–352**
 message handlers for, **557–559**
 for printing, 780–781
 in QuickWin programs, 898–899
 in split windows, 352–353
 in TEXTDEMO, **550–552**
ScrollRect class, 348
ScrollToPosition function (CScrollView), 552
ScrollWindow function, 624
SDI (single document interface) applications, 176, 394
Search dialog box for help, 17
searching
 for help, 17
 in source files, 22
seekg function (istream), 933
seekp function (ostream), 926–928
Select All command
 for MINIEDIT, 239–240, *241*, 396, *397*
 for QuickWin programs, 897
selected tool bar buttons, 493, *494*
selecting drawing tools, **612–614**
selection pointer, control palette for, *420*
SelectObject function (CDC), 530–531, 618, 729–730
SelectStockObject function (CDC), 548–549, **612–614**, 655
SendDlgItemInt function (CWnd), 441
SendDlgItemMessage function (CWnd), 441
SendDlgItemText function (CWnd), 441
sending messages to windows, 205

SendMessage function (CWnd), 557
separators in menus, 240, 264, 291
sequential file I/O, 926, 932–933
serial ports
 in MS-DOS programs, 894
 in QuickWin programs, 900–901
 and streams, 906
Serialize functions
 in CCircle, 674, 706
 in CFigure, 668–670, 701
 in CLine, 297–298, 309, 670, 702
 in CMinidrawDoc, 229–230, 278, **292–298**, 301
 in CMinieditDoc, 249, 320, 328, 393–394, 407
 in CRectangle, 671, 703
 in CRectRound, 672, 704
 in CWingreetDoc, 186
SerializeRaw function (CEditView), 320–321
serializing document data, **294–298**, **772–773**
servers in OLE, 849
Set function (CMessage), 158
Set Includes dialog box, 766, *767*
Set Tab Order command, 426
SetAmount function (CCurrency), 157
SetBkColor function (CDC), 533, 620, 650, 655
SetBkMode function (CDC), 532–533, 620, 650, 655
SetBrushOrg function (CDC), 620, 655
SetButtons function, 487
SetCapture function (CWnd), 207, 209
SetCaretPos function (CWnd), 569–570
SetCheck function (CCmdUI), 269, 493–495
SetClipboardData function (API), 831, 834, 842–844, 847–848
_setcolor function, 900
SetColor function (CBlock), 114
SetCoord function (CRectangle), 99
SetCursor function (API), 212–214
SetDefID function (CDialog), 441
SetDialogBkColor function, 452
setf function (ios), 915, 917
setfill manipulator, 914

SetIndicators function (CStatusBar), 498

setiosflags manipulator, 914–917, 919

SetMapMode function (CDC), 532–533, 620, 622, 624, 784

SetMaxPage function (CPrintInfo), 769, 775, 777

SetMenuItemBitmaps function (CMenu), 733

SetMinPage function (CPrintInfo), 777

setmode function (ofstream), 925

SetModifiedFlag function (CDocument), 299–300

SetPixel function (CDC), 625–626, 631

SetPolyFillMode function (CDC), 620, 655

setprecision manipulator, 915

SetRadio function (CCmdUI), 269, 495

SetRadius function (CRoundBlock), 116

SetROP2 function (CDC), 212–213, 620, 648–649, 655, 681–682

SetScrollSizes function (CScrollView), 345–347, 551

SetStretchBltMode function (CDC), 742

SetText function (CCmdUI), 269, 495

SetTextAlign function (CDC), 533–534

SetTextCharacterExtra function (CDC), 533

SetTextColor function (CDC), 452, 533, 546, 565

settings for projects, 20, 26

Setup program, **5–8**

SetViewportExt function (CDC), 624

SetViewportOrg function (CDC), 781

setw manipulator, **912–913**

SetWindowExt function (CDC), 624

SetWindowText function (CWnd), 320

shapes, tool bar buttons for, 476–477, *477*

SHARE program, 5

Shift key
  bit mask for, 218
  for debugging, 29
  for editing source files, 22–23
  virtual key code for, 557

shortcut keys, **240–241**
  for Clipboard commands, 826–828, *827*
  copying, 399
  identifiers for, 270–271
  for MINIEDIT, 397, 399

Show Properties command, 478

Show Topics button for help, 17

ShowCaret function (CWnd), 569–570

ShowCursor function (API), 214

showpos enumerator (ios), 917

ShowWindow function (CWnd), 391, 624

side effects, 64

significant digits in output, 916

simple combo boxes, 424

Single command in MINIDRAW, 483, *484*

single document interface (SDI) applications, 176, 394

single-line comments, **43–44**

single stepping in debugging, 31–32

Single-thickness line tool bar button, *477*

size
  of bitmaps, 478–479, 481, 728, 731, 734, **741–742**, 747
  of bounding rectangles, 357–358, 360, 668
  of buffers, 902
  of carets, 567–568
  of Clipboard memory, 832, 838
  of controls, 421–423, 425
  of drawings, for scrolling, **344–352**
  of figures, 667–668
  of fonts, 531, *532*, 546, 551
  of icons, 742
  of inline functions, 49
  of MDI windows, 386, *387*, 388
  of OLE items, 856
  of printing area, **772–773**, 775–778, 781
  of QuickWin windows, 897, 902
  of text, 531, *532*, 546, 551

SIZE structure, 345

Size To Fit command, 897

sizeof operator, C vs. C++, 43

slashes (/)
  for comments, 43–44
  as operator, overloading, 142

SMARTDrive for installation, 5

SM_CXBORDER value, 568

software requirements, **5**

Sound Recorder, 862

source files
  editing, **20–24**, **170–174**, **892–893**
  generating, **167–170**

for MINIDRAW, **202–203**
for MS-DOS programs, **892–893**
opening, 171
organizing, **97–99**
sample, 9, 11
saving, 23
for Windows programming, **167–174**
spaces
  with extraction operators, 920
  in output fields, 913
  with reference operator, 53
spacing
  identifier for, 421–422
  between lines, 534
  of text, 533
  between tool bar buttons, 487
_spawn functions, 901
speed with inline functions, 49
split bars, 352
splitting windows, **352–363**, *354*
square brackets ([]) for arrays, 70–71, 95
square cursor, 204
SRCAND raster-operation code, 738–739
SRCCOPY raster-operation code, 732,
    738, 741
SRCERASE raster-operation code, 738
SRCINVERT raster-operation code,
    738–739
SRCPAINT raster-operation code, 738
Standard Edition, components of, 11
standard streams. *See* iostream class
State menu for QuickWin programs, 897
static binding, 124
static class members, **101–104**
  constructors for, 94
  embedded, 858
static variables, 45, 58
Status Bar command in QuickWin
    programs, 898
status bars
  CCmdUI functions for, 496
  class for, 177
  for MINIDRAW, **496–499**, *496*
  for new programs, **474**, *475*, **476**
  in QuickWin programs, 897–898
STDAFX.CPP file, 179–180
STDAFX.H file, 179–180

Stdin/Stdout/Stderr window in Quick-
    Win programs, **898–899**
STDIO.H file, 906
STDLIB.H file, 83
Step Over button, 31–32, *31*
stock fonts, **548–549**, *549*
storing
  document data, **258–271**
  structures, 322
  text, **538–549**
straight lines, drawing, **646–648**
strcpy function (API), 833, 899
streams. *See* iostream class
StretchBlt function (CDC), **741–742**
  device support for, 778
  raster-operation codes for, 737–738
strikeout text
  LOGFONT field for, 539, 579
  TEXTMETRIC field for, 542, 582
string properties dialog box, 219, 292,
    399–400
string table dialog box, 219, 447
String Table option for resources, 219, 291
strings
  displaying, 910
  reading and writing, 908
strstream class, 908
struct tags, C vs. C++, **40–42**
structures, 76–77
  allocating memory for, 69
  with reference types, 56
  storing, 322
style
  of controls, 424
  of dialog boxes, 467
  of lines, 615, 648
suspending QuickWin programs, 897
Swiss font family
  LOGFONT field for, 541, 581
  TEXTMETRIC field for, 543, 583
switch statements, initializing variables
    in, 45–46
symbol character set
  LOGFONT field for, 540, 579
  TEXTMETRIC field for, 544, 584
symbol redefinition errors, 98
syntax of overloaded operators, 142

System font, bold display for, 418
system keys, 553
system menus, *175*
  class for, 177
  for MDI windows, *387*
SYSTEM_FIXED_FONT value, 549, *549*
SYSTEM_FONT value, 549, *549*

T

Tab key
  for controls, 423, **425–426**, *427*
  for editing source files, 22
  handling, 564–565
TabbedTextOut function (CDC), 535
tables of contents for help, 17
tables of virtual function addresses, 124
tabs
  with extraction operators, 920
  in source files, keystrokes for, 22
Tabstop property for controls, 423, 425
tags, C vs. C++, **40–43**
Target Directory: text box, 12
target environments, 9, 11
TECHNOLOGY index for device capabili-
    ties, 778, 785
TechNote Viewer, 8
tellg function (istream), 933
tellp function (ostream), 927
templates
  for dialog bars, 500
  document, 182, **195–196**
  for MDI programs, 393
temporary lines, 677
temporary pens and brushes, 615
TEST program, tool bars for, **474**, *475*, **476**
text, **526**
  aligning, 421–422, 434, *532*, 533–534,
    912, **914–915**
  attributes for, **532–533**
  background for, 532–533
  color of, 452, 531–533, 545–546, 565
  copying, **830–836**
  in dialog boxes, 452
  displaying, **527–535**
  finding and replacing, 469

  origins for, 340
  pasting, **836–841**
  pitch of. *See* pitch of text
  in QuickWin programs, 897
  size of, 531, *532*, 546, 551
  storing, **538–549**
text child windows in QuickWin pro-
    grams, 902
text controls
  Alt key with, 423, 426
  class for, 437
  control palette for, *420*
  properties of, 422
  using, 424
text editors. *See* MINIEDIT program
text file mode, 925
text manipulator, 925
Text menu for FONTDEMO, 444, 446, *446*
TEXTDDOC.CPP file, 576–584
TEXTDDOC.H file, 575–576
TEXTDEMO program, 526
  coding for, **527–549**
  displaying text in, **527–534**
  Font dialog box for, **535–549**
  icon for, **536–537**, *537*
  menus for, **535–536**, *536*
  program window for, *528*
  reading keyboard in, **552–566**
  scrolling in, **550–552**
TEXTDEMO.CPP file, 572–575
TEXTDEMO.H file, 571–572
TEXTDVW.CPP file, 587–592
TEXTDVW.H file, 586–587
TEXTMETRIC structure, 531, 541–544,
    547, 549, 581–584
TextOut function (CDC), 443, 534–535
thickness of lines, 648
  functions for, 488–491, 493–494, 505
  identifier for, 483, 488–489, 658
  menu for, 483, *484*, 490, **658**, *659*
  tool bar buttons for, 476–477, *477*
this pointer, **99–101**
thumbs on scroll bars, *339*
tildes (~) for destructors, 92
Tile command, 30, 898
Tile Grid option, 478–479
tiled windows, 30

for MDI, 388
for QuickWin, 898
tiny memory model, 890, 908
titles and title bars, *175*
    class for, 177
    in QuickWin programs, 897
    strings for, 219
tm fields (TEXTMETRIC), 531, *532*
TODO comments, 173
toggled keys, testing for, 557
tool bars
    CCmdUI class for, 493, **495–496**
    for Clipboard commands, 829
    coding for, **484–494**
    designing buttons for, **478–481**
    main frame window class for, 177
    for MDI programs, 394
    menus for, **482–484**
    messages for, 205, **484–494**
    for new programs, **474**, *475*, **476**
    resources for, **477–484**
Tool Options dialog box, 10
tools for drawing
    creating, **614–619**
    selecting, **612–614**
Tools installation option, 7, 10
Tools menu for MINIDRAW, 482, *483*
topics, help, 17
transferring data. *See* Clipboard; messages and message handlers; OLEDEMO program
TRANSPARENT background mode, 532, 650
Triple command in MINIDRAW, 483, *484*
Triple-thickness line tool bar button, *477*
trunc flag (ios), 927
truncation in inline functions vs. macros, 50
two-headed cursors, 204
Type: list for resources, 218–219, 240, 290
typedef, C vs. C++, **40–42**
types
    for member variables, 429
    serializing, 298

U

unary operators, overloading, **142–143**
undeclared identifier errors, 39
underlined characters
    for controls, 426
    for menu items, 239
underlined style
    data member for, 429
    identifier for, 421–422
    LOGFONT field for, 539, 579
    message handler for, 433, 438
    TEXTMETRIC field for, 542, 582
Undo command in MINIDRAW, 263–264, *264*, **268–271**
unformatted input, 921
_ungetch function, 901
union tags, C vs. C++, **40–42**
unitbuf flag (ios), 919
units
    for control size, 423
    for mapping modes, 346, 621–624
    for pen width, 615
UnrealizeObject function (CDC), 620, 655
unsetf function (ios), 917
Update command for OLE objects, 849
UPDATE_COMMAND_UI handler, 266, 268–270
    for Clipboard, 828–830, 836–838, 841, 844
    for drawings, 658, 660
    for OLE items, 859–862
    for tool bars, 488–489
update regions, 361–362, 530, 533–534
UpdateAllViews function (CDocument), 267–268
    for dialog boxes, 449
    for font display, 545
    for MDI programs, 399
    for OLE, 852, 858
    for scrolling, 551
    for split windows, 356–357, 359–362
    for storing documents, 270
    for text, 566
UpdateData function (CWnd), 428

UpdateWindow function (CWnd), 391, 437–439
updating
  dialog boxes, **442–443**
  message for, 432
  OLE items. *See* OLEDEMO program
  for scrolling, 340
  for split views, **356–363**
  view class for, 173
uppercase flag (ios), 916
Use Microsoft Foundation Classes option, 890, 895
user-defined controls
  control palette for, *420*
  using, 425
user input, 24, 424
Using Help command for QuickWin programs, 898

V

validity checks
  for control values, 431
  encapsulation for, 84–85
value, passing parameters by, 55
variable text pitch, 549, *549*
  bold display for, 418
  identifier for, 421–422
  LOGFONT field for, 540, 580
  message handler for, 433, 439
  TEXTMETRIC field for, 543, 583
Variable Type: list, 429
variables
  declaring, **44–46**
  for default function parameters, 51
  displaying, 910
  initializing, 45–46
  for instances, 78–79
  reference types for, **52–59**
  scope resolution operator for, **47–48**
  watching, 30–32, *32*
VBX controls
  class for, 437
  control palette for, *420*
  using, 425
verbs in OLE, 862

version numbers, 297, **772–773**
vertical arrow cursor, 204
vertical bars (|) with formatting flags, 917
vertical hatch patterns, *617*
vertical scroll bars, 338, *339*
  control palette for, *420*
  using, 425
vertical splitting of windows, 355–356
VERTRES index for device capabilities, 776
VERTSIZE index for device capabilities, 778
view classes, 173–174, **176–178**
  hierarchy of, 338, *339*
  for MDI programs, 390–391, *392, 393*
  message-handling by, 205–206
View menu for QuickWin programs, 897
view windows, *175, 177,* 200, **221–223**
viewpoint origin, 343
viewport origins, 340
  in mapping modes, 621
  in printing, 781, 783
ViewRect object (CRect), 349
views, 200
  messages for, **205–216**
  splitting, **352–356**, *354*
  updating. *See* redrawing
virtual functions, **120–124**
  for base classes, **127–129**
  for class objects, **125–127**
  and polymorphism, **125**
virtual key codes, **553–557**
virtual machines, 894
Visual C++ compiler, 8, 11
Visual Workbench, 8, 11
  for AppWizard, 167
  build options with, **24–26**
  building programs with, **26–27**
  creating projects with, **18–20**
  debugging programs with, **28–33**
  editing source files with, **20–24**
  running, **16**
  running programs with, **28**
  SHARE program for, 5
VK_CAPITAL virtual key code, 557
VK_DOWN virtual key code, 554
VK_END virtual key code, 554

VK_HOME virtual key code, 554
VK_LEFT virtual key code, 553
VK_NEXT virtual key code, 555
VK_PRIOR virtual key code, 554
VK_RIGHT virtual key code, 553
VK_SHIFT virtual key code, 557
VK_UP virtual key code, 554
void pointers, C vs. C++, 40

W

_wabout function, 902
warning messages, 25, 27, 913
Warnings as Errors check box, 25
Watch window, 30–32, *32*
_wclose function, 902
weight of text
  LOGFONT field for, 539, 579
  TEXTMETRIC field for, 542, 582
Welcome dialog box, 6
_wg functions in QuickWin programs, 902
WHITE_BRUSH value, 613–614
white color
  for bitmaps, 649–650, 735
  drawing functions for, 660, 663, 694
  drawing mode for, 649–650
  for pens and brushes, 613–614
WHITE_PEN value, 614
white space
  with input, 920–921
  with reference operator, 53
WHITENESS raster-operation code, 735
width
  of bitmaps, 478–479, 481, 728, 731, 734, 747
  of borders, 568
  of carets, 567–568
  of output fields, **911–913**
  of pens, 612, 614–615
  of printing area, 775–778, 781
  of text, 551
    LOGFONT field for, 539, 579
    TEXTMETRIC field for, 542, 582
width function (ios), 912
Window menu
  for MINIEDIT, 397

for QuickWin programs, 898
window procedures, 205
windows
  active, 386, 552, 902
  customizing, **221–223**
  in MDI applications, 386, *387*, 388
  messages for, **205–206**
  in QuickWin programs, **898–899**, 902
  redrawing. *See* redrawing
  in source files, 23
  splitting, 352–363, *354*
Windows .EXE targets option, 9
WINDOWS.H file, 358
Windows programs, **166–167**
  building and running, **174–176**
  classes and files for, **176–191**
  flow control in, **192–195**
  iostream class with, 908
  Microsoft Foundation Classes for, 8–9
  program window for, **174–175**, *175*
  source code for, **167–174**
Windows Sound Recorder, 862
Windows window class, 222
WINGRDOC.CPP file, 172, 177–178, 185–186
WINGRDOC.H file, 171, 177–178, 184
WINGREET program, **167**
  building and running, **174–176**
  classes and files for, **176–191**
  editing source code for, **170–174**
  flow control in, **192–195**
  generating source code for, **167–170**
  program window for, **174–175**, *175*
WINGREET.CLW file, 179
WINGREET.CPP file, 177–178, 181–183, **192–194**
WINGREET.DEF file, 179
WINGREET.H file, 177–178, 180
WINGREET.ICO file, 179
WINGREET.INI file, 176
WINGREET.MAK file, 179
WINGREET.RC file, 179
WINGREET.RC2 file, 179
WINGRVW.CPP file, 173, 177–178, 190–191
WINGRVW.H file, 177–178, 189–190
WinMain function, **194–195**

Wizards. *See* AppWizard editor; ClassWizard editor
WM_CHAR messages, **560–566**
  handlers for, **562–563**
  and virtual key codes, 555
WM_CREATE messages, 484, 567
WM_HSCROLL messages, 559
WM_INITDIALOG messages, 432
WM_KEYDOWN messages, **552–560**
WM_KILLFOCUS messages, 567
WM_LBUTTONDBLCLK messages, 862
WM_LBUTTONDOWN messages, **205–211**
WM_LBUTTONUP messages, **214–216**
WM_MOUSEMOVE messages, **211–215**, 624
WM_PAINT messages, 432, 611
WM_SETFOCUS messages, 567
WM_SIZE messages, 624, 628, 631
WM_SYSKEYDown messages, 553
WM_VSCROLL messages, 557, 559
_wmenuclick function, 902
_wopen functions, 902
WORD data type, serializing, 298
Write function (CArchive), 322

write function (ostream), 918, 925–927
WriteObject function (CArchive), 296
writing
  to arrays, 908
  blocks, 322
  document data, **294–298**
  file output, **925–928**
  to streams, 906
_wset functions, 902
_wyield function, 902
WYSIWYG principle in mapping modes, 624

X

x coordinates for drawings, 625
XOR operator with bit operations, 738

Y

y coordinates for drawings, 625
yellow drawing color, functions for, 660, 663–664, 694

AN $800 SEMINAR DISGUISED AS A BOOK

757 pp. ISBN:1259-5.

Get the same valuable information the many have paid over $800 to receive for less than $30. With *The Complete PC Upgrade & Maintenance Guide*, you'll be able to solve almost any PC problem and even supercharge your own machine.

You'll be able to use this book to install circuit boards and hard drives, increase the memory in your machine, add sound cards and other multimedia capabilities and avoid unnecessary expensive repairs.

Precise, step-by-step instructions make it easy for you to repair and upgrade your PC yourself. You'll get complete explanations of background and underlying concepts vital to PC maintenance. Armed with this information, you'll know always know what to fix, what to leave alone and when to call for help.

SYBEX. Help Yourself.

2021 Challenger Drive
Alameda, CA 94501
800-227-2346

SYBEX

SYBEX

FREE BROCHURE!

Complete this form today, and we'll send you a full-color brochure of Sybex bestsellers.

Please supply the name of the Sybex book purchased.

_____

How would you rate it?

_____ Excellent   _____ Very Good   _____ Average   _____ Poor

Why did you select this particular book?

_____ Recommended to me by a friend

_____ Recommended to me by store personnel

_____ Saw an advertisement in _____

_____ Author's reputation

_____ Saw in Sybex catalog

_____ Required textbook

_____ Sybex reputation

_____ Read book review in _____

_____ In-store display

_____ Other _____

Where did you buy it?

_____ Bookstore

_____ Computer Store or Software Store

_____ Catalog (name: _____)

_____ Direct from Sybex

_____ Other: _____

Did you buy this book with your personal funds?

_____ Yes   _____ No

About how many computer books do you buy each year?

_____ 1-3   _____ 3-5   _____ 5-7   _____ 7-9   _____ 10+

About how many Sybex books do you own?

_____ 1-3   _____ 3-5   _____ 5-7   _____ 7-9   _____ 10+

Please indicate your level of experience with the software covered in this book:

_____ Beginner   _____ Intermediate   _____ Advanced

Which types of software packages do you use regularly?

_____ Accounting   _____ Databases   _____ Networks

_____ Amiga   _____ Desktop Publishing _____ Operating Systems

_____ Apple/Mac   _____ File Utilities   _____ Spreadsheets

_____ CAD   _____ Money Management   _____ Word Processing

_____ Communications   _____ Languages   _____ Other _____
                                                              (please specify)

Which of the following best describes your job title?

_____ Administrative/Secretarial _____ President/CEO

_____ Director _____ Manager/Supervisor

_____ Engineer/Technician _____ Other _____
(please specify)

Comments on the weaknesses/strengths of this book: _____

_____

_____

_____

_____

Name _____

Street _____

City/State/Zip _____

Phone _____

PLEASE FOLD, SEAL, AND MAIL TO SYBEX

SYBEX, INC.
Department M
2021 CHALLENGER DR.
ALAMEDA, CALIFORNIA USA
94501

SYBEX

SEAL

Installation of Disk

For complete instructions on installing this disk on your computer, please refer to Chapter 1 of *Mastering Microsoft Visual C++ Programming*.

Disk Contents

This disk contains the source code for virtually every example in the book. The examples are designed to expose you to a wide range of real-world programming challenges and situations and will result in you gaining solid skills in Microsoft Visual C++ Programming.

If you need a 3½-inch disk...

To receive a 3½-inch disk, please return the original 5¼-inch disk with a written request to:

Customer Service Department
2021 Challenger Drive
Alameda, CA 94501
(800) 227-2346
Fax: (510) 523-2373

Be sure to include your name, complete mailing address, and the following reference number: 1282-X.

Otherwise, your request cannot be processed. Allow six weeks for delivery.